The SAGE Handbook of
Aging, Work and Society

The SAGE Handbook of
Aging, Work and Society

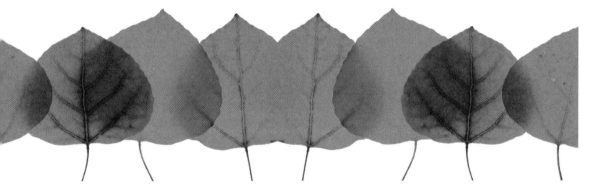

Edited by
John Field,
Ronald J. Burke and
Cary L. Cooper

Los Angeles | London | New Delhi
Singapore | Washington DC

Los Angeles | London | New Delhi
Singapore | Washington DC

SAGE Publications Ltd
1 Oliver's Yard
55 City Road
London EC1Y 1SP

SAGE Publications Inc.
2455 Teller Road
Thousand Oaks, California 91320

SAGE Publications India Pvt Ltd
B 1/I 1 Mohan Cooperative Industrial Area
Mathura Road
New Delhi 110 044

SAGE Publications Asia-Pacific Pte Ltd
3 Church Street
#10-04 Samsung Hub
Singapore 049483

Editor: Delia Martinez-Alfonso
Editorial Assistant: Colette Wilson
Production editor: Sushant Nailwal
Copyeditor: Jill Birch
Proofreader: Richard Davis
Indexer: Caroline Eley
Marketing manager: Alison Borg
Cover design: Wendy Scott
Typeset by: C&M Digitals (P) Ltd, Chennai, India
Printed in Great Britain by Henry Ling Limited, at the
Dorset Press, Dorchester, DT1 1HD

Library of Congress Control Number: 2013931191

British Library Cataloguing in Publication data

A catalogue record for this book is available from the British Library

ISBN 978-1-4462-0782-6

Contents

About the Editors

John Field is a Professor in the School of Education, University of Stirling, and Visiting Professor at Birkbeck, University of London. He has written widely on skills, knowledge and learning in both their contemporary and historical aspects, with a particular focus on the adult life course; he has also served as a adviser to government and a number of voluntary organizations. His latest book is *Working Men's Bodies: Work Camps in Britain, 1880–1939* (2013), and he has written a standard textbook on *Social Capital*. He blogs on his research interests and other matters at: http://thelearningprofessor.wordpress.com/

Ronald J. Burke is one of Canada's most prolific researchers. His work has focused on the relationship between the work environment and the individual's overall well-being, and over the past forty years he has written articles for numerous academic and professional journals. In addition to his research and teaching activities, Professor Burke was the Founding Editor of the *Canadian Journal of Administrative Sciences*. Burke has served on the editorial board of two dozen journals and has reviewed manuscripts for a dozen more journals. He has served as a member of two grants committees for the Social Sciences and Humanities Research Council of Canada, as Director of the PhD program in the School of Business at York University, and as Associate Dean Research, with the Schulich School of Business at York University. He has participated in research conferences in North and South America, the UK, Europe, Asia and Australia. He is a Fellow of the Canadian Psychological Association.

Cary L. Cooper is Professor of Organizational Psychology and Health at Lancaster University Management School and Pro Vice Chancellor at Lancaster University. He is the author/editor of over 120 books (on occupational stress, women at work and industrial and organizational psychology), has written over 400 scholarly articles for academic journals, and is a frequent contributor to national newspapers, TV and radio. He is currently Founding Editor of the *Journal of Organizational Behavior* and Editor-in-Chief of the medical journal *Stress & Health*. He is a Fellow of the British Psychological Society, The Royal Society of Arts, The Royal Society of Medicine, The Royal Society of Public Health, The British Academy of Management and an Academician of the UK's Academy of Social Sciences. He currently chairs the Academy of Social Sciences and is President of RELATE. In 2001, Cary was awarded a CBE in the Queen's Birthday Honours List for his contribution to occupational safety and health.

Notes on Contributors

Gary A. Adams is currently an endowed Professor of Human Resource Management at the University of Wisconsin Oshkosh. Dr Adams received his PhD in Industrial and Organizational Psychology from Central Michigan University, a Master's degree from Illinois State University, and BS degree from the University of Wisconsin Oshkosh. His research and consulting interests include older workers and occupational stress and health. He has published two books, several book chapters, and a number of articles in journals such as *Personnel Psychology*, *Journal of Applied Psychology*, *Journal of Occupational Health Psychology*, *American Psychologist*, *Journal of Organizational Behavior*, and *Educational and Psychological Measurement*.

Boris B. Baltes, PhD, is a Professor in the Psychology Department at Wayne State University in Detroit, Michigan (USA). His research interests include the following areas: biases in performance appraisal, age and work, and work–family balance. His work has appeared in many journals including the *Journal of Applied Psychology, Organizational Behavior and Human Decision Processes*, and the *Journal of Organizational Behavior*. He is an associate editor for the *Journal of Organizational Behavior* and is on the editorial board of various journals. He was elected a Society for Industrial and Organizational Psychology Distinguished Fellow in 2013 for his unusual and outstanding contribution to the field of industrial/organizational psychology.

Margaret E. Beier is an Associate Professor of Industrial and Organizational Psychology at Rice University in Houston, Texas. Margaret received her PhD in Industrial and Organizational Psychology from the Georgia Institute of Technology. Margaret's research is broadly focused on intellectual development through the lifespan. Specific topics include investigation of cognitive ability, age, gender, and personality and motivational traits as related to job and training performance both in organizations and educational settings. Her research combines elements of cognitive psychology, industrial/organizational psychology, and human factors. A main focus of her current research involves investigating how to best design training for older learners. Her work has been published in journals such as *Psychological Bulletin, Journal of Applied Psychology, Personnel Psychology, Journal of Personality and Social Psychology, Intelligence*, and *Psychology and Aging*.

Tommy Bengtsson is Professor of Demography and Economic History at Lund University, Sweden where he is currently Director of the Centre for Economic Demography. His research interests are in European and Asian economic and historical demography, contemporary migration, health and well-being, and population aging. Bengtsson has published on living standards in the past and present, socio-economic inequalities in health and well-being, and on how conditions in early-life affect socio-economic performance and health in later life in international journals. His book *Life under Pressure. Mortality and Living Standards in Europe and Asia, 1700–1900*, co-authored with Cameron Campbell, James Lee and others, was awarded the American Sociological Association's Award for outstanding book on Asia in 2005. He has chaired the International Union for the Scientific Study of Population's Historical Demography Committee for many years.

Todd E. Bodner is an Associate Professor in the Department of Psychology at Portland State University. His research involves the evaluation of statistical methods commonly used by practicing researchers, including the general linear model, hierarchical (multilevel) linear models, structural equation models, meta-analytic methods, and methods for handling missing data.

Stephan A. Boehm is an Assistant Professor and Director of the Center for Disability and Integration (CDI-HSG) at the University of St Gallen (Switzerland). He received a Master's (2003) and a PhD (2008) from the University of St Gallen. In 2008 and in the spring of 2009, he served as a Visiting Research Fellow at the Oxford Institute of Ageing at the University of Oxford, Great Britain. His research interests include diversity management, with a focus on the vocational inclusion of employees with disabilities and the management of demographic change as well as group-level and organizational-level processes of categorization, stereotyping, and discrimination. His work has appeared in various journals including the *Journal of Organizational Behavior*, the *Journal of Management Studies*, *Personnel Psychology*, and *Human Resource Management*.

Melissa L. Cannon is a doctoral candidate in Urban Studies and a graduate research assistant at the Institute on Aging at Portland State University. She holds a bachelor's degree in community development, and she recently completed her graduate certificate in gerontology. Her current research areas are community development and gerontology, specifically focusing on strategies for creating inclusive, age-friendly cities and communities by fostering physical and social environments that support people of all ages and abilities.

Danut A. Casoinic (PhD, University of Grenoble) is an Associate Professor of Management in the EM Strasbourg Business School, HuManiS Research Center (EA 1347), at the University of Strasbourg. His scholarly interests include, among others, age and generational stereotypes, demographic diversity, leadership behaviours and their links to various organizational outcomes. Professor Casoinic's research also focuses on the impact of age-related differences (chronological and subjective) on the quality of manager-employee work relationships, transformational leadership, and how these interactions may affect job satisfaction and organizational commitment.

Yunan Chen is an Assistant Professor in the Department of Informatics at the Donald Bren School of Information and Computer Sciences (ICS) and the Institute for Clinical and Translational Science (ICTS) at the University of California, Irvine. Her research interests lie in the intersection of human–computer interaction (HCI) and Medical Informatics. In particular, she is interested in designing and evaluating interactive systems to support clinical collaboration, patient–provider interactions and chronic care management. Her recent project explores the opportunities for game-based interventions for promoting self-care of chronic illnesses in patients' families.

Betty Eckhaus Cohen is Information Services Specialist at the Sloan Center on Aging and Work at Boston College, where she is responsible for maintaining the Center's searchable databases of Aging and Work Facts and Aging and Work Literature. She also assists in identifying and evaluating scholarly literature, reports and other sources of information that support the Center's on-going research agenda. Betty previously served for eight years heading the Social

Work Library at Boston College, and has prior experience in library management, research and teaching in public health and academic settings.

Jennifer Kane Coplon, PhD, MSW has been a clinical social worker for over 40 years, practicing in several family service and health care settings and currently working privately and at South End Community Health Center in Boston. She is also a research fellow at the Sloan Center on Aging and Work at Boston College and a scholar at the Women's Studies Research Center at Brandeis University. Passionate about understanding and advocating for disempowered people, Dr Coplon is researching marginalized elders (including the formerly homeless in Boston and Ugandan grandparents in the role of custodial parents of AIDS related orphans), conducting positive life reviews and taking photographs that capture their strength and resilience. Dr Coplon has a master's degree from Simmons College School of Social Work and a doctoral degree from the Heller School of Social Policy and Management from Brandeis University.

Sarah DeArmond is an Assistant Professor in the Department of Management and Human Resources at the University of Wisconsin Oshkosh. She earned her BA at Central Michigan University and her MS and PhD from Colorado State University. Dr DeArmond's research and consulting interests are in occupational safety and health, job performance, selection, training, and leadership. She has published a number of book chapters and her research has appeared in journals such as *Accident Analysis and Prevention*, *Public Personnel Management*, *International Journal of Selection and Assessment*, and *Journal of Applied Social Psychology.*

Paul Fairlie is a Sessional Assistant Professor in the School of Human Resource Management at York University. He received his PhD in psychology from York University. His research interests include the measurement and impact of meaningful work, and the role of personality in the workplace (e.g., perfectionism). He is also an applied consultant in industrial-organizational psychology, specializing in various forms of individual and organizational measurement, as well as organizational research. He has published in the *Journal of Personality and Social Psychology*, the *Journal of Cross-Cultural Psychology*, and in *Advances in Developing Human Resources.* He recently authored a chapter on the role of meaningful work in employee health outcomes in *The Fulfilling Workplace: The Organization's Role in Achieving Individual and Organizational Health*, edited by Ronald Burke and Cary L. Cooper (Gower Publishing, 2013).

Tara Fenwick is Professor of professional education at the University of Stirling, and Director of ProPEL [www.propel.stir.ac.uk], an international network for research in professional practice, education and learning. Her research focuses on changing knowledges, cultures and professionalisms in work, with particular interest in sociomaterial approaches to researching and conceptualising knowing-in-practice. Her most recent books include *Emerging Approaches to Educational Research: Tracing the Socio-Material* with R. Edwards and P. Sawchuk (Routledge, 2011), *Knowledge Mobilisation: Politics, Languages and Responsibilities* with L. Farrell (Routledge, 2012), with a forthcoming volume *Reconceptualising Professional Learning* with M Nerland (Routledge 2013, forthcoming).

Marvin Formosa is a Senior Lecturer within the European Centre for Gerontology, University of Malta. In 1998 and 2008, he was appointed as a lecturer by the International Institute on Ageing (United Nations – Malta) on its missions to Thailand and Qatar respectively. Dr Formosa also held the post of a Visiting Scholar at Ontario Institute for Studies in Education, University of Toronto, Toronto, Canada (2009–2010). In 2012, he was invited to join the editorial board of *Research on Ageing and Social Policy* and *International Journal on Education and Ageing*. His primary interests are older adult learning, social class dynamics, and social exclusion – subjects on which he has contributed to many edited books and journals. Recent and forthcoming works include *Lifelong Learning in Later Life: A Handbook on Older adult Learning* (with Brian Findsen, Sense Publishers, 2011), *Social Class in Later Life: Power, Identity and Lifestyle* (with Paul Higgs, The Policy Press, 2013), and *International Perspectives on Older Adult Education: Research, Policies and Practice* (with Brian Findsen, Springer, 2014).

Laura Guerrero is an Assistant Professor of Management at The University of Texas at El Paso. Her research focuses on careers and job search. She is especially interested in careers of immigrants, Hispanics, women, and other groups. Dr Guerrero has worked, studied, and lived in Mexico, the United States, and Canada. She has an undergraduate degree in economics from The University of Texas at El Paso, an MBA from Simon Fraser University, and a PhD from the Richard Ivey School of Business at the University of Western Ontario. She has published in various peer-reviewed publications including *Applied Psychology: An International Review*, *Career Development Quarterly*, and *Organizational Dynamics*. She has also co-edited *Cases in Leadership*, now available in its third edition.

Anne-Marie Guillemard is Professor of Sociology at the Faculty of Social and Human Sciences, University of Paris Descartes Sorbonne with a national research Chair (Institut Universitaire de France). Since 2011 Emeritus Professor. She is a member of the Academia Europaea. She has coordinated several European research projects in the 6th and 7th Framework Programme. Among them she was responsible for work packages in the European Network of Excellence "Civil Society and New Forms of Governance in Europe" (CINEFOGO), and the European research consortium ASPA "Activating Senior Potential in Ageing Europe" (7thFP). She sits on the editorial boards of the *Revue française de sociologie, Ageing and Society, Hallym International Journal of Aging* (Baywood Publishing Company) and *Retraite et Société*. Her work on international comparisons of welfare policies, retirement systems and employment is widely recognized. Her research focuses on questions related to age and employment, age management in public and entrepreneurial policies, the generational contract and the reform of the welfare state. Among her most recent works are the following : *Social policies and Citizenship, The Changing Landscape*, (ed) Oxford University Press, 2012, *Les défis du vieillissement, Age, Emploi, Retraite, Perspectives internationales*, Armand Colin 2010.

Leslie B. Hammer is a Professor in the Department of Psychology at Portland State University. Her research focuses on ways in which organizations can help reduce work and family stress and improve positive spillover by facilitating both formal and informal workplace supports. Dr Hammer is the Director of the Center for Work–Family Stress, Safety, and Health, Director of the Portland State Occupational Health Psychology graduate training program, and Associate Director of the Oregon Healthy Workforce Center, funded by grants from the National Institute for Child Health and Human Development and the National Institute for Occupational Safety and Health. Dr Hammer co-authored a book with Dr Margaret Neal entitled *Working Couples Caring for Children and Aging Couples: Effects on Work and Well-Being* (2007).

Apivat Hanvongse is a PhD student in the Social-Organizational Psychology Program at Teachers College, Columbia University. His primary research and scholarly interests examine how leaders help social enterprises and entrepreneurial non-profit organizations balance social and commercial value creation. Other interests include generational differences in the workplace and bilingual/bicultural issues at work. He hopes to transfer his knowledge, skills, and practice related to the field of organizational change and development to Asian and developing country contexts.

Christiane Hipp became dean of the faculty in 2011 and full professor for Organisation, Human Resource Management and General Management at the Technical University Cottbus in 2005. She received her diploma in industrial engineering in 1994 and her PhD in economics in 1999. From 1995 until 1999 Christiane Hipp was research associate at the Fraunhofer Institute for Systems and Innovation Research and from 1999 until 2005 she has been working as a senior technology manager for several companies (e.g., Vodafone) while she has continued her research at the Technical University of Hamburg-Harburg in the area of innovation management. There she received her postdoctoral lecture qualification in 2005. She was a visiting scholar at the University of Manchester's Centre for Research on Innovation and Competition. Her areas of interest include demographical change, service innovation, innovation strategies, intellectual property and innovation processes.

Carla Houkamau (PhD) is a Senior Lecturer in the Department of Management and International Business. Carla joined the Department in 2007 as a Postdoctoral Research Fellow. She completed her PhD in Psychology at The University of Auckland under the Health Research Council Scholarship program as well as a Bachelor of Commerce (Conjoint) in Management and Employment Relations. Carla specializes in the areas of personal identity and diversity management. Her current research program is concerned with the business case for diversity management: in particular, how diversity management can foster a positive work environment for individuals from diverse backgrounds while promoting employee engagement and productivity.

Yu-Shan Hsu is an Assistant Professor at the John Molson School of Business, Concordia University. She received her PhD at the University of Wisconsin-Milwaukee. Her research interests are diversity/cross-cultural management and interpersonal and interdomain relationships. Her work has been published in edited books and journals such as *International Journal of Human Resource Management and International Journal of Cross Cultural Management.*

Kerr Inkson is an Emeritus Professor at The University of Auckland Business School, New Zealand. His 48-year academic career included 25 years as full Professor, at five New Zealand universities. His main field of research is career studies. Kerr has published 17 books, and over 120 refereed journal articles and book chapters. His latest books are *Understanding Careers* (SAGE, 2007, second edition in preparation); *Cultural Intelligence* (co-authored with David C Thomas, second edition, Berrett-Koehler, 2009); *Career Studies* (4-volume collection, co-edited with Mark Savickas, SAGE, 2012); and *Managing Expatriates* (co-authored with Yvonne McNulty, Business Expert Press, 2013).

Jacquelyn Boone James is director of research at the Sloan Center on Aging & Work, and research professor in the Lynch School of Education at Boston College. She received her PhD in personality and developmental psychology at Boston University. Her research has focused on the meaning and experience of work, gender roles and stereotypes, adult development, and most recently, perceptions of older workers and emerging retirement issues. She and her colleagues have published numerous articles, opinion pieces, and four edited books. Currently, with funding from the Alfred P. Sloan Foundation, she and her director, Marcie Pitt-Catsouphes are in the process of conducting a major field experiment within a regional medical center to study the workplace impact of changes to 'time & place management' policies and programs. Recently, she was featured on CBS *Sunday Morning* to discuss issues having to do with 'the new unemployables', older workers who are having difficulty finding work. Dr James is past president of the Society for the Study of Human Development and serves on the editorial board of Research in Human Development.

Steve M. Jex is currently Professor of Industrial/Organizational Psychology at Bowling Green State University He has also held faculty positions at Central Michigan University and the University of Wisconsin Oshkosh. Dr Jex received his PhD in Industrial/Organizational Psychology from the University of South Florida and has spent most of his postdoctoral career conducting research on occupational stress. His research has appeared in a number of scholarly journals including *Journal of Applied Psychology*, *Journal of Organizational Behavior*, *Journal of Occupational Health Psychology*, *Journal of Applied Social Psychology*, and *Work & Stress*. Dr Jex is the author of two books, *Stress and Job Performance: Theory, Research, and Implications for Managerial Practice* and *Organizational Psychology: A Scientist-Practitioner Approach.*

Stina Johansson received her doctorate in Sociology at Uppsala University 1986. In 1993 she became Associate Professor in Sociology at Uppsala University, and since 1999 she is Professor in Social Work at Umeå University. During her carrier she has conducted research projects and published books and articles about professional elderly care, professionalization among care workers, informal care, old people's social networks and old people's life histories. She is also interested in comparative studies and has research collaboration with colleagues in Australia and China. Stina Johansson is also editor-in-chief for the Swedish scientific journal *Socialvetenskaplig tidskrift* (*Swedish Journal of Social Research*).

Ruth Kanfer is a Professor of Industrial and Organizational Psychology at Georgia Institute of Technology in Atlanta, Georgia, USA. Her area of expertise is work motivation, including job search and older worker reemployment, employee engagement, worker self-management, and team motivation. She is trained in clinical assessment methods and has published extensively in top-tier journals including the *Academy of Management Review*, *Academy of Management Journal*, *Journal of Applied Psychology*, and *Research in Organizational Behavior*, and has co-edited four books on motivation and emotion related to work. Her work has been funded by government and private agencies, including the National Science Foundation, the Society of Human Resource Management, the US Air Force Office of Scientific Research, the US Office of Naval Research, the National Institutes of Health/National Institute of Aging, and the Spencer Foundation. Dr Kanfer has also consulted with national organizations, state government agencies, and private companies and provided expert testimony on worker motivation in a variety of industrial sectors.

Martin Kohli is Emeritus Professor of Sociology at the European University Institute (Florence, Italy) and Professor at the Bremen International Graduate School of Social Sciences (Bremen, Germany). Previously he was at the Free University of Berlin. He is a member of the Berlin-Brandenburg Academy of Sciences and the Austrian Academy of Sciences, and from 1997–99 served as President of the European Sociological Association (ESA).

Franz Kolland is Associate Professor of Sociology at the University of Vienna. His main research focus is on social gerontology. He studies learning in later life, intergenerational learning, aging, biography, life styles and new technologies. He is Head of the working group

'Ageing and health' at the Faculty of Social Sciences of the University of Vienna. His professional activities include the co-editorship of the *International Journal of Education and Ageing*. He is board member of the Austrian Society of Gerontology and Geriatrics, the Austrian Committee on Ageing Medicine, and member of the editorial board of the German *Journal of Gerontology and Geriatrics* and the *International Journal of Education and Ageing*.

Harald Künemund is Professor of Empirical Research on Ageing and Research Methods at University of Vechta, Germany. His main topics of research are social and political participation of older people, intergenerational relations, old age and technology, and methods of social research.

Florian Kunze is a senior research associate and lecturer at the Institute for Leadership and Human Resource Management at the University of St Gallen, Switzerland. In 2012 he served as a visiting research fellow at the University of California Los Angeles (UCLA). His current research interests include consequences of the demographic change for companies, within-group processes and dynamics in work teams and organizations, discrimination and stereotyping due to demographic characteristics, and leadership research.

Christine Milligan is Professor of Health and Social Geography and Director of the Centre for Ageing Research at Lancaster University. She has published widely in the field of aging and care. Her main interests focus around aging in place and the importance of home and community in maintaining the health and well-being of older people and family care-givers. Christine has also undertaken work around active aging and is expert in qualitative and participative research methods. She works closely with public and third sector organizations as well as older people themselves.

Maggie Mort, a former journalist and health correspondent, is Reader in the Sociology of Science, Technology and Medicine and has a joint post between Sociology and Medicine at Lancaster University. She has published widely in the areas of technological change, telemedicine and telecare, innovation in health science and technology, health policy and politics, disaster and recovery studies. She works largely with ethnographic and participative methodologies.

Margaret B. Neal, PhD, is Director of the Institute on Aging and Professor of Community Health at Portland State University. She also oversees the Institute on Aging's Aging Matters, Locally and Globally Initiative, leads a service-learning program to Nicaragua, and co-directs the Oregon Geriatric Education Center. Dr Neal teaches graduate courses in gerontology and data collection methods. Her most recent research has focused on the challenges and opportunities of managing paid employment and unpaid elder care, the characteristics and creation of age-friendly cities and communities, transportation options for older adults, strategies for promoting healthy aging, and aging in developing countries. She and Dr Leslie Hammer co-authored a book entitled *Working Couples Caring for Children and Aging Couples: Effects on Work and Well-Being* (2007).

Elissa L. Perry (PhD, Carnegie Mellon University) is a Professor in the Social-Organizational Psychology Program at Teachers College, Columbia University. Her research focuses on the role of personal characteristics (e.g., age, generational membership, gender, race, disability) in human resource judgments and organizational behaviour and the effectiveness of organizational interventions (e.g., diversity training, sexual harassment awareness training) in reducing and managing discrimination. Professor Perry has published her work in journals including *Journal of Applied Psychology*, *Academy of Management Review*, and *Journal of Organizational Behavior*.

Chris Phillipson is Professor of Sociology and Social Gerontology at the University of Manchester where he co-directs the Manchester Interdisciplinary Collaboration for Research on Ageing (MICRA). He has undertaken a range of research projects in areas covering work and retirement, family and community change in later life, and the impact of social exclusion on the quality of life in old age. His publications include: *The Sage Handbook of Social Gerontology* (co-edited, Sage, 2010); *Work, Health and Well-being: The challenges of managing health at work* (co-edited, Policy Press, 2011); *Ageing* (Polity Press, 2013).

Ayala Malach Pines (deceased September 2012) received her BA at the Hebrew University and her MA and PhD at Boston University. She was a clinical, social and organizational psychologist. She served as Dean of the Guilford Glazer Faculty of Business & Management at Ben-Gurion University of the Negev in Be'er-Sheva, Israel.

Dr Pines was an internationally renowned authority in social and organizational psychology. She was a pioneer in the study of burnout and published extensively on the subject. Her Burnout Measure is being used extensively by researchers worldwide. She published 10 books on topics ranging from personal and professional burnout to romantic love and jealousy, to gender aspects and managerial issues. She published 30 book chapters and well over 100 research articles. Her books were translated into many languages, including Hebrew, French, German, Spanish, Hungarian, Greek, Turkish, Chinese, Polish, Japanese and Korean.

Above all, Professor Pines represented a rare combination of compassion, leadership and wisdom of the heart. She was a lighthouse for many patients, students and colleagues. May her memory be blessed.

Marcie Pitt-Catsouphes, PhD, is an Associate Professor in the Graduate School of Social Work and the Carroll School of Management. She directs the Sloan Center on Aging & Work at Boston College and co-directs the Center for Social Innovation. She has been the principal investigator or co-principal investigator for several large scale studies including the 2010 Generations of Talent study, an investigation which gathered data from over 11,000 employees working in eleven different countries. Dr Pitt-Catsouphes is currently co-principal investigator for a workplace intervention study, the Time and Place Management study. She was invited to the 2005 White House Conference on Aging as an issue expert and participated in the 2010 White House Forum on Workplace Flexibility.

Richard A. Posthuma is a Professor of Management at The University of Texas at El Paso. His research interests include: age stereotyping in the workplace, cross-cultural and Latin America Issues, high performance work practices, negotiations and conflict management, and higher education. He has more than 13 years of professional work experience in the public and private sectors involving: employee relations, human resource management, risk management, training, and law and has provided professional services to many public and private sector organizations. He earned his PhD in Organizational Behavior and Human Resource Management from Purdue University; JD, Cum Laude, from the Thomas M. Cooley Law School; and Masters in Labor and Industrial Relations from Michigan State University. He has numerous peer-reviewed publications in top tier journals including *Industrial Relations*, *Journal of Management*, *Journal of Organizational Behavior*, and *Personnel Psychology*. He is editor-in-chief of the *International Journal of Conflict Management*, and serves on the editorial boards of *Human Resource*

Management and the *Journal of Management*. As an attorney he is licensed to practice law in Michigan and the District of Columbia.

Margaret Richardson (PhD, University of Waikato, New Zealand) is a Research Fellow in the Management Communication Department at the University of Waikato. Her research interests include the use and rejection of computers by older people, as well as identification of the structures and practices that impact on older people's capacity to participate in and with organizations, including in their roles as workers and customers. She has published articles in *The Gerontologist*, *Research on Aging*, *Work Employment & Society*, *Communication Yearbook*, *New Media & Society*, and *Information Communication & Society*.

Celia Roberts works in the Department of Sociology, Lancaster University, with affiliations to the Centre for Science Studies and the Centre for Gender and Women's Studies. Her work focuses on new health technologies (ranging from telecare through to pharmaceuticals), embodiment and gender. She is currently working on an EU-funded project on patient activism and writing a book on early onset puberty.

Cort W. Rudolph, PhD, is an Assistant Professor of Industrial and Organizational Psychology at Saint Louis University, in Saint Louis, MO (USA), where he also serves as the Primary Investigator and Director of the Sustainable Employability Across the Lifespan (S.E.A.L.) Laboratory. Cort previously held an academic appointment at Florida International University in Miami, FL (USA). He earned his BA from DePaul University in Chicago, IL (USA), and his MA and PhD from Wayne State University, in Detroit, MI (USA), where he was a Thomas C. Rumble Research Fellow, and the recipient of the Ross & Margaret Stagner Award. Cort's research focuses broadly on issues related to aging and work processes, sustainable employability, and applications of lifespan development theory.

Malcolm Sargeant LLB, PhD is Professor of Labour Law at Middlesex University Business School, London, United Kingdom. He has written extensively on discrimination issues and, in particular on age discrimination. Books include *Age Discrimination* (Gower Publishing, 2011), *Age Discrimination and Diversity* (Ed. Cambridge University Press, 2011), and *Discrimination and the Law* (Routledge, 2013).

Heike Simone Schröder is a Postdoctoral Researcher at WU Vienna University of Economics and Business, Vienna (Austria). She received a PhD in HRM from Middlesex University Business School, London (United Kingdom) in 2011 and was a Visiting Researcher at Keio University, Tokyo (Japan) in 2009. Her research is on demographic change and workforce aging in Germany, Britain and Japan. Using institutional theory, institutional entrepreneurship and life course theory lenses, she explores how workforce aging affects and is managed by stakeholders such as the state, trade unions, firms and individual workers.

Kirk Scott is Associate Professor of Economic History at Lund University, Sweden and guest researcher in demography at the Stockholm University Demographic Unit. His research lies primarily in the intersection between immigrant integration and demography, with focuses on labor market integration in general, and its impact on demographic behavior in particular. To this end, interest has been both on the economic and demographic integration of immigrants themselves, as well as the pathways through which the children of immigrants integrate into the host society. Parallel with these studies, Scott has become increasingly interested in the economic impacts of population aging, and potential policy answers to the challenges caused by an aging population. Scott is a past president of the Swedish Demographic Association and the Nordic Demographic Association, and served as Dean of the European Doctoral School of Demography 2009–2011.

Johannes Siegrist was Professor of Medical Sociology at the Faculty of Medicine, University of Düsseldorf, until his retirement in 2012. Recently, he was awarded a Senior Professorship of Work Stress Research at this University where he continues his scientific activities, with a special focus on social determinants of healthy aging. Together with his team he developed the effort–reward imbalance model of stressful work which is applied in many investigations worldwide. He received several national and international distinctions of scholarship.

Bram Vanhoutte is a Research Associate at the Cathie Marsh Centre for Census and Survey Research of the University of Manchester. His current research focuses on aspects of inequality and gender in mental health, well-being, health and ageing. He obtained his PhD in the Social Sciences (University of Leuven), and holds MAs in Sociology (Free University Brussels) and Economy (University of Ghent).

Penny Vera-Sanso is Lecturer of Development Studies and Social Anthropology at Birkbeck, University of London. She has published widely on ageing, gender, poverty and work in urban and rural South India and is Principal Investigator of the project on which this article is based, 'Ageing, Poverty and Neoliberalism in Urban South India', (RES-352-25-0027), and of its follow-on project, 'Ageing and Poverty: the working lives of older people in India' (ES/J020788/1). Her current interest is on the invisibility of older people's work, its role in supporting the national and global economy and the means by which older people's rights as workers and citizens can be strengthened.

Birgit Verworn is a Researcher at the Helmholtz Centre for Environmental Research in Leipzig. She received her diploma in mechanical engineering in 1996 and worked as a process engineer for Procter & Gamble until 1998. From 1999 until 2004 Birgit Verworn was a researcher at the Technical University of Hamburg-Harburg and received her PhD in innovation management in 2004. In 2004 and 2005 she worked as a technology consultant and continued her research at the Technical University Cottbus in the area of innovation and human resource management. There she received her postdoctoral lecture qualification (habilitation) in 2009 and became full Professor for Organization and Management at the Dresden University of Applied Sciences. Her research areas include demographic change, innovation management and research management.

Morten Wahrendorf is a Sociologist with substantial expertise in research on health inequalities, life course epidemiology, work stress and healthy aging. He obtained his PhD in Sociology in 2009 at the Department of Medical Sociology of the University Düsseldorf, Germany. In 2011 he was awarded a postdoctoral fellowship from the German Research Foundation to work at the International Centre for Life Course Studies in Society and Health at Imperial College London.

Anna Wanka studied sociology and law at the University of Vienna. She is junior researcher and currently doing her PhD in sociology at the University of Vienna. Her research foci are aging populations and demographic change, education and spatial sociology.

Doreen Weber (née Schwarz) has been employed at the Norddeutsche Landesbank since 2011 where she works in the division of finance and risk controlling. Previously, from 2004,

Doreen Weber was a scientist at the Chair of Organization, Human Resource Management and General Management at the Brandenburg University of Technology in Cottbus, and received her PhD in economics in 2010. Her research interests still include strategic human resource management, demographic change, and the system dynamics approach. She is an expert in strategic workforce planning as well as in forecasting and measuring the value of human capital. To transfer the theoretical knowledge, she co-founded simthemis(R) in 2007 and advises private and communal companies on the effects of demographic change and their strategic course of action.

Jennica R. Webster is an Assistant Professor in the Department of Management at Marquette University. She received a PhD from Central Michigan University, a MS from the University of Wisconsin Oshkosh, and a BA from Bowling Green State University. Prior to joining Marquette University she was an Assistant Professor at Northern Illinois University. Dr. Webster's research and consulting interests lie in the areas of occupational stress, job attitudes and gender in the workplace. She has published her research in several book chapters and journals such as the *Journal of Vocational Behavior*, *Journal of Business and Psychology*, *Career Development International*, *European Journal of Work and Organizational Psychology* and *Psychology of Women Quarterly*.

Jing Wen is a postdoctoral researcher at the State Key Lab of Software Engineering, Wuhan University. She was a visiting student in the Department of Informatics at the University of California, Irvine in 2010, where she studied the use of social networking games for intergenerational relationship and family communication.

Bo Xie is an Associate Professor in the School of Nursing and School of Information at the University of Texas at Austin. She received her PhD in Science and Technology Studies from Rensselaer Polytechnic Institute, her MS in Psychology from Peking University, and her BMedSci from the West China School of Medicine in Chengdu, China. Her research focuses on health informatics interventions that can promote older adults' use of information and communication technologies for health information, communication, and decision-making (i.e., e-health literacy) that can have important implications for patient–provider relationships and health outcomes. Her research is funded by the National Institutes of Health.

Keith L. Zabel, MA, is a doctoral student at Wayne State University in Detroit, MI (USA). Keith earned his BA from Albion College in Albion, MI (USA) and his MA from Wayne State University in Detroit, MI (USA), where he is currently a National Science Foundation Graduate Research Fellow. Keith's research focuses broadly on issues related to mentoring, generational differences in the workplace, and aging and work processes.

1

The Aging Workforce: Individual, Organizational and Societal Opportunities and Challenges

Ronald J. Burke, Cary L. Cooper and John Field

Someone once said that the only sure things in life were death and taxes. We can now add a third sure thing to this list: an aging global workforce. This introductory chapter sets the context for this *Handbook* by reviewing issues contributing to, and the effects of, an aging workforce on individuals, families, organizations and societies as a whole. These issues are then addressed in significantly more detail in the chapters that follow.

The aging workforce has emerged as a major issue for individuals, organizations, and countries (Anderson, 2009; Bloom, Canning & Sevilla, 2003; Hankin, 2004; Hedge, Borman & Lammlein, 2006; Magnus, 2008; Shultz & Adams, 2007). Although interest in an aging workforce might be traced as far back as the 1950s, it has had little impact on policy and practice until recently (see Griffiths, 1997, for a review). Why haven't governments and organizations responded sooner to these demographic patterns? On the one hand, thinking about these patterns requires thinking in terms of decades rather than years. And politicians are typically concerned with the next political cycle, and business leaders with the short term. In addition, facts and information were hard to come by being spread across a range of different disciplines (e.g., sociology, psychology, gerontology, economics, public policy, business management). Thus countries and organizations are generally not well prepared for these changes (Lam, 2011). There has been some 'talk' by governments and organizations but little 'action'.

It is estimated that the world population will either peak or stabilize around 2050 after growing for hundreds of years at an increasing rate. Much of this is due to a declining birth rate in most economically developed countries. And the population will be aging because of these lower birth rates and better health care resulting in people living longer.

In the US, the senior population will represent over 20 million of the total population within the next 50 years, a dramatic increase in the number of seniors from 2000 (US Census Bureau, 2005). Between 1950 and 2000, the percentage of the world's population older than 60 grew about 8–10%; from 2000 to 2050, this figure is expected to more than double to reach 21%. In Japan and Western Europe, there they predict a 40% increase during the latter time period.

An aging workforce, a declining birth rate, and a trend to earlier retirement have come together to create skills shortage, termed a 'war for talent' by some (Michaels, Handfield-Jones & Axelrod, 2001). This is reflected in both labor shortages (loss of older employees through retirement, more difficulty recruiting younger workers, retention of current employees will be more difficult) and skills shortages (loss of experienced older employees, difficulty recruiting younger employees due to increased competition). And although Canada and the US are similar to Japan and Western Europe in terms of lower birth rates and aging populations, both Canada and the US have relatively high rates of immigration to partly offset effects of an aging population. But concerns have emerged in countries encouraging immigration in terms of assimilating immigrants, providing job opportunities for them in more difficult economic times, and addressing concerns about backlash against immigrants – particularly strong in Western Europe.

In order to address these challenges, organizations need to begin a dialogue on what strategy would work best for them, there is no 'one size fits all' approach that makes sense (Cappelli & Novelli, 2011) It should, however, start with retention planning to make sure that valuable employees remain throughout the organization, targeted selection that focuses on important knowledge and skills that fill positions in the organization, managing the culture change as older employees leave and new employees join the organization to enshrine the values deemed necessary, and starting an aging

workforce dialogue involving central organizational decision makers.

There is increasing discussion of a generation gap. Older workers are enjoying the current level of retirement benefits while younger workers are paying for these benefits. There will be a growing number of retirees and a shrinking number of workers paying for their retirement in the future – perhaps creating a growing generational divide.

In addition societies define aging differently. Are the aged seen as reliant or dependent, as poor or as filling an important place in society? Aging can be seen in some societies as a blessing rather than a problem or difficulty. But there are some obvious burdens that aging places on a society such as increasing health care needs and costs, more elder care, and greater pension demands. In addition older workers get paid more and represent higher costs than do younger workers. But the aged also can represent opportunities as there will be a need for new products and services for the aged. As the aged become a critical mass, in Europe currently a third of the population is over 65, they become a force to be reckoned with. About 90% of the elderly are healthy and they vote at a higher rate than do younger men and women.

On the organizational front, Ernst and Young has conducted surveys (their Aging Workforce Survey) among Fortune 1000 companies and concluded (1) that no single company has developed or implemented a comprehensive solution that addresses the total problem, (2) retaining key employees and maintaining intellectual capital were the human capital issues of greatest concern, increasing in importance over the two most recent surveys, and (3) the impact of the aging workforce extended beyond the executive level to middle management. Their 2007 survey showed that the aging workforce had become a more important concern among these firms: 70% now considered issues of an aging workforce to be important compared to only 38% two years earlier.

Finally, at the individual level, there is increasing evidence about the relationship of aging and cognitive and coordination skills, changes in needs and priorities, health and physical well-being, financial security and retirement. A recent longitudinal study carried out in the US using a very large sample of retirees reported that men and women who worked in some capacity following retirement fared better both psychologically and physically.

Some countries, including Singapore many states in India, have extended their retirement age. Most European countries have raised, or are in the process of raising, the age at which state pensions kick in, and while European Union (EU) legislation on age discrimination has not removed the principle of age-based retirement, it has enabled many employees to extend their working lives. Other countries, including Canada, have done away with mandatory retirement allowing individuals who want to work beyond the previously-legislated age of 65 to do so.

AGING, WORK AND SOCIETY

Aging has emerged as a major and urgent issue for individuals, organizations and governments. It is also a rapidly growing area for academic research. Current concerns focus on the implications of aging for economic competitiveness, innovation, public services, health and well-being and education, as well as the implications for relationships and financial transfers between the generations. And this is a truly global phenomenon, affecting not only North America and Europe, but also many Asian societies such as Japan, Taiwan and Hong Kong, Australasia and some Latin American societies.

The OECD, WHO and World Bank have all warned of predictable impending problems. Yet European Union policies on workforce and social aging, for example, are clearly at odds with policies designed for other domains. Public policy fears over pensions sustainability, health provision and workforce supply are nowhere matched by planned interventions and measures to deal with the problems. Where governments have tried to tackle the most significant and immediate challenges, as over public sector pensions, they have met with heated opposition.

INCREASING RESEARCH ATTENTION BEING PAID TO AGING

It should come as no surprise that increased research attention is being devoted to understanding the effects of aging, factors associated with successful aging and ways to improve the quality of life of the elderly. Here are two recent examples of this interest. First, the Canadian government is funding a large longitudinal study of factors associated with successful aging (Teotonio, 2012). It will involve 50,000 people between 45 and 65 and run over 20 years. Information collected will examine biological, behavioral, psychological, spatial, lifestyle and economic factors. Second, an International Conference on Aging, Mobility and Quality of Life was held at the University of Michigan in June 2012. The following appeared on their conference program. Since understanding aging is a multi-disciplinary effort, experts from a variety of fields presented their work: gerontologists/geriatricians; transport researchers, operators and regulators; psychologists, behavioral researchers; urban planning researchers and policy makers; safety researchers; mechanical/electrical engineers form industry and academia (vehicle design, assistive technologies); tourism/leisure researchers/industry; occupational therapists; and medical professionals. Content streams fell into two broad categories. One considered mobility-related characteristics and activities of elderly people and included spatial cognition and way finding, social participation, travel behavior, exercise and health, tourism and leisure, personal security, transport safety and aging in developing and newly industrializing countries. A second considered technological and policy responses such as building designs, urban

planning and environmental design, roadway
design, vehicle design, ICT, assistive technologies, gerontechnology, transport policy,
and community transport.

ISSUES RAISED BY AN AGING WORKFORCE: CHALLENGES AND OPPORTUNITIES

A staggering challenge

The aging population has been described in
dramatic ways by terms such as 'a demographic time bomb' and an 'old age tsunami'.
This somewhat apocalyptic language has
even become something of a cliché, but it
should not disguise the unprecedented nature
of this change. According to the United
Nations, the elderly population of the world
is growing at its fastest rate ever. By 2050,
there will be more than two billion people
aged 60 or over.

Every day, a few hundred thousand people
move into their 60s. These people have talent, experiences, skills and knowledge. There
has never been such a large group of people in
this category. Societies cannot afford to 'waste'
or 'throw away' these resources (Morrow-
Howell, Hinterlong & Sherraden, 2006). But
there is a lag between how best to capitalize
on these resources and current attitudes and
policies.

A shrinking workforce

In France, more than a million people took to
the streets in 2010 in protest over plans to
raise the retirement age from 60 to 62 in
2018. Germany's efforts to integrate 3.5 million Turkish immigrants without giving them
access to citizenship has failed to incorporate
them into German society. Both of these are
examples of responses to an aging population. As population growth rates slowed and
stopped, fewer working age people were
present. The solutions to this problem are to
raise the retirement age, encourage more
immigration, or both. By 2050, most Western

countries will spend 27–30% of their GDP
on retirees (Saunders, 2010).

A total fertility rate of 2.1 maintains a
country's population. This figure is now
lower in most industrialized countries, and
higher in some non-industrialized countries.
And 18% of US women reach the end of
their childbearing years without giving birth,
up from 10% in the 1970s. But this rate had
held steady over the past decade. More
women with advanced degrees are now having children.

The globalization of business, along with
an aging workforce, will increase demands
for talent world wide. Some countries (e.g.,
UK, US, Canada, Germany) relied on immigration to fill the need. The globalization of
business has resulted in developing countries
such as India and China now coming to these
formerly host countries for talent.

REGIONAL DIFFERENCES IN POPULATION AGING AND RETIREMENT

We must also consider regional differences
(Blossfeld, Buchholz & Kurz, 2011; Hofacher,
2010) Press, politicians and academics alike
have shown considerable interest in the pace
of economic growth in East Asia. In explaining the reasons for this Asian growth pre-
mium, though, there has been remarkably
little attention to demography. Since 1990,
Asian nations have undertaken major economic reforms in response to financial crises and other factors, and these have been
the major focus in previous studies. More
recent research suggests that demographic
change has been a major factor contributing
to cross-country differences in economic
growth through to 2005, leading to an
urgent need for policy to offset potential
negative effects of aging populations in the
future. This is likely to play out very differently in China, India, Japan and Korea,
given the very different age balances of
their respective workforces. Conventionally, Asian nations are often seen as models

of intergenerational caring, with high levels of respect for older adults in particular. Recent socio-economic changes seem to be impacting intergenerational relationships and care for older generations within Chinese families.

Contrary to popular belief, many more older people live in the developing world than in the rich north. Despite this, the condition of older people and the wider effects of population aging are still peripheral concerns in development policy. This has obvious implications for social policy, economic policy and international aid.

In some countries (US, UK, Denmark) where people retire later, 65–70% of men were still working in their early 60s; in France and Italy, 12–20% worked in their early 60s, and in Spain, 38%. Economic incentives create large differences in retirement age. Countries with early retirement have tax policies, pensions, disability and other measures that encourage people to retire at an earlier age. The 2008 economic collapse has resulted in several countries being in the process of increasing their retirement ages.

Demographic changes in the workforce can affect regional competitiveness. The aging and immigration literatures, though large, are rarely integrated. Immigration, particularly of entrepreneurs and highly skilled workers, can influence regional competitiveness. Countries need to be able to attract and select immigrants that can and will contribute, orient and socialize them to nuances of the host country, and reduce impediments to their contribution (e.g., a lack of host country experience). Poot and Strutt (2012) suggest policy and program efforts to more effectively use immigrants to both increase the size of the available labor force and add to the competitiveness of host countries.

The demographic patterns in developed and developing countries are very different. In developed countries there will be more elderly and fewer young people in the workforce. In developing countries there will be fewer elderly and more younger people in the workforce. These characteristics will continue to increase the gap between rich and poor countries as a result.

HUMAN RESOURCE MANAGEMENT POLICIES AND PRACTICES

Most workplaces and jobs have been designed without any regard to capabilities, concerns, limitations, preferences and needs associated with worker age. We need to identify risk factors that pose particular challenges to older workers, and outline strategic proposals for reducing risks to health and well-being, while helping to prolong a productive working life.

Demographic changes in the workplace will require new human resource management (HRM) strategies. As 'baby boomers' age, they will likely retire as a group causing a loss of organizational knowledge and memory and the need to recruit in a time of labor shortages (DeLong, 2004). Thus organizations need to develop long-term human resource management strategies that address an aging and shrinking workforce using a 'resource-based' view of the organization.

In addition, countries have different policies and legislation related to aging and work and these differences are reflected in HRM practices related to the employment of older workers (Schroeder, Hofacker & Muller-Camen, 2009). For example, Schroeder, Hofacker and Muller-Camen (2009) compared HRM practices in Germany and Britain as they related to employment of older workers.

The relationship between quality of work, health and retirement has also come to the fore. Increasing life expectancy, coupled with ballooning national debt and deficits, call for later retirement ages. Early retirement is caused by pension and social security arrangements, health, and employment conditions. Recent research, mainly European, has shown a strong relationship between quality of work and intended (later) retirement.

Improving work conditions seems like a viable initiative for increasing the available workforce (Ilmarinen, 2001, 2006a; Ilmarinen & Rantaqnen, 1999).

MOTIVATING WORKERS TO CONTINUE WORKING BEYOND THEIR RETIREMENT AGE

Given the looming shortage of workers it may be in some organizations' best interests to motivate employees to continue working beyond their retirement ages. A central question then becomes why do some people want to stay in the workforce after reaching normal retirement age? Some factors already identified include being in good health, having some financial need, and a high work attachment. Rousseau (2005) suggests that arrangements that employees strike with their employing organization, called i-deals (idiosyncratic deals) also can play a key role in such decisions. I-deals result in highly personalized work arrangements that meet important employee needs. Bal, De Jong, Jansen and Bakker (2012) examined the role of two types of i-deals, as well as two types of unit climates in older working employees' statements on when they planned to retire. The two types of i-deals were flexibility (e.g., choice in when one starts the work day) and development (e.g., access to training and development opportunities). The two types of work unit climates were accommodative (e.g., older workers are encouraged to retire early) and development (e.g., older workers are encouraged to develop and enhance their skills). They collected data from 1083 employees working in two units within two health care organizations. They found that the presence of flexibility i-deals was positively related to motivation to continue working and that unit climate moderated the relationship of development i-deals and motivation to continue working. One caveat is that the dependent variable was intention to continue working past normal retirement age and not actually continuing to work beyond normal retirement

age. But it seems safe to conclude that certain HR initiatives such as the opportunity to create personal i-deals and the creation of work unit climates that support development and the utilization of the skills of older workers (not the encouragement of early retirement) can impact employee continuance.

WORKPLACE CHANGES THAT ACCOMMODATE OLDER WORKERS

It is possible to design a workplace to make the environment more compatible with the abilities of older employees. These changes typically involve redesigning the physical demands of the jobs themselves using ergonomic analyses (less heavy lifting, less time pressure, avoid night work and shift work) and reducing levels of workplace stressors such as overload, ambiguity, conflict, age discrimination, work–family life difficulties often compounded by eldercare responsibilities and being in the sandwich generation.

In an aging workforce, there are significant potential efficiency gains from the use of new technologies. Guidelines for older users are now being developed by standards bodies and are implemented in domains such as Web design. Much of the focus of human factors research has been on improving efficiency in the performance of aging adults in the workforce, but reducing errors and increasing comfort and satisfaction in health-related activities should receive greater attention. Thus it is important to look at the relationship between technological change and workforce aging, and will present proposals for developing healthier and more stress-free workplaces.

Some older workers are more successful than others in maintaining high levels of functioning and contribution in spite of losses in some psychological and biological capabilities. Yet it is not clear what we can understand by career and enterprise among older workers, who frequently face barriers and challenges in maintaining productive working lives. We need to look at the prospects of employment and self-employment for older workers, in the context of developing concerns over work–life balance in the third age.

AGING AND JOB PERFORMANCE

Several literature reviews have been undertaken examining the relationship between chronological age and various indicators of job performance (e.g., Avolio & Waldman, 1994; Hedge, Borman & Lemmlein, 2006; Posthuma & Campion, 2009; Waldman & Avolio, 1986). These reviews indicated that age accounted for a relatively small amount of variance in worker cognitive, perceptual and psychomotor abilities, job attitudes and job performance. In fact the evidence seems to suggest that one's mind can function well in middle age and beyond (Strauch, 2010).

Age stereotypes

Posthuma and Campion (2009) offered an extensive review of age stereotypes as they relate to the workplace, evidence relevant to these stereotypes, and human resource management practices that can lessen the impact of these stereotypes. This issue is explored here further in the chapters by Posthuma and Guerrera and by Perry, Hanvongse and Casoinic.

Age stereotypes have relevance for human resource management and work behaviors and experiences of individuals in organizations. Age stereotypes are likely to be both more common and have wider impacts as the workforce ages. And age discrimination is likely to be subtle not flagrant. However, society will need more older workers to remain in the workforce to maintain the economy. In addition, older workers now have to work longer to compensate for pension shortfalls.

Age stereotypes result in organizations not hiring qualified and capable employees. With more older workers remaining in the workforce, it is not surprising then that age discrimination lawsuits against employers have increased. These legal challenges are costly to employers.

Posthuma and Campion (2009) define age stereotypes as 'beliefs and expectations about workers based on their age' (p. 160). Age stereotypes are typically negative, often inaccurate, and obviously distorted. Age stereotypes have consequences; older employees are less likely to be hired, less often selected for training and development and more often targeted for layoffs (Chiu, Chan, Snape & Redman, 2001).

Posthuma and Campion (2009) examine the evidence for the following age stereotypes:

1 Older workers perform less well, they have lower abilities, less motivation and are less productive.
2 Older workers are resistant to change, they are harder to train, less adaptable, and less flexible.
3 Older workers have lower ability to learn, and lower potential for development.
4 Older workers have shorter job tenures, less time to get benefits of training investments.
5 Older workers are more costly, they get higher wages, use benefits more, and are closer to retirement.
6 Older workers are more dependable, more stable, more loyal, more trustworthy, committed to their jobs, less likely to miss work, and less likely to quit.
7 Older workers get lower ratings in selection interviews and performance appraisals.
8 Older workers are more likely to also hold these age stereotypes.
9 The effects of age stereotypes tend to be reduced when job relevant information is available and used.
10 There is a perception that some jobs should be held by employees of a certain age.
11 Age stereotypes are stronger in certain industries (finance, insurance, retail, IT and computing).
12 There are wide individual differences, and there are larger differences within an age group than across age groups.

Based on their review of published research findings, they found support for the following:

1 There was no evidence that older workers perform less well, have lower levels of motivation and are less productive. In fact job performance can improve with age.
2 When declines occur (flexibility, ability to learn, return on training investments) they were found to be small.

3 Age was less important to job performance than levels of employee skill and employee health.
4 Older employees did in fact get lower ratings in selection interviews and performance appraisals.
5 Older employees did have a harder time finding jobs, keeping their jobs and getting promoted.
6 Older employees also held the same age stereotypes.
7 Job relevant information reduced the effects of age stereotypes.

Age discrimination legislation

Age discrimination legislation has been introduced in a number of countries over the last decade, with varied consequences. Only recently has it become clearer that age discrimination affects different groups in different ways (Dennis & Thomas, 2007; Powell, 2010). Recent studies suggest that the oldest and youngest workers are most affected, but women workers of all ages appear to face ageist prejudice based on physical appearance and sexuality. Sargeant's chapter in this volume explores the legal dimensions of age discrimination in greater detail, but it remains unclear how effective legislation can be in countering age discrimination in general, and in particular whether it is capable in its present form of addressing the complex patterns of age discrimination.

The end of mandatory retirement could increase age-discrimination legal cases. Some professional groups and business arrangements such as partnerships (e.g., common among accountants, lawyers, engineers) often require retirement at age 65. Employees in partnerships (usually also owners of the firm) voluntarily sign agreements stating the firm's retirement policies.

Under human rights legislation, employers may be required to accommodate age differences in the workplace just as they must accommodate the disabled. Employers get around the legislation by laying off a number of employees attributed to a restructuring or downsizing and including some younger workers.

ADDRESSING AGING WORKFORCE ISSUES IN A UNIONIZED WORKPLACE

The presence of unions, associations that have historically advocated financial benefits, due process and protection of their members, is an important factor impacting the readiness of workplaces to adapt to the aging workforce. Though labor unions continue to strive to provide important benefits to older workers (pensions, health care) they seem to be resistant to other options of interest to older workers (e.g., part-time work, flexible work hours). Several 'new' challenges facing the union movement as a result of the aging workforce and various options that these challenges present that might be satisfying to both older workers and their employing organizations.

Pitt-Catsouphes, Sano and Matz-Costa (2009), in a study of 578 US organizations employing 50 or more people, examined the effects of a union presence on aging workforce concerns. reported that a union presence was more likely to provide some benefits important to older workers, they were less likely to have a more comprehensive view of flexible work alternatives available to most of their employees. Organizations having unions were less likely to offer health insurance to all employees, and less likely to offer all of the full-time employees family health insurance. In the future, unions are more likely to be more responsive to other needs of older workers, beyond health care and pensions, to the consideration of flexible work arrangements, part-time work, and phased retirement.

ADVANTAGES OF AN AGING POPULATION

Hori, Lehmann, Wah and Wang (2010) identify some possible advantages of an aging population. These include the creation of new services, the opportunities offered by a more diverse workforce, and organizations investing differently in the development of talent.

Benefits to organizations from an aging workforce

Older workers have lots to offer (Shea & Hansen, 2006):

- 42% of boomers want to keep working because it will keep them young, not for financial reasons;
- 22% of Canadians are already working past the age of 65 (Canada Revenue Agency);
- 46% of people who retired between 55 and 60 went back to work (Statistics Canada);

Writing over 15 years ago, Griffiths (1997) proposed both national and organizational solutions such as changing management attitudes towards older workers, training of the workforce, reducing work demands for older workers, changing the work environment to make it more 'age friendly', and creating programs in the workplace and in the wider society that support health promotion.

Hedge, Borman and Lammlein (2006) suggest that organizations need to develop strategies (both policies and practices) that support an older workforce. These need to address, at a minimum, concerns about the skills and knowledge obsolescence of older employees, the development of new skills and knowledge, and ways of rewarding and motivating an older workforce. They advocate specific efforts including targeted recruitment, selection and placing older workers in jobs that fit, job redesign for older workers, the use of flexible work arrangements, flexible compensation and benefits possibilities, enhanced levels of training, a greater emphasis on performance management, supports for career management, and retirement planning seminars for older workers.

WHAT ORGANIZATIONS CAN DO TO COUNTER AGE STEREOTYPES

Posthuma and Campion (2009) suggest several initiatives to reduce the prevalence and effects of age stereotypes in the workplace. At the core of these is the creation of a friendlier climate for older workers that simultaneously reduces the effects of age stereotypes. These include:

- rewarding employees for their long tenures;
- rewarding those that are the keepers of organizational memory and knowledge;
- position older workers as a competitive advantage;
- identify areas of decision making where age stereotypes are more likely to exist;
- be alert to potential bias in employee evaluations – it is advantageous to use more 'objective' methods and processes that are less open to bias;
- use job-related information to inform perceptions and actions;
- add 'complexity' not 'simplification' to the jobs of older workers to support learning;
- be on the alert to potential age biases in selection for training and development, and promotion;
- collect and maintain employee data on attendance, cost, and performance;
- develop training offerings that deal with generational differences, age discrimination, and the benefits of an aging workforce;
- devote extra attention to areas in the workplace more likely to practice age discrimination (IT, sales).

AN EMERGING EMPHASIS ON HEALTH PROMOTION

An aging workforce has increased costs to organizations for health-related coverage and for workers becoming ill or injured and preventing them from working. To address this, employing organizations, in concert with national or local governments, are more active today in promoting the health of their workforce (Costa, Goedhard & Ilmarinen, 2005; Hayashi et al., 2010; Siegrist & Wahrendorf, 2009). This emphasis reduces health care costs, prevents chronic illness and injury, and hopefully reduces the incidence of chronic illness. These programs include smoking cessation, nutrition and exercise counselling, obesity prevention, flu vaccinations, physical health examinations, and employee assistance programs. Shepard (1997) has shown the benefits of physical activity on aging, health and well-being. In addition, physical well-being has been shown to be related to higher levels of mental capital (Cooper, Field, Goswami, Jenkins & Sahakian, 2010).

Benefits of continuing to work

Kalata (2010) reported on the results of a 13-country study showing that work provided an environment that kept individuals functioning optimally. Other evidence indicated that retired individuals did less well on cognitive tests. Why does working matter? Working maintains one's social and personality skills, the routine of getting up in the morning, dealing with other people, and being prompt, dependable and trustworthy. Adams (2011) reported that 54% of baby boomers will work part time, with 10% retiring to start their own businesses.

Factors influencing the decision to retire

As this chapter was being written, retirement was being rethought (Euwals, De Mooij & Van Vuuren, 2009; Sedlar & Miners, 2007). Factors that may have predicted employee retirement decisions twenty years ago (e.g., Feldman, 1994) may not do so today. Aging populations have put pressure on 'pay-as-you-go' pension systems suggesting a trend towards prefunded pension plans. Greater prefunding requires careful risk management, efficient regulation and supervision. More recent economic challenges are also pressing upward shifts in the age of entitlement to statutory pensions. But these attempts to shift responsibilities away from previous pensions regimes have caused enormous social tensions, not only among older adults. In addition there are wide country differences on pensions and retirement.

Most Canadians expect to continue working after retirement. Fifty-five percent of those not retired think they will have to work part time in their current field or in a different

field (Blackwell, 2011). Two-thirds of the working Canadian workforce will receive no company pension. In numbers:

70 – the age at which 20% of Canadians expect to retire;
33 – the percentage who intend to retire before 65;
5 – the percentage of employed Canadians who expect to keep working after retirement;
75 – the percentage worried they will be poor after retirement;
41 – percentage of people aged 18 to 24 who believe they will stop working completely after retirement compared to 27% of people aged 50 to 64 who believe that.

Women tend to be more satisfied with their retirements than are men. Retired individuals reported now spending more money on travel and less money on clothes.

Von Bonsdorff, Huuhtanen, Tuomi and Seitsamo (2009), in a longitudinal study, examined the relationship of personal and work-related psychological factors and the early retirement decision among older women and men. Data were collected from 1101 employees over a one-year follow-up period. Gender differences in early retirement intentions were present both at baseline and at the one-year follow-up. Negative perceptions about work and low work and general life satisfaction were associated with early retirement intentions among women. Among men, poor self-rated work ability and perceived poor health were positively associated with early retirement intentions, as were negative perceptions about work. Schultz and Wang (2007) also found that specific physical health conditions influenced retirement decisions. Thus both work- and health-related factors detected in middle age predicted later early retirement intentions.

IMPLICATIONS OF AN AGING WORKFORCE FOR ORGANIZATIONS

Ilmarinen (2006b) suggests that four fundamental changes need to be made to address issues associated with an aging workforce.

These involve societal changes in its attitudes towards aging, increasing the knowledge levels of managers and supervisors in age-related issues, changes in the nature of working life and flexible work arrangements, and changes in the health care services to meet the increasing demands of older workers. Writing elsewhere, Ilmarinen (2006a) identified three levels of intervention here: the organizational, its culture and management attitudes; the work environment, including the use of ergonomics, and analysis and reduction of job demands; and the individual, taking more responsibility for their own health through engaging in physical exercise, weight management, smoking cessation and seeking out training and educational opportunities.

An aging workforce was seen as having three major implications for organizations. First, the possibility of real culture change as older, longer-tenured people used to working in particular ways leave the workplace. Second, a loss of knowledge, talent and long-term relationships as older employees leave. And third, a loss of leadership knowledge, abilities and skills as these experienced people leave.

In order to address these challenges, organizations need to begin a dialogue on what strategy would work best for them; there is no 'one size fits all' approach that makes sense. It should however start with retention planning to make sure that valuable employees are retained, succession planning that deals with the expected loss of critical employees throughout the organization, targeted selection that focuses on important knowledge and skills that fill positions in your organization, managing the culture change as older employees leave and new employees join the organization to enshrine the values deemed necessary, and starting an aging workforce dialogue involving central organizational decision makers.

QUALITY OF WORK, HEALTH AND RETIREMENT

Siegrist and Wahrendorf (2009) reported results from the Survey of Health, Ageing, and Retirement in Europe (SHARE) study in which data was collected both before and after retirement from about 35,000 people 50 years of age or older in 15 European countries, examining the relationship between quality of work and intended retirement. They found, as have others (Tuomi, Huuhtanen, Nykyri, et al., 2001) a strong correlation between quality of work and intended retirement across the 15 countries. Good quality of work was associated with a lower percentage of intended retirements from work. This study, in line with that of Westerlund, Kivimäki, Singh-Manoux, and their colleagues (2009) indicates that poor quality of work both reduces the health and well-being of employees and increases the likelihood of their retirement, suggests that both organizational policies and actions, and national policies, need to emphasize the improvement of working life.

DO SOME PEOPLE BENEFIT FROM RETIREMENT?

Westerlund, Vahtera and Ferrie, and their colleagues (2010) found, in a large study of retired employees at a French national gas and electricity company, that retirement was associated with large reductions in mental and physical fatigue as well as smaller decreases in depression. Rates of major chronic diseases did not change with retirement. They attribute improvements with a lessening of worker fatigue.

Aging and health

We need to know more about long-term trends on health and disability among older adults, and to show how these are linked to factors such as socio-economic status, gender, financial well-being, social support and ethnicity, and to identify implications for care and for lifestyles.

As the population ages, there will be an increase in the number of cases of dementia. These individuals will require more support from caregivers for their ailing loved ones.

The costs associated with Canada's drug program, the spending on medical services and drugs, increase dramatically with age. Health care spending for those over 65 is twice as high as for those under 65, and 7.7 times as high for those aged 90 or older (National Post, 2011). There is some concern that less affluent people over 65 may be spending less on drugs and doctors visits, however, as they face rising costs and fixed incomes.

The Gallup-Healthways Well-being Index (WBI) showed that people over 65 in the US experienced the highest overall well-being. With age, Americans indicated increases in healthy behaviors, more satisfaction with their work environment, and access to necessities. Older Americans reported higher levels of emotional health, less sadness and depression. The over 65 years of age group, however, reported slightly lower levels of life satisfaction and physical health compared to other age groups in the study. Advances in medicine and increased health awareness effects are contributing to a longer life. These instill healthier behaviors to reduce obesity, and stopping smoking.

Aging and health care

In 2011, 15% of the Canadian population was 65 or older but will increase to 24% by 2036 (Statistics Canada, 2010). This will require integrated collaboration between health and social services to guarantee care for a growing group of people with multiple chronic ill health conditions (Canadian Institute for Health Information, 2011). Most Canadians believe that the demands placed on the health care system by an aging population will reduce access and lower the quality of health care. The Canadian Medical Association believes that the current health care system will be unable to meet future needs. Factors increasing demands on the health care system include: Canadians not taking responsibility for their own health (33%), an aging population (30%), higher

demands and expectations of the system by Canadians (21%), and new medical advances (16%). Thus 51% of Canadians thought that health care services would get worse in 2011, 35% thought it would get better. But it is important not to blame older people and create generational tensions.

Aging and cognitive performance

Krieger (2010) reviews studies showing that, on average, it becomes harder to multi-task or remember to complete a task after being distracted by another task as one ages. Cognitive disorders such as senility and dementia were reported by 5% of seniors over 65 according to the Agency for Health Care Research and Quality (AHRQ). Seniors aged 85 and older were more likely to have reported one or more cognitive disorders (18.4%) compared with seniors aged 75 to 84 (6%) and seniors aged 65 to 74 (1.1%). Seniors having more education and higher incomes reported having fewer cognitive impairments. Average annual health care expenses for seniors reporting one or more cognitive disorders totalled $15,549 compared to $9,019 for seniors without any cognitive disorders.

Alzheimer's and dementia

In a newly released report (2012), the World Health Organization (WHO) stated that about 36 million people currently live with dementia worldwide, more than half (58%) living in low- and middle-income countries. They estimate that this figure will rise by over 70% by 2050. Treating and caring for those with dementia currently costs more than US$604 billion per year due to loss of income of those with dementia and their caregivers, and the provision of health and social care.

Only eight countries worldwide have national programs to address dementia. Countries need to improve early diagnosis, raise public awareness of the disease and reduce its stigma, and offer more support and better care to care givers. Early diagnosis, even in wealthy countries, falls short. Only one-fifth to one-half of dementia cases are identified. Sadly, individuals with dementia and their families are typically isolated.

Strengthening care giving is vital. Most care giving is undertaken by informal caregivers-partners, children and other family members and friends. Caregivers then are also likely to suffer from depression, anxiety and reduced physical health as well. Caregivers also suffer economically. The WHO recommends developing programs to provide better support to caregivers, making community-based services available to support families so that individuals with dementia do not have to undergo expensive residential care.

Most countries have relatively few doctors that specialize in geriatrics. Among its 68,000 doctors, Canada has fewer than 300 that specialize in geriatrics. The number of people in their eighties is increasing, escalating the health care burden in Canada about $18,000 per person, a year. And 65 and over is the fastest growing age group in Canada, estimated to be 23% of the population by 2031.

Generational wars

Some have suggested that the increasing number of seniors in retirement will put additional demands on younger women and men still in the workforce to contribute additional monies to their support (Johnson, 2011; Kotlikoff & Burns, 2004). In this regard, Germany is contemplating placing extra taxes on the young to pay for the costs of supporting creasing numbers of older people, a 'demographic reserve' tax (Waterfield, 2012). It would apply to people over 25, thought to be one percent of income. This scenario suggests a generational war for resources. But viewing increased longevity as adding more years to mid-life rather than at the end might suggest a different outcome. Millions of women and men continuing to make contributions to society in their later mid-life could increase economic and psychological well-being of countries.

Generational tensions?

There may not be generational war but there seems to be generational tension. Fairlie's chapter examines claims and evidence on generational differences on the importance of work. Recent studies have shown that Generation X-ers, born between 1961 and 1981, and now in their 40s and 50s, may be getting plateaued in mid-career as baby boomers born in 1960 and earlier remain in their jobs longer and educated younger Gen Y-ers, born between 1982 and 2000, are being promoted faster (Flavelle, 2012). These findings emerged in a study of Canadian banks conducted by Price Waterhouse and Coopers. Generation X-ers comprised the largest of the three groups (60%). Twenty percent of Gen Y women and men were promoted in a three-year period (2008–2012) while only ten percent of Gen X-ers were promoted in this same time period. Although carried out in banking, these findings likely apply to other industries as well. They suggest that organizations need to pay special attention to keeping Gen Xers engaged.

'Age Rage' is a label put on negative attitudes that the young have towards seniors who are seen as getting a 'free ride' (Cravit, 2012). The reality does not seem to support this anger. First, seniors have paid taxes, and more taxes, than any other age group as well as paying into their countries' pension and old age security systems. Second, more government money allocated to pensions and health care reflects growth in the number of seniors. Third, seniors continue to make contributions through still working and taking care of the needs of their parents and children. More children are still at home living with their parents and 'multi-generational' families have increased in number as well. Thus seniors seem to be still contributing and not exploiting the young (Kohli, 2004).

INTERGENERATIONAL RELATIONSHIPS IN THE WORKPLACE

As the workforce ages, more employers will be supervising others older than they are.

Employees will have to value older workers and training younger managers on how to manage them. There will be a need to value older workers for their experience, training, mentoring, knowledge, and their workplace needs for flexibility and respect. There will also be a need to involve older workers in decision making, recognize their experience and contributions, delegate smartly. Older people's needs include feeling valued, continuing to be productive, keeping mentally strong, a flexible schedule with reduced work hours.

Generational conflicts are inevitable (Alsop, 2008; Erickson, 2009, 2008), but manageable. Individuals have different views on approaches to balancing work and life. Individuals in organizations need to listen to each other and make accommodations. Some organizational interventions have also been proposed;. These include training programs involving older and Generation Y employees, and feedback sessions in which employees are asked to identify potential issues across generations and offer suggestions for improvements.

The best is to combine the skills, experience and knowledge of older and younger employees. But there can be clashes and tensions between younger and older employees. It has been noted that some Gen X-ers, born between 1961 and 1974, can be unimpressed with older workers. It works best if the workplace becomes a democracy in that older more experienced workers do not tell younger employees what to do but instead an open dialogue is encouraged between different age groups.

DelCampo, Haggerty, Haney and Knippel (2010) explore the multi-generational workforce. They observe four distinct and different generations in the workplace. Each generation has different expectations, beliefs, values, wants and approaches to learning. As a result they work differently creating the possibility of tension and misunderstandings.

Managing these four generations raises challenges for organizations. Firms need to create coordinating processes and a culture supporting communication, cooperation among all workforce generations. Managers need to see generational differences as strengths not as liabilities. In time, the newest generation termed Gen Y or Millennials will come to change the workplace.

A new vision of aging

Advocacy groups (Canadian Association of Retired People, American Association of Retired People) have been working to foster a new vision of aging and champion the needs of the elderly. They have worked tirelessly on three fronts: Advocacy – health care, pensions, eldercare; Benefits – getting discounts on insurance, entertainment, educational offerings; and Community – social events organized by various chapters.

Freedman (2011) proposes a 'third stage', the period between middle and old age – roughly between 60 and 80 – in adult development. With people living longer, having them navigate a long period of retirement will be difficult, and a waste of talent, for both individuals and societies.

People's lives were traditionally seen as having three phases: education, work and retirement. Advances in health care have extended lives. The knowledge economy has made jobs physically easier. But retiring early may no longer be common (financial constraints, demographic factors, small company pensions).

People today are more interested in working past 'normal or expected' retirement ages due in part to better health, being in second marriages, and more having children still needing financial support.

Staying at work supports mental and physical well-being (as a result of social interactions, and a sense of meaning).

The third stage

Increasing longevity has caused experts in aging to rethink life stages. Previously, retirement followed mid-life. Now there seems to be a gap, another stage, between mid-life and retirement (Freedman, 2011). Phrases such as 'the young old', and the 'working retired' have been used to describe this period or stage. Laslett (1991) called this period the 'third age'. This stage might also last several years with millions of women and men in it. This stage is also different from the 'mid life crisis' concept in that rather than being a time of turmoil, regret and dissatisfaction, with some individuals making radical life changes (e.g., divorce, cosmetic surgery, dramatic and unpredictable changes in careers). Instead the third stage is a time for creative reinvention (Bateson, 2010; Bedell & Young, 2009; Freedman, 2007).

Millions of women and men, now in their fifties and sixties, are examining their lives and their futures, looking both back and forward. Most of these people are now free to think about what they see as important, how to use their talents and experience, rather than being assigned to retirement. Laslett (1991), in fact, describes this stage as an opportunity for fulfillment, a time for new learning, development growth, and new possibilities (Hannon, 2010). Central questions that might be considered include: Am I just getting started now or am I half finished? What might be next? How long will I continue to feel energetic and young? We don't live forever. What does it feel like to be getting older in a society that values the young? Freedman (2011) identifies two challenges for third stage women and men. One is internal – involving psychological and identity issues. The other is external – involving structural factors in society. What might we now do in a lengthening time period before retirement? Individuals at this point consider *time lived* and the experiences and skills they have accumulated in this journey; *time left to live* – this generally involves identifying what and who is important to them, what really matters, and *time beyond one's life* – the issue of generativity, how can I make the world and future better.

Freedman (2011) offers ten approaches to helping individuals in the third stage (see also Field, 2011). These involve efforts by individuals, organizations, and various levels of government.

1 *Think differently.* A need to think differently and imaginatively about the period between mid-life and old age.
2 *Create the category.* We need to give credibility to the existence of the third stage.
3 *A gap year for grown-ups.* Make time available in mid-life for reflection, renewal and new directions.
4 *Higher education.* Provide support for continued self- and human capital development.
5 *National service.* A need to create vehicles for participating in community service ventures.
6 *Elevate encore careers.* Support the notion of second careers and working longer before retiring.
7 *Revamp HR policies.* There is a need to create HR policies and programs that help employees transition to a new stage of work and life. Examples include: flextime to care for aging parents or grandchildren, part-time or part-year jobs, training to update skills, and reducing/stopping age discrimination in hiring.
8 *Individual purpose accounts. (and more).* Making money and resources available to support the transition (e.g. back to school, skills retraining).
9 *An Encore Bill.* Developing and passing legislation and policies supporting men and women in the third stage such as developing their human capital, dealing with financial concerns, and making the switch to new life and work roles.
10 *Get organized.* There is a need to develop a social movement of individuals and organizations that benefit from these changes to the third stage and support it.

AGING GRACEFULLY

Valliant (1977, 2003) reports findings from the study of Adult Development conducted at Harvard University. This study followed three separate cohorts of 824 women and men, all selected as teenagers and followed them for over 50 years. The respondents came from different social classes, races, education levels, and places of residence. The sample included 268 advantaged Harvard graduates, 456 socially disadvantaged university men (blue collar), and 90 middle class intellectually gifted women. Respondents were seen several times over this period. Data collection involved social history, childhood history, psychological and physical health assessments, work and marital experiences and satisfactions, social relationships and life satisfaction.

Here are some of the results.

- Alcohol abuse was associated with unsuccessful aging since it damages social relationships.
- Learning to play and to create following retirement, and learning how to add younger friends as older ones were lost, added more to life satisfaction than retirement income.
- Objective good physical health was less important to successful aging than subjective good health.
- A good marriage at 50 was associated with successful aging at 80 whereas low cholesterol levels were not.
- Those enjoying their lives aged more successfully.
- Individuals that accepted their lives aged more successfully.
- Individuals that helped younger people realize their goals, and those contributing to making their communities better, aged more successfully.
- Individuals that aged successfully accepted the realities of aging.
- Better physical heath was predicted by not smoking or not being a heavy smoker, not abusing alcohol, having a stable marriage, undertaking some exercise, not being overweight and having an adaptive coping style, termed mature psychological defences. Those in better physical health more often saw positives instead of negatives.

Freedman and Martin (2012), based on over 1500 people from the Terman 80-year longitudinal study at Stanford, examined predictors of a long life. People living long lives were more conscientious, worked hard and were socially connected. Conscientious people were responsible organized, pragmatic, planful, more successful in their careers, encountered fewer stressors as a result, were in more stable marriages and careers, and drank less and were less likely to smoke. All lives have Ups and Downs but perseverance is associated with a more fulfilling life experience (Wheatley, 2010). Somewhat surprisingly,

cheerful, happy-go-lucky people had the greatest risk of dying early (White, 2011). Freedman and Martin's work seems to debunk several myths about living to an old age such as the benefits of exercising, being religious, and staying married.

SOME CONCLUSIONS

A review of key demographic, health and attitude findings related to the aging workforce

- There has been a large increase in life expectancy after 1900.
- There has been a very large increase in the elderly over 65, and a decrease in individuals under 15 years of age and between 15 and 40.
- Increases in those over 65 and decreases in those under 15 are worldwide.
- Women continue to live longer than men.
- There will be more years post-retirement, estimated to be 19.0 for men and 23.1 for women.
- In 2000 the world population was relatively young but by 2025 the world population will have aged considerably (particularly among those 60 and older).
- Fewer workers to retire.
- There will likely be a labor shortage.
- Fewer elderly people now have physical or mental limitations that prevent them from working.
- Major reasons for continuing to work involve a need for money, enjoyment of the job and of working, to save money for one's retirement, and to have the resources to maintain one's health insurance.
- Four different 'generations' currently exist in the workplace: Traditionalists, born between 1928 and 1945; Baby Boomers, born between 1946 and 1964; Generation X-ers, born between 1965 and 1980; and Generation Y-ers or Millennials, born between 1981 and 2000.

Some 'big picture' issues raised in this review

- There is an urgent need to get the economy growing to deal with the aging population and the high levels of unemployment, particularly among youth.
- Most countries need to cut their budget deficits while increasing their investments in growth.

- Unfortunately all developed countries are facing large budget deficits.
- The citizens of some countries are resisting attempts by their governments to cut their budget deficits by reducing services to them, raising the age of retirement, reducing levels of pensions, and raising taxes.
- How to have an older worker population work longer without harming their health, the prospects of younger workers, and organizational productivity.
- There seem to be potential tensions or paradoxes in coming to grips with an aging workforce and aging population including: the elderly and the young, growth and budget cutting, developed countries and developing countries, global competition and international collaboration strategies, individuals and countries having higher standards of living and individuals and countries having lower standards of living, immigration and increasing unemployment levels of locals.

The need for an integrated approach to the aging population

There needs to be a worldwide collaboration if societies are to deal with an aging global population effectively. Some initiatives that have been proposed include the following.

- Creating jobs for people in their sixties and seventies.
- Developing educational programs for people in their sixties and seventis.
- Dealing with dementia and Alzheimer's.
- Offering incentives for companies to keep people working longer. For example, offering bonuses to workers staying until 70, exempt employers from paying taxes for employees beyond retirement age, more flexible work schedules, telecommuting options, and sabbaticals for education and training.
- Governments need to make the 'aging population' a priority, viewing 'aging' as a cause.
- Slow down increases in health care spending and require the elderly to pay a larger share of their own health care costs.

The chapters in this *Handbook* demonstrate the extensive range of policy initiatives being adopted to address the challenges and opportunities of societal aging, as well as summarising key areas of recent and current research in this critical area. Part 1 opens by identifying some of the key challenges for scholars and policy makers, starting with a long view of population aging in an historical perspective, and placing the issue in its wider global context. Part 2 sharpens the focus to highlight key aspects of aging within the contemporary workplace, which is followed by a series of discussions of management challenges and concerns in Part 3. The chapters in Part 4 turn the spotlight onto the wider social implications of population aging, or at any rate on what we regard as some critical examples of this broader canvas. Finally, we turn to the central policy debates in Part 5. The contributors have approached their subjects from a variety of disciplinary perspectives and national experiences, and with the aim of contributing to a debate that will continue to develop rapidly in the future.

ACKNOWLEDGEMENT

Preparation of this chapter was supported in part by York University.

REFERENCES

Adams, M. (2011) Staying alive: How Canadian baby boomers will work, play and find meaning in the second half of their adult lives. Toronto: Viking Canada.

Alsop, R. (2008) *The trophy kids grow up: How the Millennial generation is shaking up the workplace.* San Francisco: Jossey-Bass.

Anderson, K. (2009) *Reset: How this crisis can restore our values and renew America.* New York: Random House.

Avolio, B. J. & Waldman, D. A. (1994) Variations in cognitive, perceptual and psychomotor abilities across the working life-span – examining the effects of race, sex, experience, education and occupational type. *Psychology and Aging*, 9, 430–443.

Bal, P. M., De Jong, S. B., Jansen, P. g. W. & Bakker, A. B. (2012) Motivating employees to work beyond retirement: A multi-level study of the role of I-deals and unit climate. *Journal of Management Studies*, 49.

Bateson, M. C. (2010) *Composing a further life: The age of active wisdom*. New York: Alfred Knopf.

Bedell, G. & Young, R. (2009) *The new old age: perspectives on innovating our way to the good life for all*. London: National Endowment for Science, Technology and the Arts.

Blackwell, B. (2011) Most expect to continue working after retirement. *Globe and Mail*, Nov 5. B16.

Bloom, D. E., Canning, D. & Sevilla, J. (2003) *The demographic dividend: A new perspective on the economic consequences of population change*. Santa Monica, CA: The Rand Corporation.

Blossfeld, H.-P., Buchholz, S. & Kurz, K. (2011) *Aging populations, globalization and the labor market. Comparing late working life and retirement in modern societies*. Cheltenham, UK: Edward Elgar.

Canadian Institute for Health Information (2011) *Seniors and the health care system: what is the impact of multiple chronic conditions?* Toronto: Canadian Institute for Health Information.

Cappelli, P. & Novelli, W. (2011) Managing the older worker: How to prepare for the new organizational order. Boston: Harvard Business School Press.

Chiu, W. C. K., Chan, A. W., Snape, E. & Redman, T. (2001) Age stereotypes and discriminatory attitudes towards older workers: An East–West comparison. *Human Relations*, 54, 629–661.

Cooper, C. L., Field, J., Goswami, V., Jenkins, R. & Sahakian, B. (2010) *Mental capital and well-being*. London: Wiley-Blackwell.

Costa, G., Goedhard, W. J. A. & Ilmarinen, J. (2005) Assessment and promotion of workability, health and well-being of aging workers. *Proceedings of the 2nd International Symposium on Workability*, Verona, Italy 18–20 October 2004.

Cravit, D. (2012) *Beyond age rage: How the boomers and seniors are solving the war of the generations*. New York: BPS Books.

DelCampo, R. G., Haggerty, L. A., Haney, M. J. & Knippel, L. A. (2010) *Managing the multi-generational workforce*. Surrey, UK: Gower.

DeLong, D. W. (2004) *Lost knowledge: Confronting the threat of an aging workforce*. Oxford: Oxford University Press.

Dennis, H. & Thomas, K. (2007) Ageism in the workplace. *Generations*, 31, 84–89.

Erickson, T. (2009) Gen Y in the workforce. *Harvard Business Review*, February, 43–49.

Erickson, T. J. (2008) *Plugged in: The Generation Y guide to thriving at work*. Boston: Harvard Business School Press.

Euwals, R., De Mooij, R. & Van Vuuren, D. (2009) *Rethinking retirement*. The Hague: CPB Report.

Feldman, D. C. (1994) The decision to retire early: A review and conceptualization. *Academy of Management Review*, 19, 285–311.

Field, J. (2011) Lifelong learning, welfare and mental well-being into older age: trends and policies in Europe, in G. Boulton-Lewis and S. L. Tam (eds), *Active ageing, active learning: Issues and challenges*. Dordrecht: Springer, pp. 11–20.

Flavelle, D. (2012) Gen X's workplace squeeze: Invisible workers stuck between boomers who delay retiring and aggressive Gen Ys. *Toronto Star*, March 16, B1, B4.

Freedman, H. S. (2007) *Encore: Finding work that matters in the second half of life*. New York: Public Affairs.

Freedman, H. S. (2011) The big shift: Navigating the new stage beyond midlife. New York: Public Affairs.

Freedman, H. S. & Martin, L. R. (2012) *The longevity project: Surprising discoveries for health and longer life from the landmark eight-decade study*. New York: Plume.

Griffiths, A. (1997) Ageing, health and productivity: A challenge for the new millennium. *Work and Stress*, 11, 197–214.

Hankin, H. (2004) *The new workforce: Five sweeping trends that will shape your company's workforce*. New York: American Management Association.

Hannon, K. (2010) *What's next? Follow your passion and find your dream job*. San Francisco: Chronicle Books.

Hayashi, C., Olkkonen, H. Sikken, B. J., & Yermo, J. (2010) *Transforming pensions and healthcare in a rapidly changing world: Opportunities and collaborative strategies*. Pensions, 15, 161–174.

Hedge, J. W., Borman, W. C. & Lammlein, S. E. (2006) *The aging workforce: Realities, myths, and implication for organizations*. Washington, DC: American Psychological Association.

Hofacher, D. (2010) *Older workers in a globalizing world: An international comparison of retirement and late-career patterns in Western industrialized countries*. Cheltenham, UK: Edward Elgar.

Hori, Y., Lehmann, J.-P., Wah, T. M. K. & Wang, V. (2010) Facing up to the demographic dilemma. *Strategy and Business*, 58, 44–53.

Ilmarinen, J. (2001) The ageing worker. *Occupational and Environmental Medicine*, 58, 546–553.

Ilmarinen, J. (2006a) *Towards a longer work career, ageing and quality of life in The European Union*. Helsinki: Finnish Institute of Occupational Health, Ministry of Social Affairs and Health.

Ilmarinen, J. (2006b) The ageing workforce-challenges for occupational health. *Occupational Medicine*, 56, 362–364.

Ilmarinen, J. & Rantaqnen, J. (1999) Promotion of work ability during ageing. *American Journal of Industrial Medicine*, 1, 21–33.

Johnson, M. (2011) Young failed by system in need of structural adjustment. *Financial Times*, 17, 4.

Kalata, G. (2010) Retirement might slow the brain. *Toronto Star*, Oct. 14, I3.

Kohli, M. (2004) Intergenerational transfers and inheritance: a comparative view, in M. Silverstein (ed.), *Intergenerational relations across time and place*. New York: Springer, pp. 266–89.

Kotlikoff, L. J. & Burns, S. (2004) *The coming generational storm: What you need to know about America's future*. Cambridge, MA: MIT Press.

Krieger, L. M. (2010) Aging curbs ability to multitask: Study. *Toronto Star*, April 18, L3.

Lam, E. (2011) Succession plans lacking: Survey. *National Post*, June 10, FP6.

Laslett, P. (1991) *A fresh map of life: The emergence of the third age*. Cambridge: Harvard University Press.

Magnus, G. (2008) *The age of aging: How demographics are changing the global economy and our world*. New York: John Wiley.

Michaels, E., Handfield-Jones, H. J. & Axelrod, B. (2001) *The war for talent*. Boston: Harvard Business School Press.

Morrow-Howell, N., Hinterlong, J. & Sherraden, M. (2006) *Productive aging: Concepts and challenges*. Baltimore: Johns Hopkins University Press.

National Post (2011) Drug bills more onerous with age. *National Post*, May 28, FP6.

Pitt-Catsouphes, M., Sano, J. & Matz-Costa, C. (2009) Unions' responsiveness to the aging of the workforce. *Journal of Workplace Behavioral Health*, 24, 125–146.

Poot, J. & Strutt, A. (2012) International trade agreements and international migration. *The World Economy*, 33, 1923–1954.

Posthuma, R. A. & Campion, M. A. (2009) Age stereotypes in the workplace: Common stereotypes, moderators, and future research directions. *Journal of Management*, 35, 158–188.

Powell, M. (2010) Ageism and abuse in the workplace: A new frontier, *Journal of Gerontological Social Work*, 53, 654–658.

Rousseau, D. M. (2005) *I-deals: Idiosyncratic deals employees bargain for themselves*. New York: M. E. Sharpe.

Saunders, D. (2010) The incredibly shrinking workforce. *Globe and Mail*, Oct. 23, F9.

Schroeder, H., Hofacker, D. & Muller-Camen, M. (2009) HRM and the employment of older workers: Germany and Britain compared. *International Journal of Human Resources Development and Management*, 9, 162–179.

Schultz, K. S., & Wang, M. (2007) The influence of specific physical health conditions on retirement decisions. *International Journal of Aging and Human Development*, 65, 149–161.

Sedlar, J. & Miners, R.(2007) *Don't retire, REWIRE*. Indianapolis, IN: Alpha Books.

Shea, G. F. & Hansen, A. (2006) The older worker advantage: Making the most of our aging workforce. Westport, CT: Praeger.

Shepard, R. J. (1997) *Physical activity, aging and health*. Champagne, IL: Human Kinetics Publishers.

Shultz, K. S. & Adams, G. A (2007) *Aging and work in the 21st century*. Mahwah, NJ: Lawrence Erlbaum Associates Inc.

Siegrist, J. & Wahrendorf, J. (2009) Quality of work, health, and retirement. *The Lancet*, early online publication, November 9, 2009.

Statistics Canada (2010) *Population projections for Canadian Provinces and Territories*. Ottawa: Demography Division, Statistics Canada, Ministry of Industry.

Strauch, B. (2010) *The secret life of the grown-up brain: The surprising talents of the middle-aged mind*. New York: Viking.

Teotonio, I. (2012) The secret of aging well: A ground-breaking national study of 50,000 Canadians aims to unlock the mystery of a long healthy life. *Toronto Star*, April 21, L1, L6.

Tuomi, K., Huuhtanen, P., Nykyri, E., et al. (2001) Promotion of work ability, the quality of work and retirement. *Occupational Medicine*, 51, 318–324.

US Census Bureau (2005) *Statistical abstract of the United States: 2004–2005*.Washington: US Census Bureau.

Vaillant, G. E. (2003) *Aging well: Surprising guideposts to a happier life from the landmark Harvard Study of Adult Development*. Boston: Little, Brown.

Vaillant, G. E. (1977) *Adaptation to life*. Boston: Little, Brown.

von Bonsdorff, M. E., Huuhtanen, P., Tuomi, K. & Seitsamo, J. (2009) Predictors of employees' early retirement intentions: an 11-year longitudinal study. *Occupational Medicine*, 59.

Waldman, D. A. & Avolio, B. J. (1986) A meta analysis of age differences in job performance. *Journal of Applied Psychology*, 71, 33–38.

Waterfield, B. (2012) Germany proposes taxing young to help old. *Globe and Mail*, April 4, B6.

Westerlund, H., Vahtera, J., Ferrie, J. E., Kivimäki, M. & Singh-Manoux, A. (2010) Effects of retirement for major chronic conditions and fatigue: French GAZEL occupational cohort study. *British Medical Journal*, 341, 1145–1152.

Westerlund, H., Kivimaki, M., Singh-Manoux, A., Melchior, M., Ferrie, J. E., Pentti, J., Jokela, M., Leineweber, C., Goldberg, M., Zins, M. & Vahtera, J. (2009) Self-rated health before and after retirement in France (GAZEL): A cohort study. *Lancet*, 374, 1889–1996.

Wheatley, M. J. (2010) *Perseverance*. San Francisco: Berrett-Koehler.

White, N. J. (2011) Conscientiousness is the key to a long life. *Toronto Star*, Mar. 8, E1, E6.

World Health Organization (WHO) (2012) *Dementia: A public health priority*. Geneva: Switzerland: World Health Organization.

PART 1

Key Issues and Challenges

World Population in Historical Perspective

Tommy Bengtsson and Kirk Scott

Since the Second World War, the world has seen population growth which has no known precedent. When the UN, shortly after its start in 1945, collected information on the economic and social conditions of all countries of the world it became evident that the annual global population growth rate was more than 2 percent, and perhaps as much as 3 percent, and not 1 percent as previously thought. It also became evident that most of this population growth took place in poor countries and the pressing question became how the world would cope with a doubling of its population, not within 72 years, as it was predicted, but within the next 25 to 36 years. This change in the speed of population growth began much earlier, however. A hundred years previously, it was the industrializing world that saw rapid population growth, although at lower rates than those noted after the Second World War. This development marked a change in the long-term population development pattern. While historical population figures contain a fair amount of uncertainty, the best estimates available place the world population in 1500 at

under 500 million, with the planet exceeding one billion inhabitants sometime during the first half of the 19th century, a growth rate of just under 0.15 percent. The growth rate between 1850 and 1950 then increased to 0.8 percent, to reach 1.8 percent between 1950 and 2000. In 1900 the population stood at roughly 1.5 billion, and this had increased to over 6 billion by the first years of the 21st century, even though the growth rate has been falling since the mid-1970s. A rough estimation places 75 percent of the world's population growth as occurring in the 20th century. Assuming that we arbitrarily begin counting at 10,000 BCE, we can then, equally roughly, say that 75 percent of all population growth has occurred during less than one percent of our history.

The reason that the population started growing rapidly prior to industrialization was falling mortality rates among infants and children. A similar development then took place in the developing countries later on but at a much higher speed. Fertility rates began to decline by the end of the

19th century in the west, reducing population growth and, again, this process was later replicated in developing countries, but at a much higher speed. The decline in birth rates, and resulting reduction of family size, not only slowed population growth but also changed the entire age-structure of the population towards one with a higher mean age. This development was at first a blessing, since more resources could be devoted to each child and the capital–worker ratio increased, propelling economic growth. Later on, population aging was seen as a problem for two principal reasons, one being a decline in the relative size of the labour force, the other being an increasing share of elderly, which placed increasing demands on the shrinking labour force.

The fact that population growth, and population aging as well, took place in parallel with the advances of science is no coincidence, as we shall discuss later, but it did lead to an unprecedented discussion of the effects, both positive and negative, of this growth. This chapter will present an outline of population growth both from a descriptive perspective and also through an outline of the major debates surrounding population growth, how these debates arose, and their impact not only on population policy, but on the broader society as well.

THE POPULATION DEBATE

The period immediately following the Second World War saw rapid economic growth in almost all developed countries. Parallel to this economic expansion, it also saw increased awareness of the world as an interconnected entity. This awareness led the newly-formed United Nations (UN) to commission a study (UN 1952) of the living conditions of every country in the world. This study was not interested in population growth, but rather in the existence and degree of poverty and hunger. Despite some attention coming from a few demographers, the challenge of rapid population growth in

developing countries was not yet on the agenda. At the time, it was accepted that the world's population was growing at a rate of one percent per year, and that this rate would continue for the foreseeable future. The pressing challenge was providing developing countries with the tools to continue developing, both in terms of physical and human capital, but also in terms of institutions which facilitate both growth and human rights (Ohlin 1992).

One of the outcomes of this study was a realization that there was an apparent correlation between low standards of living and high population growth rates. Those countries with serious poverty concerns were growing much faster than the global average – at rates of up to 3 percent per annum. At a 1 percent growth rate, the population doubles every 72 years. At 3 percent, however, the doubling time is shortened to a mere 24 years. The obvious next question was how these already struggling countries could support a population twice the size in a mere 24 years.

In a 1953 publication on the determinants and consequences of population growth, the UN stated that '(e)specially during the last decade a number of authors have recalled the Malthusian principle of population and expressed the fear that the present population of Earth is drawing near the maximum that its resources can support' (UN 1953). This statement brings our discussion of population growth back to one of the first population theorists.

Thomas Malthus, born in 1766, is known as demographer and economist. He is most renowned, revered, and reviled for his work *An Essay on the Principle of Population* (Malthus 1798, 1826). Written at the end of the 18th century, it essentially outlined Malthus' somewhat pessimistic views of population growth based upon a combination of postulates and observations. Essentially, population growth, and especially unchecked population growth, was described by Malthus as the natural state within society. This population growth, in the face of scarce resources, could only lead to one thing – population reduction due to negative circumstances.

Malthus stated that population has a tendency to grow geometrically, but that access to resources necessary to sustain the population grows at an arithmetic rate at best. At low levels of population, with relatively abundant resources, there are no problems and population grows unchecked. As the population size nears the limits of resources, certain natural 'checks' come into play to slow or reverse population growth. These checks fall into two main categories, positive and preventive checks. Positive checks are those events which have an immediate and unwanted effect on population size. The most obvious of these checks would be starvation, when the population is simply too large to be nourished by available resources. Another check works through disease. As the population grows, population density must also increase. With people living closer together, disease spreads more easily, and outbreaks such as the bubonic plague become much more serious that otherwise. Another obvious positive check is found in war. As resources become scarce, nations may attempt to secure additional resources through land acquisition, resulting in war.

While Malthus was essentially a pessimist, he does open the door for some optimism through the concept of preventive checks. These checks are not unforeseeable, and do not lead necessarily to population reduction, but rather are planned events which slow population growth. Examples of preventive checks are increases in the age at marriage, an increase in the share of population never marrying, and methods of birth control. While showing that mankind can exert some control over rampant population growth, the basic message remained, however, that population will always tend to grow faster than resources.

If one applies Malthus' theory to human history, it can be roughly stated that during our most primitive past a regime of positive checks ruled, whereby population growth was controlled exclusively by catastrophic events which limited our ability to expand. As societies develop, they become aware of the ability to control the population through preventive checks, and therefore can avoid catastrophe, while still being subject to the same resource constraints. At the socioeconomic level, the message in a Malthusian framework is that population growth will have a negative impact on economic well-being. As populations grow the supply of workers naturally increases. With a workforce increasing faster than production, we see a lowering of real wages in a simple supply and demand model. In addition to worsening conditions for the workers, population growth may also have a negative impact on economic growth.

It is exactly the socioeconomic effects of Malthusian population growth that came into focus in the post-war period. One of the earliest and more influential arguments stating that population growth is detrimental to economic growth was formulated in the 1950s by Ansley Coale and Edgar Hoover (Coale and Hoover 1958). Coale and Hoover felt that population growth posed a great threat to economic development through its impact on capital intensity. This negative impact comes in various shapes, but all have capital scarcity as the common denominator. As the population grows, we do see a growth in the labour supply (with a lag of roughly 20 years), but there is also an increased need for investment of capital to less productive uses such as housing, education, and health. While it can be argued that investments in increased education and, to an extent, health care are productive, population growth necessitates increased investment to maintain a constant level of education and health. In addition to the investments in infrastructure depleting existing capital stocks, natural population growth implies increasing numbers of children. As the number of families with small children increase, investments required for childrearing will decrease the aggregate savings rate. This decline in savings leads to a decline in available capital for investment. These impacts on capital accu-mulation and the capital stock, coupled with an increasing workforce, must necessarily lead to a decrease in the amount of capital available per worker, and a commensurate decline in economic growth. This 'capital shallowing' caused by population growth will lead *ceteris paribus* to increasing pov-erty and greater difficulties in escaping the poverty trap.

The extent to which Coale's and Hoover's ideas were empirically supported was soon to be tested by Simon Kuznets (1966). Kuznets evaluated economic growth in a number of countries, and could find no strong evidence for a causal relationship between population growth and poor eco-nomic performance. During the period fol-lowing the beginning of industrialization, western countries entered into a period which has become widely known as *mod-ern economic growth*, defined as a long-term growth of both population and living standards. Modern economic growth is a term which grew out of an attempt to iden-tify prerequisites for economic growth dur-ing the mid-20th century. While it has now become accepted that there is no 'formula' for economic development, Simon Kuznets identified a number of factors which must be present if a society can be classified as experiencing modern economic growth. In his acceptance speech for the Prize in Eco-nomic Sciences in Honour of Alfred Nobel he identified six components which charac-terize modern economic growth. The first and most important for our purposes is that the economy must be able to simultane-ously sustain high growth rates of both population and per capita national product. This simultaneous growth, which is con-trary to Malthus' theory, is caused by shifts in economic focus from agriculture to industrialization, changing institutional structures, increased urbanization and secu-larization, and advances in transport and communication. Thus Kuznets is taking quite an optimistic view if not as optimistic as another Nobel laureate, Robert Solow,

who argues the population growth is super-seded by the inherent tendency of techno-logical change (Solow 1956).

Interestingly, the changing institutional structures which allow for economic growth, continued population growth and the ultimate escape from the Malthusian society could well be the result of popula-tion growth itself. Yet another Nobel lau-reate, Douglass North, sees population pressure acting as a catalyst (North and Thomas 1973). As the workforce grows, the cost of labour declines relative to the cost of the other two traditional factors of production – land and capital. The chang-ing relationship between these factors gives rise to new institutions which lead to increased productivity and economic growth.

Alongside Kuznets, Solow, and North, Malthusian ideas were also being chal-lenged by Esther Boserup. Boserup believed, contrary to Malthus, that food production was not constrained by arith-metic growth (Boserup 1965) and that any theory of population growth must account for the possibility of innovation. While Boserup allowed room to believe that pop-ulation would increase until checked, she did not accept the idea that once the sub-sistence barrier was reached that we would experience catastrophe. The Malthusian idea that increasing population growth leads to increasing population density and pressures on scarce resources is an obvious one, but in Boserup's view, increasing scarcity of resources would not necessarily lead to increasing mortality or decreasing fertility, but rather a shift in production techniques which allow for continued pop-ulation growth. Intensification of cultiva-tion, the use of new tools, and changing crops are all examples of how production can be increased in a non-linear manner. While Boserup was essentially an optimist, her framework must still be seen as a modification of Malthus. To the extent that innovation can continue, then the subsist-ence frontier may never be broken, but at

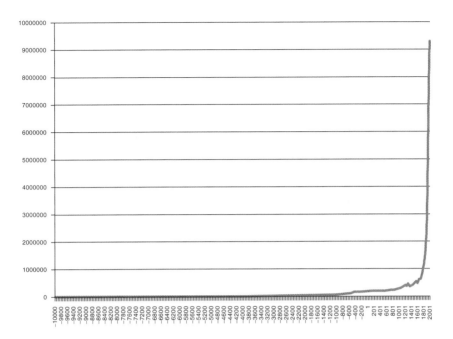

Figure 2.1   Historical Estimates of the World Population, 10 0000 BCE – 2050

Source: US Census Bureau, UN http://www.census.gov/population/international/data/worldpop/table_history.php

some point the frontier may still be reached in lack of resources.

The conflict between the pessimists and the optimists became more pronounced in the late 1960s. At that time, there was great general concern that the world was rapidly on its way to overpopulation. Looking at Figure 2.1, it is easy to understand that the exponential increase in population during the previous 150 years could lead one to worry. Not only had the world population been growing rapidly, it seemed to be growing at a rapidly accelerating rate. The world population hit 2 billion in 1925, which meant that it took roughly 125 years to increase from one to two billion. It then took only 35 years to increase to 3 billion, which occurred in 1960. Fourteen years later the population had hit 4 billion, amidst an air of panic. Nowhere was this panic more noticeable than in the works of Paul Ehrlich. Ehrlich's book, *The Population Bomb* (1968), effectively gave a voice to the general fear that unchecked population increase would lead to environmental and human disaster. In a return to Malthusian

thinking, Ehrlich predicted that overpopulation would lead to mass starvation during the 1970s and 1980s.

It was not only access to food resources which would cause problems, however. Both Ehrlich and Dennis Meadows (Meadows 1972) believed that access to land and the increasing scarcity of non-renewable resources would also work to limit both economic growth and cause poverty and starvation. While Ehrlich has publicly defended his 1968 predictions in recent years (Luiggi 2010), there is little evidence to support his claims. There were indeed cases of mass starvation during this period, but the collective evidence is that this starvation was not the result of lacking food security, but rather political instability (FAO 2000). Additionally, while many resources are indeed non-renewable, the Earth has proven to contain much greater quantities of these resources than previously believed, and technical change has often reduced demand.

Julian Simon took the opposite side of the population argument, seeing increasing population not as a threat, but rather as a resource. As population grows, it becomes easier to meet economies of scale, and it also increases the chances that a great thinker such as an Einstein or Newton will arise. In his book *The Ultimate Resource* (Simon 1981), Simon also argues that the concerns regarding scarcity espoused by Ehrlich and others need not be heeded, and we should see resources as infinite. This argument is not implying that there are infinite physical resources of a given type, but rather that mankind has always adjusted production before any actual scarcity became a threat. Here his argument is not unlike Boserup's ideas that human ingenuity can be assumed to stave off Malthusian mechanisms. Simon was so firm in this belief that he challenged Ehrlich to a bet regarding cost development of commodities. Essentially the challenge revolved around the selection of a basket of commodities that were assumed to be scarce and increasing in scarcity. If the pessimists were correct, then increasing scarcity would drive up prices. If, on the other hand, Simon was correct, then the prices should remain stable or even decline. Ehrlich and two colleagues took Simon up on the wager, selecting chromium, copper, tin, nickel, and tungsten. They then 'bought' $200 worth of each commodity, using 29 September 1980 as the purchase date. The end date of the wager was set to 29 September 1990, at which time the inflation-adjusted prices would be compared to the initial purchase prices. If the prices were higher, Simon would pay the difference between the purchase price and the current price. If the prices were lower, Ehrlich and his colleagues would cover the difference. In the end, Ehrlich wrote Simon a cheque for the amount of $576.07, which was the price decline of these five commodities during the decade.

Despite the resilience which is seen in natural resource accessibility, there are still voices calling for an active policy to prevent population pressures from negatively impacting the planet. The primary voice of today's worry is found in Herman Daly. Since the late 1980s, Daly has been vocal in opposition primarily of economic policies which he feels damage the environment (Daly and Cobb 1989). While focusing on the economy, Daly has also been critical of the impacts of population growth as well.

After this overview of the population debate at the theoretical level, we now move to a discussion of actual developments throughout time.

EARLY POPULATION GROWTH

While the period prior to the 19th century is undoubtedly important to the overall development of human society, it had very little impact on population size. Estimates for 10,000 BCE place the world population at somewhere between one and ten million, or somewhere between the size of the Glasgow and Chicago metropolitan areas. By 1800, the population was between 800 million and one billion. While this does represent respectable population growth, there is actually very little that we know about this period, with the exception of several historical records spread throughout the time, and often associated with extraordinary events such as the Black Death, or rare events such as William the Conqueror's survey of the wealth of England leading to the Domesday books.

This scarcity of information has not stopped scholars seeking to identify the existence of a Malthusian economy through examination of demographic and economic data from England during the period from roughly 1200 through 1850. The seminal work by Anthony Wrigley and Roger Schofield, *The Population History of England, 1541–1871* (Wrigley and Schofield 1981), attempted to identify the existence of a Malthusian trap through a study of economic and demographic data. Using data which was at times quite sparse and local, estimates were made of both English population development and real wages over three centuries. (Phelps

Brown & Hopkins, 1957) The fundamental assumption that Wrigley and Schofield were working under was that if Malthus was correct, and population grew faster than food production, then this should be evident in an increase in food prices.

Rising food prices would be evident in falling real wages for labourers, and the demographic responses to these falling real wages should give an idea of how Malthus' theory applied to England during its agrarian and early industrial periods. If positive checks were functioning, then one would expect to see increased mortality as a response to declining real wages. If, on the other hand, preventive checks were in action, then declining real wages should be associated not with increasing mortality, but rather with decreasing fertility. Here the mechanisms would likely be that married couples had fewer children as a response to economic constraints or that unmarried individuals lacked the means to marry, and therefore postponed marriage or remained single.

Wrigley and Schofield found that England was, indeed, living in a Malthusian world, but that the primary response to population pressures was not working via mortality, a positive check, but was rather working through reductions in fertility, a preventive check which appeared to primarily be the product of delaying marriage due to economic hardship. They also state that this Malthusian world existed only up to the years around 1800 – the time when Malthus was writing – and that after 1800 the relationship between food prices and population growth disappeared. Later studies (see Clark 2007) have attempted to refine the data used by Wrigley and Schofield, but have come to essentially the same conclusions. At some point during the late 18th century the Malthusian trap is broken to be replaced by modern economic growth.

As the western economies moved from what would today be characterized as developing to fully developed countries, we see changes not only in the economy, but also in demographic behaviour. These changes are stylized in what has become known as the theory of the demographic transition, and it is in this transition that we begin to see the process which will eventually become known as population aging.

THE DEMOGRAPHIC TRANSITION

The theory of the demographic transition was developed by Davis (1945), Notestein (1945, 1953) and others to explain the rapid population growth which was observed during the late 19th and early 20th century in Europe and North America. Essentially, the transition theory places responsibility for the rapid population growth on a situation where mortality declined rapidly, and families were slow to respond. Given the situation of the past millennia, achieving a target family size involved having more children than desired as insurance for expected death during childhood.

During the 18th and 19th centuries we begin to see a secular decline in mortality throughout Europe. The reasons for this decline are many, and not without debate, but can be grouped into five main categories. First, during the period from the Enlightenment until today there has occurred an immense progress in terms of public health and sanitation. Hand in hand with the public health improvements, there have been dramatic advances in medical science. The economic growth of the period led to a higher general standard of living and better diet than in the past, as well as improved personal hygiene. Another factor, which falls outside of man's control, is found in nature. Over the past three centuries we have experienced a general decrease in disease virulence, and this decrease would have led to declining mortality even in the face of none of the improvements mentioned above.

As mortality declined, individuals were slow to respond, leading to a situation where fertility remained at high, pre-transition levels, and mortality plummeted. This increasing disparity between fertility

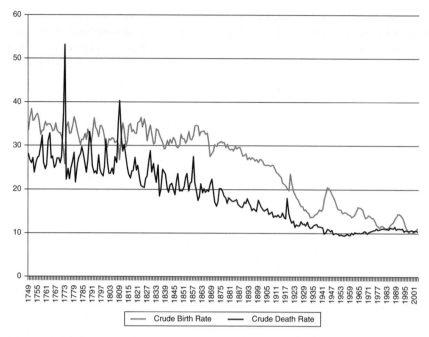

Figure 2.2   Crude birth rates and crude death rates in Sweden during the demographic transition.
Source: Statistics Sweden

and mortality led to population growth which was not necessarily desired by the individual families. Initial declines in mortality could be seen as potentially temporary, and families continued childbearing as if child mortality remained at the earlier levels. As it became obvious that mortality decline was not merely an aberration, but rather a lasting situation, families began to adjust their fertility to reflect the reality that they can achieve target family sizes without 'overproducing' children as insurance. This decline in fertility would not necessarily lead to lower population growth than before the transition, since fewer children were being born, but fewer children were also dying. Figure 2.2 shows the mortality and fertility trends for Sweden during the transition.

As seen above, birth rates and death rates were fluctuating wildly, but had a fairly constant trend through the first quarter of the 19th century. Death rates then began to fall at an almost constant rate over the next 125 years, while birth rates began to fall first in

the 1870s. It is during the period from the initial mortality decline until fertility begins to catch up with mortality developments that we see large and unprecedented population growth.

Hand in hand with this transition came a new economic regime, based largely on the successes of industrialization, in which families no longer needed to produce offspring as a source of labour or insurance against poverty in old age. As we move into the 20th century in western countries, we see that children are no longer factors of production, but they are actually becoming consumer goods. Families can have children simply for the utility they provide outside the labour market, with little or no regard to their productive capacity. As societies develop and economies become more sophisticated, it becomes possible to leverage the markets to smooth consumption over the life cycle, and families receive an incentive to limit the number of children. Since children are no longer required to smooth consumption over the life cycle, the desired family size declines, leading to the final phase of the demographic transition, which is a period of stable, and low, mortality and low fertility.

CRITICISM OF THE THEORY OF DEMOGRAPHIC TRANSITION

The demographic transition is not a universally accepted concept. As with all attempts to generalize development processes, the transition theory fails in a number of settings. Work in recent decades has focused on reconstituting population histories for a number of countries, and it has become increasingly obvious that the general pattern of the transition theory is far from universal. Examining data from France and Sweden, we see that the two countries experienced mortality decline at roughly the same time. France, however, experienced its fertility decline simultaneously with its mortality decline, while Sweden showed a lag between the times which is more in line with the theory. The result of this simultaneity is that France never experienced the period of rapid population growth which is predicted in the theory. England is another case which deviates from the theory. While mortality rates fell prior to fertility rates, the period after the onset of mortality decline was not characterized by stable fertility, but rather by increasing fertility, leading to extremely rapid population growth.

One of the key assumptions in the transition theory is that mortality in the pre-industrial period was high and reasonably constant, and the transition is essentially started with mortality decline. Data for England points to widely swinging mortality rates throughout the agrarian period, making it difficult to identify a clear breakpoint when the transition begins (Wrigley and Schofield 1981). Also notable is that there does not appear to be a strong association between standard of living and mortality, as predicted in Malthusian models. Indeed, evidence from Sweden, the Netherlands, and Canada (Bengtsson and van Poppel 2011) shows that there was very little variation in adult mortality between the social classes prior to industrialization. This lack of a connection between standard of living and mortality calls into question one of the key arguments explaining the beginnings of mortality decline. The association between economic stress and demographic behaviour appears to be more through preventive checks limiting childbirth than through mortality (Bengtsson 1993, Galloway 1988, Schofield 1984).

Delving further into the argument that increased standard of living was the cause of the initial mortality decline, Swedish data shows glaring discrepancy. First, the decline in mortality began at the end of the 18th century, while living standards did not increase notably before the mid-19th century. Additionally, the decline appears to have occurred almost simultaneously throughout Sweden, despite large regional differences in standard of living and differences in economic situation and degree of agricultural reform (Fridlizius 1984).

Turning to the other factors reportedly underlying the mortality decline we can most likely discount the medical advances made during the 19th century. Examining the effects of medical progress on mortality, McKeown and Record found very limited impact prior to the introduction of antibiotics during the first half of the 20th century – long after the beginning of the decline (McKeown and Record 1962, McKeown 1976). Other factors such as breastfeeding did have benefits for infant mortality levels, but the campaigns to increase breastfeeding did not begin until after the mortality decline.

The single explanation which seems most likely is the decline in virulence of parasites and the subsequent decline in smallpox (Fridlizius 1984, Perrenoud 1984, Schofield 1984). While this explanation is attractive, it suffers from the difficulty to measure its validity. Unlike living standards and other observable factors, virulence cannot be directly measured. The attractiveness of this explanation is that it not only accounts for mortality decline earlier than one would expect looking at the other factors, but it also accounts for the great variation in mortality observed before the decline. If virulence is not constant, and began to decline at the beginning of the transition, it could be assumed to vary before the transition as well.

This then leads us to the question of why mortality did not increase again, if the decline in virulence was not permanent. Here the other explanatory factors come into play, not so much to reduce mortality as to keep it from rising.

Turning to the fertility decline we also see discrepancies which question the generality of the transition theory. As discussed above, the theory sees fertility decline largely as a result of families adjusting to a new circumstance where large families were no longer required for economic reasons, and that decreasing infant mortality reduced the number of children required to meet the target family size. Here again, evidence from Swedish data shows that this is not the entire story (Bengtsson and Ohlsson 1994). By examining age-specific fertility rates, it can be shown that the decline in fertility did not simply lead to smaller family sizes, but led to changing childbearing behaviour. The fact that women were exposed to new options for market work during the 19th century led to a change in the timing and spacing of fertility. The fact that the fertility decline could be identified first in the urban areas while mortality decline occurred simultaneously throughout the country makes this seem entirely plausible.

Regardless of the discussions concerning the actual causes of the demographic transition, the fact still remains that most countries go through a similar process of early mortality decline, followed by fertility decline after a number of years, as a very general framework.

THE EMERGENCE OF POPULATION AGING

The demographic transition did not occur at the same time throughout the developed world. France was the forerunner of the transition, with fertility beginning to decline in the early 19th century, while other countries in Europe would wait until the late 19th or early 20th centuries to experience their transitions. The one thing that the transition did have in common for all countries was an upward shift in the mean age of the population – population aging.

Population aging became a serious issue during the last decades of the 20th century and into the 21st century, but it is by no means a new process. It essentially began during the middle of the demographic transition, when the decline in mortality was well underway, and fertility behaviour began to be adjusted downwards. In the early stages of the transition, mortality declines actually led to a population 'youthing', since most of the early progress in mortality was achieved for infant and child mortality. Increases in life expectancy do not start to have much impact on the elderly population until life expectancy surpasses 72 years (Lee 1994). Prior to the 72 year mark, most of the gains in years actually lived due to an increase in life expectancy are found below age 65. Increases in life expectancy at birth during the early stages of the transition were almost entirely due to reductions in child and infant mortality, which served to inflate the numbers of surviving children and decrease the mean age of the population.

The early stage of population aging, which we term 'the *first population aging*', was not a problem for society. The factor that caused population aging, the decline in fertility, was also its solution. First, it had positive effects on economic growth. Population growth implies capital dilution, unless additional capital is augmented, which means that per capita consumption is held back. Consequently, the larger the decline in population growth rates, the less output needs to be allocated to investment in order to keep each worker with a given amount of capital. The deceleration of population growth therefore had positive effects on the economy. Second, the reduction in fertility during the early decades of the 20th

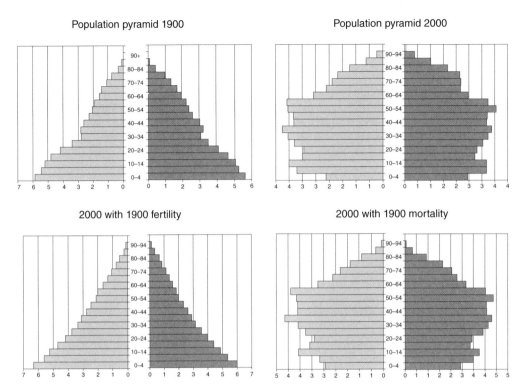

Figure 2.3 Age structure in Sweden in 2000 compared to how it would have looked if fertility/mortality had remained constant at 1900 levels throughout the 20th century. Percent of the population in each age interval, right-hand columns females (red), and left-hand columns (blue) males

Source: Own calculations using yearly data on births, deaths and migration in one-year age groups from BiSOS; Befolkning

century was so rapid that it more than compensated for the increased share of elderly. The dependency ratio – the share of the population either too young or too old to work – declined.

It is only when the transition is nearing completion that we begin to see population aging occurring to a significant extent. Here, the cause of population aging is still *not* decreasing mortality, but rather decreasing fertility. If one is to affect the mean age of a population, it can be done either through increasing the share of the population at high ages, or decreasing the share of the population at low ages. During the transition, the primary driver of population aging was simply found in the declining size of the birth cohorts.

Figure 2.3 shows a modern interpretation of an experiment first made by Ansley Coale in the mid-20th century (Coale 1957). Coale wanted to show that fertility was by far the most important factor underlying the age structure of the population. Using Swedish data, he showed that the age structure in 1950 would be essentially the same as in 1860 if fertility had remained unchanged, but mortality had been allowed to develop at the factual rate. When Coale held mortality constant at 1860 levels and allowed fertility to develop at historical rates, however, he found that the projected age structure was strikingly similar to the actual age structure in 1950. Coale's work therefore shows that the population aging that occurred throughout the first half of the 20th century was almost exclusively the result of fertility decline. While this is evidence that fertility had been the driving force until 1950, we wanted to examine the extent to which it was still the case, in light of increases in longevity which should begin to have an impact on population aging, at least in recent decades.

Figure 2.3 shows the observed age structures in Sweden in 1900 and in 2000 as well as the calculated age structure for the year 2000 under two counter-factual regimes: one where fertility is held constant at the 1900 level and mortality is allowed to change at historical rates, and one where mortality is held constant at the 1900 level and fertility is allowed to change at historical rates. The results are similar to those found by Coale; population aging in Sweden was primarily driven by the decline in fertility throughout the 20th century.

Repeating the calculations for each year from 1900 to 2000, we estimated the effect of each component of population aging, shown in Figure 2.4. When mortality was held constant, the share of people over the age of 65 was 3 percentage points lower than

the 17 percent observed in 2000. When fertility was held constant, the share of those over the age of 65 in the counter-factual was 8.4 percent, exactly the same as the percentage in 1900. This approximate level would occur regardless of whether mortality was held at the 1900 level or was allowed to develop along historical paths. Through this exercise, we show that the share of elderly in 2000 was approximately 10 percentage points higher than it would have been if family sizes had not declined during the 20th century. This implies that fertility retained its dominant position as the main determinant of age structure throughout the entire 20th century.

If fertility levels stabilize over a longer period, however, other factors, such as mortality change, will increase in importance. Average life expectancy has risen considerably during the past century. The world record in average female life expectancy has, on average, increased at an almost constant rate of three months per year from 1840 until

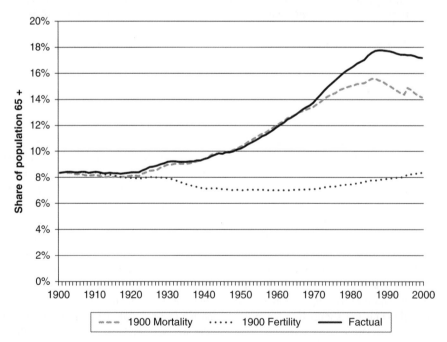

Figure 2.4   Share of the population over the age of 60, 1900-2000. Actual development and the development as it would have been with mortality held constant at 1900 levels.

Source: Own calculations using yearly data on births, deaths and migration in one-year age groups from BiSOS; Befolkning (Statistics Sweden).

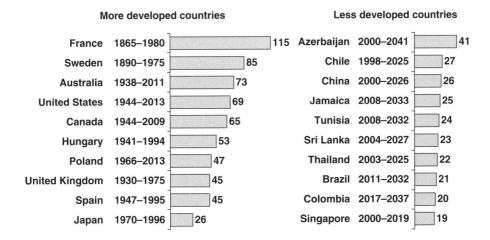

Figure 2.5   Number of years for percent of population age 65 or older to rise from 7% to 14%

Note: Dates show the span of years when percent of population age 65 or older rose (or is projected to rise) from 7 percent to 14 percent.

Source: Kinsella & Gist (1995) and Kinsella & Phillips (2005).

today, although this rate has been slightly lower for males (Oeppen and Vaupel 2002). This development means that children live roughly nine years longer than their parents, and this has continued generation after generation. The records have been held by Norway, Australia, New Zealand and a few other rather small countries including Sweden. The most recent record holder is Japan. With these high life expectancies and low fertility we have started to see declining mortality exerting an influence on the age structure in developed countries (see Preston et al. 2001).

It is when old-age mortality decline becomes the dominating factor in population aging that we enter into the period we refer to as the *second population aging*. In this period we see the old-age dependency ratio rising, with the accompanying increases in costs associated with health care and pensions. It is the shift in the age structure from lower youth dependency to higher old-age dependency that leads to the challenge of population aging.

Given that the demographic transition started at different times, and that the societal and economic conditions for fertility decline occurred much closer temporally between

countries, we see that population aging has been occurring over a long period of time, but that its speed increases as we move forward in time. Figure 2.5 shows the length of time for various countries to double the share of the population over 65 from 7 to 14 percent. France was the first country to experience fertility decline, and therefore the first country to experience population aging. The share of the population over 65 was 7 percent as early as 1865, making France the oldest country in the world at that time. It was to take 115 years for the share of elderly to increase from 7 to 14 percent (Kinsella and Gist 1995, Kinsella and Phillips 2005). Sweden was the next country to break the 7 percent barrier in 1890, but it would take only 85 more years to reach 14 percent.

By the time the development had made it to Japan, a process that took over a century for France was completed in a mere 26 years. Additionally, Japan did not hit the 7 percent mark until 1970, but by 2010 it had become the oldest country in the world, an accomplishment which should underline the dramatic speed at which aging is occurring today.

We can see this acceleration in the list of countries with the oldest populations in

Table 2.1   The 25 countries with the oldest populations 1950, 2000, 2050, ranked by share over 65 years

	1950			2000			2050	
	Land	%		Land	%		Land	%
1	France	11		Italy	18		Japan	38
2	Lithuania	11		Sweden	17		South Korea	35
3	Belgium	11		Japan	17		Macao	34
4	United Kingdom	11		Belgium	17		Spain	33
5	Ireland	11		Spain	17		Slovenia	33
6	Estonia	11		Greece	17		Martinique	33
7	Austria	10		Bulgaria	17		Singapore	33
8	Sweden	10		Germany	16		Hong Kong	33
9	Georgia	10		France	16		Italy	33
10	Luxemburg	10		Portugal	16		Dutch Antilles	32
11	Germany	10		United Kingdom	16		Cuba	32
12	Norway	10		Croatia	16		Bulgaria	32
13	Switzerland	10		Austria	15		Greece	32
14	Lithuania	9		Lithuania	15		Czech Republic	31
15	Denmark	9		Norway	15		Poland	31
16	New Zealand	9		Estonia	15		Portugal	31
17	Benin	9		Finland	15		Romania	30
18	Belarus	9		Denmark	15		Germany	30
19	Macedonia	9		Hungary	15		Slovakia	30
20	Armenia	8		Switzerland	15		Barbados	29
21	Czech Republic	8		Luxemburg	14		Bosnia & Herzegovina	29
22	USA	8		Slovenia	14		Austria	29
23	Italy	8		Ukraine	14		Croatia	28
24	Uruguay	8		Lithuania	14		Lithuania	28
25	Kirgizstan	8		Czech Republic	14		Malta	28

Source: UN 2006 Revision, United Nations Population Division

Table 2.1. France had the oldest population in the world during the 19th century, and was still leading the group in 1950. Fifty years later, France had fallen to ninth place, and is expected to be in 35th place in 2050. Sweden shows even more dramatic shifts in the ranking. Sweden had the second oldest population in 2000, but this ranking is projected to slide to 44th by 2050. Projections regarding ageing for non-European countries show that the process will take similar paths with one vital exception: they will proceed much more quickly.

RECENT DEMOGRAPHIC DEVELOPMENTS

In recent decades, demographers have begun discussing a new pattern of demographic behaviour. The theory of the demographic transition is primarily a theory explaining the movement of a population from a quasi-equilibrium position with high fertility and high mortality, through a transitory period, to a new quasi-equilibrium with low fertility and low mortality. By the last quarter of the 20th century it was becoming clear, however, that while mortality was levelling off, fertility continued to fall in many countries. Many countries in Europe were for the first time experiencing sustained fertility rates below the replacement level (Billari and Kohler 2004). Thus, the quasi-equilibrium which we expected to see at the end of the transition was rather merely a segue into a new transition.

Ron Lesthaeghe and Dirk van de Kaa (Lesthaeghe and Van de Kaa 1986) coined the concept of the second demographic transition in an attempt to explain how changes in attitudes during the post-war period had led to changes in demographic behaviour.

While seeing the first demographic transition as a general movement of the population away from a pre-industrial agrarian family model to a more 'bourgeois' model with fewer children in a nuclear family, they saw the new transition as a movement yet again, but this time towards an 'individualistic' family model. The fundamental result of this new transition was the opposite of the first transition in that it led to a weakening of the family as an institution.

Based on empirical observations during the second half of the 20th century, Van de Kaa (1997) arrived at a sequence of changes at both the institutional and the individual level which have worked together to bring about the lowest-low fertility seen in many countries today. Initially, the decline in fertility will continue due to an interrelated combination of declining fertility rates at higher ages, and reductions in higher-order childbearing.

At the same time, improved contraceptive technology and, later, increased access to induced abortions act to limit the number of pre-marital pregnancies, and, in turn, the number of 'forced' marriages. Since this allows childbearing to be postponed until after a desired marriage age, we see declines in fertility in the youngest age groups. Increasing institutional and societal acceptance of legal separation and divorce also act to reduce fertility through separation of husband and wife. The movement away from universal marriage towards cohabitation as an increasingly popular union form leads to later age at marriage, increases in pre-marital childbirth, and an increase in the mean age at first birth.

As women focus on education and careers they postpone childbearing, artificially reducing total fertility rates until postponement ceases. This leads to an increased share of lower order births occurring at higher ages. While there may be a desire to have additional children, all women may not realize their targets due to biological constraints as a result of postponement. As we reach the end of the transition, total fertility rates should stabilize, but at low levels, perhaps well below replacement fertility. Additionally, the phenomenon of voluntary childlessness becomes more accepted and important.

As mentioned above, the second demographic transition primarily emphasizes the individual's need for self-fulfilment at the expense of the family, with the result being lower fertility and more transitory union types. It should also be mentioned that, much as the previous transition theory, there has been a great deal of criticism as to the extent to which this new 'transition' is indeed a general societal movement, or simply a string of loosely related observations. Regardless of its validity, the fact remains that much of the developed world has been in a period of sustained low fertility, which shows only little sign of increasing. It is this resulting transformation into a regime characterized by below-replacement fertility that will have the most pressing impact on modern society. While changing union forms may mark a shift away from traditional and towards more modern living arrangements, it is the low fertility which will be the most difficult to manage. With smaller and smaller cohorts entering the labour force, the economic challenges of population aging will be increasingly difficult to manage.

TODAY'S POPULATION DEVELOPMENTS

Despite evidence supporting the idea that the developed countries may be in the midst of a new demographic 'transition', all countries have yet to complete their process through the first demographic transition. Indeed, many developing countries are only now experiencing the fertility decline which marks the beginning of the end of rapid population growth during the transition. The fact that fertility is declining in these countries now does a great deal to allay the worries that were rampant during the 1960s and 1970s.

There is a growing body of evidence pointing to a scenario in the 21st century where population growth will no longer be seen as a pressing political issue, but rather that population decline will be on the agenda. The European Union and Japan are already facing the real dilemma of dealing with population decline due to below-replacement fertility, and a number of the Newly Industrialized Countries (NICs) in Asia are rapidly nearing this situation. As mentioned above, developing countries are not in the position of experiencing population decline yet, but the processes are well underway. Fertility is declining in almost all countries, and, if this continues, will lead to population aging and, potentially, population decline.

Currently, however, countries in the developing world have a positive population momentum which will continue to drive population increase throughout the near future. This does not have to be a bad thing, however, since declining fertility rates will propel them into a period known as the demographic dividend (Lee and Mason 2006). This dividend describes the period when the large group of children born during the population expansion of the first demographic transition enter the labour force. Since fertility is beginning to decline, the expansion of the labour force implies a decrease in the dependency ratio and a potential for rapid economic growth. This favourable demographic situation was responsible for a good deal of the explosive economic growth in Europe during the 1950s and 1960s, in Japan during the 1970s and 1980s, in the NICs during the 1990s and 2000s, and can possibly serve as a catalyst for economic development in countries which are today struggling. Andrew Mason estimates that 25–35 percent of economic growth in east and southeast Asia in recent decades may be directly attributable to the advantageous age structure of the population which is a direct result of the first demographic transition (Lee and Mason 2006).

While the developed countries have already reaped the benefit of their first demographic dividend, and developing countries are facing the possibility of benefiting from the same, it is unsure that they will. To capture the dividend, countries need appropriate institutions in place to allow an adequate economic response to the favourable demographic situation found during the period of the first dividend. While this was the case for east and southeast Asia, it appears to be less so in Latin America, and the jury is still out on the African countries. What is certain, however, is that this dividend is transitory in nature. At some point all countries will move into the period of second population aging and the window of opportunity to benefit from the first demographic transition will close.

It is during the second population aging that the economic challenges facing society will be the greatest, but there is also a possibility that the unfavourable age structure will itself be part of the solution. Lee and Mason (2006) discuss this in terms of the second demographic dividend. This second dividend is found explicitly in the increasing share of elderly and the fact that the elderly are the one group in society which has had the most time to accumulate capital. This capital can then be invested to offset the potential production decline caused by a shrinking workforce, as well as utilized to fund retirement. Unlike the first demographic dividend, this second dividend is permanent.

All current information points to a situation where population aging will be a serious issue not only for developed countries, but more so for developing countries, and that population decline is a more imminent issue than population explosion, as already evident in some industrialized countries The manner in which countries respond to the economic and societal challenges facing them will determine the extent to which the increases in living standards gained over the past century can be defended or even potentially built upon in the future.

REFERENCES

Bengtsson, T. (1993) 'Combined Time Series and Life Event Analysis: The Impact of Economic Fluctuations and Air Temperature on Adult Mortality by Sex and Occupation in a Swedish Mining Parish, 1757–1850', in Reher, D.S. and Schofield, R.S. (eds) *Old and New Methods in Historical Demography*, Oxford: Oxford University Press, pp. 239–58.

Bengtsson, T. and Ohlsson, R. (1994) 'The Demographic Transition Revised', in Bengtsson, T. (ed.) *Population, Economy, and Welfare in Sweden*, Berlin: Springer, pp. 13–36.

Bengtsson, T. and van Poppel, F. (eds) (2011) 'Social Inequalities in Death from Past to Present. An Introduction', *Explorations in Economic History* (Special Issue on Socioeconomic Inequalities in Death), 48(3): 343–56.

Billari, F.C. and Kohler, H.P. (2004) 'Patterns of Low and Lowest-low Fertility in Europe', *Population Studies*, 58(2): 161–76.

Boserup, E. (1965) *The Conditions of Agricultural Growth: The Economics of Agrarian Change under Population Pressure*, London: Allen and Unwin.

Clark, G. (2007) *A Farewell to Alms*, Princeton: Princeton University Press.

Coale, A.J. (1957) 'How the Age Distribution of a Human Population is Determined', *Cold Spring Harbor Symposia on Quantitative Biology*, 22: 83–9.

Coale, A.J. and Hoover, E.M. (1958) *Population Growth and Economic Development in Low-Income Countries*, Princeton: Princeton University Press.

Daly, H. and Cobb, J. (1989) *For the Common Good*, Boston: Beacon Press.

Davis, K. (1945) 'The World Demographic Transition', *Annals of the American Academy of Political and Social Sciences*, 237(1): 1–11.

Ehrlich, P.R. (1968) *The Population Bomb*, New York: Ballantine.

FAO (Food and Agriculture Organization of the UN) (2000) *The State of Food and Agriculture*, Rome: UN.

Fridlizius, G. (1984) 'The Mortality Decline in the First Phase of the Demographic Transition: Swedish Experiences', in Bengtsson, T., Fridlizius, G. and Ohlsson, R. (eds) *Pre-Industrial Population Change*, Lund: Almqvist and Wicksell International, pp. 75–114.

Galloway, P.R. (1988) 'Basic Patterns in Annual Variations in Fertility, Nuptiality, Mortality and Prices in Pre-Industrial Europe', *Population Studies*, 42(2): 275–303.

Kinsella, K. and Gist, Y.J. (1995) *Older Workers, Retirement, and Pensions: A Comparative International Chartbook*, Washington, DC: Bureau of the Census.

Kinsella, K. and Phillips, D. (2005) 'The Challenge of Global Aging', *Population Bulletin*, 60(1): 5–41.

Kuznets, S. (1966) *Modern Economic Growth: Rate, Structure, and Spread*, Yale: Yale University Press.

Lee, R.D. and Mason, A. (2006) 'Reform and Support Systems for the Elderly in Developing Countries: Capturing the Second Demographic Dividend', *GENUS*, 62(2): 11–35.

Lee, R.D. (1994) 'The Formal Demography of Population Aging, Transfers, and the Economic Life Cycle', in Martin, L.G. and Preston, S.H. (eds) *Demography of Aging*, Washington: National Academy Press, pp. 8–49.

Lesthaeghe, R. and Van de Kaa, D. (1986) 'Twee demografische transities?', in Lesthaeghe, R. and Van de Kaa, D. (eds), *Bevolking: Groei en Krimp*, Deventer: Van Loghum Slaterus, pp. 9–24.

Luiggi, C. (2010) 'Still Ticking', *The Scientist*, 24(12): 26.

Malthus, Thomas Robert (1826) *An Essay on the Principle of Population*, Library of Economics and Liberty, retrieved 17 September 2012 from: http://www.econlib.org/library/Malthus/malPlong.html

McKeown, T. (1976) *The Modern Rise of Population*, London: Edward Arnold.

McKeown, T. and Record, R.G. (1962) 'Reasons for the Decline of Mortality in England and Wales during the Nineteenth Century', *Population Studies*, 16(2): 94–122.

Meadows, D.H. (1972) *The Limits to Growth. A Report for the Club of Rome's Project on the Predicament of Mankind*, New York: Universe Books.

North, D.C. and Thomas, R.P. (1973) *The Rise of the Western World: A New Economic History*, Cambridge: Cambridge University Press.

Notestein, F. (1945) 'Population – The Long View', in Schultz, T.W. (ed.) *Food for the World*, Chicago: University of Chicago Press, pp. 36–57.

Notestein, F. (1953) 'Economic Problems of Economic Change', *Proceedings of the Eighth International Conference on Agricultural Economics*, Oxford: Oxford University Press, pp. 3–31.

Oeppen, J. and Vaupel, J.W. (2002) 'Broken Limits to Life Expectancy,' *Science*, 296(10): 1030–1.

Ohlin, G. (1992) 'The Population Concern,' *Ambio*, 21(1): 6–9.

Perrenoud, A. (1984) 'The Mortality Decline in a Long Term Perspective', in Bengtsson, T., Fridlizius, G. and Ohlsson, R. (eds) *Pre-Industrial Population Change*, Lund: Almqvist and Wicksell International, pp. 41–69.

Preston, S.H., Heuveline, P. and Guillot, M. (2001) *Demography: Measuring and Modeling Population Processes*, Oxford: Blackwell.

Schofield, R.S. (1984) 'Population Growth in the Century after 1750: The Role of Mortality Decline', in Bengtsson, T., Fridlizius, G. and Ohlsson, R. (eds) *Pre-Industrial Population Change*, Lund: Almqvist and Wicksell International, pp. 17–39.

Solow, R. (1956) 'A Contribution to the Theory of Economic Growth', *Quarterly Journal of Economics*, 70(1): 65–94.

UN (1952) *Preliminary Report on the World Social Situation*, New York: UN.

UN (1953) *The Determinants and Consequences of Population Trends*, New York: UN.

Van de Kaa, D.J. (1997) 'Options and sequences: Europe's demographic patterns', *Journal of the Australian Population Association*, 14(1): 1–29.

Wrigley, E.A. and Schofield, R.S (1981) *The Population History of England, 1541–1871: A Reconstruction*, London: Edward Arnold.

3

Research on Age Diversity in the Workforce: Current Trends and Future Research Directions

Florian Kunze and Stephan A. Boehm

INTRODUCTION

A better understanding and more effective handling of diversity in the workplace have become key success factors for organizations around the world (Thomas and Ely, 1996). Due to mega-trends like increasing globalization (Rodrik, 2008; Wiersema and Bowen, 2008), the rising importance of cross-national and cross-functional work units and teams (Robinson and Dechant, 1997), and the growing labor force participation of women (Jaumotte, 2003; Juhn and Potter, 2006), workforce diversity is increasing in most organizations.

Referring to the collective amount of differences among members within a social unit (Harrison and Sin, 2006), the concept of diversity was originally applied with a focus on categories such as gender, ethnicity, and nationality (Van Knippenberg and Schippers, 2007). However, created by demographic changes in most industrialized countries, the construct of age diversity has recently garnered considerable interest from both scholars and practitioners (Shore et al., 2009). Despite several recent reviews (Jackson et al., 2003; Van Knippenberg and Schippers, 2007; Williams and O'Reilly, 1998) and meta-analytical analyses of diversity's effects in the workplace (e.g., Joshi and Roh, 2009), systematic knowledge on age diversity is still limited.

This seems rather problematic, as age diversity tends to increase even more strongly than other diversity categories. Moreover, organizations currently have only a vague idea of how age diversity will affect their internal processes and states, including their employees' well-being, commitment, and performance. Due to the relative recentness of this trend, the management of age diversity is not yet an established component of corporate training or development initiatives.

This chapter aims to close this knowledge gap by providing scholars and practitioners with insights into age diversity's distinct effects, as well as recommendations for the successful management of an age-diverse workforce. For that purpose we will first summarize different theoretical explanations for the effects of age diversity on team processes and outcomes. Thereafter we will give an overview on the empirical literature on age diversity in organization, which will be followed by an outlook on future research issues in the field and finally practical implications from a supervisor and organizational perspective.

REASONS FOR GROWING AGE DIVERSITY

Growing age diversity is a major workforce trend in most industrialized countries that is attributable to at least three factors. First, in the past decades, companies have tended to hire predominately younger employees. However, due to an expected shortage of labor in many industries (Michaels et al., 2001), companies are increasingly willing to redefine 'talent' and to recruit traditionally underrepresented groups such as older employees and employees with disabilities (Lengnick-Hall et al., 2008). Second, many companies in Western Europe engaged in early retirement programs that were also encouraged and supported by the governments. In 2001, more than 50% of German companies had no employees older than 50 years (Bellman and Kistler, 2003). Only recently have countries like Germany and Austria changed their legislation and raised the retirement age to alleviate the burden on social security systems and to attain a better ratio between taxes paid and pensions received (Gruber and Wise, 2004). As many companies followed this trend and stopped their early retirement programs (Dychtwald et al., 2004; Tempest et al., 2002), a growing number of older employees can be observed in the workplace, in turn contributing to

higher levels of age diversity. Third, at the other end of the continuum, governments try to lower the age of entry into the labor market by changing universities to bachelor-and-master systems or by reducing the required years of schooling, again contributing to higher age diversity in the workplace (Kaube, 2008).

IMPLICATIONS OF GROWING AGE DIVERSITY

With regard to potential implications for organizations, several aspects are worth mentioning. On the one hand, potential challenges might arise. As we know from research on other diversity categories such as gender and ethnicity, rising levels of age diversity might lead to communication and coordination problems among members of different generations (e.g., baby boomers, Generations X and Y) (Smola and Sutton, 2002; Twenge et al., 2010). In addition, mutual stereotypes (Posthuma and Campion, 2009) and potential sub-group formation (Tajfel and Turner, 1986) could lead to increasing levels of conflict between different age groups. For employees, such processes might lead to individual discontent, decreasing organizational commitment and job satisfaction, and higher levels of absenteeism and turnover intention. For organizations, potential effects include a loss in productivity and performance.

On the other hand, scholars have repeatedly pointed to the potentially positive aspects of diverse teams, units, and organizations, summarized by Robinson and Dechant (1997) as the 'business case for diversity'. These positive implications include a generally better use of talent, improved leadership effectiveness, an increased understanding of diverse customers, enhanced creativity, and higher problem-solving skills. Similar effects can be assumed for age diversity as teams composed of both younger and older employees should be more effective in gaining, transferring, and applying complementary knowledge, in preventing groupthink (Janis, 1972), and in identifying the needs of age-diverse customers, including the so-called 'silver market' (Kohlbacher and Herstatt, 2008). In the next paragraph, we will outline in more detail the theoretical rationale behind such seemingly contradictory effects of age diversity.

THEORETICAL RATIONALES FOR DIFFERENT EFFECTS OF AGE DIVERSITY

B. Definition and conceptualization of age diversity

To better understand the potential effects of age diversity, the construct must be clearly defined and conceptualized. Following the work of Harrison and Klein (2007), diversity can generally be defined as 'the distribution of differences among members of a unit with respect to a common attribute, X, such as tenure, ethnicity, conscientiousness, task attitude, or pay' (Harrison and Klein, 2007: 1200). Age diversity is consequently a specific form of diversity. It is a collective-level, compositional construct that reflects the age structure of a particular social entity (such as a team, a work unit, or a whole organization).

Building on this basic definition, it seems important to further differentiate between the different types or conceptualizations of age diversity that might develop within entities: separation, variety, and disparity (Harrison and Klein, 2007). Each of these types implies a different form of maximum diversity, leading to varying group processes, and, therefore, different outcomes.

Separation occurs when unit members hold opposing positions on a task- or team-relevant issue (e.g., certain values or attitudes). Regarding age diversity, a group of four might consist of two older employees (60 years) and two younger employees (20 years) who disagree in their assessment of the importance of a certain issue (e.g., punctuality or accuracy), leading to separation and potential conflict

between the younger and older employees within one unit.

Age diversity can also be conceptualized as variety, based on the different knowledge and experiences that diverse age groups might have, resulting in a fruitful pool of information regarding various tasks. For instance, age-diverse innovation teams might be composed of members from the Internet generation who have up-to-date theoretical knowledge and members from the baby boomer generation who have a substantial track record of practical technology management, thereby complementing each other and achieving better group results.

Finally, age diversity might also indicate disparity, reflecting differences in the distribution of social assets (e.g., influence, money) among group members. For example, older members in age-diverse units might possess more power and influence than younger colleagues due to their potentially higher hierarchical position, their longer tenure, or their broader social networks within the firm.

Age can lead to all three types of diversity. While variety is mostly associated with positive outcomes, separation and disparity are related to detrimental group processes and losses in effectiveness (Harrison and Klein, 2007). In the following section, the underlying psychological and sociological processes accounting for the positive effects of age diversity as variety and the negative effects of age diversity as separation and disparity will be explained.

Positive effects: the information/decision-making perspective

Scholars who argue in favor of positive diversity effects stemming from variety typically base their arguments on the so-called 'information/decision-making perspective' (Van Knippenberg and Schippers, 2007: 518). They propose that diverse unit members typically possess different knowledge bases, experiences, or skills, which might help them to devise a better solution to a problem than employees with more homogenous characteristics. In addition to their own cognitive resources, diverse members also tend to be members of different internal and external networks and have access to non-redundant information important for the group's performance (Austin, 2003). In the case of age diversity, this assumption might be particularly valid as older and younger employees tend to differ significantly in terms of interests, work experiences, education, use of technology, and social networks, for example. Such differences might stem from both membership in different age groups (and related phases of private and professional life) and different generational values or imprints (Joshi et al., 2010; Smola and Sutton, 2002). An age-diverse team or work group that uses these heterogeneous resources effectively might become an 'information processing instrument for an organization' (Harrison and Klein, 2007: 1205).

This information richness is assumed to be especially beneficial when dealing with nonroutine problems, as diverse team members can better use their additional 'sociocognitive horsepower' when working on complex tasks (Carpenter, 2002: 280). Furthermore, (age-) diverse teams seem to be more adaptive to change and might have a better understanding of diverse customers and markets. In addition, research has shown that group members with different experiences and skill sets are likely to be more creative (Burt, 2002; Jackson et al., 1995) and less endangered by the effects of groupthink (Janis, 1972) through more intense discussions with more divergent perspectives (Fiol, 1994).

In summary, scholars who adopt a variety or information/decision-making perspective presume a higher performance level of diverse teams and work groups (Bantel and Jackson, 1989).

Negative effects: the similarity-attraction paradigm, the social identity approach, token status, and perceptions of inequality

As both research and practice have demonstrated, increasing levels of diversity can also result in negative outcomes, such as higher levels of conflict and turnover and lower levels of cohesion and performance (Sacco and Schmitt, 2005). Possible explanations for such negative effects of diversity can be derived from the concepts of separation and disparity. Scholars framing diversity as separation typically rely on two underlying psychological processes that help explain the formation of sub-groups within teams and units and the consequent discrimination of certain groups of employees: the similarity– attraction paradigm (Byrne, 1971) and the social identity approach (Tajfel and Turner, 1986).

The Similarity-Attraction Paradigm

The similarity-attraction paradigm assumes that individuals prefer to interact with others who are similar to themselves (Byrne, 1971). This actual, or perceived, similarity can comprise demographic characteristics (e.g., age, gender), as well as similar values, attitudes, or beliefs (Avery et al., 2008; McPherson et al., 2001; Tsui et al., 1992). The psychological rationale for this assumption is that people seem to obtain more affirmative feedback from people who are similar to them, which in turn reduces uncertainty and creates mutual trust (Hinds et al., 2000). Interpersonal heterogeneity, on the other hand, may lead to decreased levels of communication, as well as to more communication errors (e.g., Barnlund and Harland, 1963; Zenger and Lawrence, 1989). From an empirical point of view, the effects of similarity-attraction have been shown in both friendships and voluntary interactions (Blau, 1977; McPherson and Smithlovin, 1987), as well as in work environments (e.g., Hinds et al., 2000). In the case of age diversity, one might assume that members of a team are particularly motivated to interact with other members belonging to a similar age group as they might share more values, attitudes, experiences, and interests with such individuals than with individuals belonging to different age groups (Lawrence, 1980; 1988).

The Social Identity Approach

The similarity-attraction paradigm is complemented by a second psychological process, which may also lead to separation on the basis of age group membership. Theories of social identity (Tajfel and Turner, 1986) and self-categorization (Turner, 1985) suggest that individuals tend to classify themselves, and others, into certain groups on the basis of dimensions that are relevant for them. These dimensions often include demographic categories, such as age (Avery et al., 2008; Ensher et al., 2001; Finkelstein et al., 1995; Kearney and Gebert, 2009). Individuals make use of these group classifications to differentiate between potentially similar ingroup members and different out-group members. Such group categorizations are of high importance for individuals, as they derive a large part of their social identity from membership in particular groups. Following a basic human need to maintain and strengthen their self-esteem, individuals strive to perceive their own group as superior to others (Abrams and Hogg, 1988; Hogg, 2001). Consequently, individuals tend to favor members of their own group (ingroup), which results in higher levels of trust, communication, and cooperation. Members of other groups (out-groups) may face certain forms of stereotyping and discrimination (Brewer, 1979; Brewer and Brown, 1998).

Token status

A third potential mechanism leading to separation is 'token status', as described by Kanter (1977). Based on her assumptions, minorities (usually less than 15% of the total unit) are perceived less as individuals and more as members or symbols of their respective (demographic) category (Young and James, 2001). In the case of age diversity, a small group of older employees might perceive a token status in an organization that is predominantly young, or vice versa. For instance, older employees in an information technology (IT) or start-up environment might sometimes feel like 'tokens', being reduced to their age group membership ('the old') and not being perceived as individuals with particular strengths and weaknesses. Kanter (1977) described the negative outcomes of a token status, including increased levels of stereotyping, unfair performance pressure, and the creation of interpersonal boundaries that might, in turn, negatively affect performance.

Perceptions of Inequality

Finally, the concept of age diversity will be analyzed from a disparity perspective, which also suggests primarily negative effects on group effectiveness. Having its roots in the sociological literature, disparity is often discussed under the term inequality (Blau, 1977; Blau and Blau, 1982). In the organizational literature, disparity or inequality implies that relevant or desired resources such as pay, power, status, or prestige are allocated unequally across members of a certain unit (Harrison and Klein, 2007). As a consequence of such an asymmetric distribution, certain processes might be triggered within the unit. For example, individuals with a disadvantaged status within the team (e.g., a younger team member who lacks influence) might experience feelings of dissatisfaction and a desire to leave the group. Other potential consequences include communication problems, intra-group conflicts, and drops in performance (Bloom, 1999; Pfeffer and Davis-Blake, 1990; Siegel and Hambrick, 2005).

In summary, age diversity in teams or organizations might also lead to negative effects such as feelings of detachment, discrimination, and exclusion that can arise from processes of similarity-attraction, social identity, tokenism, and inequality.

LITERATURE REVIEW

Following the theoretical explanations of positive and negative effects of age diversity in social entities in the previous sections, we will now offer a coherent overview of empirical studies that have investigated the relationship of age diversity to various team outcomes. To that end, we conducted a literature search using the *Web of Science* and *EBSCO* databases for the last 25 years within the fields of business, management, and applied psychology. With that research strategy, we felt certain that we would capture all relevant past research within the most prominent peer-reviewed journals in the last 25 years. As the following paragraphs will show in more detail, age diversity has been related to numerous team outcome variables with mixed results. We will try to cluster these findings to offer a structured picture of the existing empirical research on age diversity, starting with a summary of direct effects of age diversity and continuing with an overview of studies that also considered potential contextual factors in

the relationship between age diversity and performance.

Direct Effects of Age Diversity on Outcomes

Table 3.1 offers an overview of existing empirical studies of age diversity on team outcomes. As can be seen, we used six categories to cluster these studies: (1) the relationship between age diversity and performance in work teams, (2) the relationship between age diversity and team performance in top management teams (TMTs), (3) the relationship between age diversity and innovation, (4) the relationship between age diversity and absenteeism and turnover, (5) the relationship between age diversity and conflict, and

Table 3.1   Results of Empirical Studies on Age Diversity and Team Outcomes

Team outcomes	Study and direction of effect	
Team performance in work teams	Bell et al. (2011)	(0)
	Choi and Rainey (2010)	(0)
	Ely (2004)	(−)
	Leonard et al. (2004)	(−)
	Jehn and Bezrukova (2004)	(−)
	Joshi and Roh (2009)	(−)
	Timmerman (2000)	(−)
Performance in top management teams	Bunderson and Sutcliffe (2002)	(0)
	Kilduff et al. (2000)	(+)
	Simons et al. (1999)	(0)
	West et al. (1999)	(+)
Innovation	Bantel and Jackson (1989)	(0)
	Ostergaard et al. (2010)	(−)
	Wiersema and Bantel (1992)	(0)
	Zajac et al. (1991)	(−)
Turnover and absenteeism	Cummings et al. (1993)	(+)
	Jackson et al. (1991)	(+)
	Milliken and Martins (1996)	(+)
	O'Reilly III et al. (1989)	(+)
	Wiersema and Bird (1993)	(+)
Conflict	**Relational conflict**	
	Jehn et al. (1997)	(0)
	Pelled et al. (1999)	(−)
	Pelled et al. (2001)	(+)
	Task conflict	
	Pelled et al. (1999)	(0)
Communication/information sharing	Bunderson and Sutcliffe (2002)	(0)
	Kearney and Gebert (2009)	(0)
	Zenger and Lawrence (1989)	(−)

(6) the relationship between age diversity and communication.

Overall, no consistent findings on the relationship between age diversity and performance have been established in the literature thus far. However, almost no empirical study has reported the positive relationship between age diversity and team performance that was proposed using the information/decision-making perspective. In contrast, most studies have found either a zero or a negative relationship between age diversity and performance. Choi and Rainey (2010), for example, reported a zero relationship between age diversity and performance in 67 federal agencies. Timmerman (2000) discovered a significant negative relationship between age diversity and the success of 871 US basketball teams. Ely (2004) reported similar results related to the effect of age diversity on performance in a sample of 486 branches of a financial service company. Leonard and colleagues (2004) reported equally negative effects of age heterogeneity on sales figures in a sample of 700 retail stores. Finally, Jehn and Bezrukova (2004) found negative effects of age diversity in a sample of 1,528 teams from Fortune 500 information-processing firms.

These mostly negative findings are also backed by recent meta-analyses. Joshi and Roh (2009), for instance, reported an overall negative effect of $r = -.06$ for age diversity on team performance considering 7,217 teams. In their study, age diversity showed the strongest negative effect on performance of the six diversity types (gender, race, age, function, education, tenure). Interestingly, another meta-analysis by Bell and colleagues (2011) found no general significant effect of age diversity on performance when considering 10,646 teams. Furthermore, the meta-analysis also did not reveal any significant effect when distinguishing between different forms of operationalization of age diversity (separation, variety, disparity).

Age diversity and performance in top management teams

The research on TMT diversity is characterized by rather mixed findings. West and colleagues (1999), for example, reported in a longitudinal study with 43 UK manufacturing organizations a significant negative result on company profits as a result of age diversity in TMTs. In contrast, Kilduff and colleagues (2000) reported age diversity to be the only demographic variable that was positively related to team performance. Their results, however, have to be interpreted with caution since they were drawn from experienced managers participating in a simulated business game, which might have restricted the external validity of the findings. Bunderson and Sutcliffe (2002) reported a zero relationship between age diversity in management teams and performance of 44 business units. Likewise, Simons and colleagues (1999) showed a zero relationship between age diversity in TMTs and financial performance in 57 manufacturing companies.

Age diversity and innovation

The majority of existing studies have found no relationship between age diversity and innovative behavior in work teams. In a sample of 199 US banks, Bantel and Jackson (1989) found no relationship between age diversity of the TMT and total, technical, or administrative innovation. Other research by Wiersma and Bantel (1992) also demonstrated no significant relationship between age diversity and innovativeness. Additionally, other studies have reported a negative effect of age diversity on innovativeness. Zajac and colleagues (1991), for instance, showed a negative relationship between age diversity and innovativeness in 53 internal hospital units consisting of physicians. Recently, Ostergaard and colleagues (2010) also demonstrated a negative relationship between age diversity and innovativeness in 1,775 Danish firms. In sum, as for overall performance and innovativeness, the social categorization processes seem to dominate the information/decision-making processes, leading to zero or even negative effects on innovativeness.

Age diversity, turnover and absenteeism

Other outcome measures often studied in regard to age diversity are turnover intentions, actual turnover, and absenteeism rates. Most empirical studies have reported a positive association between age diversity and turnover in work teams (Jackson et al., 1991; O'Reilly III et al., 1989; Wiersema and Bantel, 1992; Wiersema and Bird, 1993). Additionally, other studies have inspected this relationship in more detail and discovered that those employees who differ most in terms of age from their work group are most likely to turn over (Milliken and Martins, 1996; O'Reilly III et al., 1989). Furthermore, Cummings and colleagues (1993) showed similar effects for absenteeism as an outcome variable.

Age diversity and conflict

Based on the earlier descriptions of social identity and social categorization processes (Tajfel, 1974; Tajfel and Turner, 1986; Turner, 1985), age diversity, like other types of diversity criteria, is likely to create sub-groups within teams that may get involved in mutual conflict behavior. In general, the emerging literature of conflict research differentiates between two types of conflict: task-related and relational conflict (Pelled, 1996; Pelled et al., 2001). While the former is assumed to be favorable for work group performance, since different team members engage in productive disputes on collective goals, the latter is assumed to diminish team performance, because team members engage in destructive personal disputes that distract their resources and attention from collective team goals (Jehn et al., 1999).

Overall, regarding the age diversity/conflict relationship, the findings from previous studies have been rather mixed. Pelled and colleagues (1999) reported, contrary to their expectations, that age diversity is negatively related to emotional conflict and unrelated to task conflict. The negative relationship with emotional conflict might be explained by the argument that more age similarity (e.g., less diversity) is bound to create more social comparison between colleagues in terms of career progress, which increases emotional conflict (1994). In contrast to these results and arguments, Jehn and colleagues

(1997) found in a quasi-experimental study that visible individual demographic differences in terms of age were unrelated to relationship conflicts in teams. Support for a positive relationship between age diversity and relationship conflicts comes from a study by Pelled and colleagues (2001), who found relational dissimilarity in age to be positively linked to affective conflict in a study with Mexican workers.

Age diversity and communication/ information sharing

Finally, age diversity has also been regularly investigated with regard to its relationship with group communication and information sharing, likewise with mixed results. In line with social identity theory, Zenger and Lawrence (1989) reported age diversity to be negatively related to professional communication in project groups. Bunderson and Sutcliffe (2002) found age diversity in TMTs to be unrelated to information sharing. Similarly, Kearney and Gebert (2009) did not find a main effect of age diversity on elaboration of task-relevant information in a sample of 62 research and development (R&D) teams in a multinational pharmaceutical company.

Intermediate Summary: Age Diversity and Outcome Measures

The studies presented so far have painted a mixed picture regarding the effects of age diversity on work team outcomes. In all six categories, varying results have been reported for the potential consequences of age diversity. However, overall, age diversity seems to be a factor that does not affect or impair positive team outcomes (performance, innovation, communication), but it does seem to result in an increase in negative team consequences (turnover, conflicts). Thus, the potentially negative consequences of similarity-attraction-based and social identity-based processes seem to dominate potential benefits from a broader information/decision-making perspective. Only research on TMT composition has revealed some positive effects of age diversity.

However, both from a theoretical perspective and from the perspective of practitioners in companies, these mixed and mostly negative findings on the consequences of age diversity are not satisfying. Consequently, since the end of the 1990s, a new research stream has emerged to tackle the inconsistencies in diversity research in general and in age diversity research in particular. To open the 'black box of organizational demography' (Lawrence, 1997), diversity researchers have started to investigate contextual factors that may explain the mixed findings on age diversity. This research has followed the logic that certain work-related contextual factors might be responsible for eliciting either the advantages (more cognitive information) or disadvantages (more sub-group formation leading to more conflicts and discrimination) of age diversity. Supporting this argument, Shore and colleagues stated that 'older employees are likely to have knowledge and experience that is useful within groups, but such human capital may only be utilized in an environment in which positive relations among members are conducive to appreciating different types of contributions' (2009: 121). The following section will summarize studies on the potential contextual factors of age diversity.

Moderators of the Age Diversity/Outcome Relationship

Table 3.2 offers an overview of studies that have inspected contextual factors of the age diversity/outcome relationship. The most researched contextual factors have been team processes, diversity management and human resources (HR) practices, task type, and leadership behavior.

Team processes
The study by Ely (2004) in 486 banking subsidiaries discovered team processes, and more specifically cooperation and teamwork, to be moderators of the age diversity/performance relationship. Surprisingly, under

Table 3.2 Results of Empirical Studies on Context Factors for the Age Diversity and Team Outcome Relationship

Context factors	Study
Team processes	Choi and Rainey (2010) Ely (2004)
Diversity management and HR practices	Kearney et al. (2009) Choi and Rainey (2010) Ely (2004)
Task type	Jehn and Bezrukova (2004) Timmerman (2000) Wegge et al. (2008)
Leadership behavior	Kearney and Gebert (2009) Kunze and Bruch (2010) Nishii and Mayer (2009)

conditions of high levels of cooperation and teamwork, age diversity and performance were negatively related, whereas low cooperation and teamwork were found to favor a zero or positive relationship between age diversity and branch performance. Ely (2004) speculated in light of these results that high teamwork and cooperation may suppress differences of team members, from which the collective performance might profit. Contrary to these results, Choi and Rainey (2010) found no moderation effect of team processes, measured by cooperation and communication in work units, on the relationship between age diversity and performance in 67 public agencies in the US.

Finally, Kearney and colleagues identified team need for cognition, meaning the collective actions 'to seek out and thoroughly process information in numerous domains' (2009: 583) as a factor that moderates the relationship of age diversity with elaboration of task-relevant information, collective team identification, and performance. For all three outcomes, age diversity was found to be positively related under high values of need for cognition, but negatively related under low values of need for cognition.

Diversity management and HR practices
Choi and Rainey (2010) reported diversity management in federal agencies to be a

favorable boundary condition for the age diversity/business unit relationship. Thus, if employees perceived their business unit, represented by their supervisors, as engaging in pro-diversity initiatives (e.g., policies and practices to promote diversity), the relationship between age diversity and performance was significant. Ely (2004) found no moderation effect of diversity education programs in companies in her study on the business-unit level. Likewise, Jehn and Bezrukova (2004) found no moderation effect of diversity-focused HR practices on the relationship between age diversity and group performance in a sample of 1,528 working groups.

Task type

One often researched contextual factor for the age diversity/outcome relationship is task type. Timmerman (2000), for example, found that age diversity was negatively related to performance in basketball teams, but unrelated to performance in baseball teams. From this finding, she concluded that the higher required level of task interdependence in basketball teams aggravated the negative social identity effects of age diversity. In a sample of 222 work units, Wegge and colleagues (2008) investigated the boundary role of task complexity and discovered that age diversity was only related positively to performance for groups solving complex tasks, but not for groups engaging in routine tasks. Additionally, age diversity was positively related to the unfavorable outcome of health disorders only in groups working on routine tasks. In the same study, Wegge and colleagues (2008) also inspected the role of group size as a potential moderator, but found no significant effect.

Leadership behavior

Only recently have initial studies emerged that investigated leadership behaviors as boundary conditions for the age diversity/group outcome relationship. First, Nishii and Mayer (2009) in a sample of supermarket departments discovered that overall demographic diversity, consisting of a composite measure of age, race, and gender diversity, was positively related to group turnover only when leader–member exchange (LMX) differentiation was low. Under low LMX differentiation, the relationship turned out to be non-significant. Thus, LMX seems to at least buffer the negative consequences of age diversity. Second, Kearney and Gebert (2009) reported a similar buffering effect of transformational leadership (TFL) for the relationship between age diversity and team performance. Their results showed that age diversity increased the elaboration of task-relevant information, and in turn performance, only when TFL was high. Under conditions of low TFL, they found a negative relationship between age diversity, elaboration of task-relevant information, and ultimately performance. Finally, Kunze and Bruch (2010) replicated this relationship by showing that age-based faultlines (e.g., faultlines that foster sub-group formation based on age in alignment with gender and organizational tenure) negatively relate to productive team energy only if TFL is low, but are unrelated to productive team energy if TFL is high. Hence, they assumed that TFL is a promising factor to foster the joint activation of affective, emotional, and behavioral potentials in teams with strong age-based faultlines.

FUTURE RESEARCH TRENDS

Despite the numerous recent studies on contextual factors explaining the age diversity/collective outcomes relationship, the research area still possesses many blind spots that can be addressed in future studies. In the following section, we will offer two ideas for future research trends that might help to further complement the incomplete picture on the consequences of age diversity: interaction of age with other diversity criteria in organizational faultline research and research on the organizational-level consequences of age diversity.

Age-based faultline research

In their review of diversity research in general, Joshi and Roh (2009) reported that less than 5% of the studies they initially reviewed applied an operationalization of diversity that considered several diversity facets. Similarly, Jackson and colleagues (2003) concluded in an earlier review that less than 5% of the reviewed studies integrated several diversity dimensions simultaneously.

One way to fill this research gap may be to integrate the faultline concept into diversity studies. The faultline concept was introduced by Lau and Murninghan (1998) and refers to the hypothetical dividing lines that split a group into sub-groups based on several demographic criteria that are aligned with one another. For instance, a clear-cut demographic alignment in a group (e.g., all men are old and all women are young) may strengthen coalition formation and finally result in salient group identities (a sub-group of old men versus a sub-group of young women) (Cramton and Hinds, 2005).

Strong group faultlines are generally expected, due to their polarization tendencies, to be negative for several work outcomes. In line with this expectation, prior research has shown that faultlines exhibit a negative relationship with group processes such as conflict (Li and Hambrick, 2005; Polzer et al., 2006; Thatcher et al., 2003), emergent states such as cohesion (Molleman, 2005), and behavioral/social integration (Li and Hambrick, 2005; Rico et al., 2008). However, there are also counterintuitive findings that have reported faultlines to be linked with less conflict, more team learning, psychological safety, and group learning behavior (Lau and Murnighan, 1998). These results indicated that faultlines and their relationship to team processes and outcomes are not yet fully understood (Mathieu et al., 2008).

One way to develop a better understanding of faultlines would be to examine contextual moderators that may enhance or decrease the strength and number of faultlines (Joshi and Roh, 2009). Recent studies on faultlines have investigated diversity beliefs (Homan et al., 2007), task interdependence (Molleman, 2005), and team identification (Bezrukova et al., 2009) as potential boundary conditions. Furthermore, the previously mentioned study by Kunze and Bruch (2010) found TFL to be a boundary condition for the age-based faultline/productive team energy relationship.

In sum, plenty of opportunities exist to advance the field of age diversity research in combination with faultlines. One way might be to inspect in more detail other types of diversity with which age heterogeneity has the strongest interaction in terms of faultline creation. Does age interact more with social-category facets (e.g., gender, ethnicity) or with experienced-based categories (e.g., tenure, education), or even with personality traits (e.g., big five trajectories) in faultline creation? Furthermore, like for age diversity effects, more research is needed to inspect the potential activators and deactivators of age-based faultlines in companies (e.g., training programs, proactive leadership behavior) (Thatcher and Patel, 2011).

Age diversity at the organizational level

A second fruitful area for future research might be to study age diversity not only as group-level phenomena, but also as a source for diversity-related processes throughout a company as a whole. Although age diversity possibly does not have direct performance consequences, it is likely to influence subtle and implicit processes and states within companies. After all, the negative consequences of sub-group formation and conflicts might not be limited to the group level, but might also spread throughout the company across team and unit borders.

One study found a company's age diversity to be positively related to an age discrimination climate, which in turn was negatively related to a collective affective commitment climate and ultimately also to overall company performance (Kunze et al., 2011). The authors argued that because they are in similar stages in private life and also possess historically generated similarities (Lawrence, 1980), employees from different age groups should practice more intense communication and cooperation within their own age group than between age groups (Lawrence, 1984). As a consequence, employees' formal and informal exchange and cooperation, such as joint lunches or social activities inside and outside the company, are more likely to occur between same-aged peers, even across team or unit boundaries, leading to sub-group formation and increased levels of discrimination. Additionally, increased levels of age-based discrimination might also be triggered by the violation of career time tables (Lawrence, 1984, 1988). This concept is based on the assumption that over time clear age norms develop in an organization concerning which career level an employee should reach at a given age. Based on these implicit age norms, employees are ranked on whether they have reached the adequate career level for their age group. While those employees that are 'on schedule' or even 'ahead of schedule' are not confronted with perceived discrimination, employees who fall behind the career schedule are assumed to perceive higher levels of discrimination. Increasing age diversity due to the demographic change might produce more violations of these implicit age norms (Kunze et al., 2011).

Future studies might pick up on this new level of age diversity research and investigate potential boundary conditions that help companies benefit from the potential of an age-diverse workforce. One potential boundary condition might be pro-age diversity practices, such as organizational efforts to support diversity (Triana and García, 2009; Triana et al., 2010). These pro-diversity organizational procedures and practices should help create an environment that fosters respect for all employees, regardless of their age (Hicks-Clarke and Iles, 2000; Mor Barak and Levin, 2002), and consequently reduce the evolution of an age discrimination climate, which hinders performance in age-diverse companies. Additionally, age-specific HR practices (e.g.,

Armstrong-Stassen, 2008; Boehm et al., forthcoming; Elliott, 1995) might also be perceived as a strong organizational statement that, particularly, a key goal of the organization is the avoidance of age discrimination, which in turn will potentially unlock the benefits of age diversity. Kunze and colleagues (2013) found as first study researching boundary conditions on the organizational level of analysis, that age stereotypes of the top management and diversity-friendly HR-policies play a key role for the relationship between age diversity and company performance. Finally, Choi and Rainey (2010) suggested that rewards for strong performance by employees form a necessary boundary condition for the positive linkage between age diversity and company performance.

HOW TO MANAGE AGE DIVERSITY IN THE WORKPLACE

In the last section of this chapter, we will try to translate the findings from age diversity research into concrete practical strategies for executives in companies. In particular, we will consider two levels where interventions could take place: (1) the level of team supervisor and (2) the organizational level.

Team supervisor-level strategies

First, as described in the literature review, TFL has been shown to be a positive boundary condition for both the relationship of age diversity with team outcomes (Kearney and Gebert, 2009) and for the relationship between age-based faultlines and team outcomes (Kunze and Bruch, 2010). Following these studies, leaders of age-diverse teams should aim to show high TFL behaviors at the workplace. TFL consists of six distinct sub-dimensions: acting as an appropriate role model, fostering the acceptance of common goals, identifying and articulating a clear vision for the future, setting high performance expectations, providing individualized support for followers, and providing intellectual stimulation for followers (Podsakoff et al., 1996). Through these various behaviors, team supervisors can create a common team identity that superposes all other sub-identities (e.g., those based on age) within a work group (Kunze and Bruch, 2010). Thus, strong TFL leadership behavior might be among the most promising strategies for executives to employ to benefit from their age-diverse subordinates. This is particularly interesting since numerous studies have shown that TFL is a learnable competence (Barling et al., 1996; Kelloway et al., 2000). Consequently, companies should invest in TFL leadership training for their current and future supervisors (e.g., Bass, 1990) and also treat TFL capabilities as a core requirement in recruitment and promotion decisions.

Second, leaders of age-diverse teams should also aim to create maximal interaction between employees from the different age groups. Gaertner and Dovidio (2000), for example, argued that increased interaction and task interdependence are highly likely to foster a common group identity and to lower negative consequences of diversity, such as relationship-based conflicts and decreased mutual communication (Pettigrew, 1998). Thus, team supervisors should try to incorporate the necessary interaction inherent in the task assignment. If team members perform highly interdependent tasks, they are almost forced to cooperate in a productive manner. Additionally, the workplace architecture can be designed to favor interaction. Joint coffee bars, open team offices, and other group-oriented work facilities should increase the possibility of formal and informal team interaction. Finally, off-site activities, such as outdoor trainings and joint leisure activities, can be applied to increase interaction between team members of different ages so as to foster better team outcomes.

Third, when staffing new work teams, supervisors may vary the level of age diversity depending on the type of task. While routine tasks are more efficiently accomplished with age-homogenous teams, non-routine and innovative tasks (e.g., developing new products and strategies) often require at least a certain amount of age heterogeneity. Bowers and colleagues (2000), for example, explained that complex tasks are best suited for age-diverse teams.

Organizational-level strategies

First, from an organizational-level perspective, companies should carry out age auditing procedures that employ age-profiling tools for different levels of analysis (Age-Partnership-Group, 2006). Age profiling consists of an assessment of the current age distribution throughout the company and within specific departments and teams. Based on the current situation and assumptions concerning future recruitment and retirement strategies, age profiling also allows a forward projection of 5 or even 10 years concerning the age composition of the workforce. In general, age profiling is most valuable for companies if as much detailed information on employees as possible is integrated. Instead of considering age alone, researchers may consider other socio-demographic data (e.g., gender, tenure), functional data (e.g., current position, salary amount), structural data (e.g., scope of application, growth potential), qualifications data (e.g., formal qualifications, current competencies, willingness to participate in training), and individualized data (individual career and development goals). Such specific data can substantially increase the explanatory power of an age-profiling analysis, in addition to offering companies an indication of whether age diversity might be a current or future problem for their teams, departments, or overall productivity.

Second, if age diversity is found to be present in teams or the overall organization, certain measures might be put in place to reach beneficial performance outcomes. Overall, companies should strive to develop a positive (age) diversity climate (Mor Barak et al., 1998). According to the definition offered by Gelfand and colleagues, a positive diversity climate describes 'employees' shared perceptions of the policies, practices, and procedures that implicitly and explicitly communicate the extent to which fostering and maintaining diversity and eliminating discrimination is a priority in the organization' (2005: 104). Perceptions of a strong diversity climate have repeatedly been linked to more sustainable integration and smoother collaboration among diverse employees, as well as higher levels of performance (Cox, 1994; Gonzalez and DeNisi, 2009; McKay et al., 2009; McKay et al., 2011).

Top management and the HR department play an important role in shaping such a climate. As Dychtwald and colleagues (2004) noted, HR practices in many firms are often implicitly or explicitly biased against older workers and thus create a negative age-diversity climate. Moreover, as Feldman (1994) pointed out, HR policies indicate the organization's appreciation and affirmation of its older workers and how much the company values their contribution. Thus, companies should try to establish HR measures (recruiting, training, career management) that are non-age biased. It is important that these measures target not only older workers but all age groups in the company to prevent the replacement of a discriminatory culture against older employees with a new one that discriminates against younger age groups.

CONCLUSION

The demographic change that has resulted in an aging and increasingly age-diverse workforce is one of the major challenges for organizations today and in the coming decades. Particularly, companies have to deal with growing levels of age diversity in their teams, departments, and overall organizations. This chapter has summarized recent findings concerning this pressing issue. We first contrasted the opposing theoretical rationales to explain both positive and negative consequences of age diversity, namely, the information/decision-making perspective (variety) and the processes of similarity-attraction, social identity, token status, and inequality (separation and disparity). Thereafter, we provided an overview of recent empirical studies inspecting the direct linkage between age diversity and team outcomes, as well as those considering potential boundary conditions. This chapter closed by offering perspectives for future research as well as concrete practical recommendations on how to manage age diversity in the workplace. In sum, we hope to have provided a coherent overview of the current state of the age diversity literature that will fuel both future research in the field and the productive collective engagement of all age groups in companies.

REFERENCES

Abrams, D. and Hogg, M.A. (1988) 'Comments on the motivational status of self-esteem in social identity and intergroup discrimination', *European Journal of Social Psychology*, 18(4): 317–334.

Age-Partnership-Group (2006) 'Age profiling: Monitoring the make up of your workforce', http://www.mature-project.eu/materials/Age-Profiling-v3.pdf. Accessed 16 December 2011.

Armstrong-Stassen, M. (2008) 'Organisational practices and the post-retirement employment experience of older workers', *Human Resource Management Journal*, 18(1): 36–53.

Austin, J.R. (2003) 'Transactive memory in organizational groups: The effects of content, consensus, specialization, and accuracy on group performance', *Journal of Applied Psychology*, 88(5): 866–878.

Avery, D.R., McKay, P.F. and Wilson, D.C. (2008) 'What are the odds? How demographic similarity affects the prevalence of perceived employment discrimination', *Journal of Applied Psychology*, 93(2): 235–249.

Bantel, K.A. and Jackson, S.E. (1989) 'Top management and innovations in banking – Does the composition of the top team make a difference', *Strategic Management Journal*, 10(1): 107–124.

Barling, J., Weber, T. and Kelloway, E. (1996) 'Effects of transformational leadership training on attitudinal and financial outcomes: A field experiment', *Journal of Applied Psychology*, 81(6): 827–832.

Barnlund, D.C. and Harland, C. (1963) 'Propinquity and prestige as determinants of communication networks', *Sociometry*, 26(4): 467–479.

Bass, B. M. (1990) 'From transactional to transformational leadership: Learning to share the vision', *Organizational Dynamics*, 18(3): 19–31.

Bell, S.T., Villado, A.J., Lukasik, M.A., Belau, L. and Briggs, A.L. (2011) 'Getting specific about demographic diversity variable and team performance relationships: A meta-analysis', *Journal of Management*, 37(3): 709–743.

Bellman, E. and Kistler, W.J. (2003) 'Betriebliche Sicht- und Verhaltensweisen gegenüber älteren Arbeitnehmern', *Aus Politik und Zeitgeschichte*, 20: 26–34.

Bezrukova, K., Jehn, K.A., Zanutto, E.L. and Thatcher, S.M.B. (2009) 'Do workgroup faultlines help or hurt? A moderated model of faultlines, team identification, and group performance', *Organization Science*, 20(1): 35–50.

Blau, J.R. and Blau, P.M. (1982) 'The cost of inequality: Metropolitan structure and violent crime', *American Sociological Review*, 47(1): 114–129.

Blau, Peter M. (1977) *Inequality and Heterogeneity.* New York: Free Press.

Bloom, M. (1999) 'The performance effects of pay dispersion on individuals and organizations', *Academy of Management Journal*, 42(1): 25–40.

Boehm, S., Kunze, F. and Bruch, H. (forthcoming) 'Spotlight on age-diversity climate: The impact of age-inclusive HR practices on firm-level outcomes', *Personnel Psychology.* DOI: 10.1111/peps.12047.

Bowers, C.A., Pharmer, J.A. and Salas, E. (2000) 'When member homogeneity is needed in work teams: A Meta-Analysis', *Small Group Research*, 31(3): 305–327.

Brewer, M.B. (1979) 'In-group bias in the minimal intergroup situation: A cognitive-motivational analysis', *Psychological Bulletin*, 86(2): 307–324.

Brewer, Marilynn B. and Brown, Rupert J. (1998) 'Intergroup relations', in D.T. Gilbert and S.T. Fiske (eds), *Handbook of Social Psychology*. Boston: McGraw-Hill. pp. 554–594.

Bunderson, J.S. and Sutcliffe, K.M. (2002) 'Comparing alternative conceptualizations of functional diversity in management teams: Process and performance effects', *Academy of Management Journal*, 45(5): 875–893.

Burt, Ronald S. (2002) 'The social capital of structural holes', in M.F. Guillen, R. Collins, P. England and M. Meyer (eds), *The New Economic Sociology*. New York: Russell Sage Foundation. pp. 148–189.

Byrne, Donn E. (1971) *The Attraction Paradigm*. New York: Academic Press.

Carpenter, M.A. (2002) 'The implications of strategy and social context for the relationship between top management team heterogeneity and firm performance', *Strategic Management Journal*, 23(3): 275–284.

Choi, S. and Rainey, H.G. (2010) 'Managing diversity in US Federal Agencies: Effects of diversity and diversity management on employee perceptions of organizational performance', *Public Administration Review*, 70(1): 109–121.

Cox, Taylor H. Jr. (1994) *Cultural Diversity in Organizations: Theory, Research, & Practice.* San Francisco: Berrett-Koehler.

Cramton, Catherine D. and Hinds, Pamela J. (2005) 'Subgroup dynamics in internationally distributed teams: Ethnocentrism or cross-national learning', in B. Staw and R. Kramer (eds), *Research in Organizational Behavior. An Annual Series of Analytical Essays and Critical Reviews*, Vol. 26. Oxford: Elsevier. pp. 231–263.

Cummings, A., Zhou, J. and Oldham, G.R. (1993) 'Demographic differences and employee work outcomes: Effects on multiple comparison groups', paper presented at the Annual Meeting of the Academy of Management, Atlanta, GA.

Dychtwald, K., Erickson, T. and Morison, B. (2004) 'It's time to retire retirement', *Harvard Business Review*, 82(3): 48–57.

Elliott, R.H. (1995) 'Human resource management's role in the future aging of the workforce', *Review of Public Personnel Administration*, 15(2): 5–17.

Ely, R.J. (2004) 'A field study of group diversity, participation in diversity education programs, and performance', *Journal of Organizational Behavior*, 25(6): 755–780.

Ensher, E.A., Grant-Vallone, E.J. and Donaldson, S.I. (2001) 'Discrimination on job satisfaction, organizational commitment, organizational citizenship behavior, and grievances', *Human Resource Development Quarterly*, 12(1): 53–72.

Feldman, D.C. (1994) 'The decision to retire early: A review and conceptualization', *Academy of Management Review*, 19(2): 285–311.

Finkelstein, L.M., Burke, M.J. and Raju, N.S. (1995) 'Age discrimination in simulated employment contexts: An integrative analysis', *Journal of Applied Psychology*, 80(6): 652–663.

Fiol, C.M. (1994) 'Consensus, diversity, and learning in organizations', *Organization Science*, 5(3): 403–420.

Gaertner, Sam L. and Dovidio, Jack F. (2000) *Reducing Intergroup Bias: The Common Ingroup Identity Model.* Philadelphia: Psychology Press.

Gelfand, Michele J., Nishii, Lisa H., Raver, Jana L. and Schneider, Benjamin (2005) 'Discrimination in organizations: An organizational level systems perspective', in R. Dipboye and A. Colella (eds), *Discrimination at Work: The Psychological and Organizational Bases*. Mahwah, NJ: Erlbaum. pp. 89–116.

Gonzalez, J.A. and DeNisi, A.S. (2009) 'Cross-level effects of demography and diversity climate on organizational attachment and firm effectiveness', *Journal of Organizational Behavior*, 30(1): 21–40.

Gruber, Jonathan and Wise, David A. (2004) *Social Security Programs and Retirement around the World: Micro-Estimation*. Chicago: University of Chicago Press.

Harrison, D.A. and Klein, K.J. (2007) 'What's the difference? Diversity constructs as separation, variety, or disparity in organizations', *Academy of Management Review*, 32(4): 1199–1228.

Harrison, David. A. and Sin, Hock-Peng (2006) 'What is diversity and how should it be measured?', in A.M. Konrad, P. Prasad and J.K. Pringle (eds), *Handbook of Workplace Diversity*. Newbury Park, CA: Sage. pp. 191–216.

Hicks-Clarke, D. and Iles, P. (2000) 'Climate for diversity and its effects on career and organisational attitudes and perceptions', *Personnel Review*, 29(3): 324–345.

Hinds, P.J., Carley, K.M., Krackhardt, D. and Wholey, D. (2000) 'Choosing work group members: Balancing similarity, competence, and familiarity', *Organizational Behavior and Human Decision Processes*, 81(2): 226–251.

Hogg, M.A. (2001) 'A social identity theory of leadership', *Personality and Social Psychology Review*, 5(3): 184–200.

Homan, A.C., Van Knippenberg, D., Van Kleef, G.A. and De Dreu, C.K.W. (2007) 'Bridging faultlines by valuing diversity: Diversity beliefs, information elaboration, and performance in diverse work groups', *Journal of Applied Psychology*, 92(5): 1189–1199.

Jackson, S.E., Brett, J.F., Sessa, V.I., Cooper, D.M., Julin, J.A. and Peyronnin, K. (1991) 'Some differences make a difference – Individual dissimilarity and group heterogeneity as correlates of recruitment, promotions, and turnover', *Journal of Applied Psychology*, 76(5): 675–689.

Jackson, S.E., Joshi, A. and Erhardt, N.L. (2003) 'Recent Research on Team and Organizational Diversity: SWOT Analysis and Implications', *Journal of Management*, 29(6): 801–830.

Jackson, Susan E., May, Karen E. and Whitney, Kristina (1995) 'Understanding the dynamics of diversity in decisionmaking teams', in R.A. Guzzo and E. Salas (eds), *Team Effectiveness and Decision Making in Organizations*. San Francisco: Jossey-Bass. pp. 204–261.

Janis, Irving L. (1972) *Victims of Groupthink*. Boston: Houghton Mifflin.

Jaumotte, F. (2003) 'Labour force participation of women: Empirical evidence on the role of policy and other determinants in OECD countries', *OECD Economic Studies*, 37: 51–108.

Jehn, K.A. and Bezrukova, K. (2004) 'A field study of group diversity, workgroup context, and performance', *Journal of Organizational Behavior*, 25(6): 703–729.

Jehn, K.A., Chadwick, C. and Thatcher, S.M.B. (1997) 'To agree or not to agree: The effects of value congruence, individual demographic dissimilarity, and conflict on workgroup outcomes', *International Journal of Conflict Management*, 8(4): 287–305.

Jehn, K.A., Northcraft, G.B. and Neale, M.A. (1999) 'Why differences make a difference: A field study of diversity, conflict, and performance in workgroups', *Administrative Science Quarterly*, 44(4): 741–763.

Joshi, A. and Roh, H. (2009) 'The role of context in work team diversity research: a meta-analytic view', *Academy of Management Journal*, 52(3): 599–627.

Joshi, A., Dencker, J.C., Franz, G. and Martocchio, J.J. (2010) 'Unpacking generational identities in organizations', *Academy of Management Review*, 35(3): 392–414.

Juhn, C. and Potter, S. (2006) 'Changes in labor force participation in the United States', *Journal of Economic Perspectives*, 20(3): 27–46.

Kanter, Rosabeth M. (1977) *Men and Woman of the Corporation*. New York: Basic Books.

Kaube, J. (2008) 'Schneller am Markt?', *Frankfurter Allgemeine Zeitung*. http://www.faz.net/aktuell/feuilleton/forschung-und-lehre/studiendauer-schneller-am-markt-1539810.html. Accessed 1 January 2012.

Kearney, E. and Gebert, D. (2009) 'Managing diversity and enhancing team outcomes: The promise of transformational leadership', *Journal of Applied Psychology*, 94(1): 77–98.

Kearney, E., Gebert, D. and Voelpel, S. C. (2009). When and how diversity benefits teams: the importance of team members' need for cognition. Academy of Management Journal, 52(3): 581–598.

Kelloway, E.K., Barling, J. and Helleur, J. (2000) 'Enhancing transformational leadership: The roles of training and feedback', *Leadership & Organization Development Journal*, 21(3): 145–149.

Kilduff, M., Angelmar, R. and Mehra, A. (2000) 'Top management-team diversity and firm performance: Examining the role of cognitions', *Organization Science*, 11(1): 21–34.

Kohlbacher, Florian and Herstatt, Cornelius (eds) (2008) *The Silver Market Phenomenon: Business Opportunities in an Era of Demographic Change*. Berlin, Heidelberg: Springer.

Kunze, F. and Bruch, H. (2010) 'Age-based faultlines and perceived productive energy: The moderation of transformational leadership', *Small Group Research*, 41(5): 593–620.

Kunze, F., Boehm, S.A. and Bruch, H. (2011) 'Age diversity, age discrimination, and performance consequences – A cross-organizational study', *Journal of Organizational Behavior*, 32(2): 264–290.

Kunze, F., Boehm, S., Bruch, H. (2013). 'Organizational boundary conditions to prevent negative performance consequences of age diversity', Journal of Management Studies. 50(3): 413–442.

Lau, D.C. and Murnighan, J.K. (1998) 'Demographic diversity and faultlines: The compositional dynamics of organizational groups', *Academy of Management Review*, 23(2): 325–340.

Lawrence, B.S. (1980) 'The myth of the midlife crisis', *Sloan Management Review*, 21(4): 35–49.

Lawrence, B.S. (1984) 'Age grading: The implicit organizational timetable', *Journal of Occupational Behaviour*, 5(1): 23–35.

Lawrence, B.S. (1988) 'New wrinkles in the theory of age: Demography, norms, and performance ratings', *Academy of Management Journal*, 31(2): 309–337.

Lawrence, B.S. (1997) 'The black box of organizational demography', *Organization Science*, 8(1): 1–22.

Lengnick-Hall, M.L., Gaunt, P.M. and Kulkarni, M. (2008) 'Overlooked and underutilized: People with disabilities are an untapped human resource', *Human Resource Management*, 47(2): 255–273.

Leonard, J.S., Levine, D.I. and Joshi, A. (2004) 'Do birds of a feather shop together? The effects on performance of employees' similarity with one another and with customers', *Journal of Organizational Behavior*, 25(6): 731–754.

Li, J.T. and Hambrick, D.C. (2005) 'Factional groups: A new vantage on demographic faultlines, conflict, and disintegration in work teams', *Academy of Management Journal*, 48(5): 794–813.

Mathieu, J., Maynard, M.T., Rapp, T. and Gilson, L. (2008) 'Team effectiveness 1997–2007: A review of recent advancements and a glimpse into the future', *Journal of Management*, 34(3): 410–476.

McKay, P.F., Avery, D.R. and Morris, M.A. (2009) 'A tale of two climates: Diversity climate from subordinates' and managers' perspectives and their role in store unit sales performance', *Personnel Psychology*, 62(4): 767–791.

McKay, P.F., Avery, D.R., Liao, H. and Morris, M.A. (2011) 'Does diversity climate lead to customer satisfaction? It depends on the service climate and business unit demography', *Organization Science*, 22(3): 788–803.

McPherson, J.M. and Smith-Lovin, L. (1987) 'Homophily in voluntary organizations: Status distance and the composition of face-to-face groups', *American Sociological Review*, 52(3): 370–379.

McPherson, J.M., Smith-Lovin, L. and Cook, J.M. (2001) 'Birds of a feather: Homophily in social networks', *Annual Reviews in Sociology*, 27(1): 415–444.

Michaels, Ed, Handfield-Jones, Helen and Axelrod, Beth (2001) *The War for Talent*. Boston: Harvard Business School Press.

Milliken, F.J. and Martins, L.L. (1996) 'Searching for common threads: Understanding the multiple effects of diversity in organizational groups', *Academy of Management Review*, 21(2): 402–433.

Molleman, E. (2005) 'Diversity in demographic characteristics, abilities and personality traits: Do faultlines affect team functioning?' *Group Decision and Negotiation*, 14(3): 173–193.

Mor Barak, M.E., Cherin, D.A. and Berkman, S. (1998) 'Organizational and personal dimensions in diversity climate: Ethnic and gender differences in employee perceptions', *Journal of Applied Behavioral Science*, 34: 82–104.

Mor Barak, M.E. and Levin, A. (2002) 'Outside of the corporate mainstream and excluded from the work community: A study of diversity, job satisfaction and well-being', *Community, Work & Family*, 5(2): 133–157.

Nishii, L.H. and Mayer, D.M. (2009) 'Do inclusive leaders help to reduce turnover in diverse groups? The moderating role of leader–member exchange in the diversity to turnover relationship', *Journal of Applied Psychology*, 94(6): 1412–1426.

O'Reilly III, C.A., Caldwell, D.F. and Barnett, W.P. (1989) 'Work group demography, social integration, and turnover', *Administrative Science Quarterly*, 34(1): 21–37.

Ostergaard, C.R., Timmermans, B. and Kristinsson, K. (2010) 'Does a different view create something new? The effect of employee diversity on innovation', *Research Policy*, 40(3): 500–509.

Pelled, L.H. (1996) 'Demographic diversity, conflict, and work group outcomes: An intervening process theory', *Organization Science*, 7(6): 615–631.

Pelled, L.H., Eisenhardt, K.M. and Xin, K.R. (1999) 'Exploring the black box: An analysis of work group diversity, conflict, and performance', *Administrative Science Quarterly*, 44(1): 1–28.

Pelled, L.H., Xin, K.R. and Weiss, A.M. (2001) 'No es como mi: Relational demography and conflict in a Mexican production facility', *Journal of Occupational and Organizational Psychology*, 74(1): 63–84.

Pettigrew, T.F. (1998) 'Intergroup contact theory', *Annual Review of Psychology*, 49(1): 65–85.

Pfeffer, J. and Davis-Blake, A. (1990) 'Determinants of salary dispersion in organizations', *Industrial Relations*, 29(1): 38–57.

Podsakoff, P.M., MacKenzie, S.B. and Bommer, W.H. (1996) 'Transformational leader behaviors and substitutes for leadership as determinants of employee satisfaction, commitment, trust, and organizational citizenship behaviors', *Journal of Management*, 22(2): 259–298.

Polzer, J.T., Crisp, C.B., Jarvenpaa, S.L. and Kim, J.W. (2006) 'Extending the faultline model to geographically dispersed teams: How colocated subgroups can impair group functioning', *Academy of Management Journal*, 49(4): 679–692.

Posthuma, R.A. and Campion, M.A. (2009) 'Age stereotypes in the workplace: Common stereotypes, moderators, and future research directions', *Journal of Management*, 35(1): 158–188.

Rico, R., Molleman, E., Sanchez-Manzanares, M. and Van der Vegt, G.S. (2008) 'The effects of diversity faultlines and team task autonomy on decision quality and social integration', *Journal of Management*, 34(3): 635–636.

Robinson, G. and Dechant, K. (1997) 'Building a business case for diversity', *Academy of Management Executive*, 11(3): 21–31.

Rodrik, Dani (2008) *One Economics, Many Recipes: Globalization, Institutions, and Economic Growth.* Princeton, NJ: Princeton University Press.

Sacco, J.M. and Schmitt, N. (2005) 'A dynamic multilevel model of demographic diversity and misfit effects', *Journal of Applied Psychology*, 90(2): 203–231.

Shore, L.M., Chung-Herrera, B.G., Dean, M.A., Ehrhart, K.H., Jung, D.I., Randel, A.E. and Singh, G. (2009) 'Diversity in organizations: where are we now and where are we going?', *Human Resource Management Review*, 19(2): 117–133.

Siegel, P.A. and Hambrick, D.C. (2005) 'Pay disparities within top management groups: Evidence of harmful effects on performance of high-technology firms', *Organization Science*, 16(3): 259–274.

Simons, T., Pelled, L.H. and Smith, K.A. (1999) 'Making use of difference: Diversity, debate, and decision comprehensiveness in top management teams', *Academy of Management Journal*, 42(6): 662–673.

Smola, K.W. and Sutton, C.D. (2002) 'Generational differences: Revisiting generational work values for the new millennium', *Journal of Organizational Behavior*, 23(4): 363–382.

Tajfel, H. (1974) 'Social identity and intergroup behaviour', *Social Science Information*, 13(2): 65–93.

Tajfel, Henri and Turner, John C. (1986) 'The social identity theory of intergroup behaviour', in S. Worchel and W.G. Austin (eds), *Psychology of intergroup relations*. Chicago: Nelson-Hall. pp. 7–24.

Tempest, S., Barnatt, C. and Coupland, C. (2002) 'Grey advantage – New strategies for the old', *Long Range Planning*, 35(5): 475–492.

Thatcher, S. and Patel, P.C. (2011) 'Demographic faultlines: A meta-analysis of the literature', *Journal of Applied Psychology*, 96(6): 1119–1193.

Thatcher, S.M.B., Jehn, K.A. and Zanutto, E. (2003) 'Cracks in diversity research: The effects of diversity faultlines on conflict and performance', *Group Decision and Negotiation*, 12(3): 217–241.

Thomas, D.A. and Ely, R.J. (1996) 'Making differences matter', *Harvard Business Review*, 74(5): 79–90.

Timmerman, T.A. (2000) 'Racial diversity, age diversity, and team performance', *Small Group Research*, 31(1): 592–606.

Triana, M.C. and García, M.F. (2009) 'Valuing diversity: a group value approach to understanding the importance of organizational efforts to support diversity', *Journal of Organizational Behavior*, 30(7): 941–962.

Triana, M.C., Garcia, M.F. and Colella, A. (2010) 'Managing diversity: How organizational efforts to support diversity moderate the effects of perceived racial discrimination on affective commitment', *Personnel Psychology*, 63(4): 817–843.

Tsui, A.S., Egan, T.D. and O'Reilly III, C.A. (1992) 'Being different: Relational demography and organizational attachment', *Administrative Science Quarterly*, 37(4): 549–579.

Turner, John C. (1985) 'Social categorization and the self-concept: A social cognitive theory of group behavior', in E.J. Lawler (ed.), *Advances in group processes: Theory and research*, Vol. 2. Greenwhich: JAI Press. pp. 77–122.

Twenge, J.M., Campbell, S.M., Hoffman, B.J. and Lance, C.E. (2010) 'Generational differences in work values: Leisure and extrinsic values increasing, social and intrinsic values decreasing', *Journal of Management*, 36(5): 1117–1142.

Van Knippenberg, D. and Schippers, M.C. (2007) 'Work group diversity', *Annual Review of Psychology*, 58: 515–541.

Wegge, J., Roth, C., Neubach, B., Schmidt, K.H. and Kanfer, R. (2008) 'Age and gender diversity as determinants of performance and health in a public organization: The role of task complexity and group size', *Journal of Applied Psychology*, 93(6): 1301–1313.

West, M., Patterson, M., Dawson, J. and Nickell, S. (1999) 'The effectiveness of top management groups in manufacturing organizations', *CEP Discussion Papers*, Centre for Economic Performance, London School of Economics and Political Science.

Wiersema, M.F. and Bantel, K.A. (1992) 'Top management team demography and corporate strategic change', *Academy of Management Journal*, 35(1): 91–121.

Wiersema, M.F. and Bird, A. (1993) 'Organizational demography in Japanese firms – Group heterogeneity, individual dissimilarity, and top management team turnover', *Academy of Management Journal*, 36(5): 996–1025.

Wiersema, M.F. and Bowen, H.P. (2008) 'Corporate diversification: the impact of foreign competition, industry globalization, and product diversification', *Strategic Management Journal*, 29(2): 115–132.

Williams, K.Y. and O'Reilly III, C.A. (1998) 'Demography and diversity in organizations: A review of 40 years of research', in B. Staw and R. Sutton (eds), *Research in organizational behavior*, Vol. 20. Greenwhich: JAI Press. pp.77–140.

Young, J.L. and James, E.H. (2001) 'Token majority: The work attitudes of the male flight attendants', *Sex Roles*, 45(5): 299–319.

Zajac, E.J., Golden, B.R. and Shortell, S.M. (1991) 'New organizational forms for enhancing innovation: The case of internal corporate joint ventures', *Management Science*, 37(2): 170–184.

Zenger, T.R. and Lawrence, B.S. (1989) 'Organizational demography: The differential effects of age and tenure distributions on technical communication', *Academy of Management Journal*, 32(2): 353–376.

4

Prolonging Working Life in an Aging world: A Cross-national Perspective on Labor Market and Welfare Policies Toward Active Aging

Anne-Marie Guillemard

The aging of the population and increasing longevity do not just raise questions about pensions. The major problem stemming from these trends is how to provide employment opportunities to aging wage-earners. The implications of demographic aging have been explored mainly from the angles of financially balancing the books of retirement systems or providing care for the frail elderly. These approaches are much too restrictive. The aging of the population does not just mean that the proportion of persons over the age of 60 or of the elderly is on the rise. It also affects the age pyramid of the economically active population. The aging of the workforce is a gigantic challenge for developed societies; its scope has not been sufficiently evaluated. This dimension of demographic aging and policy responses to it are the subject of this chapter.

In all developed countries, we observe an unprecedented phenomenon: the aging of the economically active population. This stems from a twofold trend. On the one hand, the large cohorts of the baby-boom generation are growing older and have swelled the ranks of 50–64 year-olds before going on retirement. On the other hand, much smaller cohorts of young people, born during a period with a lower fertility rate, are entering the labor market. Two statistics tell the story. In the European Union, 45–64 year-olds will, in 2015, make up 45% of the working-age population as compared with 35% in 1995.[1] In contrast, the proportion of 15–29 year-olds will decrease by 16% by 2015. The aging of the working-age population is a process resulting from trends affecting both the top and bottom of the age pyramid.

This chapter summarizes the research results reported in my book, *Les défis du vieillissement: Âge, emploi, retraite. Perspectives internationales* (Paris: Armand Colin 2010). The first section of this chapter will discuss senior employment as a social and a sociological problem. I describe the process that has placed this *social* problem on the political agenda and show that developed countries must address this issue in order to cope with demographic aging. A look at international data about labor force participation rates over the age of 55 and their evolution over the past 30 years will shed stark light on disparities between countries. What a contrast in the situation of 50 year-olds in Japan, Sweden and France! The first two countries have kept this group in the labor market until an advanced age, the median age of withdrawal from the labor force being at least 65. In France, this age-group has a fragile position in the labor market and is ejected early during the second part of careers, the median age of exit being barely over 58.

We thus see how relative the social definition of age turns out to be depending on the societal context. The aging wage-earner is a social construct, proof of this being the word 'senior', coined not so long ago to refer to persons who are labeled as occupationally old but are not yet classified as 'old' or 'aged'. This word brings to mind the usage in sports, where 'senior' means that one is no longer a junior but not yet a veteran. Accordingly, the same performance cannot be expected of seniors as of juniors. Take notice: the age thresholds associated with this phase of life fluctuate. For the EU, 'senior' refers to 65–79 year-olds, while 55–64 year-olds are said to be older wage-earners. For France, the word 'senior' commonly refers to 45–65 year-olds.

These observations help establish a conceptual framework for approaching 'senior' employment from a sociological angle too. International comparisons are a necessary research strategy because they provide the distance needed to 'denaturalize' definitions of age and thus shift to a relational analysis. They alone enable us to work out a theory explaining the observed disparities in occupational pathways during the second part of careers. The construction of concepts in this field of research also calls for adopting a life-course perspective in order to analyze public policies comparatively. This perspective, in line with a cognitive approach to policy analysis, focuses not just on a set of rules and models for the actions undertaken by public authorities but also on normative structures incarnating 'dominant models of interpretation of the world' (Muller 2000: 194). In other words, they are key agents in the social definition, and redefinition, of the ages of life and the age for working.

The second section of this chapter uses this framework to propose a comparative theory of economic activity during the second part of careers. It will present a typology of four configurations of labor market and welfare policies corresponding to four ideal types of occupational pathways and transitions to retirement.

In the conclusion, the results drawn from this comparative approach will serve to examine why France Belgium and Southern European countries are lagging behind in senior employment while pointing to the political strategies for catching up by adopting a new age-management. For this purpose, examples of countries that have managed to delay the age of exit from the labor market and maintain seniors in employment will be cited.

PROLONGING THE WORKLIFE: A SOCIAL AND SOCIOLOGICAL FRAMEWORK

Longevity and demographic aging force us to rework conceptions based on the traditional distribution of the time for work and non-work over the life course. This is even more so given the shortening of the worklife and the significant advances in recent decades that enable more people to live longer and in better health. As a result of this, but one generation – of median age – is working in many European countries. This means that two of the four living generations in a family line are now retired while the youngest is in school. The problem is not merely financial, as we see. It represents a major issue for society, one involving the distribution of periods for work and for inactivity over the life course.

An OECD report in 1998 drew attention to this paradoxical situation. According to it, an average man in an OECD country spent, in 1960, 50 years of his allotted 68 years of life in employment but, by 1995, was devoting only half of his life-span to work: 38 out of 76 years. The shortening of the worklife has resulted from two trends. First of all, young people are entering the labor market later in life owing to longer schooling and the difficulty of finding steady jobs. More importantly, the time spent on retirement has become much longer owing to early exit from the labor market and the rising life expectancy. In France, retirement lasted twice as long in 2010 as in 1975. For the generation that, born in 1910, left the labor force at 65 in 1975, the expected length of retirement was 10.6 years. For the generation that, born in 1950, went on retirement at 60, it amounts to 20.4 years (Conseil d'Analyse Économique 2005: 54).

This new distribution of socially defined periods of time over the life course is obviously untenable, for two reasons. In the first place, it jeopardizes the system of social transfers between generations. Will the wealth produced by an ever smaller fraction of the population suffice to guarantee a decent income to the swelling ranks of the economically inactive? Advances in productivity at the workplace will not, by themselves, solve this equation. Some

pundits have evoked the alarming possibility of 'age warfare', given that the burden of paying for pensions might corner a disproportionate share of the wealth produced by the younger generation still at work and thus imperil the principles of fairness and solidarity that govern relations between generations. In this case, social cohesion in developed countries would be menaced. In the second place, the shorter worklife forces us to ask questions about the workforce needed to produce tomorrow's wealth. The statistics are clear enough in France: persons between 25 and 54 years old hold more than 80% of jobs – a group who makes up no more than 40% of the total population. To deal with these worrisome prospects, employment opportunities must be better distributed among age-groups and generations (European Commission 2005: 94).

One of the most effective and acceptable ways to cope with preoccupations about financing welfare is, given the longevity of older age-groups, to keep people in employment longer and thus delay exit from the labor market. Making the worklife longer reaps double dividends in terms of both pensions and social expenditures: it increases the number of persons contributing to welfare (through payroll taxes) while reducing the number drawing pensions. For these reasons, the OECD in 1998 and the European Union in 1999 adopted the slogan of 'active aging' with the clear-cut goal of delaying exit from the labor market for seniors and keeping them longer in employment.[2] Accordingly, the European Strategy for Employment has included two objectives. In 2001, it set an average employment rate of 50% for 55–64 year-olds to be reached by 2010 European Council in Stocholm. In 2002, the objective of gradually raising, by approximately five years, the average age of exit from the labor market was set, too, for 2010 (European Council in Barcelone).

Unfortunately, even though the goal set for 2010 has been nearly reached in the EU-15 as a whole, it is still distant in Belgium and France, and in countries to the south, such as Italy and Spain, or east, among new member states. The employment of seniors, as well as firms and public policies for reaching this goal, poses a major challenge in countries that must deal with demographic aging.

INTERNATIONAL COMPARISONS: AN INDISPENSABLE RESEARCH STRATEGY GIVEN STRONG DISPARITIES AMONG COUNTRIES

When examining, over a long period, the economic activity of 55–64 year-olds, we notice two distinct periods, each characterized by disparity among countries. For 1980–2000, we see a 20-year decline in the employment rate after the age of 55, but variable in scope depending on the country. The employment rate of persons over 55 started decreasing in the late 1970s or early 1980s. This trend lasted until toward the end of the century. The degree of this decrease varied widely however. It was considerable on continental Europe where countries chose for at least two decades to 'save jobs' by compensating aging wage-earners for leaving the labor force via 'preretirement' or early exit schemes and other age-based measures (Kohli et al. 1991). Between 1971 and 2000, this employment rate fell by

41% in Germany, 43% in France and 36% in the Netherlands. The decrease was much smaller in Scandinavia (16% in Sweden), Japan (9%) and the United States (11%) – countries that did not heavily rely on early exit arrangements (Guillemard 2010: 43). In fact, Sweden and Japan tried to adapt to the aging of the labor force by reinforcing active employment policies and targeting aging wage-earners who were vulnerable in the labor market.

For 2000–2010, employment activity rates have risen, but variably depending on the country. As Table 4.1 indicates, the employment rate of 55–64 year-olds has been rising since the years 2000. The increase is variable however. From 1996 to 2010, it was spectacular in the Netherlands (86%) and Finland (63%), and significant for Germany (53%). The increase in other EU member states has been moderate: 35% in France and 31% in Spain, countries that have failed to reach the EU objective of 50% set for 2010. France, where less than 40% of this age-group is working, has proven unable to significantly delay the age for withdrawing from the labor market – unlike Finland and the Netherlands, where, despite a situation similar to France's in 1996, the trend has been reversed.

Table 4.1 Change in employment activity rates of 55–64 year-olds in the European Union, 1996–2011 (%)

	1996	1998	2000	2002	2004	2005	2007	2008	2009	2010	% variation	2011
Belgium	21.9	22.5	25.0	25.8	30.1	31.8	34.4	34.5	35.3	37.3	60	38,7
Denmark	49.1	50.4	54.6	57.3	60.3	59.5	58.6	57.0	57.5	57.6	17	59,5
Finland	35.4	35.7	41.2	47.8	50.9	52.7	55.0	56.5	55.5	56.2	63	57,0
France	29.4	28.3	29.4	33.8	37.5	37.9	38.3	38.2	38.9	39.7	35	41,5
Germany	37.9	37.7	37.4	38.4	41.4	45.4	51.5	53.8	56.2	57.7	53	59,9
Italy	28.6	27.7	27.3	28.6	30.5	31.4	33.8	34.4	35.7	36.6	28	37,9
Netherlands	30.5	33.0	37.9	42.0	45.2	46.1	50.9	53.0	55.1	53.7	86	56,1
Portugal	47.3	50.2	51.3	51.9	50.3	50.5	50.9	50.8	49.7	49.2	4,0	47,9
Spain	33.2	35.3	36.8	39.7	41.3	43.1	44.6	45.6	44.1	43.6	31	44,5
Sweden	63.4	62.7	64.3	68.3	69.1	69.4	70.0	70.1	70.0	70.5	14	72,3
United Kingdom	47.7	48.3	50.4	53.2	56.2	56.9	57.4	58.0	57.5	57.1	20	56,7
EU-15	36.3	36.4	37.5	39.8	42.5	44.1	46.5	47.4	48.0	48.4	35	47,4
Japan	64.2	63.8	62.8	61.6	63.0	63.9	66.1	66.3	65.5	65.2	1,6	65,1
United States	57.2	57.7	57.8	59.5	59.9	60.8	61.8	62.1	60.6	60.3	5.4	
Australia	42.4	43.9	46.2	48.6	51.7	53.5	56.6	57.4	59.0	60.6	43	

Source: Our calculations using Eurostat (EFT) and OECD data.

ADOPTING A LIFE-COURSE PERSPECTIVE TO ANALYZE PUBLIC POLICIES AND COMBINE COGNITIVE AND NEO-INSTITUTIONALIST APPROACHES

How to explain the differences observed in labor force participation rates at the end of careers in countries with rather similar demographic trends? The hypothesis underlying my interpretation is that the principal factors have to do with how a society gives meaning to the fact of growing older through its construction of the relations between age and work and its definitions of the ages to work and to stop working. These dynamic processes can be detected by analyzing the interrelations between public policies related to work, employment, training and welfare; examining the constellation of actors; and studying the normative structures that, erected by these actors, socially organize the life course.

This research adopts a life-course perspective. To understand labor force participation in the second part of careers, we must, first of all, interpret it in the light of the long, gradual process whereby wage-earners are kept in or pushed out of the labor market as they grow older. Secondly, a finding of the sociology of the life-course is that the institutionalization of welfare systems has been a powerful factor that formatted the life-course into three periods by using age as a chronological marker for setting the thresholds for passing from one age of life to the next, as pointed out by Mayer and Schoepflin (1989: 198):

> In the welfare state, the continuous flow of life is transformed into a series of situations all of which have a clear formal definition [...] Periodization of life and proliferation of sharp transitions which derive from the social insurance system combine into a life-long biographical pattern.

This biographical pattern has come undone owing to the advent of a knowledge-based society and the longer life span. Most sociologists who adopt a life-course perspective now agree that the tripartite division of the

life course, which prevailed in industrial society, has undergone deep changes and that individuals' biographies no longer fall in line with the three distinct, successive periods – education, work, leisure – that used to organize the life course (Marshall et al. 2001, Riley et al. 1994). Life-course trajectories are now 'flexible' (Best 1981), 'destandardized' (Beck 1992) and much more complex. Aging wage-earners have a harder time staying employed. Flexible work, flexible life courses, and uncertain biographical pathways are multiplying.

The concept of the life course is valuable since it allows for relating a microsociology of biographical pathways to a macrosociology of the life course as an institution that shapes career pathways and impresses upon them a relation to time and to the future that is specific to each society. This concept helps us bridge the gap between institutional changes and individuals' pathways through the world of work. It helps us better understand both the new risk profiles corresponding to individuals' life-course trajectories and the reconfigurations of welfare necessary for covering these risks. We are thus able not only to understand the new forms of vulnerability affecting the second part of careers but also to explain why certain countries have managed better than others to cope by adjusting training, employment and welfare policies.

This analysis of public policy combines the neo-institutionalist approach with a cognitive perspective. Ebbinghaus (2006: 16) has defined the first when comparing early retirement reforms in Europe, the United States and Japan:

> The study applies an institutionalist approach. The decisions of actors at the workplace level or in the social policy and bargaining arenas are embedded in institutional environments that shape actors' orientations and interests as well as the opportunity structures for the actor constellations.

To explain comparatively the contrasting pathways taken by individuals at the end of their careers, most neo-institutionalist studies have pointed to the decisive effect of the dialectics between labor market models and welfare systems. For these authors (Esping-Andersen and Sonnberger 1991, Naschold et al. 1994, Ebbinghaus 2006), this explanation involves a variable combination of push/pull factors, i.e., the arrangements in the welfare system pulling people out of the labor market and the practices in firms pushing them out of the workforce. It refers to the rules, regulations and norms of the institutions that offer to the older worker a range of opportunities for working or for exiting early from the labor force.

Ebbinghaus (2006), whose theory is the most ambitious formulation of this neo-institutionalist approach, has proposed an encompassing conceptual framework for explaining the various pathways in different countries out of the labor market during the second part of careers. It establishes a relation between, on the one hand, the dialectics of welfare regimes and labor market models and, on the other hand, the 'varieties of capitalism' described by Hall and Soskice (2001) and models of labor relations. Despite the advances made, his book has, in my opinion, two major limitations that strengthen the argument for not confining our approach to a neo-institutionalist analysis of social policies but for broadening it to include the cognitive dimension of these policies.

Our first reservation is that this theory narrowly focuses on early exit and its institutional determinants. This focus on the end of careers keeps us from understanding the whole, long process that gradually turns wage-earners into misfits at the workplace before pushing them out of the labor market. The lack of training and career prospects for wage-earners in their forties very often foretells their vulnerability in their fifties and, ultimately, determines their exit from the labor market. Some of the key factors for understanding comparatively why the ability of seniors to remain in employment differ are: the absence of programs for maintaining and updating qualifications, the lack of 'reskilling' after the age of 40, low mobility

or the scant attention paid to 'sustainable' working conditions throughout the career and not just at its end. Adopting a broader life-course perspective that envisions the whole second part of careers is absolutely indispensable for understanding the determinants of withdrawal from the labor market and the policy levers that certain countries have used to reverse the early exit trend. The short-sighted focus on the end of careers has led neo-institutionalists to underestimate the role of welfare and production regimes, the first reduced to a mere pull factor and the second to a push factor. This vision is too reductionistic and simplistic, since it fails to see that the production system might be a factor for keeping the aging in employment by, for example, providing them with attractive working conditions and career opportunities.

The second limitation of the neo-institutionalist approach is that its studies have overlooked the cognitive dimension of public policies. This blind spot keeps this approach from understanding how the rules contained in institutional arrangements gradually construct both 'differentiated age cultures' and the social definition of age that all parties in the labor market use to develop their plans of action. As a consequence, a purely neo-institutionalist approach provides but a partial understanding of the situation, since it leaves out of account both the meaning that various parties associate with institutional programs and the uses of these programs in actual practices.

Methodologically, this criticism justified our decision to adopt a qualitative approach to country case studies that concretely analyze the dynamic relation between institutional arrangements and the strategies of actors in the labor market, while paying attention to the social meanings these arrangements have for the latter. This approach to international comparisons draws on the possibilities opened by societal analysis. It pays close attention to the cluster of institutions in each national context in order to explain points of convergence and divergence among countries. A comparative societal study of education and training policies in relation to the industrial organization of Germany and France (Maurice et al. 1982, 1992) laid the foundation of this approach. It related the labor market characteristic of German firms to specific institutional arrangements in Germany, which associated a system of vocational training (apprenticeship) with a model of organization in firms (classifications and mobility). In line with this societal analysis, the life-course perspective is interested in the effects of institutional (re)configurations over the second part of career. As a consequence, it does not seem worthwhile to try to isolate each of the dimensions under consideration (welfare system and type of labor market) in order to assess their weight from a matrix of correlations between indices that have been designed separately for each of the three dimensions taken into account in Ebbinghaus's work. Loyal to a 'societal' analysis, our comparative interpretation is based on the effects of the cluster of variables that characterize each societal context.

BUILDING A COMPARATIVE THEORY OF ECONOMIC ACTIVITY DURING THE SECOND PART OF CAREERS

To explain differences in occupational pathways at the end of careers, the relevant dimensions had to be identified for constructing the configurations of social policy to be taken into account. In line with the previously mentioned Societal approach, each configuration associates a welfare regime,[3] as defined by its degree of coverage and by the compensation it provides for economic inactivity during the second part of careers, with a set of labor market policies, defined by whether or not they ensure that older wage-earners remain employable, maintain their skills and stay in the labor force.

On one level, these institutional configurations of social policy directly affect, in each country, the pathways taken by wage-earners through the labor market. Owing to the entitlements, services and status they grant (in employment or in welfare), they determine the scope of alternatives open to wage-earners: integration in employment, early exit pathways, or arrangements for accumulating wages with a pension. These configurations shape the possibilities and expectations of all persons and parties in the labor market about the prospects for senior employment.

On another level, these social policy configurations give rise to a set of meaningful normative orientations. This is their cognitive dimension. Government actions for intervening and providing protection in employment, work, training and welfare have generated age-based norms and standards. The welfare state has produced an age-based government, an 'age police' to borrow Percheron's phrase (1991).[4] In a given national context, the interactions between, on the one hand, the different sorts of 'age police' contained in welfare and labor market policies and, on the other hand, the uses made of them by various parties generate momentum. This dynamics gradually gives shape to what I have called an 'age culture' in each national context. This culture corresponds to a shared set of values and norms about how to formulate questions related to growing old and about the rights and obligations associated with each stage of life. It is grounded on principles of fairness and justice between age-groups and generations, on categorizations about age and rules of action. The policy options chosen for aging wage-earners do not just represent rules of action however. Once adopted, they act back upon the cognitive sphere. They form networks of motivations, justifications and references that shape the behavior of everyone in the labor market. This is the meaning I have given to 'age culture'. This echoes Pierre Muller's approach of public policies (2000: 194):

> One becomes aware of both the cognitive and normative nature of public authorities' actions, since the two dimensions for explaining the world and formulating norms are irreducibly related.

Each institutional configuration can thus be examined in terms of the particular age culture it promotes.

A TYPOLOGY OF OCCUPATIONAL PATHWAYS DURING THE SECOND PART OF CAREERS

To simplify, four institutional configurations of public policies were identified by crossing employment policies with the welfare policies that provide compensation for withdrawal from the labor market. Aging wage-earners, when several arrangements exist for integrating them in employment, will have more opportunities for staying in the labor market. They will, on the contrary, exit earlier if the welfare state provides generous compensation for no longer working at the end of a career. These four institutional configurations and the types of occupational pathways opened by them are presented in Table 4.2,

which also indicates the countries best exemplifying each configuration. These 'ideal types' have served as a standard for assessing the other countries in our study. This typology should not be taken statically. For example, the reforms made in the Netherlands and Finland have shifted these two countries from Type 1 to Type 2.

The empirical validation of this comparative research established tight correlations between, on the one hand, the trends in public policy configurations, along with the normative structures and age cultures they generate, and, on the other hand, the main pathways into which they channel people for entering or exiting the labor market. For each country that clearly illustrates a typical configuration, we identified the specific arrangement of social policies there over a period of twenty years and its impact on the definitions and practices of actors in the labor market.

The starting point for this analysis was to comparatively examine trends in the

Table 4.2   Four public policy configurations with impact on the second part of careers

	Level of welfare coverage[a] for economic inactivity	
Active labor market policies	Low	High
	Type 4 **Reject or retain**	**Type 1** **Depreciate and eject**
Few policy instruments for keeping aging wage-earners in the labor market	Aging wage-earners are pushed out of, or kept in, the workforce depending on the situation in the labor market. United States and United Kingdom	Aging wage-earners are depreciated and then pushed out of the labor force. France and Belgium (as well as Netherlands and Finland till 1998 and Germany till 2005)
	Type 3 **Retain**	**Type 2** **Integrate or reintegrate**
Many policy instruments for integrating or reintegrating older wage-earners in the labor force	Aging wage-earners are kept in the labor force. Japan	Aging wage-earners are kept in, or brought back into, the labor market, since welfare is tied to the beneficiary's efforts to find work. Sweden and Denmark

[a] 'Level of coverage' refers to the amount and duration of benefits as well as the range of early exit pathways out of the labor market. The factors retained for establishing this typology are not so different from those of Gallie and Paugam (2010), who have defined 'unemployment welfare regimes' by relating three dimensions: the degree of coverage of unemployment insurance, the level and duration of benefits, and the importance of active employment policies, which corresponds in this table to policies for (re)integrating older wage-earners in the labor force.

implementation of employment and welfare policies and their effects on labor participating the second part of careers. We thus came to see how, depending on the ideal type, the relations between age, work, welfare and age culture were constructed and regulated. We could also thus perceive and analyze, in this comparative framework, the diversity of national responses for dealing with the new demographic aging trends under way in all developed countries. As a result, this diversity could be not only described but also interpreted.

Type 1: Depreciate and eject

Continental Europe clearly illustrates the first public policy configuration. Countries there combine generous compensation for economic inactivity to older wage-earners with a lack of policy instruments for integrating (or reintegrating) them in the labor market. France nearly perfectly exemplifies this configuration.

With regard to the principles for legitimating the distribution of jobs and income transfers between age-groups, this first configuration gives priority to guaranteeing income, through programs that compensate aging wage-earners for the loss of jobs. Its rationale of financially making up for the loss of employment gradually generated an 'early exit culture'. These countries soon accepted the norm that wage-earners should receive social transfers instead of jobs. The French case helps us understand how an 'early exit culture' for 'inactivating' aging wage-earners has emerged out of the interplay between actors, policy instruments, norms and rules.

For nearly three decades (1977–2003), France adopted public policies that, very attractive for both firms and their employees, offered generous benefits for early exit or 'pretirement'. These benefits were usually funded directly through income taxes (under the Fonds National de l'Emploi) or indirectly through social security payroll contributions (as, for example, the Unemployment insurance granted more and more exemptions from the obligation to search for a job, these

exemptions amounting to a disguised form of preretirement). Such programs proliferated until late into the 1990s. They were costly and the expected results in terms of job openings for young people fell far short of expectations.

This first type gradually constructed a definition of aging wage-earners as persons who, vulnerable in the labor market, could not be reclassified. It was, therefore, fair and just to open access for them to social transfers. Adopting this principle led to depreciating older wage-earners; and the categories considered 'old' gradually reached down into younger generations. Once wage-earners over 55 had been deemed incapable of being reclassified and fated to ejection from the workforce,[5] employees in their fifties were then labeled as 'almost (too) old' and, therefore, vulnerable. This trend gradually reached down even into the group of 40 year-olds.

This first configuration fosters age-based discrimination in employment. A rationale of age-segmentation soon prevails as more and more age-barriers are erected. All this is built into programs with incentives for firms to treat age-groups differently: early exit schemes for their oldest employees and programs for recruiting young people.

Type 2: Integrate or reintegrate in the labor market

This second type of public policy configuration gradually constructs an age culture and a definition of older workers opposite the first type's. It concerns the Scandinavian welfare regime, which, for a long time now, has pursued active labor market policies. Providing generous welfare compensation compensation inactivity during the second part of careers goes in hand with mobilizing the labor force through an active employment policy. Welfare provisions are tied to beneficiary's efforts to activation.

This configuration favors maintaining aging wage-earners in employment through a wide range of policy instruments for integrating (or reintegrating) people in the labor market and extending employment services toward the vulnerable. The system of rules, different from the first type, tries to target vulnerable wage-earners for programs of rehabilitation and reintegration in jobs in order to respect for their right to employment. To provide equal opportunities, these countries do not just replace wages with social transfers, since this amounts, as we have seen under the continental European welfare regime, to ejecting aging wage-earners and defining them as 'unemployable'.

A preventive strategy is pursued instead. Several preventive measures for maintaining employability and fitness for work, as well as programs of rehabilitation and reintegration in employment, provide all citizens with the means for staying in employment. Aging older workers are assumed to be in jeopardy in the labor market but also to be capable of reclassification. Special programs, adequately funded, target them, like other vulnerable groups in order to preserve their right to work regardless of their age.

As my analysis of the Swedish case shows, the question of prolonging the worklife was already being debated during the second half of the 1990s, when reforms restored the work ethos, reactivated welfare and created opportunities for part-time employment at the end of careers. Gradual early retirement exit programs were restricted; and even shut down. Then, in 1999, the pension system was overhauled with the aim of providing incentives for working longer in life. The longer the wage-earner's worklife, the higher his/her pension. Furthermore, active job policies targeted aging wage-earners, among others, for rehabilitation, proposed worktime arrangements and offered incentives for reskilling throughout careers. Companies have thus been encouraged to become 'learning organizations'.

In this second type, the definition of the age to work and the rules that guide actions revolve around 'active aging', whence a 'culture of the right to employment at all ages', unlike the 'early exit culture'. Scandinavian workers during the second half of careers are offered a wide range of possibilities for remaining, fully or partially, in the labor force up until an advanced age.

Type 3: Retain in the labor market

The third public policy configuration corresponds to Japan. It offers aging wage-earners very few possibilities for receiving compensation for early exit. The older employee's obligation to work is not counterbalanced by entitlement to compensation, like in Type 2. Japanese wage-earners have no other option than active aging, regarded as positive for both person and society. However the counterpart of this socially imposed obligation to work is society's obligation to offer older workers a wide range of opportunities for staying in the labor force.

For a long time now, Japanese public policies have steadily provided motivations and justifications for keeping older employees in the workforce until an advanced age. Since the 1960s, public authorities have intervened so as to help firms keep these wage-earners in employment and encourage them to lengthen their careers. This orientation came to prevail given the very rapid aging of the Japanese population since 1980.

The 1986 act on the 'stabilization of aging workers in employment' prodded firms to defer retirement from 55 to 60. It also offered subsidies for (re)training employees over 45. In addition, public employment offices have been granted additional means for improving older workers' chances for employment, in particular through Silver Age Resource Centers. Since 1995, public interventions have aimed at prolonging the careers of 60–64 year-olds and encouraging firms to keep these employees on the workforce. Most firms have renegotiated employment contracts, in some cases with a reduction of wages, public subsidies compensating employees for the wages lost.

In Japan, the older worker has mainly been defined as someone who switches from lifelong to flexible employment. Public job policies have supported and regulated this switch by lowering this age-group's labor costs, regulating the comportment of firms or even, as a last resort, opening job opportunities in the public sector. Public regulations have related the obligation for older wage-earners to continue working to the employment obligations of firms.

Type 4: Reject or retain

The fourth public policy configuration provides limited coverage for the risk of losing a job and has few programs for keeping older workers in the labor market. These programs amount to 'welfare to work' with limited help for returning people to employment. Regulation is, in the main, left up to market forces; and older wage-earners have no choice but to stay, regardless of the 'cost' to them, in the labor market on account of the large meshes in the welfare safety net.

In Esping-Andersen's typology (1990), this configuration corresponds to the 'liberal' or 'residual' welfare state, which allows the most room for market forces. Depending on the job market, aging wage-earners are either discarded from or kept in employment. Their occupational pathways depend directly on the supply of labor and demand for it. The same holds for the definition of the aging worker. When the work force is trimmed during a recession, older workers are seen as redundant, and it is right to reject them. These 'discouraged' wage-earners are forced out of the labor market (Laczko 1987). They become unemployed with no hope of going back to work. During a labor shortage however, aging workers are remobilized for employment; and codes of good conduct are circulated to convince employers to keep, or even recruit, them. Under this fourth type, the image of older wage-earners and behaviors toward them fluctuate as a function of market requirements. Older workers form a pool of labor to be tapped when needed (Phillipson 1982).

The age culture generated by this fourth type proposes nothing other than a ban on age-based discrimination in employment, which has little effect on actual practices or, worse yet, even encourages employers to dissimulate their actions. These legal texts – the American Age Discrimination in Employment Act or the Blair government's code of good practices on Age Diversity in Employment – seek to protect aging wage-earners individually from negative forms of discrimination. However they are ambivalent since they also point a finger at potential victims (Mercat-Bruns 2002).

In line with its underlying comparative hypothesis, this research has shown that each of the four types of public policy configurations corresponds to an 'age culture' generated by a specific combination of employment and welfare policies. Each corresponds to a way of defining the relations between aging and employment as well as welfare. It has its own definition of the rights and obligations related to age, and its own principles of fairness and justice. In turn, each of these different age cultures with its image of the older worker opens specific end-of-career pathways through the labor market, ranging from rejection to reintegration. These age cultures form a framework for the actions of public authorities, employers, labor unions and wage-earners. Each age culture has its own dynamics related both to its specific institutional arrangements and to the interactions between actors to which they lead.

TAKING UP THE CHALLENGE OF PROLONGING THE WORKLIFE OF AN AGING WORKFORCE: A CROSS-NATIONAL PERSPECTIVE

The proposed comparative theory provides not only a grid for interpreting past trends and making a diagnosis of why certain European countries, as pointed out, are lagging behind in efforts to raise older wage-earners' labor force participation rates. It also helps us detect the reforms to be undertaken so that the countries still immersed in the early exit culture can break with its principle of 'inactivating' seniors and launch an unprecedented mobilization of aging wage-earners.

Given the differences in public policy configurations and their related age cultures, there is no one-size-fits-all solution for developed countries. Prolonging the worklife entails changes with a variable scope depending on the country's age culture and the participation of different age-groups in the world of work.

In Scandinavia, which has maintained a relatively high employment rate for 55–64 year-olds, as well as for young people and women, prolonging the worklife mainly calls for marginal adjustments. Occupational pathways are to be redesigned to make employment more attractive for everyone. Efforts are to be continued for 'activating' older workers and women and increasing their propensity to work. As pointed out, Sweden is already making these adjustments.

In continental Europe with its pervasive early exit culture, a literal 'cultural revolution' is necessary to increase the propensity to remain in the labor force. The behavior of all parties must undergo a deep change in order to mobilize aging wage-earners and, to a lesser extent, young people and women. Such an effort cannot be improvised. It has to be planned for the middle or long run, and should be part of a global strategy for breaking with the early exit culture and preventing the loss of fitness to work. To keep 50 year-olds in the labor market, their employability and skills have to be maintained. Furthermore, working conditions and the organization of production must be adapted to an aging workforce. This strategy calls for redesigning occupational pathways so that the experience acquired by employees be preserved and passed on during a period with a rapid turnover of generations in the workforce.

Putting an end to the early exit culture: Finland

The Finnish and Dutch cases, two exemplary European counties in this regard (See Table 4.1), reveal to us the major levers of action for boosting both the propensity of seniors to continue working but also the demand from firms for seniors. That did not just happen by itself. It followed from a middle- or long-term program and a multidimensional strategy for preventing the loss of fitness for work throughout careers.

After a long period of multiparty consultations, Finland implemented a national program (1998–2002) in favor of the employment of persons over 45. At the time, the unemployment rate stood at 9%. This five-year program sought to break with the principles and priorities set in previous public policies in favor of early exit. This strategy preventively concentrated on maintaining the ability to work throughout the second part of careers. The objective was to act on both the supply of senior labor and the demand for it. This global, integrated program operated on all dimensions: career management, training, improvement of health and working conditions, and the reorganization of work. Its more than forty coordinated measures were intended to make work more 'sustainable' in a society characterized by longevity and mobility. A major part of this national program was devoted to information and education, the objective being to change ideas about aging at work and to counter the deeply rooted bias in favor of early exit. Its slogan, 'Experience is a national asset', signaled the determination of Finnish authorities to improve public opinion's perception of older workers by presenting them as a major resource for improving the competitiveness of both firms and the country.

The second Finnish program, for 2003 to 2007, built upon and generalized the orientations of the first one. It addressed all age-groups instead of targeting just the second part of careers. VETO (its abbreviation) proposed a coordinated set of age-neutral policies for training, work and occupational health with the objective of making labor force participation more attractive to all age-groups. This new program was evidence of Finland's commitment to an integrated management of age diversity through innovative, active labor market policies.

All this is in phase with a knowledge-based society, which requires better educated, more autonomous and more mobile wage-earners. By placing the accent on developing 'human capital', Finland has renovated welfare, labor market policies and the conception of social security. Instead of a welfare that compensates for risks, this new focus on human capital opens the way toward more flexible, optional forms of social protection for individuals and toward preventive measures for making occupational itineraries more secure.

The case of Finland deserves attention for two reasons. First of all, experts have calculated that the new strategies implemented there for prolonging the worklife and boosting a new age management strategy at the workplace based on age diversity and synergy might increase the GDP by up to 5% in 2020. These prospects prove the worth of adopting such a strategy in a gloomy economic situation with little hope for growth, as in much of the eurozone. A second lesson to draw from the Finnish case is that, given the aging labor force, improving working conditions and the quality of work for all are as important as raising older workers' employment rates. Studies at the European level have detected a strong correlation between the employment rate of 55–64 year-olds and the quality of job in the country.

Levers of action for reorienting public policy toward active aging

Prolonging the worklife requires a multidimensional, preventive strategy for maintaining the fitness to work of all age-groups. Six age-neutral measures provide the main levers of action for active aging:

- Offer occupational prospects and mobility to all age-groups, in particular more opportunities for horizontal mobility. Invent a new age-management based on age diversity.
- Develop vocational training programs related to career paths, in particular after the age of 40. Life-long learning must become a reality.

- Improve working conditions and workplace health and safety in order to promote well-being at work and a longer, sustainable worklife.
- Recognize the value of experience and the importance of human capital as an asset for firms.
- Rethink the organization of the workforce so as to boost cooperation and favor the transfer of skills between generations at the workplace.
- Experiment and evaluate the actions undertaken.

To keep persons in their fifties in the labor market, it is necessary to maintain their employability and skills. It means knowing how to manage their mobility and open prospects for them at the workplace. This requires adapting working conditions and the organization to an aging workforce. On account of the rapid turnover of generations, it calls for organizing work and production so as to ensure cooperation between age-groups and the passing down of experience from one generation to the next (Guillemard 2010: Chapter 9).

In an aging society where people live longer, the worklife can be made longer only if work is bearable for a longer time. Preventive policies for improving workplace health and the quality of work can achieve this. If firms fail to take this into account, they will produce worn-out, demotivated employees; and this will negatively impact their future performance. This is even truer since the average age of the reservoir of labor from which firms draw their workforces is increasing. At the European level, proof of this can be seen in the strong correlation observed between the improved quality of work in a country and the higher employment rate of aging wage-earners there.

CONCLUSION

Hopefully, this chapter has shown that the aging of the economically active population does not signal a catastrophe that will fatally impact developed countries. Demographic aging might represent an opportunity for building a society for all ages, one with more social cohesion, solidarity and attention to diversity. The way to achieve this goal is not easy. It calls for strong determination on the part of public authorities. As this comparative analysis has shown however, the northern European countries that have taken up this challenge also have the most innovative economies. They have fully entered a new knowledge-based economy while modernizing the welfare state by promoting a social investment strategy in human capital. They have developed public policies for integrating welfare with active employment policies in the effort to support and promote the autonomy of individuals and their aptitudes throughout careers.

ACKNOWLEDGEMENT

This chapter was translated from French by Noal Mellott of the Centre Nationale de la Recherche Scientifique, Paris, France.

NOTES

1 Eurostat estimate based on assumptions of slow increases in fertility rates and life expectancy (European economic and social Council 2001).
2 Another implication of active aging is to lead seniors toward more involvement in volunteer work so that they continue contributing to society. We should not, however, underestimate the risk that this slogan will amount to no more than a command to keep on working, regardless of the cost to those concerned (Walker and Naegele 2009).
3 'Regime' in the sense given to it by Esping-Andersen (1990), who distinguished three qualitatively distinct worlds of welfare, each with its own principles of coherence. These regimes correspond to specific institutional arrangements of public policies.
4 'Police' in line with the older meaning, under the monarchy, of government as 'ruling'.
5 The term 'ejection' instead of 'rejection' has been used for continental Europe, since early exit from the labor market entails social transfers for replacing wages.

REFERENCES

Beck U., 1992, *Risk Society : Towards a new modernity*, London, Sage.
Best F., 1981, *Flexible life-scheduling: Breaking the education, work, retirement lockstep*, New York: Praeger.
Conseil d' Analyse Économique (CAE), 2005, *Les Seniors et l'emploi en France*, Paris: La Documentation Française.
Ebbinghaus B., 2006, *Reforming early retirement in Europe, Japan and the USA*, Oxford: Oxford University Press.
Esping-Andersen G., 1990, *The three worlds of welfare capitalism*, Princeton, NJ: Princeton University Press.
Esping-Andersen G. and Sonnberger H., 1991, 'The demographies of age in labor market management' in J.Myles and J.Quadagno (eds), *States, labor markets and the future of old-age policy*, Philadelphia, PA: Temple University Press, pp.227–249.
European Commission, 2005, *Face aux changements démographiques, une nouvelle solidarité entre générations*, Green paper, Brussels.
Gallie D. and Paugam S., 2000, *Welfare regimes and the experience of unemployment*, Oxford: Oxford University Press.
Guillemard A.M., 2010, *Les défis du vieillissement: Âge, emploi, retraite. Perspectives internationales*, Paris: Armand Colin.
Hall P. and Soskice D.(eds), 2001, *Varieties of capitalism: The institutional foundations of comparative advantage*, New York: Oxford University Press.
Kohli M., Rein M., Guillemard A.M., Von Gusteren H. (eds) 1991, *Time for retirement. Comparative studies of early exit from the labor force*, Cambridge: Cambridge University Press.
Laczko F., 1987, 'Older workers: Unemployment and the discouraged worker effect' in S. Di Gregorio (ed.), *Social gerontology: New directions*, London: Croom Helm, pp. 239–251.
Marshall V., Heinz W.R., Kruger H. and Verma A. (eds), 2001, *Restructuring work and the life course*, Toronto: University of Toronto Press.
Maurice M., Sellier F. and Silvestre J.J., 1982, *Politique d'éducation et organisation industrielle en France et en Allemagne*, Paris: Presses Universitaires de France.
Maurice M., Sellier F. and Silvestre J.J., 1992, 'Analyse sociétale et cultures nationales. Réponse à Philippe d'Iribarne', *Revue française de sociologie*, XXXIII–1, pp. 75–86.
Mayer K.U. and Schoepflin U., 1989, 'The state and the life course', *Annual review of sociology*, XV, pp. 187–209.
Mercat-Bruns M., 2002, 'Discrimination fondée sur l'âge et fin de carrière', *Retraite et société*, 36, Paris: La Documentation Française, pp. 112–135.
Muller P., 2000, 'L'analyse cognitive des politiques publiques: Vers une sociologie politique de l'action

publique', *Revue française de science politique*, special issue on 'Les approches cognitives des politiques publiques', 50, 2, pp. 189–207.

Naschold F., De Vroom B. and Casey B., 1994, 'Regulating employment and retirement: An international comparison between firms and countries'" in F. Naschold and B. De Vroom (eds), *Regulating employment and welfare Company and national policies of Labour force participation at the end of worklife,* Berlin: de Gruyter, pp. 434–494.

OECD, 1998, *Maintaining prosperity in an ageing society*, Paris: OECD.

Percheron A., 1991, 'Police et gestion des âges' in A. Percheron and R. Rémond (eds), *Age et politique*, Paris: Economica, pp. 111–139.

Phillipson C., 1982, *Capitalism and the construction of old age*, London: Macmillan Press.

Riley M., Johnson M. and Foner A. (eds), 1994, *Age and structural lag: Society's failure to provide meaningful opportunities in work, family and leisure*, New York: Wiley Interscience.

Walker A. and Naegele F., 2009, *Social policy in ageing societies: Britain and Germany compared*, Basingstoke: Palgrave.

5

Migration and Workforce Aging

John Field

International migration is expanding rapidly, and the experience of aging is changing with it. The Spanish sociologist Manuel Castells describes our society as dominated by a 'space of flows' arising from the rapid interchange of information and ideas through new information systems; but the movement of people throughout what Castells calls 'the space of places' is an equally striking characteristic of life in modern societies (Castells 1996, 409–15). In 1960, an estimated 77 million people emigrated; by 2010, the number of migrants reached 214 million (OECD 2012b, 16). Overwhelmingly, these are people of working age; and nearly two-thirds live in what the United Nations (UN) defines as the developed nations (UN 2010).

Migration and population aging are tightly bound together, with both developments having their origins in deeper processes of social and economic change, including such well-known features of modernity as economic globalisation, increasing material aspirations, the erosion of tradition and the transformation of family structures. From a policy

perspective, labour migration represents an important way of replacing aging retirees as they leave the workforce, as well as ensuring a steady supply of fresh labour more generally. The right of free movement of labour was one of the founding objectives of the European Union, though at no stage has labour migration within the EU matched the levels of worker mobility found in North America. And in turn, the reality of population aging and growing migration are influencing the course of social and economic development on a global basis, as well as occupying a central place in contemporary policy concerns. These have become contentious issues, as governments seek to balance economic requirements for immigrant labour against electoral demands for stronger border restrictions.

This chapter reviews recent research on migration and workforce aging, and examines the relationship between policy and practice in this contested area. It starts by looking at the general picture of migration and age. Although migrants are on average older than the rest of the world's population, they tend to be younger than the average population of the country they are entering. This reflects both the magnet effect of earnings in the richer nations, which tend to show high levels of population aging, and the consequences of policies designed to attract labour from other countries. In societies with high levels of emigration, by contrast, the effect of net migration is usually to create a bimodal population distribution, with large proportions of the young and the elderly, and governments sometimes seek to attract 'diasporic' returners. These patterns are well known, and will be summarised briefly. The rest of the chapter looks at older migrants, some of whom have 'aged in place' after migrating in their youth, while others have emigrated in later life. This is a less well-known story, and the chapter therefore pays considerable attention to this under-researched but important dimension of migration and workforce aging. It concludes with a few comments on aspects of policy towards older migrants.

DEMOGRAPHY AND MIGRATION

Workforce aging is common to all the advanced economies. Declining fertility rates and rising life expectancy rates are preoccupying academics, policymakers and managers across the globe. The 'war for talent' (surely a misleading phrase) has already led to notable increases in workforce participation rates. The proportion of women in the workforce has grown steadily, as has the proportion of older adults who are in work. In Australia, the share of all 55 to 64 year-olds who were in the workforce rose from 48% in 2000 to 56% a mere seven years later (Australian Bureau of Statistics 2007). In the USA, meanwhile, the number of over-65s in the workforce more than doubled between 1977 and 2007, a trend predicted to continue as the baby boomers join this group (US Bureau of Labor Statistics 2008). Governments in a number of countries are extending

the age of retirement; indeed, it is arguable whether, under current European employment law, it is possible in most occupations to stipulate a formal age of retirement. Again, this policy trend mirrors social trends that were already well-established, with a growing number of people in advanced countries electing to work beyond the statutory retirement age. And of course migration policy has been utilised, as one way of balancing labour supply with population aging.

As a result, most of the advanced economies expect severe labour shortages, particularly of the highly-skilled. While governments have a range of policies to deal with labour shortages, including skills training and expanding employment rates, the selective encouragement of labour immigration has long been seen as a way of solving the most pressing problems. Migration can also result from other policy decisions, including most importantly humanitarian policies on the reunification of families or the acceptance of refugees. In some countries, such as Canada, Australia and the USA, immigration has historically provided the bulk of population growth, and continues to do so today. Labour mobility was, of course, one of the founding principles of the European Union, and remains an important policy goal, albeit a controversial one in many of the member states. At present, the tendency for people to move to another EU country or within their own country remains much lower than in the USA, and net immigration rates within the EU remain lower than in the USA (Gáková and Dijkstra 2008). Nevertheless, in more recent years, immigration has also contributed more to population growth than the excess of births over deaths in a number of European countries, including Germany and – until the economic crisis of 2008 – Ireland (Coleman 2008, 454–5).

Most migrants are of prime working age. From the perspective of the receiving societies, this is primarily a question of demand. Income incentives are highest for skilled workers with experience in their profession and of prime working age; although even unskilled wages can be attractive for migrants from poor countries, most of those seeking unskilled work will be well below retirement age. As well as market factors, many governments also seek to attract immigrants who will make a sustained economic contribution. In many countries, immigration regulations are designed to ensure that immigrants do not become a drain on resources but possess the skills and abilities to contribute to the labour force. Many receiving nations have an age threshold for new immigrants, particularly if the country involved provides an age-related state pension. In Australia, for example, the upper age limit for skilled worker applicants stands at 50, while Canada's points-based system currently awards 10 points to skilled applicants aged 21–49, and a diminishing number for the over-50s, reaching zero for applicants aged 54 and over. Of course, such countries make separate provisions for family members to move, but in general policies tend more or less deliberately to promote immigration by the highly skilled and highly qualified who are not approaching retirement. As a result, much low-skill migration occurs between countries with relatively open borders, as within the EU or in several African regions (Hatton and Williamson 2003, 478). Market demand and policy do not always work hand-in-hand; in respect of skills, there is often a high demand for young unqualified workers, while immigration policies frequently seek to restrict immigration to workers with scarce skills; however, both function in such a way as to concentrate migration among those of prime working age.

This pattern is also a matter of supply. The Gallup World Survey between 2008 and 2010 asked respondents about their interest in emigrating. Overall, almost one person in four of those aged 15–24 said that they would like to emigrate if they could, along with 15% of the 25–44 age group; by contrast, 9% of 45–64 year olds wished to migrate, and only 5% of the over-65s (OECD 2012b, 34). One study of 21 African countries found that emigration rates were particularly high in those nations with a high share of population aged 15–29, particularly if opportunities for the relatively well-educated are poor (Hatton and Williamson 2003, 475–7).

This is not a new development. Most migrants, throughout modern history, have been relatively young adults, with males tending to outnumber females (Hatton and Williamson 1998, 39–42). In nineteenth-century Ireland, contemporaries widely believed that the younger and more competent men were most likely to emigrate (O'Rourke 1992, 324–5). One study suggests that even before the crisis of the 1840s, the Irish-born population in Britain were far more likely to be skilled artisans and males aged in their twenties than were those who remained at home; they also had noticeably higher literacy rates (Nicholas and Shergold 1987, 162–7).

Broadly, this skewed pattern remains equally clear in modern times. The most significant change is an increasing propensity for young women to migrate; although they are still slightly outnumbered by their male counterparts at a global level, in some countries women are now a majority of the immigrant population, while in others they predominate among the emigrant population. By 2005, internationally the proportion of women and girls among international migrants stood at nearly 50%, and were a slight majority of immigrants into European countries (UN Population Division 2006, 2–5). In the USA, by contrast, in 2011 men accounted for 59.0% of the foreign-born labour force, compared with 52.3% of native-born workers. By age, the share of 25–54-year olds in the foreign-born labour force reached 75.4%, compared with 64.5% for their native-born counterparts (US Bureau of Labor Statistics 2012). Moreover, because migrants are more likely to be of child-bearing age than the host population, they frequently tend towards larger family sizes. In contemporary Germany, for example, foreigners are on average aged 39, while people of immigrant background have an average age of 35, while those of non-immigrant background are on average aged 46 (Baykara-Krumme 2012, 9). Similar patterns can be seen elsewhere (e.g. Kaczmarczyk and Okólski 2008, 611–12).

While most migrants still tend to be better qualified than the populations they leave behind, human capital levels vary enormously. While demand may be highest for scarce skills, many receiving countries also find it difficult to fill poorly-paid low-skill jobs, such as cleaning (Wills, Datta, Evans, Herbert, May and McIlwaine 2009). And while migrants may on average possess better qualifications than their compatriots, they do not necessarily find themselves more skilled than the populations they have joined. Data from the Adult Literacy and Life Skills Survey (ALLS), conducted between 2002 and 2007 in eight countries, suggest that in most nations immigrants on average have lower levels of literacy, numeracy and problem-solving skills than the native-born. In New Zealand and Norway, established immigrants outperformed more recent arrivals; but in Australia, Canada, Switzerland and the USA, recent immigrants outperformed established immigrants on most of the scores (Statistics Canada 2011, 55–6). Even where immigrants possess educational or vocational credentials, a number of studies have shown that they may not be recognised by employers and professional associations in receiving countries, in spite of a rather large number of pilot studies and formal policy statements favouring such recognition (Andersson, Fejes and Ahn 2004; Schugurensky and Slade 2008). Even following decades of efforts by the European Commission and its agencies, migrants within the EU still often face considerable barriers to recognition of their credentials (Brockmann, Clarke and Winch 2009).

Much migration is short term, and has few, if any, lasting effects on the age structure of the population. In some cases – for example, international movement by students – it is designed to be short term, and indeed is widely understood to pose quite different issues. Throughout the 2000s in Britain, for example, short-term migration – defined as lasting between one and twelve months – remained relatively constant, and was slightly below the number of short- term emigrants who left the country during the same period. Most stayed for one to two months; for the earlier years of the decade, the largest group came from Poland, which formally joined the EU in 2004; by the end of the decade, the largest single group came from the USA. While the in-migrants were relatively young, and evenly divided between the genders, the out-migrants were more likely to be male, and were disproportionately bunched around older adults and young adults (Office for National Statistics 2012). So these groups differ slightly from longer-term migrants, and often move in order to study, or to undertake short periods of work – perhaps combined with the hope of improving one's language skills. While some may decide to stay on, they are usually a small proportion of the total, so that their influence on population structures is inconsiderable.

More long-term migration, by contrast, almost invariably impacts on the age structure of the population. In general, immigration tends to reduce the overall age structure of the population while emigration raises it. Typically, immigrants are relatively young adults, who not only swell the population in these age groups but are also likely to form families and have children. Characteristically, first generation young labour migrants who settle and raise children typically have larger family sizes than the adopted country population, though smaller than among their peers in their country of origin (Warnes, Friedrich, Kellaher and Torres 2004, 316). The exceptions are relatively few. While it is common for immigrants to be joined by their families, it is rare for these to include older people, even if they might otherwise have been cared for by the young people who have left. And while some countries attract retiree settlers, and therefore experience accelerated population aging as a result, the effects tend to be comparatively minor (Coleman 2008, 467).

For countries with an aging population, migration offers an obvious potential source of replacements. However, the fall in fertility rates is so steep in many countries that migrants are unlikely to compensate fully in the short to medium term, while in the long term immigrants will also get older (Banerjee and Robson 2009, 141–2; Coleman 2008, 459). According to one UN report, the European Union would have required 1.6 million immigrants every year up to 2050 simply to maintain existing population levels – a figure that has risen since the report was issued, because of the EU's subsequent expansion (UN Population Division 2001). Currently, it is highly unlikely that European citizens will find such levels of immigration acceptable. While attitudes vary widely by country, there is growing evidence that public opinion has become more hostile towards immigration (Eurobarometer 2010, 51–63; Favell 2010). Although it is often popular with lobbyists representing employer organisations, immigration tends to be politically controversial, particularly at times of economic crisis where the native-born are prone to resent newcomers (Wilkes 2011). Recruiting immigrants can, then, only ever be a partial solution to skills shortages; other policies are required to upskill the existing workforce, and to expand the economically active population through such measures as deferred retirement and inclusion of hitherto inactive groups such as women.

Migration policy is also potentially divisive within countries that have historically exported significant numbers of their people. In Ireland, a country with a long and charged history of emigration as a solution to poverty, landlessness and conflict, the economic growth of the later twentieth century produced both a decline in emigration rates and a massive increase in the number of immigrants, at a time when the 'natural change' in population was virtually zero (Coleman 2008, 455). With the sharp onset of economic crisis following the banking collapse of 2008, one daily newspaper opened an interactive blog under the heading 'Generation Emigration'; many of the entries referred back to the historical role of emigration in Ireland's history (http://www.irishtimes.com/blogs/generationemigration). Strong as emotions can run in European countries like Ireland, the contested nature of emigration is particularly sharp in developing countries, who stand to lose considerable numbers of highly skilled and professional workers. Recent research acknowledges that while this 'brain and skills drain' has potential benefits in terms of remittances and the acquisition of expertise, it can empty out critical parts of the workforce, particularly those whose skills have incurred significant investment, such as health professionals (Docquier, Lohest and Marfouk 2007; Mill et al. 2008; Pellegrino 2001; Zurn and Dumont 2009).

In some occupations, demographic aging is itself a significant force that is fueling demand for migrant labour. A number of studies have shown the importance of migrant workers – mainly female – for elder care (Di Rosa, Melchiorre, Luchetti and Lamura 2012; Mill et al. 2008). Some have suggested that the recruitment of immigrant women into elder care in rich nations like the USA has tended to reinforce the low status of elder care as a profession while disrupting family care traditions in the sending nations (Browne and Braun 2008). One study of migrant elder care workers in four affluent countries found that immigrants comprised around one-third of nurses in Ireland and the UK and around one-eighth in Canada and the USA, and a quarter of care assistants in Ireland and one-fifth in the other three countries. The authors also noted that most of the lower-paid group entered as family members of existing immigrants or as refugees, while qualified nurses tended to enter under skilled worker schemes (Spencer, Martin, Bourgeault and O'Shea 2010, 21–5). In all four nations, the Phillipines ranked high as a source of both nurses and care assistants, along with other relatively poor nations. Thus the recruitment of elder care workers to service the aging populations of Europe, North America, Japan and Australasia is also contributing to the drain of human resources from developing countries.

In recent years, the 'war for talent' has encouraged governments in some emigrant nations to develop strategies for attracting highly skilled leavers to return. The OECD, which in general views migration as a positive solution to skills shortages, has argued that more work is needed in the reduction of barriers to return mobility, to encourage experienced emigrants to take their skills and knowledge home, which in turn improves the stock of human capital in their countries of origin. In practical terms, OECD suggested that much could be done to facilitate this, through measures such as providing financial support to municipalities that invite returnees and provide facilities such as housing, as happens in Poland; another is to provide tax concessions to highly-skilled returnees, as in Finland, Spain and New Zealand; Estonia, meanwhile, maintains a website for putting emigrants in touch with employers back home (OECD 2012a, 51–2). There is also scope for publicity drives and other measures designed to construct a sense of diasporic group identity among emigrants, a strategy that has been very successfully exploited by recent Irish governments (Jones 2003). The Scottish Government has made the attraction of return migrants part of its immigration strategy since 2004, and in 2010 it published a Diaspora Plan that included measures to improve economic growth by 'creating conditions for members of the Diaspora to live, learn, visit, work and return to Scotland' (Scottish Government 2010, 2). Malaysia has also developed a number of programmes designed to persuade highly skilled Malaysian emigrants to return, as well as policies intended to stop them leaving in the first place (National Economic Advisory Council 2010, 125).

Whatever their economic merits, such interventions have the advantage for governments of being politically non-controversial. The return migrants are generally perceived as racial and cultural homecomers rather than as foreign immigrants competing for jobs,

housing and other resources. Yet as OECD has pointed out, such strategies are not free from difficulty (OECD 2012b, 16–17). The idea of a diaspora is hard to define in practice, and indeed some emigrants may not embrace the identity associated with ideas of diaspora. Further, those who leave a country will have reasons for doing so that may dispose them against a permanent return (such as trauma, rejection or dislike of cultural norms). Alternatively, they may have developed a romanticised view of their 'homeland' that promotes short-term tourism but can make integration a challenging and often unhappy experience. Moreover, the ability of a diaspora to contribute to social and economic development will depend on such factors as their skill mix, age composition and degree of integration into the destination country. As return migrants tend to be older than first-time migrants, their net contribution to the age structure will probably be neutral.

'AGING IN PLACE'

In many societies, the elderly were until recently a relatively homogeneous group, culturally, ethnically, religiously and linguistically. Later life has changed in many ways, and its growing diversity and heterogeneity is among these. Yet patterns and experiences of migration among older people have largely been neglected in the recent debates over migration policy. They have also been accorded relatively little attention in the research community, where studies of older migrants are either largely concerned with social policy issues (such as the specific care needs of minority ethnic elders) or planning and commerce (such as the provision of services to retirement emigrants). And barely any attention at all has been paid to the challenges facing return migrants.

Precise figures on migrant aging can be hard to come by. Most official statistics are based on the administration of immigration regulations, and these differ between countries, so that the results are rarely comparable. Even within the European Union, whose formation was based on the principle of promoting free movement of labour, goods and services across its member states, it can be very difficult to reach agreed and accurate estimates of migration (Coleman 2008, 453–4). But the broad trends are unmistakeable. To take Germany as an example once more, almost ten per cent of foreigners are aged 65 or over; while this is relatively low in comparison with the non-immigrant population, where 23.7% are aged 65 or over, it nevertheless represents a growth trend that is almost certainly unavoidable (Baykara-Krumme 2012, 9–10). In Europe, for example, post-War mass migration had led by the end of the 1970s to a large settled migrant population in a number of countries. At the time that they entered their European destinations, most immigrants were relatively young adults (White 2006, 1288). While some have since returned to their country of origin, or moved on to a third destination, in most countries the majority have remained in their new homes. In Germany, for example, the over-60s rose from 3.1% of the foreigner population in 1970 to 9.7% in 2002, while the number of over-60s rose from well under 100,000 to over 700,000 in the same period (White 2006, 1289; Baykara-Krumme 2012).

Of course, these tendencies affected different migrant groups, and different host countries, in different ways, depending on timing, scale, and the labour market characteristics of the migrant group itself, as well as on the possibilities for family reunification within the host country. And the decision to remain in place may be an incremental one, as vague aspirations are replaced by concrete plans. One interesting indicator of this is that remittance rates typically decline as retirement approaches. While this may be partly due to simple family economics, it is characteristic for remittance rates to be lower among those who have decided to settle in their country of migration than among those who plan to return to their country of origin (Makina 2012, 5–6).

For some groups, aging-in-place is a by-product of barriers to returning. Refugees are frequently unable to return to their home country, because of the very factors that drove them out in the first place. For example, the USA and some Western European countries experienced significant flows of refugees from central Europe following the Soviet occupation of 1944–5 and the periodic clampdowns that then drove dissenters – especially Jews – out of such countries as Poland, Czechoslovakia and Latvia. By the time that it was possible to return without fear of punishment, many of the emigrants were elderly, and had formed strong attachments in their new homes. Instead of returning, this cohort laid down an infrastructure of voluntary organisations, family ties and wider connections that were later used by new generations of immigrants (Kaczmarczyk and Okólski 2008, 606–7).

As migrants age in place, so their understanding of family ties and their importance may begin to change. In purely economic terms, it is probably true that subsequent generations will tend to think of family ties increasingly in terms of their relations in the country of settlement. However, some researchers have drawn attention to the continuing cultural exchanges between country of origin and the 'diaspora' of people who are descended from migrants (Joseph 2010, 60). Moreover, migrants may have ties in more than one other country; one small scale study of South Asian elders in the UK reported that as well as the country of origin, respondents had children/siblings elsewhere in Europe, as well as sometimes quite extensive family connections around the UK; conversely, the death of parents had sometimes weakened ties with the country of origin (Victor, Martin and Zubair 2012, 87). Family dispersal may, in turn, have implications for elder care, particularly if people come from a group that values family care and views state provision as somehow a sign of weakness (Victor, Martin and Zubair 2012, 90).

As well as sustaining what some have called 'transnational' networks of ties between two or more societies, migrants, and especially the first generation, may return at regular intervals to their country of origin. Caribbeans who have settled in Britain, for example, shuttle back and forth between the two communities, sometimes establishing a second home in their country of origin (Goulbourne 1999; Joseph 2010, 63). Chris Phillipson has argued that these patterns are producing 'a new kind of aging in which the dynamics of family and social life may be stretched across different continents and different types of societies' (Phillipson 2010, 21–2). In some cases, particularly among migrants with undocumented status, the capacity to maintain strong connections in their country of origin may be limited. In other cases, such as those who are immigrating into a country where there is already a well-established community of compatriots with a highly developed infrastructure of support, may find it much easier – and experience less of a sense of isolation. Nevertheless, the tendency to maintain transnational connections is a marked pattern of contemporary migration, with implications for intergenerational social support networks in both societies, as well as impacting on the self-identities of those who age-in-place.

Intergenerational ties seem to be particularly well developed among certain groups of migrants from Asian societies like China, Japan and Korea. A number of studies, usually conducted in the USA, show that Chinese and Japanese immigrants tend to preserve traditions of filial piety, and are likely to live with other family members – usually children – in older age (Kamo and Zhou 1994; MacCallum et al. 2006, 30–31). However, some researchers argue that these patterns are starting to change, as family support networks among these migrant communities are starting to loosen, and elder care is handed over more to professional services – albeit that these are sometimes provided by individuals who are presented as family members (Lan 2002; Wong, Yoo and Stewart 2006). And we should not overstate Confucian exceptionalism: it is quite common for older migrants to live close to their children's households, or even sometimes to share them (Warnes, Friedrich, Kellaher and Torres 2004, 316; White 2006, 1292).

Not all older migrants require care, of course. In the USA, for example, employment rates fall faster among the older native-born than among immigrants, though George Borjas's work provides some evidence that part of this propensity to work into old age is connected to eligibility for retirement benefits (Borjas 2011). Similar factors may be at work in France, where one survey showed that older migrants planned to retire at 60.3 years, compared with average retirement ages at the time of 58.5 for men and 59.5 for women (Vaillant and Wolff 2012). On the other hand, older migrants tend to show worse health outcomes than the native-born, which may mean that intended retirement dates are brought forward. More generally, European studies suggest that migrants who 'age in place' tend to be a highly disadvantaged group, with poor outcomes in health, housing, education and leisure; older women migrants are particularly disadvantaged, especially in respect of post-retirement income (Tucci 2012, 13–14). They are also more likely to have experienced periods of unemployment during their previous working lives (Tucci 2012, 12).

MIGRATING IN LATER LIFE

Elder migration appears to have increased considerably since 1945 (Coleman 2008, 465; Flynn, Longino, Wiseman and Biggar 1985). The majority of older migrants in most societies consist of people who have 'aged in place' – that is, they migrated and became older. The other group, which is now rapidly expanding and relatively under-researched, is made up of people who migrate in later life, many of whom are comparatively prosperous and tend to enjoy relatively high standards of income, health, and other amenities. Most of this group fall into one of three main categories: those who move to benefit from kin support, migrant retirees and return migrants. Demographers, geographers and economists have tended to ignore the migration of the elderly, concentrating mainly on labour force mobility. Yet there are important theoretical and empirical dimensions to elder migration, particularly those concerned with retirement and dependency.

Kinship migration often involves movement to live near children. Some Northern European nations have a largely unrecognised group of older migrants, who move to live near or with relatives, in the hope of receiving care in later life (Blakemore 1999, 766; Warnes, Friedrich, Kellaher and Torres 2004). Conversely, some elders migrate in order to distance themselves from their children and grandchildren. One survey of residents in Sun City, Arizona, found that many found the settlement close enough to allow for regular visits, but not so close that they became involved in family squabbles or routine babysitting (Gober and Zonn 1983, 289).

When it comes to return migration, there are relatively few reliable sets of data. While some migrants return, we are not certain whether they are a minority or a majority, and we do not really know who returns and why (Corcoran 2002, 177–8; Cassarino 2004). One Canadian study, benefiting from longitudinal data, showed that male immigrants, and highly skilled specialists and entrepreneurs in particular, can be highly mobile, with a significant proportion undertaking both return and onward migration (Aydemir and Robinson 2008). Similarly, Ní Laoire reports that even before the introduction of the Single European Market, return migration rates within Europe were relatively high, at around 70–85%; whether this was still the case subsequently is unclear (Ní Laoire 2007, 336). Moreover, it is not clear whether this high rate of return and onward migration is confined to a small group of cosmopolitan knowledge workers, or is part of an emerging pattern within a highly flexible international labour market. Paul White, on the other hand, suggests that although many migrants cling to the belief that they will 'go home' at some stage, in practice return migration rates are relatively low, partly because some retired immigrants find that they can afford to 'shuttle' between their country of origin and their country of settlement, which is usually where their children are based (White 2006, 1292). Even so, in traditional countries of emigration, return migrants sometimes make up a significant proportion of the elderly population. In Mexico, for example, it is estimated that one in every six men aged over fifty is a former emigrant to the USA (Aguila and Zissimopoulos 2009, 1).

Much return migration is inspired by deep beliefs in obligations to the maintenance of ties with kinship networks and communities of origin (Ní Laoire 2007, 336). In general, though, return migration is triggered by an exit from the labour market, and it tends to peak around the age of retirement (Aguila and Zissimopoulos 2009). A number of the elderly British Caribbeans interviewed by Ricky Joseph were considering returning in order to live with their retirement pensions on family land that they had inherited, and were planning to sell the homes that they owned in the UK (Joseph 2010, 65–7). Such plans imply a once-for-all return to the 'homeland', but an increasing number of migrants are making several returns in both directions. One study of Hong Kong citizens who had returned from Canada in early or mid-career found that a considerable proportion of those who enjoyed higher salaries in Hong Kong were thinking of moving back to Canada when they retired, usually for quality-of-life reasons (Ley and Kobayashi 2005). As throughout this chapter, then, I should emphasise the heterogeneity of this group.

Migrant retirement has increased exponentially in recent years, fueled partly by the affluence of the baby boomer generation and the spread of mass tourism associated with cheap air travel. In Germany, for example, the number of pensions paid to retirees overseas rose from around 115,000 in 1992 to 191,730 in 2009 (Schneider 2010, 8). Retirement migration tends to focus on specific areas that are attractive for reasons of climate, lifestyle and price. Within the United States, Florida dominates the states as a destination for retirement migration. It attracted over a quarter of over-60 year old inter-state migrants between 1960 and 1980 (Flynn, Longino, Wiseman and Biggar 1985, 294–5). Within Europe, southern Europe now has a large and growing population of Belgian, British, Danish, Dutch, Finnish, German, Irish, Norwegian and Swedish retirees. Migrant retirees also move between continents, with small but significant numbers of Northern Europeans retiring to the USA, Australia and Latin America, often moving to live near, or with, family members (King, Warnes and Williams 2000; Warnes, Friedrich, Kellaher and Torres 2004, 312–3).

North Americans and Northern Europeans who retire to 'sunshine' destinations typically move as part of a married or cohabiting couple (Gober and Zonn 1983, 289). One intensive study of British migrant retirees reported that over half had previously worked in managerial or semi-professional occupations, and over a quarter in clerical or other white collar jobs; half had some and one-fifth had considerable experience of international mobility and migration well before retiring to their current home (King, Warnes and Williams 2000, 74–6, 85). The destinations, such as Florida or the Mediterranean, are overwhelmingly those that became popular during the international tourist boom that took off in the 1970s and 1980s, and typically the migrants have built up connections with the area for some time (Gober and Zonn 1983, 293–4). In some cases, as the authors of one major study point out, local authorities in the destination areas deliberately marketed their resort as a retirement region after mass tourism moved on (King, Warnes and Williams 2000, 81). Some communities, such as Sun City, in Arizona, are designed and developed from the outset as retirement destinations.

Media narratives tend to focus on some of the disappointments and troubles of expatriate life. Empirical studies suggest that most expatriate retirees are able to settle relatively well in their new country; for example, a survey of British retirees in four southern European sub-belt regions reported that many experienced improvements in health, wellbeing and social engagement after moving rather than the reverse (Warnes, King, Williams and Patterson 1999). While interest in returning to Britain is stronger among those whose health no longer permits independent living, a number of voluntary organisations provide services and information to members of this group, particularly those whose social and family ties to Britain have weakened (Hardill, Spradbery, Arnold-Boakes and Marrugat 2005). A study of elderly North Americans living in Mexico reported that women found it particularly hard to adjust to living away from their grandchildren; while men shared this sense of loss (though to a lesser extent), they also felt remote from their work and work-based ties. In both cases, the researcher noted that the expatriates adapted by holding open the opportunity of return migration at some unspecified time in the future (Banks 2009).

Retirement migrants' adjustment to their new country is therefore often contingent, hedged around by qualifications and alternatives. Even though relatively few expatriates migrate back to their home country until forced to by severe incapacity or unforeseen financial circumstances, and many often vehemently deny that they wish to return to the country they have left, it seems that they value the existence of the opportunity to leave. Their adjustment is also shaped by a continuing interaction with fellow-nationals in the expatriate community, often strengthened by the choice to live in what is effectively an expatriate settlement (Banks 2009, 179). By and large, retirement migrants develop attachments in their new communities, develop new lifestyles that bridge their old and new identities and aspirations, and often adopt an explicitly critical stance towards the culture that they have left behind (Gustafson 2001).

This global movement has had a marked influence on the destination regions. Economically, the retirees are comparatively affluent, producing increased demand for a range of goods and services, from health to leisure products (Schneider 2010, 16–17). The extent to which this influence is a positive one is another matter. One study sketches a community in Spain where fewer than half of the permanent inhabitants are Spanish; during the summer season, the population triples as the permanent population is joined by holiday makers and 'seabirds' (Janoschka and Haas 2011, 297). Other destinations include 'gated communities', where the immigrant retirees live protected lives, free from the intrusions and disturbances of everyday life in Mexico or Thailand (Banks 2009). While some of these retiree migrants are 'seabirds', who move seasonally between their 'sunshine' destination and their place of origin, many remain throughout the year (Gustafson 2001; Janoschka and Haas 2011, 297–8). Some research demonstrates that permanent retired migrants can often identify strongly with their host community, and indeed *dis*-identify equally strongly with their country of origin, becoming deeply involved in local life, and contributing through volunteering and self-help services (Haas 2012).

POLICY CHALLENGES

Later life can all too easily be stigmatised as a period of woe. The dominant narrative of aging in Western societies in particular tends to present images of troubles and decline. Some may have assimilated or integrated to an extent where their situation and needs are much the same as those of all older people. And if UK evidence is anything to go by, older people's attitudes towards and experiences of age and aging seem to depend more on generation, health and socio-economic status than ethnicity,[1] as do their experiences of age-related discrimination (Sweiry and Willitts 2012, 22–8). Of course, there are often specific problems associated with the aging process, but the 'third age' can also be a period of opportunity and growth. Moving

out of full-time work, or watching one's children take responsibility for their own lives, represents for many people a liberation. The popularity of adult education movements such as the University of the Third Age, or travel holidays targeted at the retired, illustrates this neatly. Before discussing some of the problems facing older migrants, then, I will briefly examine ways in which older migrants make a positive contribution to their communities.

Probably the most important area where older adults play a distinctive and constructive role is in voluntary activity of various kinds. In Spain, for example, charitable and voluntary activities are said to be a distinctive and ubiquitous feature of the foreign retired community, with British retirees standing out in terms of the number and range of voluntary activities undertaken (Haas 2012, 3). Such activities are often focused on self-help and philanthropic initiatives, often in fields such as health and caring, but by no means confined to these. Haas suggests that these activities have a marked integrating effect, building social capital not only within the immigrant community but also between immigrants and their hosts, and also conveying various social capital benefits on the volunteers themselves (Haas 2012, 18–20). On the other hand, levels of engagement may be far lower among those who have 'aged in place'. In Germany, for example, one study showed that only ten per cent of older adults from a Turkish background are involved in voluntary activity, far lower than for people from non-migrant backgrounds; moreover, immigrants were more likely to be involved in movements that drew most of their members from their own ethnic, cultural or religious group (Huth 2012, 27).

Intergeneration practices, such as learning exchanges that bring generations together, can also provide older migrants with channels for contributing constructively to their community. The field of intergenerational practice is a new and diverse one (Springate, Atkinson and Martin 2008). Relations between the generations have become a growing focus of concern for researchers and policymakers alike. As well as the effects of demographic change and globalising tendencies, both of which are said to influence relationships between generations, it is also sometimes argued that the social and cultural distance between generations is growing, both within families and more widely in society, not least as a result of the growing ethnic and cultural diversity that is experienced by different generations. Intergenerational practice has developed rapidly in many nations, and comprises a wide range of practices. Typical policy interventions include school-based programmes, community projects, health-related projects, learning and knowledge development, mentoring activities, and also professional development and knowledge exchange. At the level of the enterprise, there is a burgeoning interest in intergenerational management, reflecting widespread belief among managers and business specialists that employees' work values and preferences – including possibly their orientations towards skills acquisition and knowledge development – are influenced by generational experiences as well as by individual employees' age (Kunze, Böhm and Bruch 2011). While this is an emerging field, and ethnicity and place are still underdeveloped aspects, intergenerational practice is increasingly attending to these dimensions (Mannion 2012).

Not all elderly immigrants, then, have particular, identifiably distinctive needs. However, there are undoubtedly some distinctive challenges and needs that are characteristically shared by some, if not all, migrants. And because of the increasing scale of global migration, as well growing policy debate over both immigration and emigration, there has been developing recognition over time of the scale, situations and needs of elderly immigrant populations. Some of these needs are shared, if not by all migrant groups, at least by a number of them. For example, many elderly primary migrants do not possess the linguistic, cultural, educational and material resources that are taken for granted by the dominant groups, and they are therefore likely to depend disproportionately on kinship networks and ethnically-specific voluntary organisations for support (White 2006, 1297; Gordo 2012, 18). Even this option can be restricted by generational changes within immigrant communities, particularly where older migrants' adult children are reluctant to provide support because they have themselves overcome the linguistic and other constraints that are limiting their parents' well-being (Ip, Lui and Chui 2007).

In many contexts, it is common for immigrant populations to experience higher than average levels of poverty as they age (White 2006, 1284). Within the European Union, poverty and other forms of exclusion are most likely to be experienced by older non-European migrants (Reijneveld 1998; Warnes, Friedrich, Kellaher and Torres 2004, 315–16).

Even within the European Union, welfare entitlements are not necessarily universal nor easily transportable between member states. Those who migrate after retirement are usually treated very differently from those migrants who work in the country before retiring; one study suggests that while the educated and linguistically competent may be able to negotiate transfers of benefits between member states, these abilities to maximise well-being are unevenly distributed across the older migrant population (Ackers and Dwyer 2004). And migrants who age in place may not be eligible for benefits as they age. In some cases, this may be because their working lives have been spent in the illicit economy, but even within the European Union, there are continuing practices of withholding full citizenship rights from legal immigrants (Warnes, Friedrich, Kellaher and Torres 2004, 321). They may also incur ill-will as a result of perceptions that some post-retirement migrants are involved in 'welfare tourism' (Timonen 1999).

Language can be problematic for a range of migrant groups. In the USA, Ikels found that many elderly immigrants are not only non-English speakers, but may also be illiterate in their native language, and therefore are not easily contacted through conventional outreach methods (Ikels 1998, 488). A number of UK studies also confirm that competence in English is relatively low among some older migrant groups, including older Asians, particularly among women (Tackey et al. 2006). Those who arrive as dependents in later life may come from a background where little or no language is spoken other than the native tongue (Blakemore 1999, 768). More generally, women migrants are less likely to encounter situations where their competence in the host language is developed; in some cases, this is intensified by constrains on women's participation in adult education (Ehrlich 1997). In cases where the primary migrants were characterised by low levels of education, their children's generation may not only have English as their main language, but may also have limited proficiency in their parent's first language (Rasinger 2012, 7–8). Some older migrants experience a diminished ability to use their native language, as a result of adaptation to the language of the host nation (Schmid and Keijzer 2009). In Israel, older Russian immigrants compensate for a lack of Hebrew competence by developing intense social ties with other Russian speakers (Remennick 2003). Some researchers recommend that second language provision should be tailored to the age-specific needs of migrant groups, particularly where older migrants have low levels of literacy and have had little or no schooling as children (Baynham et al. 2007, 30–32).

Older migrants are reportedly more likely to suffer from ill health than the host population – a pattern that appears to be explained largely by socio-economic disadvantage, sometimes reinforced by cultural and lifestyle factors (Reijneveld 1998). In general, they are more likely to report general ill health than the native-born population. In the USA, immigrants as a whole are slightly less likely to be obese than the native-born, but have lower levels of general health; however,

many of these differences decline or disappear once other factors, such as education and socio-economic status, are taken into account (Heron, Schoeli and Morales 2003, 4–6). Similarly, analysis of the European survey on aging, health and retirement has shown that migrants are more likely to suffer from debilitating illnesses and disabilities, and are also slightly more likely to be smokers than the native-born (Solé-Auró and Crimmons 2008, 870).

Older migrants can also be more likely to experience mental health problems. For example, European survey data suggest a notably higher level of depression among first-generation migrants aged 50 years or older, even after controlling for other factors that are known to cause depression in older age (Aichberger et al. 2010). UK research has also shown a greater propensity to suffer from poor mental health, including a higher incidence of dementia than can be explained by genetic risk factors (Livingston et al. 2001; Livingston and Sembhi 2003). Refugees are particularly prone to mental health problems, particularly if they have experienced severe trauma in their country of origin (Briggs 2011). Of course, these overall patterns may conceal significant variations between groups. Highly skilled migrants or affluent retirees, for example, may demonstrate better average health than their comparators among the native population. In general, though, migrant populations are more likely to experience problems with their health, physical and mental, and with support services.

Worse health standards may in turn be compounded by difficulties in accessing appropriate care. Even in societies with developed welfare states, migrants may experience difficulties in accessing health and social care. The barriers facing older migrants may include unfamiliarity with services, insufficient information about entitlements, language difficulties, and unhelpful cultural stereotypes that influence the attitudes and behaviour of service providers (Anand and Cochrane 2005). Stereotypes and popular beliefs can also limit the willingness of older migrants themselves to use public services; South Asian women, for example, may be reluctant to allow another female, however professional and well-qualified, to care for an elderly spouse (Victor, Martin and Zubair 2012, 90–91). In a multilingual and multicultural society, care providers need to develop appropriate strategies for engaging with the health and social needs of a diverse population (Brotman 2003).

To some extent, disadvantaged groups can and do draw on informal support mechanisms to complement and compensate for failings in public services. Yet although ingroup support and kinship networks are often important, access to informal social support may be problematic for some groups of older migrants. Those with the lowest levels of social support are migrants whose life histories are characterised by low rates of marriage and family formation. In the UK, older male migrants from Hong Kong have often worked long and anti-social hours, with relatively low incomes, and with little exposure to the English language, allowing them to create only very weak social networks; in some cases exposure to the illicit economy has also left them with low levels of public social protection (Warnes, Friedrich, Kellaher and Torres 2004, 317). Even among those with strong family ties, some older migrants reportedly find that their children's aspirations and values diverge from their own, leading to conflict and stress (Warnes, Friedrich, Kellaher and Torres 2004, 316). Projects to engage immigrants in voluntary activities are said to improve levels of integration and provide access to social support, particularly when such initiatives are directed towards the individual situations of elderly immigrants (Huth 2012, 29–30).

Older migrants are also more likely to face social isolation (Barrett and Mosca 2012; Saito, Kai and Takizawa 2012). One study of social capital and migration in eleven European countries, for example, found that although levels of civic association among older migrants mirrored those of the native-born,

with the highest levels for both groups being in the Nordic nations, in general the migrant populations were less active than the native-born (Berchet and Sirven 2012, 10–11). However, the longer the time spent in the host country, the more likely the individual is to become involved in civic activity; levels of social trust, on the other hand, do not vary by length of residence (Berchet and Sirven 2012, 15). Social capital, then, is not equally distributed within the immigrant population. Nevertheless, we should not rush to generalise, for in some cases, isolation is countered by other factors. Elderly Russians who emigrated to Israel in the 1990s describe the transition as difficult but positive; while they felt increasingly isolated from younger generations, they had developed strong social ties within the Russian immigrant community (Remennick 2003).

Even return migrants can experience social and cultural isolation. A number of studies explore experiences of alienation and disappointment among migrants returning to their home country (Corcoran 2002; Long and Oxfeld 2004). Studies of foreign students re-entering their home country often report a process of reverse culture shock, ranging from a lack of comfort with the home society's values and norms to fairly severe problems of psychological adjustment (Pritchard 2011). These studies, of course, involve relatively young people returning home after a relatively short period of study, but many older adult migrants return after a considerable period abroad, and the tensions and challenges can be considerably more severe. A number of studies of return migrants in Ireland have explored these issues. An analysis of longitudinal data for over-50-year olds suggested that return migrants are more likely to experience social isolation than 'stayers', particularly if they had returned after more than ten years away; but surprisingly, there was no evidence that they felt more lonely as a result (Barrett and Mosca 2012, 17). This contrast between people's positioning in relation to 'objective' measures of social isolation and their 'subjective' reporting of loneliness may be due to adaptation among return migrants, who have grown accustomed to a life with relatively few close ties or strong associational commitments (Barrett and Mosca 2012, 23).

In some respects, though, return migrants may be more socially isolated than they had been before returning. In her study of return migrants in rural Ireland, Catríona Ní Laoire reported that the people in her sample often reported difficulties in making friends, in contrast to the often open and cosmopolitan networks that they had entered as immigrants elsewhere; and they were both disappointed by what they saw as the materialism and individualism of Irish society, and resented local expectations that they conform to family and community norms that they regarded as socially conservative and oppressive (Ní Laoire 2007, 339–42). Admittedly, some of these responses may appear deeply contradictory, but they should serve to remind us that even – perhaps especially – return migrants may face difficulties of integration into the host society. In its report on diaspora populations, the OECD recommended that 'home' nations can maximise the gains from return migrants by developing reintegration programmes and counselling before and after return, as well as by promoting self-help support networks (OECD 2012b, 24). Support of this nature can help returnees make best use of their knowledge, skills and social capital, as well as avoid difficulties with financial transactions, transfer of welfare entitlements and information of employment and other opportunities.

CONCLUSIONS

This chapter has examined the nature of migration in an aging society, at a time of accelerating global exchange and influence. High levels of personal mobility are an important feature of wider tendencies towards globalisation, and indeed are a very common reaction to the pressures and opportunities that global economic and cultural trends present. In aging societies, attracting immigrant labour is a natural and obvious way of seeking to maintain skills levels and rise to the challenges of global competition. In affluent societies, emigration for retirement can be highly attractive for lifestyle reasons (and sometimes to avoid taxation in the originating nation). Yet if these patterns of mobility share some common causes, like globalisation itself they are complex and multi-facted in their working.

Above all, this chapter suggests that it is dangerous to lump all migrants into a single category, even when they share a common (if somewhat broad and poorly-defined) characteristic such as age. Rather than grouping older migrants into a single category, we need to distinguish between them. They command different linguistic, educational and material resources, and their experiences vary enormously. A world of difference separates wealthy Europeans and Americans retiring to the sunbelt and the homeless refugee in sub-Saharan Africa – and between them are just about every possible permutation of circumstances and trajectories. Moreover, this chapter has barely touched on the question of gender, which shapes experiences of migration as much as it does other social and cultural aspects of our lives.

Researchers have addressed these issues from a number of standpoints. In disciplinary terms, the topic brings together scholars from sociology, social policy, economics and history, as well as from demographics and population studies. At present, most attention has focused on the extent to which migrant labour can replenish labour stocks in aging societies, and to a lesser extent on the impact of emigration on the countries that export significant proportions of their population. There has until recently been much less focus on the experiences of older migrants, though this now appears to be changing. In part this reflects the availability of evidence. First, in most countries, migrants form a minority of the population, and they are therefore represented in survey data in relatively small numbers. They are therefore less likely to provide a simple and reliable category for analysis of longitudinal survey data, which in many other respects offer exciting prospects for research into the elderly. Second, qualitative researchers face many of the barriers of language and culture in exploring and understanding migrants' experiences that older migrants may themselves face in engaging with individuals and agencies from the host society. Nevertheless, we have an emerging body of research into the experience of migration at different stages of the life course, and we can expect that this field of research will continue to flourish and develop as public bodies, policymakers and others come to grips with the longer term effects of human mobility in modern societies.

NOTE

1 Ethnicity is not, of course, coterminous with migration status, but UK social data typically do not report separate figures for migrants.

REFERENCES

Ackers, L. and Dwyer, P. (2004) 'Fixed laws, fluid lives: the citizenship status of post-retirement migrants in the European Union', *Aging & Society*, 24(3): 451–75.

Aguila, E. and Zissimopoulos, A. (2009) *Labor market and immigration behavior of middle-aged and elderly Mexicans*. Santa Monica CA: RAND Center for the Study of Aging.

Aichberger, M., Schouler-Ocak, M., Mund, A., Busch, M., Nickells, E., Heimann, H., Ströhle, A., Reisches, F., Heinz, A. and Rapp, M. (2010) 'Depression in middle-aged and older first generation migrants in Europe: results from the Survey of Health, Ageing and Retirement in Europe', *European Psychiatry*, 25(8): 468–75.

Anand, A. and Cochrane, S. (2005) 'The mental health status of South Asian women in Britain: a review of the UK literature', *Psychology and Developing Societies*, 17(2): 195–214.

Andersson, P., Fejes, A. and Ahn, S.E. (2004) 'Recognition of prior vocational learning in Sweden', *Studies in the Education of Adults*, 36(1): 57–71.

Australian Bureau of Statistics (2007) *Australian social trends, 2007*. Accessed at http://www.abs.gov.au/socialtrends on 2 August 2012.

Aydemir, A. and Robinson, C. (2008) 'Global labour markets, return, and onward migration', *Canadian Journal of Economics*, 41(4): 1285–311.

Banerjee, R. and Robson, W. (2009) 'Immigration's impact on the growth and structure of the Canadian workforce', in H. Grubel (ed.), *The Effects of Mass Immigration on Canadian Living Standards and Society*, Vancouver: Fraser Institute. pp. 121–44.

Banks, S.P. (2009) 'Intergenerational ties across borders: grandparenting narratives by expatriate retirees in Mexico', *Journal of Aging Studies*, 23(3): 78–87.

Barrett, A. and Mosca, I. (2012) *Social isolation, loneliness and return migration: Evidence from older Irish adults*, Bonn: Forschungsinstitut zur Zukunft der Arbeit.

Baykara-Krumme, H. (2012) 'Ältere EinwanderInnen in Deutschland – ein Überblick zur demographischen Entwicklung', in E. Gregull (ed.), *Altern in der Migrationsgesellschaft*, Berlin: Heinrich-Böll-Stiftung. pp. 9–11.

Baynham, M., Roberts, C., Cooke, M., Simpson, J., Ananiadou, K., Callghan, J., McGoldrick, J. and Wallace, C. (2007) *Effective teaching and learning: ESOL*, London: National Research and Development Centre.

Berchet, C. and Sirven, N. (2012) *Cross-country performance in social integration of older migrants: A European perspective*, Paris: Institut de récherche et documentation en économie de la santé.

Blakemore, K. (1999) 'International migration in later life: social care and policy implications', *Ageing & Society*, 19(6): 761–74.

Borjas, G. (2011) 'Social security eligibility and the labor supply of older immigrants', *Industrial and Labor Relations Review*, 64(3): 485–501.

Briggs, L. (2011) 'Demoralization and psychological distress in refugees: from research to practice', *Social Work in Mental Health*, 9(5): 336–45.

Brockmann, M., Clarke, L. and Winch, C. (2009) 'Difficulties in recognising vocational skills and qualifications across Europe', *Assessment in Education*, 16(1): 97–109.

Brotman, S. (2003) 'The limits of multiculturalism in elder care services', *Journal of Aging Studies*, 17(2): 209–29.

Browne, C.V. and Braun, K.L. (2008) 'Globalization, women's migration and the long-term-care workforce', *The Gerontologist*, 48(1): 16–24.

Cassarino, J.-P. (2004) 'Theorising return migration: the conceptual approach to return migrants revisited', *International Journal on Multicultural Societies*, 6(2): 253–79.

Castells, M. (1996) *The rise of network society*. Oxford: Blackwell.

Coleman, D. (2008) 'The demographic effects of international migration in Europe', *Oxford Review of Economic Policy*, 24(3): 452–76.

Corcoran, M. (2002) 'The process of migration and the reinvention of self: the experiences of returning Irish emigrants', *Éire/Ireland: a journal of Irish studies*, 37(1–2): 172–91.

Di Rosa, M., Melchiorre, M.G., Luchetti, M. and Lamura, G. (2012) 'The impact of migrant work in the elder care sector: recent trends and empirical evidence in Italy', *European Journal of Social Work*, 15(1): 9–27.

Docquier, F., Lohest, O. and Marfouk, A. (2007) 'Brain drain in developing countries', *World Bank Economic Review*, 21(2): 193–218.

Ehrlich, S. (1997) 'Gender as social practice: implications for second language acquisition', *Studies in Second Language Acquisition*, 19(4): 421–46.

Eurobarometer (2010) *Future of Europe*, Luxembourg: European Commission.

Favell, A. (2010) 'Integration and nations: the nation-state and research on immigrants in Western Europe', in M. Martiniello and J. Rath (eds), *Selected studies in international migration and immigrant incorporation*, Amsterdam: University of Amsterdam Press. pp 371–402.

Flynn, C., Longino, C., Wiseman, R. and Biggar, J. (1985) 'The redistribution of America's older population: major national migration patterns for three census decades, 1960–1980', *The Gerontologist*, 25(3): 292–296.

Gáková, Z. and Dijkstra, L. (2008) 'Labour mobility between the regions of the EU-27 and a comparison with the USA', *Regional Focus*, 2: 1–7.

Gober, P. and Zonn, L.E. (1983) 'Kin and elderly amenity migration', *The Gerontologist*, 23(3): 288–94.

Gordo, L.R. (2012) 'Erwerbsverläufe älterer MigrantInnen', in E. Gregull (ed.), *Altern in der Migrationsgesellschaft*, Berlin: Heinrich-Böll-Stiftung. pp. 18–21.

Goulbourne, H. (1999) 'The transnational character of Caribbean kinship in Britain', in S. McRae (ed.), *Changing Britain: families and households in the 1990s*, Oxford: Oxford University Press. pp. 176–99.

Gustafson, P. (2001) 'Retirement migration and trans-national lifestyles', *Ageing & Society*, 21(3): 371–94.

Haas, H. (2012) 'Volunteering in retirement migration: meanings and functions of charitable activities for older British residents in Spain', *Ageing and Society*, First View, DOI: 10.1017/S0144686X12000669

Hardill, I., Spradbery, J., Arnold-Boakes, J. and Marrugat, M.L. (2005) 'Severe health and social care issues among British migrants who retire to Spain', *Ageing and Society*, 25(5): 769–83.

Hatton, T.J. and Williamson, J.G. (1998) *The age of mass migration: causes and economic impact*, New York: Oxford University Press.

Hatton, T.J. and Williamson, J.G. (2003) 'Demographic and economic pressure on emigration out of Africa', *Scandinavian Journal of Economics*, 105(3): 465–86.

Heron, M., Schoeni, R.F. and Morales, L. (2003) *Health status among older immigrants in the United States*, Ann Arbor MI: Population Studies Center.

Huth, S. (2012), 'Bürgerschaftliches Engagement von älteren MigrantInnen', in E. Gregull (ed.), *Altern in der Migrationsgesellschaft*, Berlin: Heinrich-Böll-Stiftung. pp. 27–31.

Ikels, C. (1998) 'Aging', in S. Loue (ed.), *Handbook of Immigrant Health*, New York: Plenum Press. pp. 477–92.

Ip, D., Lui, W.C. and Chui, W.H. (2007) 'Veiled entrapment: a study of social isolation of older Chinese migrants in Brisbane', *Ageing and Society*, 27(5): 719–38.

Janoschka, M. and Haas, H. (2011) 'Stadtentwicklung, Lokalpolitik und Ehrenamt als Experimentierfelder des alltäglichen gelebten Europas. Zur Partizipation in transnationalen Migrationsgesellschaften', in R. Johler, M. Matter and S. Zinn-Thomas (eds), *Mobilitäten – Europa in Bewegung als Herausforderung kulturanlytischer Forschung*. Münster: Waxmann.

Jones, R.C. (2003) 'Multinational investment and return migration in Ireland in the 1990s – a country-level analysis', *Irish Geography*, 36(2): 153–69.

Joseph, R. (2010) 'Globalised transmissions of housing wealth and return migration', in M. Izuhara (ed.), *Ageing and intergenerational relations: family reciprocity from a global perspective*, Bristol: Policy Press. pp. 57–76.

Kaczmarczyk, P. and Okólski, M. (2008) 'Demographic and labour market impacts of migration on Poland', *Oxford Review of Economic Policy*, 24(3): 599–624.

Kamo, Y. and Zhou, M. (1994) 'Living arrangements of elderly Chinese and Japanese in the United States', *Journal of Marriage and Family*, 56(3): 544–58.

King, R., Warnes, T. and A. Williams (2000) *Sunset lives: British retirement migration to the Mediterranean*, Oxford: Berg.

Kunze, F., Böhm, S. and Bruch, H. (2011) 'Age diversity, age discrimination, and performance consequences – a cross organizational study', *Journal of Organizational Behavior*, 32(2): 264–290.

Lan, P.-C. (2002) 'Sub-contracting filial piety: elder care in ethnic Chinese communities in California', *Journal of Family Issues*, 23(7): 812–35.

Ley, D. and Kobayashi, A. (2005) 'Back to Hong Kong: return migration or transnational sojourn?', *Global Networks*, 5(2): 111–27.

Livingston, G. and Sembhi, S. (2003) 'Mental health of the ageing immigrant population', *Advances in Psychiatric Treatment*, 9(1): 31–7.

Livingston, G., Leavy, G., Kitchen, G., Manuela, M., Sembhi, S. and Katona, C. (2001) 'Mental health of migrant elders: the Islington study', *British Journal of Psychiatry*, 179(4): 361–6.

Long, L. and Oxfeld, E. (eds) (2004) *Coming home: Refugees, migrants and those who stayed behind*, Philadelphia: University of Pennsylvania Press.

MacCallum, J., Palmer, D., Wright, P., Cumming-Potvin, W., Northcote, J., Brooker, M. and Tero, C. (2006) *Community building through intergenerational exchange programs*, Canberra: National Youth Affairs Research Scheme.

Makina, D. (2012) 'Migration and characteristics of remittance senders in South Africa', *International Migration*, Early View, DOI 10.1111/j.1468-2435.2012.00746.

Mannion, G. (2012) 'Intergenerational education: the significance of reciprocity and place', *Journal of Intergenerational Relationships*, 10(4): 1–14.

Mill, E.J., Schabas, W.A., Volmink, J., Walker, R., Ford, N., Katabira, E., Anema, A., Joffres, M., Cahn, P. and Montaner, J. (2008) 'Should active recruitment of health workers from sub-Saharan Africa be viewed as a crime?', *Lancet*, 371(9613): 685–88.

National Economic Advisory Council (2010), *New economic model for Malaysia*, Putrajaya: National Economic Advisory Council.

Nicholas, S. and Shergold, P.R. (1987) 'Human capital and the pre-Famine Irish emigration to England', *Explorations in Economic History*, 24(2): 158–77.

Ní Laoire, C. (2007) 'The "green, green grass of home"? Return migration to rural Ireland', *Journal of Rural Studies*, 23(3): 332–44.

OECD (2012a) *Better skills, better jobs, better lives: a strategic approach to skills policies*, Paris: OECD.

OECD (2012b) *Connecting with emigrants: a global profile of diasporas*, Paris: OECD.

Office for National Statistics (2012) *Short-term migration estimates for England and Wales*, London: Office for National Statistics.

O'Rourke, K. (1992) 'Why Ireland emigrated: a positive theory of factor flows', *Oxford Economic Papers*, 44(2): 322–40.

Pellegrino, L. (2001) 'Trends in Latin American skilled migration: "Brain Drain" or "Brain Exchange"?' *International Migration*, 39(5): 111–32.

Phillipson, C. (2010) 'Globalisation, global ageing and intergenerational change', in M. Izuhara (ed.), *Ageing and intergenerational relations: family*

reciprocity from a global perspective, Bristol: Policy Press. pp. 13–28.

Pritchard, R. (2011) 'Re-entry trauma: Asian re-integration after study in the West', *Journal of Studies in International Education*, 15(1): 93–111.

Rasinger, S.M. (2012) 'Language shift and vitality perceptions amongst London's second generation Bangladeshis', *Journal of Multilingual and Multicultural Development*, pre-print DOI 10.1080/01434632.2012.707202.

Reijneveld, S.A. (1998) 'Reported health, lifestyles, and use of health care of first generation immigrants in The Netherlands: do socio-economic factors explain their adverse position?', *Journal of Epidemiology and Community Health*, 52(5): 298–304.

Remennick, L. (2003) 'Retired and making a fresh start: older Russian immigrants discuss their adjustment in Israel', *International Migration*, 41(5): 153–75.

Saito, T., Kai, I. and Takizawa, A. (2012) 'Effects of a program to prevent social isolation on loneliness, depression and well-being among older adults: a randomized trial among older migrants in Japan', *Archives of Gerontology and Geriatrics*, 55(3): 539–47.

Schmid, M. and Keijzer, M. (2009) 'First language attrition and reversion among older migrants', *International Journal of the Sociology of Language*, 200: 83–101.

Schneider, S. (2010) 'Rente und Tschüss?! Deutsche Senioren verlegen ihre Ruhesitz ins Ausland', *Forschung Aktuell*, accessed on 12 February 2012 at http://hdl.handle.net/10419/57243.

Schugurensky, D. and Slade, B. (2008) 'New immigrants, volunteer work and labour market integration: on learning and re-building social capital', in D. Livingstone, P. Sawchuk and K. Mirchandani (eds), *The Future of Lifelong Learning and Work: Critical Perspectives*. Rotterdam: Sense. pp. 263–275.

Scottish Government (2010), *Diaspora Engagement Plan – Reaching out to Scotland's international family*, Edinburgh: Scottish Government.

Solé-Auró, A. and Crimmons, E.M. (2008) 'Health of immigrants in European countries', *International Migration Review*, 42(4): 861–76.

Spencer, S., Martin, S., Bourgeault, I. L. and O'Shea, E. (2010). *The Role of migrant care workers in ageing societies: report on research findings in the United Kingdom, Ireland, Canada and the United States*. Geneva: International Organization for Migration.

Springate, I., Atkinson, M. and Martin, K. (2008) *Intergenerational practice: a review of the literature*, Slough: National Foundation for Educational Research.

Statistics Canada (2011) *Literacy for Life: further results from the Adult Literacy and Life Skills Survey*, Paris: Organisation for Economic Cooperation and Development.

Sweiry, D. and Willitts, M. (2012) *Attitudes to age in Britain*, London: Department for Work and Pensions.

Tackey, N., Caebourne, J., Ashton, J., Ritchie, H., Sinclair, A., Tyers, C., Hurstfield, J., Willison, R. and Page, R. (2006) *Barriers to employment for Pakistanis and Bangladeshis in Britain*, London: Department for Work and Pensions.

Timonen, V. (1999) 'A threat to social security? The impact of EU membership on the Finnish welfare state', *Journal of European Social Policy*, 9(3): 253–61.

Tucci, I. (2012) 'Die Einkommens- und Wohnsituation älterer ImmigrantInnen', in E. Gregull (ed.), *Altern in der Migrationsgesellschaft*, Berlin: Heinrich-Böll-Stiftung. pp. 12–17.

UN Population Division (2001) *Replacement Migration: is it a solution to declining and ageing populations?*, New York: UN.

UN Population Division (2006) *International Migration Report: a global assessment*, UN, accessed on 21 September 2012 at http://www.un.org/esa/population/publications/2006_MigrationRep/report.htm.

UN (2010) *Population Facts*, 6: 1–4.

US Bureau of Labor Statistics (2008) 'Older workers: are there more older people in the workplace?', *Spotlight on Statistics*, accessed on 2 May 2012 at http://www.bls.gov/spotlight/2008/older_workers/.

US Bureau of Labor Statistics (2012) 'Labor force characteristics of foreign-born workers summary', accessed on 14 August 2012 at http://www.bls.gov/news.release/forbrn.nr0.htm.

Vaillant, N.G. and Wolff, F.-C. (2012) 'Retirement intentions of older migrant workers: does health matter?', *International Journal of Manpower*, 33(4): 441–60.

Victor, C.R., Martin, W. and M. Zubair (2012) 'Families and caring amongst older people in South Asian communities in the UK', *European Journal of Social Work*, 15(1): 81–96.

Warnes, A.M., Friedrich, K., Kellaher, L. and Torres, S. (2004) 'The diversity and welfare of older migrants in Europe', *Ageing & Society*, 24(3): 307–26.

Warnes, A.M., King, R., Williams, A.M. and Patterson, G. (1999) 'The well-being of British expatriate retirees in southern Europe', *Ageing and Society*, 19(6): 717–40.

White, P. (2006) 'Migrant populations approaching old age: prospects in Europe', *Journal of Ethnic and Migration Studies*, 32(8): 1283–1300.

Wilkes, R. (2011) 'Explaining time trends in public opinion: attitudes towards immigration and immigrants', *International Journal of Comparative Sociology*, 52(1–2): 79–99.

Wills, J., Datta, K., Evans, J., Herbert, J., May, J. and McIlwaine, K. (2009) *Global Cities at Work: New Migrant Divisions of Labour*, London: Pluto Press.

Wong, S., Yoo, G.J. and Stewart, A.L. (2006) 'The changing meaning of family support among older Chinese and Korean immigrants', *Journals of Gerontology*, Series B, 61(1): 4–9.

Zurn, P. and Dumont, J.-C. (2009) *Health workforce and international migration*, Paris: OECD

PART 2

The Aging Workforce

6

Work Performance
and the Older Worker

Margaret E. Beier and Ruth Kanfer

For the past two decades, demographers and social scientists have noted a plethora of new challenges associated with workforce aging in the US, Europe, and newly developed countries around the globe. As population and workforce aging trends up, the US and European countries have begun to re-evaluate and modify long-standing social policies and legislation regarding mandatory retirement age and the age at which benefits to older persons, such as Social Security, are provided. Workforce aging has also had an important influence in organizations, where anticipated retirements and shortages of replacement workers have led to increased adoption of changes in work design and work conditions. Flexible work policies and bridge employment opportunities represent just two of the many programs that organizations have adopted in the past 15 years or so to encourage valued older workers to remain in the job. At the individual level, recent economic turbulence, norms among workers in the Baby Boomer cohort (born 1946 to

1964), and growing scientific evidence for the role that work plays in physical and mental health have led more older workers to think about post-retirement employment and non-traditional work options, such as self-employment, part-time work, and volunteer work (Weckerle and Schultz, 1999). In the US where mandatory retirement age laws were repealed in the late 20th century, these factors have encouraged many people to work past their planned retirement age. In summary, the impact of demographic trends toward greater longevity, economic conditions, and uneven birth cohorts through the mid-to-late 20th century are having a profound effect on how nations, organizations, and individuals think about the role of work in mid- and late-life.

Evidence for workforce aging in the US and European countries is unequivocal. In the US, the US Bureau of Labor Statistics reports that workers over age 55 represent the fastest growing segment of the US workforce. The number of workers in this segment is expected to increase by 33% from 2010 to 2020. For a subset of this group, workers aged 65 to 74 (i.e., years regularly slated for retirement), participation is expected to grow by 76% over this same period (Toossi, 2012). The increased prevalence of older workers is a new reality in organizations and necessitates consideration of how to motivate and engage older workers to remain productive at work.

A coincident shift in the types of jobs available in industrialized countries has also occurred over the past few decades. In the US, jobs in the agrarian and manufacturing sectors have steadily declined as job growth increases in the service and professional/technical industry sectors (Johnson, 2004). These shifts in occupational sector job availability have complex effects on older worker employment. On the one hand, the decline in jobs that demand high levels of physical exertion affords older workers, who may experience age-related decline in physical skills, a potential advantage (Capelli, 2009). On the other hand, the growth of jobs in technical sectors that demand knowledge and skills related to new technologies (e.g., engineering processes) implies that older workers must engage in new skill learning in order to remain marketable. Age-related changes in cognitive abilities related to new skill learning and the dominance of skill training formats that capitalize on these same abilities have been argued to reduce older worker motivation for developing marketable new job skills. The problem of new skill learning among older workers is further exacerbated by changes in career patterns that necessitate continuous learning, as career histories move away from a model of life-long employment within a single organization toward a protean model of sequential career activities in different organizations across the work lifespan (Cappelli, 2009; Hall and Mirvis, 1995).

The purpose of this chapter is to examine the relationship between age and job performance within the context of age-related changes in abilities and motivation, changes in job characteristics, and broad workplace and cohort influences (such as organizational culture). We frame our discussion around two important questions: (a) what is the relationship between age and job performance? And (b) what are the individual differences and situational factors that play a role in understanding this relationship? Working from theory and research on adult development, we examine how normative, age- and cohort-related changes over the life course (intra-individual differences) may affect work motivation, workplace behaviors, and job performance. We also explore how inter-individual differences in cognitive and non-cognitive worker attributes, socio-cultural, and socio-technical factors interact with adult development and affect worker and organization outcomes. The chapter is organized into five sections. In the first section, we examine definitional issues of age and performance and provide the context for investigations of age- and cohort-influences on work outcomes. Included in this section is a review of the state of the research on the relationship between age and job performance. In the second section we provide a brief review of age-related changes associated with adult development and their impact on work outcomes, including performance. In the third section, we discuss job and work-role demands and their influence on perceptions of fit with the organization and job and important outcomes such as motivation and performance. In the fourth section, we consider contextual influences, namely age-related bias and its impact and the age–job performance relationship. In the final section, we summarize findings to date, implications for practice, and identify promising areas for future research.

Our review and analysis of age- and cohort-related influences on work outcomes stems from a multi-disciplinary perspective in which worker attributes and job demands represent the proximal determinants of job

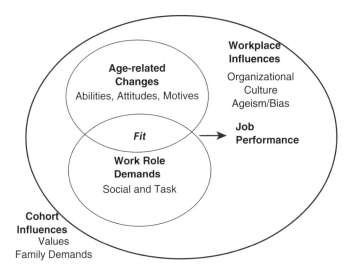

Figure 6.1   Influences on the age and job performance relationship including within-person age-related changes in KSAs, job characteristics such as task demands and motivational and social aspects of work, and contextual influences such as cohort effects and workplace influences

performance, but occur in, and are influenced by, a broader set of contextual variables including the work climate for age, and non-work influences. The model framing our discussion attempts to convey the complexity of the relationships between these factors (Figure 6.1). As shown in the figure, performance is influenced by the fit between age- and cohort-sensitive worker attributes, including knowledge, skills, abilities, and non-cognitive attributes (e.g., personality, motives) and economic- and technology-sensitive job/work role demands. Although these factors reflect the proximal determinants of work-related outcomes, they operate within the larger context of age-sensitive workplace factors such as organizational culture (including perceptions of ageism or age-related bias) and non-work influences (e.g., health, family demands). These broader contextual factors can be expected to exert indirect influence on work performance through their impact on person–job demand fit. In this chapter we examine the effects of the organizational context on

work performance (e.g., age-related bias and organizational culture), but do not address non-work contextual factors directly. Rather, their influence is discussed in the context of age-related changes in worker attributes (including motivation and values) and perceptions of fit with job/work role demands. For extensive reviews of age-related cohort influences on non-work performance see Baltes and Young (2007) and Cleveland (2008).

DEFINITIONAL ISSUES AND THE STATE OF AGE–JOB PERFORMANCE RESEARCH

Age

Age is a chronological variable that indexes life since birth. As such, it is an objective variable that can generally be reported by individuals with little error. From a psychological perspective, however, age is often used as a proxy for identifying an individual's development along one or more dimensions, including physical, cognitive, and affective. Theories and research in cognitive aging and development, such as those by Erikson (1963), Baltes and Baltes (1990), Heckhausen, Wrosch, and Schulz (2010), and Kanfer and Ackerman (2004) provide broad frameworks for understanding normative adult development on different dimensions. To investigate these normative processes, researchers typically use chronological age as a means by which to compare development at different life stages. Nonetheless, it is important to note that these theories address normative development, and do not address or refute the importance of inter-individual differences: the differences among individuals in development trajectories. Consideration of inter-individual differences in aging research is vital because people age at different rates: one person at age 50 may behave more like a 35 year old across many measured outcomes (e.g., level of activity, cognitive ability, memory), and another may behave more like a 60 year old (Hertzog, Kramer, Wilson, and Lindenberger, 2008). Similarly, people may exhibit different rates of development in different domains, such that an older person may show a less pronounced decline in memory processes than persons of a similar chronological age, but a higher level of physical decline than persons of a similar age.

Although age-related changes in cognitive and physical abilities are driven in large part by biological changes that can be usefully tracked in terms of chronological age, a growing body of research indicates that chronological age may be a less useful metric for evaluating development in terms of factors in which an individual's experiences, motives, and life tasks play a significant role in action and adjustment. In the context of work, several researchers have examined the construct of psychological age as an alternative to chronological age for predicting work outcomes (e.g., Barnes-Farrell, Rumery, and Swody, 2002; Cleveland and Lim, 2007; Kooij, de Lange, Jansen, and Dikkers, 2008). Barnes-Farrell et al. (2002), for example,

argue that psychological age may be operationalized on four dimensions: the extent to which a person reports (a) feeling older than his/her chronological age, (b) looking older than his/her chronological age, (c) acting older, and (d) holding a preference for an age older than his or her chronological age. Studies investigating the incremental validity of psychological age variables have shown that psychological age is negatively related to career development intentions and positively related to early retirement intentions after controlling for chronological age (Desmette and Gaillard, 2008). Job stress and its effects have also been examined vis-à-vis psychological and chronological age across five different countries (Barnes-Farrell et al., 2002). Chronological age was positively related to self-perceptions of competence and negatively related to work-related concerns (i.e., stressors). Psychological age was also important after controlling for chronological age. Workers who reported feeling younger than they are were less likely to report work and non-work related stresses and strain. Although this study found that the majority of workers would prefer to be younger than they are, these results suggest that older workers who feel relatively younger continue to see themselves as competent, want to continue to grow and develop in their work, and deal well with daily stressors.

Another formulation defines age along five dimensions (Kooij et al., 2008): (a) chronological age, (b) functional performance-based age (recognizing that cognitive and physical abilities may change in ways that affect performance), (c) psychosocial or subjective age (how old the person feels, looks, and acts and the age cohort with which a person identifies – most similar to the conceptualization of age examined by Barnes-Farrell et al., 2002 described above), (d) organizational age (consideration of tenure/seniority within an organization), and (e) life-span age (the lifespan stage/family status of a person). A qualitative review of the literature conducted by Kooij et al. suggests that the different conceptualizations of age matter. For instance, psychosocial age was negatively related to motivation for work, presumably because feeling older is negatively related to the desire to exert maximum effort and to try new things. Lifespan age was also negatively associated with motivation for work because of the desire for more leisure/family time in later life stages.

The recent interest in the incremental validity of psychological age measures over chronological age in predicting work outcomes reflects growing recognition of the complexity involved in delineating the role that an individual's experiences and context play in work motivation and job performance. Although chronological age clearly continues to provide value in capturing the impact of pervasive, biologically-driven processes that may impact work, psychological age appears useful in accounting for non-biological experience-based processes, such as tenure in an organization, on worker motivation and performance. Future research investigating these alternative, contextualized conceptions of development for work outcomes appears to be an important direction for future research.

Job performance

Similar to definitional issues related to age, the construct of job performance is an intuitively simple construct that is notoriously difficult to define and operationalize (Austin and Villanova, 1992; Campbell, McCloy, Oppler, and Sager, 1993). At the broadest level, job performance refers to 'the total expected value to the organization of the discrete behavioral episodes that an individual carries out over a standard period of time' (Motowidlo, 2003, p. 39). Over the past few decades, progress in understanding the structure of job performance has provided a more precise formulation of the nature of activities that contribute to organizationally-valued behaviors and outcomes. In the early 1990s, Motowidlo and his colleagues (Borman and Motowidlo, 1993) argued for a distinction

between behaviors directed toward performing tasks that contribute to the technical core of the organization (task performance), and activities that are valuable to the organization through their influence on the psychological, social, and organizational context of work (contextual performance). Task performance varies based on the requirements of the job, but is generally measured in either subjective (i.e., supervisor ratings) or objective (e.g., sales or production numbers) ways. Contextual performance includes behaviors that positively influence work environments; for example, volunteering for extra work, helping others, and following organizational rules even when they are inconvenient (i.e., organizational citizenship behaviors, OCBs). Behaviors at the opposite end of the contextual-performance spectrum include those that negatively influence work environments; for example, ignoring rules and procedures, sabotaging the work of others, and rebelling against supervision (i.e., counterproductive work behaviors, CWBs).

Numerous studies provide support for a multidimensional structure of job performance, with many showing a major distinction between worker activities directed toward accomplishment of formal, technical task work and worker activities directed toward accomplishment of informal, socially-oriented teamwork. In the context of age relationships, the more precise delineation of job performance components permits examination of the pathways and mechanisms by which age-related variables affect job performance, as well as the conditions under which age might be positively, negatively, or unrelated to different measures of job performance.

Research on age and job performance

The notion that older workers perform more poorly than younger workers is arguably one of the most widely-held beliefs in developed countries around the world. Indeed, laws about mandatory retirement age and complementary long-standing socio-cultural norms about older worker roles in society give support to the notion of a negative impact of age on work performance. Common sayings such as 'you can't teach an old dog new tricks,' reinforce stereotypes that older workers are less able to learn new skills. Nonetheless, substantial empirical evidence on the relationship between chronological age and job performance provides little evidence for the idea that older workers in general are less valuable to organizations because of poor performance.

To date, four meta-analyses have examined the relationship between age and job performance (McEvoy and Cascio, 1989; Ng and Feldman, 2008; Sturman, 2003; Waldman and Avolio, 1986). The aims of these meta-analyses have varied from investigating the influence of bias on supervisor ratings to examining a broad range of performance criteria (i.e., task and contextual performance). Overall, the results of these studies show no support for a meaningfully significant relationship between age and task performance in either a positive or a negative direction. Nonetheless, there is evidence that age is related to contextual performance *in the positive direction*. Ng and Feldman (2008) found a significant positive relationship between age and contextual measures in terms of OCBs, and a significant negative relationship between age and undesirable CWBs, such as stealing.

Although prior meta-analyses suggest that there is no reliable relationship between age and task performance, the range of correlations reported in these studies is great (e.g., in one meta-analysis the correlations ranged from $r = -.36$ to $+.39$; Sturman, 2003), suggesting the existence of moderators. Potential moderators examined to date include rating type (i.e., subjective supervisor ratings versus objective ratings), job status (i.e., professional versus non-professional), and job complexity (McEvoy and Cascio, 1989; Ng and Feldman, 2008; Sturman, 2003; Waldman and Avolio, 1986). Although there has been no compelling evidence that rating type or job status moderate the relationship between age and task performance, there is

some evidence to support job complexity as a moderator (Sturman, 2003).

In addition to the empirical support provided by Sturman's (2003) meta-analysis, there are theoretical reasons to expect that job complexity would moderate the age–job performance relationship. Because cognitive ability is related to job performance, especially in complex jobs (Schmidt and Hunter, 1998) and because cognitive abilities change with age (Cattell, 1987), the relationship between age and job performance should, theoretically, depend on job complexity. Indeed, Sturman found a significant interaction between sample mean age and job complexity such that the correlation between age and task performance increased as the mean age of the sample increased and the level of job complexity increased. This finding is somewhat surprising in that one might expect that the correlation between age and job performance would decrease as job complexity increased due to declines in some cognitive abilities with age. One explanation for this finding is that job complexity as operationalized in this study (i.e., the data dimension on the *Dictionary of Occupational Titles*; US Department of Labor, 1991) was more related to knowledge gained through experience over time, which is positively related to age, rather than memory type abilities, which are negatively related (Cattell, 1987). Perhaps a refined measure of job complexity would further elucidate the relationship between age and job performance while considering the ability demands of the job.

Taken together, the results of these meta-analyses suggest that older workers should be expected to perform job tasks at the same level as younger workers, and to contribute positively to the work environment. The research reviewed above also points to the probable existence of moderators of the age and job performance relationship; although to date the analysis of moderating variables has yielded inconsistent results. In the following section, we review age-related changes in worker attributes that may help in understanding the conditions in which age might be meaningfully related to work outcomes and performance.

ADULT DEVELOPMENT AND WORK

Although people vary considerably in the rate at which their abilities grow, stabilize, or decline with age (Hedge, Borman, and Lammlein, 2005; Hertzog et al., 2008; Kanfer and Ackerman, 2004), there are important trends in average trajectories of knowledge, skills, and abilities with age that may impact the age and job performance relation. Below we review changes in individual differences in abilities, personality, and motivational traits that occur through the lifespan and their impact on work outcomes.

Cognitive abilities and knowledge

Much research and theory has examined the underlying structure of cognitive abilities and a review of this literature is beyond the scope of this chapter (see Carroll, 1993). One organizational scheme that has gained widespread acceptance is Carroll's (1993) hierarchy of cognitive abilities. In Carroll's hierarchy, g stands at the apex, with narrower abilities at the second level. The abilities in the hierarchy most relevant to aging are fluid ability (Gf), and crystallized ability (Gc). Gf abilities are associated with novel problem solving, learning new information, and working memory abilities (working memory broadly defined as the ability to simultaneously store and process/manipulate information; Baddeley and Hitch, 1974; Cattell, 1987; Horn and Cattell, 1966). By contrast, Gc abilities are associated with the knowledge acquired through experience and education (Cattell, 1987; Horn and Cattell, 1966). Gf and Gc abilities are significantly positively correlated in samples of children and adults, and the correlations are substantial in magnitude – usually larger than .50 (Carroll, 1993). Nevertheless, these abilities show differential trajectories with age. Cross-sectional studies have shown a decline

in mean Gf scores starting in late adolescence or early adulthood and continuing at a gradual rate throughout the lifespan; these same studies also show that Gc remains relatively stable and often increases with age (Beier and Ackerman, 2001, 2005; Jones and Conrad, 1933; Miles and Miles, 1932). A similar pattern of trajectories for Gf and Gc have been obtained in longitudinal studies, although evidence for declines in Gf often appear to have a later onset in longitudinal research (Hultsch, Hertzog, Dixon, and Small, 1998; Schaie, 1996).

In the context of daily life, researchers have often explained the trajectories of Gf and Gc as a reflection of the relative necessity of these abilities at different life stages. During youth and early adulthood, for example, individuals encounter many novel tasks and allocate substantial time and effort to the development of knowledge and skills that have value for social and occupational adjustment. As people age and acquire experiences across a wide variety of situations (e.g., work, social, educational), they are less likely to encounter situations or problems that are completely novel. As such, older adults may employ acquired knowledge and experiences (e.g., Gc and job knowledge) to solve problems more efficiently. The increasing use of knowledge places less demand on the use of age-sensitive Gf abilities and allows older adults to continue to attain high levels of performance. In support of the critical importance of Gc (i.e., knowledge) for performance, Hunter (1983) and others (e.g., Schmidt, Hunter, and Outerbridge, 1986) found that job knowledge was the most direct and best predictor of job performance, and that the relationship between cognitive ability and job performance is mediated by job knowledge.

The trajectories of Gf and Gc throughout the lifespan can help explain the range of correlations found in the meta-analytic studies discussed above. In general, the decline of Gf with age may not impact job performance as people age because workers are more likely to rely on their accumulated knowledge and experience (i.e., Gc) for daily performance in most jobs (Charness, 2000). Although individual differences in Gf-type abilities continue to play a role in some aspects of many jobs, increasing job knowledge associated with age and job tenure may compensate for declines in these abilities. Thus, the compensatory role of Gc and job knowledge on job performance among older workers importantly depends on job demands. In jobs that demand high levels of Gf for daily performance, such as air traffic controller (e.g., Ackerman and Kanfer, 1993), increasing job knowledge may only partially compensate for age-related declines in memory and reasoning speed. By contrast, in jobs that demand high levels of Gc, such as tax accountants, years of job experience and greater job knowledge may sustain performance despite declines in Gf. Given the changes in abilities with age, we would expect that age would be negatively related to jobs that place extensive demands on Gf, but would be unrelated or even positively related to performance in jobs that make high demands on Gc or job knowledge. Although this makes theoretical sense, this explanation has yet to be fully supported empirically due to the current lack of a reliable means for evaluating the ability demands of jobs. It is also important to note that the ability demands of a job may influence job choice as workers craft their work roles in ways that reduce demands on age-sensitive abilities.

Speed, physical, and sensory abilities

In addition to changes in Gf and Gc, the rate of cognitive processing (perceptual speed) slows with age, which affects people's ability to carry out relatively simple tasks with speed and accuracy (e.g., checking ledgers for accuracy; Schaie and Willis, 1993). Gross physical abilities such as static strength, psychomotor abilities (e.g., tracking and manual dexterity), and sensory abilities such as hearing and sight also decline with age (Hedge et al., 2005; Warr,

2001). Although there is evidence that workers can and do develop strategies to compensate for losses in speed and psychomotor abilities with age (e.g., by looking ahead to anticipate upcoming words when typing; Salthouse, 1984), compensating for declines in gross physical strength is not as feasible (Hedge et al., 2005). In terms of sensory abilities, declines in visual acuity occur between the ages of 40 and 50 (Forteza and Prieto, 1994) and hearing loss occurs more gradually. Most age-related declines in vision and hearing can be corrected relatively easily. Nonetheless, these declines may still affect job performance when jobs rely heavily on the senses (e.g., pilot, driver, security guard; Hedge et al., 2005).

In sum, research on age-related changes in abilities paints a complex picture of how changes in cognitive and physical capacities may affect work performance in mid- and late-life. Although declines in Gf abilities are apparent starting in early adulthood, Gc abilities remain stable or even increase throughout the lifespan. Gc ability represents the knowledge acquired through experience, and is therefore a critical predictor of effective work performance. Physical abilities decline with increased age, as do sensory, speed, and psychomotor abilities, although many of these losses can be mitigated by technology-based corrections and strategy use.

Non-ability factors

Age-related changes in cognitive abilities have been studied for decades, but research investigating adult development in work-related attitudes and motives has a much shorter history. During the past decade, cross-sectional and longitudinal studies have focused on mean-level changes and intra-individual stability of the five major personality trait dimensions (i.e., extraversion, openness, agreeableness, neuroticism, and conscientiousness; Roberts and DelVecchio, 2000; Roberts, Walton, and Viechtbauer, 2006). Results of this work provide support for the notion that although mean trait scores change over the lifespan, there is relative stability in individuals' rank order. Specifically, mean levels of conscientiousness and agreeableness show slight increases as a function of chronological age, while extraversion, openness to experience, and neuroticism show slight declines in mean levels over the lifespan (Roberts et al., 2006). In the context of work, these patterns suggest that, all other things being equal, older workers can be expected to compare favorably to younger workers in jobs that place emphasis on behavioral reliability, emotional stability, and strong social skills.

Recent research examining the relationship between age, attitudes, and motivation specific to work has been couched in lifespan theories of development, one of the most prevalent being Carstensen's socio-emotional selectivity theory (Carstensen, Isaacowitz, and Charles, 1999; see Kanfer and Ackerman, 2004). Socio-emotional selectivity theory (SST; Carstensen, 1993) posits that people transition from goals related to achievement and knowledge acquisition when they are younger to goals related to emotional fulfillment during mid-life and beyond. According to SST, age-related differences in goal orientation yield different patterns and purpose of social interaction. Among young adults, social interactions are motivated by their value for providing the individual with information instrumental for increasing work-related skill learning and opportunities for advancement. Among midlife and older adults, the shift toward 'time left to live' yields goals that focus on the utilization of skills and social interactions for purposes of promoting emotional satisfaction and supporting positive self-concept.

SST also provides a framework for understanding often observed age-related differences in affective responses and attitudes. Among older adults, the emphasis placed on pursuit of socio-emotional goals is associated with higher levels of emotion regulation (Isaacowitz and Blanchard-Fields, 2012) and age-related decreases in social conflict (Blanchard-Fields, 2007). According to SST, older individuals learn how to effectively regulate their emotions and develop emotional resiliency in stressful encounters (Carstensen and Mikels, 2005). Investigations of this regulatory process further indicate age-related differences in information-processing, with older adults focusing more frequently on positive rather than negative information (i.e., the *positivity effect*; e.g. Mather and Carstensen, 2005).

Selective Optimization and Compensation is another theory that has been used to understand age-related changes in attitudes and motivation (SOC; Baltes and Baltes, 1990). SOC applies to the process of adapting throughout the lifespan, and is especially relevant in the context of aging because of cognitive and biological changes with age. In this theory, *selection* refers to the adaptive task of prioritizing the domains in which people operate to those that are most aligned with their skills, abilities, and goals. *Optimization* refers to the idea that people make efforts to augment their resources (e.g. cognitive and social) and thus engage in those behaviors that will maximize their chosen life-course. *Compensation* refers to the use of strategies and/or technology to compensate for losses in abilities (e.g., use of mnemonic devices or hearing aids would be forms of compensation). SOC theory would predict, for instance, that workers who are more embedded in an organization (e.g., due to the opportunity costs associated with turnover and job search late in life) would employ selection strategies to align their work with their skills and interests, optimization strategies directed toward improving work roles, and compensation strategies to adjust to work demands rather than to leave their current situation. Together SST and SOC theories describe aging as a lifelong process where people strive to maximize their social and emotional gains and minimize their losses. One positive byproduct of healthy aging according to these theories is that older people will gravitate toward jobs that are a good fit for their skills and personal characteristics over the course of their career, which will serve to increase positive attitudes about work.

In sum, advances in aging research and theory indicate an age-related shift from achievement-related to emotionally-relevant goals and a shift in priorities to opportunities that will optimize worker fit. Evidence associated with this developmental shift includes increased skill in emotion regulation, increased focus on positive information relative to negative, and increased resiliency to stress-inducing environments. In other words, research findings to date are consistent with widely-held beliefs that as people age, they align themselves with opportunities that support their values and needs and develop a sense of perspective that helps them to 'not sweat the small stuff.' Next, we discuss this research in the context of aging and work.

RESEARCH ON AGING AND WORK ATTITUDES

An array of work attitudes have been examined in I/O psychology, although attitudes have only infrequently been explicitly examined in the context of aging until recently. Ng and Feldman (2010) meta-analyzed the relationship between chronological age and 35 job attitudes broadly classified into three categories: task-based attitudes (e.g., job satisfaction, intrinsic work satisfaction, satisfaction with work and pay), organization-based attitudes (e.g., affective, continuance, and normative commitment, perceptions of justice), and people-based attitudes (e.g., satisfaction with co-workers and supervisors, co-worker and supervisor support). In this study, chronological age was positively related to the majority of attitudes assessed indicating that attitudes toward work become more positive with age (i.e., 27 of 35 different job attitudes overall). Age was positively related to most organizationally-based attitudes (e.g., organizational commitment, loyalty, perceptions of justice) although effect sizes (sample-weighted corrected correlations)

were somewhat small (i.e., between .10 and .24). The relationships between age and people-based attitudes were also relatively weak but in a positive direction (e.g., sample-weighted corrected correlation .12 and .10 for satisfaction with co-workers and supervisors respectively). For task-related attitudes, the sample-weighted corrected correlation between age and satisfaction with the work itself was .22, and the magnitude of the correlation was about the same, .18, for overall job satisfaction. There were some negative relationships between age and task-related outcomes. For instance, the relationship between age and satisfaction with promotion opportunities was −.31, and the relationship between age and role overload was −.30. These effects remained significant (although attenuated) after controlling for organizational tenure. In total, these results point to older workers who are relatively satisfied with most aspects of their work, but who feel somewhat overwhelmed and limited in their opportunities for growth.

Although Ng and Feldman (2010) did not find evidence for a general curvilinear relationship between age and attitudes in their study, there may be reason to believe that one exists, at least in terms of the value placed on having satisfying work. Individual studies investigating this phenomenon, for example, have found that workers place less emphasis on job satisfaction in early and late stages of their careers – although satisfaction is highly valued by mid-career workers (Li, Liu, and Wan, 2008). In sum, the most recent work on age and job attitudes generally supports SOC and SST theories in that older workers have positive attitudes toward most aspects of their jobs, presumably because they are likely to focus on the positive aspects of their environments, or because they gravitate toward and select into jobs that optimize their unique KSAOs over time.

Age and motivation

Theory and research on work-motivation and age has also been relatively scarce until recently (Carstensen et al., 1999; Kanfer and Ackerman, 2004). Similar to expectancy models of motivation (Vroom, 1964), Kanfer and Ackerman's theory of age, adult development, and work motivation posits that motivation is a joint function of age-related changes in worker competencies relative to work demands and age-related changes in the value attached to work outcomes. Kanfer and Ackerman suggest that the impact of age-related changes in abilities, knowledge, and skills on work motivation can only be understood in the context of the worker's job demands. Job characteristics, work design, and organizational responsiveness to modifying older worker roles in light of age-related changes in competencies thus play a critical role in determining work motivation. A second major influence on work motivation pertains to age-related changes in the value attached to workplace outcomes (e.g., social friendships) and organizationally-controlled work outcomes (e.g., pay and recognition). As discussed below, changes in the relative value accorded compensation over the lifespan may importantly affect work motivation and willingness to remain on the job. In this section we address these two major influences on older worker motivation.

AGE, WORK DEMANDS, AND PERSON–JOB FIT

Job characteristics refer to the objective demands that a work role places on cognitive and physical abilities and non-cognitive resources, such as temperament, social skills, and time. During the mid-to-late 20th century, the impact of job characteristics on work motivation and job performance was studied using models such as Karasek's (1979) decision latitude theory and Hackman and Oldham's (1975) job characteristics theory. According to these models, work demands such as task variety and decision latitude are proposed to influence psychological factors (e.g., psychological meaningfulness of work) that in turn affect work

motivation and job effort. Although most research on job and work design has focused on the relationship between work demands and work motivation without regard to age, there are many recent studies documenting age-related differences in work condition preferences (Boumans, De Jong, and Janssen, 2011; Sanders, Dorenbosch, Gründemann, and Blonk, 2011; Zacher and Frese, 2009). This research suggests that job characteristics are important for older workers. For example, researchers have found that jobs rated high on autonomy and co-worker support contributed to perceptions of successful aging including a personal sense of control and generativity (Sanders and McCready, 2010). Researchers have also found more generally that age moderates the relationship between a job's motivating potential score (i.e., a summed index of an assessment of the autonomy, skill variety, feedback, task identity, and task significance of the job), and motivation such that older workers benefit more than younger workers from jobs that are intrinsically challenging and fulfilling (Boumans et al., 2011).

Kooij and her colleagues (2011) have also recently pursued a motive-based approach to understanding the features of work that promote or hinder work motivation as a function of adult development. In contrast to job characteristics models, which focus on the motivating potential of the job, the motive-based approach focuses on age-related change in broad motive classes and their relationship to the value or importance attached to different work-related outcomes. Kooij et al. examined age-related differences in work-related motives organized in terms of a 2 (intrinsic or extrinsic focus) × 3 (growth, security, or affiliation target) framework. They found significant age-related differences in both focus and target motive importance, with age negatively related to growth motives such as advancement or promotion, but positively related to the importance of intrinsic work-related motives.

Consistent with SST and Kanfer and Ackerman's theory of age and work motivation

(2004), these results indicate high levels of intrinsic work motives among older workers, but lower levels of extrinsic motive strength. For instance, these results suggest that worker motives for advancement and pay decline with age, but that older worker motive strength is stronger than that of younger workers for fulfilling work, skill utilization, and autonomous work. These findings are further consistent with a large-scale cross-cultural longitudinal study conducted by Warr (2008) that showed older and younger workers similarly valued having a responsible and respectable job aligned with one's abilities, but older workers were more likely than younger workers to value having a job that contributes to society.

Results of research investigating the value of interpersonal relationships for older workers have also been intriguing. Kooij et al.'s (2011) meta-analysis on age and work motives found that age was positively related to motivation to help people and contribute to society, but it was negatively associated with working directly with other people. These findings are aligned with SST (Carstensen et al., 1999) in that not all relationships are created equal for older workers. Specifically, the networking/advancement opportunities that working with others provide seem to be devalued by older workers relative to having meaningful experiences with others (e.g., through mentoring or volunteering), which facilitate deeper emotional relationships.

Person–environment fit perspectives offer a second, less fine-grained approach to understanding the impact of aging on work motivation and performance. Fit refers broadly to the congruence of a person's KSAOs, values, and goals to those of the organization (Kristof, 1996). Multiple-levels of fit have been examined including: person–job (PJ) fit (congruence between a person's characteristics and the specific characteristics associated with the job and its tasks), person–organization (PO) fit (congruence between the employee and the entire organization), person–group (PG) fit (congruence

between the person and the work group or team they are working directly with) and person–supervisor (PS) fit (congruence in the dyadic relationship of supervisor–employee; Kristof-Brown, Zimmerman, and Johnson, 2005). SOC theory (Baltes and Baltes, 1990) suggests that workers are likely to strive to improve their fit with the work environment and job throughout their careers. Indeed, older workers report more congruence between what they want from a job in terms of opportunity, values, and goals and what the organization provides, suggesting that their experience is relatively good compared to younger workers. Furthermore, these perceptions of fit have been found to be one of the underlying drivers of the relationship between age and job satisfaction (White and Spector, 1987).

On the person side of the person–environment fit equation are traits, many of which are expected to change with age. Age would therefore be expected to influence perceptions of fit, but little research has specifically examined this relationship. The research that has been done suggests that a worker's perceptions of fit matter. For instance, fit relative to growth support was significantly predictive of job satisfaction and intentions to leave an organization for younger, but not older, workers. Furthermore, perceptions of fit relative to social interaction/cohesion were significantly predictive of satisfaction for older, but not for younger workers (Westerman and Yamamura, 2007). These findings suggest that the shift in goals suggested by SST will influence perceptions of fit differently for older and younger workers such that perception of fit will be more influenced by growth opportunities for younger workers and more influenced by social factors for older workers. Interestingly, perceptions of fit were not associated with intentions to leave an organization for older workers, but were related to intentions to leave for younger workers. This is perhaps a function of limited mobility in terms of job change for older versus younger workers. That is, factors such as perceived effort in attaining new employment, loyalty to the organization, and work becoming less central to one's identity may diminish the value placed on job change for older workers.

In sum, research to date on person–environment fit suggests that changes in KSOs through the lifespan importantly influence perceptions of fit. Job characteristics include the task demands of available jobs and therefore, the market shift from physically demanding to knowledge work over the last 30 years should benefit older workers, especially when jobs do not tax abilities that are likely to decline with age (i.e., Gf abilities). Although older workers can depend largely on the knowledge and experiences they have accumulated throughout their careers, this may not be possible in some types of jobs. From a motivational perspective, however, intrinsic motivation for performing routine tasks may decline over the lifespan, thus reducing motivation to remain in a job that affords few opportunities for full skill utilization. For workers in these jobs, work redesign that permits greater skill utilization can be expected to increase work motivation through its satisfaction of motives related to generativity and opportunities for new achievements. For example, aircraft pilots perform tasks that are age-sensitive and they may, with experience, maintain their performance using compensatory strategies. Over time, however, aircraft pilots may want to further develop their skill set and move toward alternative roles such as aircraft testing or pilot training.

It is notable that with very few exceptions (e.g., see Warr, 2008) research on aging, motivation, job attitudes, and PJ fit is cross-sectional in nature. Cross-sectional research is valuable, efficient, and a good place to start to understand how age differences affect work attitudes and motivation. Nevertheless, these studies are somewhat limited because cohort effects cannot be ruled out. A cohort effect is the influence of shared attributes of a generation of people who came of age within a socio-cultural context that potentially affects attitudes, values, and perspectives. It may be, for example, that people who grew up in the Baby Boomer generation (i.e., born 1946–1964) will have different work-related values than GenX (born 1965–1981) or Millennials (a.k.a., Generation Y and Generation ME, born 1982–1999). A specific example is the finding that older adults are more satisfied with their current jobs because they select opportunities throughout their career that optimize their KSAOs (i.e., SOC theory; Baltes and Baltes, 1990). An alternative explanation owing to cohort effects would be that older generations are simply easier to please than younger. Because this research is cross-sectional in nature, this alternative explanation cannot be ruled out.

Research does indeed show that both cohort and age influence work-related values (e.g., Smola and Sutton, 2002). A recent study by Twenge, Campbell, Hoffman, and Lance (2010) addressed the cohort versus age question by comparing the self-reported work values of graduating high school seniors in 1976 (Baby Boomers), those graduating in 1991 (GenX), and those graduating in 2006 (Millennials). Although this study is not longitudinal per se, it does address cohort issues in that each of the samples was at the same developmental age (i.e., early adulthood) when surveyed. Results showed evidence of cohort effects in values: Leisure activity as opposed to work, for example, was most valued by Millennials followed by GenX and then Baby Boomers. And although there was no difference between GenX and Baby Boomers in the value placed on interesting and meaningful work, Millennials were less likely to value work-related intrinsic rewards. Furthermore, both Millennials and GenX were more likely than Baby Boomers to value extrinsic rewards such as pay and promotion. In sum, these findings paint a picture of younger generations that are more likely than older generations to value non-work activities, status, and monetary rewards. Moreover, these findings generally suggest that longitudinal or cohort sequential designs are warranted to separate the effects of cohort from age in the study of workplace attitudes and motivation.

In sum, research on work demands and fit suggests that adult development selectively affects worker competencies and motives. Findings to date suggest that changes in work motivation pertain to changes in person–job fit, rather than as a consequence of an intrinsic change in motivation per se. Because coming of age within a socio-cultural milieu does influence attitudes about and motives for work, it is important for future research to disentangle cohort from aging effects. Future research is also needed to examine the impact of different components in work redesign efforts on older worker motivation in jobs where person–job fit may be affected by age-related changes in person competencies.

THE WORK ENVIRONMENT AND PERCEPTIONS OF OLDER WORKERS

To this point, we have discussed the impact of age on work performance in terms of age-related changes in the worker. A second, powerful impact of age on work performance pertains to the socio-cultural milieu in which the individual works. The views that others hold about a worker's competencies and performance can exert direct and indirect effects on worker performance. Research to examine these issues has occurred in the context of studies investigating the effects of age stereotypes. Age-related stereotypes are beliefs and expectations about people based on their age. These stereotypes are pervasive and can affect attitudes and perceptions about older workers that, in turn, impact organizational culture, performance ratings, opportunities for advancement, and worker withdrawal from the organization (Cheung, Kam, and Ngan, 2011). Age-related stereotypes are both positive and negative, and are thought to operate on a more subconscious level than stereotypes about race and sex, which may ultimately make them more insidious (Posthuma and Campion, 2009). On the positive side, older workers are considered to be more reliable, loyal, and productive than younger workers. At the same time, however, they are considered to be costly, inflexible, hard to train, and unable to keep up with technology. Age-related bias is defined more broadly than stereotypes and encompasses a range of perceptions and behaviors that could affect the work environment. There are three components to Finkelstein and Farrell's (2007) view of age-related bias: stereotypes are the cognitive component, prejudice is the affective component, and discrimination is the behavioral component.

Although most organizations report that the benefits of employing older workers outweigh the costs, many also indicate a preference for hiring younger over older job applicants (Johnson, 2007). Ageism research does not generally point to overt discrimination against older workers per se, but suggests that age-related bias can affect job performance both directly, through overt bias influencing subjective performance ratings, and indirectly, through the organizational culture. For instance, subjective performance ratings of older workers will be affected by stereotypes of doddering older workers who may be dependable but slow and inflexible, regardless of the worker's abilities. Rater age relative to the worker being rated will also affect performance ratings. Shore, Cleveland, and Goldberg (2003) found, for example, that a mismatch between worker and supervisor age tended to disadvantage older workers, who were less likely to be thought of as having 'potential' by younger raters, whereas older raters showed no difference in their ratings of the potential of older and younger workers. Surprisingly, this study also reported that older raters were likely to rate older workers less favorably overall than younger workers. Younger raters, by contrast, were actually likely to rate older workers more favorably than the older raters were. These puzzling findings suggest that older raters may internalize age-related stereotypes relative to poor performance. They also highlight the importance of examining both the age of the worker and the age of the rater in research on age-related bias in performance ratings.

Whereas the direct impact of age-related bias on subjective performance ratings is straightforward, research suggests that it may not be pervasive. A recent review of age-related stereotypes in the workplace identified 24 articles or book chapters that reported that performance ratings were directly affected by age-related bias (Posthuma and Campion, 2009), but roughly the same number of articles or book chapters that found little or no support for bias affecting ratings. Indeed the meta-analyses on the age and job performance relationship discussed earlier found no reliable support that rating type (i.e., subjective/supervisor rating versus objective) affected the age and job performance relationship (Ng and Feldman, 2008; Waldman and Avolio, 1986). If age-related bias were pervasive, one would expect that subjective ratings would be systematically lower for older workers than more objective ratings of job performance.

Nonetheless, the indirect effect of age-related bias on the age–job performance relationship is seen in its influence on the organizational culture, which in turn affects the behavior of older workers themselves (Greller and Stroh, 1995). Field research has shown that both younger and older people are likely to hold negative age-related stereotypes about the competence of older workers (Kite, Stockdale, Whitley, and Johnson, 2005; Posthuma and Campion, 2009). For instance, older workers' own perceptions of declining abilities and motivation with age influence their attitudes toward their own retirement and participation in development activities at work (Maurer, Barbeite, Weiss, and Lippstreu, 2008). The antecedents of these perceptions include both the older workers' personal observations of changes in their own abilities and the promulgation of age-related stereotypes that influence the organizational culture and are internalized by older employees. Recent research, including large-scale field studies further suggests that perceptions of an organizational climate of age-discrimination negatively impact affective commitment toward the organization, which in turn, will negatively affect organization performance (Kunze, Boehm, and Bruch, 2011). Perceptions of discrimination are also negatively related to motivation and perceptions of organizational support, and positively related to fear of failure (Rabl, 2010).

Recent research has examined moderators of the relationship between age-related bias and work-related outcomes; specifically, causal attributions that are made regarding performance. For instance, this work has examined whether performance errors are attributed to stable causes that are outside of the employee's control or to unstable and changeable causes (Erber and Long, 2006; Rupp, Vodanovich, and Credé, 2006). The results of this research show that people make age-related attributions that influence work-related outcomes. Rupp et al. found, for example, that raters gave harsher penalties to older targets based on bad performance because they were likely to attribute this poor performance to stable causes (i.e., age-related memory lapses). Although this research suffers from limited generalizability because it has largely been conducted with 'paper people' in a lab setting, it is an important step in further dissecting ageist attitudes that may affect the job performance of older workers.

Indeed, much of the early research on age-related bias in the applied literature (e.g., starting with Rosen and Jerdee's, 1976, first study of age-related stereotypes for working adults), suffers from a generalizability problem. These studies are usually simulations conducted in laboratory settings, where evaluators, often graduate or undergraduate students, are asked to provide opinions about training, promoting, evaluating a target person's behavior (often a written scenario). A meta-analysis by Finkelstein, Burke, and Raju (1995) for example, used exclusively simulation studies and found evidence for age-related stereotypes. Although laboratory research is beneficial because it can isolate effects that might otherwise be difficult to examine in the field, there are differences between field and lab research on age-related stereotypes, not the least of which is the limited contact college students have with older workers. Gordon and Arvey (2004) found, for instance, that studies examining age stereotypes and attitudes in the field reported significantly smaller effect sizes than those studies examining age bias in the laboratory, although notably, effect sizes in both the field and laboratory were significantly different from zero. In total, there is no argument that age-related bias exists, but there is debate about the magnitude of the effects and its impact on meaningful outcomes.

In sum, age-related bias can affect the performance of older workers both directly and indirectly. The limited research that has been conducted on how to remedy the negative effects of age-related bias suggests that the pervasive nature of stereotypes may recede somewhat as the mean age of the workforce continues to increase – that is, as older workers can increasingly identify with their work group (Garstka, Schmitt, Branscombe, and Hummert, 2004). Until then, however, age-related bias remains a potentially negative influence on older worker motivation and performance.

RESEARCH AGENDA ON AGE AND JOB PERFORMANCE

Our brief review of the age and job performance literature suggests that the relationship of chronological age to work performance is multi-determined. Job performance is not simply a function of aging, nor of any uniform age-related decline in abilities or motivation. Rather, we propose that age-related differences in work behavior and job performance stem from the joint and sometimes synergistic influences of multiple dynamic factors indicated in Figure 6.1; namely, person competencies and demands, job demands, and organizational and socio-cultural features. These factors operate in unison to influence motivation to work and motivation at work for all workers, but understanding their impact on older workers

requires identification of the changes that occur in each of these domains for older workers and their impact on motivation, performance, and worker well-being.

In this chapter we have reviewed and discussed theory and research that informs each of the relevant influences on the age and job performance relationship. The realities of the impact of aging of the workforce are upon us, and as such, researchers have recently redoubled their efforts in this area. As evidence of this, much of the research we review above has been conducted within the past decade. Nonetheless, it is clear that many unanswered questions remain. Here we outline what we consider to be the most imperative questions for future research on the age and job performance relationship.

Recommendation #1: Explore new conceptions of person attributes

There currently exists a voluminous literature on the impact of chronological age on cognitive abilities, and over the past decade, researchers have also begun investigating age-related changes in personality traits (Roberts et al., 2006), work attitudes (Ng and Feldman, 2010), and work-related motives (Kooij et al., 2011). To date, however, research has focused primarily on well-established person attributes. In the area of personality and achievement, for example, we know relatively little about the midlife emergence of generativity motives (McAdams and de St Aubin, 1992) or age-related distinctions in achievement directed toward extrinsic versus intrinsic accomplishments. Further research is needed to understand the developmental trajectories of person attributes as a function of work and non-work experiences, and how these trajectories affect the individual's navigation through work roles and impact on job performance. Individual differences in job performance over the lifespan, for example, may lie more in how workers navigate career and work roles than in age-related changes in specific abilities or traits.

Recommendation #2: Expand conceptions of work environment

Contemporary research has focused increasingly on the role that work context plays in work motivation and job performance. In the present context, older workers face diverse and distinct challenges related to age-stereotyping. Although evidence on age-related increases in conscientiousness and pro-social motivation may translate into the increased attractiveness of older workers for jobs that place heavy demands on interpersonal skills, evidence on age-related declines in fluid abilities and speed has also translated into negative age stereotypes about older worker capabilities for performing work that places high demands on memory or fast information-processing. The generalization of these findings to age stereotypes that go beyond the data can reduce older worker motivation and create artificial constraints on job performance. For example, there is little evidence on age-related differences in innovation to indicate that older workers are less innovative than younger workers. Similarly, research on age-related differences in skill training that shows longer training times for older workers does not take into account the impact of training formats that may disadvantage older workers, or differences in incentive value of training for workers at different ages. Research is needed to examine the precise mechanisms through which bias related to age stereotypes occurs in the work environment and the impact of these biases on older worker attitudes and performance. In a similar vein but from a different perspective, research is needed to examine the extent to which human resource management practices related to compensation and work role design affect older worker motivation and performance. Finally, the development of a valid and systematic way to understand contextualized ability and task demands is needed to permit a more fine-grained analysis of how job complexity moderates the age and job performance relationship and would be a potentially useful area of future research.

For example, understanding the extent to which jobs require novel problem solving and memory ability (i.e., Gf) and the extent to which they rely on knowledge and experience (i.e., Gc) will permit better placement of older workers into jobs in which they will thrive throughout their work life.

Recommendation #3: Expand the operationalization of age and utilize longitudinal design

Chronological age may not provide all of the relevant information about the psychological processes and self-perceptions associated with aging that may be relevant in the context of work. Although researchers have expanded the operationalization of age to include its psychological aspects, and have shown that psychological age and chronological age do not predict the same outcomes, it is relatively rare for researchers to include assessment of psychological age in their research studies. One of the most straightforward recommendations we have for future research is that researchers more consistently include an explicit consideration of psychological age in addition to chronological age.

The research discussed herein addresses significant gaps in our knowledge about how aging is related to work performance. Although this research is informative, most of it is limited because it is impossible to rule out cohort influences in cross-sectional research. Moreover, cross-sectional research cannot account for threats to validity such as natural selection/attrition. For instance, older workers in an organization are likely those who have thrived or at least survived there for a number of years and they are likely to be strong performers. Although selective attrition will affect the results of both cross-sectional and longitudinal research designs, longitudinal designs have an advantage in at least documenting its effect. Cross-sectional research has been effective and efficient in examining the relationship between age and job performance, but many of the questions we are now interested in asking require longitudinal methods. Longitudinal research on age and job performance will certainly not be easy, but is not impossible (Warr, 2008). The effort promises to pay off in terms of illuminating many unanswered questions about age and job performance.

CONCLUSION

This chapter was framed around two questions. What is the relationship between age and job performance? And what are the individual differences and situational factors that play a role in understanding this relationship? As of this writing, researchers are intensifying their focus on both questions, but much work remains to be done. Although there is substantial evidence for age-related changes in person attributes and age-related bias, decades of work do not show these factors affecting the relationship between age and job performance. Understanding how changes in person-related factors with age map to changes in job demands in the context of socio-cultural environment (e.g., workplace climate) affect the age–performance relationship requires that we study these variables over time and in context. Our review also suggests that future advances will require greater theoretical sophistication in understanding how the dynamics of worker, work role, and socio-environmental variables interact, with greater attention to identifying worker, job, and environment interactions that promote and hinder sustained employability in late life. We argue that such research is both timely and relevant for worker well-being, organizational productivity, and the societies in which workers and organizations are embedded.

REFERENCES

Ackerman, P. L., and Kanfer, R. (1993) 'Integrating laboratory and field study for improving selection: Development of a battery for predicting air traffic controller success', *Journal of Applied Psychology*, 78(3): 413–432.

Austin, J. T., and Villanova, P. (1992) 'The criterion problem: 1917–199', *Journal of Applied Psychology*, 77(6): 836–874.

Baddeley, A. D., and Hitch, G. (1974). Working memory. In G. H. Bower (Ed.), *The psychology of learning and motivation: Vol. 8. Advances in research and theory*. New York: Academic Press, pp. 47–89.

Baltes, P. B., and Baltes, M. M. (1990) 'Psychological perspectives on successful aging: The model of selective optimization with compensation', in P. B. Baltes and M. M. Baltes (eds), *Successful aging: Perspectives from the behavioral sciences*. New York: Cambridge University Press. pp. 1–34.

Baltes, B. B., and Young, L. M. (2007) 'Aging and work/family issues', in K. S. Shultz and G. A. Adams (eds), *Aging and work in the 21st century*. Mahwah, NJ: Erlbaum. pp. 251–275.

Barnes-Farrell, J. L., Rumery, S. M., and Swody, C. A. (2002) 'How do concepts of age relate to work and off-the-job stresses and strains? A field study of health care workers in five nations', *Experimental Aging Research*, 28(1): 87–98.

Beier, M. E., and Ackerman, P. L. (2001) 'Current-events knowledge in adults: An investigation of age, intelligence, and nonability determinants', *Psychology and Aging*, 16(4): 615–628.

Beier, M. E., and Ackerman, P. L. (2005) 'Age, ability, and the role of prior knowledge on the acquisition of new domain knowledge: Promising results in a real-world learning environment', *Psychology and Aging*, 20(2): 341–355.

Blanchard-Fields, F. (2007) 'Everyday problem solving and emotion: An adult development perspective', *Current Directions in Psychological Science*, 16(1): 26–31.

Borman, W. C., and Motowidlo, S. J. (1993) 'Expanding the criterion domain to include elements of contextual performance', in N. Schmitt and W. C. Borman (eds), *Personnel selection in organizations*. San Francisco, CA: Jossey-Bass. pp. 71–98.

Boumans, N. P. G., De Jong, A. H. J., and Janssen, S. M. (2011) 'Age-differences in work motivation and job satisfaction. The influence of age on the relationships between work characteristics and workers' outcomes', *International Journal of Aging and Human Development*, 73(4): 331–350.

Campbell, J. P., McCloy, R. A., Oppler, S. H., and Sager, C. E. (1993) 'A theory of performance', in N. Schmitt and W. C. Borman (eds), *Personnel selection in organizations*. San Francisco, CA: Jossey-Bass. pp. 35–70.

Cappelli, P. (2009) 'Trends in job demands and the implications for older workers', in S. J. Czaja and

J. Sharit (eds), *Aging and work: Issues and implications in a changing landscape*. Baltimore, MD: The Johns Hopkins University Press. pp. 107–125.

Carroll, J. B. (1993) *Human cognitive abilities: A survey of factor-analytic studies*. New York: Cambridge University Press.

Carstensen, L. L. (1993) 'Motivation for social contact across the life span: A theory of socioemotional selectivity', in J. E. Jacobs (ed.), *Nebraska Symposium on Motivation, 1992: Developmental perspectives on motivation*. Lincoln, NE: University of Nebraska Press. pp. 209–254.

Carstensen, L. L., and Mikels, J. A. (2005) 'At the intersection of emotion and cognition', *Current Directions in Psychological Science*, 14(3): 117–121.

Carstensen, L. L., Isaacowitz, D. M., and Charles, S. T. (1999) 'Taking time seriously: A theory of socioemotional selectivity', *American Psychologist*, 54(3): 165–181.

Cattell, R. B. (1987) *Intelligence: Its structure, growth, and action*. New York: Elsevier Science.

Charness, N. (2000) 'Can acquired knowledge compensate for age-related declines in cognitive efficiency?', in S. H. Qualls and N. Abeles (eds), *Psychology and the aging revolution: How we adapt to longer life*. Washington, DC: American Psychological Association. pp. 99–117.

Cheung, C., Kam, P. K., and Ngan, R. M. (2011) 'Age discrimination in the labour market from the perspective of employers and older workers', *International Social Work*, 54(1): 118–136.

Cleveland, J. N. (2008) 'Age, work, and family: Balancing unique challenges for the twenty-first century', in A. Marcus-Newhall, D. F. Halpern, and S. J. Tan (eds), *The changing realities of work and family: A multi-disciplinary approach*. Malden, MA: Blackwell. pp. 108–139.

Cleveland, J. N., and Lim, A. S. (2007) 'Employee age and performance in organizations', in K. S. Shultz and G. A. Adams (eds), *Aging and work in the 21 st century*. Mahwah, NJ: Erlbaum. pp. 109–137.

Desmette, D., and Gaillard, M. (2008) 'When a "worker" becomes an "older worker:" The effects of age-related social identity on attitudes towards retirement and work', *Career Development International*, 13(2): 168–185.

Erber, J. T., and Long, B. A. (2006) 'Perceptions of slow and forgetful employees: Does age matter?', *The Journals of Gerontology, Series B: Psychological Sciences and Social Sciences*, 61(6): 333–339.

Erikson, E.H. (1963) *Childhood and society*. New York: W. W. Norton and Co.

Finkelstein, L. M., and Farrell, S. K. (2007) 'An expanded view of age bias in the workplace', in K. S. Shultz and G. A. Adams (eds), *Aging and work in the 21st century*. Mahwah, NJ: Erlbaum. pp. 73–108.

Finkelstein, L. M., Burke, M. J., and Raju, N. S. (1995) 'Age discrimination in simulated employment contexts: An integrative analysis', *Journal of Applied Psychology*, 80(6): 652–663.

Forteza, J. A., and Prieto, J. M. (1994) 'Aging and work behavior', in H. C. Triandis, M. D. Dunnette, and L. M. Hough (eds), *Handbook of industrial and organizational psychology, Vol. 4* (2nd edn). Palo Alto, CA: Consulting Psychologists Press. pp. 446–483.

Garstka, T. A., Schmitt, M. T., Branscombe, N. R., and Hummert, M. L. (2004) 'How young and older adults differ in their response to perceived age discrimination', *Psychology and Aging*, 19(2): 326–335.

Gordon, R. A., and Arvey, R. D. (2004) 'Age bias in laboratory and field settings: A meta-analytic investigation', *Journal of Applied Social Psychology*, 34(3): 468–492.

Greller, M. M., and Stroh, L. K. (1995) 'Careers in midlife and beyond: A fallow field in need of sustenance', *Journal of Vocational Behavior*, 47(3): 232–247.

Hackman, R., and Oldham, G. R. (1975) 'Development of the job diagnostic survey', *Journal of Applied Psychology*, 60(2): 159–170.

Hall, D. T., and Mirvis, P. H. (1995) 'The new career contract: Developing the whole person at midlife and beyond', *Journal of Vocational Behavior*, 47(3): 269–289.

Heckhausen, J., Wrosch, C., and Schulz, R. (2010) 'A motivational theory of life-span development', *Psychological Review*, 11(1): 32–60.

Hedge, J. W., Borman, W. C., & Lammlein, S. E. (2005). *The aging workforce: Realities, myths, and implications for organizations*. Washington, D. C.: American Psychological Association.

Hertzog, C., Kramer, A. F., Wilson, R. S., and Lindenberger, U. (2008) 'Enrichment effects on adult cognitive development: Can the functional capacity of older adults be preserved and enhanced?', *Psychological Science in the Public Interest*, 9(1): 1–65.

Horn, J. L., and Cattell, R. B. (1966) 'Refinement and test of the theory of fluid and crystallized general intelligences', *Journal of Educational Psychology*, 57(5): 253–270.

Hultsch, D. F., Hertzog, C., Dixon, R. A., and Small, B. J. (1998) *Memory change in the aged*. New York: Cambridge University Press.

Hunter, J. E. (1983) 'A causal analysis of cognitive ability, job knowledge, job performance, and supervisor ratings', in F. Landy and J. Cleveland (eds), *Performance measurement and theory*. Hillsdale, NJ: Erlbaum. pp. 257–266.

Isaacowitz, D. M., and Blanchard-Fields, F. (2012) 'Linking process and outcome in the study of emotion and aging', *Perspectives on Psychological Science*, 7(1): 3–17.

Johnson, R. W. (2004, July) Trends in job demands among older workers, 1992-2002, *Monthly Labor Review*, 48-46. Retrieved on 22 October 2012 from the Bureau of Labor Statistics Website: http://www.bls.gov/opub/mlr/2004/07/art4full.pdf

Johnson, R. W. (2007) 'Managers' attitudes toward older workers: A review of the evidence', in S. J. Czaja and J. Sharit (eds), *Aging and work: Issues and implications in a changing landscape*. Baltimore, MD: The Johns Hopkins University Press. pp. 185–208.

Jones, H. E., and Conrad, H. S. (1933) 'The growth and decline of intelligence: A study of a homogeneous group between the ages of ten and sixty', *Genetic Psychology Monographs*, 13(3): 223–298.

Kanfer, R. and Ackerman, P. L. (2004) 'Aging, adult development, and work motivation', *Academy of Management Review*, 29(3): 440–458.

Karasek, R. A. (1979) 'Job demands, job decision latitude, and mental strain: Implications for job redesign', *Administrative Science Quarterly*, 24(2): 285–308.

Kite, M. E., Stockdale, G. D., Whitley, B. E., Jr., and Johnson, B. T. (2005) 'Attitudes toward younger and older adults: An updated meta-analytic review', *Journal of Social Issues*, 61(2): 241–266.

Kooij, D., de Lange, A., Jansen, P., and Dikkers, J. (2008) 'Older workers' motivation to continue to work: five meanings of age. A conceptual review', *Journal of Managerial Psychology*, 23(4): 364–394.

Kooij, D. T. A. M., de Lange , A. H., Jansen, P G. W, Kanfer, R., and Dikkers, J. S. E. (2011) 'Age and work-related motives: Results of a meta-analysis', *Journal of Organizational Behavior*, 32(2): 197–225.

Kristof, A. L. (1996), 'Person-organization fit: An integrative review of its conceptualizations, measurement, and implications', *Personnel Psychology*, 49(1): 1–49.

Kristof-Brown, A. L., Zimmerman, R. D., and Johnson, E. C. (2005), 'Consequences of individuals' fit at work: A meta-analysis of person-job, person-organization, person-group, and person-supervisor fit', *Personnel Psychology*, 58(2): 281–342.

Kunze, F., Boehm, S. A., and Bruch, H. (2011) 'Age diversity, age discrimination climate and performance consequences – a cross organizational study', *Journal of Organizational Behavior*, 32(2): 264–290.

Li, W., Liu, X., and Wan, W. (2008) 'Demographic effects of work values and their management implications', *Journal of Business Ethics*, 81(4): 875–885.

Mather, M., and Carstensen, L. L. (2005) 'Aging and motivated cognition: The positivity effect in attention and memory', *Trends in Cognitive Sciences*, 9(10): 496–502.

Maurer, T. J., Barbeite, F. G., Weiss, E. M., and Lippstreu, M. (2008) 'New measures of stereotypical beliefs about older workers ability and desire for development: Exploration among employees age 40 and over', *Journal of Managerial Psychology*, 23(4): 395–418.

McAdams, D.P., and de St. Aubin, E. (1992) 'A theory of generativity and its assessment through self-report, behavioral acts, and narrative themes in autobiography', *Journal of Personality and Social Psychology*, 62(6): 1003–1015.

McEvoy, G. M., and Cascio, W. F. (1989) 'Cumulative evidence of the relationship between employee age and job performance', *Journal of Applied Psychology*, 74(1): 11–17.

Miles, C. C., and Miles, W. R. (1932) 'The correlation of intelligence scores and chronological age from early to late maturity', *The American Journal of Psychology*, 44, 44–78.

Motowidlo, S. J. (2003) 'Job performance', in I. B. Weiner, W. C. Borman, D. R. Ilgen, and R. J. Klimoski (eds), *Handbook of psychology: Industrial and organizational psychology* (Vol. 12). Hoboken, NJ: Wiley and Sons. pp. 39–53.

Ng, T. W. H., and Feldman, D. C. (2008) 'The relation of age to ten dimensions of job performance', *Journal of Applied Psychology*, 93(2): 392–423.

Ng, T. W. H., and Feldman, D. C. (2010) 'The relationship of age with job attitudes: A meta-analysis', *Personnel Psychology*, 63(3): 677–718.

Posthuma, R. A., and Campion, M. A. (2009) 'Age stereotypes in the workplace: Common stereotypes, moderators, and future research directions', *Journal of Management*, 35(1): 158–188.

Rabl, T. (2010) 'Age, discrimination, and achievement motives', *Personnel Review*, 39(4): 448–467.

Roberts, B. W., and DelVecchio, W. F. (2000) 'The rank-order consistency of personality traits from childhood to old age: A quantitative review of longitudinal studies', *Psychological Bulletin*, 126(1): 3–25.

Roberts, B. W., Walton, K. E., and Viechtbauer, W. (2006) 'Patterns of mean-level change in personality traits across the life course: A meta-analysis of longitudinal studies', *Psychological Bulletin*, 132(1): 1–25.

Rosen, B., and Jerdee, T. H. (1976) 'The nature of job-related age stereotypes', *Journal of Applied Psychology*, 61(2): 180–183.

Rupp, D. E., Vodanovich, S. J., and Credé, M. (2006) 'Age bias in the workplace: The impact of ageism and causal attributions', *Journal of Applied Social Psychology*, 36(6): 1337–1364.

Salthouse, T. A. (1984) 'The skill of typing', *Scientific American*, 250(2): 128–135.

Sanders, M. J., and McCready, J. W. (2010) 'Does work contribute to successful aging outcomes in older workers?', *International Journal of Aging and Human Development*, 71(3): 209–229.

Sanders, J., Dorenbosch, L., Gründemann, R., and Blonk, R. (2011) 'Sustaining the work ability and work motivation of lower-educated older workers: Directions for work redesign', *Management Revue*, 22(2): 132–150.

Schaie, K. W. (1996) 'Intellectual development in adulthood', in J. E. Birren, K. W. Schaie, R. P. Abeles, M. Gatz, and T. A. Salthouse (eds), *Handbook of the psychology of aging* (4th edn.). San Diego, CA: Academic Press. pp. 266–286.

Schaie, K. W., and Willis, S. L. (1993) 'Age difference patterns of psychometric intelligence in adulthood: Generalizability within and across ability domains', *Psychology and Aging*, 8(1): 44–55.

Schmidt, F. L., and Hunter, J. E. (1998) 'The validity and utility of selection methods in personnel psychology: Practical and theoretical implications of 85 years of research findings', *Psychological Bulletin*, 124(2): 262–274.

Schmidt, F. L., Hunter, J. E., and Outerbridge, A. N. (1986) 'Impact of job experience and ability on job knowledge, work sample performance, and supervisory ratings of job performance', *Journal of Applied Psychology*, 71(3): 432–439.

Shore, L. M., Cleveland, J. N., and Goldberg, C. B. (2003) 'Work attitudes and decisions as a function of manager age and employee age', *Journal of Applied Psychology*, 88(3): 529–537.

Smola, K. W., and Sutton, C. D. (2002) 'Generational differences: Revisiting generational work values for the new millennium', *Journal of Organizational Behavior*, 23(4): 363–382.

Sturman, M. C. (2003) 'Searching for the inverted u-shaped relationship between time and performance: Meta-analyses of the experience/performance, tenure/performance, and age/performance relationships', *Journal of Management*, 29(5), 609–640.

Toossi, M. (2012, January) 'Employment outlook: 2010–2020: Labor force projections to 2020: A more slowly growing workforce'. *Monthly Labor Review*, 43–64. Retrieved on 22 October 2012 from the Bureau of Labor Statistics Website: http://www.bls.gov/opub/mlr/2012/01/art3full.pdf

Twenge, J. M., Campbell, S. M., Hoffman, B. J., and Lance, C. E. (2010) 'Generational differences in work values: leisure and extrinsic values increasing, social and intrinsic values decreasing', *Journal of Management,* 36(5).

US Department of Labor (1991) *Dictionary of Occupational Titles* (4th edn). Retrieved on 22 October 2012 from http://www.oalj.dol.gov.

Vroom, V. H. (1964) *Work and Motivation*. John Wiley: New York.

Waldman, D. A., and Avolio, B. J. (1986) 'A meta-analysis of age differences in job performance', *Journal of Applied Psychology*, 71(1): 33–38.

Warr, P. (2001). Age and work behavior: Physical attributes, cognitive abilities, knowledge, personality traits and motives. In C. L. Cooper & I. T. Robertson (Eds.), *International Review of Industrial and Organizational Psychology, Vol. 16*. Chichester, UK: Wiley, pp. 1–36.

Warr, P. (2008) 'Work values: Some demographic and cultural correlates', *Journal of Occupational and Organizational Psychology*, 81(4): 751–775.

Weckerle, J. R., and Shultz, K. S. (1999) 'Influences on the bridge employment decision among older USA workers', *Journal of Occupational and Organizational Psychology*, 72(3): 317–329.

Westerman, J. W., and Yamamura, J. H. (2007) 'Generational preferences for work environment fit: Effects on employee outcomes', *Career Development International*, 12(2): 150–161.

White, A. T., and Spector, P. E. (1987) 'An investigation of age-related factors in the age-job-satisfaction relationship', *Psychology and Aging*, 2(3): 261–265.

Zacher, H., and Frese, M. (2009) 'Remaining time and opportunities at work: Relationships between age, work characteristics, and occupational future time perspective', *Psychology and Aging*, 24(2): 487–492.

7

Age and Work Motives

Cort W. Rudolph, Boris B. Baltes
and Keith L. Zabel

AGE AND WORK MOTIVES

Despite seemingly limitless admonitions regarding the aging of the world's population (e.g. United Nations, 2009), research on aging and work has only recently begun to directly consider the implication of such trends on workplace processes, such as the influence of an aging workforce on work motivation. Despite recent reviews (Kooij, de Lange, Jansen, and Dikkers, 2007; Kooij et al., 2011), primary research has yet to adequately address this topic directly, and of the literature that has in some way considered age along with motivational variables, certain methodological concerns may limit our ability to effectively draw conclusions about the influence of developmental processes in later life on work motivation.

Indeed, most of the research that can inform our understanding of the role of aging in work motivation has measured chronological age as a cross-sectional control variable. Thus, most research cannot distinguish between 'true' developmental effects and ones that are due to cohort differences.

Despite these limitations, the present chapter seeks to review the existing body of research concerning the influence of age on work motivation. Methodological limitations aside, given the impending shifts in workplace age demographics, it is imperative that we coalesce our understanding of the ways in which age may influence work motivation to inform the design of interventions to engage an aging workforce.

Only recently has research begun to understand that the relationship between age and many workplace variables tends to be dynamic as opposed to static. In this vein, Kanfer and Ackerman (2004) developed a theoretical framework from which to approach the relationship between workplace motives and age. Kanfer and Ackerman (2004) argue that changes which occur as individuals age (i.e., loss, growth, reorganization, exchange) impact psychological variables, which in turn impact motivational processing. In addition, Kanfer and Ackerman (2004) posit that age-related decreases in fluid intelligence and increases in crystallized intelligence change the way in which individuals are motivated. For instance, as individuals age, they may have higher levels of motives that act as a compensatory mechanism to make up for their decreasing fluid intelligence. In essence, Kanfer and Ackerman's model posits that motives are dynamic and that as individuals age some workplace motives increase and others decrease.

Although a great deal of empirical research has focused on the effects of both aging (e.g., Cron and Slocum, 1986; Warr, 1992) and motivation (e.g., Lilly, Duffy, and Virick, 2006; Steers, 1975) on workplace outcomes, with few exceptions (e.g., Adler and Aranya, 1984; Inceoglu, Segers, Bartram and Vloeberghs, 2009) almost no empirical studies have been primarily interested in how workplace motives change as a function of aging. Thus, nearly all the studies we review below examined the relationship between age and motives without that relationship being the primary interest of their research.

A second problem with the current state of the age-motive literature is that almost every study that has examined the relationship between age and motives has used a cross-sectional design. Indeed, we could only locate two studies that have examined the relationship between age and motives using a longitudinal design (Bateman and Strasser,

1984; Rentsch and Steel, 1998). Given that the research we discuss below has found several meaningful relationships between age and workplace motives, these two issues need to be addressed by future research to advance our knowledge of the dynamic relationship between aging and work motivation.

As a means to organize the present chapter, we rely on a model of work motives that crosses three levels of needs (growth, social, and security) with two loci (intrinsic and extrinsic; Deci and Ryan, 1985). This model, depicted in Table 7.1, allows us to focus narrowly on very specific intersections of needs and their locus, and is consistent with recent scholarship that has attempted to summarize the various ways in which age intersects with motivation (see Kanfer and Ackerman, 2004; Warr, 2001). The following review is thus split into sections that focus on (a) the relationship between age and both intrinsic (e.g., need for achievement) and extrinsic (e.g., promotion) growth needs, (b) both intrinsic (e.g., need for affiliation) and extrinsic (e.g., need for recognition) social needs, and (c) both intrinsic (e.g., job security) and extrinsic (e.g., pay) security needs. Each section is anchored by a summary of the major theoretical perspectives on lifespan development that may inform our understanding of the dynamics of work motives.

Table 7.1   Conceptual Work-Motive Framework

	Intrinsic	Extrinsic
Growth	• Need for Achievement • Need for Autonomy • Need for Feedback • Career Motivations • Need for Growth/Growth Need Strength • Self-esteem • Need for Mastery	• Promotion Related
Social	• Need for Affiliation • Control of others • Trust • Support • General Social Motivation	• Need for Recognition
Security	• Existence Needs • Need for Security • Job Security • Need for Control • Need for Prevent Loss	• Need for Pay • Economically Related Needs

Then, a more in depth summary of the findings of individual studies are offered to serve as a comprehensive overview of the extant literature. Finally, we finish with a discussion of the present review in the larger context of work and aging literature, noting – where appropriate – directions for future research, and suggestions for furthering the scientific study of age and working.

GROWTH MOTIVES

Generally speaking, growth motives are aimed at reaching higher levels of functioning. As such, it should not be surprising that growth needs encompass a wide range of motivations – with both intrinsic (e.g., need for achievement) and extrinsic (i.e., promotion-related) foci (see Table 7.1). From a lifespan perspective, there are several theories that describe the age-related dynamics of growth motives. Once such theory, Selection, Optimization, and Compensation (SOC: see Baltes and Baltes, 1990) suggests that developmental gains are maximized by a process of *selecting* viable goals, *optimizing* resources to obtain those goals, and *compensating* for resource losses that serve as barriers to goal attainment. As individuals age, this regulation process changes to accommodate resource gains and losses; likewise, SOC predicts that growth-related work motives decline as one ages, and that motives related to maintenance and regulation of work-related losses will increase.

Intrinsic Growth

As suggested, the lifespan theory of SOC (Baltes, Staudinger, and Lindenberger, 1999) predicts that age-related declines in growth motives occur because, as we age, orientations shift to emphasize motives related to maintenance and regulation of losses over the attainment of new skills. As evidence for this, Freund (2006) found that younger adults focus more on growth-relevant optimization goals, whereas older adults focus more on goals directed toward prevention of resource losses. This general pattern is also offered by Kanfer and Ackerman (2000), who suggest that younger adults' desire to learn was higher than older adults'.

Need for Achievement

Need for achievement has been characterized as 'the personal striving of individuals to attain goals within their social environment' (Cassidy and Lynn, 1989, p. 301). First conceptualized by McClelland (1961), need for achievement was described as competition against a standard of excellence, and it has been postulated that employees who are very focused on goal achievement have more long-term work orientations and plans, which may subsequently lead to increased career commitment.

As suggested above, lifespan theories generally predict declines in intrinsic growth motives with age. Despite these predictions, recent meta-analytic evidence (Kooij et al., 2011) suggests a small, albeit significant, positive relationship between age and achievement needs ($\rho = .06$), indicating that on average, achievement needs increase with age. While this result is seemingly contrary to expectations based upon theory, by focusing on the results of various primary studies that have measured both age and various types of intrinsic growth motives (e.g., need for achievement), one finds a great deal of variation in the relationship between these two variables that might help explain this result.

Indeed, despite the fact that lifespan theories predict that achievement needs should be less important as one ages, only two studies have demonstrated significant negative relationships between age and need for achievement. For example, Treadway, Hochwarter, Kacmar, and Ferris (2005) studied correlates of political skill and behavior within organizations, including age and need for achievement. Using a sample of 193 working adults with at least 5 years of full-time experience, age was negatively related to need for achievement, such that older individuals had lower levels of need for achievement ($r = -.18$) than younger individuals.

In the second study to find this negative relationship, Churchill, Ford, and Walker (1979) used a VIE (Valence-Instrumentality-Expectancy) framework (Vroom, 1964) to understand the relationship between sales-people's personal characteristics and desires for various rewards. Chronological age was negatively related to rewards that emphasize a sense of accomplishment, a factor that closely maps onto the concept of need for achievement. In this study, older individuals demonstrated a lower valence for accomplishment-based rewards.

Many studies that have measured both age and need for achievement have found non-significant relationships between these two variables. For example, Bateman and Strasser (1984) employed a longitudinal design and found that there was no evidence for a direct relationship ($r = .06$) between age and need for achievement. Similarly, Inceoglu et al. (2009) conducted a study of work motivations in a large northern European sample ($n = 7644$). When controlling for many other variables (e.g., participant demographics) there was no evidence for a direct relationship between chronological age and need for achievement.

Tang and Ibrahim (1998) investigated a number of the antecedents of organizational citizenship behaviors in two cultures including age and need for achievement, and concluded that there is no relationship between chronological age and need for achievement in either an American ($r = .02$) or Middle Eastern sample ($r = .10$). Likewise, in a study of individual factors that contribute to career commitment, Goulet and Singh (2002) surveyed 278 employees and found that cross-sectional chronological age was unrelated to need for achievement ($r = .04$).

Loon and Casimir (2008) focused on the moderating role of need for achievement in the relationship between job-demand for learning and job-related learning in a sample of 153 working adults. In terms of the present review, need for achievement was not significantly related to age ($r = -.02$). However, interestingly, age was negatively related to job-related learning ($r = -.14$), suggesting that older individuals perceive that they acquire fewer job-relevant skills than younger individuals. Fagenson (1992) compared protégés' and non-protégés' level of need for achievement in a sample of 169 employees (46% of which were protégés) from two service organizations. Age was unrelated to need for achievement for both protégés ($r = -.02$) and non-protégés ($r = -.15$). Similarly, McNeese-Smith and Crook (2003) surveyed 412 nurses, and found there was no relationship between age and need for achievement.

Schaubroeck, Ganster, and Jones (1998) studied factors that influence the attraction-selection-attrition process, including age and need for achievement, across five organizations ($n = 681$). In this study, age was unrelated to need for achievement ($r = .05$). Similarly, in Frew and Bruning's (1987) investigation of various precursors of work stress and strain in a sample of 62 employees at a manufacturing firm, age was unrelated to need for achievement ($r = -.10$). Similarly, Zhu, Luthans, Chew, and Li (2006) investigated personal characteristics that related to the willingness of accepting expatriate assignments – including age and need for achievement. This study broadly sampled engineers and managers ($n = 357$), working at various levels at international firms in Singapore. Once again, the bivariate relationship between age and need for achievement ($r = .03$) was not significant.

In a longitudinal study of the relationship between job characteristics and absenteeism, Rentsch and Steel (1998) investigated the moderating role of growth need strength, including need for achievement over a six-year period. Using a sample of civilian personnel working for the US Department of Defense ($n = 332$), the results of this investigation suggest that there is no effect of age on need for achievement ($r_{time-1} = -.01$; $r_{time-2} = .05$), and that longitudinally, there is no appreciable (i.e., statistically significant) effect of age on need for achievement. Byrne, Kacmar, Stoner, and Hochwater (2005) similarly found that age was unrelated to need for achievement ($r = -.08$). Finally, in a now classic investigation of the role that need for achievement plays in job design, Steers and Spencer (1977) utilized a sample of 115 managers from a large manufacturing firm and found no relationship between need for achievement and age ($r = -.09$) or tenure ($r = .03$).

Finally, some studies have found a positive relationship between age and need for achievement. Steers (1975) found that chronological age was positively related to need for achievement ($r = .21$, $p < .05$), such that older individuals had higher levels of need for achievement than younger individuals. Similarly, Rowe and Snizek (1995) found that preferences for feelings of accomplishment (i.e., a factor relevant to need for achievement) were significantly – and positively – related to age, although the magnitude of this effect was quite small (i.e., about .004% of the variance could be explained by cross-sectional chronological age).

In another study, Tang, Singer, and Roberts (2000) found that need for achievement was not related to age for females ($r = -.06$), but was for males ($r = .13$); older males had higher levels of need for achievement than younger males. Similarly, Rotondo (1999) investigated the relationship between a number of individual difference variables – including age and need for achievement – and career-related coping. In this study, need for achievement was significantly and positively related to age, such that older individuals had higher levels of need for achievement ($r = .21$) than younger individuals. Likewise, Young and Perrewe (2004) found that age was significantly, and positively related to need for achievement for protégés; older protégés had higher levels of need for achievement ($r = .12$) than younger protégés. Interestingly, this relationship was not significant for mentors ($r = .03$). Finally, studies outside of the traditional realm of organizational research have also found positive relationships between age and need for achievement.

For example, Ehigie, Kolade, and Afolabi (2006) studied how various personality factors influence politicians' attitudes towards the wellbeing of their constituents, concluding that age was positively related to need for achievement ($r = .19$).

Taking a closer look at the research it is clear that a majority of studies have found no relationship between age and need for achievement. Indeed, studies with very high levels of statistical power (e.g., Inceoglu et al., 2009; Schaubroeck et al., 1998), multi-cultural samples (e.g., Tang and Ibrahim, 1998), and including samples with large age ranges (e.g., Byrne et al., 2005) have found no relationship between age and need for achievement. In addition, while very few age–work motive studies have used a longitudinal design in general, two studies utilizing a longitudinal designs found no relationship between age and need for achievement (Bateman and Strasser, 1984; Rentsch and Steel, 1998). Thus, the majority of evidence suggests there is no relationship between age and need for achievement.

Even though the majority of studies have found no relationship between age and need for achievement, there exists a handful of documented studies that have found a positive relationship between age and need for achievement, and at least two studies that found a negative relationship between age and need for achievement. However, even in the rare case that a significant relationship has been found between age and need for achievement, age has explained, at most, just over 4% of the variability in need for achievement. Thus, even when age is a significant predictor of need for achievement, the practical significance of age as a predictor seems weak at best.

Need for Autonomy

Self-determination theory (Deci and Ryan, 1985) suggests that individuals' experience of autonomy fosters high quality forms of motivation and engagement for activities, including enhanced performance. Indeed, need for autonomy is an intrinsic growth factor that has been posited to vary with age (e.g., Vallerand, O'Connor, and Hamel, 1995). As suggested above, lifespan theories generally posit that intrinsic growth motives will decline with age. However, not surprisingly, there has been a great deal of variability in the results of studies that have measured both age and need for autonomy; studies that have found positive, negative, and no effects of age on need for autonomy are reviewed below. The Kooij et al. (2011) meta-analysis found a significant, positive relationship between age and need for autonomy ($\rho = .27$). Interestingly, this was the strongest relationship between age and work motives found in this review.

Indeed, only one study has actually garnered support for the notion that autonomy needs are negatively related to age. Adler and Aranya (1984) compared work needs, attitudes, and preferences among accountants at various stages of their careers. Need for autonomy was found to be highest in the 'maintenance' career stage and lowest in the 'preretirement' career stage. Overall, the pattern of results suggests that need for autonomy increases from the 'establishment' stage of one's career to the 'advancement' stage, plateauing during the 'maintenance' stage, and dropping off significantly during the 'preretirement' stage.

Contrary to theory, a far more common conclusion is that age is positively related to need for autonomy. Indeed, Inceoglu et al. (2009) examined the cross-sectional relationship between age and need for autonomy, and found that older individuals had higher need for autonomy than younger individuals. The magnitude of this effect, however, was quite small (i.e., age accounted for 2% of the variance in need for autonomy). Furthermore, this study found evidence for a nonlinear relationship between age and need for autonomy, suggesting that need for autonomy may plateau as we age. In a similar vein, Fagenson (1992) compared protégés' and non-protégés' levels of need for autonomy, finding that age was positively related to need for autonomy for protégés ($r = .29$),

suggesting that older protégés have higher levels of need for autonomy than younger protégés. However, this effect was not significant for non-protégés ($r = -.11$). Similar effects have also been found by Ehigie et al. (2006) and by Lefkowitz (1994). In their longitudinal study of the relationship between job characteristics and absenteeism, Rentsch and Steel (1998) found that need for autonomy was positively and significantly related to age ($r = .16$).

A good deal of research has concluded that age and need for autonomy are unrelated. For example, in Frew and Bruning's (1987) investigation of manufacturing firm employees ($n = 62$), age was unrelated to need for autonomy ($r = .20$). Given the small sample used in this study, however, the lack of statistical significance could be attributed to a lack of statistical power. Similarly, Mudrack and Naughton (2001) and Steers and Spencer (1977) found no relationship between need for autonomy and age. Sverke and Sjoberg (1994) studied various factors that predict commitment to unions in a sample of unionized Swedish public sector employees ($n = 257$). This research likewise found no relationship between age and job autonomy ($r = .01$).

Kidd and Green (2004) investigated the various factors that influence research scientists' commitment to their fields, and turnover intentions. Using a sample of research scientists from a variety of subfields in biology ($n = 220$), this research found no relationship between age and need for autonomy ($r = -.07$). Similarly, Lang and Carstensen (2002) investigated the role that future time perspectives (i.e., a facet of socio-emotional selectivity theory) play in social motivations, and the quality of personal networks, and concluded that age was unrelated to need for autonomy ($r = -.09$).

Payne (1970) examined the relationship between various work behaviors and extraversion. Using a sample of 113 female employees, both discrepancies in need for autonomy ($r = -.07$) and the importance ($r = -.18$) of need for autonomy were found to be unrelated to age. Similarly, Naus, van Iterson, and Roe (2007) used a sample of 174 Dutch workers, and found that job autonomy and age were unrelated. Finally, in their study of gender as a moderator of job satisfaction, Neil and Snizek (1988) found no relationship between age and perceived job autonomy across multiple samples of Australian government workers.

Reviewing the studies above, it is clear that a majority of these investigations have found either no relationship, or a positive relationship between age and need for autonomy. Given that only one known study has found a negative relationship between age and need for autonomy, this might call into question whether or not intrinsic growth motives related to autonomy decrease with age. Perhaps one reason for inconsistent findings regarding the age–need for autonomy relationship is the finding that the relationship may be non-linear in nature (i.e., Adler and Aranya, 1984). Specifically, Adler and Aranya (1984) found that need for autonomy was highest in the 'maintenance' career stage and lowest in the 'pre-retirement' career stage. Given that the majority of studies do not include many individuals in the pre-retirement stage in their sample, the inconsistent findings with respect to the significance of relationships, and the sheer number of positive significant relationships between age and need for autonomy may make sense.

Feedback and Career-Related Motivation

Feedback can be generally conceived of as actions taken by an external agent to provide information regarding some aspect of one's performance (Kluger and Denisi, 1996). Task-focused feedback has been linked to increased task-motivation (Kluger and Denisi, 1996). Likewise, career motivation is a complex, multidimensional construct consisting of both individual characteristics (e.g., career identity, career insight, and career resilience) and broader career decisions and behaviors (e.g., career decisions

and behaviors) (London, 1983). Given their relevance to workplace processes in general, it is perhaps not surprising that feedback and career motivation have also been studied as intrinsic growth factors related to age. As suggested, intrinsic growth factors are predicted to be negatively related to age; however, the results of a variety of studies have consistently shown that age is unrelated to both feedback and career motivation. For example in their longitudinal investigation, Rentsch and Steel (1998) found that aging has little effect on need for feedback, in that the influence of age on the need for feedback was non-significant, and constant across time ($r_{time1} = .01$, $r_{time2} = .00$). Likewise, Steers and Spencer (1977) and Frew and Bruning (1987) found no relationship between need/desire for feedback and age.

Beyond studies of feedback, very few studies have investigated the relationship between age and career motivation. One study that approximates this (Wolf, London, Casey, and Pufahl, 1995) used an aggregate variable representing career experience (i.e., an aggregate of age, length of career, and number of jobs held) and found that career experience was unrelated to career motivation in a sample of 72 unemployed engineers ($r = .06$). However, because age was not directly linked to career motivation, it is difficult to tell whether or not age is related to career motivation.

Need for Growth and Growth Need Strength

The job characteristics model proposed by Hackman and Oldham (1976) suggests that the potency of growth needs strength is key to understanding the link between job characteristics and work outcomes, such as performance. Broadly defined, growth needs can be conceptualized as needs for personal challenge and accomplishment, for learning, and for professional development. Need for growth and Growth Need Strength (GNS) are intrinsic growth factors that have been studied in a number of domains. Again, lifespan theories generally suggest that age should be negatively related to intrinsic social motives, such as those relevant to growth. However, given that growth needs are strongly related to achievement needs, it is again not surprising that there have been very mixed results with respect to the relationship between age and growth variables. Interestingly, and in line with theory, Kooij et al. (2011) found a very small, albeit significant, negative relationship between age and growth outcomes ($\rho = -.14$), suggesting that in the aggregate, age accounts for about 1% of the variance in such outcomes.

Some evidence for this notion can also be gleaned from primary investigations. For example, Hackman and Oldham (1976) investigated the influence of demographic variables on GNS, and found a negative relationship between age and GNS. Additionally, Inceoglu et al. (2009) examined the relationship between age and need for personal growth, finding evidence for a relationship between chronological age and personal growth, such that older individuals have lower levels of need for personal growth than younger individuals.

Contrary to theory, some studies have found a positive relationship between age and growth. For example, within Churchill et al.'s (1979) VIE framework, chronological age was found to be positively related to rewards that emphasize personal growth, a factor that closely maps onto the concept of need for growth. Older individuals were more likely to hold a higher level of valence with respect to growth-based rewards. Similarly, Cook and Wall (1980) found age to be positively related with higher order need strength, such that older individuals were more likely to perceive that their higher order needs had been fulfilled compared to younger individuals.

Complicating the issue further, still more studies have found no relationship between age and growth. For example, Schmitt, White, Coyle, and Rauschenberger (1979) investigated various factors that predict life satisfaction in retirement and found that age was unrelated to growth needs ($r = .00$).

Likewise, Saavedra and Kwun (2000) found that GNS was unrelated to age ($r = -.03$). Similar results have been garnered from other investigations as well. For example, Phillips and Bedeian (1994) found that GNS was unrelated to age ($r = .07$). Tharenou and Harker (1982) also found no relationship between age and GNS, as did Coyle-Shapiro and Morrow (2003) in their investigation of the role that individual differences play in the adoption of total quality management orientations. Finally, Ingram and Bellenger (1983) investigated organizational and personal variables – including age and growth needs – and their relative effects on the reward valences of salespeople. Like the other studies reviewed above, this study found no relationship between chronological age and personal growth.

One very plausible explanation for the variability in the effects of age on growth could be the presence of moderators – be they measured or, as we have seen thus far, likely unmeasured. Given that a majority of studies that have measured age along with motives have not been designed to assess the impact of age on such outcomes, it is not surprising that differences in the directionality and significance of these effects exist. However, we can get a better picture of when we would expect age to have an influence by understanding the conditions under which age does relate to work motives.

For example, Ebner, Freund, and Baltes. (2006) investigated developmental changes in personal goal orientations from young to late adulthood across several studies. The results of this investigation suggest that the relationship between age and growth orientations is moderated by resource demands (i.e., having the resources necessary to achieve one's goals). Specifically, older adults were found to have lower levels of growth goal orientations than younger adults, regardless of resources demands (i.e., equal vs unequal). However, younger adults who had equal levels of expected resource demands for goals were much more likely to have high growth goal orientations. Likewise, Adler and Aranya's (1984) longitudinal investigation of work needs across the work lifespan found that need for esteem increased from early to late-middle career stages, where it plateaued.

Ford, Walker, and Churchill (1985) investigated various personal factors that are related to performance for salespersons, including age and the valence of personal growth. Interestingly, salespeople had stronger desires for personal growth during the early stages of their careers; younger salespeople (i.e., under 35 years) with lower tenures had the highest valence for personal growth. Finally, Aldag and Brief (1979) investigated various correlates of the Job Diagnostic Survey's higher order needs measure, including age, in a variety of professional samples. Age was significantly, and negatively related to higher order needs strength for nursing aides and manufacturing employees, but not for correctional employees, hospital employees, or police officers. The significant negative correlation between age and higher order needs for nursing and manufacturing employees suggests that for these groups, older individuals have lower higher order needs than younger individuals.

Taken together, these studies suggest very inconsistent results regarding the directionality of the relationship between age and growth-related motives. Some studies have found a positive relationship (e.g., Churchill et al., 1979), whereas others have found a negative relationship (e.g., Aldag and Brief, 1979) and others have found no relationship (Schmitt et al., 1979). As suggested, one explanation for these inconsistent results is the presence of moderators. For example, Ford et al. (1985) found the relationship between age and GNS was strongest among those salespeople that had low levels of job tenure. Given many of the studies examining the relationship between age and GNS measured age chronologically as opposed to using job tenure, perhaps more studies should examine job tenure in relation to GNS to see if stronger relationships can be distinguished between job tenure and GNS as opposed to chronological age and GNS.

Self-esteem

Self-esteem is a ubiquitous psychological construct, which while stable, has been generally thought to follow a developmental trajectory in which declines are experienced between middle and late adulthood (Trzesniewski, Donnellan, and Robbins, 2003). This evidence aligns well with the lifespan perspective that the intrinsic growth factors decline with age. Furthermore, given that self-esteem is a pervasive life force, it is not surprising that it has been studied within the realm of the workplace. Indeed, several studies within this literature support the idea that self-esteem declines with age. For example, Mudrack and Naughton (2001) found that self-esteem was negatively related to age in a sample of full-time workers from a variety of industries ($n = 183$). Older individuals had lower levels of self-esteem than younger individuals ($r = -.14$). Likewise, Cook and Wall (1980) found a negative relationship between age and self-esteem need non-fulfillment – younger individuals were more likely to perceive that their self-esteem was unfulfilled compared to older individuals. However, as with much of the evidence for the relationship between age and intrinsic growth factors, there has been a great deal of variability in the results of such studies.

Some studies have found that age and self-esteem are unrelated. For example, in their study of the organizational correlates of self-esteem, Tharenou and Harker (1982) found a significant positive relationship between age and self-esteem, and it is worthwhile to note that the magnitude of this effect was respectable ($r = .23$). Lefkowitz (1994) found a similar significant relationship between age and self-esteem need fulfillment in a study of 732 managers and staff members of a YMCA ($r = .19$).

Finally, several investigations have found that age is not related to self-esteem. In this regard, Tang and Ibrahim (1998) found no relationship between chronological age and self-esteem or organization-based self-esteem, either in an American or Middle-Eastern Sample. Likewise, Schaubroeck et al. (1998)

used a sample consisting of individuals from five different organizations ($n = 681$), and found no relationship between chronological age and personal self-esteem. Furthermore, Frew and Bruning (1987) found that age was unrelated to self-esteem. Finally, Payne (1970) found no relationship between age and self-esteem in a sample of graduate business school students; however, given the narrow range of ages studied here, this may not be that surprising.

Need for Mastery

Mastery orientation is defined as one's desire to be proficient in topics to the best of their ability. Mastery orientation has been associated with deeper engagement with work tasks and greater perseverance in the face of setbacks (Ames, 1992). Much like need for achievement, lifespan theories (e.g., SOC) would predict that mastery goal orientations may become less important as one ages, and defaults to goal orientations aimed at managing developmental declines (i.e., compensation). Despite this intuitive link, need for mastery has seen relatively little attention with respect to age, and the results of studies investigating these phenomena have been largely equivocal. For example, Caldwell, Herold, and Fedor (2004) investigated the relationships among organizational change, individual differences, and changes in person–environment fit. Age was positively related to need for mastery ($r = .15$), such that older individuals had higher levels of need for mastery than younger individuals. However, Kanfer and Ackerman (2000) found the opposite effect, finding that age was unrelated to a desire to learn ($r = -.01$), and was negatively related to mastery ($r = -.17$) such that older individuals had lower levels of mastery than younger individuals.

Similar to most of the relationships between age and intrinsic growth factors, there has generally been mixed evidence for the relationship between age and both self-esteem and need for mastery, with a nearly equal number of studies finding a positive relationship, negative relationship, and no relationship.

However, fewer studies have examined the relationship between age and self-esteem and age and need for mastery opposed to other intrinsic growth factors (e.g., need for achievement, need for autonomy). Given the inconsistent empirical findings in the few studies that have examined the relationship between age and self-esteem, and age and need for mastery, there is clearly a need for more careful investigation into the relationship between age and these two intrinsic growth factors.

Extrinsic Growth

Extrinsic growth outcomes are generally those related to promotion or advancement at work. Several theoretical perspectives inform predictions about the relationship between age and such outcomes. For example, the Life Span Theory of Control (Heckhausen and Schulz, 1995) posits that age-related shifts in primary control mechanisms drive individuals to use fewer strategies directed at modifying external circumstances as they age. This might suggest that older employees are less likely to be motivated by a desire to pursue extrinsically oriented growth outcomes, such as promotions or other opportunities to advance at work. Furthermore, Kanfer and Ackerman (2004) posit that the salience of extrinsic work-related outcomes, such as promotions, decline with age. This has been explained by evidence for age-related shifts in temporal perspective, which serve to reduce the salience and attractiveness of such job features among older workers. These ideas might collectively predict that older workers value promotion outcomes less than younger workers. Despite this, Kooij et al. (2011) found a small, non-significant negative relationship between age and prestige and status outcomes ($\rho = -.02$); however, there was a significant negative relationship between age and extrinsic motives in general ($\rho = -.10$).

Promotion Related Outcomes

Promotion related outcomes generally refer to the valence placed upon opportunities for advancement in the workplace. Given that developmental theories generally posit that extrinsic growth motives decline with age, it is not surprising that research has generally confirmed this. For example, in a study using a sales context, Ingram and Bellenger (1983) found that salespeople have higher valences for promotion when they are younger. Similarly, Rowe and Snizek (1995) found that age was negatively related to preferences for advancement, although the magnitude of this effect was quite small. Markham, South, Bonjean, and Corder (1985) investigated, among other things, the relationship between age and the importance of promotions. This study found a negative relationship between age and the importance of promotions – older individuals viewed promotions as less important than younger individuals.

Inceoglu et al. (2009) examined the relationship between age and need for progression, finding a relationship between chronological age and personal growth such that older individuals have lower levels of need for progression than younger individuals. Furthermore, Lefkowitz (1994) found a significant negative relationship ($r = -.11$) between age and the importance of advancement, once again suggesting that advancement is more important for younger workers than older workers.

Finally, studies by Churchill et al. (1979) and Ford et al. (1985) provide conflicting results with respect to the relationship between age and promotion outcomes. First, Churchill et al. (1979) found age to be positively related to the valence for promotion-based rewards; older individuals were more likely to hold a higher level of valence with respect to promotions than younger individuals. However, in their study of personal factors that are related to performance for salespersons, Ford et al. (1985) found that younger individuals have higher valences for promotion than older individuals – suggesting that promotions may be more important during the early stages of one's career, and relatively less important as one ages.

At least one study has found no relationship between age and promotion-related outcomes.

Specifically, Ornstein, Cron, and Slocum (1989) investigated how career stage relates to a number of organizational variables, including promotion satisfaction – which was found to be unrelated to career stage and age. Given that the dependent variable of interest here was promotion satisfaction, and not valence for promotions, this null result may not be surprising.

With respect to age and extrinsic growth factors, a majority of studies have found weak negative relationships (e.g., Inceoglu et al., 2009; Markham et al., 1985). Thus, supporting the lifespan perspective, it seems that with age, extrinsic growth factors become less important. Furthermore, in line with SOC theory, this evidence suggests that as individuals age, their perspective may change to accommodate resource gains and losses. Thus, growth-related work motives such as need for promotion or advancement decrease as motives switch from needs that support advancement to needs that support the maintenance and regulation of developmental losses.

SOCIAL MOTIVES

Social motives encompass a range of motives relevant to social interactions. As before, we have classified social motives as either intrinsic or extrinsic. Both intrinsic social needs (e.g., need for affiliation) and extrinsic social needs (e.g., need for recognition) encompass a diverse array of motives (see Table 7.1). One noteworthy lifespan development theory, Socio-emotional Selectivity Theory (SEST, Carstensen, 1992), suggests that as we age, we become increasingly selective in our investment of resources in emotionally meaningful goals and activities. One manifestation of this 'selectivity' is a withdrawal from broader social networks in favor of a narrower range of social interactions that maximize positive emotional experiences (i.e., as a means of mitigating emotional risks). In essence, this theory predicts shifts in social motives that are directly related to aging.

With regard to intrinsic social motives, the Kooij et al., (2011) meta-analysis found a weak negative correlation between need for affiliation and age ($\rho = -.07$), suggesting that older workers have lower levels of need for affiliation than younger workers. However, this relationship was very weak, with age accounting for less than 0.5% of the variance in need for affiliation. As one might expect given this meta-analytic finding, some studies have found a negative relationship between age and need for affiliation (e.g., Fagenson, 1992), while others have found a positive relationship between age and need for affiliation (e.g., Payne, 1970). Still more have found no significant relationship between age and need for affiliation (Schmitt et al., 1979; Tang et al., 2000).

Intrinsic Social Motives

Need for affiliation describes a person's need to feel a sense of involvement and belonging within a social group. Given that SEST suggests that we begin to withdraw from social relationships as we age, one might expect age to be negatively related to social motives, such as need for affiliation. Indeed, several studies have garnered evidence in support of this notion. For example, Mudrack and Naughton (2001) found a negative relationship between need for affiliation and age ($r = -.25$), suggesting that as individuals age, their need to be affiliated with others decreases. Fagenson (1992) likewise found that there was a negative correlation between both age and need for affiliation ($r = -.37$) and job tenure and need for affiliation ($r = -.43$) in a sample of protégés. A study by Payne (1970) found a negative relationship between age and the importance of making friends ($r = -.27$). Similarly, Cook and Wall (1980) developed new measures of social need fulfillment, organizational commitment, and trust in a sample of British blue-collar workers ($n = 260$). They found a significant negative correlation between age and personal need non-fulfillment ($r = -.30$), but not social need non-fulfillment ($r = -.13$).

Still, several studies have found that need for affiliation is unrelated to age. For example, Tang et al. (2000) measured need for affiliation using the MNQ (Steers and Braunstein, 1976). They found no relationship between need for affiliation and age, regardless of gender ($r = .11$ for men, $r = -.05$ for women). However, there was a significant relationship between need for affiliation and job tenure for women ($r = -.17$), but not men ($r = -.08$). Schmitt et al. (1979) examined the relationship between retirement and life satisfaction in a sample of individuals that took a Civil Service exam ($n = 353$). Relatedness needs were uncorrelated with age ($r = .02$) but significantly correlated with job tenure ($r = .11$). Likewise, Ehigie et al. (2006) found no relationship between need for affiliation and age ($r = .10$). Churchill et al. (1979) measured need for affiliation as the amount of additional satisfaction participants reported they would feel by a '10% increase in the amount of liking and respect received from other people the salesperson has contact with on the job' (p. 51). Results suggested age and job tenure were unrelated to the valence for need for affiliation.

At least one study has found that need for affiliation is positively related to age. Specifically, Inceoglu et al. (2009) defined need for affiliation as 'opportunities for interaction with other people at work' (p. 63). They found a significant positive correlation between need for affiliation and age. However, it is worth noting that the correlation was small, and may be attributed to statistical power from a large sample.

Taking stock of studies in this area, a majority have found a negative relationship between age and need for affiliation. Such results support Carstensen's (1992) SEST theory, which posits that with age, we strategically reduce the number of interactions we have with others in order to 'maximize social and emotional gains and minimize social and emotional risks' (p. 331). Indeed, Carstensen (1992) found that individuals typically minimize the number of interactions they have with acquaintances and close friends rather early in adulthood, but increase the number of interactions they have with their spouse and siblings during that same time.

Trust

Trust can be conceived of as 'a willingness of a party to be vulnerable to the actions of another party based on the expectation that the other will perform a particular action important to the trustor, irrespective of the ability to monitor or control that party' (Mayer, Davis, and Schoorman, 1995, p. 712). Although trust is an oft-cited antecedent of a variety of organizational outcomes, it has also been conceived specifically as a motivational antecedent (Dirks, 1999). Given that trust is conceived of here as an intrinsic social motive, one might expect levels of trust to decline with age. However, with respect to age and trust, Coyle-Shapiro and Morrow (2003) found that trust in colleagues was unrelated to both age ($r = -.02$) and job tenure ($r = -.17$).

Social Support

Social support has been defined broadly as 'the availability of helping relationships and the quality of those relationships' (Leavy, 1983, p. 5). Indeed, social support has been cited as an important factor in mitigating work-stress (Viswesvaran, Sanchez, and Fisher, 1999). SEST suggests that the scope of, and our involvement in social relationships change across the lifespan. This might suggest that broad social support may become less important with age in favor of a narrower range of social support, which leads to the prediction that there is a negative relationship between age and social support. At least two studies have investigated the relationship between social support and age. For example, Byrne et al. (2005), in a sample of undergraduate students ($n = 173$), found that perceived organizational support was unrelated to age ($r = -.06$). Contrary to this, Rotondo (1999) examined the relationship between individual difference variables and coping strategies for individuals that have reached career plateaus in a sample of workers from a water treatment facility ($n = 120$) and

found social support was negatively correlated with age ($r = -.29$), but not with job tenure. Given the range restriction in age in Byrne et al., (2005) study the conclusions drawn by Rotondo are probably more realistic.

Extrinsic Social Motives

For much the same reason that intrinsic social motives are posited to decline with age, it has been suggested by several theories that extrinsic social motives will likewise decay. Supporting this notion, Kooij et al., (2011) found a small negative correlation between need for recognition and age ($\rho = -.13$), such that older workers tend to have lower levels of need for recognition than younger workers. However, as with many of the relationships reviewed here, previous research has found inconsistent relationships between need for recognition and age.

Need for Recognition

Need for recognition can be conceptualized as the extrinsic manifestation of need for achievement. Although developmental theories would generally suggest that extrinsic motives decline with age, the results of several primary studies that have measured age and need for recognition have found generally equivocal results, which do not necessarily support this prediction. For example, Inceoglu et al. (2009) defined need for recognition as 'praise and other outward signs of recognition for achievement' (p. 63), and found a significant positive relationship between need for recognition and age. Other studies have found no relationship between age and need for recognition. For example, Ingram and Bellenger (1983) examined how organizational characteristics and demographic variables were related to reward valences in a sample of salespeople ($n = 241$), concluding that need for recognition was unrelated to both age and job tenure. Likewise, Churchill et al. (1979) found that age and job tenure were unrelated to the valence of need for recognition.

Clearly, the existing research that links age and extrinsic social motives suggests there is a great deal of variability in this relationship across studies. Most studies have found no relationship between age and need for recognition (e.g., Ingram and Bellenger, 1983). Interestingly, only one known study has found a negative relationship between age and need for recognition (Inceoglu et al., 2009). Given our review suggested nearly all studies that examined the need for recognition-age relationship found no relationship between the variables, it is difficult to draw any certain conclusions with respect to the relationship between age and need for recognition.

SECURITY MOTIVES

Security motives can be both intrinsic (e.g. need for job security, need to prevent loss) and extrinsic (e.g., valence of pay or promotion; see Table 7.1), and theory as well as empirical findings would suggest that the levels of importance for these two types of security needs, in terms of work motives, will differ with age. For example, the framework developed by Kanfer and Ackerman (2004) would suggest that increased effort needed for certain tasks requiring fluid intelligence (which declines with age) would make certain tasks and job features less attractive for older workers. One could argue that these types of tasks would be more related to extrinsic rewards such as pay and promotion. Indeed, meta-analytic findings suggest that a small, negative relationship exists between age and compensation/benefits ($\rho = -.10$; Kooij et al., 2011).

Another theory put forth by Warr (2001) uses the idea of habituation effects to suggest much the same. That is, familiarity with extrinsic rewards makes them less attractive such that they will decline in importance over time. In sum, we would expect extrinsic security rewards to decline in importance as a motive for work as one ages. On the other hand, tasks or job features that require crystallized intelligence (i.e., which does not

decline and can actually increase with age) may become more attractive. Examples of these would be tasks such as mentoring which includes affective or intrinsic rewards. Indeed, recent scholarship concerning generativity motives suggests that this may by a key predictor in understanding older workers' motivation to continue working (e.g., Templer, Armstrong-Stassen, and Cattaneo, 2010).

In addition, several theories would posit that older workers also want to protect their self-concept and prevent losses (e.g., Ebner at al., 2006; Kanfer and Ackerman, 2004). For example, Ebner and colleagues used the SOC model (Baltes and. Baltes, 1990; Freund and Baltes, 2000) to propose that as workers age, they make use of strategies that maximize growth and gains, while minimizing losses. As resources (i.e., both physical and mental) are reduced with age, there is a shift from promotion (i.e., growth-related) strategies to prevention (i.e., loss-related) strategies. This shift is likewise reflected in an individual's personal goal orientation. For example, an individual's focus on a need to prevent loss (e.g., job security) may become more salient. In contrast, a person's goal orientation towards growth (e.g., extrinsic security rewards) would decrease. Thus, we would expect the importance of intrinsic security needs, as a motive to work, to increase as one ages. Indeed, meta-analytic findings suggest that a small, positive relationship exists between age and need for security ($\rho = .06$; Kooij et al., 2011).

Intrinsic Security Motives

Several now-classic theories that view motivation as a set of progressive needs suggest that existence needs serve as the basis for the fulfillment of higher order needs (e.g., Alderfer, 1972; Maslow, 1943). Despite what developmental theories would predict (i.e., an increase in intrinsic security needs), Schmitt et al. (1979) found that age was uncorrelated with existence needs. This is perhaps not surprising however, given the sample used (i.e., retirees), in that one might not expect the importance of this type of work-centric existence need to matter to such individuals.

Job security generally refers to one's confidence in their ability to maintain a desired employment arrangement. Job insecurity (i.e., concerns about the expected continuity of one's employment arrangement) has been linked to a number of detrimental organizational outcomes, such as more negative job and organizational attitudes, individual health, and people's behavioral relationship with their organization (Sverke, Hellgren, and Naswall, 2002). In a broader sense than job security, need for security, like other basic needs, generally refers to the need to feel safe and free from danger.

Like other intrinsic security motives, both job security and need for security are posited to increase with age. Indeed, several empirical studies have shown evidence for this. For example, Rowe and Snizek (1995) used data from twelve national samples contained in the General Social Survey (gathered from 1973 to 1990, $n = 7436$) and found that age correlated positively with preference for job security, $r = .05$. This effect is small and likely driven by the power inherent in the large sample utilized. Likewise, Markham et al. (1985) found a small but significant ($r = .14$) correlation between need for job security and age. Finally, Ingram and Bellenger (1983) found that age was related to an increased valence (preference) for job security ($r = .19$).

Other studies have found no relationship between age and job security/security needs. For example, Ford et al. (1985) found no differences between older and younger workers in terms of their preferences for job security. Similarly, Goulet and Singh (2002) conceptualized job security and fear of job loss as situational variables, suggesting that certain practices affect individuals' job security, which in turn influences their commitment. Indeed, job insecurity was uncorrelated with both age and job tenure ($r = -.02$). Likewise, Churchill et al. (1979) found that job security was unrelated to both age and tenure,

as did Andolsek and Stebe (2004) in a cross-cultural study with samples from Hungary and Germany. Inceoglu et al. (2009) combined need for security and job security, a construct they refer to as 'ease and security', but found no relationship between ease and security and age or between ease and security and tenure.

Payne (1970) utilized two samples; the first sample included female employees at a packaging manufacturer ($n = 81$), where no relationship was found between age and need for security. Similarly, there was no relationship between need for security and tenure. However, when considering the second sample of management students ($n = 106$), there was a positive correlation ($r = .17$) between age and need for security, suggesting that older individuals were higher in need for security than younger individuals. It should be noted that one possible explanation for the discrepancy in these findings is the low power in the first sample.

Additionally, at least one study, Lefkowitz (1994), found age to be negatively related to security needs. In this investigation, a diverse set of participants (e.g., managers, staff members of a YMCA, undergraduates, hospital workers, $n = 732$) were sampled to test for gender differences in job-related attitudes. In this investigation, need for security was negatively correlated with age ($r = -.11$), and uncorrelated with tenure.

Finally, some evidence suggests that security needs vary in accordance to one's career stage, relative to age. Applying Maslow's need hierarchy theory (1954) and Hall's career stages model (1976), Adler and Aranya (1984) predicted that security needs would be highest in the preretirement stage (beyond age 60). In a sample of male accountants ($n = 744$), the results suggest that security needs were the highest in the preretirement stage and were significantly higher than the establishment (<30) and advancement (30–45) stages, but not significantly higher than the maintenance stage (45–60).

One last intrinsically oriented security motive warrants consideration, namely strivings toward loss prevention. Within a lifespan framework, loss generally refers to a developmentally-based decrement in resources (e.g., cognitive, social, or physical). Brandtstädter (1999) suggests that as we age, a focus on preserving resources and counteracting developmental losses becomes a dominant concern. To this end, Ebner et al. (2006) utilized a sample comprising 49 younger (18–26 years), 43 middle-aged (40–59 years), and 41 older adults (65–84 years), and found that the older adults reported a stronger focus on maintaining their status quo and preventing losses than did younger adults.

Considering the results presented here, it is clear that the relationship between age and security needs is rather inconsistent. Several studies have found a negative relationship between age and need for security (e.g., Markham et al., 1985), whereas others have found no relationship between age and need for security (e.g., Churchill et al., 1979). Similar to a variety of other workplace motives, there seem to be inconsistent results on how age impacts the need for security. However, given the majority of studies have found weak, positive relationships, one might provide a theoretically justified argument that a positive relationship exists between age and need for security.

Extrinsic Security Motives

Extrinsic security motives refer to economically derived motives, which according to theory (e.g., Kanfer and Ackerman, 2004), are generally predicted to decline with age. In this vein, Oliver (1977) examined selected antecedents of the valence (desirability) of pay and the instrumentality (attainability) of performance for pay. These constructs were combined into an integrative framework and investigated in a study of 92 male life insurance agents. Age was negatively related to both valence ($r = -.34$) and instrumentality ($r = -.34$). Similarly, Rowe and Snizek (1995) found that age correlated negatively with preference for higher income ($r = -.03$). However, the magnitude of this effect was quite small.

Despite the notion that extrinsic motives decline with age, many studies fail to find this relationship. For example, Churchill et al. (1979) found no relationship between the attractiveness of pay and age, and Lefkowitz (1994) likewise found no relationship between the need for money and age or tenure. Similarly, Ford et al. (1985) found no differences between older and younger workers in terms of pay security. Likewise Ingram and Bellenger (1983) also concluded that age was unrelated to an increased or decreased valence (preference) for pay. Dendinger, Adams, and Jacobson (2005) investigated reasons for working among older retired adults and found that age was not related to any of the examined reasons for working. This may not be surprising given that motives for working after retirement may be very different than those for working before retirement.

At least one study has found a positive relationship between age and pay-related outcomes. Pappas and Flaherty (2006) examined the influence of company reward systems on motivation levels in a sample of 214 salespeople, finding that some salespeople respond better with fixed salary plans and some with incentives. Age was correlated positively with pay reward valence ($r = .36$) and instrumentality ($r = .27$).

Taken together, these studies suggest that the relationship between age and extrinsic security motives (e.g., pay) is multifaceted. Indeed, the majority of studies we examined found no relationship between age and extrinsic security motives (e.g., Churchill et al., 1979; Leftkowitz, 1994). In addition, one study found a moderate positive relationship and one found a moderate negative relationship. Given the majority of studies found no relationship between age and extrinsic security motives, it is difficult to make any conclusions about the magnitude and direction of the relationship between age and extrinsic security motives.

DISCUSSION

The purpose of this chapter is to coalesce a body of empirical work regarding the relationship between age and work motives. In the following paragraphs, we provide a broad summary of our findings regarding the relationship between age and the various facets of work motives we have discussed (e.g., need for achievement for growth needs, need for affiliation for social needs, need for security for security needs). These findings are summarized in Table 7.2. In addition, we will compare our findings to recent meta-analytic findings (Kooij et al., 2011), pointing out similarities and differences. Where appropriate, we will discuss possible reasons for differences between our conclusions, and those of Kooij et al. (2011). Furthermore, when applicable, we will discuss possible theories (e.g., SOC) that help to explain the pattern of results we found. Finally, we conclude with some commentary on the overall state of this area of research and suggestions that may benefit aging and work motive research in the future.

Growth Needs

Our review suggests that the majority of studies have found no relationship between age and need for achievement, and our conclusions generally support Kooij et al.'s (2011) meta-analysis, which found a small positive relationship between age and need for achievement ($\rho = .06$). Given these meta-analytic results, and our findings, there is really little evidence to suggest an appreciable relationship exists between age and need for achievement. However, it is worthwhile to note that the vast majority of these studies rely on cross-sectional evidence to describe a longitudinal (i.e., developmental) phenomenon.

Furthermore, the majority of studies have found either no relationship between age and need for autonomy or a positive relationship between age and need for autonomy, suggesting that our conclusions are somewhat similar to results from Kooij et al.'s (2011) meta-analysis, which found a moderate positive relationship between age and need for autonomy ($\rho = .27$). However, given that Adler and Aranya (1984) found a non-linear relationship between need for autonomy and age such that need for autonomy was highest in the 'maintenance' career stage and lowest in the 'preretirement' career stage, this suggests that different conceptualizations of age may be a promising way to study the need for autonomy–age relationship in the future.

Our review of the relationship between age and GNS found very inconsistent results regarding the directionality of this relationship.

Table 7.2   Summary of Lifespan Theory Predictions and Results of the Current Review

Theory	Prediction of Theory	Results from Our Review
SOC (P. B. Baltes et al., 1999)	• Intrinsic and Extrinsic Growth Motives <u>decrease</u> with age. • Extrinsic Social and Security Motives <u>decrease</u> with age. • Intrinsic Security Motives <u>increase</u> with age.	• Age is negatively related to need for advancement/promotion. • Support for the relationship between age and extrinsic motives is largely mixed. • Age is positively related to need for security.
Kanfer & Ackerman (2004)	• Intrinsic and Extrinsic Growth Motives <u>decrease</u> with age. • Extrinsic Social and Security Motives <u>decrease</u> with age. • Intrinsic Security Motives <u>increase</u> with age.	• Age is negatively related to need for advancement/promotion. • Support for the relationship between age and extrinsic motives is largely mixed. • Age is positively related to need for security.
SEST (Carstensen, 1993)	• Intrinsic and Extrinsic Social Motives <u>decrease</u> with age.	• Age is negatively related to need for affiliation.

The results of our review are somewhat similar to results from Kooij et al.'s (2011) meta-analysis, which found a weak, negative relationship between age and GNS ($\rho = -.14$). Similar to the relationships between age and several other intrinsic growth factors, results suggest there are weak, practically non-significant relationships between age and need for feedback, need for self-esteem, and need for mastery. Given very few studies have examined the relationship between age and these three motives, more research needs to be conducted to determine if the few results found in previous studies can be replicated.

In addition to intrinsic growth factors, extrinsic growth factors (e.g., need for promotion and need for advancement) have been studied in regards to age. The majority of studies have found a weak negative relationship between age and extrinsic growth factors (e.g., Inceoglu et al., 2009; Markham et al., 1985). Indeed, the conclusions from our review are very similar to those of Kooij et al.'s (2011) meta-analysis, which found a moderate negative relationship between age and need for promotion or advancement ($\rho = -.23$). This relationship generally supports the SOC theory, which suggests that as we age, motives adapt from a focus on growth to a focus on the maintenance and regulation of developmental losses.

Social Needs

Regarding the relationship between age and need for affiliation, our review suggests that the majority of studies have found a negative relationship between age and need for affiliation. Results from our review support Kooij et al.'s (2011) meta-analysis, which found a negative relationship between age and need for affiliation ($\rho = -.07$). Beyond need for affiliation, our review of the relationship between age and need for recognition suggests there is no appreciable relationship between age and need for recognition. However, our conclusions are somewhat different than those of Kooij et al.'s (2011) meta-analysis,

which found a negative relationship between age and need for recognition ($\rho = -.13$). Given our review suggests that nearly all studies examining the need for recognition–age relationship found no relationship between the variables and Kooij et al.'s (2011) meta-analysis found a small, negative relationship, it is clear that while this effect may be present in the aggregate, any single study may be underrepresenting the true relationship between age and need for affiliation. Taken collectively, these conclusions generally support Carstensen's (1992) SEST theory, which posits that as individuals age, they strategically reduce the number of interactions they have with others. Thus, it seems that Carstensen's SEST (1992) theory is a useful framework from which to explain what seem to be conclusive findings in regards to age and social needs.

Security needs

Similar to conclusions drawn by Kooij et al. (2011; $\rho = .06$), we suggest that the relationship between age and need for security is positive, yet small. This consistency can be explained by using the SOC framework, and the notion that with age, growth-related goals shift in favor of those directed at the prevention of loss. To the extent to which job security signifies the prevention of a loss-related strategy as one ages, SOC theory is a useful framework from which to explain the job security–age relationship. Despite promise for intrinsic security needs, our review suggests that there is practically no significant relationship between age and extrinsic security motives (e.g., pay). Furthering our confidence in this conclusion, Kooij et al., (2011) found a weak, negative relationship between age and compensation and benefits ($\rho = -.10$).

Again, this finding can be explained by SOC theory, which posits that shifts in prevention of promotion orientations are representative of changes in individual's personal goal orientation. For example, an individual's focus on a need to prevent loss (e.g., job security) would become more salient. In contrast, a persons' goal orientation towards growth (e.g., extrinsic security rewards) may decrease. Given that pay is a growth-related strategy, the negative relationship found in Kooij et al.'s (2011) meta-analysis supports SOC theory, although we found more evidence in our review for no meaningful relationship between extrinsic motives and age.

FUTURE RESEARCH

Using longitudinal designs

In our literature searches we found only two studies that employed longitudinal designs (Bateman and Strasser, 1984; Rentsch and Steel, 1998). Specifically, Bateman and Strasser (1984) examined the relationship between two conceptualizations of age (i.e., chronological age and job tenure) and need for achievement using a longitudinal design. Results suggested that the relationships between need for achievement and age and need for achievement and job tenure were stronger at Time 2 (five months after the original survey was given) than Time 1 (the time at which the first survey was given). Similarly, Rentsch and Steel (1998) found the relationship between need for achievement and age was stronger at Time 2 than Time 1. However, Rentsch and Steel (1998) found the relationship between need for achievement and job tenure was stronger at Time 1 than Time 2. However, one may criticize even these studies for not using a longitudinal design that considers measurements beyond two time points as a means to assess developmental change. Despite this, given that only two studies have employed any type of longitudinal design in examining the age–workplace motives relationship and that no known studies have used a longitudinal study in examining any motive except need for achievement in relation to age, future research must use longitudinal designs to examine the relationship between age and all workplace motives.

Indeed, there are numerous advantages to using longitudinal designs, especially in research where the goal is to capture developmental

phenomena (e.g., changes in work motives that accompany aging). Given the inconsistent findings across the vast majority of studies presented here, it is imperative that future studies adopt more advanced longitudinal designs to rule out the influence of confounds associated with the cross-sectional operationalization of age (e.g., cohort effects).

Testing for non-linearity

Another possible explanation for the small relationships and inconsistent findings presented here may be that these relationships tend to be non-linear in nature. At least two studies have conceptualized age using a variable besides self-reported chronological age (e.g., career stage) and found a non-linear relationship between age and workplace motives (i.e., Adler and Aranya, 1984; Inceoglu et al., 2009). Thus, it seems that it may be worthwhile for researchers to investigate how operationally defining age as career stage can be used as a way to test for non-linearity in the relationship between all workplace motives and age. Given that few studies have adopted this approach and the ones that have found novel results, this direction for future research is well-warranted.

Testing for moderators and other process/outcome variables

Another consideration for future research in this area is the need to test for moderators of the age–motive relationship, and the need to conceptualize age and work motives within a larger process framework that emphasizes antecedents, process variables, and outcomes. Indeed, while the present review sheds light on the idea that conceptually, age and motives should covary, the tenuous strength of this relationship suggests that other variables may be co-acting with age and work motives. As we saw from the Ebner et al. (2006) study, the relationship between age and growth orientations may be moderated by resource demands. This is just one example of a myriad of individual difference (e.g., changes in fluid intelligence, meaning of working, work ethic, future time perspective, regulatory focus) and contextual factors (e.g., job demands, climate for aging, national or organizational policies) that may independently – or in tandem – affect the relationship between age and work motives. This idea is complicated further by the notion that changes in work motives are assumed to follow a developmental trajectory. Thus, these moderating factors must be considered over time, along with work motives, to gain a true picture of the condition of changes in motives over time.

As a separate-but-related issue, research has generally failed to consider both the antecedents to developmental changes in work motives, and the outcomes of such changes on workplace processes. Beyond this, the impact of variability in motives over time on work outcomes has neither been formally considered, nor explored. Indeed, a thorough understanding of the mechanisms that drive changes in work motives, and the impact of dynamic work motives on workplace outcomes at the individual (e.g., job attitudes, continuance intentions, retirement decision making) and aggregate level (e.g., performance, culture) has yet to be undertaken. Such an investigation would proffer a better understanding of the developmental process in terms of shifts in motivational orientations, particularly as applied to the workplace.

Using different conceptualizations of age

Kooij et al. (2007) describe five conceptualizations of age, including chronological age, functional or performance-based age, psychosocial or subjective age, organizational age, and the lifespan concept of age. As we have documented, nearly all studies that have examined the relationship between age and workplace motives have defined age using chronological age. Given that Kooij et al. (2007) report weak to strong intercorrelations between the different conceptualizations of age, it is likely that examining all conceptualizations of age with workplace motives would add utility towards examining the age–workplace motive relationships as opposed to only examining age from the chronological point of view. Given that no known studies have examined the age–workplace motive relationship from the functional age, psychosocial age, and lifespan concept of age points of view, and only a few studies have examined the age–workplace motive relationship from the organizational age point of view (i.e., career stage – see Adler and Aranya, 1984; Inceoglu et al., 2009), we suggest future studies should examine the age–workplace motive relationship from a conceptualization of age other than chronological age.

CONCLUSIONS

Our review of the relationship between age and workplace motives suggests that consistently, studies have found negative relationships between age and the need for promotion or advancement and age need for affiliation. In addition, our review suggests that consistently, studies have found a positive relationship between age and need for security. Even though our review and previous meta-analytic work (Kooij et al., 2011) suggests the three effects are weak, the three consistent findings in regards to the age–workplace motive relationships support SOC Theory (Baltes et al., 1999), Kanfer and Ackerman (2004), and Carstensen's (1992) SEST theory. Additionally, for the most part, our conclusions support findings from Kooij et al.'s (2011) meta-analysis. Future research should examine the relationships between age and workplace motives using longitudinal designs, testing for non-linearity, and using conceptualizations of age other than chronological. Until this literature begins to use more rigorous designs (e.g., longitudinal), and measures age using different conceptualizations (e.g., psychosocial), it will be difficult to gain any additional insight into the relationship between age and workplace motives.

REFERENCES

Adler, S., and Aranya, N. (1984), 'A comparison of the work needs, attitudes, and preferences of professional accountants at different career stages', *Journal of Vocational Behavior*, 25(1): 45–57.

Aldag, R. J., and Brief, A. P. (1979), 'Examination of a measure of higher-order need strength', *Human Relations*, 32(8): 705–718.

Alderfer, C. P. (1972), *Existence, relatedness, and growth: Human needs in organizational settings*. New York: Free Press.

Ames, C. (1992), 'Classrooms: Goals, structures, and student motivation', *Journal of Educational Psychology*, 84(3): 261–271.

Andolsek, D. M., and Stebe, J. (2004), 'Multinational perspectives on work values and Commitment', *International Journal of Cross Cultural Management*, 4(2): 181–209.

Baltes, P. B., and Baltes, M. M. (1990), 'Psychological perspectives on successful aging: The model of selective optimization with compensation', in P. B. Baltes and M. M. Baltes (eds), *Successful aging: Perspectives from the behavioral sciences*. New York: Cambridge University Press. pp. 1–34.

Baltes, P. B., Staudinger, U. M., and Lindenberger, U. (1999), 'Lifespan psychology: Theory and application to intellectual functioning'. *Annual Review of Psychology*, 50: 471-507.

Bateman, T. S., and Strasser, S. (1984), 'A longitudinal analysis of the antecedents of organizational commitment', *Academy of Management Journal*, 27(1): 95–112.

Brandtstädter, J. (1999), 'Sources of resilience in the aging self: Toward integrating perspectives', in T. M. Hess and F. Blanchard-Fields (eds), *Social cognition and aging*, San Diego, CA: Academic Press. pp. 123–141.

Byrne, Z. S., Kacmar, C., Stoner, J., and Hochwarter, W. A. (2005), 'The relationship between perceptions of politics and depressed mood at work: Unique moderators across three levels', *Journal of Occupational Health Psychology*, 10(4): 330–343.

Caldwell, S. D., Herold, D. M., and Fedor, D. B. (2004), 'Toward an understanding of the relationships among organizational change, individual differences, and changes in person-environment fit: A cross-level fit', *Journal of Applied Psychology*, 89(5): 868–882.

Carstensen, L. L. (1992), 'Social and emotional patterns in adulthood: Support for socioemotional selectivity theory', *Psychology and Aging*, 7(3): 331–338.

Cassidy, T., and Lynn, R. (1989), 'A multifactorial approach to achievement motivation: The development of a comprehensive measure', *Journal of Occupational Psychology*, 62(4): 301–312.

Churchill, G. A., Jr., Ford, N. M., and Walker, O. C. (1979), 'Personal characteristics of salespeople and the attractiveness of alternative rewards', *Journal of Business Research*, 7(1): 25–50.

Cook, J., and Wall, T. (1980), 'New work attitude measures of trust, organizational commitment and personal need non-fulfillment', *Journal of Occupational Psychology*, 53(1): 39–52.

Coyle-Shapiro, J. A. M., and Morrow, P. C. (2003), 'The role of individual differences in employee adoption of TQM orientation', *Journal of Vocational Behavior*, 62(2): 320–340.

Cron, W. L., and Jr., Slocum, J. W. (1986), 'The influence of career stages on salespeople's job attitudes, work perceptions, and performance', *Journal of Marketing Research*, 23(2): 119–129.

Deci, E. L., and Ryan, R. M. (1985), *Intrinsic motivation and self-determination in human behavior*. New York: Plenum.

Dendinger, V. M., Adams, G. A., and Jacobson, J. D. (2005), 'Reasons for working and their relationship to retirement attitudes, job satisfaction and occupational self-efficacy of bridge employees', *International Journal of Aging and Human Development*, 61(1): 21–35.

Dirks, K.T. (1999), 'The effects of interpersonal trust on work group performance', *Journal of Applied Psychology*, 84(3): 445–455.

Ebner, N. C., Freund, A. M., and Baltes, P. B. (2006), 'Developmental changes in personal goal orientation from young to late adulthood: From striving for gains to maintenance and prevention of losses', *Psychology and Aging*, 21(4): 664–678.

Ehigie, B. O., Kolade, I. A., and Afolabi, O. A. (2006), 'Personality factors influencing politicians' attitudes toward wellbeing of citizens: A study in southwest Nigeria', *International Journal of Public Sector Management*, 19(5): 428–446.

Fagenson, E. A. (1992), 'Mentoring – Who needs it? A comparison of protégés and nonproteges needs for power, achievement, affiliation, and autonomy', *Journal of Vocational Behavior*, 41(1): 48–60.

Ford, N. M., Walker, O. C., and Churchill, G. A. (1985), 'Differences in the attractiveness of alternative rewards among industrial salespeople: Additional evidence', *Journal of Business Research*, 13(2): 123–138.

Freund, A. M. (2006), 'Age-differential motivational consequences of optimization versus compensation focus in younger and older adults', *Psychology and Aging*, 21(2): 240–252.

Freund, A. M., and Baltes, P. B. (2000), 'The orchestration of selection, optimization, and compensation: An action-theoretical conceptualization of a theory of developmental regulation', in W. J. Perrig and

A. Grob (eds), *Control of human behavior, mental processes, and consciousness: Essays in honor of the 60th birthday of August Flammer*. Mahwah, NJ: Lawrence Erlbaum Associates Publishers. pp. 35–58.

Frew, D. R., and Bruning, N. S. (1987), 'Perceived organizational characteristics and personality measures of as predictors of stress/strain in the work place', *Journal of Management*, 13(4): 633–646.

Goulet, L. R., and Singh, P. (2002), 'Career commitment: A reexamination and an extension', *Journal of Vocational Behavior*, 61(1): 73–91.

Hackman, J. R., and Oldham, G. R. (1976), 'Motivation through the design of work: Test of a theory', *Organizational Behavior and Human Performance*, 16(2): 250–279.

Hall, D. T. (1976), *Careers in organizations*. Glenview, IL: Scott, Foresman.

Heckhausen, D., and Schulz, R. (1995), 'A life-span theory of control', *Psychological Review*, 102(2): 284–304.

Inceoglu, I., Segers, J., Bartram, D., and Vloeberghs, D. (2009), 'Age differences in work motivation in a sample from five Northern European countries', *Zeitschrift fiir Personalpsychologie*, 8(2): 59–70.

Ingram, T. N., and Bellenger, D. N. (1983), 'Personal and organizational variables: Their relative effect on reward valences of industrial salespeople', *Journal of Marketing Research*, 20(2): 198–205.

Kanfer, R., and Ackerman, P. L. (2004), 'Aging, adult development and work motivation', *Academy of Management Review*, 29(3): 440–458.

Kanfer, R., and Ackerman, P. L. (2000), 'Individual differences in work motivation: Further explorations of a trait framework', *Applied Psychology: An International Review*, 49(3), 470–482.

Kidd, J. M., and Green, F. (2004), 'The careers of research scientists: Predictors of three dimensions of career commitment and intention to leave science', *Personnel Review*, 35(3): 229–251.

Kluger, A. N., and Denisi, A. (1996), 'The effects of feedback interventions on performance: A historical review, a meta-analysis, and a preliminary feedback intervention theory', *Psychological Bulletin*, 119(2): 254–284.

Kooij, D., de Lange, A., Jansen, P., and Dikkers, J. (2007), 'Older workers' motivation to continue to work: Five meanings of age', *Journal of Managerial Psychology,* 23(4): 364–394.

Kooij, D. T. A. M., de Lange, A. H., Jansen, P. G. W., Kanfer, R., and Dikkers, J. S. E. (2011), 'Age and work-related motives: Results of a meta-analysis', *Journal of Organizational Behavior*, 32(2): 197–225.

Lang, F. R., and Carstensen, L. L. (2002), 'Time counts: Future time perspective, goals, and social relationships', *Psychology and Aging*, 17(1): 125–139.

Leavy, R. L. (1983), 'Social support and psychological disorder: A review', *Journal of Community Psychology*, 11(1): 3–21.

Lefkowitz, J. (1994), 'Sex-related differences in job attitudes and dispositional variables: Now you see them,…', *Academy of Management Journal*, 37(2): 323–349.

Lilly, J. D., Duffy, J., and Virick, M. (2006), 'A gender-sensitive study of McClelland's needs, stress, and turnover intent with work-family conflict', *Women and Management Review*, 21(8): 662–680.

London, M. (1983), 'Toward a theory of career motivation', *Academy of Management Review*, 8(4): 620–630.

Loon, M., and Casimir, G. (2008), 'Job-demand for learning and job-related learning', *Journal of Managerial Psychology*, 23(1): 89–102.

Markham, W. T., South, S. J., Bonjean, C. M., and Corder, J. (1985), 'Gender and opportunity in the federal bureaucracy', *American Journal of Sociology*, 91(1): 129–150.

Maslow, A. H. (1943), 'A theory of human motivation', *Psychological Review,* 50(4): 370–396.

Maslow, A. H. (1954), 'The instinctoid nature of basic needs', *Journal of Personality*, 22(3): 326–347.

Mayer, R. C., Davis, J. H., and Schoorman, F. D. (1995), 'An integrative model of organizational trust', *Academy of Management Review*, 20(3): 709–734.

McClelland, D. D. (1961), *The achieving society.* Princeton, NJ: Van Nostrand.

McNeese-Smith, D. K., and Crook, M. (2003), 'Nursing values and a changing nurse workforce: Values, job, and job stages', *Journal of Nursing Administration*, 33(5): 260–270.

Mudrack, P. E., and Naughton, N. J. (2001), 'The assessment of workaholism as behavioral tendencies: Scale development and preliminary empirical testing', *International Journal of Stress Management*, 8(1): 93–111.

Naus, F., van Iterson, A., and Roe, R. A. (2007), 'Value incongruence, job autonomy, and organization-based self esteem: A self-based perspective on organizational cynicism', *European Journal of Work and Organizational Psychology*, 16(2): 195–219.

Neil, C. C., and Snizek, W. E. (1988), 'Gender as a moderator of job satisfaction', *Work and Occupations,* 15(2): 201–219.

Oliver, R. L. (1977), 'Antecedents of salesmen's compensation perceptions: A path analysis interpretation', *Journal of Applied Psychology*, 62(1): 20–28.

Ornstein, S., Cron, W. L., and Slocum, J. W. (1989), 'Life stage versus career stage: A comparative test of the theories of Levinson and Super', *Journal of Organizational Behavior*, 10(1): 117–133.

Pappas, J. M., and Flaherty, K. E. (2006), 'The moderating role of individual-difference variables in compensation research', *Journal of Managerial Psychology*, 21(1): 19–35.

Payne, R. (1970), 'Factor analysis of a Maslow-type need satisfaction questionnaire', *Personnel Psychology*, 23(2): 251–268.

Phillips, A. S., and Bedeian, A. G. (1994), 'Leader–follower exchange quality: The role of personal and interpersonal attributes', *Academy of Management Journal*, 37(4): 990–1001.

Rentsch, J. R., and Steel, R. P. (1998), 'Testing the durability of job characteristics as predictors of absenteeism over a six-year period', *Personnel Psychology*, 51(1): 165–190.

Rotondo, D. (1999), 'Individual-difference variables and career-related coping', *The Journal of Social Psychology*, 139(4): 458–471.

Rowe, R., and Snizek, W. E. (1995), 'Gender differences in work values: Perpetuating the myth', *Work and Occupations*, 22(2): 215–229.

Saavedra, R., and Kwun, S. K. (2000), 'Affective states in job characteristics theory', *Journal of Organizational Behavior*, 21(2): 131–146.

Schaubroeck, J., Ganster, D. C., and Jones, J. R. (1998), 'Organization and occupation influences in the attraction-selection-attrition process', *Journal of Applied Psychology*, 83(6): 869–891.

Schmitt, N., White, J. K., Coyle, B. W., and Rauschenberger, J. (1979), 'Retirement and life satisfaction', *Academy of Management Journal*, 22(2): 282–291.

Steers, R. M. (1975) 'Effects of need for achievement on the job performance-job attitude relationship', *Journal of Applied Psychology*, 60(6): 678–682.

Steers, R. M., and Braunstein, D. N. (1976), 'A behaviorally-based measure of manifest needs in work settings', *Journal of Vocational Behavior*, 9(2): 251–266.

Steers, R. M., and Spencer, D. G. (1977), 'The role of achievement motivation in job design', *Journal of Applied Psychology*, 62(4): 472–479.

Sverke, M., and Sjoberg, A. (1994), 'Dual commitment to company and union in Sweden: An examination of predictors and taxonomic split methods', *Economic and Industrial Democracy*, 15(4): 531–564.

Sverke, M. Hellgren, J., and Naswall, K. (2002), 'No security: A meta-analysis and review of job insecurity and its consequences', *Journal of Occupational Health Psychology*, 7(3): 242–264.

Tang, T. L., and Ibrahim, A. H. S. (1998), 'Antecedents of organizational citizenship behaviors revisited: Public personnel in the United States and in the Middle East', *Public Personnel Management*, 27(4): 529–550.

Tang, T. L., Singer, M. G., and Roberts, S. (2000), 'Employees' perceived organizational instrumentality: An examination of the gender differences', *Journal of Managerial Psychology*, 15(5): 378–406.

Templer, A., Amstrong-Stassen, M., and Cattaneo, J. (2010), 'Antecedents of older workers' motives for continuing to work', *Career Development International*, 15(5): 479–500.

Tharenou, P., and Harker, P. (1982), 'Organizational correlates of employee self-esteem', *Journal of Applied Psychology*, 67(6): 797–805.

Treadway, D. C., Hochwarter, W. A., Kacmar, C. J., and Ferris, G. R. (2005), 'Political will, political skill, and political behavior', *Journal of Organizational Behavior*, 26(3): 229–245.

Trzesniewski, K.H., Donnellan, M.B., and Robbins, R. W. (2003), 'Stability of self-esteem across the lifespan', *Journal of Personality and Social Psychology*, 84(1): 205–220.

United Nations (2009) *World Population Prospects: The 2008 Revision*. CD-ROM Edition – Extended Dataset, United Nations.

Vallerand, R. J., O'Connor, B. P., and Hamel, M. (1995), 'Motivation in later life: Theory and assessment', *International Journal of Aging and Human Development*, 41(1): 221–238.

Viswesvaran, C., Sanchez, J., and Fisher, J. (1999), 'The role of social support in the process of work stress: A meta-analysis', *Journal of Vocational Behavior*, 54(2): 314–334.

Vroom, V. H. (1964), *Work and motivation*. New York: Wiley.

Warr, P. (1992), 'Age and occupational well-being', *Psychology and Aging*, 7(1): 37–46.

Warr, P. (2001), 'Age and work behaviour: Physical attributes, cognitive abilities, knowledge, personality traits and motives', in C. L. Cooper, and I. T. Robertson (eds), *International review of industrial and organizational psychology*. New York: John Wiley and Sons. pp. 1–36.

Wolf, G., London, M., Casey, J., and Pufahl, J. (1995), 'Career experiences and motivation as predictors of training behaviors and outcomes for displaced engineers', *Journal of Vocational Behavior*, 67(3): 316–331.

Young, A. M., and Perrewe, P. L. (2004), 'The role of expectations in the mentoring exchange: An analysis of mentor and protégé expectations in relation to perceived support', *Journal of Managerial Issues*, 16(1): 103–126.

Zhu, W., Luthans, F., Chew, I. K. H., and Li, C. (2006), 'Potential expats in Singaporean organizations', *Journal of Management Development*, 25(8): 763–76.

8

New Patterns of Late-Career Employment

Kerr Inkson, Margaret Richardson
and Carla Houkamau

INTRODUCTION

A major tradition in career studies is the notion of the career as an age-related cycle. Levinson, Darrow, Klein, Levinson and McKee (1978) wrote a book called *The Seasons of a Man's Life* and Levinson and Levinson (1996) *The Seasons of a Woman's Life*, and, based on intensive data from small samples of men and women, posited intricate patterns of career and personal development – such as 'mid-life crisis' – that mapped precisely against individuals' ages. The metaphoric notion of a life, and a career, having 'seasons' – predictable patterns involving growth, flowering, harvest and decline is attractive and lines up with much everyday experience of others' lives.

Donald Super (1957, 1990), the dominating figure in career development research in the twentieth century, similarly suggested four stages of career development, each with its key preoccupation and label, and each with a particular framing in terms of age: exploration (age 15–24); establishment (age 25–44); maintenance (age 45–64); and disengagement (age over 64), in each of which the individual is attempting to implement a self-concept. While the theory provides a good retrospective explanation of many careers, most experience their careers as a gradual flow of development, with different tasks gradually acquiring and losing salience at different times rather than as a sequence of stages. Additionally, careers nowadays seem more erratic, and less predictable. Regarding aging and older workers, both Super's and Levinson's theories appear to confirm ageist stereotypes. Indeed, Super originally named his final career stage 'decline', and he only changed it to 'disengagement' when he himself began to approach it. Even then Super didn't disengage, but continued in his career as an academic, continuing to publish until his death in 1994, aged 83. A premise of this chapter is that 'disengagement' (apparently meaning disengagement from paid employment), if it occurs, may occur gradually, may take place at any age or across any range of ages, and may be accompanied by 're-engagement' in other forms of activity.

A common problem occurs when aging workers experience a career 'plateau', that is, a point where hierarchical advancement ceases, the career 'flattens out', and the chances of additional hierarchical advancement or increased responsibility decline (Feldman & Weitz, 1988). If the individual has expectations of continuing career progress, this can be very frustrating, but in other cases workers adapt well to the plateau, accepting that there are many other means of fulfillment for them, such as continuing to perform their role well and taking more of an interest in their fellow workers and in family and leisure activities (Feldman & Weitz, 1988). Organizations however have a responsibility to recognize that even plateaued workers often have greater potential than their current jobs permit them to utilize, and significant needs for continuing career development (Smith-Ruig, 2009).

Nowadays vocational psychologists talk more about the 'cycles within cycles' of careers, for example, 'a mini-cycle of growth, exploration, establishment, management and disengagement occurs .... each time an individual's career is destabilized by socio-economic and personal events' (Savickas, 2002: 156). Productive cycles can apply to discrete events within the bigger cycle of the whole career. And while many older workers practise career 'disengagement', not all do so; many do so gradually rather than suddenly, and others commence new careers in the voluntary sector. The issue of prolonging careers through, and despite, the process and social institution we call 'retirement' is therefore important, not only for older workers themselves but for their employers, their potential employers, their families and society as a whole.

RETIREMENT VERSUS LATE-CAREER EMPLOYMENT: THE PROBLEM

A Maori professor in a New Zealand University told us this story. One day he suggested to his 84-year-old father, a small farmer who still worked his own land, that he should retire. But the old man recognized that if he retired, because of the Maori concept of *mahi aroha,* or voluntary work, and his status as a *kaumatua,* or elder, in his tribe, he would be responsible for much management and mentorship within the tribe. 'No, no', he said. 'I can't retire – I'd never have time.'

The conventional, Western notion of retirement increasingly seems a distinctly odd one. In this view, an individual works in full-time employment until, at some apparently arbitrary age, perhaps 60 or 65, his or her employer or government offers a pension which absolves the employee from the need for a salary, and therefore from the need to work. The employee walks out of the workplace, never to return, goes home and devotes the rest of his or her life to leisure activities. The underlying assumption is: why would one work, if one didn't have to? Is this a functional model for a modern society? Is it sensible to conclude that the older are economically unproductive, and to encourage them in that belief? Is the assumption that the only reason people continue to work is because they need the money tenable? Is spending all one's time in leisure activities a healthy and satisfying option anyway?

Fortunately, both historically and in contemporary society, retirement tends not to happen according to its stereotype. Michelangelo was appointed as chief architect at St Paul's Cathedral in Rome at the age of 71, and continued in that role until he died at the age of 89. The newspapers are full of stories about politicians, business moguls, film actors and writers working on and on, into their 70s, 80s and 90s. Others, particularly women, who are supposedly retired, work on tirelessly in the voluntary sector, providing services on which society vitally depends, on a voluntary basis (Erlinghagen & Hank, 2006), apparently to their own advantage in terms of health and well-being (McMunn et al., 2009).

While the availability or otherwise of a pension is a powerful influence on people's decisions about whether and where to continue in paid work, it is far from the only consideration. So the retirement stereotype is flouted by many, both employers, employees, and the self-employed: but it may still influence all these groups, and government officials as well, to retain ageist policies and activities which are out of kilter with changing social conditions. Public discourse about a 'retirement age' is misleading, since what is actually being talked about is usually a 'pension age' or 'pensionablity age', the age at which an individual is entitled to receive a State or employment pension, which need have no necessary effect on employment. It would be helpful to creating more positive attitudes to extending work careers if this terminology were changed to reflect its true meaning more accurately.

'It's time', according to Dychtwald et al. (2004: 48), 'to retire retirement.' Dychtwald et al. based their argument primarily on the view that in a situation where fewer and fewer employed will be expected to support more and more non-employed economically, it makes no sense to encourage – and in some cases force – people with economically valuable energy and skills, to leave the workforce. As the world moves more and more towards economies based on knowledge and experience rather than physical muscle and raw undeveloped talent, employers increasingly recognize that they can add value by retaining the services of their most knowledgeable and experienced workers. In the smaller arena of the organization too, older, long-service workers are often key repositories of the core knowledge and skills, as well as the institutional history, culture, and external networks that continue to make the organization viable. At the same time, there is no denying that as people age they lose physical and sometimes mental energy, and often experience health problems, so that although many older workers still have a contribution to make, it cannot continue to be the same contribution that they made when they were at their peak.

From the individual point of view, many older workers find their paid work an increasing burden and would welcome the opportunity to find more time to devote to family, leisure and other pursuits. But they may not wish to give work up altogether, in one fell swoop: a sudden departure from work that they find stimulating and in which they are knowledgeable, and from the social networks that help to sustain their day-to-day lives, may not be a welcome proposition. Also, economic considerations have to be factored in: many might *like* to retire, but can't afford to do so until they have worked long enough to save enough of a 'nest egg.'

THIS CHAPTER

In this chapter, we suggest that the key to creating win-win solutions to the employers' and the workers' problems, is *flexibility*. In particular, both groups, and society as a whole, need to recognize that while for some employees and their employers 'once-for-all' retirement may be the best solution, for many – perhaps a majority – it is not.

In the following sections we therefore seek to background 'retirement' as a phenomenon in our society, and note the forces impinging on it – political, social, economic, and psychological – and its consequent susceptibility, as a social institution, to variance and diversity. Next, we consider the case for extending the careers of older workers beyond the 'normal' retirement age, and conclude that doing so may not only be necessary due to demographic changes, but may also be 'good business' for organizations that promote such policies. We then consider four increasingly popular versions of more flexible retirement options – namely phased retirement, bridge employment, self-employment and encore careers, noting the nature, benefits and problems of each and the necessity for appropriate 'meso-level' (organizational) and macro-level (societal) policies to support them. Throughout, we illustrate our propositions with research and case material from our own country, New Zealand, and elsewhere.

RETIREMENT: ITS NATURE AND CONSEQUENCES

Defining retirement

The literature on retirement has recently been summarized by Wang and Shultz (2010). Retirement is commonly understood as permanent exit from the workforce due in part to aging. Retirement is commonly treated as an economic phenomenon (Richardson, 1993): for example, nearly all of the *Wikipedia* entry on retirement deals with the financial implications of retirement for retirees and for society. The conventional wisdom about retirement consequently focuses issues such as the employed/not employed dichotomy, and the provision of pensions (O'Rand & Henretta, 1999). In this chapter however, we show that because of the existence of various semi-employed, semi-retired options, the blurring of work and leisure, and the feminization of the workforce, dichotomies are becoming less and less appropriate (Beehr, Glazer, Nielson & Farmer, 2000; O'Rand & Henretta, 1999). Also, retirement is a social as well as an economic institution, and has psychological as well as financial implications for retirees (Hyde et al., 2004).

Retirement can be defined from different perspectives. Economic definitions are the most common (Richardson, 1993). But alternative definitions of retirement may stress the subjective side, indicating the meaning of retirement for individuals. Identity may undergo substantial shifts, or become ambiguous. Where an official form requires a semi-retired professor to enter his or her 'occupation', what does s/he write? 'Retired'? 'Semi-retired'? 'Semi-retired professor'? Or 'professor'? Retirement can be viewed by different people – prospective as well as actual retirees – either as a time of increasing debilitation, as a state of idleness and non-contribution, as a welcome relief from the unwanted imperatives of employment, as 'time for the family', or as a period of renewed self-development (Wahrendorf & Siegrist, 2010). Levinson and Wofford (2000),

perhaps a little optimistically, characterized retirement as the 'flexibility phase' of the career, providing the individual with maximum autonomy in terms of location, control of time, and choice of activities.

Factors affecting retirement

Like most career phenomena, retirement can be considered in terms of a balance between social and economic structures that impose themselves upon the individual and his or her choices; and individual agency that enables individuals to make their own decisions and initiate their own actions within structural constraints (Peiperl & Arthur, 2000).

The societal forces impinging on retirement are dictated by the diversity of stakeholder interests in it as an institution. These include the wider society and its government (which often has to pay much of the financial cost of retired people), political interests (which may represent particular ideological views such as individual self-sufficiency versus welfare state), private and public sector work organizations (which may need either to rid themselves of surplus or inappropriate employees, or alternatively to retain the valued skills of older workers); and of course retirees and potential retirees themselves. In any society each group will have its own agenda relating to issues such as mandatory retirement age, pension provision and encouragement of phased retirement: such issues will be played out in political venues. In New Zealand, for example, 'Grey Power' (www.greypower.co.nz) is an important lobby group open to all citizens over 50, which claims substantial success in influencing various items of legislation relevant to older and retired workers.

As a historical institution, retirement had an original purpose of avoiding the presumed deficiencies of older workers by removing them from the workforce (Richardson, 1993). The outcome was often a mandatory retirement age accompanied by complementary social security provisions (Litwin, 2007). More recently, a changing dynamic has been driven by increasing recognition that for many older workers skill decrements are slight (Avolio and Waldman, 1994) and are compensated for by advantages in experience and commitment (Brimeyer et al., 2010); that the life expectancy and health of older workers have recently increased (Baltes & Smith, 2003); and that skills shortages, both immediate and forecast, increasingly make some older workers attractive as continuing employees (Callanan & Greenhaus, 2008; Collins, 2003). As a result, governmental policies and organizational strategies regarding retirement have been changed.

Notwithstanding such enlightened thinking, there are currently countervailing concerns that globalizing processes, the tendency of older workers to expect 'seniority' pay premiums, and ageist devaluation of their skills is leading to increasing numbers retiring early (Hofacker, 2010). Such phrases as 'the decision when to retire' may suggest a degree of agency and autonomy that some in society cannot realize (Beehr et al., 2000), making retirement 'an unaffordable luxury' (McManus et al., 2007). Ageist stereotypes also play a part (Callanan & Greenhaus, 2008). Agency cannot be guaranteed. Many workers retire early, involuntarily rather than voluntarily, through downsizing and layoffs (Dorn & Souza-Posa, 2010). These accounts indicate the power of societal, economic, and political forces over individuals' retirement decisions.

In many countries, however, State pension provisions provide for a basic income for all citizens over a specified age, often 65, giving many greater flexibility over their retirement-related decisions. There is currently much concern that the aging of populations in developed countries will eventually make such pensions economically unsustainable, resulting in pressures to reduce the costs of pensions by raising the 'retirement age' at which individuals become eligible (OECD, 2011). Some workers, through personal circumstances such as inheritances or participation in company pension schemes, have additional flexibility in their decision making (McKelvey, 2009). In many countries political instability and economic cycles create additional uncertainty in the decision-making context.

Individuals' consideration of retirement occurs over a long period of their lives. Pre-retirement planning, and discussion with others, are desirable, though negative attitudes can cause procrastination (Richardson, 1993). Both financial and psychological issues should be considered, but the literature on retirement planning is almost exclusively about financial considerations. According to Kim and Feldman (2000), the typical decision process does indeed involve a first 'feasibility' phase when calculation of financial contingencies – for example, likely savings accumulation, pensions, inflation, taxation, and future expenditure – take precedence; and a second phase when individuals weigh their current health and fitness, job satisfaction, work ethic, non-work interests, family circumstances (e.g. spouse's employment status).

Research attention to the consequences of retirement for retirees has focused on their adjustment to retirement – for example their mental health, satisfaction, social integration and leisure activities – or on the intermediate, semi-retirement options we have noted. Adjustment is a dynamic process (Jonsson et al., 2000), where adjustment, stablization and readjustment may repeat in cyclic manner. Adjustment is aided by control over the actuality and timing of retirement (Wong & Earl, 2009). Involuntary retirement in particular has been shown to lead to negative outcomes (Shultz et al., 1998). The good news is that overall retirement more often than not turns out to be a positive experience for those going through it (Bosse et al., 1991).

The diversity of contemporary retirement

Thus, there is a complex set of contextual and personal factors influencing the decision to retire, or to semi-retire, and the situation may be complicated by additional options for phased retirement, bridge employment, part-time employment or self-employment (to be discussed later in this chapter). Such variances and uncertainties set new challenges not only for retirees but also for researchers seeking to determine general statements about retirement. Although, overall, positive financial well-being and poor physical health are strong predictors of retirement, pathways to retirement are increasingly diverse (O'Rand & Henretta, 1999). For example, retirement can be voluntary or involuntary, planned or unplanned, gradual or sudden. Subjectively it can be based on different sets of motives and represent a host of different meanings to the retiree (Beehr, 1986; O'Rand & Henretta, 1999).

Both academic considerations of retirement and observation of current patterns increasingly therefore lead us to the view that retirement is a process rather than an event, is multifaceted and complex, has psychological as well as financial consequences, and is often gradual rather than sudden.

THE CASE FOR EXTENDING THE CAREERS OF OLDER WORKERS

Reviews of academic literature around aging and ageism show that, while older workers are sometimes perceived in a positive light, negative perceptions tend to predominate (Taylor & Walker, 1998; Pickersgill et al., 1996; Johnson & Neumark, 1997). In our country, for example, McGregor and Gray (2002) found in a sample of 1,012 New Zealand employers that while older workers were seen as loyal, conscientious and reliable, they were also seen as more expensive to employ, harder to train, less physically capable and less likely to work longer hours when required. This aligns with international research which indicates that employers assume older workers are less adept than their younger counterparts, take more time off work due to illness and injury and are less productive due to a lack of drive and enthusiasm (Pickersgill et al., 1996). Not only do these perceptions discourage older job seekers who may have to contend with age discrimination (Wilson & Kan, 2006)

they may also deter employers from effectively preparing for the inevitable shifts in the age demographics of the workforce (Murray & Syed, 2005).

Notwithstanding employers' perceptions of weaknesses in older workers as employees, and despite variability between countries, such workers are becoming more and more numerous. Other authors in this book have demonstrated that future societies are likely to have an ever-increasing number of older citizens who will potentially become more and more of an economic burden on a declining number of economically productive younger citizens. In our country, New Zealand, for example, the number of younger workers entering the workforce is decreasing while, at the same time, a relatively larger percentage of the workforce is approaching the New Zealand 'retirement age' of 65, when a universal State pension is paid (McGregor & Gray, 2002). By 2020, it is anticipated that one in four New Zealand workers will be 55 or older, and by 2021, workers aged 65 and over are expected to increase from 2% to 4% of the workforce (Statistics New Zealand, 2006). By 2051 workers aged 40–64 years will make up 52 percent of all working-age people, compared with 44 percent in 1999 (Statistics New Zealand, 2000; Boyd & Dixon, 2009). These trends, alongside a growing skills shortage mean that we can no longer question that older people comprise an important part of the workforce. Indeed, if all workers were to retire when they are Super's (1957, 1990) disengagement age of 64, the result could well be an overall shortage of highly skilled and experienced workers available to meet the needs of businesses. The reality of this social change will influence the way we see conventional career trajectories and workers in their 'prime'.

While it seems vital for employers to prepare for the anticipated changes in the age make-up of the workforce, many are reticent to put any specific policies in place to accommodate or entice employees to stay at work after retirement age. In a survey of 696 organizations in the United States Pitt-Cat-souphes et al. (2009) found that even though four out of ten employers anticipated that the aging of the workforce would have a significant impact on their business over the following three years due to skills shortages, approximately one-third also reported not having enough programmes in place for the recruitment and training of older workers. The New Zealand Equal Employment Opportunities Trust (2008) found a similar trend in a study of 26 New Zealand organizations: while many employers believed older employees were stable and conscientious workers few were well prepared for the aging workforce or had specific policies or practices related to employing older people. Because a major challenge for employers in the future will be to overcome challenges posed by the inevitable aging of the population a revaluation of the value of older workers is overdue.

A growing number of researchers have turned their attention to exploring the economic benefits of hiring and retaining older workers (Arrowsmith & McGoldrick, 1997; Brooke, 2003; Jorgensen & Taylor 2008; Taylor, 2008; Taylor et al., 2010; White 1999). While as people age they tend to lose physical and sometimes mental energy, experience health problems, the contributions that older workers can still make may well outweigh the costs incurred from their physical decline.

A growing body of research contests the view that older workers are less enthusiastic about their jobs or that they represent an increased cost to their employers. For example, a US study of 2001 employees aged between 50 and 70 found that the majority of respondents intended to continue working in their 'retirement', and that 30% reported that they would do so out of choice rather than necessity. Those older respondents tended to have a very positive attitude about the workplace and reported they approached work with enthusiasm because they appreciated the stimulation and opportunity to make a valuable contribution (Brown, 2003).

Empirical research has also highlighted that older workers often have accumulated knowledge and a range of interpersonal skills which can benefit their employers. For example, in a survey of over 6,000 workers, the New Zealand Equal Opportunities Trust found that older workers were seen as having better communication skills than their younger counterparts as well as the ability to train and mentor others. These skills were seen as adding value to organizations and more than made up for any physical decline that might occur (EEO Trust, 2006). Similarly in a survey of 500 UK organizations, Taylor and Walker (1994) found that 74% of employers perceived older workers as having more sophisticated institutional knowledge as well as deeper understanding of their organizations' values and culture.

Such employee attributes can translate into tangible benefits in several ways. For example UK research has found that in cases of organizational downsizing older workers' familiarity with their organizations' cultural history and customer base enables them to preserve, maintain and transmit important aspects of corporate culture to younger employees (Employers' Forum on Age & Age Concern, 1997) thereby providing a buffer against threats to organizational culture and morale.

Employers also need to keep in mind the significant costs and risks associated with replacing workers. Contrary to the stereotype that older workers are more expensive to employ than younger employees, several studies indicate that, since older workers stay longer in their jobs, they save businesses money in recruitment and training costs. In an often cited study on American hotel chain Days Inn, McNaught and Barth (1992) found that 87% of older workers who had completed training and induction courses were still employed by Days Inn a year after being hired compared to a mere 30% of younger workers. The researchers concluded that although the costs of recruiting and hiring were the same for every employee, older employees were less costly hires because of their loyalty to their employer. Similar data have been gathered in the UK (Employers Forum on Age & Age Concern, 1997). In a recent Australian study, Brooke (2003) analysed the costs involved in recruitment; training, absenteeism and work injuries of employees from 187 companies employing 484,070 employees and found that older workers were less expensive to employ than younger employees due to lower turnover and their slightly higher costs of absenteeism and work injuries.

In the next section we consider alternative options to once-and-for-all retirement, their operationalization by organizations and individuals, and their likely consequences for all stakeholders.

NEW PATTERNS OF CAREER EXTENSION

Empirical studies have identified, for older people, a positive association between work and well-being (e.g. Cameron & Waldegrave, 2009; Warr et al., 2004) and a specific link between work, paid or unpaid, and self-esteem and self-efficacy (e.g. Morrow-Howell et al., 2009; Moen & Fields, 2002). In addition, being forced into retirement and having long periods outside the workforce can detract from life satisfaction (Calvo et al., 2009; Koopman-Boyden & Waldegrave, 2009). While the importance of work to older people is thus recognized, so is a desire for flexibility if they are to continue working beyond the traditional retirement date (e.g. Owen & Flynn, 2004). This section of the chapter explores the issue of career extension and the options increasingly available to those who can, want, or need to work during or after 'retirement'.

Types of career extension

The literature indicates several pathways through which older workers can extend their careers, including phased retirement, bridge employment, self-employment, and encore careers. We discuss each of these options below, then examine public and organizational policies and programmes that facilitate and/or inhibit the take-up of options to full retirement.

Phased retirement

Phased retirement has been defined as 'a broad range of employment arrangements, formal and informal, that allow an employee who is approaching normal retirement, to continue working, usually with a reduced workload, in transition from fulltime work to fulltime retirement' (Brainard, 2002: 1). Phased retirement has benefits for employers and employees. For employers these include the ability to retain valued employees with specialized knowledge of their job and of the wider organization, to transfer knowledge from older to younger workers through mentoring, and to reduce the costs associated with hiring and training personnel to replace retiring workers (Brainard, 2002; Hutchens, 2007). For employees, phased retirement offers the opportunity to reduce their work activity gradually, to pursue leisure and family activities, to exercise skills developed earlier in the career, to transition to retirement without sacrificing valued social networks, and to supplement future retirement income (Brainard, 2002; Davey & Cornwall, 2003).

Despite such advantages, phased retirement arrangements are not currently widely available, and are more likely to be on offer in large, 'white-collar' establishments, such as those in education and the public sector, which have an existing culture of part-time work and job-sharing. Such opportunities are more often taken up by highly educated workers and those on higher incomes (Brainard, 2002; Chen & Scott, 2006; Hutchens, 2007; Hutchens & Grace-Martin, 2006).

For informal phased retirement offers, employers, often concerned with issues of productivity, commitment, and the successful integration of part-timers into work teams (Clark, 2007), tend to select employees with long tenure, a record of high performance, and little need for supervision (Hutchens, 2007; Hutchens & Grace-Martin, 2006). Such selectivity can produce problems for managers and cause resentment among workers, particularly if allocation is based on the grace and favour of managers and lacks the transparency of firm-wide policies. Such issues can, however, be worked through by employers (Hutchens, 2007) and employer advisory groups, and it is widely expected that in response to growing organizational needs to retain long-term personnel, and workers' demands for more flexible arrangements, phased retirements will increase into the future (Hutchens, 2007).

While phased retirement remains an under-researched area in terms of verifiable measures of effectiveness (Clark, 2007), there are case study reports that this option provides value to those who take it up. For example, CentrePort, a New Zealand transport services company, introduced phased retirement through a firm-wide policy allowing everyone with more than 30 years' service to reduce to 24 hours a week, while still receiving a full-time contribution to their superannuation scheme plus a lump sum payment on retirement. CentrePort management is clear that the benefits of this policy outweigh the costs (CentrePort, 2008). This phased retirement programme is transparent, includes blue-collar as well as white-collar workers, and operates in a highly competitive commercial environment.

Bridge employment

A second way in which older workers can extend their careers is through bridge employment, which is defined as 'employment that takes place after a person's retirement from a fulltime position but before the person's permanent withdrawal from the workforce' (Kim & Feldman, 2000: 1195). Bridge employment can be in the form of contract work, part-time work, or temporary work. Bridge employment can be taken up by retirees in the organization from which they retired, or a different organization in the same career field, or in a different organization or a different career field.

For older workers, many of the benefits of bridge employment are similar to the benefits of phased retirement, including mediation of the transition from full-time work to full-time retirement with resultant mental health benefits (Kim & Feldman, 2000). However, bridge employment in a non-career field does not have the same beneficial effects on mental health as bridge employment in a career field, partly because of the stress involved in adjusting to a new work environment and role identity (Zhan et al., 2009). Also, job satisfaction in career bridge employment has been found to be greater than in bridge employment in a different field (Wang et al., 2009). These results suggest that bridge employment can have beneficial effects on retirees' mental and physical health, but caution is also needed in presuming that bridge employment is a panacea ensuring healthy outcomes. For instance, some part-time bridge employment can be insecure, low quality, and poorly paid (Owen & Flynn, 2004). Also, there is evidence that older people, once out of work, can take significantly longer to re-enter the workforce than younger workers (e.g. Berger, 2009; OECD, 2006), suggesting that if quality work is wanted, a bridge job should be organized prior to retirement, because it may well be difficult to take up post retirement.

The benefits of bridge employment for employers are similar to those gained from phased retirement: access to workers with known skills, experience, and knowledge of the organization's systems and culture. However, companies can be more open to 'retire-rehire' arrangements that enable them to be selective in those they offer contracts to without being criticized of discriminatory practice; and the workers so contracted can be more easily dismissed when no longer needed (Kim & Feldman, 2000; Ulrich, 2003).

Thus, bridge employment can be a valuable, fluid, and cost-effective solution to staffing problems and, because short fixed-term contracts may well suit some workers, such as retired professionals, such employment can be seen as an attractive and popular win-win option (Owen & Flynn, 2004). In New Zealand, for example, bridge employment, in the form of contract, temporary employment, and casual work, is high amongst older workers aged 65–69 and is a preferred option for lifestyle reasons (Boyd & Dixon, 2009). In the US, Cahill et al. (2005) have found bridge employment to be common for older workers, and have suggested that traditional retirement in the sense of complete and sudden withdrawal from the workforce may become the exception rather than the rule.

Examples of bridge employment programmes include Monsanto's 'Resource Re-entry' programme where retirees are brought back to work on various projects for durations of a week to a year (Lindorff, 2006); MITRE's 'Reserves at the Ready', a cadre of retired technical, administrative, and support staff available to assist with projects on an as-needed basis (Albright & Cliff, 2005); and CVS Pharmacy's 'Snowbird Scheme' which allows its employees to transfer to different CVS pharmacies on a seasonal basis, while the company manages the swell of business in certain stores at particular times of the year (Abelson, 2006). Each of these programmes recognizes the mutually beneficial aspects of a contingent workforce, and offers an innovative way forward in adjusting to and maximizing the potential of an aging workforce.

Self-employment

A third way in which some older people choose to work during and after retirement is through self-employment. A self-employed person can be defined as one 'who operates his or her own economic enterprise or engages independently in a profession or trade (including partnerships)' (Statistics New Zealand website).

Self-employment is potentially attractive to older individuals because it offers flexibility, particularly the opportunity to be one's own boss and set one's own time schedules and thus the possibility of accommodating changing preferences for work, leisure, and other commitments, as well as the ability to adjust workload to changing health and life circumstances (Johnson, 2009; Karoly & Zissimopoulos, 2004). However, because business failures can undermine income security (Johnson, 2009), as well as health and confidence levels, it is also an inherently risky enterprise; a situation which may be particularly problematic in the self-employed person's later years when he/she may have less time and energy to recover and re-build.

While the push and pull factors of autonomy and risk partly explain older individuals' interest in self-employment, other factors are also influential. They include health, resources, and risk profiles – with poor health decreasing the probability of moving into self-employment (Parker & Rougier, 2007). Those with money, connections and skills are more disposed to self-employment (Hochguertel, 2010; Platman, 2003), and those with a high need for security being less disposed (Zissimopoulos & Karoly, 2009).

Countries differ in terms of the numbers of older workers who switch to self-employment. For example, in England, Curran and Blackburn (2001) found only a moderate level of interest in self-employment among the 50–75 age group, with concerns for security being among the top reasons for preferring not to be self-employed. In the same country, Parker and Rougier (2007) found that many older employees switching to self-employment do so as a last resort. In contrast, studies in the US have found that post-career transitions into and out of self-employment are common amongst older Americans (Giandrea et al., 2008), while in New Zealand, self-employment is an increasingly favoured option amongst older workers (Boyd & Dixon, 2009). Thus, while self-employment may appeal as a way for some older retirees to continue working, perceived risks associated with it may limit its universal take-up (Parker & Rougier, 2007).

Encore careers

A fourth way in which retirees and those in, or approaching, retirement can continue to engage productively in society is through an encore career. Freedman (2006/7; 2007) discussed 'social purpose' encore careers as the pursuit of purpose-driven work in the second half of life. Such work centres on 'the chance to be of service and contribute to the betterment of others' (Freedman, 2007: 141). President Obama described it as an activity undertaken by those who, instead of transitioning into retirement, 'come back for an encore, plowing a lifetime of experience into helping people in need' (Bank, 2009). In Freedman's book, *Encore: Finding work that matters in the second half of life*, he recounts stories about people who have left their careers, often corporate careers, to engage in work that they find meaningful and that makes a social impact. Just one example is that of Ed Speedling who, after 30 years as a hospital executive and academic, left to work with the homeless in Philadelphia. These stories are inspiring and celebrate passionate people committing to particular issues in order to make a difference.

Other forms of encore career include Sullivan et al's. (2003) notion of 'career recycling' and Ibarra's (2004) strategies for career reinvention. While the labels may vary, these encore careers all share a common motivation to seek out deep change, personal renewal, and meaningful work rather than focusing on work, principally, as a means to social status and financial reward. Importantly, also, they involve a forward momentum, including movement towards the goal of self-knowledge and self-actualization and, thus, a re-negotiation of one's role in and contribution to society and the economy rather than a concern with 'downshifting' (Ibarra, 2004), and disengagement.

An encore career can include involvement in paid and unpaid work, such as formal volunteering activities in which many older people engage in their retirement years. Such work is described by Burr et al. (2005) as a type of structured helping typically undertaken as a discretionary activity, usually without monetary reward, and in a public setting, such as a not-for-profit organization, for the benefit of third parties – persons other than family or friends. Such work is recognized as beneficial in terms of the contribution it makes to the health and well-being of individuals, communities, and nations (Meadows, 2004; Narushima, 2005).

While this broader notion of the social purpose encore career includes many older people engaged in community work, it can also inadvertently exclude others for whom there appears little alignment between the concept and their way of life. It is therefore sobering to note how culturally bound this concept may be. For example, for New Zealand Maori, unpaid work, *mahi aroha*, performed by elders and others according to the values and principles of *tikanga*, correct behaviour, is not a *voluntary* exercise it is a duty, the fulfilment of a cultural obligation. Examples of *mahi aroha* include attendances at marae events such as celebrations and funerals, involvement in Maori education and development programmes, and advice to government and other mainstream agencies on Maori protocols. *Mahi aroha* is also not considered *helping,* rather it is based on being a member of a group and contributing, as expected, to the well-being of that group. Such unpaid work is one of the activities in which Maori elders engage extensively, formally and informally, and it is through elders that the traditions and practices of *mahi aroha* are learned and passed on to future generations (Durie, 1999; OCVS, 2007). Thus, *mahi aroha* is not just about *doing good work*, it is also a cultural imperative, a key way to maintain and retain a distinctive Maori cultural identity and way of life.

Although similarities and differences in the concepts of encore careers, volunteering, and *mahi aroha* are evident, all reflect important ways in which societies organize to allocate responsibilities and negotiate expectations of one another (Anheier & Salamon, 1999) including recognizing, respecting, and valuing the lived and work-related experiences of older people. Such organizing utilizes policies and practices in individual workplaces, as well as being a basis for the broad social systems and moral orders within which organizations operate, and which set the parameters for the changing nature of the age–work relationship (Roberts, 2006). It is to these meso- and macro-level contexts and the frameworks that facilitate and/or inhibit career extension options that we now turn.

Meso-level policies and programmes

Options for extending careers, such as those discussed above, are enabled by organizational environments conducive to good practices in age management – that is, policies and programmes that promote positive attitudes towards aging and older people (age awareness), develop the skills and employability of older workers, and adapt working conditions and employment opportunities to an age-diverse workforce (Naegele & Walker, 2006). Naegele and Walker's research into age management best practice across the European Union indicates that, in relation to career development, good practice includes providing older employees with opportunities to progress, and to maintain as well as to enlarge their skills and knowledge. Initiatives along these lines include the development of competence databases, the precise matching of job specifications with work-related performance changes over the course of a career, and the integration of training opportunities into career planning strategies. One example identified by Naegele and Walker was Achmea, a large financial services company in the Netherlands, in which career advice is provided to employees every five years after the age of 45, and older workers are provided with assistance and paid leave to study. Another example is that of a manufacturing company in Latvia, Rigas Elektromasinbuves Rupnica, whose human resource policies aim to extend employees'

working lives and attract retirees back to the workforce by combining active recruitment methods, bonuses and benefits for older employees, and social support throughout the process.

While such initiatives are designed to attract and maintain the employability of older workers and enhance their career progression, they are also designed to benefit organizations by preventing the loss of older workers' skills and experience. In addition, investing in the training of older workers can produce better employee retention than training invested in younger workers (CentrePort, 2008).

The success of strategies for career development guided by age management, and other initiatives designed to maximize the potential of an aging workforce, depends on their being seen as a joint effort. That effort involves managers' committing to age management programmes and embedding them in the organization's strategies, systems, policies, and culture; workers' supporting such programmes and being prepared to take advantage of all opportunities to improve their workability; and governments' developing public policy frameworks that create an environment conducive to the retention of mature workers, and to good age management practice (Business of Ageing, 2011; Naegele & Walker, 2006; Walker, 2006).

Macro-level policies and programmes

In relation to the aging workforce, governments are key players whose involvement is crucial in setting out fresh maps that will not only shape the behaviour of managers and older workers but also bring about significant cultural change (Taylor, 2006). Governments' roles include enacting anti-age discrimination legislation, removing institutionalized obstacles such as automatic pay increases for seniority, reversing existing policies that favour early retirement, providing financial incentives for the recruitment, retention, and training of older workers, and conducting public education programmes to counteract negative images of older workers (Naegele & Walker, 2006; Vodopivec & Dolenc, 2008). While many such programmes are in place, there is still much work to be done if those individuals who need to, want to, and can work beyond the usual date of retirement are able to do so in pursuit of flexible, meaningful, and stimulating careers.

REFERENCES

Abelson, J. (2006, March 1). Snowbirds at work: Employers allow winter time transfers. *The Boston Globe*. http://www.globalaging.org/elderrights/us/2006/snowbird.htm (retrieved 25 May 2011).

Albright, W. D., & Cliff, G. A. (2005). Ahead of the curve: How MITRE recruits and retains older workers. *Journal of Organizational Excellence*, 24, 53–63.

Anheier, H. K., & Salamon, L. M. (1999). Volunteering a cross-national perspective: Initial comparisons. *Law and Contemporary Problems*, 62, 43–65.

Arrowsmith, J., & McGoldrick, A. E. (1997). A flexible future for older workers? *Personnel Review*, 26(4), 258–273.

Avolio, B. J., & Waldman, D. A. (1994). Variations in cognitive, perceptual, and psychomotor abilities across the life span: Examining the effects of race, sex, experience, education and occupation. *Psychology and Aging*, 9, 430–462.

Baltes, P. B., & Smith, J. (2003). New frontiers in the future of aging: From successful aging of the young old to the dilemmas of the fourth age. *Gerontology*, 49(2), 123–135.

Bank, D. (2009). *President Obama champions social innovation and encore careers.* http://www.encore.org/news/encore-campaign/president-calls-all-ages (retrieved 27 May 2011).

Beehr, T. A. (1986). The process of retirement: A review and recommendations for future investigation. *Personnel Psychology*, 39(1), 31–55.

Beehr, T. A., Glazer, S., Nielson, N. L., & Farmer, S. J. (2000). Work and nonwork predictors of employees' retirement ages. *Journal of Vocational Behavior*, 57(2), 206–225.

Berger, E. D. (2009). Managing age discrimination: An examination of the techniques used when seeking employment. *The Gerontologist*, 49(3), 317–332.

Bosse, R., Aldwin, C., Levenson, M., & Workman-Daniels, K. (1991). How stressful is retirement? Findings from a normative ageing study. *Journal of Gerontology*, 46, 9–14.

Boyd, S., & Dixon, S. (2009). *The working patterns of older workers*. Wellington, New Zealand: Department of Labour.

Brainard, K. (2002). *Phased retirement overview: Summary of research and practices*. Baton Rouge, LA: National Association of State Retirement Administrators. http://www.nasra.org/resources/Phased%20Retirement%20Overview.pdf (retrieved 25 May 2011).

Brimeyer, T. M., Perrucci, R., & Wadsworth, S. M. (2010). Age, tenure, resources for control and organizational commitment. *Social Science Quarterly*, 91(2), 511.

Brooke, L. (2003). Human Resource costs and benefits of maintaining a mature age workforce. *International Journal of Manpower*, 24 (3), 260–283.

Brown, S. K. (2003). *Staying ahead of the curve 2003: The AARP working in retirement study*. Washington, DC: AARP.

Burr, J. A., Choi, N. G., Mutchler, J. G., & Caro, F. G. (2005). Caregiving and volunteering: Are private and public helping behaviours linked? *The Journals of Gerontology*, 60B, S247, 52–56.

The Business of ageing: Realising the economic potential of older people in New Zealand: 2011–2051. (2011). Wellington, New Zealand: Ministry Social Development. http://www.msd.govt.nz/documents/about-msd-and-our-work/publications-resources/research/business-of-ageing/business-of-ageing.pdf (retrieved 26 May 2011).

Cahill, K. E., Giandrea, M. D., & Quinn, J. F. (2005). *Are traditional retirements a thing of the past? New evidence on retirement patterns and bridge jobs.* BLS Working Paper 384. US Department of Labor Bureau of Labor Statistics. http://www.bls.gov/ore/pdf/ec050100.pdf (retrieved 26 May 2011).

Callanan, G. A., & Greenhaus, J. H. (2008). The baby boom generation and career management: A call to action. *Advances in Developing Human Resources*, 10(1), 70–85.

Calvo, E., Haverstick, K., & Sass, S. A. (2009). Gradual retirement, sense of control and retirees' happiness. *Research on Aging*, 31(1), 112–135.

Cameron, M. P. & Waldegrave, C. (2009). Work, retirement and wellbeing among older New Zealanders. In P. Koopman-Boyden and C. Waldegrave (eds), *Enhancing wellbeing in an ageing society (EWAS) Monograph No. 1*, pp. 67–81. Hamilton and Lower Hutt: University of Waikato; Family Centre Social Policy Research Unit.

CentrePort (2008). *Valuing experience: A practical guide to recruiting and retaining older workers.* http://www.neon.org.nz/eeogroups/valuingexperience/ (retrieved April 2011).

Chen, Y-P., & Scott, J. (2006). *Phased retirement: Who opts for it and toward what end?* Washington, DC: AARP Public Policy Institute. http://assets.aarp.org/rgcenter/econ/inb113_retire.pdf (retrieved 25 May 2011).

Clark, R. L. (2007). *The emergence of phased retirement: Economic implications and policy concerns.* Paper presented at the John Deutsch Institute Conference, Retirement Policy Issues in Canada, October 26–27 at Queens University. http://jdi-legacy.econ.queensu.ca/Files/Conferences/Retirementconferencepapers/Clark.pdf (retrieved 25 May 2011).

Collins, G. A. (2003). Rethinking retirement in the context of an aging workforce. *Journal of Career Development,* 30(2), 145–157.

Curran, J., & Blackburn, R. A. (2001). Older people and the enterprise society: Age and self employment propensities. *Work, Employment & Society,* 15(4), 889–902.

Davey, J. A. & Cornwall, J. (2003). *Maximising the potential of older workers.* Wellington, New Zealand: New Zealand Institute for Research on Ageing.

Dorn, D., & Sousa-Posa, A. (2010). 'Voluntary' and 'involuntary' early retirement: an international analysis. *Applied Economics,* 42(4), 427–438.

Durie, M. H. (1999). Kaumatautanga reciprocity: Maori elderly and whanau. Aoteaora. *New Zealand Journal of Psychology,* 28, 102–106.

Dychtwald, K., Erickson, T., & Morison, B. (2004). It's time to retire retirement. *Harvard Business Review,* 82(3), 48–57.

Employers Forum on Age & Age Concern (1997). Age, employment & business success. Getting the balance right in recruitment. HRM Consulting Pty Ltd in association with the global Saratoga network produced the Australian Human Resource Benchmarking Report 1999 Edition.

Equal Employment Opportunities Trust (2006). EEO Trust Work & Age Survey Report 2006. http://www.eeotrust.org.nz/research/index.cfm?cache=120912 (retrieved 14 July 2011).

Equal Employment Opportunities Trust (2008). Older workers: Employers speak out . http://www.eeotrust.org.nz/research/index.cfm?cache=120912 (retrieved 14 July 2011).

Erlinghagen, M., & Hank, K. (2006). The participation of older Europeans in volunteer work. *Ageing and Society,* 26, 567–584.

Feldman, D. C., & Weitz, B. A. (1988). Career plateaus reconsidered. *Journal of Management,* 14, 69–80.

Freedman, M. (2006/2007). The social-purpose encore career: Baby boomers, civic engagement, and the next stage of work. *Generations,* 30(4), 43–46.

Freedman, M. (2007) *Encore: Finding work that matters in the second half of life.* New York: Public Affairs.

Giandrea, M. D., Cahill, K. E., & Quinn, J. F. (2008). *Self employment transitions among older American workers with career jobs.* Chestnut Hill, MA: Boston College Department of Economics. URL: http://www.bls.gov/ore/pdf/ec080040.pdf (retrieved 26 May 2011).

Hochguertel, S. (2010). *Self employment around retirement age.* www.tinbergen.nl (retrieved 26 Mary 2011).

Hofacker, D. (2010). *Older workers in a globalizing world: An international comparison of retirement and late career patterns in Western industrialized countries.* Cheltenham, UK: Edward Elgar.

Hutchens, R. (2007). *Phased retirement: Problems and prospects.* URL: http://crr.bc.edu/images/stories/Briefs/wob_8.pdf (retrieved 25 May 2011).

Hutchens, R., & Grace-Martin, K. (2006). Employer willingness to permit phased retirement: Why are some more willing than others? *Industrial Labor Relations Review,* 59, 525–546.

Hyde, M., Ferrie, J., Higgs, P., Mein, G., & Nazroo, J. (2004). The effects of pre-retirement factors and retirement route on circumstances in retirement: Findings from the Whitehall II study. *Ageing & Society,* 24(2): 279–296.

Ibarra, H. (2004). *Working identity: Unconventional strategies for reinventing your career.* Boston , MA: Harvard Business School Press.

Johnson, R. W. (2009). Employment opportunities at older ages: Introduction to the special issue. *Research on Aging,* 31(1), 3–16.

Johnson, R. W., & Neumark, D. (1997). Age discrimination, job separations, and employment status of older workers: evidence from self-reports. *Journal of Human Resources,* 32(4), 779–811.

Jonsson, H., Borell, L., & Sadlo, G. (2000). Retirement: An occupational transition with consequences for temporality, balance and meaning of occupations. *Journal of Occupational Science,* 7(1): 3–16.

Jorgensen, B., & Taylor, P. (2008) .Older workers, government and business: Implications for ageing populations of a globalising economy. *Economic Affairs,* 28(1): 18–23.

Karoly, L. A., & Zissimopoulos, J. (2004). Self employment among older U. S. workers. *Monthly Labor Review,* 127(7), 24–47.

Kim, S., & Feldman, D. C. (2000). Working in retirement: The antecedents of bridge employment and its consequences for quality of life in retirement. *Academy of Management Journal*, 43(6), 1195–1210.

Koopman-Boyden, P., & Waldegrave, C. (2009). *Enhancing wellbeing in an ageing society: 65–84 year olds in New Zealand, 2007*. Hamilton and Lower Hutt: University of Waikato; Family Centre Social Policy Research Unit.

Levinson, D. J., & Levinson, J. D. (1996). *The seasons of a woman's life.* New York: Knopf.

Levinson, D. J., Darrow, C. N., Klein, E. B., Levinson, M. H., & McKee, B. (1978). *The seasons of a man's life.* New York: Knopf.

Levinson, H., & Wofford, J. C. (2000). Approaching retirement as the flexibility phase. *Academy of Management Executive*, 14(2), 84–95.

Lindorff, D. (2006). The old folks are coming! The old folks are coming! *Treasury and Risk Management*, 16, 40–44.

Litwin, H. (2007). Does early retirement lead to longer life? *Ageing & Society*, 27(5), 739–754.

Office for the Community and Voluntary Sector (OCVS) (2007). *Mahi Aroha: Maori perspectives on volunteering and cultural obligation*. Office for the Community and Voluntary Sector. Wellington, New Zealand. www.ocvs.govt.nz (retrieved 18 July 2009).

McGregor, J. and Gray, L. (2002). Stereotypes and older workers: The New Zealand experience. *Social Policy Journal of New Zealand*, 18.

McKelvey, J. B. (2009). Globalization and ageing workers: constructing a global life course. *International Journal of Sociology and Social Policy*, 29(1/2), 49–59.

McManus, T., Anderberg, J., & Lazarus, H. (2007). Retirement – an unaffordable luxury. *Journal of Management Development*, 26, 484–492.

McMunn, A., Nazroo, J., Wahrendorf, M., Breeze, E., & Zaninotto, P. (2009). Participation in socially-productive activities, reciprocity and well-being in later life: Baseline results in England. *Ageing and Society*, 29, 765–782.

McNaught, W. & Barth, M.C (1992). Are older workers "Good Buys?" - A case study of Days Inns of America. *Sloan Management Review, Spring , 33 (3)* 53-63.

Meadows, P. (2004). *The economic contribution of older people: a Report for Age Concern England*. http://www.ageconcern.org.uk/AgeConcern/Documents/regions_economic_contribution_report_o758.pdf (retrieved 10 October 2008).

Moen, P., & Fields, V. (2002). Midcourse in the United States: Does unpaid community participation replace paid work? *Ageing International,* 27(3), 21–48.

Morrow-Howell, N., Hong, S.I. and Tang, F. (2009). Who benefits from volunteering? Variations in perceived benefits. *The Gerontologist*, 49(1), 91–102.

Murray, P., & Syed, J. (2005). Critical issues in managing age diversity in Australia. *Asia Pacific Journal of Human Resources*, 43(2), 210–224. United States: Australian Human Resources Institute. Retrieved from http://dx.doi.org/10.1177/1038411105055059

Naegele, G., & Walker, A. (2006). *A guide to good practice in age management*. Luxembourg: Office for Official Publications of the European Communities. http://www.eurofound.europa.eu/pubdocs/2005/137/en/1/ef05137en.pdf (retrieved 31 May 2011).

Narushima, M. (2005). Payback time: Community volunteering among older adults as a transformative mechanism. *Ageing and Society*, 25, 567–584.

OECD (2006). *Live longer, work longer.* Paris: OECD.

OECD (2011). *Pensions at a Glance 2011: Retirement-Income Systems in OECD and G20 Countries*. http://www.oecd.org/els/social/pensions/PAG (retrieved 4 June 2011).

O'Rand, A. M. and Henretta, J. C. (1999). *Age and inequality: Diverse pathways through later life*. Boulder, CO, US: Westview Press.

Owen, L., & Flynn, M. (2004). Changing work: Mid- to late-life transitions in employment. *Ageing International*, 29(4), 333–350.

Parker, S. C., & Rougier, J. (2007). The retirement behaviour of the self employed in Britain. *Applied Economics*, 39, 697–713.

Peiperl, M. A., & Arthur, M. P. (2000). Topics for conversation: career themes old and new. In M. A. Peiperl, M. B. Arthur, R. Goffee, & T. Morris (eds) *Career frontiers: New conceptions of working lives* (pp. 1–19). Oxford, UK: Oxford University Press.

Pickersgill, R., Briggs, C., Kitay, C., O'Keefe, S., & Gillezeau, J. (1996). *Productivity of mature and older workers: Employers' attitudes and experiences*. Sydney: University of New South Wales. Australian Centre for Industrial Relations, Research and Teaching (ACIRRT). Monograph 13.

Pitt-Catsouphes, M., Sweet, S., Lynch, K., & Whalley, E. (2009). Talent management study: The pressures of talent management (Issue Brief No. 23). Chestnut Hill, MA: Sloan Center on Aging and Work at Boston College. Retrieved from http://agingandwork.bc.edu/documents/IB23_TalentMangmntStudy_2009-10-23.pdf

Platman, K. (2003). The self-designed career in later life: A study of older portfolio workers in the United Kingdom. *Ageing & Society*, 23, 281–302.

Richardson, V. E. (1993). *Retirement counseling: A handbook for gerontology practitioners.* New York: Springer.

Roberts, J. (2006). Taking age out of the workplace: Putting older workers back in? *Work, Employment and Society*, 20(1), 67–86.

Savickas, M. L. (2002). Career construction: A developmental theory of vocational behavior. In D. Brown & Associates, *Career choice and development* (4th edn, pp. 149–205). San Francisco: Jossey-Bass.

Shultz, K.S., Morton, K. R., & Weckerle J. R. (1998). The influence of push and pull factors on voluntary and involuntary early retirees' retirement decision and adjustment. *Journal of Vocational Behavior*, 53(1), 45–57.

Smith-Ruig, T. (2009). Exploring career plateau as a multi-faceted phenomenon: Understanding the types of career plateaux expereiened by accounting professionals. *British Journal of Management*, 20(4), 610–622.

Statistics New Zealand (2000). Changing Face of New Zealand's Population (accessed 27 July 2005)]

Statistics New Zealand (2006). *2006 Census of Population and Dwellings: National Summary*. Wellington: Statistics New Zealand.

Statistics New Zealand website (2011). http://www.stats.govt.nz/browse_for_stats/work_income_and_spending/employment_and_unemployment/LEED-reports/person-level-statistics/self-employment.aspx (retrieved 26 May 2011).

Sullivan, S. E., Martin, D. F., Carden, W. A., & Mainiero, L. A. (2003). The road less travelled: How to manage the recycling career stage. *Journal of Leadership and Organizational Studies*, 10(2), 34–42.

Super, D. E. (1957). *The psychology of careers*. New York: Harper & Row.

Super, D. E. (1990). A life-span, life-space approach to career development. In D. Brown, L. Brooks & Associates, *Career choice and development* (2nd edn, pp. 197–261). San Francisco: Jossey-Bass.

Taylor, P. (2006). *Employment initiatives for an ageing workforce in the EU15*. Luxembourg: Office for Official Publications of the European Communities.

Taylor, P. (ed.) (2008) *Ageing Labour Forces: Promises and Prospects*. Edward Elgar Publishing Inc: Northampton.

Taylor, P., & Walker, A. (1994). The ageing workforce: Employers' attitudes towards older people, *Work, Employment and Society*, 8 (4), 569–591.

Taylor, P., & Walker, A. (1998). Employers and older workers: attitudes and employment practices). *Ageing and Society*, 18, 641–658.

Taylor, P., Brooke, L., McLoughlin, C., & Di Biase, T. (2010). Older workers and organizational change: corporate memory versus potentiality, *International Journal of Manpower*, 31 (3), 374–386.

Ulrich, L. B. (2003). *Older workers and bridge employment: an Exploratory study*. Unpublished doctoral thesis. Blacksburg, VA: Virginia Polytechnic Institute and State University.

Vodopivec, M., & Dolenc, P. (2008). *Live longer, work longer: Making it happen in the labour market*. Washington: The World Bank SP Discussion Paper 0803. http://siteresources.worldbank.org/SOCIAL PROTECTION/Resources/SP-Discussion-papers/Labor-Market-DP/0803.pdf (retrieved 20 May 2011).

Wahrendorf, M., & Siegrist, J. R. (2010). Are changes in productive activities of older people associated with changes in their well-being? Results of a longitudinal European study. *European Journal of Ageing*, 7(2), 59–68.

Walker, A. (2006). Active ageing in employment: Its meaning and potential. *Asia Pacific Review*, 13(1), 78–93. http://www.eurofound.europa.eu/pubdocs/2006/39/en/1/ef0639en.pdf (retrieved 25 May 2011).

Wang, M., Adams, G. A., Beehr, T. A., & Shultz, K. S. (2009) Bridge employment and retirement: Issues and opportunities during the latter part of one's career. In S. G. Baugh & S.E. Sullivan (eds), *Maintaining focus, energy, and options through the life span* (pp. 135–162). Charlotte, NC: Information Age.

Wang, M., & Shultz, K. S. (2010). Employee retirement: A review and recommendations for future investigation. *Journal of Management*, 36(1), 172–206.

Warr, P., Butcher, V., Robertson, I., & Callinan, M. (2004). Older people's well-being as a function of employment, retirement, environmental characteristics and role preference. *British Journal of Psychology*, 95(3), 297–324.

White, J. (1999). *Midwinter Spring: Smart Business and Older Workers: New Zealand Guide to Best Practice for Employers in an Ageing Population*, EEO Trust, Auckland.

Wilson, M., & Kan, J. (2006). *Barriers to entry for the older worker*. Research Report, Auckland, New Zealand: The University of Auckland Business School.

Wong, J. Y., and Earl, J. K. (2009). Towards an integrated model of individual, psychosocial, and organizational predictors of retirement adjustment. *Journal of Vocational Behavior*, 75(1), 1–13.

Zhan, Y., Wang, M., Liu, S., & Shultz, K. S. (2009). Bridge employment and retirees' health: A longitudinal investigation. *Journal of Occupational Health Psychology*, 14(4), 374–389.

Zissimopoulos, J. M., & Karoly, L. A. (2009). Labor-force dynamics at older ages: Movements into self employment for workers and nonworkers. *Research on Aging*, 31(1), 89–111.

9

Care Work and New Technologies of Care for Older People Living at Home

Celia Roberts, Maggie Mort and Christine Milligan

THE PROBLEM OF CARE WORK

I've had carers ... saying 'I've told Social Services, I'm off!' And they've never come back 'cause they've just been pushed right to the far end, often because the person they care for isn't appreciative of what they're doing. And some times you get a bit of pay back for something in the past and they say 'Well I've had enough of you, I'm off!' (Interview, Carer Support Officer, 2009)

In this extract, a Carer Support Officer describes serious breakdowns in the provision of care for older people living at home: in his experience, looking after older relatives can be highly fraught. Indeed, care work more generally, both paid and unpaid, is often both emotionally and physically challenging. In the case of older people living at home, new technologies are currently being enlisted to help with this problem. In this chapter we examine the complexities of this 'solution', arguing that new care technologies reconfigure rather than reduce the challenges of caring.

Social research has much to offer in addressing the problems of care work. In a special issue of *Sociology* entitled *Rethinking the Sociology of Work*, Halford and Strangleman (2009) describe the range of research undertaken in the second part of the 20th century, and promote a return to work as a core topic for sociology, calling for interdisciplinary engagement to reinvigorate the field. Work on and with bodies is a key area here. Building on a widespread interest in care, researchers have recently focused on the labour involved in looking after young, aging and/or unwell bodies. A special issue of *Sociology of Health and Illness* (2011), for example, brings together papers on what editors Julia Twigg et al. call 'body work'. These highlight the significance of co-presence and physical touch in health and social care work, and describe the significant temporal and spatial reorderings that occur when paid care workers enter care recipients' homes (see also Angus et al., 2005; Milligan at al., 2010; Willems, 2010). Research on care also highlights the significance of emotions in body work. As body work, care necessarily involves physical intimacies of lesser or greater degrees, depending on the body parts involved and the kinds of bodies being worked on. It also often involves highly charged emotional relations: intimate physical care, as Twigg et al. (2011) argue, evokes experiences of childhood, illness and sexual interactions, all of which are emotionally laden (see also England and Dyck, 2011). Body work is always gendered, involving relations of power. In the case of older people these relations are complex. Like other care recipients, some older people refuse care practices and make the carers' work very difficult to do. 'Nonetheless,' Twigg et al. write, '... as Lee-Trewick's (1996) study of residential care suggested, care workers have plenty of opportunities to retaliate, including the withdrawal of emotional support' (2011: 180). These power relations differ according to whether the care work is undertaken by paid formal carers or by family and friends in informal care arrangements; significant bodies of work describe this (see Milligan, 2009).

In more formal care arrangements, questions of power also revolve around social and employment status. Recent studies of 'global care chains' (Hochschild, 2003), for example that by Lyon and Glucksmann (2008), indicate that paid care work in Europe and resource rich countries is increasingly undertaken by women from less developed parts of the world. This racialized division of labour builds on historical class divisions in which the labour of tending to the bodies of others was delegated to those of lower social status. Hands-on care work, and particularly caring for aging bodies, has long been figured as 'dirty work' (Twigg et al., 2011: 174). One of the key problems for this kind of work is timing. Bodies do not fit well into bureaucratic or scientific models of labour management or profit maximization:

> Body time fits poorly with 'clock time' (Simmonds, 2002). Whereas clock time, the commodity against which capitalist wage-labour is reckoned ... is abstract, accountable and exchangeable, bodily rhythms are individual and variable, the times and duration of bodily need unpredictable and expansive. (Twigg et al., 2011: 177)

This poor fit leads to a demand for flexible bodies and flexible workers, but also to strenuous attempts to fit the care of older bodies into tightly regulated time management schemes, with often negative results for both workers and care recipients (see Wibberley, 2011; BBC *Panorama*, 2009). As Twigg et al. argue:

> demand spikes are inevitable. When these occur, unless staffing levels are 'unprofitably' high, a decreasing likelihood given the dominance of the profit-motive in the social organization of body work, some demand is likely to go unmet; patients, clients or service users are left waiting. (Twigg et al., 2011: 177)

TELECARE FOR OLDER PEOPLE LIVING AT HOME

One widespread response to this problem in the case of older people living at home has been to provide '24–7' services that claim to provide 'care at a distance' and 'peace of mind' through information and communication technologies.[1] Known as 'telecare', these services – although quite varied in their specificities – aim to fill the temporal gaps usually involved in the provision of hands-on care, with the explicit aim of assisting older people to remain in their own homes as long as possible. (Department of Health, 2005)

In this chapter we discuss data from a three-year ethnographic study of telecare, funded by the European Commission under the Framework 7 'Science in Society' programme. The project, 'Ethical Frameworks for Telecare Technologies', observed the implementation and use of telecare systems for older people living at home in four countries: England, Norway, Spain and the Netherlands. The study also involved a deliberative axis in which older people and carers came together in a series of citizens' panels in each country to discuss the current state and potential futures of telecare. Meeting twice over 18 months, these panels debated the nature of 'good care' and how telecare technologies might or might not have a role in providing this.[2] In this chapter we explore findings from the English study, focusing on one essential, yet undervalued element of telecare provision: the work undertaken by operators in remote monitoring centres. Describing this work ethnographically allows us to think critically about the meaning of care for older people living at home, and to contribute a fresh perspective to sociological debates about the nature of contemporary care work.

Part of broader policy drives promoting 'aging in place' (Audit Commission, 2004; Milligan et al., 2010), telecare discourses promise these systems will support older people's independence, increase their safety and security, and provide swift responses in emergency situations. In England, 'telecare' refers to a range of technologies and associated services: at its most basic, an alarm worn around the neck or wrist connected to a 'hub' linked to the telephone line in the home and thence to a remote monitoring centre. When the 'user' presses the alarm, an alert is registered on screen in the monitoring centre and a teleoperator contacts the user's home and organizes help if required. Supplementing this personal alarm, contemporary telecare systems often involve environmental monitors that warn of gas leaks, smoke or extreme temperatures and mobility-related devices (falls monitors, bed sensors, door sensors) which are triggered if the user does something outside of an established set of behavioural parameters: gets out of bed too often, goes outside at night, falls down. (In 'Northshire', our research area, 'telecare' consists of a personal alarm and at least two other sensors.) In England, systems are widely promoted to older people who are encouraged to accept them as one element of a 'package of care' assembled by social workers and funded in relation to the individual's income.

The care package most often also involves physical care (washing, dressing, toileting, help with meals and mobility). Telecare commissioners and providers often stress that telecare should not be a substitute for hands-on care, but rather supplement it. Such assertions sometimes fail to reassure: many older people and social workers we met viewed the promotion of telecare as a vehicle for cost-cutting through reducing allocations of hands-on care and, as we describe elsewhere (Milligan et al., 2011), saw telecare as heralding a dangerous, dehumanizing loss of 'real' care.

Given recent growths in system installations, the question becomes in what ways can telecare be construed as care? If carers cannot always be co-present, is there any way in which telecare systems might fill this care gap? Despite sharing respondents' concerns about reductions in hands-on care, we wanted to remain open to the question of what counts as care, and to look for moments and places where care might happen in and through technological systems. Inspired by work in science and technology studies, we refused to assume that care technologies fall somehow outside humanity (and are cold, hard, unfeeling) but preferred to see the care arrangements and practices involved in telecare as machine-human collectives that might produce something that could be called and experienced as care (see also Mol et al., 2010: 14; Pols and Moser, 2009).

Somewhat surprisingly perhaps, we found such collectives taking shape in monitoring centres. Relatedly, in getting close to the work undertaken in monitoring centres and spending time with the operators, we also came to understand a key paradox of telecare: these systems, intended to work at a distance and to be of particular help to people who do not have robust networks of co-present caring others, only function well *when they are situated within such networks*. Although designed to provide care at distance, telecare works best when care is close at hand. These two findings indicate that care at a distance (or 'disembodied' care) both shares some elements of body work and, rather than a supplement or opposite, is inextricable from or inter-implicated with it.

ETHICAL FRAMEWORKS FOR TELECARE TECHNOLOGIES: METHODOLOGY

In the wider project, partner research teams undertook ethnographies of telecare systems and facilitated citizens' panels, firstly to discuss existing and proposed telecare systems and latterly to consider our ethnographic findings. In England our ethnography focused on the implementation of the government's telecare strategy in 'Northshire' during 2008 to 2010. This research involved observations in service management meetings, social work offices, older people's homes, housing association offices and 'smart homes', practitioner training meetings and telecare monitoring centres. We undertook interviews with managers, workers, older people and their families. In this chapter we focus on data from seven visits to two very different monitoring centres in Northshire: one large centre operated by a not-for-profit housing association covering a wide geographical zone, and a much smaller more locally oriented centre run by a district council. In each case we were present for several hours at various times of the day and night, observing operators taking calls, making decisions and implementing actions. In between calls we talked with operators about their work and sometimes recorded these discussions with the consent of workers and their managers: calls with clients were not recorded.[3] Extensive field notes were written after each visit.

Audio recordings were fully transcribed and field notes and transcriptions analysed for recurring themes. This analysis was further developed in international data workshops in which each research partner presented

translations of raw data and preliminary analyses from their ethnographies. The key themes arising from these workshops are described in several project reports and in other publications.[4, 5] Preliminary analyses were also fed back to the second round of citizens' panels, giving older people and carers an opportunity to comment and make further contributions.

WHAT KIND OF WORK IS TELECARE MONITORING?

In many ways, telecare operators are archetypal of the contemporary labour market. As service workers who can be located 'anywhere', require little training, often work to highly controlled practice protocols, and who are time-managed through computerized performance monitoring and call recording, they can be relatively easily globally outsourced and are usually poorly paid. Their jobs are precarious, yet demanding. A body of sociological literature demonstrates that such workers are often poorly treated by clients, subject to verbal abuse and complaint, and have inadequate supervision to manage these difficulties (e.g. Deery at al., 2002; Grebner et al., 2003; Korczynski, 2009; Mulholland, 2002). Teleoperators usually have to rely on (largely unrecognized and undervalued) personal skills and proximal social networks to cope with the emotional difficulties of their work (Korczynski, 2003).

Working in a Northshire telecare monitoring centre involves undertaking multiple tasks: telecare is only one part of what operators do. After 5pm, both monitoring centres also field general calls for their organization. This means responding to issues ranging from blocked drains to unemptied rubbish bins, oil spills on roads or other emergencies (such as flooding or accidents), and individual housing emergencies (e.g. homeless people seeking temporary accommodation). This is mostly triage work – teleoperators are provided with a list of agencies to contact in each situation – but the issues covered are sometimes serious and callers are often distressed or angry.

The key function of telecare monitoring is to mediate between clients (older people living at home mostly alone), informal and formal carers and emergency services. Operators have to assess each situation (a call from a user or an alarm), work out which alarm has been triggered (the computer cannot distinguish) and decide who needs to become involved. Their first response is to try to contact the client directly (the call can go through the client's telephone or, more usually, through 'the hub' that is installed next to their landline and which the client should be able to hear from any room). If the client does not answer, operators must decide whether it is best to go straight to emergency services or instead involve those named on the client's file as a nearby informal carer (family member, friend or neighbour). If these 'contacts' are not available or refuse to help, and emergency services are not required, the operator can request a visit from the care company. This can be difficult: contract carers must interrupt their busy routines to make additional visits. In some cases, the operator may agree that the worker will simply check the situation when undertaking their scheduled face-to-face visit.

As illustrated below, teleoperators have to work with uncertainty and indeterminacy. The information they receive in any one call or alarm event is very limited (the person may be unable to communicate clearly; an alarm may mean many different things). Although clients' files automatically appear on screen as the call or alarm comes through, the information is limited, consisting of basic medical and social information and list of contacts. This means that operators use incrementally acquired knowledge about the clients and their support networks, their homes and wider social environments in making decisions. Such information may not be 'on the database' but exists in a shared social memory or emerges in conversations held in the monitoring centre. Although essential to telecare's smooth operation, such

knowledge is not formally valued in any accounting process.

Finally, we want to suggest that teleoperators do a kind of 'repair work' in which they attempt to refashion forms of social relationships for older people who are living in relative isolation. Stitching together fragments of information and connection, teleoperators provide a service that is better recognized as care work than seen as (merely) technical, triaging labour. Although often reported as personally rewarding, this work has significant psychological costs for teleoperators: costs that should be acknowledged and accounted for in evaluations of telecare services.

CARING AND CO-PRESENCE IN TELEWORK

Working in the monitoring centre involves building relationships with people whom the operator cannot see or touch and whom they have rarely met face to face (although it should be noted that in both monitoring centres studied here, some operators may also work as telecare installers, and so may have met some clients at home; some had a background in local care home or warden work). Building relationships is done through careful listening and the use of flexible conversational protocols. Although operators are trained to answer calls in particular ways, we found that each had their own 'style' and moved off a standard script quite quickly after the initial introductory exchanges. In the larger monitoring centre the manager showed us a thick file of printouts containing protocols for each type of call. Flicking through the pages she pointed out the numerous handwritten notes suggesting alterations for future editions: protocols are constantly under review.

While spatially remote, telecare is strongly dependent on face-to-face contact arranged by the operator. Often a telephone call is not enough to meet a client's need or to reassure the operator that everything is satisfactory.

Telecare clients are often classified as highly vulnerable: many suffer from forms of dementia and are physically very frail. One operator put it succinctly: 'When it gets to telecare you know that they're a whisker away from not being able to look after themselves.' In the following extract, another operator, Carol, describes how she manages this sense of vulnerability by almost always getting someone to visit the older person when an alarm is triggered:

Researcher:	So if a call comes through and you're not sure how the person is – they're confused – how do you deal with that? Because you can't see them, you can't touch them, you can't – how do you manage?
Carol:	Listen to the conversation and make my mind up what is going on, and then nine times out of ten I would get someone to go and check on them. I would never leave an elderly person, because they're a little bit like a child.[6] They say things and you can't really ... take it for granted they'll be all right – in case – I never leave a call, I always get someone ... it's not worth it.

As hinted here, a substantial part of monitoring work involves managing 'false alarms' and distinguishing these from real emergencies. Some sensors produce frequent false alarms: falls monitors worn around the waist, for example, may trigger an alarm if the person slumps over whilst sleeping in a chair; some users in our study reported repeated false alarms from bed sensors designed to trigger if someone does not return to bed after a set period. Teleoperators decide about such calls through talking with the clients and must also mediate the effects of false alarms: it can become very irritating to clients and families to be repeatedly called when nothing is wrong. Here Carol compares the pendant alarm system ('Lifeline'), which the client presses to request help, with more complex telecare systems relying on sensors:

> The Lifeline system's fabulous, it's great that. It's really like having a friend in the house. I think it's a fantastic thing. But a lot of the telecare I think,

'Poor people!' You know, just the fall detector for instance ... never in all the time we've done telecare have we had a one that's been genuine, they're all false calls.

Another operator told a related story about a woman who had been fitted with a fall detector. When she fell asleep in her chair, her body would tilt and trigger the alarm. This was happening up to 10 times a night. When the operators contacted her to check whether she had fallen, she would – with some justification – complain that they were 'keeping her awake all night!'.

As is evident in the following field note, decisions about apparently false alarms are often based on acquired knowledge of the particular client.

> A call comes through. The teleoperator can work out through a process of elimination and knowing the client, that it's the medication dispenser, it comes as 2 calls, about 5 minutes apart. He tries to speak to the client (Edward) but there is no answer. He says 'This is Peter from the call centre. Just phoning to remind you to take your medication.' Still no answer. Whilst he is 'offline', I talk to Peter – asking him what's going on. He tells me he did the installation and knows that Edward is a rather unusual man. He lives alone in a house that 'he shouldn't be allowed to live in, it's so filthy.' ... He doesn't bother to talk to the call centre and it's unclear whether or not he will take the medication. The dispenser will eventually stop 'binging', whether he's taken the medication or not. As Peter says, 'he might take it later, or he might throw it out'. The teleoperators can't make anyone take the medication. I ask Peter how he feels about Edward not speaking to him. Peter says he doesn't mind – he knows Edward and understands that 'he's not really up for speaking to anyone'. (Field note, April 2009)

Teleoperators also encountered the opposite kind of problem, where users would (operators claimed) deliberately trigger alarms in order to have the chance to talk to someone. This field note describes the workers' relationships to clients who are 'excessively' reliant on telecare contact:

> All the calls are fully audio-recorded and put on the database. The two operators and the manager showed me the files of the most 'impressive'

clients in terms of numbers of calls. Some of these account for up to 10 calls a day for months. They are clearly fond of these clients despite the high demand they constitute and were eager to talk about them in relatively personal terms. The manager got out the file of one man who had since moved into care and then died. His file had been printed out for storage and was several inches thick. She flicked through the file with a kind of rueful pride. (Field note, October 2008)

As we discuss elsewhere (EFORTT Project Team, 2009: 34), this form of telecare use was described by Northshire care managers in team meetings as a 'mis-use' of the service that should be 'stamped out' if possible.

Alongside 'false alarms', there are many problems that operators cannot easily help clients with. Teleoperators have to use verbal skills to deal with this situation, coaxing the older person to get out of bed and to reach the toilet safely on their own:

> You feel so helpless through the night if you get a call and suddenly they'll say 'I want a wee'. Well you can't get the paramedics to go and get them out to have a wee and they might not have any – I mean we've got key safes to let paramedics and that in, but sometimes there is nothing you can do! There isn't, is there? There's nothing you can do, but try and talk them into getting out of bed. I've done that before today. (Bev)

Such attempts to 'talk people into' doing something hint at the skills operators have in producing a kind of virtual co-presence: skills that are most useful in dealing with very vulnerable and confused clients. Bev and Anita describe how they use voice and a form of projection of self to reassure the client and address the problem. The tone of this approach could be seen as infantilizing: when we discussed this material with the citizens' panels, some members were concerned by it, but it is clearly intended to be caring. Anita's use of the term 'we' is important: it produces a kind of alignment with the client, reducing the social and physical space between them.

> Anita: ... same with the bed sensor, it tells you when they get out, and you do try and speak to the people just to make sure they

haven't fallen ... There's one lady, she wanders all night long, just moving herself. She has bad nights, she doesn't sleep very well.

> Bev: We should sing lullabies to her. I usually say 'It's too early now, get back into bed, night night, God bless' and they like you to talk to them like that, [when] ... you're lovely with them. You can talk to her.
> Anita: You say, 'We're having a bad nightmare, let's have a brew!' [chuckles]
> Bev: Yes, she'll go and – because she's capable – make herself a cup of tea.

Formal training received by telecare operators is very brief; the job is mostly learned through co-working and mentoring. This story demonstrates the role of gradually accrued knowledge of clients: both operators know that this particular woman is capable of making a cup of tea, so they use this as a calming strategy.

Teleoperators attempt to build relationships via the system and when there is a requirement to make weekly test calls to make sure the equipment is working, this can lead to formation of emotional attachments. This regular, mundane contact allows for familiarity to develop:

> Researcher: And are there some people that you get to know in a sense?
> Liz: Yes. You get attached to some of them as well, even from just like doing the weekly test calls. I know when I used to do a lot of helping out in the days I'd get to know, even down to getting to know the wardens when they come through [on the phones].[7] They like that as well, [you're] not just a voice, they send you Christmas cards.

Her colleague told us, however, that these weekly calls are now being phased out, because of higher numbers of clients on the system. This means fewer opportunities for building meaningful relationships with clients, even those classed as 'vulnerable':

> Well, we had a lot of weeklies – they were the vulnerable ones – but they try to get everyone to test monthly now, we have hardly any on the weekly now. (Carol)

When calls are thought to be real emergencies, teleoperators can experience substantial anxiety about clients with whom they have built these fragile relationships. Limited to following a 'procedure', teleoperators sometimes worry about what the outcome will be: they have no control over the face-to-face encounter that they put in train. They cannot know, for example, how long emergency services will take to arrive and whether the right decision has been made about whom to send:

> The most difficult calls for me are the telecare and the fire and the CO_2 or gas detectors, they worry me no end. I really don't like them. When they come through I do tend to think [gasp] 'God!' We have a procedure, but I think how long will it take to get someone there? Invariably everything's okay but ... but I do worry about that. (Carol)

Joanne graphically describes the anxieties produced when a client does not respond to her call after an alarm has been triggered. She phones the client's 'contacts', who also do not respond, and then has to go to emergency services. In all this, she tells, time feels like it's slipping away, and the client may be 'on the floor', but there is nothing else she can do:

> ... basically the alarm's gone off, you can't hear anything from them [the client], you've rung them back after a certain time of buzzing them, turning up the volume and speaking, there's no reply still. You ring perhaps the one contact, or maybe two, you can't get them, it's an answer phone. You think 'Right, okay, I'm not happy.' You try ringing them again, you ring the contacts again, and this is like 10 minutes. So you think 'Right, I need to get some help.' So the first thing we have to go to is the police. Well the police will go on the odd occasion, [but] where it's one they've been to a few times they don't prioritize it. So you just hope everything's okay. Anyway then you're having to wait ... while you're waiting for the police to go, and you ask them to come back to you and let you know, you're still trying the contacts and leaving messages, just in case they're listening and don't pick up.
>
> And that can go on till the police get there and they say 'We can't hear anything, the door's locked, we can't see anything, there's no lights on' and it's –. Then it's the ambulance as well. Well

they have to break in, they have to get permission to break in then, and occasionally they are there on the floor, but they've had to break in because the contacts haven't been available. Well, all that can take, as you can imagine, a good hour or so. And you're thinking 'Well if they are in need of help, you know' – but what else can you do?

Neither telecare technologies nor monitoring centre workers provide hands-on, physical care for older people. Their role is to mediate between the older people and those who are morally or economically contracted to provide such care: what they call 'the contacts'. This can involve families, friends, neighbours, care organizations and emergency services. Some of these contacts work better than others; some family members, for example, are seen as helpful and others not (they live too far away or are not responsive). Some operators told us there had been complaints from emergency services that telecare was increasing their workloads. So, as Joanne states, 'telecare's only as good as the contacts we've got'. For people who have 'nobody', telecare provides little. Although technically there should always be a 'live' contact (in the final instance this would be a contract agency worker), the operators felt it was much easier to effectively help those with a list of reliable contacts than those with none. In other words, telecare depends on 'old-fashioned' social networks of potentially co-present carers that can be mobilized in instances of uncertainty:

> Joanne: You know a lot of the Alzheimer's, things like that where their memory's going ... I mean we've got gas detectors in and you go through and you're talking to them and you say 'Can you smell any gas? Can you check your cooker for me?' [They say] 'I haven't got a gas cooker' and they have, you know ... So you just have to get someone [to go out] ... I've always said, telecare's only as good as the contacts we've got. If you can't get somebody to go and check on that, you know, you're really struggling, because the police don't want to know every few minutes [or] to be going. So the

more contacts we can get with the telecare the better, because that's what we have to rely on you see.

Researcher: So it's about the network –

Joanne: It is

Researcher: – around that person?

Joanne: Yes. Then we've got one or two ... that have got nobody.

Despite the helplessness produced by not being able physically to help someone in distress, and having to rely on contacts who may or may not be interested or able to help, teleoperators have a significant role in a crisis, which is to 'stay on the line' with the older person until help arrives. In some cases, this means being 'with' the person as they die. This is clearly a traumatic experience of closeness-despite-distance, and one that does not appear to be formally recognized in the monitoring centres we visited.

Emma: ... and when someone's got dementia and they're very upset you don't know [if the alarm signals a real emergency or not]: it can be real; it can be just in their minds. But you can't take that chance. I've had people die on me which to this day upsets me, because I couldn't be with her, and I knew when she came on to me she'd die – and it still upsets me. [She is upset at this point and gets up.]

Researcher: It's hard, it's hard. I'm sorry. Thank you very much.

Here, Anita confirms that even after dealing with death or major local emergencies, there has been no (formal) counselling offered to workers.

Anita: [This] isn't necessarily a criticism against my employers, but we've had some hairy things go on in here.

Researcher: I can imagine.

Anita: And there's no offer of counselling afterwards.

Researcher: Isn't there? No, right. Even if someone died while you're talking to them or –?

Anita: No, there's no offer of counselling. Or even major emergencies, because we also deal with – we're the first port of call for major emergencies.

Workers also reported that when clients die, they are often not informed, and these could be people with whom they have built fragile relationships over many years. In one case Anita discovered by reading the local paper's obituaries (which she was doing when we arrived) that one of her clients had died. She dealt with her feelings about this through talking with her co-worker about the client and her death. On other days, or on the night shift, there may be no other workers present.

So no there is actually very little sort of support, and I suppose some of it ... like the lady I've taken off this morning and I've only learned that she's passed away because her name's in the newspaper. (Anita)

Monitoring centre work focuses on very frail and elderly people, which demands a certain philosophical approach. As Anita said, 'You know these people are not going to get better': they are either going to die at home or move into residential care. Anita made this remark in response to Bev's description of the anxiety she experienced, particularly when working alone at night:

Bev: I found it was worse through the night when you were learning [how to do the job]. Here you can always ask somebody if you're on days but through the night, ... I used to find it – until I got used to everything – quite frightening, not knowing. Because you can't be getting people up and ringing through the night really can you? I found that really frightening.

Researcher: It's a lot of responsibility.

Bev: It is ... You used to think 'Do I get them out or is it County? Do I do this? Do I do that?' And it really was quite nerve-wracking. I used to think '8 hours, 6 to go and I've survived'. I did at the beginning when I first worked here, I did. I do think it's a big responsibility, I do think we are responsible.

Anita: I suppose it's [hesitation] trying to keep your distance and understand it's a job, and that's the end of it, and you know these people are not going to get better. And of course you rationalize in that respect.

The teleoperators we observed undertake multiple, complex tasks in their attempts to repair or reshape social relationships through the telephone and computer technologies available to them: they provide essential social contact for those who 'have nobody'; they provide preliminary verbal care in situations where the need does not justify calling on a different carer; they take care of people in crisis until help arrives; and they mediate between kinds of carers involved in any particular person's life. Providing this kind of care-at-a-distance costs a lot emotionally. As is evident above, sometimes this distress was re-activated through our conversations, and the absence of formal counselling was also noted. However, as has been shown in other stressful occupations (Mort and Smith, 2009), it was clear that peer support was helpful. Perhaps unsurprisingly, the ways in which workers build meaningful if fragile relationships also mean that many of these causes of stress (death, crises, worry) are also what make the job feel worthwhile for respondents. Indeed, it is this combination of experiences – the building of meaningful relationships and the modes of responding in a crisis – that seemed to constitute this work as 'care' for the operators:

> Anita: I think to treat it just as a job is treating people like pieces of meat. These are somebody's Mum. You know, it could be my Mum, your Mum. It could be our parents, it could be our children!
>
> Bev: I think all of us go to a lot of extreme lengths to sort things out – we never leave anything – to find things out for people. We all do, don't we?

Although graphically describing the stresses of her job, Joanne also affirmed its value:

> Researcher: [There] are the times when perhaps you lose someone, but other times you can make a difference, can't you?
>
> Joanne: Well yes, they've come back and sent a little card since saying 'Thank you, if you hadn't been so quick in getting help they wouldn't be here today.' ... That's why I like it. You feel like you're doing something needed don't you, in the community?

THE INTER-IMPLICATION OF EMBODIED AND 'DISEMBODIED' CARE

Our observations of monitoring centre work demonstrate that telecare relies on 'old-fashioned' networks of people and embodied practices of caring. It is not enough for the older person to put through a call: there must be someone who can respond quickly. Promoters of telecare would agree and say that this is the key role of the service, and argue that telecare is precisely indicated for people who do not have robust social networks. Our research uncovered something else – operators needed to be able to call the 'contacts' when something was unclear or ambiguous; informal contacts are required for the (frequent) occasions in which the demand is not urgent but none the less pressing (when it is not appropriate to call the police or the ambulance, for example). We learned just how many ambiguities arise when alarms are triggered, and how often it is unclear what is happening in the older person's home. In many such cases, only co-presence will do.

Much critical thinking around telecare, including concerns about it expressed by relevant workers (social workers in particular) in our broader ethnographic study, focuses on the ways in which telecare might (or is seen to) replace other forms of (hands-on) care. We have made a related argument ourselves (Roberts and Mort, 2009). In investigating the practices of monitoring centre workers, however, we are prompted to suggest that rather than care being diminished, it might be better understood as being reshaped. Teleoperators go to significant effort to ensure that older people living at home benefit from accepting telecare technologies into their homes and certainly do undertake care work in relation to their clients. This is of course a substantially different kind of care from that provided, for example, by a home visit or in a day centre, but to characterize it as *not-care* misses too much care work.

Important policy implications arise from this finding: we suggest that telecare services should value and promote the formation of friendly relationships between teleoperators and clients. This could mean, for example, maintaining weekly test calls (which allow for short interactions in non-stressful times) and promoting some personalization of the work (one of the centres we spent time in, for example, sent out a newsletter with photographs of teleoperators to clients, to assist them to 'put a face to a name'). More significantly, our findings about the nature of telecare work hold implications for the recruitment of teleoperators. Most of the workers we met had experience in older people's care and had good local knowledge of the area their clients were living in. They were able to use appropriate language and conversational styles with clients, to understand issues relating to place and thus in many cases to form meaningful relationships. Telecare services, we suggest, would do well to continue employing such workers, rather than moving monitoring work outside local areas or appointing operators who do not have backgrounds in working with older people.

The work undertaken in call centres is often invisible in policy or managerial discussion of telecare: teleoperators themselves, for example, did not attend Northshire's regular 'Telecare Steering Group' meetings, where key decisions were made about the service. While social workers and their lesser paid counterparts (review assessment and support officers) were present, telecare installers and teleoperators were absent (though their managers attended). In this, it seems, teleoperators are positioned as 'mere' technicians who should (rather automatically) deliver a service that has been shaped by more qualified care experts. Our research challenges this understanding of telecare, suggesting that teleoperators (and indeed, installers – see Mort, Roberts and Callén, 2012) play a highly significant role in providing care. This work should, we suggest, be recognized and supported: at a minimum,

telecare operators should be offered more training and be able to access appropriate debriefing after dealing with crises. It is important to note here that during the period of our study, a pay harmonization process within the district council running one of the monitoring centres led to a significant decrease in pay for operators: this work is not well remunerated despite the hard-won skills that are needed. As our Spanish colleagues also discovered in their study of a Catalan homecare service, such skill draws on experience (often figured merely as 'intuition'). As Lopez et al. (2010: 83) insist, 'it must be cautioned that experience and intuition are not acquired individually, eventually becoming internal capabilities. Instead they are practices developed in operators' everyday work.' The knowledge used by operators to provide 'disembodied' care is collaborative and cumulative: 'It takes a lot of time to become acquainted with this practice of caring' (2010: 84).

Contemporary sociology, and particularly work from science and technology studies, highlights the ways in which new information and communication technologies are reshaping the everyday lives of people in developed countries. Older people are no exception here: although often figured as resistant to or unable properly to understand these systems, older people encounter a wide range of such technologies on a daily basis. In response to government policy, many are encouraged to accept telecare systems into their homes, to be monitored and assessed by them, and to learn how to interact with unknown others via them.[8] These are powerful and for some, rather daunting, expectations. The motivation to get involved, however, is often strong: often older people are offered telecare as a 'last ditch' effort to prevent admission to residential care. Sociologically, the push towards telecare could be framed as dehumanization or diminution of care. Here, we have argued instead that telecare involves two rather counterintuitive elements of care: first, those who are supposed 'merely' to triage care services (the teleoperators) provide various forms of care (literally 'hands-off' but not actually disembodied); and second, that high-tech 'care-at-a-distance' is dependent on and inextricably bound up with hands-on body work. Technological care can also be intimate (Mort and Smith, 2009). Telecare thus highlights the complexity of contemporary care scenarios. It shows *both* that systems involving sensors and alarms can, because they are 'done' by people on the end of phone lines, involve caring practices, *and* that such systems are not an adequate substitute for social networks around individuals: the latter remain highly significant in providing quality of life and safety for older people living at home.

What this means for sociological research on care work, we suggest in agreement with our colleagues, is that 'Instead of casting care and technology in contrast with each other, we [need] ... to rethink and reframe them together' (Mol et al., 2010: 15). This suggestion adds something significant to Halford and Strangleman's (2009) call to reinvigorate the sociology of work: whilst we agree that interdisciplinary collaboration will enhance this broad project, we would also emphasize the importance of analysing technologies in their dynamic relations with human and non-human actors and social arrangements and practices. Science and technology studies has much to offer in this regard, both methodologically and theoretically, and is a resource that could be much more deeply drawn upon in researching work.

ACKNOWLEDGEMENTS

This work was funded by the European Commission under the FP7 'Science in Society' programme. The study is entitled 'Ethical Frameworks for Telecare Technologies' (Project no: 217787). We would like to acknowledge the work of all of our colleagues on this project: their intellectual contributions to this work are inestimable. We would also like to thank Josephine Baxter for her contributions, both practical and intellectual.

NOTES

1 There are of course other forms of 'care at a distance', including the work undertaken by families to arrange and coordinate proximate care (see Milligan and Wiles, 2010: 740–2).
2 We ran 22 citizens' panels in total: eight in England, four in Spain, five in the Netherlands and five in Norway.
3 Approval was granted under Northshire County Council's Research Governance Framework, and all researchers obtained Criminal Record Bureau clearance. Information about the research was widely disseminated amongst relevant actors, and team members became familiar faces at Northshire Telecare Steering Group meetings. We met with workers at all levels of the service to explain our work. When workers and older people participated in recorded interviews they read project information sheets and signed consent forms. It was not practical to request consent from clients during a call (which, as explained below, are often times of great confusion) and it was impossible to predict who would call on any particular day. Thus we do not report here on what was said by clients during calls.
4 http://www.lancs.ac.uk/efortt/
5 Of most relevance here is our Spanish colleagues' analysis of a Catalan Home Care Service (Lopez et al., 2010), which, although making a different argument about safety and security, reports very similar findings about the work of telecare operators.
6 This reference to the older person being 'like a child' indicates a potentially paternalistic power relationship between this teleoperator and her clients. While apparently well-meaning, this kind of figuration of the older person is out of touch with contemporary approaches to caring for older people and is indicative of the low levels of training undertaken by telecare operators. Most operators undergo a brief training period and then 'learn on the job'. As described in more detail below, this produces dependence on co-workers and, for some, high levels of anxiety when first working at night, when they can be alone in the monitoring centre.
7 Wardens are responsible for looking after older people living in sheltered accommodation. During the day alarms from community alarm systems go through to their phones rather than to the monitoring centre. When they end their shifts they contact the monitoring centre to pass over responsibility for monitoring the clients' alarms.
8 For an analysis of how older people are subject to government policy more broadly in terms of 'better aging' see Pickard, 2009.

REFERENCES

Angus, J., Kontos, P., Dyck, I., McKeever, P. and Poland, B. (2005) The personal significance of home: habitus and the experience of receiving long-term home care. *Sociology of Health and Illness* 27(2): 161–87.

Audit Commission (2004) *Implementing Telecare*. London: Audit Commission.

BBC *Panorama* (2009) Britain's Homecare Scandal, 9 April.

Deery, S., Iverson, R. and Walsh, J. (2002) Work relationships in telephone call centres: understanding emotional exhaustion and employee withdrawal. *Journal of Management Studies* 39(4): 471–96.

Department of Health (2005) *Building Telecare in England*. London: Department of Health.

EFORTT Project Team (2009) *Work Package 4 Report: The Data Clinic*. Available at: http://www.lancs.ac.uk/efortt/work%20packages.html

England, K. and Dyck, I. (2011) Managing the body work of home care. *Sociology of Health & Illness* 33: 206–19.

Grebner, S., Semmer, N., Lo Faso, L., Gut, S., Kälin, W. and Elfering, A. (2003) Working conditions, wellbeing and job-related attitudes among call centre agents. *European Journal of Work and Organizational Psychology* 12(4): 341–65.

Halford, S. and Strangleman, T. (2009) In search of the sociology of work: past, present and future. *Sociology* 43(5): 811–28.

Hochschild, A.R. (2003) Love and gold. In: Ehrenreich, B. and Hochschild, A.R. (eds) *Global Woman: Nannies, Maids and Sex Workers in the New Economy*. London: Granta Books, 15–30.

Korczynski, M. (2003) Communities of coping: collective emotional labour in service work. *Organisation* 10(1): 55–79.

Korczynski, M. (2009) The mystery customer: continuing absences in the sociology of service work. *Sociology* 43(5): 952–7.

Lee-Trewick, G. (1996) Emotion Work, Order and Emotional Power in Care Assistant Work, in V. James and J. Gabe (eds) *Health and the Sociology of Emotions,* Oxford: Blackwell

Lopez, D., Callen, B., Tirado, F. and Domenech, M. (2010) How to become a guardian angel: providing safety in a home telecare service. In: Mol, A., Moser, I. and Pols, J. (eds) *Care in Practice: On Tinkering in Clinics, Homes and Farms*. Bielefeld: Transcript, 73–91.

Lyon, D. and Glucksmann, M. (2008) Comparative configurations of care work. *Sociology* 42(1): 101–18.

Milligan, C. (2009) *There's No Place like Home: People, Place and Care in an Ageing Society*. Aldershot: Ashgate.

Milligan, C., Mort, M. and Roberts, C. (2010) Cracks in the door? Technology and the shifting topology of

care. In: Schillmeier, M. and Domenech, M. (eds) *New Technologies and Emerging Spaces of Care*. Farnham: Ashgate.

Milligan, C., Roberts, C. and Mort, M. (2011) Telecare and older people: who cares where? *Social Science and Medicine* 72(3): 347–54.

Milligan, C. and Wiles, J. (2010) Landscapes of care. *Progess in Human Geography* 34(6): 736–54.

Mol, A., Mose,r I. and Pols, J. (2010) Care: putting practice into theory. In: Mol, A., Moser, I. and Pols, J. (eds) *Care in Practice: On Tinkering in Clinics, Homes and Farms*. Bielefeld: Transcript, 7–25.

Mort, M., Roberts, C. and Callén, B. (2012) Aging with telecare: care or coercion in austerity? *Sociology of Health and Illness*, Early view DOI: 10.1111/j.1467-9566.2012.01530.x

Mort, M. and Smith, A. (2009) Beyond information: Intimate relations in sociotechnical practice. *Sociology* 43(2): 215–31.

Mulholland, K. (2002) Gender, emotional labour and teamworking in a call centre. *Personnel Review* 31(3): 283–303.

Pickard, S. (2009) Governing old age: the 'case-managed' older person. *Sociology* 43(1): 67–84.

Pols, J. and Moser, I. (2009) Cold technologies versus warm care: on affective and social relations with and through care technologies. *Alter: European Journal of Disability Research* 3(2): 159–78.

Roberts, C. and Mort, M. (2009) Reshaping what counts as care: older people, work and new technologies. *ALTER: European Journal of Disability Research* 3(2): 138–58.

Simmonds, W. (2002) Watching the clock: keeping time during pregnancy, birth, and postpartum experiences. *Social Science & Medicine* 55 (4): 559–570

Twigg, J., Wolkowitz, C., Cohen, R.L. and Nettleton, S. (2011) Conceptualising body work in health and social care. *Sociology of Health and Illness* 33(2): 171–88.

Wibberley, G. (2011) The invisibility and complexity of domiciliary carers' work, around, in and out of their labour process. Unpublished PhD thesis, Lancaster University.

Willems, D. (2010) Varieties of goodness in high-tech home care. In: Mol, A., Moser, I. and Pols, J. (eds) *Care in Practice: On Tinkering in Clinics, Homes and Farms*. Bielefeld: Transcript Verlag. pp 257–75.

10

Aging, Work and the Demographic Dividend in South Asia

Penny Vera-Sanso

South Asia is experiencing demographic change generated by declining fertility, reduced mortality and lengthening life expectancy.[1] The outcome is a rapidly shifting population structure with a narrowing base, a youth bulge, an accelerating increase in the older population, especially in the oldest old, and an increasing feminisation of old age, again, especially in the oldest old.[2] This is happening in the context of low productivity in the two sectors of the economy in which the largest number of people are employed, the agricultural and informal sectors; for the vast majority of people neither sector allows for income smoothing over the life course through savings. Further, societal aging is happening in the context of political economies that provide no, or negligible, social pensions.

Much current interest in South Asia's population structure focuses on the 'working generation', usually defined as 15–59 years or 15–64 years, and particularly on the 'youth' who could potentially deliver a 'demographic dividend', thereby solving the conundrum of population aging in developing economies.[3] In contrast to this idea and the related one underlying a wide range of development strategies, that reductions of poverty at younger ages will have a meaningful impact on poverty in old age, this chapter will demonstrate, first, that older people's paid and unpaid work is needed to realise the demographic dividend, second, that older people already play an important role in reducing family poverty and sustaining national economies and, third, that *only* age-specific policies can address poverty in old age. To do this the chapter will describe the demography, labour market, and intergenerational relations in a number of South Asian countries, using analyses largely based on national survey data and my own ethnographic research conducted over the past two decades in urban and rural Tamil Nadu, India.

DEMOGRAPHIC STRUCTURE

The demographic picture across South Asia is varied. The most recent comparative demographic source is the UN population projections, 2010 revision. According to the trends identified by the UN, Sri Lanka reached replacement level fertility in 2000 and reached a life expectancy at birth of over 74 years by 2010 (see Table 10.1 below).[4] At the other extreme Pakistan will continue to have a high fertility rate until after 2040 and had a life expectancy of about 64 years at birth in 2010. Replacement level fertility will be achieved in Bangladesh shortly after 2010, in India in 2020 and Nepal will achieve replacement level fertility shortly after 2025. India is the country with the lowest overall life expectancy, particularly for men – reflecting the wide regional disparities within India's experience of demographic change. In South Asia if someone reaches the age of 60 they can expect a further 16–22 years of life.

Table 10.1 demonstrates that in all countries women's life expectancy is greater than men's and that at age 60 it is either greater than or equal to men's life expectancy. The life expectancy at age 60 bunches around 17 to 18 years for all countries barring India which has the lowest male life expectancy of 16 years and Sri Lanka which has the highest male life expectancy of 19 and a female life expectancy of 22 years which is significantly higher than any other life expectancy in South Asia. In other words men in India who

reach 60 will on average live to age 76 while women who reach 60 in Sri Lanka will on average live to age 82. Table 10.2, when combined with Table 10.1, demonstrates both women's greater life expectancy and their greater longevity in South Asia, especially in Nepal and Sri Lanka. The male domination of the sex ratio that we are aware of in terms of the phenomenon known as 'missing females' (Sen, 1990; Croll, 2001) reflects anti-female practices in early life. By age 60 in all countries except Pakistan the sex ratio is very definitely in women's favour, especially in Nepal and Sri Lanka, and the decline in male numbers dwindles further in the over 80 age band; resulting in what might be called 'missing men'.[5] In other words women dominate the 60+ age band in most South Asian countries, a significant proportion of whom will be widows. Further, their dominance deepens in the 80+ band, which is also the fastest growing of all age bands projections for India, for example, suggest that by 2051 the 80 and above age bands will be four times its 2001 size (Tyagi 2010).

While at the upper age bands people are living longer and their absolute numbers are significant and rapidly increasing, their proportion in the population is currently comparatively small because of the youth bulge. Table 10.3 sets out the projected acceleration of the growth of the over 60 population between 2010 and 2050. The UN World Population Prospects, 2008 revision, which vary slightly from the 2010 revision

Table 10.1 Life expectancy at birth and at age 60[1]

	Years of life expectancy at birth (2005–10)		Years of life expectancy at age 60 (2010–15)	
Country	Male	Female	Male	Female
Bangladesh	67.4	68.3	18	18
India	62.8	65.7	16	18
Nepal	66.7	68	17	18
Pakistan	63.8	65.4	17	18
Sri Lanka	71.2	77.4	19	22

Source: *World Population Prospects: the 2010 revision* (United Nations, 2011)

1 National figures can hide significant variations within countries, especially the larger ones, such as India, where fertility and mortality rates vary considerably between states.

Table 10.2   Sex ratio at birth, age 60: men to 100 women

Country	Total sex ratio (year 2005–10)	Sex ratio in 60+ age group (year 2011)
Bangladesh	105	96
India	108	92
Nepal	105	81
Pakistan	105	106
Sri Lanka	104	85

Source: World Population Prospects: the 2010 revision (United Nations, 2011)

Table 10.3   Percentage of age 60+ in the population

Country	2010 %	2050 %
Bangladesh	6.7	22.2
India	7.8	19.1
Nepal	6.4	16.9
Pakistan	6.4	15.8
Sri Lanka	12.6	27.4

Source: World Population Prospects: the 2010 revision (United Nations, 2011)

Table 10.4   Percentage of age 15–59 in the population

Country	2011 %	2050 %
Bangladesh	62.7	61.8
India	62.0	61.9
Nepal	58.2	63.6
Pakistan	58.6	64.0
Sri Lanka	62.5	55.0

Source: World Population Prospects: the 2010 revision (United Nations, 2011)

figures set out above, suggests that as the youth bulge ages the 60+ population in South Asia will broadly grow by 50% between 2010 and 2025 and then double between 2025 and 2050. A comparison of what is known as the 'working age' band of 15–59 for 2011 and 2050 in Table 10.4 demonstrates that the youth bulge will continue to be expanding the 'working age' population in Nepal and Pakistan but by 2050 will have swelled the 60+ age band in Sri Lanka. The Bangladesh and Indian cases are the most interesting; while the proportion of children decline and that of 60+ increase, the proportion of people aged 15–59 remain more or less the same. The classification of 15–59 as the working age band is more wishful thinking than empirically correct, as this chapter will demonstrate. What is happening then, is an aging of the workforce as the numbers of potential child workers drop and the number of people aged 60+ increases.

Taken together with the trends on male to female ratios, we can see that South Asia is aging at an accelerating pace, that life expectancy is rising and those that reach 60 years can expect to live to 79–82, that women dominate the upper end of the age spectrum, that the 80+ age band is growing the fastest and that the population structure is shifting from early to later years.

LABOUR MARKETS, YOUTH BULGE AND REALISING THE DEMOGRAPHIC DIVIDEND

The demographic dividend hypothesis starts with the assumption that workers, or at least productive workers, are to be found in the 'working age' population (15–59 or 15–64) and that economic development relies on raising the country's per capita productivity. This requires a larger and more educated workforce, expansion of employment and higher levels of savings for old age and investment in the economy (Bloom, Canning and Sevilla, 2001). The hypothesis is that when the 'working age' population reaches 65% the demographic window opens for rapid economic expansion and will then close when that percentage falls as the population continues to age. From this perspective the middle of the century will be the period when most South Asian countries will have the potential to reap the demographic dividend. Sri Lanka, having started the demographic transition earliest, will fall out of the window of opportunity by 2025, prior to Pakistan entering it after 2030. India as a whole, would have a longer window, from 2011 to 2061, but the demographic benefit would be small (by comparison with China and East Asia) because of the variation in demographic transition across India's states. The states of Kerala and Tamil Nadu had already reached the 65% mark in 2001 while Bihar, Rajasthan and Uttar Pradesh, being amongst the last to reach 65%, will have a shorter duration of dividend potential (Kulkarni, 2010).

Converting the youth bulge from a demographic product of fertility and mortality decline into a demographic dividend relies on policies that will realise the potentials of a proportionately large 'working age' population. Policies to expand employment, increase productivity, raise human capital and draw women into the labour force are seen as critical (World Bank, 2008); others also argue for facilitating older people's labour force participation (Arunatilake, 2010). While increasing the size of the workforce would increase the per capita productivity by reducing the worker:dependent ratio, that is not the same as increasing each worker's productivity.

The reality is that South Asian countries rely heavily on agriculture for employment and the overwhelming majority of working people are engaged in informal employment (Nayar et al, 2012). Agricultural employment accounts for 31%–73% of all employment in the region and informal employment for between 71% and 95% (see Table 10.5). Neither agriculture nor the informal economy are noted for a capacity to raise worker productivity while expanding employment. Rather their *modus operandi* is the shedding and take up of workers in rapid response to short-term demand. What is more, the trend is towards informalisation of work, short-term contracts and the maintenance of low wages in the state and private sectors and the erosion of labour rights in order to attract foreign investment. Many people working in the formal private and state sectors as well as those within the contracted out/privatised state sector are now employed as casual workers with significant impact on their earnings and

livelihood security in the short and long term. In India, for example, casual workers earn 45% less than regular employees (International Labour Organisation, 2008: 115) while wages for urban casual work in Bangladesh and India is no better than for casual agricultural work (Nayar et al, 2012: 102) demonstrating that for the vast majority of the South Asian population urbanisation does not necessarily improve incomes.[6] In rural areas there are wage differentials: non-farm work commands a higher wage than agricultural work.

Investment in services and manufacturing divides, in descending order, between strategies that rely on cheap, low-productivity labour or higher-productivity labour on short-term contracts and highly capital-intensive production systems, such as car manufacturers' reliance on robots. In places there has been some success in raising productivity by exploiting the declining working age population in developed countries through technology intensive and labour absorbing services, such as the high-profile Indian IT and IT-enabled-services (ITES) sectors. However, these two sectors employ less than 1% of the population in India, are geographically concentrated, rely on short-term contracts and have proven vulnerable to the contraction of the global economy. They would not be able to produce a demographic dividend, within the demographic time-frame, through increased worker productivity alone.

An enlarging labour force will increase competition for work and lower wages and, while it is unlikely to reduce chronic poverty and may even deepen it, a larger workforce could expand national economies; with the result that without redistributive policies, the demographic dividend is likely to increase poverty and inequality. The evidence in South Asia indicates a disconnect between GDP growth and poverty reduction or inequality outcomes (Papola, 2010). The largest challenge for poverty reduction is 'working poverty', particularly, but not exclusively the income differentials between the formal and informal economies and their reflection in consumption inequities (Alam, 2010; Papola, 2010) and the vulnerability of the informal

Table 10.5   Employment

Country	Informal employment (all sectors) %	Agricultural employment %
Bangladesh	87	39
India	86	50
Nepal	95	73
Pakistan	89	43
Sri Lanka	71	31

Source: Nayar et al (2012), informal employment: Figure 3.11; agricultural employment: Table 3.4[1]

1 The data is based on national evidence and their collection varies: the agriculture employment data was collected between 2008 (Nepal and Sri Lanka) and 2010 (India) and the informal employment was collected between 2005 (Bangladesh) and 2010 (India).

economy to changes in the global and local economy (Unni, 2001). The western financial crisis of late 2008–9 and subsequent recovery in India demonstrates the way economies reliant on a large informal economy rapidly shed labour in a downturn. By December 2008 the downturn in a number of Indian industries created further pressure on employment and incomes throughout the economy. The burden of job losses in the informal economy was six times greater than in the formal (Government of India, 2009), yet the recovery was concentrated in the small graduate-employing ITS/BOP sectors (Government of India, 2011).

Increasing per capita productivity could be achieved by drawing more people into the workforce and a number of policy initiatives are in place to encourage such (most ubiquitous being microfinance). Increasing the size of the workforce will not of itself result in an expansion of decent work, including higher incomes, security of work and adequate savings for old age; nor will it increase worker productivity. Whether growth through an enlarged workforce, that is a demographic dividend, is realised or not, redistributive policies are needed to counteract the income effects of extensive and expanding informality and, as will be seen below, of age discrimination in the labour market.

AGE- AND-GENDER-SEGMENTED LABOUR MARKET

There are clear continuities in the patterns of labour force participation (LFP) of all age groups across South Asia that reveal the role poverty and the lack of pensions have in older people's LFP.[7] Here I demonstrate the age- and-sex-segmented nature of the labour market in South Asia as well as the complementarity between men's and women's work roles.

There is a declining share of younger workers (in the 15–24 age band) in all South Asian countries (Islam, 2010; Rahman, 2010; Durr-e-Nayab, 2010) and a rising number of workers in the 25–54 age bands in all countries (Islam, 2010). Between 1980 and 2006 in the age band of 55+ the number of men working went down in all countries whereas women's participation went up in India, Pakistan and Sri Lanka but not in Bangladesh where older women's participation went down (Islam, 2010; World Bank, 2008). However, this drop in older women's work in Bangladesh may be more of a function of what is being classified as work. Sixty-three per cent of all workers in Bangladesh, irrespective of age, are engaged in self-employment or unpaid family employment; the latter was the only growing employment status in Bangladesh between 1996 and 2006, and accounts for 34% of older women's work (Rahman, 2010). Qualitative evidence suggests that older women's unpaid work in family businesses may be under-enumerated due to families characterising such work as 'helping out' or 'passing time' rather than working (Vera-Sanso, 2012)[8]

The declining male LFP and increasing female LFP in the older age bands reflects the tendency for South Asian women to join the labour force later in life in order to subsidise or replace male incomes especially in the face of age discrimination and male morbidity and mortality. Even so older working men tend to out-number older working women by 2:1. For example, in Pakistan, male employment is nearly full between the ages of 25–49, the peak being reached between 30–34 years (Durr-e-Nayab, 2010). Women's LFP rate is generally half that of men's, never going beyond 54%, and peaking, at age 40–44, ten years later than men, which is shortly before men start leaving the labour force in greater numbers. Between 1980 and 2006 older women's LFP rate rose by 50% in Pakistan (from 12% to 19%) but this would not have compensated for the decline from 60% to 47% in older men's LFP rate; Durr-e-Nayab (2010) finds Pakistani women are entering the labour force to compensate for male unemployment due to the youth bulge and 38% of elderly women are unable to find employment.

There are, however, variations from this general pattern. For instance, Nepal's rate of older men and women's employment is very high at age 60–64. According to the 2001 Census, in Nepal 82% of men aged 60–64 work and 60% are still working aged over 65. Unusually the percentage of women aged 60–64 working, at 78%, was very close to the men's rate but declined to 34% for those 65 and over (Shrestha, 2010). In Sri Lanka, where 50% of men aged 60–69 work as do 20% in the age group over 70, the percentage of older men working is lower than the percentage in India, Bangladesh and Pakistan. Yet Sri Lanka's older women's LFP rate is similar to that of India and Pakistan. In Sri Lanka only 14% of women aged 60–69 worked and 3% of women aged over 70 worked (World Bank, 2008). While the Sri Lankan pattern reflects the common higher LFP of men, it is not common for men to leave the workforce a decade later than women, that is at age 60–69. Arunatilake (2010) attributes the working age pattern to the shortage of part-time work for older people.[9] Older people either retired overnight, when they reached 60, or continued to work between 36 hours (part-time) and 48 hours (full-time) per week until they were forced out of work by ill-health.

Older men and women are concentrated in the lower reaches of the labour market and there are clear gender divisions in older people's work. Most older people are located in rural areas and do the lowest paid work, that is agricultural work, as there is less opportunity for alternatives. Older women living in rural areas are more likely to work than those living in urban areas. In urban areas older men are most likely to be in semi-skilled and unskilled work and older women in unskilled work. Not only do older people face age-discrimination in urban and rural labour markets but the sex-segregated nature of work further limits older people's capacity to find age-appropriate work. For instance, in Bangladesh over 70% of men aged 55+ are self-employed, while over 70% of women aged 55+ are more or less evenly split between self-employment and non-salaried household employment. Of the remainder, women are more likely to be employed on an irregular/casual basis than are men (Rahman, 2010). This contrasts with 15–59 age groups which have a higher share of regular and casual employment. Older people are less able to access regular or casual waged work and must either create their own economic niche or, as in the case of women, support someone else's work through their unpaid labour. Access to waged work is not the only issue. Wages decline with age, so the older workforce suffer less disadvantage in the case of self-employment and it allows lower hours of employment for the upper age brackets (Rahman, 2010).[10]

There is currently little evidence of the impact of age discrimination on income differentials as most analyses are framed by the assumption that older people do not or should not work. What evidence there is suggests that wage differentials for older people are likely to be widespread. In India a survey of wage differentials in the registered slums of four Indian cities in 2006–7 found that people under the age of 25 and over the age of 59 receive markedly lower average incomes than do people in the age band 25–59 (Ghosh et al., 2010). A similar pattern is also to be found in Sri Lanka where people aged over 60 are paid much less than younger people, though the decline starts at age 50 for women in the private sector, (Arunatilake, 2010). Qualitative research I undertook in the South Indian state of Tamil Nadu in 2000 found that while in formal terms older men and women did not earn less than the casual day rates of younger people, farmers' unwillingness to employ older workers outside the high season's labour bottlenecks made the latter vulnerable to masked wage cuts. In the low season older workers would follow younger ones who had been called to a field for casual work and beg the farmer to hire them. At the end of the day they might be given two-thirds of the wage and asked to return the next morning for the remainder; leaving them to weigh up whether they would do better to forego the shortfall and seek more casual work or vice versa.

In Sri Lanka 50% of older workers are self-employed (this rises to 90% of the workers aged 80) and 43% of workers over 60 are casual workers, leaving 2% who are regular employees and 5% who are employers (Arunatilake, 2010). Evidence from Sri Lanka demonstrates the importance of self-employment as an old age safety-net in the absence of any, or adequate, state provision. Not only are the majority of older workers self-employed and this proportion rises with age, reflecting the well-known difficulties of securing and sustaining casual work with increasing ill-health and frailty, but most had been regular employees in the informal economy. In Sri Lanka informal workers do not have pensions and continue to work past their 70th birthday, retiring due to ill-health, while formal sector workers retire overnight at around 60 years (Arunatilake, 2010). The World Bank's (2008) and Arunatilake's (2010) data on working hours demonstrates that even though self-employment does provide flexibility in terms of hours, the 'active' elderly work long hours: for men 47 hours per week in their early sixties dropping to 36 hours in the 72–75 age band, and for women dropping from 35 to 29 hours respectively. The need for most older people to earn at least some money is further demonstrated by the fact that the 'average' hours of

self-employment for men aged 72–75 is 10 hours and for women is 2 hours (World Bank 2008). This life-course work pattern is a broadly familiar one for India, where men and, especially, women are more commonly in the informal economy and more likely to resort to self-employment as compared to younger people or, as shall be demonstrated below, to work as unpaid helpers supporting younger people's self-employment.[11]

In an already crowded informal economy, swollen by the influx of formal sector workers at retirement and by the processes of privatisation and sub-contracting of formal and public sector work, urban and rural labour markets are not age-friendly. Older people find it difficult to secure an adequate quantum of casual work or equal wages for such. Many turn to self-employment and work in family business and can work extremely long hours; though there is greater opportunity in self-employment to tailor the intensity and length of work to physical capacity and income needs than in waged work. Older men are reported everywhere as having a higher labour force participation rate than women and a greater tendency to self-employment. In part this may reflect gender biases in reporting arising from differential status in relation to assets and other livelihood inputs as well as women's greater responsibility for domestic work which position men as workers and women as dependants. Even so, it is clear that women are entering the labour force later than men and are doing so to off-set the effects of age discrimination in employment and incomes.

INTERGENERATIONAL RELATIONS

Intergenerational relations can be analysed at two levels: the societal and the familial. In South Asia care and support of the old is firmly placed on the shoulders of 'the family'. Politicians', journalists' and academics' unremitting iteration of the responsibilities of children (sons especially), of 'traditional values' and of blaming the 'breakdown of family' and 'loss of tradition' on a range of causes from westernisation to filial indifference allows South Asian states to evade responsibility for their older poor. This discourse of a South Asian 'tradition' or culture of support for parents elides the difference between economic, emotional and physical support and misrepresents custom and law on financial support. Sons are obliged to support their parents only *if* and *when* parents are no longer able to support themselves, to the *extent* that parents need it and to the *extent* that sons are able to do so, bearing in mind their primary responsibilities to their wive(s) and children and their joint responsibility with their brothers (Vera-Sanso, 2005). Adding wealth and poverty to the mix means that wealthier parents and those with impoverished sons would or could not expect economic support from their children. Many of the remainder would have struggled with the ambiguities of timing, need and economic capacity that are necessarily embedded in a social norm that must cover a wide range of economic and demographic contexts.[12] Despite misrepresenting 'traditional' values and practices, this public re-defining of tradition creates an aura of legitimacy for a number of legal and policy measures including negligible or no old age provision for the vast majority of older people.[13]

We have already seen that South Asian countries have large and growing informal economies and these are characterised by insecurity, low wages and no pensions, and frequently insufficient surplus income to save for old age. In order to determine the extent to which South Asian states are absolving themselves of a responsibility towards the vast majority of their population we need a comparison with other developing countries (see Table 10.6).[14] Bolivia is a lower middle income country, as is India, Pakistan and Sri Lanka. It provides a universal pension to people aged 60 providing an income of $60 per month at purchasing power parity (PPP) that is 158% of the international poverty line at a cost of 1.06% of GDP that is, 15% of per capita GDP.[15] India's social pension is

means-tested and cash-capped, targeted at the poor aged 60 and over. India's social pension provides an income of $10 per month PPP, representing 33% of the international poverty line and costs 0.04% of GDP or 3% of per capita GDP. The current level of India's national social pension of Rs200 per month was set in November 2007 and has not been raised since for people aged below 80 despite significant inflation, especially in food stuffs. The paucity of the pension's value is clear when we consider that in November 2008 97% of rents in Chennai's slums were significantly over Rs300 per month (Vera-Sanso, 2010). Amongst the 'below poverty line' households that do qualify for a pension most households do not have one pension, rarer still is for households containing more than one older person to have two social pensions. Nepal, a low-income country, manages to provide a universal pension, covering people aged 70 and over; this is one of the most generous pensions in the region, set at $15 PPP, 40% of the international poverty line and costing the country 0.35% of GDP or 14% GDP per capita. Bangladesh, another low-income country manages to provide a means-tested pension for men aged 65+ and women aged 62+ at $10 PPP, 29% of the poverty-line, at the cost of 0.9% of GDP, 7% of GDP per capita. Sri Lanka and Pakistan are both lower middle income countries and provide no social pension at all.

In the context of the paucity of pension support and other safety-nets and the extent of under-nutrition that those living in poverty endure, it is indisputable that older people will need to contribute to the family income as much as they are able.[16] In Pakistan, for instance, older people's monetary contributions, especially those of older men, are vital for keeping the household budget positive; in rural areas nearly half of elderly workers bring in 51–100% of household income (Durr-e-Nayab, 2010). This study also found that the key factor in determining whether older people worked was how many other earners were in the family and the balance

Table 10.6   Non-contributory social pensions

Country	National Income	Pension at PPP p/month	% of international poverty line	Pension age	% of GDP	% of GDP per capita
Bolivia	Lower Middle	$60	158	60	1.06	15
India	Lower Middle	$10	27	60	0.04	3
Pakistan	Lower Middle	0	–	–	–	–
Sri Lanka	Lower Middle	0	–	–	–	–
Bangladesh	Low	$10	26	65/men 62/women	0.9	7
Nepal	Low	$15	40	70	0.35	14

Source: Social Pension Database, HelpAge International, accessed 10 July 2013 (http://www.pension-watch.net/download/50585e09cffca)

between income and expenditure (see also Rahman, 2010 on Bangladesh). Hence, in Pakistan, 30% of older men living in joint/ extended households are working and 45% of elderly women workers in rural households are sole earners while many other older women workers do not work for money but for kind or as unpaid workers.

In addition, my own research in rural and urban South India finds a complex set of arrangements where older women regularly take on the domestic and caring work of younger female relatives, who may or may not live in the same household, in order to enable the younger women to work (Vera-Sanso, 2012). This, as well as income transfers from older people to their younger relatives, demonstrates that family-based intergenerational support by no means inevitably flows up the generations as discourses of old age dependency suggest.

Where society-based intergenerational relations of support are weak and there is widespread poverty it is inevitable that older people will need to work into very late old age and many will work until they die. It is also inevitable that many will be supporting younger relatives in a complex set of exchanges that may include paid and unpaid labour, transfers in money or kind or the underwriting of loans, provision of assets for pawning and so on.

AGING AND WORK IN SOUTH INDIA

This section uncovers the ways in which older people contribute to the economy. Older people are not acknowledged as contributing to the economy, as having rights as workers or as having a right to work. Instead either their work is positioned as inconsequential or marginal or they are positioned as victims of negligent children, poverty or widowhood. This failure to recognise older people as workers runs from the top, where State institutions produce schemes, policies and plans for a growing 'working age' group defined as aged 15–59 to the bottom of society, where older people's labour is devalued and often unpaid. A key strategy in belittling labour is to define the skill as negligible or natural, to define the work as marginal, private, easy, arising from love, a domestic chore, helping out, passing time or as trifling.

To demonstrate the ways in which older people contribute to the economy I draw on two decades of research in the South Indian State of Tamil Nadu. Mixed methods research I undertook in Chennai, the capital of the Tamil Nadu and India's fourth largest metropolis, in 1989, 1990–2 and 2007–10 and for 9 months in two villages in Western Tamil Nadu in 2000.[17] The focus has been the urban and rural poor living in Chennai's slums and the *cheries* of two villages. *Cheries* are the neighbourhoods in which castes once known collectively as Untouchables live. In this case the people were Chakkliyars, the caste considered the lowest caste of all. Research in Chennai's slums was undertaken amongst a variety of slums, some officially notified by the government as slums, hence receiving some infrastructural inputs (public water pumps, street lighting) and 'unnotified slums' which received the most minimal government inputs, if any.[18] Slum residents comprised a mix of the lower end of the caste hierarchy, including a much higher proportion of castes once known as Untouchables than is present in the city's overall population.

The cherie dwellers were concentrated at the lower end of the labour market. Their casual work was characterised by low wages, insecurity, irregularity and scarcity. In the *cheries* most people worked as agricultural labourers who were called for work as local farmers needed them. However, work was on a downward trend as farmers were switching from grains and vegetables to the less labour intensive produce (coconut, teak, banana and chicken rearing) and as young men formed work gangs to undertake piece rate (*mottam*) contracts that excluded all but the most vigorous men (Vera-Sanso, 2007). Some young men were able to off-set some of the low season with road building work during the dry season. With low and irregular incomes it was necessary that everyone who could work did so whenever work was available. By 2000 this no longer included children, most of whom went to school, partly spurred by a free midday meal (which could be their only meal in the low season) and partly by the decline in bondage as landowners preferred the limited contractual relations of casual labour to the on-going ties of bondage.[19] It was only in the peak season that farmers and labour contractors were willing to hire older people. Often the work was organised in such a way that excluded older people – for instance, while older people could dig out onions they could not carry filled sacks to the collection point. Older people reported that they sought work as they could outside the peak season, cajoling or begging landowners and contractors

for work, often having to endure a public shaming in the process (Vera-Sanso, 2007). As work peaks varied from village to village, depending on their water source, older people would stay with sons and daughters and sometimes other relatives hoping to extend their access to work during high labour demand. Couples who were too old to work intensively would alternate rest and work days in the peak season and people, particularly women, who were unable or less likely to secure agricultural work would take up the heavy domestic and childcare roles in order to release a younger woman for agricultural work. As stated earlier, in formal terms older people received the same wages as younger people, though some farmers made older people return the next day for their wages. In a context where incomes are almost entirely spent on food and where under-nutrition is extreme, having to walk 3 km to the field to pick up yesterday's wages undermined the value of a day's work and would significantly impinge on older people's capacity to access work that day.

If we step back from the experience of older people as agricultural workers and look at their contribution to the agricultural economy it is clear that they act as a reserve army of labour, increasing the supply of labour during peak season. We can also see that older people are helping to increase per capita productivity by reducing the worker:consumer ratio; they do this by working themselves and by taking on the unpaid but necessary reproduction of labour work, that is domestic and care work, in order to release a younger women into the workforce. Since the introduction in 2005 of the National Rural Employment Guarantee Scheme (NREGS), that provides for a maximum of 100 days workfare for each household and which is designed to improve agricultural infrastructure, older people have taken up this work where they are allowed to do so by local officials.[20] In directly participating in the agricultural economy as workers and as labourers on the NREGS, or indirectly through their unpaid domestic and caring work, older people are expanding the current agricultural work-force, participating in the improvement of local infrastructure and contributing to the production of future workers. Older people are making these contributions with neither recognition nor effective assistance from the State. While the State of Tamil Nadu, unlike other States, raised its Old Age Pension to Rs1,000 per month, in April 2011, the extreme mismatch between the number entitled to the pension and the number of pensions available meant that the pre-existing social, physical and financial costs in securing a pension remained, thereby forcing the poorest to continue working.

Chennai's slum dwellers are similarly concentrated at the lower end of the urban labour market. In 1989/early 1990s there were a number of slum dwellers working in the State sector as regular employees of the post office, public buses and hospitals and as canteen staff, warehousemen and street sweepers. By early 2008 the numbers of slum dwellers working in the State sector had declined with contracting out and privatisation. In both the early 1990s and the late 2000s most slum dwellers and all older people worked in the informal economy working as casual or regular workers and in self-employment. Additionally, older people worked as unpaid family labour. In both periods men started work shortly before marriage and continued until they were no longer able to or no longer given work, while women started working in their 30s or later to subsidise or replace men's incomes which begin to decline in their 40s (Vera-Sanso, 2010, 2012).

In early 2008 our survey of 800 households in five of Chennai's central and southern slums found that 28% of people aged 60+ and 20% of people aged 70–79 were reported by themselves or their families as working. However, intensive further research with 179 households as well as observations of a central Chennai street market between 2007 and 2010 revealed a significant number of older people playing extensive, unpaid 'helper' roles in a son's or daughter's petty business. Many of these businesses, particularly

in the case of street vending, were effectively someone else's in name only; proven by the closing of the business when the older person was ill or injured and its complete abandonment when they died. A comparison of older people's reported work participation with that of younger people reveals that older people are more likely to be working than are younger people. In early 2008 under 24% of 15–19 year olds were working compared to 28% of people aged over 60. There were twice as many women in the workforce aged 60 and over than women/girls aged under 20 and slightly more men aged 60 and over than men/boys under 20.[21] In fact, the percentage of 15–19 year olds working was close to the percentage of 70 to 74 year olds working. These younger people were either in education or looking for work that they and their families considered appropriate to their education, status and aspirations. This is no coincidence; these work patterns are closely inter-related. The need to contribute to family budgets either to support education objectives directly or indirectly, by freeing families of the need to support older relatives, is one of the most common reasons older women cite for undertaking paid work. Clearly, defining the 'working age population' as 15–59 does not reflect the realities of the labour market and when policies are made on this basis, they are likely to disenfranchise a significant section of the labour force.

Within the five slums older people were engaged in more than 40 occupations, yet this did not exhaust the full range of work that older people could be seen to be doing on the streets of Chennai. Older people are working in every sector of the urban economy. They link the agricultural economy with the urban economy through retailing agricultural produce (vegetables, fruit, coconuts, banana leaves, flowers) which they or others source from the wholesale market and sell in street markets across the city. A number of older people act as wholesalers in central Chennai, buying from the wholesale market outside the city and selling on to retailers from a smaller wholesale market in central Chennai. Others process grains and make snacks and *tiffin* (light meals) for breakfast, lunch and supper for workers and school children. They also sell fish they have sourced from Chennai's fishing boats and have a major role in delivering Aavin milk door to door. Aavin milk is the successful outcome of the huge European Union funded World Food Programme and Government of India collaboration of the 1970s, known as Operation Flood, set up to develop the dairy industry and increase farmer incomes by cutting out the middle man. Older people, mostly women, provide the low-cost interface that links this major international project to the endpoint in the distribution chain, the urban domestic consumer. Older men are engaged in the low-cost end of transportation: pulling cycle rickshaws full of children to and from school or delivering parcels for shopkeepers; others load and unload bullock carts, or pull carts themselves, taking stock from workshop and factory to retailers while others deliver newspapers by cycle. Older people sell small manufactured goods made of paper, plastic, metal and knitted cotton. They provide cleaning and security services to offices, businesses, blocks of flats and middle class homes as well as security at ATM machines and at peri-urban railway stations where they secure commuters' bikes and motorbikes. In construction older men do repairing and replacement work and men and women break bricks to make foundations for building construction and road laying. Older men do a wide range of repair work, on shoes, bicycles, watches, small household equipment and so on. This is by no means an exhaustive list and men and women are distinctively positioned within these occupations; men being more likely to work as casual workers and regular wage workers and women are more likely to work as self-employed, unpaid family workers or regular wage workers.

Older people are filling critical gaps in the labour market created by younger people vacating the most poorly paid, insecure and low-status work. This is reflected in income differentials: this study found the average

monthly income for slum dwellers under 60 is 50% more than the average for slum dwellers over 60 (Harriss-White et al, 2013). Despite being low status the work undertaken by older people is by no means marginal; it is critical to distributing the products of an economic sector, agriculture, that employs 50% of India's population to one of its largest markets, India's fourth largest metropolis, Chennai. They do the same for a number of other industries. Further, they keep production costs down by directly providing low-cost services and materials to a range of sectors or indirectly by providing low-cost services to workers. This contributes to the greater competitiveness of industries operating in the global market place. Further, older women who take on the domestic and caring work of related and unrelated women (either as unpaid domestic duties or as paid domestic work) in order to release a younger woman on to the labour market are helping to expand the workforce, often grounding a chain of women that leads to the export market.[22] In a country that massively under provides to poorer populations the basic infrastructural requirements needed to make the combining of paid work alongside domestic and caring work feasible, it is essential that older women take on the domestic duties of younger women in order to realise a demographic dividend.[23] Or, to put it in more theoretical terms, under the current infrastructural provision the reproduction of the low income labour force on a daily and generational basis cannot be feasibly combined with 'productive' work; new, even lower-cost replacement labour is needed.

The lack of recognition of older people's contribution to the economy prevents the State from protecting or developing the livelihoods of older people. Rather, State schemes to provide work or protection, such as insurance and pensions through occupational Welfare Boards, frequently exclude people over the age of 59. There is also the danger that an expanded social pension might be seen as satisfying the State's responsibilities to older people and may even make older people's work appear to lack legitimacy, further undermining their rights as workers. Not only would this deprive many people of work that they need to do in order to contribute to fragile household budgets or to input into family networks, it could deprive them of the work they *wish* to do because of the independence, status, sense of self-worth and sociality it provides or because they do not want to take on physically demanding domestic work. As one woman who goes from office to office cleaning telephones and computers put it, 'I will always have to work. If I'm not doing this work then I must work at home and I prefer to work out of the house'. Pensions set at a level to cover basic living and housing costs will provide choice; they will allow older people to decide whether and how much work they will do and, most importantly, they will enable older people to reject the most demeaning, onerous and poorly paid work open to them.

CONCLUSIONS

The chapter has illustrated the assumptions and blindspots that the demographic dividend hypothesis carries. These include the assumption that only 'working age populations' (aged 15–59) make a significant contribution to the economy, that the production and maintenance of workers through domestic and caring work can be treated as external to the economy, that workers are not linked in a chain of labour that distributes the label and rewards of 'worker' status unequally across age groups and that increasing the worker:consumer ratio will necessarily increase economic growth and wealth rather than deepen inequality by lowering incomes through increased competition. Clearly redistributive policies will be critical to counteract the negative impacts of an enlarging workforce on inequality, especially inequalities between classes and age bands.

At present there is very little research available on older people's work in developing countries and this chapter on South Asia has been made feasible by a regional conference held in Delhi in 2008 organised by the Institute of Economic Growth, Delhi and since published (Alam and Barrientos, 2010). Several papers at this conference drew on national survey data to disclose whose work is ignored when official summary statistics and analyses discuss the labour force and 'working population'. It is now becoming clear that people working over the age of 59 and into late old age is widespread in South Asia, and is likely to be widespread anywhere else where deep poverty is not countered by adequate safety nets. The mixed methods research undertaken in South India extends our understanding, not just of the under-reporting of older people working and their conditions of work but also the significance of their work. We can now see that older people are not just supporting themselves and their families but are contributing to the wider economic strategy needed to realise the demographic dividend by increasing human capital to raise productivity, joining the workforce and releasing a chain of younger women into the labour market. Some of these younger women go directly into production for the global economy (textiles, pharmaceuticals) but most take on the domestic and caring responsibilities of others in the global economy. An examination of the forward and backward linkages of older people's work in the informal economy and their role in agriculture demonstrates their important but unrecognised role in supporting the national (and hence the global) economy, often taking on the work that younger people have largely vacated. Older people play an essential role in agricultural production; directly, as agricultural labourers of last resort they relieve critical seasonal bottlenecks, and indirectly through their street vending in urban areas, where they are indispensable to the distribution of agricultural produce. Older women provide the interface that links the major international project, Operation Flood, to domestic consumers and it is likely that as further research is undertaken into older people's economic roles more of this interface work will be uncovered. Older people are to be found in the lowest reaches of all sectors of the economy from banking (as security) to the booming construction industry (breaking coal to make bricks and breaking bricks to make rubble for foundations and roads). They keep capital's costs down by providing cheap inputs and by providing cheap services to the working population. They also subsidise capital and the State through their unpaid work in helping to reproduce labour on a day-to-day and generational basis.

Most academic, policy and campaign interest in older people in developing countries focuses on their need for pensions. It would be a great disservice to older people if the discursive space this occupies precludes them from exercising the choice to work if they need and wish to and if it deters pressure towards the realisation and extension of older people's rights to work and as workers. What older people need is a pension that enables them to choose whether and how much work they wish to do and that will allow them to refuse the most onerous, low-paid and menial work that many are now forced to undertake.

NOTES

1   For the purposes of this chapter reference will only be made to Sri Lanka, Pakistan, Nepal, India and Bangladesh.

2   Except for Nepal where the ratio of men to women followed the general pattern until 1981, since when older men outnumber older women (Shrestha, 2010).

3   There is a wide variation in the definition of youth. The UN defines it as 15–24, Nepal starts it from age 10 and India stretches it to age 35 (Atal, 2005).

4   Replacement level fertility depends on local mortality rates, so the global replacement level fertility of 2.33 is used here, rather than the standard used for developed countries of 2.1.

5   The significance in this reversal becomes striking when we consider that the total sex ratio is an *average* that includes an early life sex ratio strongly dominated by males and a later life sex ratio strongly dominated by females.

6   In Nepal and Pakistan wages for urban casual work is only 20–30% higher than for casual agricultural work (Nayar et al, 2012: 102).

7   Studies of older people generally take the age of either 60 or 65 as denoting older people or 'elders' and a few use the age of 55 or more. Older people frequently do not know their age so exactitude regarding age is unachievable. More relevant than concerns about comparability and determining what threshold to use is understanding that people who rely on selling their manual labour tend to underestimate factors that would reduce their standing in the labour market, such as their age or their able-bodied-ness (Erb and Harriss-White, 2002). It may be that age levels are often higher in the 55–69 age band than declared.

8   In 2004–5, for the first time the Government of India (NSS, 2007) attempted to tackle the underenumeration of female economic activities. 'Women' (defined as aged over 5) who are normally classified as 'usually engaged in domestic duties' were asked if they engage in a limited range of other economic activities from which their households benefit. This raised the reported female work participation rate in rural areas from 37% to over 53% and the urban rate from 18% to 23%.

9   It might also reflect the heavy domestic burden that those living in poverty have to carry or a lower availability of regular work for middle aged and older women.

10   See also Vera-Sanso (2010) and Harriss-White et al (2013).

11   In India the share of older people in self-employment is about 50% higher than the 15–59 year age band and this employment status has been growing (from 76% in 1983 to 82% in 2004–5) while casual labour and regular employment have declined (Rajan, 2010). By contrast the 'working age' population are more likely to be involved in casual labour or regular employment.

12   See India's recent summarising of custom and law in one act, The Maintenance and Welfare of Parents and Senior Citizens Act 2007. See Shah (1996) on the 'traditional' joint households as having increased in India since 1820 except for a particularly vocal urban, educated, professional class that is driving the 'loss of tradition' discourse.

13   Since May 2012 a widespread and high profile campaign, the Pension Parishad, is now positioning the State as duty bearers of citizen's rights to life and dignity in old age – this is a radical revisioning of the Indian State's role which had been seen as no more than forcing children to support parents and providing small charitable contributions to a portion of older people living below the poverty line.

14   See HelpAge International's Pension Watch (http://www.pension-watch.net/) for globally comparative data on old age pensions. Data for this chapter was taken from the 7 July 2012 revisions.

15   The international poverty line is $1.25 a day at purchasing power parity.

16   Direct figures on adult under-nutrition are not readily available but nutritional poverty levels can be discerned through infant nutrition and birth-weights, especially at term. The percentage of children under 5 in South Asia suffering from under-nutrition is 42% (15% are severely undernourished) and 48% are stunted, based on figures for 2003–9 (UNICEF, 2011). One-third of India's children are born each year with low-birth weights, accounting for

26% of the global total; the majority of these children are born at term (Paul et al., 2011).

17 For the 1990–2 research I was ably assisted by Marlia Hussain and in 2000 by Radha Viswanathan. The 2007–10 research project was undertaken in collaboration with V. Suresh, Marlia Hussain, Henry Joe and Arul George from the Centre for Law, Policy and Human Rights, Chennai. I am grateful to a number of generous funders including the University of London for their funding of the 1989–92 research (Central Research Fund and University Postgraduate Studentship) and the Arts and Humanities Research Council, Biotechnology and Biological Sciences Research Council, Engineering and Physical Sciences Research Council, Economic and Social Research Council and Medical Research Council for funding the 2007–10 research project (RES-352-25-0027) through The New Dynamics of Ageing Programme.

18 In India 'slum' is both a technical and legal term and people living in what is classed as 'notified slums', notified by state and local government as slums, had greater legal protection and greater access to state resources than those that have not been notified. The municipal government, the Corporation of Chennai, first notified 1,202 slums in 1971 and added 17 more slums in 1985. The failure to notify more slums is one of the foci of Chennai slum dweller associations' current campaigns.

19 There were divergent opinions in the *cheries* about the value of bondage (Vera-Sanso, 2007).

20 Implementation of the NREGS varies from village to village and in some no people over 60 are allowed to participate and in others they are. In some they receive equal wages and in some they do not. Similarly the effectiveness of NREGS for improving agricultural infrastructure varies from village to village. In 2009 NREGS was renamed the Mahatma Gandhi National Rural Employment Guarantee Scheme.

21 There was a gender difference between males and female working under the age of 20; males were more likely to be in apprenticeships and females were more likely to be 'earning more than learning'. No children under the age of 10 worked and only 2% of children between the ages of 11–14 were working.

22 In the slums older women frequently take on the work of daughters or daughters-in-law who either work directly in export production themselves or who work as cleaners for people who work in export or IT/BOP.

23 This lack of infrastructure ranges from insufficient or total lack of drainage, water and electricity, morning announcements of school closures and under-supply of medical care to no nursing and food in public hospitals. The paucity of basic infrastructure for slum dwellers reproduces poverty and deepens inequality.

REFERENCES

Alam, M. (2010) 'Demographic ageing, consumption poverty and later life health: an exploration of South Asian nations with special reference to India', in Alam, M. and A. Barrientos (eds) *Demographics, Employment and Old Age Security: Emerging Trends and Challenges in South Asia*, Macmillan, Delhi.

Alam, M. and A. Barrientos (eds) (2010) *Demographics, Employment and Old Age Security: Emerging Trends and Challenges in South Asia*, Macmillan, Delhi.

Arunatilake, N. (2010) 'The labour market institutions, ageing and elderly welfare in Sri Lanka', in Alam, M. and A. Barrientos (eds) *Demographics, Employment and Old Age Security: Emerging Trends and Challenges in South Asia*, Macmillan, Delhi.

Atal, Y. (2005) 'Youth in Asia: An Overview', in Fahey, S. and F. Gale (eds) *Youth in Transition: The Challenges of Generational Change in Asia*, Proceedings of the 15th Biennial General Conference, Association of Asian Social Science Research Councils, UNESCO, Bangkok, pp. 9–21.

Bloom, D., D. Canning and J. Sevilla (2001) *Economic Growth and Demographic Transition*, National Bureau Economic Research, Working Paper Series, Working Paper 8685, Cambridge, Massachusetts.

Croll, E. (2001) 'Amartya Sen's 100 Million Missing Women', *Oxford Development Studies*, 29(3): 225–244.

Durr-e-Nayab (2010) 'Demographic transition in Pakistan: implications for old age employment and economic security', in Alam, M. and A. Barrientos (eds) *Demographics, Employment and Old Age Security: Emerging Trends and Challenges in South Asia*, Macmillan, Delhi.

Erb, S. and B. Harriss-White (2002) *Outcaste from Social Welfare: Adult Disability, Incapacity and Development in Rural South India*, Books for Change, Bangalore, India.

Ghosh, N., B.N. Goldar and A. Mitra (2010) 'Population ageing and its implications on the labour market: the South Asian experience', in Alam, M. and A. Barrientos (eds) *Demographics, Employment and Old Age Security: Emerging Trends and Challenges in South Asia*, Macmillan, Delhi.

Government of India (2009) *Report on the Effect of Economic Slowdown on Employment in India (October–December 2008)*, Ministry of Labour and Employment, Labour Bureau, Chandigarh.

Government of India (2011) *Report on the Effect of Economic Slowdown on Employment in India (July–September 2011)*, Ministry of Labour and Employment, Labour Bureau, Chandigarh.

Harriss-White, B., W. Olsen, P. Vera-Sanso and V. Suresh (2013) *Multiple shocks and slum household economies in South India*, Economy and Society Special Issue, Corbridge, S. and A. Shah (eds), 42(3): 400–431.

HelpAge International. *Social Pension Database*, http://www.pension-watch.net/download/50585e09cffca (accessed 10 July 2013).

International Labour Organisation (2008) *World of Work Report 2008: Income Inequalities in the Age of Financial Globalisation, ILO*, Geneva.

Islam, R. (2010) 'The role of human resource in sustaining economic growth in South Asia', in Alam, M. and A, Barrientos (eds) *Demographics, Employment and Old Age Security: Emerging Trends and Challenges in South Asia*, Macmillan, Delhi.

Kulkarni, P.M. (2010) 'Demographic changes, opportunities and challenges for India', in Alam, M. and A. Barrientos (eds) *Demographics, Employment and Old Age Security: Emerging Trends and Challenges in South Asia*, Macmillan, Delhi.

Nayar, R., P. Gottret, P. Mitra, G. Betcherman, Y.M. Lee, I. Santos, M. Dahal, and M. Shrestha. (2012) *More and Better Jobs in South Asia*, World Bank, Washington.

NSS (National Sample Survey) (2007) *Participation of Women in Specified Activities along with Domestic Duties, 2004–5, 61st round*, National Sample Survey Organisation, Government of India.

Papola, T.S. (2010) 'Economic growth under globalization: employment and poverty reduction in South Asian countries', in Alam, M. and A. Barrientos (eds) *Demographics, Employment and Old Age Security: Emerging Trends and Challenges in South Asia*, Macmillan, Delhi.

Paul, V.K., H.S. Sachdev, D. Mavalankar, P. Ramachandran, M.J. Sankar, Nita Bhandari, V. Sreenivas, T. Sundararaman, D. Govil, D. Osrin and B. Kirkwood (2011) 'Reproductive health, and child health and nutrition in India: meeting the challenge', *The Lancet*, 377(9762): 35–52.

Rahman, R.I. (2010) 'Labour market response to demographic changes in Bangladesh: a focus on ageing of the labour force', in Alam, M. and A. Barrientos (eds) *Demographics, Employment and Old Age Security: Emerging Trends and Challenges in South Asia*, Macmillan, Delhi.

Rajan, I. (2010) *Demographic Ageing and Employment in India*, ILO Asia-Pacific Working Paper Series, International Labour Organisation, Bangkok.

Sen, A. (1990) 'More than a 100 million women are missing', *The New York Review of Books*, Dec 20, 1999.

Shah, A. (1996) 'Is the joint household disintegrating?', *Economic and Political Weekly*, 31(9):537–542.

Shrestha, D.P. (2010) 'Demographic and socio-economic dimensions of the elderly population in Nepal', in Alam, M. and A. Barrientos (eds) *Demographics, Employment and Old Age Security: Emerging Trends and Challenges in South Asia*, Macmillan, Delhi.

Tyagi, R.P. (2010) 'From a deficit to a surplus: changing female–male ratios in younger and older ages in India – lessons for South Asia', in Alam, M. and A. Barrientos (eds) *Demographics, Employment and Old Age Security: Emerging Trends and Challenges in South Asia*, Macmillan, Delhi.

UNICEF (2011) *The State of the World's Children*, http://www.unicef.org/sowc2011/statistics.php (accessed on 12 August 2012).

United Nations (2009) *World Population Prospects: the 2008 Revision*, United Nations Population Division, United Nations, New York.

United Nations (2011) *World Population Prospects: the 2010 Revision*, United Nations Population Division, United Nations, New York.

Unni, J. (2001) 'Gender and informality in labour market in South Asia', *Economic and Political Weekly*, 36(26): 2360–2377.

Vera-Sanso, P. (2005) 'They don't need it and I can't give it: filial support in South India', in P. Kreager and E. Schroder-Butterfill (eds) *The Elderly Without Children*, Berghahn Press, Oxford, pp.77–105.

Vera-Sanso, P. (2007) 'Increasing consumption, decreasing support: a multi-generational study of family relations among South Indian Chakkliyars', *Contributions to Indian Sociology*, 41 (2): 225–48.

Vera-Sanso, P. (2010) 'Gender and ageing in India: conceptual and policy issues', in Sylvia Chant (ed.) *Elgar International Handbook on Gender and Poverty*, Edward Elgar, Aldershot, pp. 220–25.

Vera-Sanso, P. (2012) 'Gender, poverty and old age livelihoods in urban South India in an era of globalisation', *Oxford Development Studies*, 40:3, pp 324-430

World Bank (2008) *Sri Lanka: Addressing the Needs of an Aging Population*, World Bank, Report No. 43396-LK, Human Development Unit, South Asia Region.

11

Age and Generational Differences in Work Psychology: Facts, Fictions, and Meaningful Work

Paul Fairlie

AGE AND GENERATIONAL DIFFERENCES IN WORK PSYCHOLOGY: FACTS, FICTIONS, AND MEANINGFUL WORK

Currently, over 40 million people in the United States are 65 years of age or older. This number is expected to more than double by 2050 (Jacobsen et al., 2011). Similar trends are expected in many European countries (Lanzieri, 2011). In the following decade, the proportion of adults between 65 and 74 years of age will grow significantly (Vincent & Velkoff, 2010). The labour force will continue to age as a result (Toossi, 2009). Paradoxically, the growing prevalence of older workers also spells massive workforce reductions in the future as a function of retirement, decreasing birth rates, and lower generational replacement. By the end of 2013, the proportion of the US population over age 65 will surpass the proportion under 15 years of age (Vincent & Velkoff, 2010). In Europe, the population

under 15 years of age is projected to decline gradually from 2020 onwards (Carone & Eckefeldt, 2010).

The demographic trends, above, suggest that employers need to understand older workers in order to best leverage the largest proportions of their workforces. However, they also need to understand younger workers in order to prepare and support them for the workplaces that they stand to inherit in much smaller numbers. Two areas of understanding will be essential: 1) what younger and older workers *want* (motives, needs, values), and 2) what they *have*, in terms of perceived work characteristics that may satisfy their motives, needs, and values. A third area of understanding relates to knowing their differences in reported levels of critical employee outcomes (e.g., job satisfaction, organizational commitment, work engagement).

Older workers are important to understand not only because of their increasing proportions in the workforce, but also for the unique benefits that they confer to employers. Older workers have ample skills, experience, corporate memory, and a history of creative problem-solving (Warr, 1996). Older adults also tend to have higher levels of agreeableness and conscientiousness (Anusic et al., 2011; Lucas & Donnellan, 2011), and lower levels of neuroticism (Allemand et al., 2007). Perhaps as a result, older adults have a lower prevalence of anxiety, mood, impulse-control, and substance use disorders (Gum et al., 2009). Older adults also report higher levels of subjective well-being than younger adults (Diener et al., 1999). Subjective well-being includes positive affect, which is associated with lower levels of depression (American Psychiatric Association, 1994), is considered to broaden and build thought and action repertoires (Fredrickson, 2001), and is linked to higher job performance (Wright & Staw, 1999). Thus, older workers are an essential organizational resource as a function of personality and well-being.

The motives, needs, and values of older workers must be understood in order to motivate this age group and leverage their strengths. As a result, organizational researchers have focused a great deal of attention on this subject (Kanfer & Ackerman, 2004; Warr, 2001). If older workers are not properly supported and motivated, the number of retirees per worker could double over the next five decades (OECD, 2006). To highlight this point, older workers report that they are more likely to quit working if they won a lottery (Highhouse et al., 2010). Thus, employers must have policies in place to maximize the motivation and engagement of older workers (Barnes-Farrell and Matthews, 2007).

Age and generational differences in the workplace

The growing interest to understand younger and older workers is reflected in a great deal of internet activity. A conservative Google web search returned nearly 230 million hits on this topic.[1] There has also been a proliferation of popular books on how to manage younger workers (Alsop, 2008; Espinoza

et al., 2010; Marston, 2007; Tulgan, 2009) older workers (Cappelli & Novelli, 2010; Leibold & Voelpel, 2006), and their presumed differences and conflicts (Johnson & Johnson, 2010; Lancaster & Stillman, 2003; Zemke et al., 1999). Yet, many age and generational differences have been challenged as mythical and/or based on hearsay rather than rigourous research (Deal, 2012; Giancola, 2006; Hedge et al., 2006). Predictably, the 'gray literature' on these differences has been rife with contradictory findings.

For example, younger workers are reported to be both more happy and less happy at work, relative to older workers (Mercer, 2011; Net Impact, 2012). Different consulting firms and think tanks have reported different work motives for the same age group or generation (Krywulak & Roberts, 2009; Mercer, 2011; Net Impact, 2012; Towers Perrin, 2009). Some of the gray literature findings are at odds with peer-reviewed research. For example, educational institutions (Levit & Licina, 2011) and private research organizations (Net Impact, 2012) claim that younger workers value meaningful work over compensation. The opposite conclusion has reached by academic researchers (Twenge, 2010; Twenge et al., 2010; Twenge et al., 2012).

A review of the published literature suggests only small differences among age groups and generations in work psychology variables. This includes personality traits (Wong et al., 2008), work attitudes (Kowske et al., 2010), and work motives (Finegold et al., 2002; Wong et al., 2008; Yang & Guy, 2006). Three recent meta-analyses have especially clarified our knowledge in this area. Ng and Feldman (2010) found weak to moderate relationships, at best, between age and 35 work attitudes. However, they did find that older workers were slightly more satisfied with most aspects of their jobs (work itself, pay, co-workers, supervisors) with the exception of promotions. Older workers reported slightly more job control, intrinsic motivation, job involvement, and organizational commitment in the jobs. They also reported fewer job demands, as well as less role ambiguity, conflict, and overload.

In a second meta-analysis, Kooij and colleagues (2010) found that older workers were slightly more satisfied and committed when strong HR *maintenance* practices were present (performance management, intrinsic rewards, information sharing, teamwork, flexibility). Younger workers were more satisfied and committed when strong HR *development* practices were present (promotion). In a follow-up meta-analysis (Kooij et al., 2011) age was positively related to intrinsic motives (autonomy, achievement, development or challenging work assignments, interesting work, working with or helping people, job security), and negatively related to growth and extrinsic motives (salary, benefits, career advancement, recognition, organizational status). Motives for prestige or status were unrelated to age. Yet, the mean estimated age effect in this study was 0.08 across work motives.

Overall, it would appear that age and/or generational differences in work perceptions, attitudes, and motives are small to moderate, at best (Macky et al., 2008). Such differences may be larger in the context of moderating variables. For example, age differences in work attitudes are larger in the context of higher tenure and lower education (Ng Feldman, 2010). The results are mixed with race and gender (Ng & Feldman, 2010). Tenure has been controlled to clarify age-related relationships among perceptions of HR practices, organizational commitment, and job satisfaction (Kooij et al., 2010). Age differences in work motives are also moderated by occupation, cohort, and categorical age groups (Kooij et al., 2011). Finally, age has been found to moderate relationships among perceptions of HR practices, organizational commitment, and job satisfaction (Kooij et al., 2010). The range and diversity of moderating effects reported in these studies may account for some of the equivocal findings

in the gray literature, as well as disparities in peer-reviewed findings.

A NEW PROGRAM OF RESEARCH

More research is needed to clarify the nature of age and generational differences in the workplace, particularly as they relate to differences in perceived work characteristics, differences in work motives, needs, and values, and differences in levels of employee outcomes. To address this need, the author summarizes the results of a recent program of research based on a national sample in America (Fairlie, 2010) with supplemental results from a convenience sample of North Americans (Fairlie, 2011b), and a single organization. The following four questions were addressed through one or more samples.

1 *Is age related to reported levels of work characteristics and employee outcomes?* In other words, do people at different age levels report similar or different levels of positive work characteristics? Do they also report similar or different levels of work adjustment, as a composite of employee outcomes (e.g., overall job satisfaction, organizational commitment, turnover cognitions, exhaustion)?

2 *Are there generational differences in reported levels of work characteristics and employee outcomes?* In other words, do Boomers, Generation X, and Generation Y report similar or dissimilar levels of positive work characteristics and work adjustment, as a composite of employee outcomes?

3 *What has the strongest relationships with employee outcomes: Age, generations, or work characteristics?* This question was addressed by looking at the effects of age and generational membership on employee outcomes, over and above perceived work characteristics. There was also an interest to determine if *any* age break was effective at accounting for levels of work adjustment, apart from common generational groupings (Boomers, Generation X, and Generation Y).

4 *Are different generations motivated by similar or different work characteristics?* This question was addressed by comparing the magnitudes of correlations and regression coefficients among perceived work characteristics and employee outcomes for different generations. Different magnitudes were

taken to suggest different work motives, needs, and/or values. Age and generational membership were also explored as moderators of relationships among work characteristics and several employee outcomes.

The current program of research is believed to contribute to the clarification of age and generational differences in several ways. First, the program involved the comprehensive measurement of over 30 work characteristics, factored into eight global dimensions (Fairlie, 2010). Second, age and generational differences were explored in the context of six employee outcomes (overall job satisfaction, organizational commitment, turnover cognitions, exhaustion, work engagement, discretionary effort). Third, the results were based on three samples, including one national (between-organization), and one derived from a single organization (within-organization) for multiple replications in different data contexts.

The current research program was also predicated on the measurement of meaningful work. Research suggests that meaningful work is a 'sleeping giant' of work motivation. Compared to other work characteristics, meaningful work characteristics are more strongly linked to job satisfaction and organizational commitment (Fairlie, 2010; Fairlie, 2011b), as well as work engagement and discretionary effort (Fairlie, 2011b). They also relate more strongly to lower turnover cognitions (Fairlie, 2010; 2011b), physical and mental health symptoms (Fairlie, 2010), and symptoms of stress, burnout, and depression (Fairlie, 2011b). Yet, these results were derived from total sample analyses. Little is known about the impact of meaningful work for different age groups and generations. Given the importance of meaningful work, and the growing age-related challenges that are faced by organizations, the data from the above studies were re-analyzed to determine whether meaningful work could be a resource for motivating and leveraging some or all age groups and generations in the workplace.

The interest in meaningful work as a possible leverage point for different age groups and generations is heightened by the findings of other studies. As mentioned earlier, few substantive age and generational differences have been found in perceptions of work characteristics, work motives, and links among work characteristics and employee outcomes (Macky et al., 2008; Kooij et al., 2010; Kooij et al., 2011; Ng & Feldman, 2010). Yet, the work characteristics that have been measured in past studies have been limited in breadth and diversity. While there are many models of work characteristics (Campion & Thayer, 1985; Hackman & Oldham, 1975; Parker & Wall, 1998) and satisfaction with work characteristics (Balzer et al., 2000; Spector, 1997), few of these models include work characteristics that are aligned with models of psychological meaning.

What is meaningful work?

Meaning entails issues of 'life meaning, purpose, and coherence' (Ryff, 2000:132). Additionally, '…having meaning is viewed as a feature of optimal human functioning, which involves having goals, being engaged, and possessing inner strength in the face of life's obstacles. But to live without meaning is to experience despair, alienation, and confusion' (Ryff, 2000:132). Baumeister (1991) identified four main needs for meaning as purpose (including goals and fulfillments), values, efficacy, and self-worth.

While there are individual differences in what people find meaningful, researchers have identified several common dimensions, including having purpose, values, and goals, spirituality, relationships, service, autonomy, commitment, challenge, achievement, competence, and self-realization (Antonovsky, 1990; Baumeister, 1991; Ebersole, 1998; Emmons, 1999; Frankl, 1992; Kobasa, 1979; Maslow, 1970; Nakamura & Csikszentmihalyi, 2003; Ryan & Deci, 2000; Ryff & Keyes, 1995; Wong, 1998). Many of these themes are inherent in personal strivings (Emmons, 1991), current concerns (Klinger, 1998), personal projects (Little, 1983), life longings (Kotter-Grühn et al., 2009), self-determination (Ryan & Deci, 2000), and conceptions of the 'good life' (King & Napa, 1998).

Meaningful work is defined as *job and other workplace characteristics that facilitate the attainment or maintenance of one or more dimensions of meaning* (Fairlie, 2010). The concept of meaningful work is not new. Both Maslow (1965) and Alderfer (1972) described work characteristics that promote self-actualization. McGregor (1960) described work that allows for imagination, ingenuity, and creativity. The 'motivator factors' in Herzberg's Motivator-Hygiene Theory (Herzberg et al., 1959) have been identified elsewhere as meaningful work. Locke (1976) claimed that job satisfaction results from doing things that are personally valued. Finally, meaningfulness of work is an aspect of the Job Characteristics Model (Hackman & Oldham, 1975). What has been lacking, historically, are comprehensive models and measures of meaningful work characteristics.

Samples and measures

The research program involved three samples and studies. Sample One ($n = 1,000$) consisted of full-time, working Americans from 50 U.S. states that completed a web survey as members of a paid, online panel. Sample Two ($n = 574$) was a convenience sample of working Americans and Canadians that accessed the website of a Canadian leadership training and development company to complete a web survey in exchange for score feedback. Sample Three ($n = 578$) consisted of employees of a Canadian not-for-profit organization that completed a web survey battery as their employer's employee survey. Participants in Samples Two and Three were at least part-time employed.

The modal profiles across samples were female (56–71 per cent), non-supervisory (59–77 per cent; except for Sample Two, 39 per cent), with one to five years of tenure (38 per cent and 38 per cent where measured). Sample One and Two participants were at least 18 years of age. The mean ages in Samples One and Two were 42.60 and 46.42, respectively. Age in Sample Three was measured in ordered categories, with modal age categories of 45–54, and 55–64 years of age. Birth year was measured only in Samples One and Two, enabling the identification of Boomers (31 and 37 per cent), Generation X (56 and 55 per cent), and Generation Y (12 and 7 per cent; see Strauss and Howe, 1991).

All samples completed the Meaningful Work Inventory (MWI; Fairlie, 2010), a comprehensive employee survey of evidence-based work characteristics (linked to employee outcomes in past research) and work characteristics aligned with models of psychological meaning. The MWI contains over 30 specific work characteristics scales that factor into eight global work characteristics scales: meaningful work, leadership and organizational features, supervisory relationships, co-worker relationships, intrinsic rewards, extrinsic rewards, organizational support, and work demands and balance (see Table 11.1). Reliability and validity information is available elsewhere (Fairlie, 2010; 2011a; 2011b; 2012).

While each MWI global scale contains varying amounts of meaningful work content, the *meaningful work* global scale is perhaps most aligned with dimensions of meaning. It contains four facets: *self-actualizing work* (realizing one's full potential, purpose, values, and goals through one's job and organization), *social impact* (having a positive impact on people and things through one's job and organization), *personal accomplishment* (feelings of personal accomplishment from one's job), and *career advancement* (belief that one can achieve one's highest career goals in one's current organization).

Several employee outcomes were also measured. Four items were developed by the author to measure overall job satisfaction, organizational commitment, turnover cognitions, and the exhaustion component of burnout in Sample One. This was

Table 11.1   Meaningful Work Inventory (MWI) global work characteristics scales

Scale	Facets
Meaningful work	• Self-actualizing work (e.g., job enables one to fulfill one's potential and become a fully-functioning person) • Social impact (legacy, generativity, 'mattering') • Job enables one to fulfill one's life purpose, goals, and values • Feelings of personal accomplishment • Belief in achieving one's highest career goals in one's organization
Leadership and organizational features	• Integrity (fair, honest, trustworthy, respectful, democratic) • Authenticity (consistent words and actions) • Clear communication of goals and direction • Corporate social responsibility (protects and maintains human rights and the environment)
Supervisory relationships	• Integrity (fair, honest, trustworthy, respectful, accountable, democratic) • Social support (emotional, appraisal) • Feedback • Recognition • Communicates the importance of one's job
Co-worker relationships	• Integrity (trustworthy, respectful) • Social support (emotional, instrumental)
Intrinsic rewards	• Autonomy • Skill utilization • Task variety • Task identity • Creative freedom • Involvement and participation • Job-induced self-efficacy (e.g., job enables one to discover one's strengths) • General opportunities for growth and development
Extrinsic rewards	• Fair pay • Perks • Other rewards for one's efforts.
Organizational support	• Efficient operations (policies, procedures) • Resources (people, things, training) • Communications • Role clarity
Work demands and balance	• Work demands (realistic) • Work-life balance

expanded to twelve items in Sample Two, and reduced to seven items in Sample Three. Based on factor analyses, most or all of the items were positively-scaled and summed to form a *work adjustment* composite variable in each sample (see Fairlie, 2010; 2011b). Participants in Sample Two also responded to a discretionary effort item (i.e., extra-role behaviour), the Utrecht Work Engagement Scale (UWES-9; Schaufeli et al., 2006; Shimazu et al., 2008) and the Oldenburg Burnout Inventory (OLBI; Demerouti & Bakker, 2008; Demerouti et al., 2003).

RESULTS AND DISCUSSION

This chapter focuses primarily on results obtained from Sample One, since it was the largest, and perhaps most representative sample. The results obtained from Samples Two and Three are reported and discussed more briefly with respect to replication and/ or when the results involve different measures. The results are also grouped by research question to maximize continuity, especially when similar variables were examined across samples and studies. Not all results are tabled for space considerations.

Are there age differences in reported levels of work characteristics and work adjustment?

Only three global work characteristics were weakly and positively correlated with age in Sample One, including perceptions of meaningful work, intrinsic rewards, and extrinsic rewards (see Table 11.2). Age was also positively related to work adjustment. The most variance that was accounted for by age in any of the measured variables was less than 2 per cent. Similar, but stronger correlations were found between age and meaningful work, intrinsic rewards, and work adjustment in Sample Two (see Table 11.3). Only perceptions of organizational support and positive co-worker relationships were related to age in the organizational sample in Sample Three. In short, *there were very small relationships among age and levels of both perceived work characteristics and employee outcomes.*

Are there generational differences in reported levels of work characteristics and work adjustment?

Boomers, Generation X, and Generation Y were compared in their perceptions of work characteristics and reports of work adjustment in Sample One. A multivariate analysis of variance (MANOVA) was performed with generation as the independent variable and eight global work characteristics and work adjustment as the dependent variables.

There was an overall significant difference among the generations. More specifically, and compared to Generation Y, Boomers reported higher levels of meaningful work and work adjustment. Yet, the overall effect of generational differences on the combined dependent variables was small (partial $\varepsilon^2 = 0.03$). Smaller still were the generational differences in meaningful work and work adjustment (both partial $\varepsilon^2 = 0.01$). Finally, these small differences disappeared when tenure was controlled. Age was

correlated with tenure in this sample, consistent with other studies (Bedeian et al., 1992; Hunt & Saul, 1975).

A similar analysis was conducted in Sample Two, with the additional consideration of work engagement and exhaustion as dependent variables. Since the generational samples were very unequal, and the equality of covariance matrices was threatened, the number of Boomers and Generation X were randomly reduced to nearly equal the number of Generation Y for this analysis ($n = 37$–41). The dependent variables were reduced to only those correlated with age. Overall generational differences approached significance, with univariate differences in meaningful work and work adjustment, similar to those found in Sample One.

In summary, it would appear that Boomers report slightly more meaningful work and higher levels of work adjustment than Generation Y. But in general, *there were very small generational differences in levels of both perceived work characteristics and employee outcomes.*

What has larger effects on critical employee outcomes: age, generations, or work characteristics?

Common age and generation breaks

A multiple regression analysis was conducted on Sample One to estimate the amount of variance that could be accounted for in levels of work adjustment by both age and generational membership, after controlling for perceived work characteristics (see Table 11.4). The first block of eight global work characteristics accounted for 66 per cent of the variance in work adjustment. The second block of age and two generational contrast variables accounted for only 1 per cent of additional variance in levels of work adjustment.[2] In fact, seven of the eight work characteristics variables remained significant in the final equation, with perceptions of meaningful

Table 11.2 Sample One: Psychometric properties and correlations among age, work characteristics, and work adjustment

	Mean	S.D.	Alpha	Correlations
				Age
Meaningful work	45.65	13.43	.95	.10**
Leadership and organizational features	45.23	13.59	.96	−.04
Supervisory relationships	44.31	12.46	.96	−.03
Co-worker relationships	26.81	5.43	.93	−.04
Intrinsic rewards	44.47	10.09	.90	.07*
Extrinsic rewards	13.64	4.42	.87	.09**
Organizational support	29.14	6.84	.87	.00
Work demands and balance	9.85	2.64	.76	−.02
Work adjustment	19.56	5.27	.83	.14***

$N = 867$ to 999. $*p < .05$. $**p < .01$. $***p < .001$.

Table 11.3 Sample Two: Psychometric properties and correlations among age, work characteristics, and employee outcomes

	Mean	S.D.	Alpha	Correlations
				Age
Meaningful work	46.90	14.00	.94	.19***
Leadership and organizational features	46.65	13.69	.95	.06
Supervisory relationships	43.60	13.20	.94	−.04
Co-worker relationships	27.44	6.08	.94	.07
Intrinsic rewards	39.87	11.00	.92	.14***
Extrinsic rewards	14.23	4.61	.83	.04
Organizational support	28.52	7.45	.85	.04
Work demands and balance	9.76	2.77	.62	−.01
Work adjustment	49.74	15.86	.93	.16***
UWES total engagement	44.92	12.29	.95	.19***
OLBI exhaustion	18.48	4.15	.84	−.18***
Discretionary effort	5.40	1.42	–	.13***

$N = 509$ to 573. $***p < .001$.

work and work demands and balance having the strongest unique effects. Age, but not generational contrasts, remained significant. Adding tenure as an additional first block did not appreciably change the results.[3]

Similar regression analyses on work adjustment were conducted in Samples Two and Three. Generational variables were not included. In Sample Two, the eight global work characteristics accounted for 67 per cent

of the variance in work adjustment (see Table 11.5). Age accounted for less than 1 per cent of the remaining variance. Four of the eight work characteristics variables remained significant in the final equation, with perceptions of meaningful work and leadership and organizational features having the strongest unique relationships with work adjustment. Age remained significant with a small effect in the final equation. Nearly identical results

Table 11.4 Sample One: Multiple regression analysis: incremental validity of age and generations predicting work adjustment

Variable	B	SE B	β	r^2	Δr^2
Step 2				.67	.01***
Meaningful work	3.95	.47	.29***		
Leadership and org. features	.94	.43	.07*		
Supervisory relationships	1.13	.46	.08*		
Co-worker relationships	.46	.80	.01		
Intrinsic rewards	2.91	.68	.16***		
Extrinsic rewards	3.22	1.27	.08*		
Organizational support	2.18	1.01	.08*		
Work demands and balance	15.82	2.04	.23***		
Age	2.17	.74	.13**		
Boomers vs. other gen.'s	5.89	5.37	.04		
Gen X vs. Gen Y	2110.09	1573.73	−.04		

$N = 741.$ *$p < .05.$ **$p < .01.$ ***$p < .001.$

Table 11.5 Sample Two: Multiple regression analysis: incremental validity of age predicting work adjustment

Variable	B	SE B	β	r^2	Δr^2
Step 2				.67	.00*
Meaningful work	.44	.05	.38***		
Leadership and org. features	.39	.05	.32***		
Supervisory relationships	.12	.05	.10*		
Co-worker relationships	−.04	.08	−.01		
Intrinsic rewards	.09	.08	.06		
Extrinsic rewards	.60	.13	.18***		
Organizational support	−.05	.10	−.02		
Work demands and balance	−.30	.20	−.05		
Age	.09	.05	.06*		

$N = 405.$ *$p < .05.$ **$p < .01.$ ***$p < .001.$

were obtained from a similar analysis in Sample Three, with meaningful work, leadership and organizational features, and age significant in the final equation.

Similar regression analyses were conducted in Sample Two with work engagement and exhaustion as outcome variables (see Table 11.6). The eight work characteristics accounted for 59 per cent of the variance in work engagement, with an additional 1 per cent of variance accounted for by age. Meaningful work and intrinsic rewards remained

significant. Age also remained significant with a small effect. For exhaustion, work characteristics accounted for 43 per cent of the variance, with age contributing a further 3 per cent, leaving meaningful work, work demands and balance, and age significant in the final equation (see Table 11.7).

In Sample Two, work characteristics contributed 26 per cent of the variance in discretionary effort (see Table 11.8). Age had no effect after controlling for work characteristics. Of the five work characteristics that

Table 11.6   Sample Two: Multiple regression analysis: incremental validity of age predicting work engagement

Variable	B	SE B	β	r^2	Δr^2
Step 2				.60	.01*
Meaningful work	.57	.05	.63***		
Leadership and org. features	−.08	.04	−.09		
Supervisory relationships	.03	.04	.03		
Co-worker relationships	−.05	.08	−.02		
Intrinsic rewards	.20	.07	.17**		
Extrinsic rewards	−.05	.12	−.02		
Organizational support	.10	.09	.06		
Work demands and balance	−.01	.17	.00		
Age	.09	.04	.07*		

$N = 406$. $^*p < .05$. $^{**}p < .01$. $^{***}p < .001$.

Table 11.7   Sample Two: Multiple regression analysis: incremental validity of age predicting exhaustion

Variable	B	SE B	β	r^2	Δr^2
Step 2				.46	.03***
Meaningful work	−.09	.02	−.29***		
Leadership and org. features	.01	.02	.03		
Supervisory relationships	−.03	.02	−.09		
Co-worker relationships	−.01	.03	−.02		
Intrinsic rewards	−.01	.03	−.02		
Extrinsic rewards	.08	.05	.08		
Organizational support	−.02	.04	−.03		
Work demands and balance	−.69	.07	−.45***		
Age	−.07	.02	−.17***		

$N = 409$. $^*p < .05$. $^{**}p < .01$. $^{***}p < .001$.

remained significant in the final equation, the strongest unique effects were reserved for meaningful work and intrinsic rewards. In Sample Three, work characteristics accounted for a similar 23 per cent of the variance in discretionary effort. Meaningful work and work demands and balance remained significant in the final equation.

Alternative age and generation breaks

The above analyses returned few substantive differences for age and 'typical' generations (Boomers, Generation X, and Generation Y). However, there may be other age and generational breaks that are more predictive of employee outcomes. The birth years used to define the generations were based on a sociocultural theory of recurring 'mood eras' in society (Howe & Strauss, 1997; Strauss & Howe, 1991). Other theorists have identified key historical events that shape the development of individuals within generations (Rogler, 2002). Alternatively, government census bureaus have used population trends to defined generations (Crowley, 2003). Regardless of how generations are defined, individuals within generations

Table 11.8   Sample Two: Multiple regression analysis: incremental validity of age discretionary effort

Variable	B	SE B	β	r²	Δr²
Step 2				.26	.00
Meaningful work	.04	.01	.37***		
Leadership and org. features	.01	.01	.09		
Supervisory relationships	−.01	.01	−.13*		
Co-worker relationships	−.01	.01	−.04		
Intrinsic rewards	.03	.01	.27***		
Extrinsic rewards	−.05	.02	−.16**		
Organizational support	.01	.01	.05		
Work demands and balance	−.11	.03	−.21***		
Age	.00	.01	.01		

$N = 414$. *$p < .05$. **$p < .01$. ***$p < .001$.

are often found to be heterogeneous with respect to their social attitudes and values (Popiel & Fairlie, 1996).

Additional analyses were undertaken to identify the age breaks and/or generational boundaries that *best* predict employee outcomes. In other words, age groups and generations would be empirically-derived based on their relationship with such outcomes. To this end, a chi-squared automatic interaction detection (CHAID) analysis was conducted on Sample One, with age predicting levels of work adjustment (overall job satisfaction, organizational commitment, turnover cognitions, exhaustion).

CHAID is a robust, non-parametric method of exploring data (Kass, 1980). It forms post hoc interactions among predictor and outcome variables by maximizing chi-square statistics and statistical significance. It also creates groupings based on these interactions. Levels of predictor variables (e.g., age) are merged if they are not significantly different with respect to the outcome variable (e.g., work adjustment). In a CHAID analysis, the age groups that emerge would be maximally-different in their levels of work adjustment. For the current analysis, conservative parameters were set for maximum tree growth, node size, and cross-validation.

The results of the CHAID analysis suggested that three age groups best describe the

relationship between age with levels of work adjustment. These groups were: under 27 years of age, between 27–42 years of age, and over 42 years of age. Based on birth years and data collection dates, the birth year boundaries for these 'alternative' generations were: before 1968, between 1968–1983, and after 1983.

Although this new generational membership variable was empirically-derived to have the largest possible association with work adjustment, its effect on work adjustment was still minimal in a follow-up MANOVA (partial $\epsilon^2 = 0.02$ compared to 0.01 for Boomers, Generation X, and Generation Y). Additionally, in a follow-up regression analysis, this generational membership variable, together with age, predicted only 2 per cent of the variance in work adjustment after controlling for work characteristics. The unique effects of work characteristics remained largely unaltered. Thus, even when generations are optimally-constructed to predict work adjustment, their effect on levels of work adjustment are negligible when compared to work characteristics. Overall, in this section, *work characteristics had far stronger relationships with a broad range of employee outcomes when compared to age and generational membership, regardless of how the generations are defined. Additionally, meaningful work appears to be an important condition for these outcomes, for all age groups and generations.*

Are different generations motivated by similar or different work characteristics?

There was also an effort to determine whether different age groups or generations possess different work motives, needs, and values. Locke and Latham (2004:388) view work motives as 'internal factors that impel action and to external factors that can act as inducements to action.' Work needs may be 'partially non-conscious drivers of preferences for particular job characteristics and work outcomes' (Kooij et al., 2011:199). A work value is 'an objective, either a psychological state, a relationship, or a material condition, that one seeks to attain or achieve' (Super, 1980: 82). Work values typically describe the value or importance that individuals place on outcomes obtained at work (Sagie et al., 1996).

Unlike past studies (Hansen & Leuty, 2012; Kooij et al 2011; Wong et al., 2008), the above variables were not directly measured.[4] Rather, they were inferred from the strengths of relationships among perceived work characteristics and employee outcomes. This indirect method of inferring motives and similar variables is aligned with views that such variables operate, to a large extent, at an unconscious level outside of awareness (Baard et al., 2004). Thus, they may not always lend themselves to reliable and valid self-report. This is consistent with research suggesting that many individuals cannot identify, on a conscious level, what makes them truly happy or satisfied (Gilbert, 2006).

Since these variables were indirectly measured, there is no way to determine whether a motive, need, and/or value was operating in any particular relationship in the studies. It is also possible that more than one variable was operating at one time. For example, work values are believed to operate as secondary drivers at the service of work needs (Kalleberg, 1977; Latham & Pinder,

2005; Ronen, 1994; Steel and Konig, 2006). Emerging approaches tend to view work motivation as encompassing unconscious needs, motivational orientations, and conscious values with respect to particular work characteristics and outcomes (Latham & Pinder, 2005; Sagie et al., 1996). Thus, any or all types of drivers may have been operating in these studies.[5]

Correlations were computed among the eight global work characteristics and work adjustment for each generation in Sample One (see Table 11.9). All work characteristics were significantly correlated to work adjustment for all generations, with effect sizes that were medium to large (Cohen, 1992). On average, work characteristics were correlated with work adjustment at 0.64, 0.62, and 0.53 for Boomers, Generation X, and Generation Y, respectively. Work characteristics that were strongly-correlated with work adjustment across generations were meaningful work (mean $r = 0.70$), intrinsic rewards (mean $r = 0.68$) and organizational support (mean $r = 0.67$). Overall, correlations among work characteristics and work adjustment were smallest for Generation Y, suggesting that positive work characteristics, while critical for higher work adjustment for most individuals, nonetheless have a weaker 'driver' effect for Generation Y.

Generational differences in work adjustment drivers were also explored in separate regression analyses for each generation in Sample One (see Table 11.10). The unique beta weights were explored across analyses. First, a greater number of work characteristics emerged as unique predictors of work adjustment for Boomers and Generation X, together, compared to Generation Y. This suggests that older generations have a greater number of separate work motives, needs, and/or values. It may also suggest that for older generations, there are several 'routes' to higher levels of work adjustment. Alternatively, younger generations may not make as many distinctions between various aspects of their work. Their perceptions of each work characteristic may be more inter-dependent

Table 11.9   Sample One: Correlations among work characteristics and work adjustment by generation

	Correlations with work adjustment		
Work characteristics	Boomers (*n* = 272 to 311)	Generation X (*n* = 488 to 560)	Generation Y (*n* = 100 to 122)
Meaningful work	.71	.71	.68
Leadership and org. features	.64	.61	.50
Supervisory relationships	.67	.65	.47
Co-worker relationships	.49	.35	.29†
Intrinsic rewards	.72	.70	.62
Extrinsic rewards	.58	.61	.52
Organizational support	.67	.71	.63
Work demands and balance	.61	.63	.54

All *r*'s $p < .001$ except † $p < .01$.

Table 11.10   Sample One: Work characteristic predictors of work adjustment by generation

	Standardized regression coefficients (Betas) with work adjustment		
Work characteristics	Boomers (*n* = 219)	Generation X (*n* = 432)	Generation Y (*n* = 88)
Meaningful work	.26***	.30***	.41***
Leadership and org. features	.12*	.04	.07
Supervisory relationships	.17**	.06	−.07
Co-worker relationships	.03	−.01	.05
Intrinsic rewards	.27***	.13*	.00
Extrinsic rewards	.04	.10*	.16
Organizational support	−.09	.15**	.15
Work demands and balance	.24***	.23***	.18

$*p < .05$. $**p < .01$. $***p < .001$.

in response to work events and experiences. Finally, the lack of significant, unique beta weights for Generation Y may also be due to lower sample size and statistical power.

The largest unique effects for Boomers were related to intrinsic rewards, meaningful work, and work demands and balance. For Generation X, they were meaningful work, work demands and balance, and organizational support. Only meaningful work emerged as a unique predictor of work adjustment for Generation Y. Thus, meaningful work had some of the strongest, unique relationships with work adjustment across generations, signaling that this work characteristic may be important for all generations. Additionally, the unique link between meaningful work and work adjustment increased from older to younger generations, suggesting either a singular importance of this work characteristic for Generation Y, or that younger generations perceive most work characteristics as connected in some way to meaningful work.

Some results of the current research program would suggest that work characteristics have stronger effects on work adjustment than age and generational membership. Yet, the results of this section, thus far, also suggest that age and/or generational membership may moderate relationships among one or more work characteristics and work adjustment. Such interactions have been found in recent meta-analyses of work characteristics, age, and employee outcomes (Kooij et al, 2010; Kooij et al, 2011; Ng & Feldman, 2010). However, there were too many plausible hypotheses and interactions to test through regression analysis in the current studies. Thus, a further CHAID analysis was performed on Sample One to explore the presence of interactions among any work characteristics, age, and generational membership in predicting levels of work adjustment.

CHAID analysis has fewer statistical assumptions than linear regression analysis (Kass, 1980). At each step in the analysis, CHAID chooses the predictor variable (e.g., age, generational membership, work characteristic) that has the strongest interaction with the outcome variable (i.e., work adjustment). This process continues until a decision tree is formed. Given that CHAID forms post hoc interactions among variables based on chi-square statistics and statistical significance, it is the most idealistic way of detecting possible interactions among predictors, and among predictors and outcomes.

In the results, meaningful work and extrinsic rewards were the only variables that significantly interacted with levels of work adjustment. Additionally, meaningful work and extrinsic rewards were the only predictor variables that interacted with one another to predict levels of work adjustment. Thus, even with opportunistic, post hoc analyses, age and generational membership did not emerge as significant predictors of work adjustment. Nor did they emerge as significant moderators of work characteristics in their prediction of work adjustment. This analysis was repeated with more liberal growth limits (5 levels) and varying numbers of

cross-validating folds (5 to 25), each time arriving at an almost identical decision tree. Similar CHAID results were found for work adjustment in Sample Two, with meaningful work and extrinsic rewards emerging as the only predictors of work adjustment. In Sample Three (the organizational sample), meaningful work and organizational support emerged as the sole predictors of work adjustment.

CHAID analyses were also conducted with other outcome variables. In Sample Two, only meaningful work emerged as a sole predictor of work engagement. Work demands and balance emerged as the most significant predictor, in interaction with meaningful work, in predicting exhaustion. For discretionary effort, only meaningful work emerged as a predictor. In Sample Three, meaningful work interacted with organizational support to predict discretionary effort.

In summary, the results in this section suggest that while each generation was somewhat motivated by a different number of different work characteristics, in general, work characteristics had very similar motivating effects for all age groups and generations. Additionally, meaningful work appears to be an important source of work motivation for all age groups and generations.

GENERAL DISCUSSION

The results from three samples show few substantive age and generational differences in work psychology variables. Specifically, age was not strongly related to reported levels of work characteristics and work adjustment. There were also small generational differences in these variables. This suggests that workers of all ages and generations perceive similar levels of positive work characteristics in their jobs and workplaces and experience similar levels of work adjustment. Compared to their younger counterparts, older workers and generations did report slightly higher levels of meaningful work (i.e., self-actualizing work, social impact, personal accomplishment, career advancement) and work adjustment (i.e., job satisfaction, organizational commitment, turnover cognitions, exhaustion). However, these differences were very small.

The studies also found work characteristics to be much stronger predictors of employee outcomes than age and generational membership. This was true regardless of whether the outcome was work adjustment, work engagement, discretionary effort, or exhaustion. Age and generational membership, alone or in combination, never accounted for more than 3 per cent of the variance in these outcomes. These results suggest that the positive work characteristics are almost equal in their importance for workers of all ages and generations (regardless of how generations are defined). Finally, while there were differences among generations in the number of individual work characteristics that related to work adjustment, as well as the magnitude of those relations, meaningful work was one of the stronger correlates and predictors across generations. Thus, all generations appear to value meaningful work. It also appears to be a condition for positive employee outcomes for workers of all ages and generations.

General implications

The most salient implication of the current findings is that age and generational differences in the workplace may have been overstated, particularly in the popular media, business press, and other gray literature sources. Another implication is that meaningful work may be a valuable resource for managing all age groups and generations. Not only does meaningful work appear to be motivating for all workers, but it also has some of the strongest links, relative to other work characteristics, with employee outcomes that employers seek to increase (e.g., job satisfaction, organizational commitment, work engagement, discretionary effort) or decrease (e.g., exhaustion, turnover cognitions). This flies in the face of stereotypes

suggesting that younger workers are more desiring of meaningful work (Curtis, 2012; Salzberg, 2012). These stereotypes are perpetuated by opinion polls that have been conducted only among younger workers and students (Levit & Licina, 2011). Furthermore, workers of all ages and generations appear to report similar levels of meaningful work, suggesting that no one age group or generation is particularly at risk with respect to the associated outcomes of meaningful work.

Meaningful work should also be important for organizations. Dimensions of meaning are closely-tied to what people most desire in life (King & Napa, 1998; Kotter-Grühn et al., 2009) and what makes them happiest (Sheldon et al., 2001). Perceived meaning is also linked to higher well-being (Keyes, 2007; McKnight & Kashdan, 2009; Ryan & Deci, 2000; 2001; Ryff & Keyes, 1995). While individuals in Western society appear to be attaching more importance to interesting and socially-useful work (Davis et al., 2009), their levels of job satisfaction and work ethic have declined (England, 1991; Highhouse et al., 2010; Twenge et al., 2010; Weaver, 1997). Fairlie (2010; 2011b; 2013) has also shown meaningful work to be one of the strongest factors implicated in several employee outcomes. In short, meaningful work is both desirable and healthy for workers, and potentially productive and profitable for organizations.

Some of the current findings suggest that there is some merit to the idea of age and/or generational differences in work motives, needs, and values. For example, the correlations among some work characteristics and work adjustment decreased with each successive generation. Specifically, it would appear that older generations are more motivated by leadership and organizational features, supervisory relationships, co-worker relationships, and intrinsic rewards than younger generations. Additionally, work demands and balance appear to be more important to Boomers and Generation X. Some of these differences make sense in light of life-span developmental theories.

The Selection, Optimization, and Compensation theory (Baltes et al., 1999) maintains that successful development involves both the maximization of gains and the minimization of losses. As individuals age, they allocate fewer resources to attaining growth (optimization) and more resources toward the regulation of loss (compensation). Needs for self-actualization and growth should decrease with age, while security needs should increase. As work characteristics, leadership and organizational features, and supervisory relationships both involve relying on individuals in power to act with high integrity (e.g., fair, honest, democratic). These accountabilities may provide a sense of security to older workers. They may also signal continued access to resources that they strive to protect and maintain. However, according to this theory, older generations should also place *less* value on meaningful work, since it includes a facet of self-actualizing work.

Similarly, Socioemotional Selectivity Theory (Carstensen, 1995) suggests that as time horizons shrink, aging individuals come to invest more resources in emotionally meaningful goals and activities. They also begin to eschew knowledge-related goals (e.g., gaining knowledge, career planning) in favour of emotion-related goals and emotionally gratifying experiences in the present. As a result, older adults tend to spend more time with familiar individuals with whom they have had rewarding relationships. This could also account for the relatively higher importance of supervisory and co-worker relationships for older generations, as well the higher importance of intrinsic rewards, which include 'enjoyable' work characteristics (e.g., autonomy, skill utilization, task variety, creative freedom). The importance of enjoyable work characteristics for older generations also makes sense in relation to the Life Span Theory of Control (Heckhausen & Schulz, 1995). This theory assumes that as individuals age, they engage in more secondary control behaviour (addressing one's mental states and emotions) and less primary control behaviour (directed at the external world) in order to protect motivational resources against increasing failures and losses.

Practical implications

The current studies, together with past studies, suggest that there are few differences among age groups and generations in work psychology variables. Yet, also similar to past studies (Wong et al., 2008), very small age effects emerged in some analyses. If employers do wish to focus on age in the workplace, then life-span models of development may be utilized to better understand employees at different ages (Macky et al., 2008). Similarly, it may be prudent to understand differences in life stage-related events that may be occurring in employees' non-work lives (e.g., paying off student loans versus putting kids through college).

Some effort could be expended to involve younger and older workers in team-building events to build a shared identity around their similar work motives, needs, and values. Research suggests that each generation holds stereotypical views of other generations (Lester et al., 2012). Once these perceived differences are minimized, actual differences in knowledge, skills, and abilities could be leveraged across age groups on cross-generational teams. Reverse mentoring programs could also be implemented (Chaudhuri & Ghosh, 2012). Additionally, focus groups could be used to determine how younger and older workers wish to address their similar motives, needs, and values. For example, with respect to meaningful work, older employees may wish to have social impacts through mentoring. Younger workers may prefer to engage in employer-sponsored volunteer work.

Since different age groups and generations appear to value similar work characteristics, and that work characteristics appear to be more predictive of employee outcomes, one overarching practical implication of the current findings is that organizations could focus more attention on improving working conditions for employees of all ages, rather than formulating age-specific management strategies. A 'one size fits all' approach to work motivation may be both economical and pervasive in its impacts on critical employee outcomes. The eight global work characteristics measured in the current studies could inform this approach, with particular emphases on meaningful work, intrinsic rewards, and to a lesser extent, leadership and organizational features, and work demands and balance.

Since meaningful work was found to be exceptionally impactful for all age groups and generations, these particular work features warrant their own practical considerations. For example, meaningful work characteristics should be represented on employee surveys. Existing opportunities to experience meaningful work should also be clearly communicated to employees. Since employees' job perceptions may be inaccurate (Spector, 1992), such opportunities may go 'unused'. Specifically, managers could better explain to employees how their actions connect to the vision and mission of the organization. Since social impact is a key facet of meaningful work, programs could be implemented to create stronger bonds between employees and clients (e.g., client testimonials, 'twinning' employees and customers). In general, employees could experience greater exposure to the human recipients of their work. These and several other recommendations for promoting meaningful work have been presented in more detail elsewhere (Fairlie, 2011b).

Limitations and future directions for research

The current studies were not without limitations. First, they were based on convenience samples that were overweighted by females and employees in supervisory positions. Future research should take advantage of probability sampling (Kidder & Judd, 1986). The results should also be replicated with other measures, since some study measures were comprised of single items. Several other inventories could be used to measure work characteristics and employee outcomes (Parker & Wall, 1998; Spector, 1997). The examination of age and generational differences in the workplace could also be expanded to include other variables such as occupational stress and stressors (Vagg & Spielberger, 1998; Williams & Cooper, 1998). Also, work motives, needs, and values were not directly measured. Rather, they were inferred from relationships among levels of perceived work characteristics and employee outcomes. Future studies could include self-report measures of these variables to assess their actual moderating effects (Amabile et al., 1994; Gay et al., 1971; Macnab et al., 1987; Pryor, 1981).

The current studies also relied on self-report data, which may be associated with response sets (Crocker & Algina, 1986) and method variance effects (Spector & Brannick, 1995). Future studies could be conducted with other methods of data collection (e.g., behavioral observation, ratings). The research was also cross-sectional in nature, which limits causal interpretations. The separate effects of age and generation, in particular, cannot be disentangled. These two variables are presumed to have different impacts. Aging refers to changes in biological, psychological, social functioning that are associated with changes in chronological age (Baltes et al., 1999). Generations are identifiable groups sharing similar birth years and significant life events at critical stages of development (Kupperschmidt, 2000). Longitudinal methods are needed to more accurately assess changes in employee outcomes as a function of age, generations, and work characteristics. Specifically, cohort analyses could be conducted to cross-control for age and generational membership (Glenn, 2005).

Another limitation concerns the definitional boundaries of each generation. The current studies used birth years suggested by Strauss and Howe (1991). However, Boomers have been variously defined as beginning between 1940 and 1946, and ending between 1960 or 1964. The boundary years for Generation X have been quoted as starting in the early 1960's, and ending anywhere from the mid 1970s to 1982 (Adams, 2000; Jurkiewicz and Brown, 1998; Karp et al., 1999; Kupperschmidt, 2000; O'Bannon, 2001; Scott, 2000). Despite this variance in definitions, it is worth remembering that few generational differences were found in the current studies, even when generations were empirically-derived. As an aside, the current studies were also limited by low sample sizes obtained for Generation Y. Therefore, some caution is warranted in drawing firm conclusions about this generation. However, the replication of some generational findings across samples offers some assurance in the validity of the findings.

CONCLUSIONS

As populations continue to age, so too will workforces around the world. Yet, the growing prevalence of older workers in organizations will eventually be halted and reversed in the wake of mass retirements and generational replacement by much younger, and less numerous cohorts. These trends behoove organizational researchers and employers to understand and motivate all age groups and generations in the workplace to fully leverage their knowledge, skills, and abilities. Much of the current understanding in this area has relied on opinion and hearsay emanating from a variety of dubious sources. The current program of research was an attempt to supplement a growing body of more rigorous research on age and generational differences in perceived work characteristics, levels of critical employee outcomes, and work motives, needs, and values. The overarching conclusion from the current program is that age and generational differences are quite small.

In particular, meaningful work emerged as perhaps the most important work characteristic for most employee outcomes, and for all age

groups and generations. Additionally, all age groups and generations reported similar levels of this critical feature of work in their current jobs and workplaces. In short, it would appear that all age groups and generations *have* and want meaningful work. Ironically, meaningful work is still under-represented in models of work characteristics, on employee surveys, and in research on organizational behaviour (Campion & Thayer, 1985; Hackman & Oldham, 1975; Parker & Wall, 1998; Spector, 1997). This observation, together with the current findings, suggest that meaningful work is an overlooked resource, and a possible competitive advantage for employers. Employers may benefit from offering work that enables both younger and older workers to realize their full potential, purpose, values, and goals, to have significant social impacts, to feel a regular sense of accomplishment, and to achieve their highest career goals.

NOTES

1 Derivations of 'generation', 'work', 'age', 'young' and 'old', appearing together, were searched for on June 25, 2012.
2 Two orthogonal, dichotomous contrast variables were created to compare 1) Boomers to other generations, and 2) Generation X to Generation Y. The presence of age and generational contrast variables in the equation did not exceed tolerance limits (Fox, 1991).
3 The sample was large enough to test for small effects with 12 predictor variables (Green, 1991). A categorical regression analysis was also performed with global work characteristics, age, and generational membership (as an optimally-scaled nominal variable) predicting work adjustment. The results were similar.
4 However, the range of work motives that have been directly measured in the past has been narrow. Smola and Sutton (2002) focused largely on aspects of protestant work ethic. Yang and Guy (2006) used items from the General Social Survey (GSS) that were more suggestive of employee outcomes than work motives (e.g., job involvement, job satisfaction, extra-role behaviour).
5 As an aside, many measures of work needs (e.g., Alderfer, 1972; Gay et al., 1971; Herzberg et al., 1959; McClelland & Winter, 1971), values (e.g., Macnab et al., 1987; Super, 1970; Taylor & Thompson, 1976), preferences (e.g., Amabile et al., 1994; Fineman, 1975; Pryor, 1981), and concerns (Roberson, 1989) share similar content, further blurring their separate conceptualization and measurement.

REFERENCES

Adams, S.J. (2000). Generation X: how understanding this population leads to better safety programs. *Professional Safety*, 45, 26–29.

Alderfer, C.P. (1972). *Existence, relatedness, and growth: Human needs in organizational settings.* New York: Free Press.

Allemand, M., Zimprich, D., & Hertzog, C. (2007). Cross-sectional age differences and longitudinal age changes of personality in middle adulthood and old age. *Journal of Personality*, 75, 323–358.

Alsop, R. (2008). *The trophy kids grow up: how the millennial generation is shaking up the workplace.* New York: John Wiley & Sons.

Amabile, T.M., Hill, K.G., Hennessey, B.A., & Tighe, E.M. (1994). The Work Preference Inventory: Assessing intrinsic and extrinsic motivational orientations. *Journal of Personality and Social Psychology*, 66, 950–967.

American Psychiatric Association. (1994). *Diagnostic and statistical manual of mental disorders: DSM-IV* (4th ed.). Washington: American Psychiatric Association.

Antonovsky, A. (1990). Personality and health: Testing the sense of coherence model. In H.S. Friedman (Ed.) *Personality and disease, Wiley series on health psychology/behavioral medicine* (pp. 155–177). Oxford: John Wiley & Sons.

Anusic, I., Lucas, R.E., & Donnellan, M.B. (2011). Cross-sectional age differences in personality: Evidence from nationally representative samples from Switzerland and the United States. *Journal of Research in Personality*, 46, 116–120.

Baard, P.P., Deci, E.L., & Ryan, R.M. (2004). Intrinsic need satisfaction: A motivational basis of performance and well-being in two work settings. *Journal of Applied Social Psychology*, 34, 2045–2068.

Baltes, P.B., Staudinger, U.M., & Lindenberger, U. (1999). Lifespan psychology: Theory and application to intellectual functioning. *Annual Review of Psychology*, 50, 471–507.

Balzer, W.K., Kihm, J.A., Smith, P.C., Irwin, J.L., Bachiochi, P.D., Robie, C., Sinar, ... & Parra, L.F. (2000). Users' manual for the Job Descriptive Index (JDI; 1997 version) and the Job in General scales. In J.M. Stanton and C.D. Crossley (Eds.), *Electronic resources for the JDI and JIG*. Bowling Green, OH: Bowling Green State University.

Barnes-Farrell, J., & Matthews, R. (2007). Age and work attitudes. In K. Shultz, & G. Adams (Eds), *Aging and work in the 21st century* (pp. 139–162). Mahwah: LEA Laurence Erlbaum Associates.

Baumeister, R. (1991). *Meanings of life.* New York: Guilford Press.

Bedeian, A.G., Ferris, G.R., Kacmar, K.M. (1992). Age, tenure, and job satisfaction: A tale of two perspectives. *Journal of Vocational Behavior*, 40, 33–48.

Campion, M.A., & Thayer, P.W. (1985). Development and field evaluation of an interdisciplinary measure of job design. *Journal of Applied Psychology*, 70, 29–43.

Cappelli, P., & Novelli, B. (2010). *Managing the older worker: how to prepare for the new organizational order.* Boston: Harvard Business Press.

Carone, G., & Eckefeldt, P. (2010, April). Making use of long-term demographic projections in multilateral policy coordination in the European Union. European Commission, Directorate General for Economic and Financial Affairs of the European Commission (DG ECFIN). Luxembourg: Eurostat.

Carstensen, L.L. (1995). Evidence for a life span theory of socioemotional selectivity. *Current directions in Psychological science*, 4, 151–156.

Chaudhuri, S., & Ghosh, R. (2012). Reverse mentoring: A social exchange tool for keeping the boomers engaged and millennials committed. *Human Resource Development Review*, 11, 55–76.

Cohen, J. (1992). A power primer. *Psychological Bulletin*, 112, 155–159.

Crocker, L., & Algina, J. (1986). *Introduction to classical and modern test theory.* Fort Worth: Harcourt, Brace & Jovanovich.

Crowley, M. (2003, June 17). *Generation X speaks out on civic engagement and the decennial census: An ethnographic approach* (Census 2000 Ethnographic Study). Washington: U.S. Census Bureau. Retrieved from: http://www.census.gov/pred/www/rpts/Generation%20X%20Final%20Report.pdf.

Curtis, L. (2012, May 2). *The millennial dilemma: Just a job or truly meaningful work?* Retrieved from: http://www.forbes.com/sites/85broads/2012/05/02/the-millennial-dilemma-just-a-job-or-truly-meaningful-work/.

Davis, J.A., Smith, T.W., & Marsden, P.V. (2009). General Social Surveys, 1972–2008: Cumulative codebook. Chicago: National Opinion Research Center.

Deal, J.J. (2012, Spring). Five millennial myths: Forget what you think you know about your employees. *Strategy+Business*, 66, 1–3.

Demerouti, E., & Bakker, A.B. (2008). The Oldenburg Burnout Inventory: A good alternative to measure burnout and engagement. In J. Halbesleben (Ed.), *Stress and burnout in health care* (pp. 65–78). Hauppage, NY: Nova Sciences.

Demerouti, E., Bakker, A.B., Vardakou, I., & Kantas, A. (2003). The convergent validity of two burnout instruments: A multitrait-multimethod analysis. *European Journal of Psychological Assessment*, 19, 12–23.

Diener., E., Suh, E.M., Lucas, R.E., & Smith, H.L. (1999). Subjective well-being: Three decades of progress. *Psychological Bulletin*, 125, 276–302.

Ebersole, P. (1998). Types and depth of written life meanings. In P.T.P. Wong & P.S. Fry (Eds), *The human quest for meaning: A handbook of psychological research and clinical applications* (pp. 179–191). Mahwah, NJ: Erlbaum.

Emmons, R.A. (1991). Personal strivings, daily life events, and psychological and physical well-being. *Journal of Personality*, 59, 453–472.

Emmons, R.A. (1999). *The psychology of ultimate concerns: Motivation and spirituality in personality*. New York: Guilford Press.

England, G.W. (1991). The meaning of working in the USA: Recent changes. *European Work and Organizational Psychologist*, 1, 111–1124.

Espinoza, C., Ukleja, M., & Rusch, C. (2010). *Managing the millennials: Discover the core competencies for managing today's workforce*. New York: John Wiley & Sons.

Fairlie, P. (2010, August). *The Meaningful Work Inventory: Development and initial validation*. Paper presented at the 118th. Annual Convention of the American Psychological Association, San Diego, CA.

Fairlie, P. (2011a, August). *Meaningful work: A sleeping giant of work motivation in the context of other job characteristics, employee engagement, and employee outcomes*. Paper presented at the 119th. Annual Convention of the American Psychological Association at Washington, DC.

Fairlie, P. (2011b). Meaningful work, employee engagement, and other key employee outcomes: Implications for human resource development. *Advances in Developing Human Resources,* 13, 504–521.

Fairlie, P. (2012). *The Meaningful Work Inventory Technical monograph*. Toronto, Ontario, Canada: Author.

Fairlie, P. (2013). Meaningful work is healthy work. In R.J. Burke & C.L. Cooper (Eds), *The fulfilling workplace: The organization's role in achieving individual and organizational health* (pp. 87-205). Surrey, England: Gower Publishing.

Finegold, D., Mohrman, S., & Spreitzer, G.M. (2002). Age effects on the predictors of technical workers' commitment and willingness to turnover. *Journal of Organizational Behavior*, 23, 655–674.

Fineman, S. (1975). The Work Preference Questionnaire: A measure of managerial need for achievement. *Journal of Occupational Psychology*, 48, 11–32.

Fox, J. (1991). *Regression diagnostics: An introduction*. Newbury Park, CA: Sage Publications.

Frankl, V. (1992). *Man's search for meaning* (4th ed.). Boston: Beacon Press.

Fredrickson, B.L. (2001). The role of positive emotions in positive psychology: The broaden-and-build theory of positive emotions. *American Psychologist*, 56, 218–226.

Gay, E.G., Weiss, D.J., Hendel, D.D., Dawis, R.V., & Lofquist, L.H. (1971). *Manual for the Minnesota Importance Questionnaire*. Minneapolis, MN: Industrial Relations Center, University of Minnesota.

Giancola, F. (2006). The generation gap: More myth than reality? *Human Resource Planning*, 29, 32–37.

Gilbert, D. (2006). *Stumbling on happiness*. New York: Random House.

Glenn, N.D. (2005). *Cohort analysis* (2nd ed.). Thousand Oaks, CA: Sage Publications.

Green, S.B. (1991). How many subjects does it take to do a regression analysis? Multivariate Behavioral Research, 26, 499–510.

Gum, A.M., King-Kallimanis, B., & Kohn, R. (2009). Prevalence of mood, anxiety, and substance-abuse disorders for older Americans in the National Comorbidity Survey Replication. *American Journal of Geriatric Psychiatry*, 17, 769–781.

Hackman, J.R., & Oldham, G.R. (1975). Development of the Job Diagnostic Survey. *Journal of Applied Psychology*, 60, 159–170.

Hansen, J.C., & Leuty, M.E. (2012). Work values across generations. *Journal of Career Assessment*, 20, 34–52.

Heckhausen, J., & Schulz, R. (1995). A Life-span theory of control. *Psychological Review,* 102, 284–304.

Hedge, J.W., Borman, W.C., & Lammlein, S.E. (eds). (2006). *The aging workforce: Realities, myths, and implications for organizations*. Washington, DC: American Psychological Association.

Herzberg, F., Mausner, B., & Snyderman, B. (1959). *The motivation to work*. New York: Wiley.

Highhouse, S., Zickar, M.J., & Yankelevich, M. (2010). Would you work if you won the lottery? Tracking changes in the American work ethic. *Journal of Applied Psychology*, 95, 349–357.

Howe, N., & Strauss, W. (1997). *The fourth turning*. New York: Broadway Books.

Hunt, J.W., & Saul, P.N. (1975). The relationship of age, tenure, and job satisfaction in males and females. *Academy of Management Journal*, 18, 690–702.

Jacobsen, L.A, Kent, M., Lee, M., & Mather, M. (February, 2011). America's aging population.

Population Reference Bureau, 66 (1). Retrieved from: http://www.prb.org/pdf11/aging-in-america.pdf.

Johnson, M., & Johnson, L. (2010). *Generations, Inc.: From Boomers to Linksters – Managing the friction between generations at work*. New York: Amacom.

Jurkiewicz, C. E., & Brown, R.G. (1998). GenXers vs. boomers vs. matures: Generational comparisons of public employee motivation. *Review of Public Personnel Administration*, 18, 18–37.

Kalleberg, A.L. (1977). Work values and job rewards: A theory of job satisfaction. *American Sociological Review*, 42, 124–143.

Kanfer, R., & Ackerman, P.L. (2004). Aging, adult development, and work. *Academy of Management Review*, 29, 440–458.

Karp, H., Sirias, D., & Arnold, K. (1999). Teams: Why generation X marks the spot. *The Journal for Quality and Participation*, 22, 30–33.

Kass, G.V. (1980). An exploratory technique for investigating large quantities of categorical data. *Applied Statistics*, 29, 119–127.

Keyes, C.L.M. (2007). Promoting and protecting mental health as flourishing: A complementary strategy for improving national mental health. *American Psychologist*, 62, 95–108.

Kidder, L.H. & Judd, C.M. (1986). *Research methods in social relations*. New York: Holt, Rinehart & Winston.

King, L.A., & Napa, C.K. (1998). What makes a life good? *Journal of Personality and Social Psychology*, 75, 156–165.

Klinger, E. (1998). The search for meaning in evolutionary perspective and its clinical implications. In P.T.P. Wong & P.S. Fry (Eds), *Handbook of personal meaning: Theory, research, and application* (pp. 27–50). Mahwah, NJ: Erlbaum.

Kobasa, S.C. (1979). Stressful life events, personality, and health: An inquiry into hardiness. *Journal of Personality and Social Psychology*, 37, 1–11.

Kooij, D.T.A.M., de Lange, A.H., Jansen, P.G.W., Kanfer, R., & Dikkers, J.S.E. (2011). Age and work-related motives: Results of a meta-analysis. *Journal of Organizational Behavior*, 32, 197–225.

Kooij, D.T.A.M., Jansen, P.G.W., Dikkers, J.S.E., & de Lange, A.H. (2010). The influence of age on the associations between HR practices and both affective commitment and job satisfaction: A meta-analysis. *Journal of Organizational Behavior*, 31, 1111–1136.

Kowske, B.J., Rasch, R., & Wiley. J. (2010). Millennials' (lack of) attitude problem: An empirical examination of generational effects on work attitudes. *Journal of Business and Psychology*, 25, 265–279.

Kotter-Grühn, D., Wiest, M., Zurek, P.P., & Scheibe, S. (2009). What is it we are longing for? Psychological

and demographic factors influencing the contents of Sehnsucht (life longings). *Journal of Research in Personality*, 43, 428–437.

Kupperschmidt, B.R. (2000). Multigeneration employees: Strategies for effective management, *The Health Care Manager*, 19, 65–76.

Krywulak, T., & Roberts, M. (2009). *Winning the 'generation wars': Making the most of generational differences and simulations in the workplace*. Toronto: Conference Board of Canada.

Lancaster, L.C., & Stillman, D. (2003). *When generations collide: Who they are. why they clash. how to solve the generational puzzle at work*. New York: HarperCollins.

Lanzieri, G. (2011, March 31). The greying of the baby boomers: A century-long view of ageing in European populations. *Eurostat, Statistics in focus 23/2011*. Luxembourg: Eurostat.

Latham, G.P., & Pinder, C.C. (2005). Work motivation theory and research at the dawn of the twenty-first century. *Annual Review of Psychology*, 56, 485–516.

Leibold, M., & Voelpel, S.C. (2006). *Managing the aging workforce: Challenges and solutions*. New York: John Wiley & Sons.

Lester, S.W., Standifer, R.L., Schultz, N.J., Windsor, J.M. (2012). Actual versus perceived generational differences at work: An empirical examination. *Journal of Leadership & Organizational Studies*, 19, 341–354.

Levit, A., & Licina, S. (2011). *How the recession shaped millennial and hiring manager attitudes about millennials' future careers*. Commissioned by Career Advisory Board. Presented by DeVry University. Retrieved from: http://newsroom.devry.edu/images/20004/Future%20of%20Millennial%20Careers%20Report.pdf.

Little, B.R. (1983). Personal projects: A rationale and method for investigation. *Environment and Behavior*, 15, 273–309.

Locke, E.A. (1976). The nature and causes of job satisfaction. In M.D. Dunnette (Ed.), *Handbook of industrial and organizational psychology* (pp. 1297–1343). Chicago: Rand McNally.

Locke, E.A., & Latham, G.P. (2004). What should we do about motivation theory? Six recommendations for the twenty-first century. *Academy of Management Review*, 29, 388–403.

Lucas, R.E., & Donnellan, M.B. (2011). Personality development across the life span: longitudinal analyses with a national sample from Germany. *Journal of Personality and Social Psychology*, 101, 847–61.

Macnab, D., Fitzsimmons, G., Casserly, C. (1987). Development of the Life Roles Inventory-Values Scale. *Canadian Journal of Counselling*, 21, 86–98.

Macky, K., Gardner, D., & Forsyth, S. (2008). Generational differences at work: Introduction and overview. *Journal of Managerial Psychology*, 23, 857–861.

Marston, C. (2007). *Motivating the 'what's in it for me' workforce: Manage across the generational divide and increase profits*. New York: John Wiley & Sons.

Maslow, A.H. (1965). *Eupsychian management*. Chicago: Irwin-Dorsey.

Maslow, A.H. (1970). *Motivation and personality* (2nd ed.). New York: Harper and Row.

McClelland, D.C., & Winter, D.G. (1971). *Motivating economic achievement*. New York: Free Press.

McGregor, D. (1960). *The human side of enterprise*. New York: McGraw-Hill.

McKnight, P.E., & Kashdan, T.B. (2009). Purpose in life as a system that creates and sustains health and well-being: An integrative, testable theory. *Review of General Psychology*, 13, 242–251.

Mercer (2011, June). *Inside employees' minds (U.S. survey summary)*. Retrieved from: http://new-rules-of-engagement.mercer.com/New%20Rules%20US/Inside%20Employees%27%20Minds%20-%20US.

Nakamura, J., & Csikszentmihalyi, M. (2003). The construction of meaning through vital engagement. In C.L.M. Keyes & J. Haidt (Eds), *Flourishing: Positive psychology and the life well-lived* (pp. 83–104). Washington: American Psychological Association.

Net Impact (2012, May). *Talent report: What workers want in 2012. Executive summary*. Retrieved from: http://netimpact.org/docs/NetImpact_WhatWorkersWant2012.pdf.

Ng, T.W.H., & Feldman, D.C. (2010). The relationships of age with job attitudes: A meta-analysis. *Personnel Psychology*, 63, 677–718.

O'Bannon, G. (2001). Managing our future: the generation X factor. *Public Personnel Management*, 30, 95–109.

OECD. (2006). *Live longer, work longer: A synthesis report*. Retrieved from: http://www.oecd.org/document/42/0,3746,en_2649_33927_36104426_1_1_1_1,00.html.

Parker, S., & Wall, T. (1998). *Job and work design: Organizing work to promote well-being and effectiveness*. Thousand Oaks, CA: Sage Publications.

Popiel, S., & Fairlie, P. (1996). Generation X: The social values of Canadian youth. *Canadian Journal of Marketing Research*, 15, 11–22.

Pryor, R.G. (1981). Tracing the development of the Work Aspect Preference Scale. *Australian Psychologist*, 16, 241–257.

Roberson, L. (1989). Assessing personal work goals in the organizational setting: Development and evaluation of the Work Concerns Inventory. *Organizational Behavior and Human Decision Processes*, 44, 345–367.

Rogler, L.H. (2002). Historical generations and psychology: The case of the Great Depression and World War II. *American Psychologist*, 57, 1013–1023.

Ronen, S. (1994). An underlying structure of motivational need taxonomies: A cross-cultural confirmation. In M. Dunnette, & L. Hough (eds), *Handbook of industrial and organizational psychology* (pp. 241–269). Palo Alto, CA: Consulting Psychologists Press.

Ryan, R.M., & Deci, E.L. (2000). Self-determination theory and the facilitation of intrinsic motivation, social development, and well-being. *American Psychologist*, 55, 68–78.

Ryan, R.M., & Deci, E.L. (2001). On happiness and human potentials: A review of research on hedonic and eudaimonic well-being. *Annual Review of Psychology*, 52, 141–66.

Ryff, C.D. (2000). Meaning of life. In A.E. Kazdin (Ed.), *Encyclopedia of psychology*. Oxford: Oxford University Press.

Ryff, C.D., & Keyes, C.L.M. (1995). The structure of psychological well-being revisited. *Journal of Personality and Social Psychology*, 69, 719–727.

Sagie, A., Elizur, D., & Koslowsky, M. (1996). Work values: A theoretical overview and a model of their effects. *Journal of Organizational Behavior*, 17, 503–514.

Salzberg, B. (2012, July 3). *What millennials want most: A career that actually matters*. Retrieved from: http://www.forbes.com/sites/forbesleadershipforum/2012/07/03/what-millennials-want-most-a-career-that-actually-matters/.

Schaufeli, W.B., Bakker, A.B., & Salanova, M. (2006). The measurement of work engagement with a short questionnaire – A cross national study. *Educational and Psychological Measurement*, 66, 701–716.

Scott, J. (2000). Is it a different world to when you were growing up: generational effects on social representations and child-rearing values. *British Journal of Sociology*, 51, 355–376.

Sheldon, K.M., Elliot, A.J., Kim, Y., & Kasser, T. (2001). What is satisfying about satisfying events? Testing 10 candidate psychological needs. *Journal of Personality and Social Psychology*, 80, 325–339.

Shimazu, A., Schaufeli, W.B., Kosugi, S., Suzuki, A., Nashiwa, H., Kato, A., ...Goto, R. (2008). Work engagement in Japan: Validation of the Japanese version of the Utrecht Work Engagement Scale. Applied Psychology: An International Review, 57, 510–523.

Smola, K. W., & Sutton, C. (2002). Generational differences: Revisiting generational work values for the new millennium. *Journal of Organizational Behavior, 23*, 363–382.

Spector, P.E. (1992). A consideration of the validity and meaning of self-report measures of job conditions. In C.L. Cooper and I.T. Robertson (Eds), *International review of industrial and organizational psychology* (Vol. 7, pp. 123–151). New York: Wiley.

Spector, P.E. (1997). *Job satisfaction: Applications, assessment, causes, and consequences*. Thousand Oaks, CA: Sage.

Spector, P.E., & Brannick, M.T. (1995). The nature and effects of method variance in organizational research. In C.L. Cooper & I.T. Robertson (Eds.), *International review of industrial and organizational psychology* (pp. 249–274). West Sussex, England: Wiley.

Steel, P., & Konig, C.J. (2006). Integrating theories of motivation. *Academy of Management Review, 31*, 889–913.

Strauss, W., & Howe, N. (1991). Generations. New York: William Morrow and Company.

Super, D.E. (1970). *The Work Values Inventory*. Boston: Houghton Mifflin.

Super, D.E. (1980). A life span, life space, approach to career development. *Journal of Vocational Behavior, 16*, 282–298.

Taylor, R.N., & Thompson, M. (1976). Work value systems of young workers. *Academy of Management Journal, 19*, 522–536.

Toossi, M. (2009, November). Labor force projections to 2018: Older workers staying more active. *Monthly Labor Review*. Retrieved from: http://www.bls.gov/opub/mlr/2009/11/art3full.pdf.

Towers Perrin (2009). *Closing the engagement gap: A road map for driving superior business performance (Towers Perrin Global Workforce Study 2007–2008)*. Retrieved from: http://www.towersperrin.com/tp/getwebcachedoc?webc=HRS/USA/2008/200803/GWS_Global_Report20072008_31208.pdf.

Tulgan, B. (2009). *Not everyone gets a trophy: How to manage Generation Y*. New York: John Wiley & Sons.

Twenge, J.M. (2010). A review of the empirical evidence on generational differences in work attitudes. *Journal of Business and Psychology, 25*, 201–210.

Twenge, J.M., Campbell, W.K., & Freeman, E.C.. (2012). Generational differences in young adults' life goals, concern for others, and civic orientation, 1966–2009. *Journal of Personality and Social Psychology, 102*, 1045–1062.

Twenge, J.M., Campbell, S.M., Hoffman, B.J., & Lance, C.E. (2010). Generational differences in work values: Leisure and extrinsic values increasing, social and intrinsic values decreasing. *Journal of Management, 36*, 1117–1142.

Vagg, P.R., & Spielberger, C.D. (1998). Occupational stress: Measuring job pressure and organizational support in the workplace. *Journal of Occupational Health Psychology, 3*, 294–305.

Vincent, G.K., & Velkoff, V.A. (2010). *The next four decades: The older population in the United States: 2010 to 2050 (Current Population Report P25–1138)*. Retrieved from: http://www.census.gov/prod/2010pubs/p25-1138.pdf.

Warr, P. (1996). Younger and older workers. In P. Warr (Ed.), *Psychology at work* (4th ed., pp. 308–332). London: Penguin.

Warr, P. (2001). Age and work behaviour: Physical attributes, cognitive abilities, knowledge, personality traits and motives. In C.L. Cooper, & I.T. Robertson (Eds), *International review of industrial and organizational psychology* (Vol. 16, pp. 1–36). New York: John Wiley & Sons.

Weaver, C. N. (1997). Has the work ethic in the USA declined? Evidence from nationwide surveys. *Psychological Reports, 81*, 491–495.

Williams, S., & Cooper, C.L. (1998). Measuring occupational stress: Development of the Pressure Management Indicator. *Journal of Occupational Health Psychology, 3*, 306–321.

Wong, M., Gardiner, E., Lang, W., & Coulon, L. (2008). Generational differences in personality and motivation: Do they exist and what are the implications for the workplace? *Journal of Managerial Psychology, 23*, 878–890.

Wong, P.T.P. (1998). Implicit theories of meaningful life and the development of the Personal Meaning Profile. In P.T.P. Wong & P.S. Fry (Eds), *The human quest for meaning: A handbook of psychological research and clinical applications* (pp. 111–140). Mahwah, NJ: Erlbaum.

Wright, T.A., & Staw, B.M. (1999). Affect and favorable work outcomes: two longitudinal tests of the happy-productive worker thesis. *Journal of Organizational Behavior, 20*, 1–23.

Yang. S. M., & Guy, M. E. (2006). GenXers versus Boomers: Work motivators and management implications. *Public Performance & Management Review, 29*, 267–284.

Zemke, R., Raines, C., & Filipczak, B. (1999). *Generations at work: Managing the clash of Veterans, Boomers, Xers, and Nexters in your workplace*. New York: AMACOM.

PART 3

Managing an Aging Workforce

12

Comparative Age Management: Theoretical Perspectives and Practical Implications

Stephan Alexander Boehm,
Heike Simone Schröder, and Florian Kunze

INTRODUCTION

The average age of the population will increase substantially in most industrialized countries over the next 50 years due to increasing life-expectancies and decreasing fertility rates (OECD, 2006). This demographic change has negative implications on the sustainability of social security systems, on the availability of adequately-qualified labor (Auer and Fortuny, 2000; Börsch-Supan, 2002) and on economic growth (Feyrer, 2007). Demographic change also confronts organizations with various challenges, including the simultaneous retirement of large groups of employees (stemming from the baby boomer generation), a potential lack of skilled job candidates, as well as an increase in the average age of the workforce (Dychtwald, Erickson and Morison, 2004).

Despite the demographic trends and economic implications, Human Resource Management (HRM) at the organizational-level is often tailored towards young individuals, rather than employees from all age groups. Previous studies have observed direct and indirect discrimination against older individuals with regard to hiring, promotion, training, and redundancies, as well as workplace and working-time designs (Wood, Wilkinson and Harcourt, 2008). This is the case, even though the literature discusses the negative implications of (perceived) age discrimination. These negative implications include a loss of skills and experience, a poor return on investment in human capital (Taylor and Walker, 1998), and a decrease in company performance (Kunze, Boehm and Bruch, 2011; 2013). Demographic, labor market and firm-level challenges therefore require the implementation of human resource management (HRM) measures that help to better integrate individuals of all age groups in the workforce.

The alternative to an HRM approach that primarily focuses on young individuals is the concept of age management. Age management is defined as 'the various dimensions by which human resources are managed within organizations with an explicit focus on aging and, also, more generally, to the overall management of workforce aging via public policy or collective bargaining' (Walker, 2005: 685). Age management is holistic, intergenerational and life-phase oriented. It suggests practical organizational-level measures, such as a systematic change of positions over the life-course; a job design that takes account of different age profiles; life-long learning; active health and safety management; and flexible working-time options that enable individuals of different ages to work based on life-course-related requirements. Furthermore, age management guidelines recommend measures to actively recruit and retain older workers (Flynn and McNair, 2007; Naegele and Walker, 2006).

In this chapter, we discuss organizational-level age management policies and practices from a multi-level and interdisciplinary perspective. We will first apply a *macro-level* perspective based on comparative age management research that discusses whether and how firm-level age management differs across countries and industrial sectors. In doing so, we outline international and national pressures for the introduction of firm-level age management. We then apply a *micro-level* perspective and discuss how age management policies in companies should be tailored to better capture the potential of an aging workforce and of age-diverse work teams. In the penultimate section of the chapter, we highlight why and how individuals and organizations can profit if age management is stringently introduced and the corporate culture is adapted accordingly. Overall, we aim to provide a coherent description of the current research on age management in companies by integrating macro and micro-level research.

The consequences of demographic change, and the resulting need for the proactive management of an aging workforce, have received attention in the fields of management, sociology, psychology, social policy, economics, law and gerontology in the Americas, Europe and Asia (Armstrong-Stassen, 2008; Duncan, 2008; Hedge, 2008; Riach, 2009; Yamada, 2010). Muller-Camen et al. (2011a), however, suggest that, even though macro-level research has provided comparative perspectives on how national environments influence older workers' employment and retirement transitions and trajectories (Ebbinghaus, 2006; Maltby, De Vroom, Mirabile and Overbye, 2004), age management literature rarely considers national-level policy differences that filter international convergence pressures, such as globalization and European legislation. This lack of research exists even though it is expected that national institutional pressures lead to the development of country-specific HRM (Muller-Camen et al., 2004). As such, this section considers change pressures at the international and national level that affect organizations' age management. We argue that, despite international convergence factors, the national institutional context matters in relation to how and why organizations design their HRM approaches.

INTERNATIONAL DRIVERS FOR AGE MANAGEMENT

Previous studies have discussed factors that influence organizational age management approaches similarly across national contexts at the international level. The first factor is the process of globalization, which has caused a tertiarization of the economy in industrialized countries. Consequently, the service sector gains in influence due to its increasing size, while the primary and secondary sectors lose their former importance (Castells, 2000). As a consequence, industries, such as mining, ship building or textiles, in which older workers were previously employed, are either in decline or production is shifted to low labor-cost countries (Buchholz, Hofäcker and Blossfeld, 2006). Hence, work opportunities for older workers in such industries in industrialized countries are decreasingly available. Secondly, technological progress results in a change in the qualification profiles required by many occupations. Information and communication technology skills are increasingly important (Castells, 2000), which, however, (some) older workers might not (yet) possess (Buchholz et al., 2006). Hence, older workers who lack required technological skills might no longer be considered employable (Fortuny, Nesporova and Popova, 2003; Loretto and White, 2006). These two trends have in the past led to an increasing and premature externalization of older workers from the labor market.

Nevertheless, there are also international trends that push national policy-makers and organizations towards extending older workers' working lives. In Europe, one such factor is the European Union (EU) framework directives aimed at increasing the labor market participation of those aged 55plus (EC, 2000, 2001), as well as to abandoning age discrimination in employment (Sargeant, 2008). This legislation is based on further international trends, such as demographic change, the aging labor force and the sustainability of social security systems (OECD, 2006), as discussed previously. Policy-makers and organizations are therefore faced with contradictory pressures. On the one hand, older workers might not be adequately prepared for today's labor market. On the other hand, policy-makers and organizations have to adhere to legislation by increasing older workers' labor market participation; they can no longer externalize older workers on grounds now covered by anti-age discrimination legislation.

The question that now remains is whether these pressures lead to the implementation of similar or different organizational HRM policies across countries. Convergence theory argues that (HR) management practices converge across countries due to the increasing importance of international trends (Kerr, Dunlop, Harbison and Myers, 1960). Contrary to this, institutional theory argues that organizational policies remain different across countries, because of the influence of national institutions (Hall and Wailes, 2009).

THE ROLE OF INSTITUTIONAL THEORY IN ACCOUNTING FOR NATIONALLY-DISTINCT MODELS OF AGE MANAGEMENT

International and comparative HRM research employs institutional theory to assist in identifying differences in organizational policies across countries and explaining differences in the role of the institutional context (Hall and Wailes, 2009). Institutional theory stipulates that national institutions influence how organizations design HRM policies (Hall and Soskice, 2001). Institutions have the function of regulating the behavior of organizations and can be formal, such as laws, or informal, such as conventions (North, 1994).

In contrast to convergence theory, institutional theory suggests that each national context consists of institutions that impact the organizational structure and behavior distinctively, regardless of similar global change pressures (McGaughey and De Cieri, 1999). This hypothesis is underpinned by the 'National Business Systems' (Whitley, 1999) and 'Varieties of Capitalism' (VoC) (Hall and Soskice, 2001) literature. Previous studies have found differences between various national institutional contexts (Mayer and Whittington, 2004), leading to variations in (HR) management practices (Bowen, Galang and Pillai, 2002; Kostova, Roth and Dacin, 2008). Hence, HRM policies at the firm-level are assumed to differ between countries.

Considering comparative age management, the discussion of the effects of different VoCs upon the management of older workers is taken up by Ebbinghaus (2006). He found that, despite global change pressures, countries display different age management approaches, resulting in divergent retirement timing outcomes. These outcomes range from early retirement to working beyond the national retirement age, depending on the national institutional policies that support one or the other retirement timing model. Similarly, Schroder, Hofäcker and Muller-Camen (2009) illustrated that age management differs between the 'liberal market economy' of Britain and the 'coordinated market economy' of Germany. This is the result of differences in their institutional environments, such as their labor market policies.

Lain (2012) furthermore suggested that age management might differ between similar VoC regimes. He found that national policies towards working past retirement, including the existence of a default retirement age (DRA), influence work opportunities for those aged 65plus in Britain and the United States of America (USA). Even though both countries are considered 'liberal market economies', the existence of a DRA in Britain has resulted in less qualified work opportunities for those past retirement age in Britain in comparison to the USA, where anti-age discrimination legislation has prohibited that employers automatically retire employees when they reach pension age.

This discussion suggests that national institutions exist that influence age management. Such institutions include: the pension system; the availability of early retirement pathways; the structure of the labor market (internal versus external) (Blossfeld, Buchholz and Hofäcker, 2006); the role of the state (interventionist versus non-interventionist) (Hall and Soskice, 2001); and the access to life-long learning (Taylor, Brooke and Biase, 2010).

Hofäcker and Pollnerová (2006) suggested that the employment rate of individuals aged 50 and over is mediated by the respective national context's design of work and retirement incentives. They found that countries with low welfare incentives for early retirement, such as social-democratic and liberal countries (e.g., Norway, Sweden, the USA and the United Kingdom (UK)), experience a relatively high labor market participation of those aged 50 and over. In contrast, countries with strong (state-financed) early exit options and welfare subsidies experience lower labor market participation rates. These countries primarily belong to the conservative welfare state

cluster, and include Germany, Italy and Spain.

Hofäcker and Pollnerová (2006) also found a systematic relationship between the degree of employment regulations, such as employment protection, and labor market participation rates. Countries with medium to high employment protection, such as conservative and Southern European countries, show lower employment rates of individuals aged 50 and over than do countries with low employment protection, such as liberal welfare states (e.g., UK and USA). This is because high employment protection regulations might deter organizations from hiring unemployed older individuals, as it might be difficult to lay them off again.

Hofäcker and Pollnerová (2006) further discussed the effects of national active employment policies upon the employment rates of older workers. They found that countries with a higher public expenditure on active labor market programs (measured as a percentage of national Gross Domestic Product) tended to show higher employment rates of those aged 50 and over. Such active labor market policies were primarily found in Denmark and Sweden. However, even though liberal welfare states, such as the UK and USA, tend to leave employment regulation to the market and tend not to engage in active labor market policies, they have a similarly high old age employment rate. This indicates that, in these cases, the role of the state in intervening in labor market processes is mediated by the existence, or lack, of welfare state provisions in supporting older unemployed workers, thereby pushing such individuals back into the labor market.

Fourthly, Hofäcker and Pollnerová (2006) discussed the role of life-long learning opportunities upon the employment rate of older workers. They found that countries in which life-long learning plays a significant role, such as in liberal and social-democratic countries, exhibit higher labor market participation rates of those aged 50 and over than countries in which life-long learning is less prevalent, such as conservative and

Southern European countries. This is because life-long learning is directly linked with the updating of skills relevant to maintaining productivity.

While institutional theory suggests that organizational policies vary between countries, it assumes that organizations within the same context implement similar policies. There are multiple pressures within an institutional environment that result in relative organizational convergence, leading to a potentially path-dependent behavior where organizations tend to follow the path prescribed by national institutions, such as the labor market or the welfare state system (Sydow, Schreyögg and Koch, 2009). Path-dependency reduces organizational uncertainty and promotes stability within the institutional context (Scott, 1987). However, institutions are not stable, but evolving (Greenwood, Suddaby and Hinings, 2002). Therefore, comparative age management research in Britain and Germany found the emergence of new institutions in influencing age management. Even though age management was found to be largely path-dependent, Muller-Camen et al. (2011a) discovered that trade unions in Germany and age lobbyists in Britain influenced employers' age management option exploration within institutionally-set boundaries.

INSTITUTIONAL CHANGE AND THE ROLE OF HUMAN AGENCY IN MEDIATING THE INFLUENCE OF NATIONAL INSTITUTIONS: THE EXAMPLE OF AGE MANAGEMENT

Institutional theory therefore also discusses the establishment of new institutions and the destabilization of old ones. Dacin, Goodstein and Scott (2002: 45) suggested that 'institutions change over time, are not uniformly taken-for-granted, have effects that are particularistic, and are challenged.' Consequently, institutional change leads to a break with existing institutions within a national context (Schneiberg, 2007).

With regard to age management, pressures leading to the destabilization of old institutions include demographic change, the aging workforce, the sustainability of social security systems, globalization, and legal changes. As a result of these exogenous drivers, national institutions, such as the labor market and pension systems, are adapted to accommodate such changes. Consequently, employers and other actors are expected to adjust their age management approaches (Flynn, Upchurch, Muller-Camen and Schroder, 2013).

Changes to the institutional context based on exogenous factors that lead to breaks with existing institutions furthermore suggest that there might be increasing diversity within institutional contexts, where organizations are assumed to have 'space' to deviate from established practices (Almond et al., 2005). Indeed, studies have found that institutional contexts have internal diversity (Wood, Croucher, Brewster, Collings and Brookes, 2009). Similarities between HRM practices have also been found between organizations operating in different VoC regimes (Croucher, Gooderham and Parry, 2006).

These findings propose that there might be more diversity within, and more convergence between, national systems than assumed by institutional theory. Such findings are also emerging in the comparative age management literature.

Muller-Camen et al. (2011b) argue that sectoral peculiarities and organizational-level pressures lead to differences in age management among organizations in the same context, while organizations in different contexts might exhibit similarities. This was the case in a comparison of organizations in Britain and Germany, where retail firms had implemented similar practices based on sectoral and organizational change pressures, despite different institutional forces. This implies that endogenous, or firm-specific, factors should be taken into account when studying age management. This is supported by Walker (2005: 685), who postulated that the 'key internal aspects of organizations, especially the human resource and development culture and the existence of high profile sponsors, are crucial in progressing successful age management initiatives.'

Diversity within countries might occur because the institutional context possibly affords organizations space to maneuver (Almond et al., 2005) and because high profile sponsors push policies that might go beyond the space provided by the context (Walker, 2005). Such options call into question the overly determining role of institutions, as postulated by institutional theory, and highlight the role of rational choice, or human agency, in the organizational decision-making processes. The concept of human agency denotes that individuals have the capacity to exercise control over the nature and quality of their lives by acting intentionally, by applying forethought and by reflecting about their capabilities in light of socio-structural influences (Bandura, 2001). While early works in institutional studies primarily considered the influence of the context upon organizations and individual actors, institutional entrepreneurship literature integrated a theory of action into institutional theory (Heugens and Lander, 2009). The theory of action was applied to eliminate the assumption of organizations and individuals as being 'overly socialized and slavishly devoted to the reproduction of habits' (Battilana, Leca and Boxenbaum, 2009: 67).

While the role of institutional entrepreneurs has been explored in a variety of (management) fields (Maguire, Hardy and Lawrence, 2004), the approach has so far not been applied with regard to comparative age management. However, the study of how institutional entrepreneurs overcome institutional barriers in designing age management will shed some light on how endogenous factors and the influence of high profile sponsors can alter age management, despite constraining national institutions. This is because organizations and individual actors realize that age management can act as a competitive advantage.

In the next section, we will discuss how HR managers, as examples of institutional entrepreneurs, can design and execute different

types of HRM strategies to gain this competitive advantage.

MICRO-LEVEL AGE MANAGEMENT IN COMPANIES: POTENTIAL DIMENSIONS AND DESIGNS

As we defined in the introduction of this chapter, the term 'age management' refers to the organizational HRM dimensions employed to manage human resources with an explicit focus on the demands of an aging workforce. Having established the *macro* role of the international and institutional contexts in influencing age management, the following section elaborates on the *micro* organizational-level motivations and change pressures to implement age management, as well as on the actual HRM dimensions suggested to satisfy the challenges posed by demographic change and the aging workforce. While institutional theory assumes that the design and implementation of HRM should be context-specific, the literature has, across countries, formulated best practice guidelines with regard to age management (Armstrong-Stassen and Templer, 2006; Naegele and Walker, 2011; Patrickson and Hartmann, 1995). These best practice guidelines are introduced in more detail subsequently.

Such best practices should be adapted to local institutional demands prior to the design and implementation of specific organizational policies. As outlined in the previous section, however, organizations and individual agents might have space to formulate HRM policies that do not 'slavishly' follow institutional conventions, but that take divergent organization-specific requirements and philosophies into account.

Scholars have proposed different HRM fields of activity within age management, however, in most cases, there is a significant overlap. Casey Metcalf and Lakey (1993) and Walker (2005) mention job recruitment (and) exit; training; development and promotion; flexible working practices; ergonomics and job design; and changing attitudes towards aging workers, as the most important domains of age management in the European Union. Similarly, Naegele and Walker (2011) developed a list of the primary dimensions of age management: job recruitment; learning, training and life-long learning; career development; flexible working practices; health protection and promotion and workplace design; redeployment; employment exit and transition to retirement. This approach is consistent with the work of Armstrong-Stassen and colleagues (Armstrong-Stassen, 2008; Armstrong-Stassen and Lee, 2009; Armstrong-Stassen and Templer, 2006; Armstrong-Stassen and Ursel, 2009), who focused on the Canadian context and proposed flexible working options; training and development; job design; recognition and respect; performance evaluation; compensation; and pre/post-retirement options as the typical components of age management. Other scholarly works, such as Patrickson and Hartmann's (1995) study of the Australian context and Boehm, Kunze and Bruch's (forthcoming) study of the German context identify and build upon similar clusters.

For our review, we strive to display a holistic picture, taking into account as many relevant dimensions as possible. Building upon and consolidating the theoretical and empirical work mentioned previously, we subsequently discuss the dimensions of *recruiting, training and life-long learning, career management and redeployment, flexible working times and alternative work arrangements, health management and workplace accommodations, performance measurement and remuneration, transition to retirement,* as well as *integrated age management approaches.* For each of these dimensions, we outline organizations' motivations to engage in such practices, as well as examples of concrete HRM activities.

RECRUITING

Referring to the definition by Walker (1996: 3), good practice in the dimension of age-related recruiting ensures 'that older workers have either equal or special access to the available job and that potential applicants are not discriminated against either directly or indirectly'.

Advantages of age-related recruiting practices

Organizations have a motivation to engage in age-related recruiting practices for a variety of reasons. The first reason is that national economies have to deal with simultaneously shrinking and aging labor forces, potentially leading to a 'war for talent' (Michaels, Handfield-Jones and Axelrod, 2001). For Germany, demographers have projected a workforce decline of 10 million workers by 2050, equaling 20 percent of the total workforce (Deutsches Statistisches Bundesamt, 2009). For countries like the USA, with comparably high birth rates, the impending retirement of the over-proportionally large baby boomer generation will cause problems in relation to filling open job positions (Dychtwald, Erickson and Morison, 2004). This is especially true for potentially missing younger job applicants, as the gap between labor needed and labor available is going to widen continually. Consequently, organizations should 'redefine talent' and actively recruit older employees to broaden their hiring pool (Armstrong-Stassen and Templer, 2005).

The second reason is that older job entrants might possess better complementary skills, knowledge, and expertise when compared to younger employees, enabling a more fruitful intergenerational discussion, joint problem-solving, and the prevention of group think (Austin, 2003; Harrison and Klein, 2007; Janis, 1972). The active recruitment of individuals aged 50 and over has additional advantages for firms. Employees who are of a similar age as their customers should have a better understanding of their customers' behavior and preferences (Jackson and Alvarez, 1992; Cox, 1993). This is of importance for companies, as consumers between the ages of 40 and 70 will become a major customer group – both in terms of quantity (due to their growing number) and purchasing power (due to their high savings) (GFK, 2008; Kohlbacher and Herstatt, 2009).

The final reason is that actively recruiting older individuals might positively affect the internal perceptions of diversity (Kossek, Lobel and Brown, 2006; Kossek, Markel and McHugh, 2003) and the external image of the organization.

Forms and examples of age-related recruiting practices

The active and targeted recruitment of applicants aged 50 and over is a comparably innovative approach, given the long history of early retirement in most industrialized countries (Harris, 1991; Patrickson and Hartmann, 1995). However, to implement such strategies, certain basic prerequisites have to be met. These include the abolishment of implicit and explicit age limits in job advertisements, job descriptions, and career paths. Job advertisements could be designed and communicated in an age-neutral way or even targeted at older age groups. In addition, job interviewers and interview procedures should focus on experiences and skills, instead of chronological age. Recruiters should also ascertain that they do not use selection methods which are inherently negatively biased against older workers (Patrickson and Hartmann, 1995; Salthouse, 1990).

The absence of negative stereotypes and prejudices based on workers' age among potential interviewers, HRM, top management, and leadership personnel is another critical pre-condition (Gordon and Arvey, 2004; Lin, Dobbins and Farh, 1992; Posthuma and Campion, 2009). In their study of 493 HR managers in Canada, Armstrong-Stassen and Templer (2005) found that approximately 20 percent of the companies they investigated had already implemented practices to attract older employees. Furthermore, about 50 percent of the remaining organizations indicated that they were expecting to implement such practices in the future.

Organizations can choose among different recruiting strategies to attract older individuals. On the one hand, companies can recruit older personnel who have not been previously employed by the company. Besides their normal recruiting methods, they can set up special job campaigns or use databases and online portals focused on older experts. In some cases, the help of external recruiting agencies or government institutions also seems advisable (Naegele and Walker, 2011). One the other hand, they can engage in activities to re-recruit retired employees. The period of vocational adjustment is comparably short for these employees, as they have job-relevant knowledge and skills, and the right cultural fit. Employers can rehire their former staff on the basis of contract or consulting work, or they can offer them full- or part-time positions.

In a comparative survey of employers in Greece, Hungary, Spain, the Netherlands, and the UK, Van Dalen and colleagues (2010) found that British (42 percent) and Hungarian employers (31 percent) were more likely to recruit older workers than Greek (8 percent), Dutch (8 percent), or Spanish firms (7 percent). Furthermore, they found a consistent pattern, indicating that re-recruiting retired employees is about half as likely as the recruitment of new older individuals.

TRAINING AND LIFE-LONG LEARNING

Age-related training and life-long learning practices assure that older employees are not disadvantaged with regard to training access throughout their life-course and that training practices accommodate the specific needs of older individuals (Walker, 1996).

Advantages of age-related training and life-long learning practices

Historically, training in organizations was often targeted at young employees in their early career stages, as firms expected a longer period of amortization (Van Yoder, 2002). In addition, widespread stereotypes existed that older employees were less intelligent (Raza and Carpenter, 1987), had less potential for development, (Duncan, 2001; Wrenn and Maurer, 2004), and were less trainable than their younger colleagues (Brooke and Taylor, 2005; Rosen and Jerdee, 1989). Consequently, in the past, organizations were less willing to invest in the training of older employees (Rosen and Jerdee, 1976); hence, older employees had less access to training (Barth, McNaught and Rizzi, 1993; Rix, 1996; Taylor and Urwin, 2001).

In contrast to such common age-related prejudices, research has demonstrated that older workers are able to acquire new skills and technologies (Sterns and Doverspike, 1988). In addition, research in developmental psychology shows that there is no general decline in intellectual capabilities during the aging process (Cunningham, 1987; Kanfer and Ackerman, 2004), especially with regard to crystallized intelligence that builds upon and includes educational and experiential knowledge, extent of vocabulary, verbal comprehension and communication skills (Cattell, 1987).

While training and learning might be more time consuming for older employees (Kubeck, Delp, Haslet and McDaniel, 1996; Birren and Fisher, 1995), it is still possible and is also an organizational necessity (Warr, 2001). In times of the fast-paced, technology-driven economy and aging workforces, companies cannot risk creating a vicious circle of a lack of training and eroding vocational and learning skills. Consequently, it seems advisable for companies to invest in training activities for employees of all age groups to raise the qualification level of employees with potentially positive implications for firms' overall productivity and performance. Besides skill improvement, such training and development activities for both younger and older workers should also have a motivational effect. By investing in training, employers express a form of acknowledgement for all employees and demonstrate the company's reliance upon everybody's full participation until retirement.

Forms and examples of age-related training and life-long learning practices

Armstrong-Stassen and Templer (2006) investigated the level of engagement in age-related training practices among 493 Canadian public and private sector organizations. They found that almost 50 percent of the organizations did not engage in life-long learning to update current skills, as well as convey new skills and expertise. About 10 percent of the organizations reported that they were engaged in these practices, while close to 40 percent indicated that they were somewhat engaged. Close to 70 percent stated that they provided older employees with access to new technologies.

Naegele and Walker (2011) provided further examples of age-related training practices, such as targeted skills assessments and competence databases, in order to keep track of organizations' overall skill levels, as well as its age distribution. Furthermore, job rotations with related on-the-job-training was described as an effective training strategy. Research has also proposed that tailored training programs for specific age groups seem to be reasonable.

The industrial gerontology model suggests that five factors are particularly important when designing trainings for older learners (Belbin and Belbin, 1972; Sterns and Doverspike, 1988; 1989). These are motivation, structure, familiarity, organization, and time. With regard to all of these five dimensions, certain adaptations seem advisable that account for important physical and cognitive aging effects of older learners (Birren and Fisher, 1995). For instance, older training participants should get sufficient time to finish the training successfully and should be able to link the new information to existing, job-related knowledge (Sterns and Doverspike, 1988). Based on these considerations, training adaptations with regard to instructional methods and instructional factors seem essential.

With regard to instructional methods, especially modeling (where learners observe another person executing a behavior) and active participation (where learners perform the focal task themselves) were proposed as being effective, while traditional lecturing (with a unidirectional flow of information) was regarded as less suitable. In a meta-analysis including 41 studies, Callahan, Kiker and Cross (2003) found that all three lecturing types explained unique variance in observed training performance for older participants. Consequently, an effective training for older employees might use a multi-method approach, combining all three types of knowledge transfer.

With regard to further instructional factors, Callahan and colleagues (2003) meta-analytically investigated the role of supplementary materials, feedback, pacing, and group size. Again, based on potential deficits in attentional memory processes and a reduced learning speed, one might expect that older learners' training success is more dependent on written course materials (references guides, etc.), support and feedback from the trainer, more time and the option for self-pacing, as well as a smaller group size (with more trainer interaction and more psychological safety). In contrast to their hypotheses, Calahan and colleagues (2003) only found support for the importance of self-pacing and group size while the other two factors were unrelated to training success. Self-pacing showed by far the largest relationship with training success, indicating the need to avoid time pressure for older learners and providing them with the opportunity to assume responsibility for their learning progress. This seems especially relevant when they are confronted with new technologies (Gist, Rosen and Schworer, 1988).

An adjustment in the training methods for the needs and learning styles of older workers was also investigated by Armstrong-Stassen and Templer (2006) in their Canadian study. They found that only about 10 percent of companies already engaged in these practices. As for other age management dimensions, organizations should not make the mistake of focusing their training activities solely on older employees. It is necessary to invest in training for all age groups and to adapt training measures to specific needs and preferences throughout the life-course (Beaver and Hutchings, 2005).

CAREER MANAGEMENT AND REDEPLOYMENT

Naegele and Walker (2011) and Armstrong-Stassen and Ursel (2009) state that age-related career management involves practices that foster employees' chances to progress within the organization, irrespective of age. In this way, they obtain developmental opportunities, including life-long learning, throughout their careers. If employees' capability profiles no longer match their current task or job descriptions, redeployment may become a promising intervention strategy.

Advantages of age-related career management and redeployment

As Patrickson and Hartmann (1995) point out, career management differs between age groups, as long-term career perspectives might be more important for younger employees than for older ones. Nevertheless, older employees' remaining working lifetime has increased over the last few decades (Rix, 1990; Buoncore, 1992). As such, it is more important to provide employees aged 50 and over with a realistic and promising picture of their developmental perspectives within the firm (Sheppard, 1988; Siegel 1993). The introduction of new career models, as well as concrete career planning activities, seem to be key in successfully employing older workers' competencies. Moreover, firms can systematically check and align employees' abilities with the requirements of their workplaces to spur performance and prevent potential health problems (Ilmarinen, 2005). Active career management might also positively affect employees' intrinsic job motivation, as they perceive themselves as having a future in the organization; this includes potential promotions and new job opportunities.

Forms and examples of age-related career management and redeployment

A good starting point for age-related career management is the introduction of regular career talks in which employees' expectations and managers' appraisals are compared and discussed. Based on these evaluations, concrete career plans can be developed. In addition, special career consultations, such as career development workshops, for employees above a certain age, can be introduced. As the primary goal of such discussions, both the organization and the employee should strive for a clarification of each others' expectations and for an agreement on future development paths.

In cases where older workers have no ambition or possibility of striving for promotions, alternative career models might be a solution. These models include sideways career movements, project work assignments and downshifting (Hall, 1985; Sundstrom, 1992). Firms should also take into account the specific competencies of older employees and look for roles or tasks where they can best possibly use their skills and experiences. Patrickson and Hartmann (1995) mention 'sounding board' roles or functions, such as coaching and mentoring, where they can provide emotional support for younger colleagues.

Related to such career development initiatives is the topic of redeployment, defined as a compensatory measure in response to performance constraints, where employees enter new workplaces that assure a better fit between work demands and individuals' achievement potentials (Naegele and Walker, 2011). If managed properly, such redeployments can positively affect employees' motivation, health, and performance, and assure employment until retirement age. As Armstrong-Stassen and Templer (2006) show, such job reassignments and job transfers are comparably widespread, as more than 55 percent of the studied organizations indicated that they were somewhat or highly engaged in these activities.

To be successful in career management and career redeployment, companies must know their employees' abilities and health profiles, as well as their workplaces' requirements (in terms of physical and psychological constraints). It is also important that all organizational stakeholders, such as the management, HRM, employees, unions, and company physicians, collaborate effectively to achieve the best possible fit between the job and the job holder. Finally, it seems important to link activities in career management and redeployment with other dimensions of age management, such as training, working-time practices or workplace accommodations that all have important interfaces with one another.

FLEXIBLE WORKING TIME AND ALTERNATIVE WORK ARRANGEMENTS

Flexible working time practices provide employees with greater flexibility concerning contractually-agreed working hours and work scheduling in order to reflect employees' changing work preferences over their life-course (Naegele and Walker, 2011; Walker, 1996).

Advantages of flexible working time and alternative work arrangements

The importance of working time flexibility at the macro level was highlighted by Vaupel and Loichinger (2006), who described the need to fundamentally rethink the current practices of working time distribution over an individual's life span. They emphasize that individuals experience a significant concentration of tasks between age 20 and 40, including education, work, child rearing, and leisure. The option of part-time employment for employees, including older workers, would enable a better distribution of work over the life time. Also, on the micro level, working time flexibility is associated with positive outcomes, such as increased motivation and performance from a better work-life balance, as well as better health levels, reduced sick leaves, and a better utilization of labor resources (Fevre, 1991; Naegele and Walker, 2011). As with other dimensions of age management, such flexibility does not only serve older workers, but equally serves individuals of all ages with, for example, caring responsibilities.

Forms and examples of flexible working times and alternative work arrangements

Flexible working time practices can comprise different working time arrangements, such as flexible work schedules or starting times. In their study on Canadian organizations, Armstrong-Stassen and Templer (2006) report such flexible schedules as the most prevalent working time practice, with 20.7 percent of the studied organizations being highly engaged and 39.7 percent being somewhat engaged in doing so. Moreover, firms can introduce part-time employment such as a reduced workweek. This practice was already popular with the firms (9.7 percent highly engaged, 33.7 percent somewhat engaged) (Armstrong-Stassen and Templer, 2006). Moreover, there seems to be a trend towards even more flexibility, as 68.4 percent of the organizations indicated increasing engagement in the future.

If organizations want to allow for longer periods of absence, and compensate for work peaks, they can introduce sabbatical systems, working time accounts, or annual working hours. Working at home is another way to create more working time flexibility, allowing employees to balance work needs with family responsibilities. Job sharing might also be an option, where more than one person shares a workplace or job function. Finally, flexible time arrangements can be supplemented by special incentives, like eldercare unpaid leave. For working time practices, such as a home office, job sharing, and unpaid leaves, Armstrong-Stassen and Templer (2006) report comparably high values, with about 50 percent of organizations already having implemented such schemes.

HEALTH MANAGEMENT AND WORKPLACE ACCOMMODATIONS

Age-related health management and respective workplace accommodations relate to both an introduction of corporate health initiatives, as well as an optimal organization and (re-)design of work processes and workplaces to ensure employees' long-term health and capacity to work (Naegele and Walker, 2002).

Advantages of health management and workplace accomodations

It is a fact that both physical and psychological skills change over the course of a person's life. There is evidence that a person's sensory functions (auditory and visual senses), motor functions (e.g., physical strength), and cardiorespiratory functions tend to decline with age (Ilmarinen, 1994, 2001; Kemper, 1994; Robinson, 1986; Spirduso and MacRae, 1990; Robertson and Tracy, 1998). However, it is necessary to stop perceiving age as a form of disease. Age is a biological process that starts at birth. Workers aged 50 and over generally do not receive more injuries or take more sick leave than their younger co-workers. However, once older workers are injured or become ill, their recovery times are significantly longer than that of younger individuals (Wieland, 2010; Dychtwald et al., 2006; Patrickson and Hartmann, 1995). In addition, perceived health problems are a primary predictor of older workers' early retirement decisions (Mein, Martikainen, Stansfeld, Brunner, Fuhrer and Marmot, 2000) and a source of performance differences between younger and older workers (McCann and Giles, 2002). Hence, an aim of age management must be to prevent (chronic) health problems among employees, to maintain their productivity and working ability. Such an approach should not focus exclusively on older employees, but target all employees.

Forms and examples of health management and workplace accommodations

A variety of health management and work-place accommodations can lead to a more productive and successful workplace. A pro-active health management system should be based on providing safe working conditions that prevent accidents, workplace injuries, and occupational diseases. As Neville (1998) estimates, up to 85 percent of all workplace injuries might be avoided by providing appropriate training and implementing safe workplace practices.

Research has also indicated clear links between health promotion programs, including health education, screening and interventions, fitness programs, as well as stress management, and employees' health, reduced absenteeism, and increased motivation and job satisfaction (Conrad, 1988a, 1988b; Daley and Parfitt, 1996). The positive impact of health promotion programs upon key financial indicators has been studied extensively (Aldana, 2001; Heaney and Goetzel, 1997; Pelletier, 2001). If organizations want to retain their older personnel and maintain their work ability, they should implement preventive health promotion programs throughout an employee's entire professional life. As such, employees' health conditions should be evaluated regularly, and, depending on these assessments, preventive measures may be taken (Danna and Griffin, 1999). If necessary, organizations can also adjust individuals' workloads, job descriptions, and workplaces. In order to do so, companies must systematically analyze and document potential health risks associated with certain workplaces (Naegele and Walker, 2011).

Organizations might also have to implement specific workplace accommodations, such as ergonomic seating, which might help prevent health problems among older employees and/or vulnerable occupational groups. That being said, an ergonomic (re-)design of workplaces is an effective method to prevent health problems and increase performance for all workers, including younger employees and white collar workers. As Bell (2007) reports, 71 percent of necessary workplace accommodations cost less than 500 USD per case, while 20 percent of recommended accommodations do not cost anything.

Another organizational characteristic that firms should foster is a health-oriented culture. To accomplish this, they might introduce incentive and bonus programs that reward health-conscious behaviors, such as participating in sports or voluntary health checks, organizing special health events (e.g., a breast cancer day), providing healthy food options on-site, and giving line managers the means to actively foster the health levels of their team, for example, by structuring the workload and engaging in early intervention behaviors in the case of a long-term absence.

Companies should also be aware of the rising importance of psychological health. As recent data for Germany indicates, the number of days absent due to psychological disorders rose from 33.6 million in 2001 to 53.5 million in 2010 (Handelsblatt, 2012). Similar trends are reported by Barmer GEK (Wieland, 2010), an organization with more than 8.6 million customers, making it one of Germany's largest health insurers. According to their data, psychological health problems account for 17.6 percent of all days absent (rank 2 overall), with an average absence of 40.5 days per case. Organizations should react to these challenges by training managers in regard to dealing with psychological disorders and by monitoring and reducing employees' occupational stress levels.

PERFORMANCE MEASUREMENT AND REMUNERATION

Age-related performance measurement and remuneration refer to a fair, non-discriminatory, and potentially age-specific assessment and rewarding of employees' accomplishments (Patrickson and Hartmann, 1995).

Advantages of age-related performance measurement and remuneration

It is a prevalent age stereotype that older employees might show lower job performance than their younger colleagues, due to declining mental or physical abilities, or increasing resistance to change (Cuddy and Fiske, 2002; Gordon and Arvey, 2004; McCann and Giles, 2002; Rosen and Jerdee, 1976). Empirical evidence supporting this poor performance stereotype is, however, scarce (Ferris and King, 1992; Reio, Sanders-Rejo and Reio, 1999). In contrast, meta-analytical results show no relationship between age and performance (McEvoy and Cascio, 1989, Ng and Feldman, 2008), or even a positive relationship when job performance was measured by productivity or peer evaluations (Waldman and Avolio, 1986). Nevertheless, Waldman and Avolio (1986) illustrated that employees' performance decreases with age, if measured by supervisor evaluations. More recent research, however, did not fully support this finding (Liden, Stilwell and Ferris, 1996). In fact, supervisors' subjective appraisals of employee performance might be prone to age bias (Sterns and Alexander, 1988). In addition, forced ranking appraisal systems might increase bias against older workers due to social comparison processes (Osborne and McCann, 2004; Shore and Goldberg, 2005). Consequently, for organizations, it seems key to find ways to evaluate employees' performance in a non-discriminatory way, irrespective of age.

Performance has to be rewarded fairly. There are stereotypes that older employees are more costly than younger colleagues due to higher wages and more generous financial benefits (Capowski, 1994), leading to perceptions of lower economic value (Finkelstein and Burke, 1998; Ostroff and Atwater, 2003). Empirical studies of this stereotype are limited, with some evidence that salaries increase until the age of 50, but flatten out afterwards (Hedge, Borman and Lammlein, 2006). Other studies report no significant cost differences between younger and older workers (Broadbridge, 2001).

Forms and examples of age-related performance measurement and remuneration

To find fair methods of evaluating and rewarding employees of all age groups, organizations have to decide if they want to adjust appraisals for potential age-related differences in employee performance. For instance, if only quantity is taken into account, older employees' performance might decrease. However, if quality is considered, older employees' performance might increase. Consequently, organizations have to decide what constitutes 'good' performance (Patrickson and Hartmann, 1995).

Organizations have multiple options regarding the actual performance assessment. First, they can rely on traditional supervisor evaluations; however, they should ascertain that supervisors are aware of common stereotypes and are trained to evaluate employees' performance fairly. Second, to make supervisors' evaluations more comparable and fair across the organization, standardized systems, such as measures of competence or structured reviews (e.g., Management by Objectives-systems) might be introduced. In doing so, potential influences of age bias might be reduced as evaluators focus more on individual abilities and accomplishments instead of age group membership (Fiske and Neuberg, 1990; Posthuma and Campion, 2009). Third, organizations could complement supervisor's assessments with additional sources of information, such as 360 degree peer evaluation systems.

With regard to remuneration, organizations have to overcome traditional seniority-based compensation systems that couple higher age with higher wages and salaries. While it seems reasonable to reward experience, an automatic increase irrespective of performance gains seems unsuitable. Therefore, organizations have started to replace regular salary increases by broader pay bands with fewer levels within each band (Patrickson and Hartmann, 1995; Selby-Smith, 1994). To introduce 'pay-for-performance' philosophies, organizations have to negotiate with relevant stakeholders, especially in highly unionized contexts.

TRANSITION TO RETIREMENT

At some point in an employee's career, retirement is the logical next step. To enable a smooth transition between working life and retirement is beneficial for both the organization and the employees.

Advantages of a smooth transition to retirement

For employees, a smooth transition to retirement facilitates their acclimatization to this new life phase. The smooth transition is recommended, as an abrupt transition to retirement can be problematic. Both sociological role theory (Kim and Moen, 2001) and continuity theory (Richardson and Kilty, 1991) emphasize potentially negative effects of retirement for subjective well-being, as employment typically holds a prominent role within an individual's self concept (Pinquart and Schindler, 2007; Reitzes and Mutran, 2002). The abrupt loss of this role might cause psychological distress with potentially negative effects on well-being, satisfaction, or health (Pinquart and Schindler, 2007). In contrast, a gradual retirement might enable individuals to better cope with the new situation by identifying new roles and activities. These might include a stronger focus on private and family life or the development of new interests, such as a hobby or volunteer activity (Wu, Tang and Yan, 2005).

For organizations, gradual retirement processes seem equally advantageous. One reason is that companies do not lose their crucial knowledge 'over night'. Instead, knowledge can be transferred to potential job successors through means of intergenerational teams. Another reason is that a smoother and better-planned retirement process might enable companies to stay in contact with pensioners, even after the final retirement day, to draw on their competencies for special projects.

Finally, an employee-friendly and supporting retirement process might also positively affect the internal and external image of the organization (Naegele and Walker, 2011).

Forms and examples of a smooth transition to retirement

Since organizations can pursue different activities to provide employees with a more gradual transition to retirement, Armstrong-Stassen and Templer (2006: 252) explored the prevalence of three basic options in the Canadian context for gradual retirement transitions, namely 'providing partial or phased retirement', 'providing trial retirement' (giving retirees the opportunity to return to work after a specific time period), and 'providing retirement with call-back arrangements (re-employment of retirees)'. They found that retirement with call-back arrangements and partial retirement were much more common than trial retirement. For all three options, however, companies expected an increase in future engagement. Additional activities include preparatory measures for future retirees, such as workshops or counseling facilities, focusing on the job-retirement transition.

It is important to note that the economic, legal, and labor market context plays an important role in the design of retirement transition activities (Naegele and Walker, 2011). Organizations might have a limited sphere of influence, making it necessary to design options in light of legislation and in collaboration with social partners. Nevertheless, even under similar external conditions, companies have space in how they design their retirement programs.

Table 12.1 offers an overview of the different HR dimensions and related HR practices.

INTEGRATED AGE MANAGEMENT APPROACHES

While the introduction of particular age management strategies with regard to health management, training, or retirement might

Table 12.1

HR dimension	Definition	Advantages for companies	Forms and examples of age-related HR practices
RECRUITING	Equal or special access to jobs for older employees; no direct or indirect discrimination of older applicants.	– Enlarged **hiring pool** by considering older applicants; – Unique **skills, knowledge**, and **expertise** of older employees: joint problem-solving, prevention of group think; – **Customer orientation** through fit with age of major customer group; – Diversity-friendly **image** (internal and external) of the company.	– **Age-neutral** job advertisements, job descriptions, career paths; – Focus on experiences and skills (not age) in **job interviews**; – **No negative stereotypes** among responsible personnel (HR, line management); – Use of **recruitment instruments** (job campaigns, databases, online portals) targeting older employees; – **Re-recruitment** of retired employees (short adjustment phase, job-relevant knowledge and skills, cultural fit).
Training and life-long learning	Equal access to trainings throughout employees' work life; consideration of specific needs of older employees.	– Increased **qualification level** of employees improves productivity and performance; – Training as a form of acknowledgement has a **motivational effect**.	– Update of **existing skills** vs. acquiring **new skills**; – **Competence databases** (organizations' overall skill levels); – **Job rotation** with related on-the-job-training; – Principles for designing **trainings for specific age groups**: motivation, structure, familiarity, organization, and time; – Adaptation of **instructional methods**: modeling, active participation, multi-method approaches.
Career management and redeployment	Career management: Equal opportunities to progress within the organization, irrespective of age. Redeployment: Relocation of employees as a response to performance constraints to attain a better person-job-fit.	Career management: – **Fit** of employees' abilities and workplace requirements: Increased **performance** and prevention of **health** problems; – Increased intrinsic job motivation (focus on new job opportunities). Redeployment: – Increased **motivation, health**, and **performance**; – Assure employment until retirement age.	Career management: – Regular career talks or **career development workshops**; – **Alternative career models**: Lateral career moves, project work assignments, downshifting; – "**Sounding board**" and mentoring roles for older employees. Redeployment: – Ensure **fit** between employees' abilities and health profiles and workplaces' requirements; – Link career management / redeployment with **other age** management activities (e.g., training, accommodations).
Flexible working time and alternative work arrangements	Enabling employees to be flexible regarding their working hours and work scheduling compliant with changing work preferences during their work life.	– Increased employee **motivation**; – Increased **performance**; – Better **work-life balance**, **health** levels, and reduced sick leaves; – Better utilization of **labor resources**.	– **Flexible work schedules** or starting times; – **Part-time employment**, e.g. reduced workweek; – **Sabbatical systems**, **working time accounts**, **annual working hours**; – **Working from home**; – **Job sharing**; – **Special incentives**, e.g. eldercare unpaid leaves.

HR dimension	Definition	Advantages for companies	Forms and examples of age-related HR practices
Health management and workplace accommodations	Organizational actions for fostering employees' long-term health and work ability, esp. company health initiatives and (re-)design of work processes and workplaces.	– Prevention of longer **recovery times**; – Avoidance of **early retirement** decisions; – Reduced **performance differences** between younger and older workers; – Maintained **productivity** and **working ability**; – Improved health, reduced **absenteeism**, increased **motivation** and job **satisfaction**.	– Ensure **safe working conditions**; – **Health promotion programs** (health education, screening programs, stress management); – Adjustment of **individuals' workloads** and work tasks; – **Workplace accommodations**: e.g. ergonomics; – **Health-oriented culture**: Incentive systems for health-conscious behavior (on-site sports, health checks); – Foster **psychological health**.
Performance measurement and remuneration	Fair, non-discriminatory, and potentially age-specific assessment and rewarding of employees' accomplishments.	– **Fair reward** of performance, **fair methods** of evaluating and rewarding employees of all age groups; – Overcoming age-related performance **stereotypes**.	Performance assessment: – **(Re-)define "good" performance** (quantity vs. quality); – Performance assessment: **Supervisor evaluations** (evaluation training), **standardized systems** (reducing age bias), additional **information sources** (360 degree evaluation). Remuneration: – Reward of **performance gains**, not experience gains; – Broader **pay bands**; – **"Pay-for-performance"** philosophy.
Transition to retirement	Enabling a smooth transition between working life and retirement.	– Gradual retirement: No sudden loss of **crucial knowledge**; – **Transfer** of knowledge to job successors; – Keep contact to pensioners to turn to their **competencies** for special projects; – Internal and external **company image**.	– Different forms of **gradual transition**: Provide **partial or phased retirement**, **trial** retirement, retirement with **call-back arrangements** (re-employment of retirees); – **Preparatory measures** for future retirees: workshops, counseling activities.

already provide organizations with a certain advantage in managing the demographic change, it is important to note that only integrated and comprehensive approaches enable companies to fully respond to the needs of different age groups in the workplace (Naegele and Walker, 2011; Walker, 1999). While corporate examples of such fully-developed age management strategies are still rare, they implicate a number of advantages. On the one hand, they potentially meet the needs of all employees and are not focused solely on the aging workforce. On the other hand, they are more consistent, as most dimensions are strongly interrelated. For instance, postponing retirement is only an effective strategy if employees stay healthy (health management dimension) and have up-to date knowledge (training dimension). Overall, employees' long-term motivation depends on a variety of factors and can be best sustained and improved by providing a holistic age management framework taking into account all of the dimensions previously described.

Our second section presented the institutional-theoretical background for age management. The third section described the various dimensions of age management practices. This section will be devoted to the consequences of these practices in organizations. We will structure the results on two levels: the individual level and the organizational level. This section will close with a discussion of the boundary conditions favoring the successful dissemination of age management.

INDIVIDUAL-LEVEL EFFECTS OF AGE MANAGEMENT

There is a well-developed stream of literature investigating how certain bundles of well-developed HR practices (often subsumed under the term 'high performance work practices' or 'HPWP') may impact organizational outcomes (see Combs, Liu, Hall, and Ketchen, 2006 and Lepak, Liao, Chung, and Harden, 2006 for theoretical and empirical reviews). While the majority of this literature focused on the organizational-level consequences of effective HR practices such as productivity and financial performance (see e.g. Huselid, 1995; MacDuffie, 1995), a limited number of studies have also looked at the individual outcomes of HPWP, such as turnover intentions, job satisfaction, organizational commitment, and organizational citizenship behaviors (Kehoe and Wright, 2013; Whitener, 2001). What most of these studies have in common is that they largely neglect the construct of age. They neither investigate age-specific HR practices nor do they explicitly account for age as a potential boundary condition in the HPWP-outcome relationship.

An exception is the work by Kooij, Jansen, Dikkers and De Lange (2010) who investigated the influence of age on the associations between HR practices and both affective commitment and job satisfaction. In a meta-analysis of 83 studies, they investigated the individual-level consequences of different types of commitment-based HRM practices, ranging from performance and rewards systems over work life policies to flexible work schemes. For all of these measures, they received support for a positive relationship with both individual job satisfaction and individual affective commitment.

Their theoretical reasoning for these effects is twofold. First, they argue that commitment-based HRM practices favor the social-exchange relationship of individual employees with their organization (Eisenberger, Huntington, Hutchison and Sowa, 1986). More specifically, if individual employees perceive strong support from the organization through commitment-based HRM practices, they will reciprocate that by showing stronger feelings of obligations for the employer. Second, arguing with signaling theory (Casper and Harris, 2008), commitment-based HRM practices are considered a positive signal from the organization in that it values and supports its employees, which further increases the level of satisfaction and emotional attachment of their employees.

For our purpose, it is of interest as to whether age-related HRM practices also have these positive effects on individual performance. Interestingly, Kooij and colleagues (2010) found a moderation of age, for several relationships between different HRM practices and the two individual outcomes. As an overall picture for older employees maintenance-oriented HRM practices (e.g., performance management, rewards, information sharing, teamwork, and flexibility) seem to be more effective, whereas younger workers favor development-oriented practices (e.g., promotion). Similarly, Conway (2004) reports a moderation of age for the relationship between several HRM practices (career development, employability, and job design) and normative commitment.

These results indicate a need for the age-adjustment of HRM practices to reach better individual outcomes. Only HRM practices that consider the strengths and needs of different age groups, as outlined in section 3, can help increase performance of all age groups. The research on the individual efficiency of these factors is, however, still in its infancy, and future studies should especially focus on rigorous evaluation studies to reach a broader acceptance of these measures, both in theory and practice.

ORGANIZATIONAL-LEVEL EFFECTS OF AGE MANAGEMENT

In addition to individual-level effects, age-related HRM practices are also bound to affect collective processes and, ultimately, organizational performance. Again, literature on HPWP has extensively researched how general HRM practices affect organizational performance. Huselid (1995) for example reports positive effects of HPWP on short and long-term corporate financial performance in an US-based sample of more than 1,000 companies. Likewise Delany and Huselid (1996) report a positive relationship between HRM practices, such as staffing, training, incentive compensation, and grievance procedures and

perceptual measures of organizational performance in 590 organizations.

Little research has so far explored if these effects also hold for the association between age-related HR practices and performance. To our knowledge, only one study by Boehm, Kunze and Bruch (forthcoming) has investigated a relationship between age management and firm performance.

The authors propose that companies should introduce bundles of age-inclusive HR practices that do not focus solely on older employees but equally foster all age groups' (1) knowledge, skills, and abilities, (2) motivation and effort, as well as (3) opportunities to contribute. More specifically, such age-inclusive HR practices might include age-neutral recruiting policies, equal access to training for all age groups, age-neutral career and promotion systems, initiatives to educate managers about leading age-diversity in the workplace, as well as the promotion of an age-inclusive corporate culture. As shown by Boehm and colleagues (forthcoming) in a sample of 93 German companies, such age-inclusive HR practices might contribute to the development of an organization-wide age-diversity climate, which in turn should be directly related to increased perceptions of social exchange and indirectly to firm performance and employees' aggregated turnover intentions. We strongly encourage further research on this relationship, because as for the relationships on the individual level, establishing a positive relationship between age management and organizational performance is a key factor for the broad dissemination of these factors within companies in the future.

BOUNDARY CONDITIONS FOR EFFECTIVE AGE MANAGEMENT

Beyond the proposed effects of age management on the individual and organizational level, there might also be several boundary conditions that favor or disfavor this relationship. First, as Kossek, Lobel and Brown (2006) argue, the top management plays a crucial role for the success or failure of organizational diversity initiatives. Ideally, the members of the top management team should show role model leadership behavior, for example by integrating age management in their daily leadership behavior. If any diversity change-effort, and especially those for age diversity, lacks the support of the top management its impact is likely to be very limited (Nkomo and Kossek, 2000). For ethnic-diversity this assumption received support by the study of Thomas and Gabarro (1999), who found that several diversity efforts were only successful if a critical mass of senior executives supported the initiatives.

Second, age management can only have a positive relationship with positive organizational outcomes, if it is backed-up and disseminated in the daily leadership relationships within the organization (Naegele and Walker, 2011). If a company formally offers career perspectives and training for employees of all age groups, but especially older employees are not encouraged by their direct supervisors to participate in these programs, the initiatives are likely to fail. Additionally, direct leadership relationships are also one key area in organizations shaping a pro-diverse organizational culture. If leadership relationships are on average characterized by mutual distrust between supervisors and subordinates from different age groups or discrimination based on age takes place, even optimally designed age-related HRM practices will not have a positive impact on performance. Consequently, it is of key importance that the implementation of age management is accompanied by age-diversity training offered to top and line managers.

Third, in line with Cox (2001), age management can only be successful, if organizations incorporate formal measurement systems for the application of practices and their relationship to an age-diversity culture within a company. Thus employers need to regularly conduct employee opinion surveys on the application of age management and about attitudes of employees from different age groups. These surveys should allow to

assess if the implemented practices have the desired effect, or need to be adjusted. Furthermore, surveys should allow monitoring the process of cultural change initiated by age management.

No empirical study known to us has addressed these potential boundary conditions for age management/outcome relationships to date. For the future development of this area of research we strongly encourage to do so.

CONCLUSION AND AREAS OF FUTURE RESEARCH

This chapter offers a coherent and interdisciplinary perspective of the current state of knowledge with regard to HRM strategies for an aging workforce. We applied a multi-level perspective to capture this phenomenon. First, using a macro-level perspective, we reviewed how the comparative HRM literature uses institutional theory to explain differences in age management approaches in different national contexts by highlighting the role of the institutional determinants of organizational age management. Second, by applying a micro-level perspective, we reviewed the applied HRM literature that discussed the practical dissemination of age management in companies and its potential consequences at the individual and organizational level.

On both levels of analysis, research on age management was found to be in the early stages of development. Consequently, there are many potential venues for future research. Regarding comparative age management research, for example, a knowledge gap exists regarding the role of institutional entrepreneurs and how they might influence the dissemination of age management policies beyond the restriction of national institutions. Additionally, most research on age management on both levels has considered organizational policies as reported by employers. However, there might be a gap between formal policies and implemented practices (Cunningham, James and Dibben, 2004), where line managers with HRM responsibilities might deviate from formal policies because of a lack of support, a lack of knowledge regarding formal HRM policies, or specific attitudes held towards older workers. As a result, it would be of interest to further explore whether and how age management is actually implemented at the workplace level. Finally, on the micro level of analysis, the performance consequences of age management need to be researched in more detail, particularly to increase their acceptance by practitioners in companies. In summary, this chapter provides a basis for macro-level, micro-level and inter-disciplinary research on successful age management in companies.

REFERENCES

Aldana, S.G. (2001) 'Financial impact of health promotion programs: A comprehensive review of the literature', *American Journal of Health Promotion*, 15(5): 296–320.

Almond, P., Edwards, T., Colling, T., Ferner, A., Gunnigle, P., Muller-Camen, M., Quintanilla, J. and Wächter, H. (2005) 'Unraveling home and host country effects: An investigation of the HR policies of an American multinational in four European countries', *Industrial Relations Journal*, 44(2): 276–306.

Armstrong-Stassen, M. (2008) 'Organisational practices and the post-retirement employment experience of older workers', *Human Resource Management Journal*, 18(1): 36–53.

Armstrong-Stassen, M. and Lee, S.H. (2009) 'The effect of relational age on older Canadian employees' perceptions of human resource practices and sense of worth to their organization', *The International Journal of Human Resource Management*, 20(8): 1753–1769.

Armstrong-Stassen, M. and Templer, A.J. (2005) 'Adapting training for older employees. The Canadian response to an aging workforce', *Journal of Management Development*, 24(1): 57–67.

Armstrong-Stassen, M. and Templer, A.J. (2006) 'The response of Canadian public and private sector human resource professionals to the challenge of the aging workforce', *Public Personnel Management*, 35(3): 247–260.

Armstrong-Stassen, M. and Ursel, N.D. (2009) 'Perceived organizational support, career satisfaction, and the retention of older workers', *Journal of Occupational and Organizational Psychology*, 82(1): 201–220.

Auer, P. and Fortuny, M. (2000) *Ageing of the Labour Force in OECD Countries: Economic and Social Consequences*. Geneva: International Labour Organization.

Austin, J.R. (2003) 'Transactive memory in organizational groups: The effects of content, consensus, specialization, and accuracy on group performance', *Journal of Applied Psychology*, 88(5): 866–878.

Bandura, A. (2001) 'Social cognitive theory: An agentic perspective', *Annual Review of Psychology*, 52(1): 1–26.

Barth, M.C., McNaught, W. and Rizzi, P. (1993) 'Corporations and the aging workforce', in P. Mirvis (ed.), *Building the Competitive Work Force*. New York: Wiley. pp. 156–200.

Battilana, J., Leca, B. and Boxenbaum, E. (2009) 'How actors change institutions: Towards a theory of institutional entrepreneurship', *The Academy of Management Annals*, 3: 65–107.

Beaver, G. and Hutchings, K. (2005) 'Training and developing an age diverse workforce in SMEs. The need for a strategic approach', *Education + Training*, 47(8/9): 592–604.

Belbin, E. and Belbin, R. (1972) *Problems in adult retraining*. London: Heinemann.

Bell, M.P. (2007) *Diversity in Organizations*. Mason: South-Western Cengage Learning.

Birren, J. and Fisher, L. (1995) 'Age and speed of performance: Possible consequences for psychological functioning', *Annual Review of Psychology*, 46: 329–353.

Blossfeld, H.-P., Buchholz, S. and Hofäcker, D. (eds.) (2006) *Globalization, Uncertainty and Late Careers in Society*. New York: Routledge.

Boehm, S., Kunze, F. and Bruch, H. (forthcoming) 'Spotlight on age-diversity climate: The impact of age-inclusive HR practices on firm-level outcomes', *Personnel Psychology*, in press.

Börsch-Supan, A. (2002) *Labor Market Effects of Population Aging*. Mannheim: Mannheim Research Institute for the Economics of Aging (MEA).

Bowen, D.E., Galang, C. and Pillai, R. (2002) 'The role of Human Resource Management: An exploratory study of cross-country variance', *Human Resource Management*, 41(1): 103–122.

Broadbridge, A. (2001). 'Ageism in retailing: Myth or reality?' in I. Golver and M. Branine (eds.), *Ageism in work and employment*. Burlington, VT: Ashgate. pp. 153–174.

Brooke, L. and Taylor, P. (2005) 'Older workers and employment: Managing age relations', *Aging & Society*, 25(3): 415–429.

Buchholz, S., Hofäcker, D. and Blossfeld, H.-P. (2006) 'Globalization, accelerating economic change and late careers – A theoretical framework', in H.-P. Blossfeld, S. Buchholz and D. Hofäcker (eds.), *Globalization, Uncertainty and Late Careers in Society*. London: Routledge. pp. 1–23.

Buoncore, A.J. (1992) 'Older and wiser: Senior employees offer untapped capabilities', *Management Review*, 81(7): 49–52.

Callahan, J.S., Kiker, D.S. and Cross, T. (2003) 'Does method matter? A meta-analysis of the effects of training method on older learner training performance', *Journal of Management*, 29(5): 663–680.

Capowski, G. (1994) 'Ageism: The new diversity issue', *Management Review*, 53: 10–15.

Casey, B., Metcalf, H. and Lakey, J. (1993) 'Human resource strategies and the Third Age: policies and practices in the UK', in P. Taylor, A. Walker, B. Casey, H. Metcalf, J. Lakey, P. Warr and J. Pennington (eds.), *Age and Employment: Policies, Attitudes and Practice*, London: Institute of Personnel Management. pp. 43–74.

Casper, W.J. and Harris, C.M. (2008) 'Work-life benefits and organizational attachment: Self-interest utility and signaling theory models', *Journal of Vocational Behavior*, 72(1): 95–109.

Castells, M. (2000). *The Rise of the Network Society, The Information Age: Economy, Society and Culture*. 2nd edn. Oxford: Blackwell. (1st edn, 1996.)

Cattell, R.B. (1987) *Intelligence: Its Structure, Growth, and Action*. Amsterdam: North Holland Press.

Combs, J., Liu, Y., Hall, A. and Ketchen, D. (2006) 'How much do high performance work practices matter? A meta analysis of their effects on organizational performance', *Personnel Psychology*, 59(3): 501–528.

Conrad, P. (1988a) 'Health and fitness at work: A participants' perspective', *Social Science & Medicine*, 26(5): 545–550.

Conrad, P. (1988b) 'Worksite health promotion: The social context', *Social Science & Medicine*, 26(5): 485–489.

Conway, E. (2004) 'Relating career stage to attitudes towards HR practices and commitment: Evidence of interaction effects?', *European Journal of Work and Organizational Psychology*, 13(4): 417–446.

Cox, T. (1993) *Cultural Diversity in Organizations: Theory, Research and Practice*. San Francisco: Berrett-Koehler Publishers.

Cox, T. (2001) *Creating the Multicultural Organization: A Strategy for Capturing the Power of Diversity*. San Francisco: Jossey-Bass.

Croucher, R., Gooderham, P. and Parry, E. (2006) 'The influences on direct communication in British and Danish firms: country, ‚strategic' HRM or unionization?', *European Journal of Industrial Relations*, 12(3): 267–286.

Cuddy, A.J. and Fiske, S.T. (2002) 'Doddering but dear: Process, content and function in stereotyping of older persons', in T. Nelson (ed.), *Ageism: Stereotyping and Prejudice against Older Persons*. Cambridge, MA: MIT Press. pp. 3–26.

Cunningham, I., James, P. and Dibben, P. (2004) 'Bridging the gap between rhetoric and reality: Line managers and the protection of job security for ill workers in the modern workplace', *British Journal of Management*, 15(3): 273–290.

Cunningham, W.R. (1987) 'Intellectual abilities and age', in: K.W. Schaie (ed.), *Annual Review of Gerontology and Geriatrics*. Vol. 7. New York (NY): Springer Publishing Company. pp. 117–134.

Dacin, M.T., Goodstein, J. and Scott, W.R. (2002) 'Institutional theory and institutional change: Introduction to the special research forum', *Academy of Management Journal*, 45(1): 45–57.

Daley, A.J. and Parfitt, G. (1996) 'Good health – Is it worth it? Mood states, physical well-being, job satisfaction and absenteeism in members and non-members of British corporate health and fitness clubs', *Journal of Occupational and Organizational Psychology*, 69(2): 121–134.

Danna, K. and Griffin, R.W. (1999) 'Health and well-being in the workplace: A review and synthesis of the literature', *Journal of Management*, 25(3): 357–384.

Deutsches Statistisches Bundesamt (2009) *Bevölkerung Deutschlands bis 2060*, Report. Retrieved on 20 July 2010 from: http://www.destatis.de/jetspeed/portal/cms/Sites/ destatis/Internet/DE/Presse/pk/2009/Bevoelkerung/pressebroschuere__bevoelkerungsentwicklung2009,property=file.pdf

Duncan, C. (2001) 'Ageism, early exit, and the rationality of age-based discrimination', in I. Golver and M. Branine (eds.), *Ageism in work and employment*. Burlington, VT: Ashgate. pp. 25–46.

Duncan, C. (2008) 'The dangers and limitations of equality agendas as means for tackling old-age prejudice', *Ageing & Society*, 28(8): 1133–1158.

Dychtwald, K., Erickson, T.J. and Morison, B. (2004) 'It's time to retire retirement', *Harvard Business Review*, 82(3): 48–58.

Dychtwald, K., Erickson, T.J., and Morison, B. (2006) *Workforce Crisis. How to Beat the Coming Shortage of Skills and Talents*. Boston: Harvard Business School Press.

Ebbinghaus, B. (2006) *Reforming Early Retirement in Europe, Japan and the USA*. Oxford: Oxford University Press.

EC (2000) *Lisbon European Council 23 and 24 March 2000 – Presidency Conclusions*. Retrieved on 28 May

2012 from http://www.europarl.europa.eu/summits/lis1_en.htm.

EC (2001) *Stockholm European Council 23 and 24 March 2001 – Presidency Conclusion*. Retrieved on 28 May 2012 from http://www.consilium.europa.eu/ueDocs/cms_Data/docs/pressData/en/ec/00100-r1.%20ann-r1.en1.html.

Eisenberger, R., Huntington, R., Hutchison, S. and Sowa, D. (1986) 'Perceived organizational support', *Journal of Applied Psychology*, 71(3): 500–507.

Ferris, G.R. and King, T.R. (1992) 'The politics of age discrimination in organizations', *Journal of Business Ethics*, 11(5–6): 341–350.

Fevre, R. (1991) 'Emerging alternatives to full time and permanent employment', in P. Brown and R. Scase (eds.), *Poor Work: Disadvantage and the Division of Labour*. Milton Keynes: Open University Press. pp. 56–70.

Feyrer, J. (2007) 'Demographics and productivity', *Review of Economics and Statistics*, 89(1): 100–109.

Finkelstein, L.M. and Burke, M.J. (1998) 'Age stereotyping at work: The role of rater and contextual factors on evaluations of job applicants', *Journal of General Psychology*, 125(4): 317–345.

Fiske, S.T. and Neuberg, S. (1990) 'A continuum of impression formation, from category-based to individuation processes: Influences of information and motivation on attention and interpretation', *Advances in Experimental Social Psychology*, 23(1): 1–74.

Flynn, M. and McNair, S. (2007) *Managing Age – A Guide to Good Employment Practice*. London: Chartered Institute for Personnel and Development/Trades Union Congress.

Flynn, M., Upchurch, M., Muller-Camen, M. and Schroder, H. (2013) 'Trade union responses to ageing workforces in the UK and Germany', *Human Relations*, 66(1): 45–64.

Fortuny, M., Nesporova, A. and Popova, N. (2003) *Employment Promotion Policies for Older Workers in the EU Accession Countries, the Russian Federation and Ukraine*. Geneva: International Labour Organization.

GfK (2008) *GfK Purchasing Power Study*. Retrieved on 20 July 2010 from: http://www.gfk.com/group/investor/key_figures_and_publications/investor_relations_news/news/002428/index.de.html.

Gist, M., Rosen, B. and Schworer, B. (1988) 'The influence of training method and trainee age on the acquisition of computer skills', *Personnel Psychology*, 41(2): 255–265.

Gordon, R.A. and Arvey, R.D. (2004) 'Age bias in laboratory and field settings: A meta-analytic investigation', *Journal of Applied Psychology*, 34(3): 468–492.

Greenwood, R., Suddaby, R. and Hinings, C.R. (2002) 'Theorizing change: The role of professional associations in the transformation of institutionalized fields', *Academy of Management Journal*, 45(1): 58–80.

Hall, D.T. (1985) 'Project work as an antidote to career plateauing in a declining engineering organisation', *Human Resource Management*, 24(3): 271–292.

Hall, P.A. and Soskice, D. (2001) *Varieties of Capitalism: The Foundation of Comparative Advantage*. Oxford: Oxford University Press.

Hall, R. and Wailes, N. (2009) 'International and comparative Human Resource Management', in A. Wilkinson, N. Bacon, T. Redman and S. Snell (eds.), *The Sage Handbook of Human Resource Management*. Los Angeles: Sage. pp. 115–132.

Handelsblatt (2012) *Anteil der Fehltage wegen Stress schnellt an*. Retrieved on 30 April 2012 from http://www.handelsblatt.com/unternehmen/buero-special/arbeitsbelastung-anteil-der-fehltage-wegen-stress-schnellt-an/6575178.html.

Harris, C.C. (1991) 'Recession, redundancy and age', in P. Brown and R. Scase (eds.), *Poor Work: Disadvantage and the Division of Labour*. Milton Keynes: Open University Press. pp. 103–115.

Harrison, D.A. and Klein, K.J. (2007) 'What's the difference? Diversity constructs as separation, variety, or disparity in organizations', *Academy of Management Review*, 32(4): 1199–1228.

Heaney, C.A. and Goetzel, R.Z. (1997) 'A review of health-related outcomes of multi-component worksite health promotion programs', *American Journal of Health Promotion*, 11(4): 290–307.

Hedge, J.W. (2008) 'Strategic Human Resource Management and the older worker', *Journal of Workplace Behavioral Health*, 23(1/2): 109–123.

Hedge, J.W., Borman, W.C. and Lammlein, S.E. (2006) *The Aging Workforce: Realities, Myths, and Implications for Organizations*. Washington, DC: American Psychological Association.

Heugens, P.P. and Lander, M.W. (2009) 'Structure! Agency! (and other quarrels): A meta-analysis of institutional theories of organization', *Academy of Management Journal*, 52(1): 61–85.

Hofäcker, D. and Pollnerová, S. (2006) 'Late careers and career exits. An international comparison of trends and institutional background patterns', in H.-P. Blossfeld, S. Buchholz and D. Hofäcker (eds.), *Globalization, Uncertainty and Late Careers in Society*. London: Routledge. pp. 25–53.

Huselid, M.A. (1995) 'The impact of human resource management practices on turnover, productivity, and corporate financial performance', *Academy of Management Journal*, 38(3): 635–672.

Ilmarinen, J. (1994) 'Aging, work and health', in J. Snel and R. Cremer (eds.), *Work and Aging: A European Perspective*. London: Taylor and Francis Ltd. pp. 47–63.

Ilmarinen, J. (2001) 'Aging workers', *Occupational and Environmental Medicine*, 58(8): 546–552.

Ilmarinen, J. (2005) *Towards a Longer Worklife. Ageing and the Quality of Worklife in the European Union*. Helsinki: Finish Institute of Occupational Health.

Jackson, S.E., and Alvarez, E.B. (1992) 'Working through diversity as a strategic imperative', in: S.E. Jackson (ed.), *Diversity in the Workplace: Human Resources Initiatives*. New York: The Guilford Press. pp. 13–29.

Janis, I. (1972) *Victims of Groupthink: A Psychological Study of Foreign-Policy Decisions and Fiascoes*. Boston: Houghton Mifflin.

Kanfer, R. and Ackerman, P.L. (2004) 'Aging, adult development, and work motivation', *Academy of Management Review*, 29(3): 440–458.

Kehoe, R.R. and Wright, P.M. (2013) 'The impact of high-performance human resource practices on employees' attitudes and behaviors', *Journal of Management*, 39(2): 366-391.

Kemper, H.C.G. (1994) 'Physical work and the physiological consequences for the aging worker', in: J. Snel and R. Cremer (eds.), *Work and Aging: A European Perspective*. London: Taylor and Francis Ltd. pp. 31–46.

Kerr, C., Dunlop, J.T., Harbison, F.H. and Myers, C.A. (1960) *Industrialism and Industrial Men. The Problems of Labor and Management in Economic Growth*. Cambridge: Harvard University Press.

Kim, J.E. and Moen, P. (2001) 'Is retirement good or bad for subjective well-being?' *Current Directions in Psychological Science*, 10(3): 83–86.

Kohlbacher, F. and Herstatt, C. (2009) *The Silver Market Phenomenon: Business Opportunities in an Era of Demographic Change*. Berlin, Heidelberg: Springer.

Kooij, D.T.A.M., Jansen, P.G.W., Dikkers, J.S.E. and De Lange, A.H. (2010) 'The influence of age on the associations between HR practices and both affective commitment and job satisfaction: A meta-analysis', *Journal of Organizational Behavior*, 31(8): 1111–1136.

Kossek, E.E., Lobel, S.A. and Brown, J. (2006) 'Human resource strategies to manage workforce diversity: Examining the "business case"' in A.M. Konrad, P. Prasad and J.K. Pringle (eds.), *Handbook of Workplace Diversity*. London: Sage. pp. 53–74.

Kossek, E.E., Markel, K.S. and McHugh, P.P. (2003) 'Increasing diversity as an HR change strategy', *Journal of Organizational Change Management*, 16(2): 328–352.

Kostova, T., Roth, K. and Dacin, M.T. (2008) 'Institutional theory in the study of multinational corporations: A critique and new direction', *Academy of Management Review*, 33(4): 994–1006.

Kubeck, J.E., Delp, N.D., Haslet, T.K. and McDaniel, M. (1996) 'Does job-related training performance decline with age?' *Psychology and Aging*, 11(1): 92–107.

Kunze, F., Boehm, S.A. and Bruch, H. (2011) 'Age diversity, age discrimination climate and performance consequences - A cross organizational study', *Journal of Organizational Behavior*, 32(2): 264–290.

Kunze, F., Boehm, S.A. and Bruch, H. (2013) 'Organizational performance consequences of age diversity: Inspecting the role of diversity-friendly HR policies and top managers' negative age stereotypes', *Journal of Management Studies*, 50(3): 413–442.

Lain, D. (2012) 'Working past 65 in the UK and the USA: segregation into 'Lopaq' occupations?', *Work, Employment and Society*, 26(1): 78–94.

Lepak, D.P, Liao, H., Chung, Y., and Harden, E.H. (2006) 'A conceptual review of human resource management systems in strategic human resource management research' in J.J. Martocchio (ed.), *Research in personnel and human resources management*. (Vol. 25). Oxford, UK: Elsevier. pp. 217–271.

Liden, R.C., Stilwell, D. and Ferris, G.R. (1996) 'The effects of supervisor and subordinate age on objective performance and subjective performance ratings', *Human Relations*, 49(3): 327–347.

Lin, T.R., Dobbins, G.H. and Farh, J.L. (1992) 'A field study of race and age similarity effects on interview ratings in conventional and situational interviews', *Journal of Applied Psychology*, 77(3): 363–371.

Loretto, W. and White, P. (2006) 'Employers' attitudes, practices and policies towards older workers', *Human Resource Management Journal*, 16(3): 313–330.

MacDuffie, J.P. (1995) 'Human resource bundles and manufacturing performance: Organizational logic and flexible production systems in the world auto industry', *Industrial and Labor Relations Review*, 24(2): 197–221.

Maguire, S., Hardy, C. and Lawrence, T.B. (2004) 'Institutional entrepreneurship in emerging fields: HIV/AIDS treatment advocacy in Canada', *Academy of Management Journal*, 47(5): 657–679.

Maltby, T., De Vroom, B., Mirabile, M.L. and Overbye, E. (eds.) (2004) *Ageing and the Transition to Retirement:*

A Comprehensive Analysis of European Welfare States. Aldershot: Ashgate.

Mayer, M. and Whittington, R. (2004) 'Economics, politics and nations: Resistance to the multidivisional form in France, Germany and the United Kingdom, 1983–1993', *Journal of Management Studies*, 41(7): 1057–1082.

McCann, R. and Giles, H. (2002) 'Ageism in the workplace: A communication perspective', in T. Nelson (ed.), *Ageism: Stereotyping and Prejudice Against Older Persons*. Cambridge, MA: MIT Press. pp. 163–199.

McEvoy, G.M. and Cascio, W.F. (1989) 'Cumulative evidence of the relationship between employee age and job performance', *Journal of Applied Psychology*, 74: 11–17.

McGaughey, S.L. and De Cieri, H. (1999) 'Reassessment of convergence and divergence dynamics: Implications for international HRM', *International Journal of Human Resource Management*, 10(2): 235–250.

Mein, G., Martikainen, P., Stansfeld. S.A., Brunner, E.J., Fuhrer, R. and Marmot, M.G. (2000) ‹Predictors of early retirement in British civil servants›, *Age and Ageing*, 29(6): 529–536.

Michaels, E., Handfield-Jones, H. and Axelrod, B. (2001) *The War for Talent*. Boston: Harvard Business School Press.

Muller-Camen, M., Croucher, R., Flynn, M. and Schroder, H. (2011a) 'National institutions and employers' age management practices in Britain and Germany: 'Path dependence' and option exploration', *Human Relations*, 64(4): 507–530.

Muller-Camen, M., Flynn, M. and Schroder, H. (2011b) The management of an aging workforce: An assessment of organizational policies in Germany and the UK, paper presented at Academy of Management annual meeting, San Antonio.

Muller-Camen, M., Tempel, A., Almond, P., Edwards, T., Ferner, A., Peters, R. and Wächter, H. (2004) *Human Resource Management in US Multinationals in Germany and the UK*. London: Anglo-German Foundation.

Naegele, G. and Walker, A. (2002) 'Altern in der Arbeitswelt – Europäische "Leitlinien einer guten Praxis" (good practice) für die Gleichbehandlung älterer Arbeitnehmer/innen in der betrieblichen Sozialpolitik', in B. Badura et al. (eds.), *Fehlzeiten-Report 2002. Demographischer Wandel*. Berlin: Springer. pp. 225–234.

Naegele, G. and Walker, A. (2006) *A Guide to Good Practice in Age Management*. Dublin: European Foundation for the Improvement of Living and Working Conditions.

Naegele, G. and Walker, A. (2011) 'Age management in organisations in the European Union', in M. Malloch, L. Cairns, K. Evans and B.N. O'Connor (eds.), *The Sage Handbook of Workplace Learning*. London: Sage. pp. 251–267.

Neville, H. (1998) 'Workplace accidents: They cost more than you might think', *Industrial Management*, 40: 7–9.

Ng, T.W.H. and Feldman, D.C. (2008) 'The relationship of age to ten dimensions of job performance', *Journal of Applied Psychology*, 93: 392–423.

Nkomo, S. and Kossek, E. (2000) 'Managing diversity: Human resource issues', in E. Kossek and R. Block (eds.), *Managing Human Resources in the 21st Century: From Core Concepts to Strategic Choice*. Cincinnati: Southwestern. pp. 9.1–9.22.

North, D.C. (1994) 'Economic performance through time', *American Economic Review*, 84(3): 359–369.

OECD (2006) *Ageing and Employment Policies: Live Longer, Work Longer*. Paris: OECD.

Osborne, T. and McCann, L.A. (2004) 'Forced ranking and age-related employment discrimination', *Human Rights*, 31(2): 6–9.

Ostroff, C. and Atwater, L.E. (2003) 'Does whom you work with matter? Effects of referent group gender and age composition on managers' compensation', *Journal of Applied Psychology*, 88(4): 725–740.

Patrickson, M. and Hartmann, L. (1995) 'Australia's ageing population: Implications for human resource management', *International Journal of Manpower*, 16(5/6): 34–46.

Pelletier, K.R. (2001) 'A review and analysis of the clinical and cost-effectiveness studies of comprehensive health promotion and disease management programs at the worksite: 1998–2000 update', *American Journal of Health Promotion*, 16(2): 107–116.

Pinquart, M. and Schindler I. (2007) 'Changes of life satisfaction in the transition to retirement: A latent-class approach', *Psychology and Aging*, 22(3): 442–455.

Posthuma, R.A. and Campion, M.A. (2009) 'Age stereotypes in the workplace: Common stereotypes, moderators, and future research directions', *Journal of Management*, 35(1): 158–188.

Raza, S.M. and Carpenter, B.N. (1987) 'A model of hiring decisions in real employment interviews', *Journal of Applied Psychology*, 72(4): 596–603.

Reio, T.G., Sanders-Rejo, J. and Reio, T. (1999) 'Combating workplace ageism', *Adult Learning*, 11(1): 10–13.

Reitzes, D.C. and Mutran, E.J. (2002) 'Self-concept as the organization of roles: Importance, centrality, and balance', *Sociological Quarterly*, 43(4): 647–667.

Riach, K. (2009) 'Managing 'difference': Understanding age diversity in practice', *Human Resource Management Journal*, 19(3): 319–335.

Richardson, V. and Kilty, K.M. (1991) 'Adjustment to retirement: Continuity vs. discontinuity', *International Journal of Aging and Human Development*, 33(2): 151–169.

Rix, S.E. (1990) *Older workers*. Santa Barbara, CA: ABC-CLIO.

Rix, S.E. (1996) 'Investing in the future: What role for older worker training?', in W.H. Crown (ed.), Handbook on Employment and the Elderly. Westport, CT: Greenwood Press. pp. 304–323.

Robertson, A. and Tracy, C.S. (1998) 'Health and productivity of older workers', *Scandinavian Journal of Work, Environment and Health*, 24(2): 85–97.

Robinson, P.K. (1986) 'Age, health, and job performance', in J.E. Birren, P.K. Robinson and J.E. Livingston (eds.), *Age, Health, and Employment*. Englewood Cliffs (NJ): Prentice-Hall. pp. 63–77.

Rosen, B. and Jerdee, T.H. (1976) 'The influence of age stereotypes on managerial decisions', *Journal of Applied Psychology*, 61(4): 428–432.

Rosen, B. and Jerdee, T.H. (1989) 'Investing in the older worker', *Personnel Administrator*, 34(1): 70–74.

Salthouse, T.A. (1990) 'Cognitive competence and expertise in aging', in J.E. Birren and K.W. Schaie (eds.), *Handbook of the Psychology of the Aging*, 3rd edn., San Diego, CA: Academic Press. pp. 310–319.

Sargeant, M. (ed.) (2008) *The Law on Age Discrimination in the EU*. Aspen: Kluwer.

Schneiberg, M. (2007) 'What's on the path? Path dependence, organizational diversity and the problem of institutional change in the US economy, 1900–1950', *Socio-Economic Review*, 5(1): 47–80.

Schroder, H., Hofäcker, D. and Muller-Camen, M. (2009) 'HRM and the employment of older workers: Germany and Britain compared', *International Journal of Human Resources Development and Management*, 9(2–3): 162–179.

Scott, W.R. (1987) 'The adolescence of institutional theory', *Administrative Science Quarterly*, 32(4): 493–511.

Selby-Smith, C. (1994) 'Restructuring office work in the public service', in M. Patrickson, V. Bamber and G. Bamber (eds.), *Organizational Change Strategies: Case Studies of Human Resource and Industrial Relations Issues*. Melbourne: Longman Cheshire. pp. 115–128.

Sheppard, H. (1988) 'Work continuity versus retirement: Reasons for continuing work', in R. Morris and S. Bass (eds.), *Retirement Reconsidered: Economic and Social Roles for Older People*. New York: Springer. pp. 129–147.

Shore, L.M. and Goldberg, C.B. (2005) 'Age discrimination in the workplace', in R.L. Dipboye and A. Colella (eds.), *Discrimination at Work*. Mawhaw, NJ: Lawrence Erlbaum. pp. 203–225.

Siegel, S.R. (1993) 'Relationships between current performance and likelihood of promotion for old versus young workers', *Human Resource Development Quarterly*, 4(1): 39–50.

Spirduso, W.W. and MacRae, P.G. (1990) 'Motor performance and aging', in J.E. Birren, K.W. Schaie (eds.), *Handbook of the Psychology of Aging*. 3rd edn. San Diego, CA: Academic Press. pp. 183–200.

Sterns, H.L. and Alexander, R.A. (1988) 'Performance appraisal of the older worker', in H. Dennis (ed.), *Fourteen Steps in Managing an Aging Work Force*. Lexington, MA: Lexington Books. pp. 85–93.

Sterns, H.L. and Doverspike, D. (1988) 'Training and developing the older worker: Implications for human resource management', in H. Dennis (ed.), *Fourteen Steps in Managing an Aging Work Force*. Lexington, MA: Lexington Books. pp. 97–110.

Sterns, H.L. and Doverspike, D. (1989) 'Aging and the training and learning process', in I. Goldstein and Associates (eds.), *Training and development in organizations*. San Francisco, CA: Jossey-Bass. pp. 299–331.

Sundstrom, D. (1992) 'Downshifting: The new career management', *The International Journal of Career Management*, 2(2): 3–7.

Sydow, J., Schreyögg, G. and Koch, J. (2009) 'Organizational path dependence: Opening the black box', *Academy of Management Review*, 34(4): 689–709.

Taylor, P., Brooke, E. and Biase, T. (2010) 'European employer policies concerning career management and learning from a life-span perspective', In G. Naegele (ed.), *Soziale Lebenslaufpolitik*. Wiesbaden: VS Verlag für Sozialwissenschaften. pp. 474–497.

Taylor, P. and Urwin, P. (2001) 'Age and participation in vocational education and training', *Work, Employment and Society*, 15(4): 763–779.

Taylor, P. and Walker, A. (1998) 'Policies and practices towards older workers: A framework for comparative research', *Human Resource Management Journal*, 8(3): 61–77.

Thomas, D. and Gabarro, J. (1999) *Breaking Through: The Making of Minority Executives in Corporate America*. Boston: Harvard Business School Press.

Van Dalen, H.P., Henkens, K., Henderikse, W. and Schippers, J. (2010) 'Do European employers support later retirement?', *International Journal of Management*, 31(3): 360–373.

Van Yoder, S. (2002) 'Coping with the graying workforce', *Financial Executive*, 18(1): 26–28.

Vaupel, J.W. and Loichinger, E. (2006) 'Redistributing work in aging Europe', *Science*, 312(5782): 1911–1913.

Waldman, D.A. and Avolio, B.J. (1986) 'A meta-analysis of age differences in job performance', *Journal of Applied Psychology*, 71(1): 33–38.

Walker, A. (1996) *Combating Age Barriers*. Dublin: European Foundation for the Improvement of Living and Working Conditions.

Walker, A. (1999) 'Combating age discrimination at the workplace', *Experimental Aging Research*, 25: 367–377.

Walker, A. (2005) 'The emergence of age management in Europe', *International Journal of Organisational Behaviour*, 10(1): 685–697.

Warr, P.B. (2001) 'Age and work behaviour: Physical attributes, cognitive abilities, knowledge, personality traits and motives', in C.L. Cooper and I.T. Robertson (eds.), *International Review of Industrial and Organizational Psychology*. Palo Alto: Consulting Psychology Press. pp. 1–34.

Whitener, E.M. (2001) 'Do "high commitment" human resource practices affect employee commitment?', *Journal of Management*, 27(5), 515–535.

Whitley, R.D. (1999) *Divergent Capitalisms: The Social Structuring and Change of Business Systems*. Oxford: Oxford University Press.

Wieland, R. (2010) 'Barmer Gesundheitsreport 2010'. Berlin: Barmer.

Wood, G., Croucher, R., Brewster, C., Collings, D.G. and Brookes, M. (2009) 'Varieties of firm: Complementarity and bounded diversity', *Journal of Economic Issues*, 43(1): 239–258.

Wood, G., Wilkinson, A. and Harcourt, M. (2008) 'Age discrimination and working life: Perspectives and contestations – A review of the contemporary literature', *International Journal of Management Reviews*, 10(4): 425–442.

Wrenn, K. A. and Maurer, T.J. (2004) 'Beliefs about older workers' learning and development behavior in relation to beliefs about malleability of skills, age-related decline, and control', *Journal of Applied Social Psychology*, 34(2): 223–242.

Wu, A.S., Tang, C.S. and Yan, E.C. (2005) 'Post-retirement voluntary work and psychological functioning among older Chinese in Hong Kong', *Journal of Cross-Cultural Gerontology*, 20: 27–45.

Yamada, A. (2010) 'Labor force participation rates of older workers in Japan - Impacts of retirement policy, steep age-wage profile and unionization', *Japanese Economy*, 37(1): 3–39.

13

Demographic Challenges for Human Resource Management: Implications from Management and Psychological Theories

Birgit Verworn, Christiane Hipp and Doreen Weber

INTRODUCTION

The world's population is aging rapidly, and due to this demographic change, the personnel structure in organizations will change considerably over the next decades (Verworn and Hipp, 2009). Furthermore, organizations may be confronted with skill shortages and the loss of knowledge due to the mass retirement of the baby-boom generation (Buyens et al., 2009). Human Resource Management (HRM), therefore, is facing challenges in the areas of employability and motivation, strategic human resource planning, recruitment, retirement and knowledge management (Claes and Heymans, 2008; Gellert and Kuipers, 2008; Inceoglu et al., 2009; Korff et al., 2009). There is little

managerial experience or empirical evidence to fall back on regarding changing workforce demographics. Many of the recommendations for organizations concerning these changes lack a theoretical foundation and seem to be based only on common sense (Verworn et al., 2009). The aim of this chapter is to discuss a possible theoretical foundation by describing the possible contribution of selected management and psychological theories. Managerial implications for HRM are derived. The theories considered in this chapter have their roots in strategic management, psychology and social psychology (more precisely, the resource-based theory), cognitive psychology, industrial psychology, developmental psychology and literature on age stereotypes.

IMPLICATIONS FROM MANAGEMENT THEORY: THE RESOURCE-BASED THEORY OF THE FIRM

A theory suitable for discussing HRM strategies to adapt to demographic changes is the resource-based theory of the firm, which emphasizes 'the way strategic resources are developed over time through opportunities that do not necessarily repeat themselves' (Boxall, 1996: 65; see also Barney et al., 2011). The resource-based theory explains companies' success through superior resources compared to competitors. Organizational superior resources at a given time are defined as the strengths of a given firm or as input factors – human or nonhuman – that are owned or controlled by the firm (Wernerfelt, 1984; Lado and Wilson, 1994). Barney (1991) characterizes superior resources with the help of four different resource characteristics: valuable, rare, inimitable, and nonsubstitutable.

Researchers have applied the resource-based theory of the firm to different management fields (see Acedo et al., 2006), one of those being HRM (e.g., Autier and Picq, 2005; Colbert, 2004; Lado and Wilson, 1994; Lepak and Snell, 1999; Wright and McMahan, 1992; Wright et al., 2001). The focus so far has been on HRM issues without considering the challenges of changing workforce demographics. The current chapter contributes to filling that gap by building heavily on a publication of Verworn et al. (2009), which expands the management-oriented theoretical considerations of Lado and Wilson (1994) into the specific challenges of demographic changes. Lado and Wilson (1994) focused on human resource (HR) systems and their ability to create sustainable competitive advantage, classifying four categories of organizational competencies: managerial, input-based, transformational and output-based. Managerial competencies include, for example, strategic leaders' capabilities to enact a beneficial firm–environment relationship (Lado and Wilson, 1994). Input-based competencies encompass physical and capital resources as well as human resources, knowledge and skills (Lado and Wilson, 1994). Transformational competencies enable organizations to advantageously convert input resources into output (Lado and Wilson, 1994). Output-based competencies refer to corporate reputation and similar invisible strategic assets.

Managerial competencies

Lado and Wilson (1994) focused in their approach on the possibilities of managerial competencies to influence firms' successes and failures. The authors especially emphasized that HR managers and professionals can support or hinder the strategic decision-making process. In this context managerial competencies include inimitable abilities to formulate and accomplish a *strategic vision*. This unique competence helps the whole organization to prioritize activities and deploy scarce resources. Due to an unreasonable use of stereotyping thinking, older, but experienced, employees are often neglected within organizational decision making (Patrickson and Ranzijin, 2005; Wood et al., 2008). In the case of an aging workforce, an active integration of experienced and aged employees could support formulating a valuable and nonsubstitutable strategic vision for the organization. The experience of these employees on different hierarchical levels helps to maintain a unique combination of top down and bottom up approaches and to formulate and communicate strategies and visions in a firm-specific and realizable manner (Leibold and Voelpel, 2006). These arguments are also supported by Lado and Wilson (1994), who highlighted that articulating a strategic vision is inherently tacit and firm-specific to the historical context. It also requires complex interactions among the organization's key actors to allow for a sustained competitive advantage. Here, more than ever, aged employees and troupers – but also already retired employees and alumni – can play an unrivaled role.

Lado and Wilson (1994) also emphasized the importance of *enacting the organizational environment.* Following the approach that organizations and their members are enacted through a collective way of thinking, reasoning, and behavior, a competitive advantage can be derived based on the inimitable way different organizational members work together to build commonly shared ways of thinking and acting over the years (Weick, 1979 and 2001). Lado and Wilson (1994) assumed that the process of enacting is idiosyncratic (interpretation of organizational-specific symbols and knowledge), imaginative (unique search for strategic possibilities), and evolutionary (processes of variation, selection, und retention). In the light of demographic change, an older workforce – and especially a workforce that is mainly socialized within one organization over the years – is a unique accumulation of people with a broad and common understanding of the organization and the environment. HR managers are called to identify and use this specific accumulation of knowledge, values, and beliefs to identify possible implementation barriers in times of change. Innovation managers are called to develop and improve distinctive products, processes and services while mirroring and shaping them with aged and knowledgeable employees. It might also be possible to establish a unique and effective process to more easily integrate a younger or new workforce by actively using the common memory, values, and shared organizational interpretation of the environment. This could be realized by age-diverse teams that integrate experienced employees with just-hired people from outside the organization.

Input-based competencies

The first input-based competency proposed by to Lado and Wilson (1994) was to *exploit the imperfections in the labor market.* Given the increasing share of people aged 45 and older and the decreasing share of the younger labor force, organizations could recruit and try to make better use of older employees with unique knowledge, skills or abilities.

The organizations that exploit this potential in times of 'war for talents' might achieve sustained competitive advantage if organizational culture, processes and training adapt accordingly (Hodgkinson et al., 1996). Recognizing the difficulty of recruiting different age groups, Haesli and Boxall (2005) suggested, for example, making use of specialized recruitment agencies. In addition to recruiting older employees, employees with unique knowledge, skills or abilities who are approaching retirement might be offered tailored, end-of-career arrangements like part-time work or job sharing (Buyens et al., 2009; Claes and Heymans, 2008; Hedge et al., 2006). Retirees possessing unique knowledge, skills or abilities could be rehired on a part-time or temporary basis (Purcell, 2000) or utilized as interim managers, coaches and mentors (Leibold and Voelpel, 2006).

The second input-based competency described by Lado and Wilson (1994) was to *create internal labor markets,* meaning that job positions would be filled with internal candidates. By offering key employees a career path within the organization, firm-specific knowledge, skills and abilities can be tied to the firm (Lazear and Oyer, 2004; Windolf, 1986). If employees leave, the investment in human capital might decrease and, additionally, the replacement of firm-specific knowledge, skills and abilities could involve costs for the organization (Lado and Wilson, 1994). Grimshaw and Rubery (1998) pointed out that the implementation of the internal labor market concept as an HRM strategy has been underutilized or ignored so far, particularly by management. Due to skill shortages, it will become increasingly difficult to replace key employees with candidates from the external labor market, so internal labor markets will probably gain importance for HRM.

Lado and Wilson (1994) suggested a third input-based competency: *investing in firm-specific human capital* (e.g., recruitment and selection, performance appraisal, and training). Such an investment should be taken into consideration for resources that are not widely available in the external labor market and cannot be readily and cost-efficiently substituted by other resources (Lado and Wilson, 1994). The mass retirement wave of the Baby Boom generation might be a replacement issue related to demographic change. Organizations should be aware of a potential loss of firm-specific human capital if a disproportionately high number of employees retire simultaneously so they can develop knowledge transfer strategies to mitigate these losses (Argote et al., 2000; Argote and Ingram, 2000; Goh, 2002). In this context, Stamov-Roßnagel and Hertel (2010) emphasized diagnostic tools for optimizing team building in age-diverse teams.

Furthermore, due to the decreasing potential labor force, training is an important investment to enable employees to adjust to new equipment and procedures, adapt to changing environments and continue to enhance their job-related skills (Hedge et al., 2006). Older workers may suffer more from skill or knowledge obsolescence than younger workers, because their training is often more out of date or they may be victims of stereotypes, denying them opportunities to reverse their obsolescence (Hedge et al., 2006).

Transformational competencies

According to Lado and Wilson (1994), *harnessing innovation and entrepreneurship* is an important transformational competency of a firm. The role of HRM in this context is to identify and develop entrepreneurial talents (Shipton et al., 2006). So far, entrepreneurial talent has often been associated with youth. Older employees were believed to be less capable of acquiring new skills, absorbing new knowledge and producing new ideas (Shearring, 1992) although there is no clear empirical evidence for this assumption (Verworn, 2010; Verworn and Hipp, 2009). Furthermore, there is evidence that creativity training and challenging tasks foster creative thinking and innovation and enable workers to maintain their innovativeness as they age (Hedge et al., 2006; Shearring, 1992). Especially in dynamic and fast changing

environments, as well as for jobs with a high proportion of changing and innovative tasks, an age- and risk-sensitive (but not discriminating) learning and motivation strategy must be developed and implemented. New skills and knowledge should no longer be associated with youth and hiring new employees, as fewer and fewer qualified young employees are available in the labor market.

A second transformational competency is *fostering organizational learning*, which is more than the sum of each member's individual learning. Organizations develop and maintain learning systems that influence their current members and are transmitted to new hires by organization histories and norms (Fiol and Lyles, 1985).

However, an aging workforce with a more homogeneous age structure and fewer new hires could negatively impact organizational learning. Older workers are often perceived as having certain undesirable characteristics, including low trainability and inflexibility (Arrowsmith and McGoldrick, 1995; Chiu et al., 2001). Other stereotypes about aging suggest that older employees stick to routines and have more problems adapting to change than younger employees (Chiu et al., 2001). Yet, older employees have more experience and 'wisdom' and might reflect upon their work and work environment at a higher level than less experienced employees (Moberg, 2001; Sterns and Miklos, 1995), thereby fostering organizational learning. However, bearing in mind the probable retirement waves and, thus, a loss of an entire (key) work group, significant damage could be done to organizational memory (Alvesson, 2000; Haesli and Boxall, 2005).

A third transformational competency proposed by Lado and Wilson (1994) was the *promotion of organizational culture*, a term introduced by Pettigrew (1979). According to Hofstede et al. (1990), organizational culture manifests itself in symbols, heroes, rituals and values. An important task of HRM with regard to the aging workforce is to create an organizational culture free of age stereotypes and age discrimination. Although the organizational culture regarding older workers cannot be changed overnight, HRM policies and practices can begin to alter culture (Hedge et al., 2006). The findings of Chiu et al. (2001) have suggested that anti-age discrimination policies can have a positive impact on the beliefs and attitudes about the adaptability of older workers and of providing them with training.

Output-based competencies

Output-based competencies include all intangible assets that are interlinked with the quality of products and services, corporate reputation or image, and customer loyalty (Lado and Wilson, 1994). Although these resources are intangible and difficult to measure, they often require long-term and huge investments in human, technical, and organizational assets. These assets are not freely tradable and can be the source of a competitive advantage (Lado and Wilson, 1994). Furthermore, these output-based competencies signal an optimal and well-organized use of organizational resources, making the firm attractive to all kinds of stakeholders, such as suppliers and R&D innovation partners. Different leverage effects can be identified in the context of an aging society and an aging workforce. Walker (2006) argued that a strategy of an age-sensitive HR management – which would include the reduction of stereotyping thinking and discrimination, improving the appreciation of the older workforce, and providing access to learning – has the potential to optimize the use of human capital. Such a strategy encourages aging employees to exert a stronger influence not only over their later life careers but also over their health and well-being. This is a second step to create a motivated and responsible, age-sensitive workforce and additionally supports employee branding and corporate reputation building. In a third step, even positive effects on the quality of products and services can be derived, as Hackman and Oldham (1976) showed the positive interrelation between motivational aspects

and output performance issues (see also Oakland and Oakland, 1998). In this respect it is also important to highlight that experience is a better predictor of performance than age itself (Avolio et al., 1990). For HR management and managers, this means allowing all employees, from hiring and beyond retirement age, to learn and to experiment, in combination with individually adopted motivation instruments to facilitate and ensure output-oriented performance.

IMPLICATIONS FROM DEVELOPMENT PSYCHOLOGICAL THEORY: THE SOC THEORY

Korff et al. (2009) suggested adopting a lifespan psychology perspective on age-related changes. The SOC theory (Baltes, 1997) is based on the premise that successful personal development (including aging) comprises three components, *Selection, Optimization, and Compensation (SOC)*, which minimize losses and maximize gains (Freund and Baltes, 2000). The SOC theory posits that people *Select* by narrowing the range of alternatives from the available options, *Optimize* their strategies for goal attainment, and *Compensate* for age-related losses to maintain a given level of functioning (Freund and Baltes, 2000). The SOC theory implies that the skills and needs of older employees are more heterogeneous than those of younger employees. Furthermore, Stamov-Roßnagel and Hertel (2010), who combined different motivational theories with a lifespan perspective, proposed considering individual work tasks rather than entire jobs as the level of analysis, as motivation might differ markedly between different tasks: 'As a result of selection, optimization, and compensation processes (...), workers are likely to develop motivation profiles instead of one single motivation for an entire job' (Stamov-Roßnagel and Hertel, 2010: 895). The findings of Armstrong-Stassen and Schlosser (2008) suggested that to retain older workers, employers need to ensure that older workers' tasks promote personal development and that their work assignments include adequate opportunities to learn new knowledge and skills. Older workers should be integrated, motivated, and trained without discrimination. For organizations to achieve this, they should redesign their human resource strategy and personal development activities to ensure a generation-wide integration of employees and adopt age-sensitive incentives and motivation systems that foster individual selection, optimization and compensation processes. This would require companies to leave current, common practices of HRM and to motivate researchers to develop diagnostic tools and HRM instruments to adequately measure age-sensitive personal characteristics and foster age-sensitive motivational aspects at the individual and task-based level (Maurer et al., 2008).

IMPLICATIONS FROM COGNITIVE PSYCHOLOGICAL THEORY: THE THEORY OF FLUID AND CRYSTALLIZED INTELLIGENCE

Aside from formal qualifications and motivation, the cognitive capacities of employees determine organizational outcomes (Korff et al., 2009). The theory of fluid and crystallized intelligence, introduced by Cattell (1971) and Horn (1976), describes two important cognitive capacities. 'Fluid intelligence (Gf) describes adaptive mental behavior in unfamiliar situations. Gf represents different forms of reasoning including abstracting, forming, and using concepts (classification), perceiving and using relations, identifying correlates, maintaining awareness in reasoning, and abstracting ideas, especially from figural and nonverbal, symbolic and semantic content' (Jonassen and Grabowski, 1993: 53). 'Crystallized intelligence (Gc) consists of those cognitive performances that have been habituated or crystallized (…) as a result of previous learning experiences' (Jonassen and Grabowski, 1993: 53). Several researchers analyzed lifetime changes in fluid and crystallized intelligence or the level of fluid and

crystallized intelligence of particular age groups (e.g., Baltes and Lindenberger, 1997; Baltes et al., 1980; Lee et al., 2005). Although aging is an individual process, some average tendencies can be observed. There is support for an increase in fluid intelligence until the cessation of neural maturation, generally during adolescence, which is followed by a decline (Cunningham et al., 1975; Korff et al., 2009). In contrast, crystallized intelligence is believed to increase steadily across the adult age span (Cunningham et al., 1975; Korff et al., 2009) and decline after the typical retirement age. Henseke and Tivig (2008) and Weinberg (2004) provided empirical evidence to support this belief. Especially in experience-based fields, like agriculture and metallurgy, the first peak of inventors occurs at around age 48, and the second peak at around 60 years, while in fast-changing fields, like information and communication technologies, younger workers adopt technological knowledge more rapidly compared to older workers.

HR practices that take age-related changes in fluid and crystallized intelligence into account can optimize the fit between job demands and personal abilities (Korff et al., 2009). Adequate job design and training ensure compatibility between employees' cognitive resources and their task assignments (Korff et al., 2009). Older workers with an assumed higher proportion of experience-based, crystallized intelligence must especially be motivated and integrated into innovation and change management. Principally in fields in which incremental and continuous changes are necessary to remain competitive (e.g., in many service industries), older employees can highly contribute to improve processes, products, and services. It is also important to motivate and integrate older employees if whole and complex systems of products, technologies, and processes have to be maintained and improved. Here, the experiences over the years help to get a 'deep', often tacit, understanding of what is possible and not possible (Gellert and Kuipers, 2008), but disruptive and radical change that is based on analogies and experiences in different industries or topics can also be initiated by creative older employees. People like Steve Jobs are creative and remain so over the years. It is important to identify these employees through HR management practices to ensure an environment and a working context in which these people can keep and enhance their creativity over their working life.

IMPLICATIONS FROM AGE STEREOTYPE THEORY: THE THEORIES ABOUT THE LINK BETWEEN ATTITUDES AND BEHAVIOR

Several theories link attitudes to behavioral intentions or behavior. Two wide-spread examples are Rosenberg and Hovland's model of attitude (Rosenberg and Hovland, 1960) and the theory of planned behavior (Ajzen, 1991). Attitudes are typically defined as predispositions to respond in a particular way toward a specified class of objects (Rosenberg and Hovland, 1960). In the case of aging workforces, the class of objects is older workers. According to Rosenberg and Hovland (1960), the types of response fall into three major categories: cognitive, affective, and behavioral. Negative or positive attitudes towards older employees fall mainly into the category of cognitive response, but they can also influence behavior. When such negative or positive beliefs regarding the characteristics of older employees are widely held, they are defined as age stereotypes (Rosen and Jerdee, 1977). Examples of such stereotypical views of age include depicting older employees as less capable, efficient, creative, and less able to learn or to cope with future challenges (Posthuma and Campion, 2009; Rosen and Jerdee, 1977). Age stereotypes can have a significant influence on the expectations of performance, the performance itself and how the performance is evaluated (Hedge et al., 2006). The myths of aging are often reinforced by HRM policies and practices (Hedge et al., 2006). The result can be discrimination against older workers with regard to recruiting, selection for training or

layoffs (Chiu et al., 2001; Finkelstein et al., 2000; Posthuma and Campion, 2009). Age stereotypes and myths also influence older employees' perceptions and expectations of aging and might, therefore, discourage them and hamper their job performance (Buyens et al., 2009; Hedge et al., 2006). That may lead older workers to avoid precisely those tasks (e.g., creative tasks) that society expects them to fail at (Buyens et al., 2009).

An implication would be, again, to ensure HR practices free of age discrimination, e.g., installing age-independent HR practices of recruitment, promotion and training. HR should support a work climate free of age stereotypes (Claes and Heymans, 2008). Although age stereotypes develop during childhood and are resistant to change, it is possible to alter them in adult life (Lippmann, 1922). Age stereotypes can be the result of insufficient knowledge about aging (Tornstam, 2007) or of insufficient or negative experiences with older employees (Maurer et al., 2008). Thus, HR can not only offer management guidelines and management training, but it can also foster age-diverse team work or 'tandems' between an older employee close to retirement and younger employees or new hires. The findings of Gellert and Kuipers (2008) led to the same conclusion; they found that teamwork and team performance may benefit from older workers.

IMPLICATIONS FROM INDUSTRIAL PSYCHOLOGICAL THEORY: THE DEPRECIATION AND DEFICIT MODELS

The so-called 'depreciation model' or 'deficit model' proposes that older workers' added value to an organization declines as they reach the retirement age (Claes and Heymans, 2008; Hedge et al., 2006; Yeatts et al., 1999). Compared to those who are younger, older people lose important features, showing defects and deficits that hamper their performance and innovativeness (Meyer, 2011). According to a meta-analysis by Waldman and Avolio (1986), chronological age accounts only for a small percentage of the variance in performance, contradicting the deficit model. Regarding innovation, empirical findings are more heterogeneous. Research findings by Meyer (2011) and Rouvinen (2002) support the assumption of the deficit model that age is negatively related to technology adoption and innovation. In contrast, Verworn (2010) analyzed ideas submitted through suggestion systems and found no evidence for a decline in the quantity or quality of ideas in terms of the submitter's age. Verworn and Hipp (2009) found no effect of there being a high share of older employees in German manufacturing companies' innovation output.

Overall, the depreciation and deficit models have been the basis for HR practices for decades (Claes and Heymans, 2008). Meta-analyses and recent findings suggest that these models are a foundation of age stereotypes rather than contributing constructively to HRM. They tend to emphasize losses without considering gains across the life-span

(Korff et al., 2009). Negative effects of age stereotypes have already been discussed in connection with Rosenberg and Hovland's model of attitude, and the main implication for HRM is to skip the depreciation and deficit model (Claes and Heymans, 2008).

SUMMARY

Table 13.1 summarizes implications from the theories discussed in this chapter. With this effort we contribute to a theoretical foundation for often recommended approaches to cope with demographic changes. Some of the implications are derived from more than one of the theories, an indication of their appropriateness. However, some implications seem rather contradictory. While theories about the link between attitudes and behavior and research on age stereotypes suggest installing age-independent HR practices of recruitment, promotion and training, SOC theory suggests age-sensitive and task-based HR practices.

Table 13.1 Theories and implications for HRM considering demographic changes

Theory	Implications for HRM considering demographic changes
Resource-based theory of the firm	
Managerial competencies	
Articulating a strategic vision	• Integrate older and qualified employees into the strategy building and communication process
Enacting organizational environment	• Use the common memory, values, and shared organizational interpretation of the environment to more easily integrate younger workforce members • Communicate and discuss organizational changes to identify possible implementation barriers • Discuss new products and services with aged and experienced staff to mirror and improve them
Input-based competencies	
Exploiting imperfections in the labor market	• Recruit older qualified people • Offer part-time work arrangements for older workers • Utilize retirees as interim managers, coaches and mentors
Creating an internal labor market	• Create internal labor markets for all age cohorts • Offer career planning for all age cohorts
Investing in firm-specific human capital	• Foster knowledge transfer from older to younger employees • Initiation succession planning for Baby Boomers

(Continued)

Table 13.1   (Continued)

Theory	Implications for HRM considering demographic changes
Transformational competencies	
Harnessing innovation and entrepreneurship	• Stop acquiring new skills and new knowledge by only hiring young employees • Smart allocation of HR to enable workers to maintain their creativity and innovativeness
Fostering organizational learning	• Foster organizational learning
Promoting organizational culture	• Prevent age discrimination based on negative age stereotypes • Promote new managerial mindsets with regard to older employees
Output-based competencies	• Apply age-sensitive HR management practices to support the well-being and motivation of employees (and increase employee branding and output performance of the organization)
SOC theory	• Apply age-sensitive and task-based HR practices • Assign tasks that promote personal development, including adequate opportunities to learn new knowledge and skills
Theory of fluid and crystallized intelligence	• HR practices optimize the fit between job demands and personal abilities (in terms of job design and training) • Support experience-building • Identify and motivate creative employees through the whole working life
Theories about the link between attitudes and behavior	• Apply age-independent HR practices of recruitment, promotion and training • Prevent age discrimination based on negative age stereotypes • Promote new managerial mindsets with regard to older employees, e.g., by managerial guidelines or management training
Research on age stereotypes	• Foster age-diverse teams work or 'tandems' with an older employee close to retirement and a young employee
Depreciations and deficit model	• Stop using assumptions of the models as a justification for HR practices which favor younger employees (e.g., recruitment, task assignment)

This potential contradiction might be resolved by age-sensitive HR practices that are free of age stereotypes, e.g., that neither favor nor discriminate against older employees, instead of practices that focus on advancing individual employees. In sum, especially HR managers can help to sensitize top and middle management to specific managerial, age-sensitive instruments and competencies.

REFERENCES

Acedo, F.J., Barroso, C. and Galan, J.L. (2006) 'The resource-based theory: dissemination and main trends', *Strategic Management Journal*, 27(7): 621–636.

Ajzen, I. (1991) 'The theory of planned behavior', *Organizational Behavior and Human Decision Processes*, 50(2), 179–211.

Alvesson, M. (2000) 'Social identity and the problem of loyalty in knowledge-intensive companies', *Journal of Management Studies*, 37(8): 1101–1123.

Argote, L. and Ingram, P. (2000) 'Knowledge transfer: A basis for competitive advantage in firms', *Organizational Behavior and Human Decision Processes*, 82(1):150–169.

Argote, L., Ingram, P., Levine, J.M. and Moreland, R.L. (2000) 'Knowledge transfer in organizations: learning from the experience of others', *Organizational Behavior and Human Decision Processes*, 82(1):1–8.

Armstrong-Stassen, M. and Schlosser, F. (2008) 'Benefits of a supportive development climate for older workers', *Journal of Managerial Psychology*, 23(4): 419–437.

Arrowsmith, J. and McGoldrick, A.E. (1995) 'HRM service practices: flexibility, quality and employee strategy', *International Journal of Service Industry Management*, 7(3): 46–62.

Autier, F. and Picq, T. (2005) 'Is the resource-based "view" a useful perspective for SHRM research? The case of the video game industry', *International Journal of Technology Management*, 31(3–4): 204–222.

Avolio, B.J., Waldman, D.A. and McDaniel, M.A. (1990) 'Age and work performance in nonmanagerial jobs: The effects of experience and occupational type', *The Academy of Management Journal*, 33(2): 407–422.

Baltes, P.B. (1997) 'On the incomplete architecture of human ontogeny: selection, optimization, and compensation as foundation of developmental theory', *The American Psychologist*, 52(4): 366–380.

Baltes, P.B. and Lindenberger, U. (1997) 'Emergence of a powerful connection between sensory and cognitive functions across the adult life span: A new window to the study of cognitive aging?', *Psychology and Aging*, 12(1): 12–21.

Baltes, P.B., Reese, H.W. and Lipsitt, L.P. (1980) 'Life-span developmental psychology', *Annual Review of Psychology*, 31: 65–110.

Barney, J.B. (1991) 'Firm resources and sustained competitive advantage', *Journal of Management*, 17: 99–120.

Barney, J.B., Ketchen, D.J., Jr. and Wright, M. (2011) 'The future of resource-based theory: Revitalization or decline?', *Journal of Management,* 37: 1299–1315.

Boxall, P. (1996) 'The strategic HRM debate and the resource-based view of the firm', *Human Resource Management Journal*, 6(3): 59–75.

Buyens, D., Van Dijk, H., Dewilde, T. and De Vos, A. (2009) 'The aging workforce: Perceptions of career ending', *Journal of Managerial Psychology*, 24(2): 102–117.

Cattell, R.B. (1971) *Abilities: Their structure, growth, and action*. Boston: Houghton Mifflin.

Chiu, W.C.K., Chan, A.W., Snape, E. and Redman, T. (2001) 'Age stereotypes and discriminatory attitudes towards older workers: An East–West comparison', *Human Relations*, 54(5): 629–661.

Claes, R. and Heymans, M. (2008) 'HR professionals' views on work motivation and retention of older workers: a focus group study', *Career Development International*, 13(2): 95–111.

Colbert, B.A. (2004) 'The complex resource-based view: Implications for theory and practice in strategic human resource management', *Academy of Management Review*, 29(3): 341–358.

Cunningham, W.R., Clayton, V. and Overton, W. (1975) 'Fluid and crystallized intelligence in young adulthood and old age', *Journal of Gerontology*, 30(1): 53–55.

Finkelstein, L.M., Higgins, K.D. and Clancy, M. (2000) 'Justifications for ratings of old and young job applicants: An exploratory content analysis', *Experimental Aging Research*, 26(3): 263–283.

Fiol, C.M. and Lyles, M.A. (1985) 'Organizational learning', *The Academy of Management Review*, 10(4): 803–813.

Freund, A.M. and Baltes, P.B. (2000) 'The orchestration of selection, optimization, and compensation: An action-theoretical conceptualization of a theory of developmental regulation', in W.J. Perrig and A. Grob (eds.), *Control of human behaviour, mental processes, and consciousness*, Mahwah: Lawrence Erlbaum Associates. pp. 35–58.

Gellert, F.J. and Kuipers, B.S. (2008) 'Short- and long-term consequences of age in work teams: An empirical exploration of ageing teams', *Career Development International*, 13(2): 132–149.

Goh, S.C. (2002) 'Managing effective knowledge transfer: An integrative framework and some practice implications', *Journal of Knowledge Management*, 6(1): 23–30.

Grimshaw, D. and Rubery, J. (1998) 'Integrating the internal and external labour markets', *Cambridge Journal of Economics*, 22: 199–220.

Hackman, J.R. and Oldham, G.R. (1976) 'Motivation through the design of work: Test of a theory', *Organizational Behavior and Human Performance*, 16(2): 250–279.

Haesli, A. and Boxall, P. (2005) 'When knowledge management meets HR strategy: An exploration of personalization-retention and codification-recruitment configurations', *International Journal of Human Resource Management*, 16(11): 1955–1975.

Hedge, J.W., Borman, W.C. and Lammlein, S.E. (2006) *The aging workforce: Realities, myths, and implications for organizations*. Washington, DC: American Psychological Association.

Henseke, G. and Tivig, T. (2008) 'Demographic change and industry-specific innovation patterns in Germany', in M. Kuhn and C. Ochsen (eds.), *Labor markets and demographic change*. Wiesbaden: VS Research. pp. 122–136.

Hodgkinson, G.P., Snell, S., Daley, N. and Payne, R.L. (1996) 'A comparative study of knowledge of changing demographic trends and the importance of HRM practices in three European countries', *International Journal of Selection and Assessment*, 4(4): 184–194.

Hofstede, G., Neuijen, B., Ohayv, D.D. and Sanders, G. (1990) 'Measuring organizational cultures: A qualitative and quantitative study across twenty cases', *Administrative Science Quarterly*, 35(2): 286–316.

Horn, J.L. (1976) 'Human abilities: A review of research and theory in the early 1970s', *Annual Review of Psychology*, 27: 437–485.

Inceoglu, I., Segers, J., Bartram, D. and Vloeberghs, D. (2009) 'Age differences in work motivation in a sample from five Northern European countries', *Zeitschrift für Personalpsychologie*, 8(2): 59–70.

Jonassen, D.H. and Grabowski, B.L. (1993) *Handbook of individual differences, learning, and instruction*. New Jersey: Lawrence Erlbaum Associates.

Korff, J., Biemann, T., Voelpel, S., Kearney, E. and Stamov-Roßnagel, C. (2009) 'HR Management for an aging workforce: A life-span psychology perspective, *Zeitschrift für Personalpsychologie*, 8(4): 201–213.

Lado, A.A. and Wilson, M.C. (1994) 'Human resource systems and sustained competitive advantage: a competency-based perspective', *The Academy of Management Review*, 19(4): 699–727.

Lazear, E.P. and Oyer, P. (2004) 'Internal and external labor markets: a personnel economics approach', *Labour Economics*, 11(5): 527–554.

Lee, J.-Y., Lyoo, K., Kim, S.-O., Jang, H.-S., Lee, D.-W., Jeon, H.-J., Park, S.-C. and Cho, M.J. (2005) 'Intellect declines in healthy elderly subjects and cerebellum', *Psychiatry and Clinical Neurosciences*, 59(1): 45–51.

Leibold, M. and Voelpel, S. (2006) *Managing the Aging Workforce: Challenges and Solutions*. Erlangen: Publicis, Wiley.

Lepak, D.P. and Snell, S.A. (1999) 'The human resource architecture: Toward a theory of human capital allocation and development', *Academy of Management Review*, 24(1): 31–48.

Lippmann, W. (1922) *Public opinion*. New York: Macmillan Company.

Maurer, T.J., Barbeite, F.G., Weiss, E.M. and Lippstreu, M. (2008) 'New measures of stereotypical beliefs about older workers' ability and desire for development: Exploration among employees age 40 and over', *Journal of Managerial Psychology*, 23(4): 395–418.

Meyer, J. (2011) 'Workforce age and technology adoption in small and medium-sized service firms', *Small Business Economics,* 37(3): 305–324.

Moberg, D.J. (2001) 'The aging workforce: implications for ethical practice', *Business and Society Review*, 106(4): 315–329.

Oakland, J.S. and Oakland, S. (1998) 'The links between people management, customer satisfaction and business results', *Total Quality Management*, 9(4–5): 185–190.

Patrickson, M. and Ranzijn, R. (2005) 'Workforce ageing: The challenges for 21st century management', *International Journal of Organisational Behaviour*, 10(4): 729–739.

Pettigrew, A.M. (1979) 'On studying organizational cultures', *Administrative Science Quarterly*, 24(4): 570–581.

Posthuma, R.A. and Campion, M.A. (2009) 'Age stereotypes in the workplace: Common stereotypes, moderators, and future research directions', *Journal of Management*, 35(1): 158–188.

Purcell, P.J. (2000) 'Older workers: employment and retirement trends', *Monthly Labor Review*, 123(10): 19–31.

Rosen, B. and Jerdee, T.H. (1977) 'Too old or not too old', *Harvard Business Review*, 55: 97–106.

Rosenberg, M.J. and Hovland, C.I. (1960) 'Cognitive, affective and behavioral components of attitudes', in C.I. Hovland and M.J. Rosenberg (eds.), *Attitude organization and change*. New Haven: Yale University Press. pp. 1–14.

Rouvinen, P. (2002) 'Characteristics of product and process innovators: some evidence from the Finnish innovation survey', *Applied Economics Letters*, 9(9): 575–580.

Shearring, H.A. (1992) 'Creativity and older adults', *Leadership & Organization Development Journal*, 13(2): 11–16.

Shipton, H., West, M.A., Dawson, J., Birdi, K. and Patterson, M. (2006) 'HRM as a predictor of innovation', *Human Resource Management Journal*, 16(1): 3–27.

Stamov-Roßnagel, C. and Hertel, G. (2010) 'Older workers' motivation: Against the myth of general decline', *Management Decision*, 48(6): 894–906.

Sterns, H.L. and Miklos, S.M. (1995) 'The aging worker in a changing environment: organizational and individual issues', *Journal of Vocational Behavior*, 47(3): 248–268.

Tornstam, L. (2007) 'Stereotypes of old people persist'. *International Journal of Ageing and Later Life*, 2(1): 33–59.

Verworn, B. (2010) 'Does age have an impact on having ideas? An analysis of the quantity and quality of ideas submitted to a suggestion system', *Creativity and Innovation Management*, 18(4): 326–334.

Verworn, B. and Hipp, C. (2009) 'Does the ageing workforce hamper innovativeness of firms? (No) evidence from Germany', *International Journal of Human Resources Development and Management*, 9(2/3): 180–197.

Verworn, B., Schwarz, D. and Herstatt, C. (2009) 'Changing workforce demographics: Strategies derived from the resource-based view of HRM', *International Journal of Human Resources Development and Management*, 9(2/3): 149–161.

Waldman, D.A. and Avolio, B.J. (1986) 'A meta-analysis of age differences in job performance', *Journal of Applied Psychology*, 71(1): 33–38.

Walker, A. (2006) 'Active ageing in employment: Its meaning and potential', *Asia-Pacific Review,* 13(1): 78–93.

Weick, K.E. (1979) *The social psychology of organizing*. 2nd edn. Reading, MA: Addison-Wesley.

Weick, K.E. (2001) *Making sense of the organization*. Malden, MA: Blackwell Publishers.

Weinberg, B.A. (2004) *'Experience and technology adoption'*, IZA Discussion Paper No. 1051. Bonn: Institute for the Study of Labor.

Wernerfelt, B. (1984) 'A resource-based view of the firm', *Strategic Management Journal*, 5(2): 171–180.

Windolf, P. (1986) 'Recruitment, selection, and internal labour markets in Britain and Germany', *Organization Studies*, 7(3): 235–254.

Wood, G., Wilkinson, A.J. and Harcourt, M. (2008) 'Age discrimination and working life: Perspectives and contestations a review of the contemporary literature', *International Journal of Management Reviews*, 10(4): 425–442.

Wright, P.M. and McMahan, G.C. (1992) 'Theoretical perspectives for strategic human resource management', *Journal of Management*, 18(2): 295–320.

Wright, P.M., Dunford, B.B. and Snell, S.A. (2001) 'Human resources and the resource based view of the firm', *Journal of Management*, 27(6): 701–721.

Yeatts, D.E., Folts, W.E. and Knapp, J. (1999) 'Older workers' adaptation to a changing workplace: Employment issues for the 21st century', *Educational Gerontology*, 25(4): 331–347.

14

Age Stereotypes in the Workplace: Multidimensionality, Cross-cultural Applications, and Directions for Future Research

Richard A. Posthuma and Laura Guerrero

INTRODUCTION

All too often employers use negative age stereotypes unfairly to limit employment opportunities for older workers (The Economist, 2006). Negative age stereotypes create discrimination against older workers, resulting in the underutilization of this valuable human resource (*EEOC* v. *Town of Huntington*, 2008; Finkelstein, 2011; Roscigno, Mong, Byron, & Tester, 2007). As a result, organizations fail to utilize the full potential of older workers even though they could provide valuable contributions that would improve organizational performance. Therefore, it is important to understand workplace age stereotyping to help managers find ways to reduce negative consequences.

Moreover, the problem of age stereotyping in the workplace has been recognized in many

countries around the world (Lokenhoff, et al., 2009). In response to this widespread problem, the European Union has promoted active aging as a way to combat negative age stereotypes in the workplace (European Union Legislation, 2011). Nevertheless, the effects of age stereotyping are likely to differ significantly across countries and cultures. For example, research suggests that Asian cultures may be less likely to discriminate against older workers (Posthuma, Roehling, & Campion, 2011).

Ironically, everyone gets older and aging eventually affects everyone, yet there has been less research on age stereotyping compared to race and gender stereotypes. To address this gap in the literature and to enhance our understanding of age stereotypes, we need more research on the causes and consequences of age stereotyping in the workplace. This chapter builds on previous research related to age stereotyping by developing further a structured meta-theoretical framework to guide future research (Posthuma & Campion, 2009; Posthuma, Wagstaff, & Campion, 2012). Research following this framework will enable the creation of an integrated body of knowledge to enhance our understanding of the multiple dimensions of age stereotyping and of similarities and differences in age stereotyping across cultures. It will also provide guidance to practitioners as they seek to avoid age stereotyping in their workplaces.

DEFINITIONS

Age stereotypes

In general, stereotypes are traits that are ascribed to a group and by extension to each individual within that group (Fiske & Neuberg, 1990; Sherman, 1996). Thus, workplace age stereotypes are stereotypes that are ascribed to employees based on their age (Levy, 2009). Stereotypes are considered unfair to individuals because they make judgments based on a group characteristic.

The negative effects of judging individual older workers based on stereotypes about all older workers can happen in two ways. First, the stereotype about older workers as a group may be false and therefore result in false conclusions about individuals within the group of older workers. Thus, stereotypes can be studied according to their veracity: true or false. For example, a common stereotype is that older workers are less motivated and more detached from their work (Posthuma & Campion, 2009). However, research shows that the opposite tends to be true because older workers are usually more motivated, satisfied, and committed to their work (Ng & Feldman, 2010). Nevertheless, if managers accept the truth of this stereotype, either explicitly or implicitly, they may falsely presume that individual older workers are less motivated and therefore make decisions about

their work assignments that negatively affect individual workers.

Secondly, a stereotype about older workers may generally be true for many, but not true for individuals within the group of older workers. While it may be true that as people age they tend to gradually lose muscle strength and elasticity, not all individuals lose it at the same rate. In fact, individuals over the age of 65 who exercise regularly may be stronger than younger individuals who do not exercise at all. For example, a stereotype about older workers could be that workers over age 65 are less likely to be physically able to perform certain types of work. While this may be true for some types of jobs, e.g., airline pilot, it may not hold true for all workers who are over the age of 65 or for all jobs. It is noteworthy, however, that stereotypes that are true, will have words that contain qualifying words or phrases such as 'usually' 'more often' 'less likely' and the like. Thus, the stereotype would be false if stated in an absolute fashion as applicable to all older workers but true because of the qualifying words and phrases.

Moreover, worker age stereotypes can be either positive or negative. Thus, stereotypes can be studied according to their polarity: positive versus negative. A positive stereotype would ascribe a generally favorable characteristic to older workers. For example, a positive stereotype about older workers is that they are more dependable (Posthuma & Campion, 2009). A negative stereotype would ascribe a generally unfavorable characteristic to older workers. For example, a negative stereotype about older workers is that they will have shorter job tenure and therefore, fewer years in which the employer can reap the benefits of training older workers (Posthuma & Campion, 2009).

The interplay between the truth and falsity of age stereotypes with the positive and negative aspects of age stereotypes can be used to create four categories of stereotypes, as illustrated in Figure 14.1. This interplay reveals important directions for future research. In this figure, the truth or falsity of

Veracity	Polarity	
	Negative	Positive
False	I. Negative and False	II. Positive and False
True	III. Negative and True	IV. Positive and True

Figure 14.1   Interplay of False vs. True and Negative vs. Positive Workplace Age Steretypes

the stereotypes is represented on the vertical axis and the negativity versus positivity on the horizontal axis. Type I age stereotypes are false and negative. This type is probably the most common. Type II stereotypes are false but positive. Type III stereotypes are true, but negative. Type IV stereotypes are true and positive.

Future research should aim to answer important questions about these four different types of stereotypes. For example, is it the case that Type I stereotypes are the most common, and if so, why and what can be done to counteract them? Moreover, is it possible that in some circumstances, Type II stereotypes offset the negative affect of Type I stereotypes such that even though they are both false, the negative effects on older workers are diminished? Additional questions that compare, contrast, and integrate these four types of stereotypes will provide useful directions for future research.

Comparatively, there is less research on stereotypes that are considered generally true. Nevertheless, important research questions about true stereotypes should be explored. For example, do true negative stereotypes have less negative effect on individual older workers compared to false negative stereotypes because they are sufficiently qualified such that managers will treat the older workers as individuals and make judgments about them based on their own characteristics? For example, if a true stereotype is that workers over 65 are less likely to be able to perform the tasks of physically demanding jobs, when, where, and why will employers judge individual

workers based solely on their age, or judge them based on their own individual physical abilities? Alternatively, will true positive stereotypes offset the negative effect of false negative stereotypes in some contexts? If so, when, where, and why?

Another possible area of research is whether the impact of false stereotypes is more damaging than the impact of true stereotypes. Although it may seem that negative stereotypes are likely to be more damaging than positive ones, this needs to be investigated empirically. For instance, if older workers are stereotyped as being more dependable, an individual worker may be assigned undesirable tasks based on the perception that he or she is less likely to complain or leave the organization.

The classification of age stereotypes along these two dimensions of veracity and polarity should not preclude consideration of the possibility that stereotypes may not be either absolutely true or false or absolutely negative or positive. Rather, it is likely that some stereotypes may be measured by the degree of their truth and the degree of their negativity. Thus, future research should be open to the possibility that these categories are not absolute but more like continuous variables that can be further conceptualized and measured in degrees using multi-item scales with Likert type response formats.

Nevertheless, all too often an unfortunate outcome of age stereotypes is that individual employees are judged based on their age rather than on their own job-related knowledge, skills, and abilities. This can result in age discrimination.

Age discrimination

Age discrimination in the workplace results when people make unlawful decisions about employees based upon their age. Those decisions could result in older workers not being hired, not receiving training, being downsized, laid off, etc. Often, age discrimination is caused by negative age stereotypes about older workers (*Kentucky Retirement Systems* v. *EEOC*, 2008). Thus, age stereotypes are often the cause and age discrimination is the effect. For example, in one case a youth counselor was replaced with someone younger because of the supervisor's stereotyped belief that older workers cannot relate as well to young people (*EEOC* v. *Town of Huntington*, 2008). That case is consistent with the research that shows how negative stereotypes about older workers (e.g., they would have less 'drive' and be less attractive to younger customers) lead to lawsuits based on age discrimination (Roscigno, Mong, Byron, & Tester, 2007).

Legislation in the US provides few exceptions under which discrimination is allowed. One such exception is a bona fide occupational qualification (BFOQ), which allows for situations where it is necessary to hire a person based on their gender, religion, national origin or age. Thus, there are a few circumstances in which age could be considered a bona fide occupational qualification, suggesting that decisions about individuals based on their age are lawful. The case of commercial airline pilots is one example. The US Federal Aviation Administration established a rule that pilots over age 60 flying commercial airplanes must retire because of the perceived risk to passengers. Nevertheless, this standard was modified when a law was passed in 2007 that permitted pilots aged 60 to 64 to serve as pilots on multi-crew operations (Carswell v. Airline Pilots Association, 2008).

Age bias

Age bias exists when there are erroneous judgments about workers based on their age. Age stereotypes can be a cause of age bias. These errors in judgment about workers based on their age could be positive or negative (Clapham & Fulford, 1997; Gordon & Arvey, 2004). Typically, however, age bias consists of negative evaluations of older workers.

Ageism

Whereas age bias occurs when there are erroneous judgments, ageism includes both prejudice and discrimination that harms older workers (Posthuma & Campion, 2009; Rupp, Vodanovich, & Crede, 2005). Thus, ageism is a broader term that incorporates both age bias and age discrimination. Age stereotypes are often a cause of ageism.

The concepts of age stereotypes, age discrimination, age bias, and ageism are key components that explain the relationships of workers' age with age stereotypes and important outcomes for employees and employers. Previous work has explicated a meta-framework for understanding these relationships (Posthuma & Campion, 2009; Posthuma, Wagstaff, & Campion, 2012). This chapter builds on the foundation established by this work. Here, the previously developed model is updated with recent research and refined to further elaborate the multi-dimensional nature of age stereotypes and make much needed connections to national culture models in order to encourage cross-cultural comparison research.

ADVANCING A META-FRAMEWORK FOR AGE STEREOTYPES RESEARCH

In the typical theoretical model, expected relationships among constructs are hypothesized and tested. However, to guide future research on a broad topic, such as age stereotyping, an overarching conceptual framework is needed to incorporate many different types of studies that contain different theories and hypothesized relationships while simultaneously enabling the integration of those multiple theories, measures, and results into a coherent framework. Previous work has provided a broad meta-theoretical framework that serves as a template for theoretical development of specific research propositions related to age stereotyping (Posthuma & Campion, 2009; Posthuma, Wagstaff, & Campion, 2012). This chapter shows how that broad framework can serve as a template for incorporating multiple dimensions of age stereotypes and extending them to multi-cultural settings. We also show how age stereotypes can be conceptualized and measured not just by categories of types of stereotypes, but also through multiple dimensions (Coutant, Worchel, Bar-Tal, & van Raalten, 2011). This chapter also shows the way in which the cultures of different countries can moderate the relationships within this model.

This meta-theoretical framework includes several different categories of constructs: (1) worker age, (2) outcomes of age stereotypes, (3) age stereotypes, (4) upstream moderators, and (5) downstream moderators. Age stereotypes appear at the center of this model. The model illustrates the relation between age stereotypes and other categories of constructs. This model can be thought of as a meta-theory, since it includes categories of constructs and not just the constructs themselves. A more complete explication of this model is provided in previous work (Posthuma & Campion, 2009, Posthuma, Wagstaff, & Campion, 2012). This model is well-suited to act as a guide for future research by providing a framework within which other researchers can use their own wisdom and insights to identify, create, explore, and test more specific constructs within these categories. This should encourage a more coordinated and more rapid development of knowledge about age stereotypes in the workplace.

MULTIDIMENSIONALITY OF WORKPLACE AGE STEREOTYPES

Despite the usefulness of this meta-framework, stereotypes are frequently studied as distinct and unrelated concepts, impeding the advancement of research in the field. This is not surprising since real world phenomena often do not fit neatly into theoretical models. For example, prior research identified many different stereotypes about older workers in terms of poorer performance, resistance to change, lower ability to learn, shorter tenure, and increased cost (Posthuma & Campion, 2009). These stereotypes can be thought of as bundles of words and phrases that constitute different and often unrelated cognitions. This broad and varied kaleidoscope of cognitions makes it difficult for researchers to conduct research in this area.

Similarly, recent research on ethnic stereotypes has criticized the prior conceptualization of ethnic stereotypes as consisting of bundles of phrases and adjectives (Coutant, Worchel, Bar-Tal, & van Raalten, 2011). That research demonstrated the usefulness of an alternative conceptualization of multiple dimensions of stereotypes. That conceptualization proposes that stereotypes can be measured along five dimensions: evaluation, saliency, homogeneity, uniqueness, and perceived consensus (Coutant, Worchel, Bar-Tal, & van Raalten, 2011). Research on workplace age stereotypes could utilize the same type of multidimensional perspective. Moreover, this dimensionalization of age stereotypes can be particularly useful in cross-cultural settings because it includes dimensions that capture differences across ethnicities, which reflect, to some degree, cultural differences.

For example, some researchers focus on resistance to change stereotype, suggesting that older workers are more resistant to change (Figure 14.2). Research could examine the extent to which this stereotype is positive, negative (evaluation), or salient (i.e., how much do people pay attention to it). The tendency to resist change could be positive because older workers have more work experience and have seen many workplace fads come and go over their careers. Thus, they may be less likely to get caught up on a fad that would turn out to be unproductive. The tendency of older workers to resist

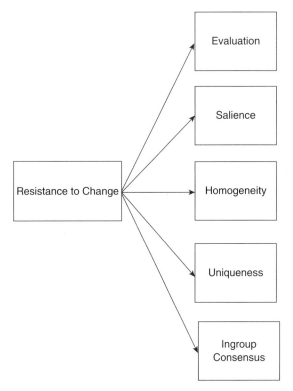

Figure 14.2   Dimensions of Age Stereotypes Using the Resistance to Change Example

change may held by many people, but not be very salient if people don't rely on it to make decisions about individual older workers. Researchers could also study the degree of homogeneity of resistance to change among all older workers, its uniqueness or universality, and consensus about trait (i.e., does everybody agree with it). Moreover, this multidimensional approach to research on workplace age stereotypes can be particularly useful in examining differences across countries and cultures because dimensions like consensus and homogeneity can be measured at the group level comprising people in different countries.

For example, an expatriate may perceive that in her home country the stereotype of older workers having lower learning abilities is not salient, not homogeneous, somewhat unique (other workers are also expected to have learning difficulties), and may not be held by the majority of people

(lack of consensus). In contrast, the same expatriate manager may perceive that in the host country the same stereotype is salient, homogeneous, somewhat unique, and held by the majority of people (consensus). An area of future research would be to investigate to what extent the behaviors of expatriates are impacted by the perceptions of these dimensions of the stereotype in the host country in comparison to their own values about discrimination in the workplace or in comparison to how they would behave in the home country.

Figure 14.3 illustrates the relation of these multiple dimensions of workplace age stereotypes with other elements in the meta-framework. The numbered paths in the model represent the expected cause and effect relationships in the model.

Path 1 indicates that workers' age can relate directly to outcomes for both individual workers and the organization. For example,

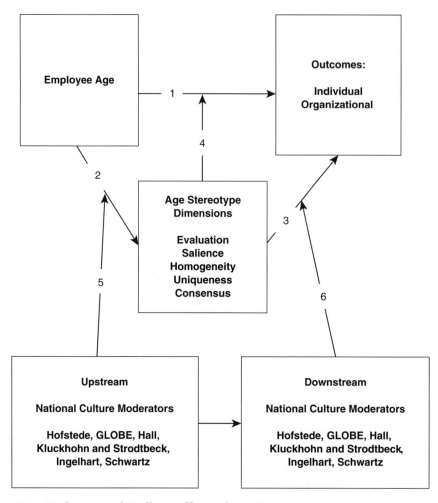

Figure 14.3   Moderator and Mediator Effects of Age Stereotypes

older workers may be discriminated against because of their age (*EEOC* v. *Town of Huntington*, 2008; Roscigno, Mong, Byron, & Tester, 2007). Older workers may also enhance organizational performance because of their more positive work attitudes (Ng & Feldman, 2010). Path 1 may be thought of as the baseline or control condition that does not include the effects of age stereotypes.

Path 2 indicates the relationship between employees' age and age stereotypes. In other words, as the employees age, they are more likely to be impacted by age-related stereotypes. A unique aspect of this path between employee age and age stereotype is that some employees may be able to conceal the signs

of aging to some extent, which is often not an option to individuals who are likely to be impacted by racial or gender stereotypes. As an example, older workers may be perceived as more resistant to change. However, this resistance to change stereotype can be assessed along the five dimensions of evaluation, salience, homogeneity, uniqueness, and consensus. The resistance to change stereotype will likely have a negative evaluation and even though it exists, it may be more or less salient depending on the circumstances. In addition, the resistance to change stereotype may not be homogeneous or may vary in its uniqueness. Lastly, the resistance to change stereotype may lack consensus. This same type of analysis can be applied to other workplace age stereotypes.

Path 3 indicates the relationship between the various dimensions of age stereotypes and outcomes for individuals and organizations. Thus, for example, the extent to which the resistance to change stereotype is perceived as salient may influence the likelihood that it will have actual effects on the individual and the organization. Moreover, the path from 2 through age stereotypes and then through 3 to outcomes suggests the possibility that age stereotypes may at least partially mediate the relationship between employee age and outcomes. The extent to which age stereotypes mediate the relationship between worker age and outcomes serves as an explanation for the relationship between workers' age and outcomes.

However, this meta-framework conceptualizes age stereotypes as both mediators and moderators of the relationship between worker age and individual outcomes (Baron & Kenny, 1986). Path 4 indicates the moderating effects of age stereotypes on the relationships between worker age and outcomes for individual workers. Thus, each of the proposed five dimensions of age stereotypes can act as moderators of the relationship of workers' age with individual and organizational outcomes. This suggests that when age discrimination exists, it can have a direct effect on outcomes (Path 1), which the five dimensions of age stereotypes can enhance or diminish. For example, when the resistance to change stereotype is perceived to be less salient, the discrimination against individual older workers may be diminished. In this application of the meta-framework, paths 5 and 6 relate to the moderating influence of national culture, as explained in detail in the following section.

CROSS-CULTURAL RESEARCH ON WORKPLACE AGE STEREOTYPES

Age stereotypes

While most research on age stereotypes has been conducted in Anglo-American countries, recent research has identified the relevance of this issue in other countries. Unfortunately, cross-cultural research on workplace age stereotypes is lacking in two respects.

First, much research on age stereotypes has focused on a single country. For example, one study found age stereotypes and age discrimination resulting in fewer training opportunities for employees in Italy (Lazazzara & Bombelli, 2011). Another study found significant workplace age stereotyping in Romania (Gherasim-Ardelean & Goras, 2011). However, these studies did not measure national culture. Future research will need to design studies that would incorporate more than one country and measure national culture in order to gain a better understanding of the influence of the cultures on workplace age stereotypes.

Second, the cross-cultural research on age stereotypes tends to focus on general age stereotypes and not stereotypes relevant to the workplace. Nevertheless, this research is important because it illustrates the universal applicability of age stereotypes and their different dimensions in different countries and cultures. Several studies compared age stereotypes across two countries. For example, one study found that young people in both Canada and South Korea held a negative stereotype about the decline in memory of individuals as they age (Ryan, Jin, & Anas, 2009). In France and Morocco both negative and positive stereotypes about aging were found (Macia, Lahmam, Baali, Boetsch, & Chapuis, 2009). Another study found that in China and in the US, people tended to believe that older people experience a decline in mental and physical abilities (Boduroglu, Yoon, Ting, & Park, 2006). These studies illustrated both the similarities and differences in age stereotypes across countries. In general, age stereotypes tend to be negative rather than positive, although some studies suggest that in some countries, older people may be perceived more positively (e.g., China and Morocco).

However, a more comprehensive study (Lockenhoff et al., 2009) of collated data across 26 countries found similarities and differences in general age stereotypes, although it did not focus on workplace age stereotypes. One of the findings that is generalizable across countries is a negative stereotype that older people tend to be less attractive and unable to perform and learn. Another generalizable positive stereotype appears to be that older people tend to have greater wisdom and that they are worthy of respect. Nevertheless, some differences across countries in certain age related stereotypes also emerged. Some countries were found to have more positive general views about aging (e.g., China and India) than others (e.g., Serbia, UK and Argentina).

These multi-country studies contribute to our understanding of age stereotypes by collecting data from more than one country, thereby enabling cross-country comparisons. However, the causes of these differences remain unclear because not all of these studies used cultural measures to determine if culture was the explanatory mechanism for these differences. In addition, because there can be variation within cultures, individual-level values should also be considered. In summary, it is recommended that future research include measures of national culture and individual-level values when doing cross-cultural comparative research. In addition, other context-related measures should be considered such as percentage of the population over the age of 65. For instance, Lockenhoff et al., (2009) found a negative relationship between this percentage and general attitudes towards aging. When doing multi-country studies, it may be necessary to establish what age is considered 'older' given that different countries have different life expectancies using the traditional Western age of retirement may not be relevant in a country with a life expectancy in the 40s. Another limitation is that to date, these multi-country studies have not specifically measured work-related age stereotypes. Therefore, future cross-cultural research should concentrate on work-related age stereotypes.

Another method to conduct cross-cultural research is to collect data from countries with similar cultures. Several researchers have clustered multiple countries into culturally similar groups (e.g., Ronen & Shenkar, 1985). We conducted an exploratory analysis to determine the viability of clustered country analyses of workplace age stereotypes.

In that exploratory study, we used an online survey tool to ask respondents to write both positive and negative statements about older workers. We then grouped their responses into two country clusters: Asian and Anglo-American. Countries in the Asian group included: China, Japan, Singapore, Taiwan, and Philippines. Countries in the Anglo-American cultures included: Australia, Canada, New Zealand, and United Kingdom. The statements are reported in Table 14.1. These statements provide examples of the groupings of words and phrases that typify much of the actual cognitions that people express about age stereotypes.

In Asian countries, people reported positive stereotypes about older workers, stating that they were clever and wise, loyal, and dependable. In Asian cultures, negative stereotypes included older worker reluctance to change, lack of enthusiasm, and too much whining. The findings also indicated that overall, Asians reported more positive age stereotypes compared to Anglo Americans. In Anglo-American countries, people reported positive stereotypes about older workers, including being patient, reliable, and having common sense. On the contrary, negative stereotypes included being too set in their ways, taking longer to grasp new ideas and being inflexible and stubborn. As an example, a respondent said, 'Older employees have less energy than the younger ones. They don't seek new ways to do things. They tend to be comfortable only with their peers. Just by being grey-haired, balding, overweight, and unable to dunk a basketball, they drag the whole company down.'

Age discrimination

Age stereotypes can lead to age discrimination, so future research needs to examine the manifestation of this phenomenon across

Table 14.1   Positive and Negative Workplace Age Stereotypes: Asian vs. Anglo-American Cultures

National Culture Group	Age Stereotypes about Older Workers	
	Positive	Negative
Asian	Very clever and wise.	They whine too much.
	They have enough experience and are highly skilled.	Higher salary for their level of performance.
	Valuable experience and loyalty.	Reluctant to change.
	They can work longer hours because their children are older.	Inertia against change.
	Most of them are no longer financially burdened because the children have finished schooling.	Lack of enthusiasm toward innovation.
		Do not want to discover new methods because they are comfortable with what they are doing.
	Work experience will help them deal with any problems that crop up.	
	Most older workers are dependable.	
	They do not need acknowledgment for good work done because they are usually more content with their lives and just want to give back.	
Anglo-American	A lot of experience.	Too set in their ways.
	Not so many personal issues (e.g., kids) that keep them from doing the job.	They can be too set in their ways. Just because something worked 20 years ago doesn't mean it's the best way now.
	Street smart, seasoned, risk averse.	
	Expertise, patience.	They might take longer to grasp new concepts.
	Common sense.	Sometimes they expect unwavering respect even though they have not earned it or they have done things to lose it.
	Patience.	
	Reliable.	
	Depth of knowledge, industry contacts, ability to deal with difficult situations.	Conservatives, slow, do not listen to younger employees.
	Maturity, stability, commitment.	Most of them are not ready to get changed with the new things (modern technology).
	They don't do everything by the book, they can think for themselves. By gaining life experience and not just what is taught in school and university, they are better equipped to deal with the day-to-day mishaps and unexpected items.	More serious and long term absence/ Demographic challenges which may impact on recruiting younger people and attrition rates/ Difficulty of assessing when they can no longer do the job and exiting people with dignity.
	Loyalty, experience, knowledge of the organization's ethos.	Illness, depending on job may not be as able.
	Experiences/Discretion/Knowledge/Loyalty.	Inflexibility/Afraid of change and new developments/IT knowledge.
	They seem to have a better work ethic compared to younger employees. They have vast experience and knowledge because they have been working for much longer and can therefore assist.	It is harder to keep up with the new technologies, maybe needed more support/ investment than with younger employees.
	The obvious life experiences to draw from. Set higher standards. Are role models for younger colleagues. Considerably more reliable and literate.	See many situations as "black & white/right & wrong" when today's world presents us with so many shades of gray.
	Steady calmer temperament and experience. In small firms, women of child bearing age who need maternity leave present a difficulty for management. With older ladies this is no longer an issue.	Tend to be inflexible and lack creativity.
		Older employees have less energy than the younger ones. They don't seek new ways to do things. They tend to be comfortable only with their peers. Just by being grey-haired, balding, overweight, and unable to dunk a basketball, they drag the whole company down.
	They are more relaxed about issues that would cause stress in young employees. They have a routine that allows them to be more productive than the employee that is still chasing new experiences. They often call on experience to get their work done in much shorter timeframes than younger employees require. They're reliable.	Mainly "my way or the highway" mentality. Stubbornness.

different countries and cultures. Since age stereotypes often lead to discrimination against older workers, the US outlawed discrimination based on age many years ago. More recently, countries in the European Union have also either enacted or upgraded their laws to prohibit discrimination based on age (Lahey, 2010). Nevertheless, the actual enforcement of these laws varies across countries (Lahey, 2010). There has been a paucity of cross-cultural research on the relationships between age stereotypes, age discrimination, and the legal ramifications of this phenomenon. More research is needed to determine how different countries and cultures address the effects of age stereotypes on discrimination of older workers through legal or other channels.

APPLICATIONS OF CULTURE MODELS TO WORKPLACE AGE STEREOTYPES

Organizational researchers tend to utilize seven popular models of national culture. In this section, we briefly describe those models and illustrate the ways in which they can be integrated into the workplace age stereotype research in order to gain a better understanding of the effects of different country cultures.

We propose that various aspects of these seven models of national cultural values can function both as upstream and as downstream moderators (Figure 14.3). Upstream moderators influence the relationship between worker age and age stereotypes (Path 5). Downstream moderators influence the relationship between workplace age stereotypes and the outcomes of those stereotypes (Path 6). We discuss these relationships using seven popular national culture models. These applications are intended to be illustrative and not exhaustive with an aim to encourage and motivate future research to consider conceptualizations provided here. For each of these cultural frameworks, we introduce the dimensions of national culture contained in that framework. We then show how those dimensions of culture can act as moderators of the

relationship between employee age and dimensions of age stereotypes (upstream moderators: Path 5) and how dimensions of culture can also act as moderators of the relationships between dimensions of culture and outcomes (downstream moderators: Path 6).

Hofstede

The Hofstede model defines five dimensions that differentiate national cultures: Power Distance, Individualism, Masculinity, Uncertainty Avoidance, and Long-term Orientation (Hofstede, 1980, 2001). Several of these five dimensions have the potential to moderate the relationship between worker age and the five dimensions of workplace age stereotypes.

Lockenhoff et al. (2009) found that participants from cultures with greater uncertainty avoidance (Hofstede, 1980) were more likely to have negative views about aging. Participants from countries with lower levels of power distance noted less favorable views of age-related changes in knowledge and wisdom. Future research should consider other possible moderating relationships of these cultural dimensions. For example, in cultures that emphasize long-term orientation, the salience and homogeneity of positive age stereotypes (e.g., wisdom) may be enhanced. By contrast, in cultures that emphasize masculinity, that is, achievement, assertiveness, and competition, the negative evaluation of the older workers' poor performance stereotype may be exacerbated. Other dimensions of Hofstede's model can be applied similarly in new and creative ways.

GLOBE

The GLOBE model includes nine dimensions that differentiate national cultures: Performance Orientation, Future Orientation, Gender Egalitarianism, Assertiveness, Humane Orientation, In-Group Collectivism, Institutional Collectivism, Power Distance, and Uncertainty Avoidance (House et al., 2004). Several of these nine dimensions have the potential to moderate the relationship between worker age and the five dimensions of workplace age stereotypes.

For example, in cultures with higher levels of Humane Orientation, the salience of negative age stereotypes may be diminished. Moreover, in cultures that value a higher level of individualism, it may be less likely that even a high consensus around negative age stereotypes would actually lead to age discrimination because employers would be more likely to consider employees as individuals as opposed to members of a group of older workers.

Hall

The Hall model incorporates three factors: Context, Space, and Time (Hall, 1966, 1976). In this model, the meaning of communication in high-context cultures is influenced to a great degree by the situation and to a lesser degree by the actual content of the message. Cultures also differ in their perceptions of the appropriateness of intimate versus public and social spaces as well as in the degree to which they tend to be mono-chronic, focusing on one thing at a time, or poly-chronic, which is akin to multi-tasking. These dimensions of culture have the potential to influence the five dimensions of workplace age stereotypes.

For example, a culture valuing context and poly-chronic time orientation may be more likely to encourage a more negative evaluation of the older workers' performance in contexts in which the job has multiple competing demands. Alternatively, cultures valuing context will be less likely to let a high level of consensus about a stereotype have in negative impact on older workers, since they are more likely to seek out individualized context specific information about individuals and the situation as opposed to relying just on a general stereotype.

Ingelhart

Ingelhart's model contains two dimensions, Traditional/Secular and Survival/Self-expression (Inglehart, 1997; Ingelhart & Baker, 2000;

Ingelhart, Basanez, Diez-Medrano, Halman, & Luijkx, 2004; Iglehart & Welzel, 2005). The Traditional dimension focuses on the degree to which individuals value tradition and religion, contrary to the Secular in which tradition and religion are less valued. Survival focuses on hard work and materialistic concerns, contrary to Self-expression, which values subjective well-being and quality of life. Both of these dimensions of culture have the potential to influence the five dimensions of workplace age stereotypes.

Lockenhoff et al. (2009) found that participants from cultures high in secular-rational values indicated more negative views towards new learning in advanced age. Other relationships between Ingelhart's dimensions and age stereotypes should be considered in future research. For example, a culture that is more traditional may not evaluate older employees negatively because it would associate traditions with older individuals. Alternatively, cultures that are higher on self-expression may be more accepting of the uniqueness of individual older workers and therefore less likely to use negative evaluations of all older workers to discriminate against them.

Kluckhohn and Strodtbeck

Kluckhohn and Strodtbeck's (1961) model contains six dimensions of culture. The first dimension describes individual's relationship to nature, which can reflect dominance, subjugation, or harmony. The second dimension involves the relationships between people, which can be characterized by individualism, collectivism, or hierarchy. The third dimension is time orientation, which can include a focus on the present, past, or future. The fourth dimension reflects the nature of human activity, focusing on being, doing, or thinking. The fifth dimension concerns assumptions about human nature, which can be good, bad, or a combination of both. The sixth dimension refers to the conception and preferences regarding space, which can be private, public, or a mixture of both. Several of these six dimensions of culture have the potential to influence the five dimensions of workplace age stereotypes.

For example, a culture valuing a higher level of dominance and subjugation may be more likely to view the negative age stereotypes about older workers' poor performance or their decreased ability to learn, because positive perceptions could interfere with the ability to dominate and subjugate older workers. Alternatively, cultures that perceive human nature as generally good may enhance the positive evaluation of the stereotype that older workers are wiser, and thereby reduce the likelihood of negative outcomes for older workers.

Schwartz

The Schwartz model contains ten dimensions of culture: Achievement, Benevolence, Conformity, Hedonism, Power, Security, Self-direction, Stimulation, Tradition, and Universalism (Schwartz, 1992, 1994). Achievement oriented cultures value being influential, ambitious, and capable. Benevolent cultures value being forgiving, honest, and loyal. Conformity oriented cultures value being obedient, polite, and self-disciplined. Hedonistic cultures value pleasure and enjoying life. Power oriented cultures value authority and social power. Security oriented cultures value national security, family security, and a sense of belonging. Self-direction oriented cultures value independence, freedom, and curiosity. Stimulation oriented cultures value daring, exciting, and varied life. Traditional cultures value accepting one's position, devoutness, and humbleness. Universalism oriented cultures value equality, broadmindedness, and social justice. Several of these ten dimensions of culture have the potential to influence the five dimensions of workplace age stereotypes.

For example, a culture that is high on universalism would be less likely to permit negative evaluations of older workers' capabilities because such culture values equality and social justice. Alternatively, a society high on security and tradition would be less likely to permit the negative evaluation of older workers' poor performance and actual age discrimination.

Trompenaars

The Trompenaars model contains seven dimensions of culture: Universalism, Individualism, Neutrality, Specificity, Achievement, Sequentiality, and Internality (Trompenaars, 1993; Hampden-Turner & Trompenaars, 1994). Universalism focuses on the degree to which things are universally true, e.g., reflect general rules, as opposed to individual consideration, which is more particularistic. Individualism focuses on the importance of individuals as opposed to groups. Neutrality focuses on the degree to which persons are detached and non-emotional. Specificity focuses on the degree to which things like work and private life are kept in specific realms as opposed to a greater integration of them in more diffused and public cultures. Achievement focuses on the degree to which it is believed people should earn status through achievement as opposed to ascription. Sequentiality focuses on the degree to which things are done one at a time versus simultaneously. Internal focuses on the degree to which people think they should control their environment as opposed to environment controlling them. Several of these seven dimensions have the potential to moderate the relationship between workers' age and the five dimensions of workplace age stereotypes.

For example, in cultures that are higher on universalism, it may be more likely that the age of employees would result in a consensus about stereotypes about older workers. In a more particularistic culture, age would be less likely to be important or at least there would be less likely to be consensus about the stereotype. Alternatively, cultures higher on an ascription orientation (less achievement oriented) may be inclined to support positive stereotypes, such as older workers being wiser, making elderly respected and rewarded in the workplace.

OTHER AVENUES FOR FUTURE RESEARCH

In addition to studying the topics outlined above, researchers are encouraged to pursue other lines of inquiry using the meta-framework outlined in this chapter. Three promising areas are: (1) recruiting older workers, (2) decision making regarding older workers, and (3) business ethics.

There is very little research on the effectiveness of recruiting older workers. Even though older workers may be one of the most qualified groups in terms of experience and job knowledge, employee recruiting research has tended to focus too much on recruiting college students (Barber, 1998). This may be because college students are a convenient sample to study. However, it is likely that the most effective methods for recruiting college students (e.g., on campus interviews and placement centers) are generally unavailable to older workers. Therefore, more research is needed to guide organizations who will want to hire older workers.

The decision making literature also provides numerous theories that can be useful in studying how organizations make decisions about older workers (Beach, 1997). For example, it has been noted that managers make less than optimal decisions for a variety of reasons. These can include unfounded age-related stereotypes. Future research could adapt and refine these theories to study how age related stereotypes are used and how organizations can overcome them. For example, it has been shown how organizations can make downsizing decisions in a way that will be fair to all workers and reduce the likelihood that negative stereotypes will enter into the decision making process (Campion, Guerrero, & Posthuma, 2011).

The ethics literature also provides a variety of useful avenues for future research regarding age stereotypes. Moreover, given the challenges that businesses face because of high profile corruption scandals, the importance of business ethics research is increasing. Within this literature, one of the more popular frameworks describes stages of moral development (Kohlberg, 1981; Kohlberg, Levine, & Hewer, 1983). This theory is derived from developmental psychology and posits that as people mature, they pass through various stages that increase in their level of moral sophistication. This model suggests that as workers age, they may sometimes become more ethical. However, more research is needed to determine the extent to which this may be true for individual older workers. Other business ethics theoretical perspectives are also likely to be applicable to workplace age stereotype research.

CONCLUSION

This chapter advances the development of a meta-framework that guides future studies on stereotypes about older people in the workplace. The purpose of this meta-framework is to facilitate a more rapid advancement of knowledge, while enabling researchers to develop their own theoretical perspectives.

This chapter also encourages researchers to move beyond identification of words and phrases that constitute stereotypical statements about older workers and to adopt multi-dimensional measures of different facets of age stereotypes. In addition, there is a need for more cross-cultural comparative research to facilitate a better understanding of the similarities and differences in age stereotypes across different countries and cultures. Specific examples were provided, showing how several dimensions of seven popular cultural frameworks can be used to study the moderating effects of culture on several different facets of age stereotypes.

REFERENCES

Barber, A. (1998). *Recruiting Employees: Individual and Organizational Perspectives*. Thousand Oaks: CA: Sage Publications.

Baron, R. M., & Kenny, D. A. (1986). The mediator–moderator variable distinction in social science research: Conceptual, strategic, and statistical considerations. *Journal of Personality and Social Psychology, 51*, 1173–1182.

Beach, L. R. (1997). *The Psychology of Decision Making: People in Organizations*. Thousand Oaks: Sage Publications.

Boduroglu, A., Yoon, C., Ting L., & Park, D. C. (2006). Gerontology. Age-related stereotypes: A comparison of American and Chinese cultures. *Gerontology, 52*, 324–333.

Campion, M. A., Guerrero, L., & Posthuma, R. A. (2011). Reasonable human resource practices for making employee downsizing decisions. *Organizational Dynamics, 40*, 174–180.

Carswell v. Airline Pilots Association, F. Supp. 2d 107 (D.C., 2008).

Clapham, M. M., & Fulford, M. D. (1997). Age bias in assessment center ratings. *Journal of Managerial Issues, 9*, 373–87.

Coutant, D., Worchel, S., Bar-Tal, D., & van Raalten, J. (2011). A multidimensional examination of the "Stereotype" concept: A developmental approach. *International Journal of Intercultural Relations, 35*, 92–110.

E.E.O.C. v. Town of Huntington, 2008 WL 361136, (No. 05 CV 4559 (DRH) (WDW), E.D.N.Y., Feb. 8, 2008).

European Union Legislation (2011). *Decision No. 940/2011/EU of the European Parliament of the Council of 14 September 2011 on the European Year for Active Ageing and Solidarity between Generations (2012)*. Westlaw OJ 2011 L246/5.

Finkelstein, Lisa M. 2011. Overqualified as a euphemism for too old? *Industrial & Organizational Psychology, 4*, 250–251.

Fiske, S.T., & Neuberg, S. (1990). A continuum of impression formation, from category-based to individuation processes: Influences of information and motivation on attention and interpretation. *Advances in Experimental Social Psychology, 23*, 1–74.

Gherasim-Ardelean, S., & Goras, M. (2011). Stereotypes and prejudices in HR industry in Romania. *Applied Medical Informatics, 28*, 53–61.

Gordon, R. A., & Arvey, R. D. (2004). Age bias in laboratory and field settings: A meta-analytic investigation. *Journal of Applied Psychology, 34*, 468–492.

Hall, E.T. (1966). *The Hidden Dimension*. New York: Doubleday.

Hall, E.T. (1976). *Beyond Culture*. New York: Anchor Books/Doubleday.

Hofstede, G. (2001). *Culture's Consequences* (2nd ed.). Thousand Oaks, CA: Sage.

House, R. J., Hanges, P. J., Javidan, M., Dorfman, P. W., & Gupta, V. (2004). *Culture, leadership, and organizations: The GLOBE study of 62 societies*. Thousand Oaks, CA: Sage.

Inglehart, R. (1997). *Modernization and postmodernization: Cultural, economic, and political change in 43 societies*. Princeton: Princeton University Press.

Inglehart, R. & Baker, W. (2000). Modernization, cultural change, and the persistence of traditional values. *American Sociological Review, 65*, 19–51.

Inglehart, R., Basanez, M., Diez-Medrano, J., Halman, L., & Luijkx, R. (2004). *Human values and beliefs*. Mexico City: Siglo XXI Editores.

Inglehart, R., & Welzel, C. (2005). *Modernization, cultural change, and democracy: The human development sequence*. Cambridge: Cambridge University Press.

Hampden-Turner, C., & Trompenaars, F. (1994). *The Seven Cultures of Capitalism*. London: Piatkus.

Hofstede, G. (1980). *Cultures consequences: International differences in work-related values*. Beverly Hills, CA: Sage.

Hofstede, G. (2001). *Culture's Consequences: Comparing Values, Behaviors, Institutions, and Organizations across Nations* (2nd ed.). Thousand Oaks, CA: Sage.

Kentucky Retirement Systems v. E.E.O.C., 128 S. Ct. 2361 (2008).

Kluckhohn, F.R., & Strodtbeck, F.L. (1961). *Variations in Value Orientations*. Evanston, IL: Row, Peterson.

Kohlberg, L. (1981). *Essays on Moral Development, Vol. I: The Philosophy of Moral Development*. San Francisco, CA: Harper & Row.

Kohlberg, L., Levine, C., & Hewer, A. (1983). *Moral stages: A Current Formulation and a Response to Critics*. Basel, NY: Karger.

Lahey, J. N. (2010). International comparison of age discrimination laws. *Research on Aging. 32*, 679–697.

Lazazzara, A., & Bombelli, M. C. (2011). HRM practices for ageing Italian workforce: The role of training. *Journal of European Industrial Training, 35*, 808–825.

Levy, B. 2009. Stereotype embodiment: A psychosocial approach to aging. *Current Directions in Psychological Science, 18*, 332–336.

Lockenhoff, C. E., De Fruyt, F., Terracciano, A., McCrae, R., R., De Bolle M., Costa, P. T., ..., & Yik, M. (2009). Perceptions of aging across 26 cultures and their culture level associates. *Psychology and Aging, 24*, 941–954.

Macia, E., Lahman, A., Baali, A., Boetsch, G., & Chapuis-Lucciani, N. (2009). Perception of Age Stereotypes and Self-Perception of Aging: A Comparison of French and Moroccan Populations. *Journal of Cross-Cultural Gerontology, 24*, 391–410.

Ng, T. W. H., & Feldman, D. C. 2010. The relationships of age with job attitudes: A Meta-analysis. *Personnel Psychology, 63*, 677–718.

Posthuma, R. A., & Campion, M. A. (2009). Age stereotypes in the workplace: Common stereotypes, moderators, and future research directions. *Journal of Management, 35*, 158–188.

Posthuma, R. A., Roehling, M. V., & Campion, M. A. (2011). Employment Discrimination Law Exposures for International Employers: A Risk Assessment Model. *International Journal of Law and Management, 53*, 281–298.

Posthuma, R. A., Wagstaff, M. F., & Campion, M. A. (2012). Age stereotypes and workplace age discrimination: A framework for future research. In Jerry W. Hedge and Walter C. Borman (Eds.), *The Oxford Handbook of Work and Aging* (pp. 298–312). New York: Oxford University Press.

Ronen, S., & Shenkar, O. (1985). Clustering countries on attitudinal dimensions: A review and synthesis. *Academy of Management Review, 10*, 435–454.

Roscigno, V. J., Mong, S. Byron, R., & Tester, G. (2007). Age discrimination, social closure, and employment. *Social Forces, 86*, 313–334.

Rupp, D. E., Vodanovich, S. J., & Crede, M. (2005). The multidimensional nature of ageism: Construct validity and group differences. *Journal of Social Psychology, 145*, 335–362.

Ryan, E. B., Jin, Y-S., & Anas, A. P. (2009). Cross-cultural beliefs about memory and aging for self and others: South Korea and Canada. *International Journal of Aging & Human Development, 68*, 185–194.

Schwartz, S. (1992). Universals in the content and structure of values: Theoretical advances and empirical tests in 20 countries. In M. Zanna (Ed.), *Advances in experimental and social psychology* (Vol. 25, pp. 1–65). New York: Academic.

Schwartz, S. (1994). Beyond individualism-collectivism: New cultural dimensions of values. In U. Kim, H. C. Triandis, C Kagitçibasi, S. C. Choi, & G. Yoon, (Eds.), *Individualism and collectivism: Theory, method and applications* (pp. 85–119). London: Sage.

Sherman, J. W. (1996). Development and mental representation of stereotypes. *Journal of Personality and Social Psychology, 70*, 1126–1141.

The Economist (1996). Older workers: How to manage an aging workforce (February 16). *The Economist*, p. 11.

Trompenaars, F. (1993). *Riding the Waves of Culture: Understanding Diversity in Business*. London: Economist Books.

15

Older Workers, Occupational Stress and Safety

Gary A. Adams, Sarah DeArmond,
Steve M. Jex and Jennica R. Webster

OLDER WORKERS OCCUPATIONAL STRESS AND SAFETY

A series of well-established demographic trends such as increased life expectancies and changing patterns of birthrates are bringing about an aging of the world's population (Kinsella & He, 2009). One of the key issues stemming from population aging is the aging of the workforce and older people's continued participation in paid work. Continued workforce participation among aging workers is currently being encouraged by a number of forces including social concerns, the needs of employing organizations and older workers themselves. At a societal level retaining older people in the workforce is at least partially driven by economic concerns about the viability of old age social insurance programs (e.g., The Economist, 2011). At an organizational level, employers are interested in retaining older workers as a means to avoid potential skills shortages and the loss of organizational specific knowledge that can occur when older

workers leave the workforce (Burke & Ng, 2006; DeLong, 2004; Manpower Group, 2011). Older workers themselves express interest in continued work owing to financial concerns as well as the desire to remain active, maintain social relationships and other non-financial returns from work (Dendinger, Adams, & Jacobson, 2005; Loi & Shultz, 2007). The combined effect of these trends is an increasingly older workforce.

The aging of the workforce brings with it a number of issues which are explored among the various chapters that comprise this *Handbook*. Among these issues are the topics of occupational stress and safety. Despite the fact that the workplace has become safer in many regards and that, in general, continued work is associated with better physical and mental health (Yeomans, 2011); the workplace can still be hazardous to one's health (International Labour Organization, 2011). These hazards stem from (1) occupational stress issues arising mainly from the psychosocial work environment and (2) safety issues arising mainly from accident/injuries (Wegman & McGee, 2004). Although difficult to quantify, occupational stress hazards (often referred to as stressors) have been shown to be related to various indicators of poor mental and physical health, absenteeism, healthcare utilization and decreased productivity (European Agency for Safety and Health at Work, 2009; International Labour Organization, 2011; Jex & Crossley, 2005; Leka & Jain, 2010). With regard to accidents/injuries, in the US alone, the Centers for Disease Control and Prevention (2011) reported that there were more than 1.2 million non-fatal work-related injuries and illness resulting in time away from work in 2009 and approximately 17% of these were workers over the age of 55. The CDC (2011) also reported 4,551 fatal workplace injuries in 2009. Of these, approximately 31% were among those over the age of 55. Clearly, occupational stress and safety are important concerns for all workers. They are especially important for aging workers because of the increasing number of older workers, because they limit workforce participation, and because the aging process itself may be related to the nature, type, and consequences of occupational stress and safety.

The purpose of this chapter is to explore the role of chronological age in the areas of occupational stress and safety among older workers. We begin by briefly presenting a conceptual model identifying the possible relationships linking age to variables commonly studied in the area of occupational stress and safety. Then, we provide a review of representative research examining these linkages, incorporating relevant theory and highlighting the fact that the knowledge-base regarding these linkages is scant. We recognize that while there is some convergence between the two areas, research about occupational stress and safety grew out of two separate research traditions. Research on occupational stress has focused on the relationship between the psychosocial environment and wellbeing, whereas safety research has focused on accidents/injuries. Accordingly we

divide the review along these two lines. We conclude with suggestions for future research.

CONCEPTUAL MODEL LINKING AGE TO OCCUPATIONAL STRESS AND SAFETY

Figure 15.1 presents a conceptual model linking age to concepts in the occupational stress and safety literatures. To begin, the model recognizes that chronological age is most often used as a proxy for more substantive age-related changes (most commonly losses) in physical and mental abilities that are thought to impair functioning at work as well as age-related changes (gains) in adaptive resources that allow older workers to maintain and even improve functioning at work (Salthouse & Maurer, 1996; Warr, 1994). Next, it identifies the main antecedents and individual outcomes found in the occupational stress and safety literatures (Barlow & Iverson, 2004; Kahn & Byosiere, 1992, Sonnentag & Frese, 2003). These antecedents include stressors as well as safety-related attitudes and behaviors of the workers. The negative outcomes include physical, psychological and behavioral outcomes as well as occupational injuries and accidents. Finally, the model shows three possible relationships between age (via age-related losses and gains), antecedents, and outcomes. The first possible relationship is a direct relationship between age and antecedents. The second is a direct relationship between age and outcomes. These direct relationships suggest that as people get older they are more or less likely to experience certain types or amounts of antecedents and outcomes. The third type of relationship age might have is a moderating effect. This means that the relationship between antecedents and outcomes is different for workers of different ages. More specifically, this could mean one of two things. First, age could attenuate relationships between some antecedents and outcomes; that is, increased age could be a *protective* factor. Secondly, age could strengthen relationships

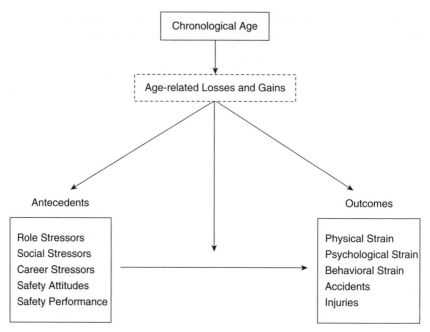

Figure 15.1   Conceptual model linking age to concepts in the occupational stress and safety literatures

between antecedents and outcomes; that is, increased age could be a *vulnerability* factor. In the sections that follow we review the theoretical and empirical arguments linking age to occupational stress and safety.

AGE AND OCCUPATIONAL STRESS

Within the occupational stress literature the term *stressor* is used to indicate characteristics of the work environment that prompt a negative reaction on the part of the worker experiencing it. The term *strain* refers to the negative reaction that comes as a result of a stressor (Jex & Beehr, 1991). In terms of Figure 15.1, stressors are antecedents and strains are outcomes. In this section we begin by describing the relationships among age and stressors followed by age and strains.

Age and stressors

A great deal of research has examined stressors in the workplace (Kahn & Byosiere, 1992).

Relatively few studies, however, have examined the relationship between age and workplace stressors. This is unfortunate because there are a number of good reasons to believe that age is directly related to the stressors older workers experience. A myriad of workplace stressors have been identified in the occupational stress literature (Sonnentag & Frese, 2003). In this section we review theory and research on the relationship between age and a number of commonly identified stressors. These include: (1) role stressors, (2) social stressors, and (3) career-related stressors.

Role stressors

Role stressors, which consist of role ambiguity, role conflict, and role overload (Katz & Kahn, 1978), are three widely studied stressors in the occupational stress literature. Role ambiguity exists when there is a lack of clarity about the prescribed roles of the job and role conflict occurs when there are incompatible role expectations. Role overload refers to situations when the expectations of the role cannot be met. Research tends to find negative relationships between age and both role ambiguity and role conflict (Jackson & Schuler, 1985; Ng & Feldman, 2010). This suggests that older workers report experiencing lower levels of these stressors than younger workers. There are two possible explanations for these findings. First, as workers age they accumulate more work experiences acquiring more occupational expertise and wisdom (Kaufman & Lichtenberger, 2002; Schaie, 1996), which may act as a resource when dealing with role-related stressors. Second, older workers are more likely to be in high status positions with certain characteristics including job control, flexible work schedules, and access to support from the job environment. These job characteristics may reduce employee exposure to stressors such as role ambiguity and role conflict (Zacher & Frese, 2009; Zacher, Heusner, Schmitz, Zwierzanska, & Frese, 2010).

Role overload occurs when the physical and/or cognitive demands of the work role exceed the worker's capacity to fulfill them. There are two competing arguments on the possible relationship between age and overload. The first stems from the 'decrement' model of aging (Giniger, Dispenzieri, & Eisenberg, 1983). It argues that the loss of physical and cognitive abilities associated with the aging process ultimately lead to poor functioning at work. Physical losses include decreased aerobic ability, physical strength and endurance, balance, manual dexterity and tolerance for heat (Maertens, Putter, Chen, Manfred, & Huang, in press), which would seem to make it more likely that older workers would experience more physical overload compared to younger workers. For example, loss of muscle mass makes it more difficult to lift heavy objects; the loss of endurance reduces the ability to carry out tasks involving sustained or repetitive physical effort. Cognitive ability losses occur in the area of fluid intellectual abilities including processing speed, working memory, attention, and abstract reasoning (Park, 2000). Because of these age-related cognitive declines it may be

more difficult for older adults to complete tasks that require the retention of large amounts of information or vigilant monitoring of the environment (Wang & Chen, 2006). These would seem to make it more likely that older workers would experience more cognitive overload compared to younger workers.

A second perspective argues that older workers are better at managing their physical and cognitive resources and are therefore less likely to experience overload. The theory of selective optimization with compensation (SOC) is based on the assumption that people have a limited number of resources (physical and cognitive) and have to choose how to allocate those resources (Baltes, 1997; Baltes & Baltes 1990; Freund & Baltes, 2002). Selection refers to a strategy where people utilize their strengths by focusing on tasks (or jobs) on which they already perform well, for example, by transitioning into jobs that better match their abilities (Ackerman, Beier, & Bowen, 2002; Warr, 1997). Optimization strategies include strengthening skills needed to complete tasks or putting more time/effort into completing a task. Compensation strategies refer to the use of external and internal aids to help overcome declining abilities. External aids such as new technologies including voice recognition software and larger font sizes can help older workers adapt to some of the age-related losses they experience (Charness, Czaja, & Sharit, 2007). Older workers may also use 'internal' aids. For example, they may rely on crystallized intelligence including job expertise, job-related problem solving abilities, and a wide-range of life experiences to compensate for declines in fluid intelligence (Kanfer & Ackerman, 2004). There is growing empirical evidence suggesting that SOC strategies can help older workers maintain job performance (Yeung & Fung, 2009).

In summary, it appears that older workers may be at lower risk for experiencing role ambiguity and role conflict provided that they are able to leverage their acquired resources (e.g., expertise) and are in environments that provide them with control, flexibility and support. While there are competing arguments for the relationship between age and role overload there is too little empirical evidence to determine which of those arguments is most strongly supported. We suspect that, like role ambiguity and role conflict, the risk for role overload depends on the ability and opportunity older workers have to leverage their resources in order to offset their losses.

Social stressors

Social stressors consist of poor social interactions with people inside the organization (e.g., co-workers and supervisors) or outside the organization (e.g., customers; Sonnentag & Frese, 2003). Several types of social stressors have been identified in the work stress literature including bullying (e.g., Rayner, 1997), incivility (e.g., Andersson & Pearson, 1999), interpersonal conflict (e.g., Spector & Jex, 1998), and abusive supervision (e.g., Tepper, 2000). Although there are subtle differences among these types of social stressors they are similar in that they are forms of interpersonal mistreatment that target an individual (Hershcovis, 2011).

Although most workers are likely to experience social stressors in their work environment, not all workers will experience these stressors equally. Older adults, for example, are not as likely to report emotional distress due to social tensions compared to younger adults (Birditt & Fingerman, 2003). This is consistent with socioemotional selectivity theory (SST), which argues that as people age they realize a shorter lifespan horizon and become more selective with how they invest their time and resources (Carstensen, Isaacowitz, & Charles, 1999). More specifically, as people begin to perceive they have less time to live they focus their energy in meaningful relationships, and maximize the experience of positive emotions (Ready & Robinson, 2008). For example, in order to gain positive emotions, older adults surround themselves with people with whom they have rewarding relationships. Because older adults tend to spend more time with these people it is less likely that they will be exposed to interpersonal mistreatment. In addition, in order to increase positive emotions, older adults develop emotional regulation strategies that filter negative information (Mather & Carstensen, 2005). This type of emotional regulation strategy helps older adults to effectively manage interpersonal conflict situations (Birditt & Fingerman, 2005). Some evidence for this in a work setting comes from a study by Dahling and Perez (2010); they found that older workers express more positive affect and naturally felt emotions.

Older workers, however, are more likely to experience social stressors stemming from ageism compared to younger workers. Ageism is the 'systematic stereotyping of and discrimination against older people because they are old' (Butler, 1989, pp. 139). Age stereotypes are the beliefs and expectations people have about older workers that are often negative and inaccurate (Fiske & Neuberg, 1990). Several different types of stereotypes about older workers have been noted in the literature including the belief that older workers are inflexible and unwilling (or not able) to adapt to change, less able to learn new skills, less productive, and more expensive compared to younger workers (Brooke & Taylor, 2005; Kite & Johnson, 1988). Negative stereotypes about older workers are widespread in organizations and are often assumed to be the cause of age discrimination albeit research shows only a modest relationship (Finkelstein & Farrell, 2007; Shore & Goldberg, 2004). Age discrimination exists when an employee is treated unfairly due to his/her age and is shown to be a major issue in US organizations. In 2010, the US Equal Employment Opportunity Commission (2011) received over 23,263 complaints of age discrimination. Empirical studies have shown that older workers receive more negative hiring, promotion, and performance appraisal evaluations (Gordon & Arvey, 2004) compared to younger workers and harsher consequences for those poor performance ratings (e.g., transfer, request for resignation, demotion; Rupp, Vodanovich, & Crede, 2006). Thus, while older workers are less likely to experience generalized mistreatment, they are more likely to experience mistreatment based on ageism.

Career-related stressors

Career-related stressors include those that can hinder or threaten the progression of one's career. Types of career-related stressors that are commonly studied in the organizational literature include job insecurity and skill obsolescence. Job insecurity occurs when workers feel threatened by potential job loss (Probst, 2004). Downsizing, mergers, and acquisitions have led to increased feelings of job insecurity for all workers, especially those who are older (Armstrong-Stassen & Cattaneo, 2010). Skill obsolescence refers to the depreciation of knowledge or skills needed to effectively perform in a current or future work role. Older workers are especially vulnerable to skill obsolescence and job insecurity compared to younger workers owing to the negative effects of ageism. The evidence suggests that older workers are less likely to receive support for (Greller & Simpson, 1999; Maurer, Weiss, & Barbeite, 2003) or seek out training (Colquitt, LePine, & Noe, 2000; Warr & Birdi, 1998). Older workers also have fewer developmental opportunities such as challenging job assignments (Maurer, 2007; Wrenn & Maurer, 2004). Employers are less likely to offer training and developmental to older workers because older workers are perceived to be more expensive and to have a shorter career horizon decreasing the possibility for a return on investment (Simpson, Greller, & Stroh, 2002; Taylor & Urwin, 2001). This lack of investment in training is likely to lead to greater skill obsolescence thereby decreasing older workers' employability and making them more susceptible to losing their jobs.

Another career-related stressor that is unique to older employees is retirement. According to Jex and Grosch (in press) as well as Adams and Rau (2011), there is a great deal of variability in the extent to which employees plan for retirement; for some employees the years leading up to retirement may be viewed as quite stressful due to uncertainty about finances, ability to maintain one's health, and how to structure one's time after one is no longer working full-time. Furthermore, the transition into retirement is especially difficult for those who are highly involved in their jobs (Beehr, Glazer, Nielson, & Farmer, 2000). Fortunately, the weight of the evidence suggests that most people ultimately adjust well to retirement (Beehr & Adams, 2003; Wang, Henkens, & Van Solinge, 2011; Wang & Shultz, 2010).

Age and strain

As noted earlier, a *strain* is a negative response that results from exposure to a stressor. Given the wide range of stressors that may be present in the workplace, it should come as no surprise that there are also a vast number of strains. In order to keep this number manageable, occupational stress researchers have typically grouped strains into three relatively exclusive categories: (1) physical, (2) psychological, and (3) behavioral. In the section that follows we review the literature, first regarding the direct relationship between age and strain, and then as a potential moderator of the relationship between stressors and strains.

Physical strains

Physical strains include reactions to stressors that reflect an employee's physical health and wellbeing. Strains that fall under this category are of considerable importance to both individual employees and also to organizations; in the former case this is due to the potential impact on wellbeing, while in the latter case it is likely due to the impact on health care and related costs (Manning, Jackson, & Fusilier, 1996). By far the most common method of measuring physical strain has been through the use of self-report physical symptom inventories (e.g., Spector & Jex, 1998). In some cases, however, researchers have utilized more rigorous methods such as physiological measurement (e.g., Schaubroeck, Jones, & Xie, 2001). With respect to physical strain, it is well established that the human body undergoes a number of physical changes as one ages (Maertens et al., in press). As a result, it should not be surprising that age has a direct relationship with many of the commonly used measures of physical strain. For example, age has been shown to be positively related to number of physical symptoms (Spector & Jex, 1998), as well as physiological measures such as blood pressure (Fox, Dwyer, & Ganster, 1993). It has also been shown, as would be expected, that age is positively related to doctor visits and other indicators of healthcare utilization (Ford et al., 2004).

Psychological strains

Psychological strains typically include emotional/affective reactions to stressors including anxiety, frustration, depression, and anger (Spector & Jex, 1998). It is worth noting that occupational stress researchers have typically examined what may be described as *subclinical* levels of the aforementioned affective/emotional states; however, it is certainly possible that stressors in the workplace could contribute to clinically significant anxiety disorders or depressive episodes. The direct relationship between age and psychological strain is somewhat more complex than that for physical strains. For example, it has been shown that the prevalence of clinical depression declines across adulthood (Gatz, 2000). However, it has also been shown that the relation between age and clinical depression may not be linear; specifically, the highest rates appear to be among young adults and those over 75 years of age. Because occupational stress researchers are almost always interested in the assessment of *sub-clinical* levels of depression, it is unclear whether the existence of age differences in clinically significant depression generalizes to less serious levels. Our own perusal of the occupational literature indicates that age is very weakly related to depression and other negative

psychological strains such as anxiety and frustration (Spector & Jex, 1998), and in fact many studies do not report relations between age and these strains. This suggests age does not have a strong direct relationship with most of the psychological strains measured in the occupational stress literature, and more generally that findings in the clinical literature may not generalize to the measurement of sub-clinical aversive psychological states.

Despite the lack of evidence for a relation between age and psychological strain, there is evidence that age is *positively* related to positive psychological states such as job satisfaction and organizational commitment (Ng & Feldman, 2010; Meyer, Stanley, Herscovitch, & Topolnytsky, 2002). These positive relations are generally explained in one of two ways. First, as people get older it is more likely they have acquired jobs with characteristics (e.g., higher salary, higher-levels jobs) that lead to satisfaction and commitment. Secondly, increased satisfaction and commitment with age may simply be a way to justify one's long tenure with an organization or the fact that one's job prospects are limited with increasing age. While positive outcomes are not considered to be strains per se (Jex & Beehr, 1991), they are still important to consider because they are often used as proxy measures of psychological strains in occupational stress research. On a more substantive level, these findings also suggest that as employees get older they may face stressors with a reserve of positive affect.

Behavioral strains

Behavioral strains represent reactions to stressors that directly or indirectly impact employees' on-the-job behaviors. Perhaps the most common behavioral strain in occupational stress research is job performance, despite the fact that research investigating the relationship between stressors and performance has been quite mixed (Jex, 1998). In addition to performance, other common behavioral strains examined in occupational stress research include turnover intentions (Jamal, 1990), accidents (Greiner, Kraus,

Ragland, & Fischer, 1998), and counterproductive work behaviors (Spector & Fox, 2005). When we consider the direct relationship between age and behavioral strains, empirical evidence is again quite mixed. For example, while there is considerable evidence for the existence of age-related declines in job-related tasks that require speed of processing (Salthouse, 1996) and physical exertion (Seitsamo & Martikainen, 1999), the evidence regarding other types of job tasks is less clear. Thus, it is difficult to make a general statement of whether age has a detrimental effect on performance. If one looks at other types of potential behavioral reactions to stressors, such as accidents and counterproductive behaviors, there is evidence that age is negatively related (Ng & Feldman, 2008; Ng & Feldman, 2010; Sprung, 2011).

Age as a moderator between stressors and strain

As stated earlier, if age is viewed as a moderator variable this means that the strength of the relationship between stressors and strains differs at different age levels. As with the evidence for a direct relationship, the evidence for age as a moderator variable is quite mixed. For example, utilizing a sample of firefighters, electricians, and managers, Mayes, Barton, and Ganster (1991) found that role conflict and underutilization of skills had a stronger negative effect, both in terms of psychological and physical strain, on older employees. Conversely, in this same sample it was found older employees responded *positively*, in terms of all outcomes, to responsibility for others, role ambiguity, and leader production emphasis. These findings suggest that balancing multiple role demands may be more difficult for older employees, perhaps due to cognitive changes associated with increased age. It may also be the case when older employees feel underutilized this is particularly stressful since their future job prospects may be less certain than their younger colleagues. The other findings from the Mayes et al. (1991) study, however, suggests that increased age can be a resource in

helping employees cope with certain types of stressors. As Jex, Wang, and Zarubin (2007) point out, older employees have more varied job experiences and therefore may have acquired more effective coping responses when faced with some stressors.

In addition to directly moderating stressor–strain relationships, it is also possible that age may serve as a higher-order moderator in the stress process. Recently, Shultz, Wang, Crimmins, and Fischer (2010) examined whether age moderated the interaction between job demands and job control which is proposed by the well-known Demands-Control model of stress (Karasek, 1979). These researchers found only one demand–control interaction among younger employees; specifically having more time to complete tasks buffered the impact of problem solving demands. For older employees, however, they found three demand–control interactions. Specifically, having both sufficient time and job autonomy both buffered the impact of time deadlines; in addition, scheduling flexibility buffered the impact of problems solving demands. The overall implication of this study is that age may impact how employees use job-related control, and which types of control are the most important. Since this study was done very recently there have not as yet been any replications, however, this would certainly be a fruitful topic for future research in the moderating effects of age.

Overall, it appears that age does have a direct relationship with a number of stressors and strain outcomes. What is less clear and consistent, however, is the strength and direction of these effects. Age also appears to act as a moderator and a higher order moderator of the relationship between stressors and strains. Thus, researchers would be well advised to study it more closely or at least use age as a control variable.

AGE AND SAFETY

Research in the area of workplace safety grew out of the health- and engineering-related fields where there is a long tradition of attempting to identify and mitigate physical hazards in the workplace. Much of this work has focused on physical controls (e.g., hearing protection, machine guarding, ergonomic design, etc.) to reduce or eliminate accidents and injuries. These are beyond the scope of our review. Rather, we focus our attention on the growing stream of research that examines the role of employee attitudes and behaviors as antecedents to accidents and injuries.

Safety attitudes

An attitude is an evaluation of a person, entity or idea that has some impact on behavior (Eagly & Chaiken, 1993). It is important to study attitudes in relation to occupational safety because it has long been recognized that attitudes are linked to behavior (Kim & Hunter, 1993), and existing models of occupational safety include attitudes as distal predictors of accidents and injuries (Christian, Bradley, Wallace & Burke, 2009). In a safety context, one would anticipate if someone had a more positive attitude toward occupational safety he/she would be more apt to engage in positive safety performance which hopefully would lead to fewer accidents and injuries (Christian et al., 2009).

There are a number of theories which help to explain why age might be related to job attitudes, including attitudes toward safety. One such theory is socioemotional selectivity theory (Carstensen, 1991). As noted earlier, this theory suggests that people consciously and subconsciously monitor the amount of time they have left in the world, and try to maximize their social and emotional gains and minimize their losses. Therefore, older adults want to and do have more positive emotional experiences than negative emotional experiences (Gross, Carstensen, Tsai, Skorpen, & Hsu, 1997). Older workers experience more positive emotional states, and they are expected to have more positive attitudes in general. When one investigates the research literature on age and job attitudes, one finds support for this idea. Indeed, a recent comprehensive meta-analysis of age and job attitudes found that in general older people tend to have more positive job attitudes than younger people (Ng & Feldman, 2010).

There is little research on age and safety attitudes; however, the research that does exist seems to suggest that older workers have more positive safety attitudes than younger workers. For instance, Siu, Phillips, and Leung (2003) conducted a study with Chinese construction workers. The results indicated that the older workers had more positive attitudes toward safety. Similarly, Gyekye, and Salminen (2009) and Parkes (2003) found that older workers had more positive perceptions of safety than younger workers in samples of Ghanaian industrial workers and people working on oil and gas installations in the North Sea. This general finding was further supported by Grosch and Pransky (2009) in a qualitative review which noted that older workers have significantly higher pre-injury job satisfaction, are more satisfied with the response of their employers, and report fewer problems returning to work. This research is consistent with the idea that age has a positive direct relationship with safety attitudes.

Safety performance

Safety performance is a term that has been used to reference both safety-related behavior at work and safety-related outcomes such as accidents and injuries. For our purposes, safety performance refers to job-related behavior that promotes the health and safety of workers, clients, the public, and the environment (Burke, Sapry, Tesluk, & Smith-Crowe, 2002; Christian et al., 2009; Griffin & Neal 2000; Hofmann, Morgeson, & Gerras, 2003). Safety performance has been conceptualized as a multi-dimensional construct, and Griffin and Neal (2000) differentiated between safety compliance and safety participation. Safety compliance refers to core safety activities that need to be carried out by individuals to maintain workplace safety (e.g., following safety policies and procedures). Safety participation refers to behavior which indirectly contributes to workplace safety by helping to develop an environment that promotes safety (e.g. attending voluntary safety meetings and training). We focus on safety performance because there seems to be a clear relationship between safety performance and accidents and injuries (Christian et al., 2009).

Like many of the other antecedents in Figure 15.1, there are two competing arguments for the relationship between age and safety performance. One argument is that age-related losses of physical (Maertens et al., in press) and fluid cognitive abilities (Park, 2000) will lead to poor job performance among older workers, including poor safety performance. The second is that older workers are able to adapt to these losses by using the selection, optimization, and compensation strategies (Freund & Baltes, 2002) described earlier and by leveraging gains in crystallized intelligence (i.e., accumulated knowledge or wisdom) (Kanfer & Ackerman, 2004). SOC theory suggests that older people aiming at successful job performance are going to compensate for age-related declines by allocating more resources to maintenance and regulation of loss activities than growth activities. If this is true, older people may have better safety performance than younger people.

Similar to safety attitudes little empirical research has explored the relationship between age and safety performance. This is clearly seen in a recent meta-analysis of the relationship between age and job performance (Ng & Feldman, 2008). These authors included safety performance; however they only found five studies to analyze. These all focused on safety compliance. That meta-analysis found the sample-size weighted corrected correlation was $r = .10$. This is not terribly different than what has been found when investigating the relationship between age and job performance in general. Both Ng and Feldman's (2008) quantitative review and Warr's (1994) qualitative review result in similar conclusions: there seems to be a small direct relationship between age and performance.

Occupational accidents and injuries

As compared to safety attitudes and performance, there is substantially more research which has explored relationships between age and accidents and injuries. Generally, older workers are thought to have lower accident rates than younger workers (Crawford, Graveling, Cowie, Dixon, & MacCalman, 2010; Jex et al., 2007). There has been some variability in empirical findings. For instance, Siu et al. (2003) found that age was not related to accident rates. Gyekye and Salminen (2009) found that older workers had the lowest accident involvement rate. However, it has been suggested that these inconsistencies could be due to differences in industries and age cohorts. Butani (1988) has also suggested that accident frequency actually varies more by experience than age.

With regard to injuries, research clearly indicates that the findings vary depending on whether the injuries are non-fatal or fatal. A majority of studies show that older workers have fewer non-fatal injuries than younger workers (Hansson, DeKoekkoek, Neece, & Patterson, 1997; Ng & Feldman, 2008). A recent qualitative review suggests that this relationship is curvilinear (Grosch & Pransky, 2009). Grosch and Pransky (2009) cite statistics from the United States Bureau of Labor Statistics which indicate that the rate of non-fatal injuries/illnesses gradually declines with age until it levels off for workers 65 years and older.

Grosch and Pransky (2009) suggested a number of reasons that older workers may experience fewer non-fatal injuries and illnesses than older workers. These authors suggested that older workers may actually be in positions which call for less exposure to hazards due to seniority and having greater control over their work. These findings also might be the result of age often being related to experience. It may be that significant experience and knowledge helps older workers avoid these injuries (Butani, 1988). Finally, Grosch and Pransky (2009) also suggest that the difference between the injury rates of younger and older workers might be driven by the 'healthy worker selection effect'. In other words, workers who are more prone to injuries may no longer be employed or at the very least workers who are more prone to injuries in specific jobs may have opted to pursue less hazardous work. These assertions seem consistent with what SOC theory would suggest. Older workers may be compensating for age-related declines in abilities by focusing on different outcomes (i.e., selecting different jobs) or by allocating more resources to maintenance and regulation of loss activities such as safety performance which could lead to fewer injuries.

Empirical findings exploring the relationship between age and fatal injuries are substantially different than those for non-fatal injuries. A majority of studies find that younger workers have less fatal injuries than older workers. In fact the fatality rate for those over 65 in the US is three times that of younger workers (Crawford et al., 2010). Similarly, Grosch and Pransky (2009) noted that there seems to be a dramatic increase in fatal injuries for workers 65 and older. These findings are consistent with those exploring the connection between age and injury severity. This research seems to suggest that older workers sustain more severe injuries and miss more work due to injuries (Crawford et al., 2010; Grosch & Pransky, 2009; Hansson et al., 1997; Liao, Arvey, Butler, & Nutting, 2001).

The age-related differences in fatal occupational injuries and injury severity have been explained in a number of ways. Some have suggested that older workers are more susceptible to more severe and fatal injuries due to lower baseline functioning (Brorsson, 1989; Grosch & Pransky, 2009). There is significant research indicating that there are age-related declines in reaction time, vision, aerobic capacity, muscular strength, and endurance to name a few (Crawford et al., 2010). Research has also suggested age-related declines in hardiness and recovery speed (Butler, Hartwig, & Gardner, 1997). All of these could be connected to increases

in fatal injuries. Grosch and Pransky (2009) suggest that these differences could also be due to age-related differences in the cumulative effect of repeated exposures to hazards. For instance, employees may engage in improper lifting practices throughout their employment yet not see the effects of doing so until later in life. Further, employees may be able to cut corners and recover when younger but be less capable of doing so later in life (e.g., falling and catching themselves). These explanations are consistent with the idea that age acts as a moderator, in this case a vulnerability factor, in the relationship between working conditions and safety outcomes.

In summary, it appears that age does have a direct positive relationship with safety attitudes and performance but its relationship to outcomes depends on the type of accident or injury. Older workers have fewer accidents and non-fatal injuries but more severe and fatal injuries. Thus, researchers would be well advised to study it more closely or at least use age as a control variable.

FUTURE RESEARCH DIRECTIONS

In reviewing this literature it becomes clear that there are significant gaps in our understanding of the connection between age and occupational stress and safety. We believe three needs stand out above some others. Perhaps the most pressing needs are the theoretical development and empirical research aimed at reconciling the competing predictions of the loss-based and gain-based views for the role of age in the occupational stress and safety processes.

One way to begin would be for researchers to consider alternative measures of age rather than focusing solely on chronological age. Some other measures of age in the workplace that would seem especially relevant include functional age and social age (Sterns & Doverspike, 1989; Cleveland & Lim, 2007). Functional age measures are intended to capture a person's standing on age-related changes in physical and cognitive ability, which may more clearly address the losses and gains than chronological age (e.g., the work ability index, Toumi, Ilmarinen, Katajajarinne, & Tuki, 1998). Social age measures are intended to capture how one's age is perceived by others. These measures would seem relevant for studying stressors arising from ageism. Another approach would be to examine the conditions under which losses and gains are more (or less) likely to impact occupational stress and safety. As a starting point this research could begin by adapting Warr's (1994) model relating age to job performance to the study of occupational stress and safety (Laflamme & Menckel, 1995). In this model predictions about the impact of gains and losses associated with aging depend on the type of task performed on the job. It would seem that this model is readily adaptable to the study of the types of antecedents and outcomes found in the occupational stress and safety literatures. It also seems that because jobs are embedded in organizations which are then embedded in industries more multi-level research should be conducted.

A second area for future research would be to examine the joint effects of age and factors that co-vary with other demographic characteristics such as gender and ethnicity. The workforce is not only growing older but more diverse and mounting evidence suggests that occupational stress and safety can vary depending on these other characteristics. For example, with regard to gender, there is evidence that the difference in non-fatal injuries between young and old men is greater than the difference between young and old women. There is data from the United Kingdom which reveals that older males (over 55) had the lowest rate of reportable non-fatal injuries where females had the highest rate (Crawford et al., 2010). Some have suggested that these differences might be due in part to women's greater vulnerability to arthritis and other autoimmune diseases and osteoporosis and also the negative effects of stress on menopausal and postmenopausal health (Granville & Evandrou, 2010; Payne & Doyal, 2010).

Some have also suggested that this might be the result of women and men doing different work. It has been noted that women are more often in lower paid, lower status jobs, more likely to engage in part-time work, and may do more unpaid work at home than men (Granville & Evandrou, 2010; Payne & Doyal, 2010).

A third area where there is a pressing need is intervention research (Crawford et al., 2010; Grosch & Pransky, 2009). The existing research on age and occupational stress and safety in general is somewhat limited. However, research which explores how the effectiveness of interventions might vary in relation to age is extremely limited. Grosch and Pransky (2009) noted that few public policy strategies aimed at encouraging people to remain in the workforce longer actually are evaluated in terms of what this policy would do to worker safety. This is viewed as a significant limitation, and one that research should not ignore. It seems that age-related physical and mental declines could negatively impact occupational stress and safety outcomes, however, empirical evidence seems to suggest that there are positive relationships between age and stressors, safety attitudes and performance in addition to negative relationships between age and at least some outcomes (i.e., non-fatal injuries). This suggests that older workers are compensating in some way for negative changes in ability and that many of them are being successful in doing so. This may offer insight in how to create more effective safety interventions.

CONCLUSION

This review demonstrates that age plays an important role in the occupational stress and safety process. It may have a direct positive or negative relationship to specific antecedents and outcomes and it may influence the relationship between those antecedents and outcomes. It is also clear that age reflects more than simply a number of years. However, given the competing predictions as well as the scant and often conflicting empirical results found in the literature, it is clear that there is much more work to be done. A better understanding of the role of age in the occupational stress and safety process is imperative to achieving a healthy workplace not just for older workers, but ultimately for all workers.

REFERENCES

Ackerman, P.L., Beier, M.E., & Bowen, K.R. (2002). What we really know about our abilities and our knowledge. *Personality and Individual Differences, 33*, 587–605.

Adams, G.A., & Rau, B.L. (2011). Putting off tomorrow to do what you want today: Planning for retirement. *American Psychologist, 66*, 180–192.

Andersson, L.M., & Pearson, C.M. (1999). Tit for tat? The spiraling effect of incivility in the workplace. *The Academy of Management Review, 24*, 452–471.

Armstrong-Stassen, M. & Cattaneo, J. (2010). The effect of downsizing on organizational practices targeting older workers. *Journal of Management Development, 29*, 344–363.

Baltes, P.B. (1997). On the incomplete architecture of human ontogeny: Selection, optimization, and compensation as foundation of developmental theory. *American Psychologist, 52*, 366–380.

Baltes, P.B., & Baltes, M.M. (1990). Psychological perspectives on successful aging: The model of selective optimization with compensation. In P.B. Baltes & M.M. Baltes (Eds.), *Successful aging: Perspectives from the behavioral sciences* (pp. 1–34). New York: Cambridge University Press.

Barlow, L., & Iverson, R.D. (2004). Workplace safety. In J. Barling, E.K. Kelloway, & M.R. Frone (Eds.), *Handbook of work stress* (pp. 247–266). Portland, OR: Book News, Inc.

Beehr, T.A., & Adams, G.A. (2003). Introduction and overview of current research and thinking on retirement. In G.A. Adams & T.A. Beehr (Eds.), *Retirement: Reasons, processes, and results* (pp. 1–15). New York: Springer Publishing Company.

Beehr, T.A., Glazer, S., Nielson, N.L., & Farmer, S.J. (2000). Work and non-work predictors of employees' retirement ages. *Journal of Vocational Behavior, 57*, 206–225.

Birditt, K.S., & Fingerman, K.L. (2003). Age and gender differences in adults' descriptions of emotional reactions to interpersonal problems. *Journal of Gerontology: Series B: Psychological Sciences and Social Sciences, 58*, 121–128.

Birditt, K.S., & Fingerman, K.L. (2005). Do we get better at picking our battles? Age differences in descriptions of behavioral reactions to interpersonal tensions. *Journals of Gerontology, Psychological Sciences and Social Sciences, 60*, 121–128.

Brooke, L., & Taylor, P. (2005). Older workers and employment: Managing age relations. *Ageing & Society, 25*, 415–249.

Brorsson, B. (1989). The risk of accidents among older drivers. *Scandinavian Journal of Public Health, 17*, 253–256.

Burke, M.J., Sapry, S.A, Tesluk, P.E., & Smith-Crowe, K. (2002). General safety performance: A test of a grounded theoretical model. *Personnel Psychology, 55*, 429–457.

Burke, R., & Ng, E. (2006). The changing nature of work and organizations: Implications for human resource management. *Human Resource Management Review, 16*, 86–94.

Butani, S.J. (1988). Relative risk analysis of injuries in coal mining by age and experience at present company. *Journal of Occupational Accidents, 10*, 209–216.

Butler, R. (1989). Dispelling ageism: The cross-cutting intervention. *Annuals of the American Academy of Political and Social Science, 503*, 138–147.

Butler, R.J., Hartwig, R.P., & Gardner, H.H. (1997). HMO's, moral hazard, and cost shifting in workers' compensation. *Journal of Health Economics, 16*, 191–206.

Carstensen, L.L. (1991). Selectivity theory: Social activity in life-span context. *Annual Review of Gerontology and Geriatrics, 11*, 195–217.

Carstensen, L.L., Isaacowitz, D., & Charles, S.T. (1999). Taking time seriously: A theory of socioemotional selectivity. *American Psychologist, 54*, 165–181.

Centers for Disease Control and Prevention (2011). *Nonfatal Occupational injuries and illnesses among older workers: United States 2009.* Retrieved 12/28/2011 from: http://www.cdc.gov/mmwr/preview/mmwrhtml/mm6016a3.htm

Charness, N., Czaja, S., & Sharit, J. (2007). Age and technology for work. In K.S. Shultz, G.A. Adams, K.S. Shultz, G.A. Adams (Eds.), *Aging and work in the 21st century* (pp. 225–249). Mahwah, NJ US: Lawrence Erlbaum Associates Publishers.

Christian, M., Bradley, J., Wallace, C., Burke, M. (2009). Workplace Safety: A Meta-Analysis of the Roles of Person and Situation Factors. *Journal of Applied Psychology, 94*, 1103–1127.

Cleveland, J.N., & Lim, A.S. (2007). Employee age and performance in organizations, in Shultz, K.S. and

G.A. Adams (Eds), *Aging and Work in the 21st Century*, Lawrence Erlbaum Associates, Mahwah, NJ, pp. 109–38.

Colquitt, J.A., LePine, J.A., & Noe, R. (2000). Toward an integrative theory of training motivation: A meta-analytic path analysis of 20 years of research. *Journal of Applied Psychology*, 85, 678–707.

Crawford, J.O., Graveling, R.A., Cowie, H., Dixon, K., & MacCalman, L. (2010). The health, safety and health promotion for older workers. *Occupational Medicine*, 60, 184–192.

Dahling, J.J., & Perez, L.A. (2010). Older worker, different actor? Linking age and emotional labor strategies. *Personality And Individual Differences*, 48(5), 574–578.

DeLong, D. (2004). *Lost knowledge: Confronting the threat of an aging workforce*. New York: Oxford University Press.

Dendinger, V., Adams, G., & Jacobson, J. (2005). Reasons for working and their relationship to retirement attitudes, job satisfaction and occupational self-efficacy of bridge employees. *International Journal of Aging & Human Development*, 61, 21–35.

Eagly, A.H., & Chaiken, S. (1993). *The Psychology of Attitudes*, Orlando, FL US: Harcourt Brace Jovanovich College Publishers.

The Economist (2011). *Special report: Pensions falling short*. London, UK: The Economist Newspaper Limited.

Equal Employment Opportunity Commission (2011). Age Discrimination in Employment Act (includes concurrent charges with Title VII, ADA and EPA) FY 1997–FY 2010. Washington, DC: Author. Available at: www.eeoc.gov/eeoc/statistics/enforcement.adea.cfm

European Agency for Safety and Health at Work. (2009). *Outlook 1: New and emerging risks in occupational safety and health*. Luxembourg: Office of Official Publications of the European Communities.

Finkelstein, L.M., & Farrell, S.K. (2007). An expanded view of age bias in the workplace. In K. Shultz and G. Adams (Eds.), *Aging and Work in the 21st Century* (pp. 73–108). Hillsdale, NJ: Lawrence Erlbaum.

Fiske, S.T., & Neuberg, S.L. (1990). A continuum of impression formation, from category-based to individuating processes: Influences of information and motivation on attention and interpretation. In M.P. Zanna (Ed.), *Advances in experimental social psychology* (Vol. 23, pp. 1–74). New York: Academic Press.

Ford, J.D., Schnurr, P.P., Friedman, M.J., Green, B.L., Adams, G.A., & Jex, S.M. (2004). Posttraumatic stress disorder symptoms, physical health, and health care utilization fifty years after repeated exposure to a toxic gas. *Journal of Traumatic Stress*, 17, 185–194.

Fox, M.L., Dwyer, D.J., & Ganster, D.C. (1993). Effects of stressful job demands and control on physiological and attitudinal outcomes in a hospital setting. *Academy of Management Journal*, 36, 289–318.

Freund, A.M., & Baltes, P.B. (2002). Life-management strategies of selection, optimization, and compensation: Measurement by self-report and construct validity. *Journal of Personality & Social Psychology*, 82, 642–662.

Gatz, M. (2000). Variations on depression in later life. In S.H. Qualls & N. Ables (Eds.), *Psychology and the aging revolution: How we adapt to longer life* (pp. 239–254). Washington, DC: American Psychological Association.

Giniger, S., Dispenzieri, A., & Eisenberg, J. (1983). Age, experience and performance on speed and skill jobs in an applied setting. *Journal of Applied Psychology*, 68, 469–475.

Gordon, R.A. & Arvey, R.D. (2004). Age bias in laboratory and field settings: A meta-analytic investigation. *Journal of Applied Social Psychology*, 34, 1–27.

Granville, G., & Evandrou, M. (2010) Older men, work and health. *Occupational Medicine*, 60, 178–183.

Greiner, B.A., Kraus, N., Ragland, D.R., & Fisher, J.M. (1998). Objective stress factors, accidents, and absenteeism in transit operators: A theoretical framework and empirical evidence. *Journal of Occupational Health Psychology*, 3, 130–146.

Greller, M.M., & Simpson, P.A. (1999). In search of late career: A review of contemporary social science research applicable to the understanding of late career. *Human Resource Management Review*, 9, 309–347.

Griffin, M.A., & Neal, A. (2000). Perceptions of safety at work: A framework for linking safety climate to safety performance, knowledge, and motivation. *Journal of Occupational Health Psychology*, 5, 347–358.

Grosch, J.W., & Pransky, G.S. (2009). Safety and health issues for an aging workforce. In S.J. Czaja, J. Sharit, & J. Sharit (Eds.), *Aging and work: Issues and implications in a changing landscape* (pp. 334–358). Baltimore, MD US: Johns Hopkins University Press.

Gross J.J., Carstensen L.L., Tsai J., Skorpen C.G., & Hsu A.Y.C. (1997). Emotion and aging: Experience, expression, and control. *Psychology and Aging*, 12, 590–599.

Gyekye, S.A., & Salminen (2009). Age and workers' perceptions of workplace safety: A comparative study. *International Journal of Aging and Human Development*, 68, 171–184.

Hansson, R.O., DeKoekkoek, P.D., Neece, W.M., & Patterson, D.W. (1997). Successful aging at work: Annual review, 1992–1996: The older worker and transitions to retirement. *Journal of Vocational Behavior, 51*, 202–233.

Hershcovis, M.S. (2011). Incivility, social undermining, bullying ... oh my!: A call to reconcile constructs within workplace aggression research. *Journal of Organizational Behavior, 32*, 499–519.

Hofmann, D.A., Morgeson, F.P., & Gerras, S.J. (2003). Climate as a moderator of the relationship between leader–member exchange and content specific citizenship: Safety climate as an exemplar. *Journal of Applied Psychology, 88*, 170–178.

International Labour Organization. (2011). *ILO introductory report: Global trends and challenges in occupational safety and health.* XIX World Congress on Safety and Health at Work. International Labour Office. Geneva, ILO.

Jackson, S.E., & Schuler, R.S. (1985). A meta-analysis and conceptual critique of research on role ambiguity and role conflict in work settings. *Organizational Behavior and Human Decision Processes, 36*, 16–78.

Jamal, M. (1990). Relationship of Type-A behavior to employees' job satisfaction, organizational commitment, psychosomatic health problems, and turnover motivation. *Human Relations, 43*, 727–738.

Jex, S.M. (1998). Stress and job performance: Theory, research, and Implications for managerial practice. Thousand Oaks, CA: Sage.

Jex, S.M., & Beehr, T.A. (1991). Emerging theoretical and methodological issues in the study of work-related stress. In K. Rowland & G. Ferris (Eds.), *Research in Personnel and Human Resources Management* (Vol. 9, pp. 311–365). Greenwich, CT: JAI Press.

Jex, S.M., & Crossley, C.D. (2005). Organizational consequences. In J. Barling, E.K. Kelloway & M. Frone (Eds.), *Handbook of work stress* (pp. 5–599). Thousand Oaks: Sage Publications.

Jex, S.M., & Grosch, J. (in press). Retirement decision making. In M. Wang (Ed.), *The Oxford Handbook of Retirement.*

Jex, S.M., Wang, M., & Zarubin, A. (2007). Aging and occupational health. In K.S. Shultz & G.A. Adams (Eds.), *Aging and work in the 21st century: Applied psychology series* (pp. 199–223). Mahwah, NJ, US: Lawrence Erlbaum Associates Publishers.

Kahn, R.L., & Byosiere, P. (1992). Stress in organizations. In M.D. Dunnette & L.M. Hough (Eds.), *Handbook of industrial and organizational psychology* (2nd ed., Vol. 2, pp. 571–650). Palo Alto, CA: Consulting Psychologists Press.

Kanfer, R., & Ackerman, P.L. (2004). Aging, adult development and work motivation. *Academy Of Management Review, 29*(3), 440–458. doi:10.5465/AMR.2004.13670969

Karasek, R.A. (1979). Job demands, job decision latitude, and mental strain: Implications for job re-design. *Administrative Science Quarterly, 24*, 285–306.

Katz, D., & Kahn, R.L. (1978). *The social psychology of organizations* (2nd ed.). New York: Wiley.

Kaufman, A.S., & Lichtenberger, E.O. (2002). *Assessing adolescent and adult intelligence* (2nd ed.). Boston: Allyn & Bacon.

Kim, M., & Hunter, J. (1993). Attitude–behavior relations: A meta-analysis of attitudinal relevance and topic. *Journal of Communication, 43*, 101–142.

Kinsella, K., & He, W. (2009). *An aging world: 2008.* US Census Bureau, International Population Reports. Washington, DC: US Government Printing Office.

Kite, M.E., & Johnson, B.T. (1988). Attitudes toward older and younger adults: A meta-analysis. *Psychology and Aging, 3*, 233–244.

Laflamme, L., & Menckel, E. (1995). Aging and occupational accidents: A review of the literature of the last three decades. *Safety Science, 21*, 145–161.

Leka, S., & Jain, A. (2010). *Health impact of psychosocial hazards at work: An overview.* World Health Organization. University of Nottingham.

Liao, H., Arvey, R.D., Butler, R.J., & Nutting, S.M. (2001). Correlates of work injury frequency and duration among firefighters. *Journal of Occupational Health Psychology, 6*, 229–242.

Loi, J., & Shultz, K. (2007). Why older adults seek employment: Differing motivations among subgroups. *Journal of Applied Gerontology, 26*, 274–289.

Maertens, J., Putter, S., Chen, P.Y., Manfred, D., Huang, Y.H. (in press). Physical capabilities and occupational health of older workers. In J.W. Hedge and W. C. Borman (Eds), *Oxford handbook of work and aging.* New York, NY: Oxford University Press.

Manning, M.R., Jackson, C.N., & Fusilier, M.R. (1996). Occupational stress, social support, and the costs of health care. *Academy of Management Journal, 39*, 738–750.

Manpower Group (2011). *Talent shortage survey results.* Milwaukee, WI: Manpower Group. Retrieved from: http://us.manpower.com/us/en/multimedia/2011-Talent-Shortage-Survey.pdf

Mather, M., & Carstensen, L.L. (2005). Aging and motivated cognition: The positivity effect in attention and memory. *Trends in Cognitive Science, 9*, 496–502.

Maurer, T. (2007). Employee development and training issues related to the aging workforce. In K. Shultz &

G. Adams (Eds.) *Aging and work in the 21st century*. New Jersey: Lawrence Erlbaum Associates.

Maurer, T., Weiss, E., & Barbeite, F. (2003). A model of involvement in work-related learning and development activity: The effects of individual, situational, motivational, and age variables. *Journal of Applied Psychology*, 88, 707–724.

Mayes, B.T., Barton, M.E., & Ganster, D.T. (1991). An exploration of the moderating effect of age on stressor-employee strain relationships. *Journal of Social Behavior and Personality*, 6, 389–398.

Meyer, J.P., Stanley, D.J., Herscovitch, L., & Topolnytsky, L. (2002). Affective, continuance, and normative commitment to the organization: A meta-analysis of antecedents, correlates, and consequences. *Journal of Vocational Behavior*, 61, 20–52.

Ng, T.H., & Feldman, D.C. (2008). The relationship of age to ten dimensions of job performance. *Journal of Applied Psychology*, 93(2), 392–423.

Ng, T.W.H., & Feldman, D.C. (2010). The relationships of age with job attitudes: A meta-analysis. *Personnel Psychology*, 63, 677–718.

Park, D.C. (2000). The basic mechanisms accounting for age-related decline in cognitive function. In D.C. Park and N. Schwarz (Eds.), *Cognitive aging: A primer* (pp. 3–21). Philadelphia PA: Psychology Press.

Parkes, K.R. (2003). Shiftwork and environment as interactive predictors of work perceptions. *Journal of Occupational Health Psychology, 8*, 266–281.

Payne, S., & Doyal, L. (2010). Older women, work and health. *Occupational Medicine*, 60(3), 172.

Probst, T.M. (2004). Job insecurity: Exploring a new threat to employee safety. In J. Barling, M.R. Frone, J. Barling, M.R. Frone (Eds.), *The psychology of workplace safety* (pp. 63–80). Washington, DC: American Psychological Association.

Rayner, C. (1997). The incidence of workplace bullying. *Journal of Community & Applied Social Psychology*, 7, 199–208.

Ready, R.E., & Robinson, M.D. (2008). Do older individuals adapt to their traits?: Personality-emotion relations among younger and older adults. *Journal of Research in Personality, 42*, 1020–1030.

Rupp, D.E., Vodanovich, S.J., & Crede, M. (2006). Age bias in the workplace: The impact of ageism and causal attributions. *Journal of Applied Social Psychology*, 36, 1337–1364.

Salthouse, T.A. (1996). The processing-speed theory of adult age differences in cognition. *Psychological Review*, 103, 403–428.

Salthouse, T.A., & Maurer, T.J. (1996). Aging, job performance, and career development. In J.E. Birren, K. Schaie, R.P. Abeles, M. Gatz, T.A. Salthouse, J.E.

Birren, T.A. Salthouse (Eds.), *Handbook of the psychology of aging* (4th ed.) (pp. 353–364). San Diego, CA US: Academic Press.

Schaie, K.W. (1996). Intellectual development in adulthood. In J.E. Birren & K.W. Schaie (Eds.), *Handbook of the psychology of aging* (4th ed.) (pp. 266–286). San Diego: Academic Press.

Schaubroeck, J., Jones, J.R., & Xie, J.L. (2001). Individual differences in utilizing control to cope with job demands: Effects on susceptibility to infectious disease. *Journal of Applied Psychology*, 86, 265–278.

Shultz, K.S., Wang, M., Crimmins, E., & Fisher, G.F. (2010). Age differences in the Demand–Control Model of work stress: An examination of data from 15 European countries. *Journal of Applied Gerontology*, 29, 21–47.

Seitsamo, J., & Martikainen, R. (1999). Changes in capability in a sample of Finnish aging workers. *Experimental Aging Research, 1*, 345–352.

Shore, L.M., & Goldberg, C.B. (2004). Age discrimination in the workplace. In R.L. Dipboye & A. Colella (Eds.), *Discrimination at work: The psychological and organizational bases* (pp. 203–222). London: Lawrence Erlbaum Associates.

Simpson, P.A., Greller, M.M., & Stroh, L.K. (2002). Variation in human capital investment activity by age. *Journal of Vocational Behavior*, 61, 109–138.

Siu, O., Phillips, D.R., & Leung, T. (2003). Age differences in safety attitudes and safety performance in Hong Kong construction workers. *Journal of Safety Research, 34*, 199–205.

Sonnentag, S., & Frese, M. (2003). Stress in organizations. In W.C. Borman, D.R. Ilgen, & R.J. Klimoski (Eds.), *Comprehensive handbook of psychology: Industrial and organizational psychology* (Vol 12., pp. 453–491). New York: Wiley.

Spector, P.E., & Fox, S. (2005). A model of counterproductive work behavior. In S. Fox & Spector, P.E. (Eds.), *Counterproductive workplace behavior: Investigations of actors and targets* (pp. 151–174). Washington, DC: American Psychological Association.

Spector, P.E., & Jex, S.M. (1998). Development of four self-report measures of job stressors and strain: Interpersonal Conflict at Work Scale, Organizational Constraints Scale, Quantitative Workload Inventory, and Physical Symptoms Inventory. *Journal of Occupational Health Psychology*, 3, 356–367.

Sprung, J. (2011). Work locus of control as a moderator of the relationship between work stressors and counterproductive work behavior. Unpublished master's thesis, Bowling Green State University, Bowling Green, OH.

Sterns, H.L., & Doverspike, D. (1989). Aging and the retraining and learning process in *organizations*.

In I. Goldstein & R. Katzel (Eds.), *Training and development in work organizations* (pp. 229–332). San Francisco, CA: Jossey-Bass.

Taylor, P., & Urwin, P. (2001). Age and participation in vocational education and training. *Work, Employment & Society, 15,* 763–779.

Tepper, B.J. (2000). Consequences of abusive supervision. *Academy of Management Journal, 43,* 178–190.

Wang, M., & Chen, Y. (2006). Age differences in attitude change: Influences of cognitive resources and motivation on responses to argument quantity. *Psychology and Aging, 21,* 581–589.

Wang, M., & Shultz, K.S. (2010). Employee retirement: A review and recommendations for future investigation. *Journal of Management, 36,* 172–206.

Wang, M., Henkens, K., & van Solinge, H. (2011). Retirement adjustment: A review of theoretical and empirical advancements. *American Psychologist.* Advance online publication. doi: 10.1037/a0022414.

Warr, P. (1994). Age and employment. In H.C. Triandis, M.D. Dunnette, L.M. Hough (Eds.), *Handbook of industrial and organizational psychology* (Vol. 4, pp. 485–550). Palo Alto, CA US: Consulting Psychologists Press.

Warr, P. (1997). Age, work, and mental health. In K.W. Schaie & C. Schooler (Eds.), *The Impact of work on older adults* (pp. 252–296). New York: Springer.

Warr, P., & Birdi, K. (1998). Employee age and voluntary development activity. *International Journal of Training and Development, 2,* 190–204.

Wegman, D.H., & Mcgee, J.P. (2004). *Health and safety needs of older workers.* Washington, DC: The National Academic Press.

Wrenn, K.A., & Maurer, T.J. (2004). Beliefs about older workers' learning and development behavior in relation to beliefs about malleability of skills, age-related decline, and control. *Journal of Applied Social Psychology 34* 223–242.

Yeomans, L. (2011). *An update of the literature on age and employment.* Health and Safety Executive, Buxton, Derbyshire: Harpur Hill.

Yeung, D.Y., & Fung, H.H. (2009). Aging and work: How do SOC strategies contribute to job performance across adulthood? *Psychology and Aging, 24,* 927–940.

Zacher, H. & Frese, M. (2009). Remaining time and opportunities at work: Relationships between age, work characteristics, and occupational future time perspective. *Psychology and Aging, 24,* 487–493.

Zacher, H., Heusner, S., Schmitz, M., Zwierzanska, M.M., & Frese, M. (2010). Focus on opportunities as a mediator of the relationships between age, job complexity, and work performance. *Journal of Vocational Behavior, 76,* 374–386.

16

Training Older Workers: A Review

Yu-Shan Hsu

INTRODUCTION

The aging workforce is an emerging phenomenon around the world, especially in industrialized countries. Almost one-third of the working-age population in developed countries will be aged 50 or over by 2050 (United Nations, 2007). Over the next 30 years, Europeans over the age of 60 will grow by 50% and the number of adults aged 20 to 59 will fall by 6%. The numbers of those aged 20 to 29 will fall by 9 million. These figures indicate a continuous aging of the workforce among European Union (EU) countries (Krenn and Oehlke, 2001). According to the Australian Bureau of Statistics (ABS), labor force participation rate among the 55 to 64 years age group increased from 48% in 2000 to 56% in 2005 (ABS, 2007). The American workforce is aging as well (Hartley and Biddle, 2002). The Bureau of Labor Statistics (BLS, 2010) has projected that by 2018 there will be 40 million workers 55 years of age or older in the United States. This is approximately 23.9% of the US workforce. The

number of workers age 55 years and older will increase by 43%, while the number of workers age 25 to 54 years will increase by only 1.5% (BLS, 2010). By 2020, more than half of the workforce will be age 40 or older (Beatty and Visser, 2005). Recent studies of older workers by Association for the Advancement of Retired Persons (AARP) also indicate that many Americans are choosing to work beyond the traditional retirement age (Gornick, 2005). With the rapidly changing work environment and emergence of technology, helping older workers remain vital within their organization is a critical issue (Callahan, Kiker, and Cross, 2003).

According to Sparrow and Davies (1988), training is an important vehicle for enhancing the performance of older workers. Implementing training and development practices targeting older workers are important to perceptions of organizational support and career satisfaction and ultimately to the retention of older workers (Armstrong-Stassen and Ursel, 2009). However, even though research results have suggested that job performance does not decline with age (Waldman and Avolio, 1986), there are many negative stereotypes regarding the 'trainability' of older workers, which may reduce the training access and the training effectiveness of older workers. Compared to younger workers, older workers are perceived to have lower potential for development (Rosen and Jerdee, 1976a), to learn less quickly, to be less able to grasp new ideas (Perry and Varney, 1978), and to be less flexible and more likely to become weary than their younger colleagues (Stagner, 1985; Warr, 1994). Employers are often reluctant to train older employees because they are simply too valuable in their current jobs to warrant the lost productivity associated with training or development (Andrisani and Daymont, 1987; Straka, 1992). These costs, along with a supposedly shorter payback period, lead employers to avoid making human capital investments in their older workers (Rix, 1996).

Are these stereotypes justified? To clarify these potential misconceptions, I review published research on the training and learning issues of older workers. With this review, I seek answers to these questions: (1) Is older workers' training performance worse than that of younger workers? (2) Are older workers less willing to participate in training than younger workers? (3) Are employers/peers less willing to train older workers than younger workers? Based on my assessment of these issues, I then provide some recommendations for the training of older workers and discuss future research directions.

TRAINING OF OLDER WORKERS: WHERE ARE WE NOW?

This review focuses on published research on the training and learning issues of older workers in the workplace context. Articles were collected through an extensive computer literature search. The computerized data bases that were searched included PsycINFO and the Social Science Citation Index. These data bases included journals from the

disciplines of organizational behavior, industrial/organizational psychology, cognitive psychology, and educational gerontology. Example keywords used were: training, older worker, age, and aging.

Definition of 'older worker'

Before addressing the focal research questions, I consider the definition of an 'older worker'. There is no universal operationalization of this term. Legally, an older worker is defined as anyone in the workforce at or above the age of 40 (Age Discrimination in Employment Act). However, in the research literature, the definitions are much more varied, from 40 and over (Gist, Rosen, and Schwoerer, 1988), 44 and over (Wallen and Mulloy, 2006), 50–65 (Simpson, Greller, and Stroh, 2002) to 55–67 (Elias, Elias, Robbins, and Gage, 1987). Many studies compare the training outcomes of younger and older workers without identifying the definition of younger and older workers or without explicitly stating the rationale for using a particular age range. In a review of 105 studies, Ashbaugh and Fay (1987) found that the average chronological age of an older worker was 53.4 years. Thus, perhaps this can serve as a reasonable lower bound for the term 'older worker,' although what is considered old may depend on the context (Maurer, Wrenn, and Weiss, 2001).

Research has suggested that there is a common belief that older workers have less potential for learning and development (Maurer et al., 2001). In this section, I review current literature regarding the comparison of older and younger workers' training performance and then look more closely at individual differences that may account for reported differences.

In comparison with younger workers, groups of older workers seem to have much more variability in training performance (Kubeck, Delp, Haslett, and McDaniel, 1996). In an analysis of results from several studies published in *Psychology and Aging* and the *Journal of Gerontology*, Morse (1993) reported that older adults as a group are more variable than younger groups in basic and general abilities. This increased variability may be due to several factors: (1) the combined effects of individuals' unique experiences over more years, (2) genetically based differences have more time to be expressed, and (3) older people, somewhat freer of social constraints, are more likely to choose their own courses of action. Warr, Allan, and Birdi (1999) found that knowledge gain scores before and after training were associated with age ($r = -.24, p < .01$), but they found no age differences in later behavior on the job in terms of frequency of use of the learned technology, a goal of training.

An implication of the variability of performance among older workers is that individual differences may play an important role. For example, if individual qualities such as pre-training competence and other training-relevant characteristics are taken into consideration when selecting workers for training, the negative age effects suggested in prior research may be significantly smaller. From my review of the literature, I identified four relevant individual differences: physical and cognitive changes in older workers, self-efficacy, anxiety, and pre-test mastery of training material.

Physical and cognitive changes in older workers

The age-related change with the greatest effect on learning may be the decrease in fluid intelligence, which is associated with declining working memory function (Van Gerven, Pass and Schmidt, 2000). Working memory, previously called short-term memory, is the portion of the cognitive processing system used to process incoming information and transfer it to long-term memory. Working memory function has been shown to decline with age. Therefore, older adult workers encode new materials more slowly and have a delayed ability to retrieve information because of the slowed processing speed (Ford and Orel, 2005). Older adults may miss relevant details of the training program because

of slower processing rates and a reduced working memory capacity, leading to poorer comprehension of material (Warr, 1994). The decrement of cognitive response is slight for simple tasks but increases monotonically as task complexity increases (Spirduso and MacRae, 1990). Novel tasks which make heavy information-processing demands are performed less well by older people (Salthouse, 1989). Myers and Conner's (1992) laboratory investigation of this phenomenon indicated that older workers were able to achieve similar levels of task performance to younger workers during both practice and transfer of the experiments but older workers appeared restricted to tasks drawn from the same semantic domain.

Older adults also appear to have greater difficulty filtering out irrelevant information. Some have argued that this problem corresponds with a decline in the efficiency of what has been identified as 'inhibitory attention mechanisms' (Hasher and Zacks, 1998), but others have offered a more positive view. Older adults may have more difficulty ignoring extraneous thoughts simply because their comparatively greater breadth and scope of experience leads to a broader activation of stored material when presented with a stimulus (Jones and Bayen, 1998).

Kubeck et al.'s (1996) meta-analysis examined the question, 'Does job-related training performance decline with age?' and the results showed poorer training performance for older adults. Older adults, relative to younger adults, showed less mastery of training material ($k = 48, n = 4389, r = -.26$), completed the final training task more slowly ($k = 9, n = 842, r = .28$), and took longer to complete the training program ($k = 5, n = 194, r = .42$). However, the authors found the magnitude of relationships between age and training performance varies across studies. Additionally, recent research has indicated that the delayed retrieval exhibited by some older adults may not be the result of slowed processing speed but instead may represent an older adult's heightened concern with accuracy. Older adults in their desire to be correct will take longer to complete tasks (Backman, Small, and Wahlin, 2001).

In addition to cognitive ability, when it comes to computer-based learning, age-related decrements in visual-spatial processing and control (Dywan and Murphy, 1996), auditory selective attention (Barr and Giambra, 1990), and memory (Kirasic, Allen, Dobson, and Binder, 1996) impede the learning speed of older workers. The literature on learning, memory, comprehension, and problem-solving suggests that older cohorts are less well-equipped to acquire the skills necessary for effective word processing (Botwinick, 1984). Older trainees perform less well than younger trainees using microcomputers due to greater ability decrements (Elias et al., 1987).

Having said that, recent research (Vance, Heaton, Fazeli, and Ackerman, 2010) shows that cognitive ability such as speed of processing can be improved by specially designed exercises that are tailored to the individual's performance. Therefore, having older workers gone through this speed of processing training might help alleviate worse training performance due to decreasing cognitive ability.

Self-efficacy

Reed, Doty, and May's (2005) research examined the importance that self-efficacy played in training performance, specifically in computer skill acquisition. Their results indicated that computer self-efficacy mediates the negative relationships between age and computer skill acquisition. Chronological age alone offers a poor predictor of technical learning capacity. This result implies that when it comes to older workers, training may not be a matter of skill training, but also a consideration of antecedents affecting self-efficacy for that particular task. Effective training for older workers should extend beyond training methods to examine age-related influence factors on self-efficacy.

Anxiety

Research showed that the older the trainee, the greater the anxiety related to the training

context (Baracat and Marquie, 1994). Older workers may experience more anxiety in learning situations (Rebok and Offerman, 1983). Older employees have themselves expressed anxiety about their retraining capabilities, especially in comparison to younger workers and when the focus of skills acquisition is the new technologies (Costello, 1997; Knowles, 1973). However, this result differs from the observation of Warr and Bunce (1995), perhaps because in their case they were dealing with open learning, which is assumed to be less stressful than traditional training courses. Similarly, in the work done by Charness, Schumann, and Boritz (1992), no difference in the level of anxiety was found between young and older trainees learning how to use word processing software. Because this was an experimental study, the lack of professional implication may explain the lack of difference in emotional terms as a function of age. Delgoulet and Marquie (2002) suggested that in some cases older trainees experience higher learning anxiety, perhaps because they perceive a bigger gap than younger people between their capabilities and training requirements, or requirements for tasks to be performed during the training.

Although Delgoulet and Marquie's (2002) study found greater anxiety in the older trainees, this greater level of anxiety had no significant effect on their training performance. This can be explained in several ways. First, it is possible that the level of anxiety reached was insufficient to affect performance (Mueller, 1992), or that the age-related differences in anxiety observed at the beginning of the course then disappeared during the training course. Another possible explanation is suggested by results obtained in the study by Laguna and Babcock (1997) on the relationship between computer anxiety and age-related differences in performance on computer-based cognitive tasks. These authors found no relation between anxiety and performance measured in terms of errors but did find a positive relationship with the time taken to perform the task.

Baracat and Marquie (1994) showed that there were differences in the decision-making criteria adopted by young and older trainees during tests on the retrieval of previously learned information. These decision-making criteria revealed that older people were much more reluctant to commit an action when they were not completely sure that the procedure was the right one. This attitude had been interpreted as showing a higher level of anxiety in the learning situation when compared with young people (Delgoulet and Marquie, 2002).

Pre-test mastery of training material

Sterns and Gray (1999) have observed that one of the problems for older employees was less pre-test mastery of training material, thus putting them at a disadvantage compared to younger employees at the beginning of training (Gray, Boyce, Hall, and McDaniel, 1996). The study also more precisely examined how the effects of age might change in the presence of essential controls. Results confirmed that age differences in post-training knowledge were, at least in part, a function of parallel differences in pre-training knowledge. Further, the portion of age differences that could not be explained by pre-training knowledge differences were significantly decreased once education was included as a control. Factors relating to the unique life experiences of individuals from different generational cohorts appear to also play a role in the age differences. Charness, Kelly, Bosman and Mottram's (2001) word-processing application training study indicated that there are strong direct effects of experience as well as its interactive role on training performance, which are important signals to managers that an older trained workforce can remain a cost-effective workforce when given the opportunity to retrain. It will probably take them longer to retrain, but their performance at the end of training can be equivalent to that of younger workers, both for effectiveness and efficiency.

In sum, although working memory declines with age, which may slow the learning speed of older workers, from the discussion above, we may notice that the poorer training performance is confounded with other factors, such as self-efficacy, higher concern with accuracy, pre-training knowledge, education; age actually has a small effect size on training performance. In addition, there is large within group variability which further decreases the strength of the conclusion drawn from several researches that 'older workers' as a group perform less well than younger workers. Therefore, we can conclude that older workers are trainable.

Are older workers less willing to participate in training than younger workers?

Training is desired when we want to help narrow the gap between a job's requirements and the skills and needs of an older worker (Abraham and Hansson, 1995). However, stereotypes suggest that older employees lack both the motivation and capacity to take advantage of training opportunities. For example, Rosen and Jerdee (1976a) identified job-related age stereotypes depicting older employees as rigid and resistant to change, less receptive to new ideas, and less capable of learning compared with younger employees. Capowski (1994) describes research which showed that 57% of businesses claim that older employees show resistance to training.

The results above show that older workers are perceived to be less motivated to learn than younger workers. Some research has empirically examined the truth regarding those perceptions of older workers. McEnrue (1989) found that younger employees were more willing to engage in self-development than older employees. Some research of organizational behavior has suggested that as employees get older, they tend not to be involved in training and development activities as much as younger employees (Birdi, Allan, and Warr, 1997; Cleveland and Shore, 1992). In the workplace, older adults are said to avoid retraining because they fear competition, doubt their abilities, and question the benefits of such training (Sterns, 1986). At least for on-the-job training, most previous empirical research conducted in the United States confirmed that older workers did indeed train comparatively less (Booth, 1993; Frazis, Gittleman, and Joyce, 1998; Lynch, 1992; Royalty, 1996). However, some of this literature suggests that older workers might be sometimes excluded or may be influenced by stereotypical beliefs held by decision-makers or older worker themselves (Maurer et al., 2001). This is another related issue that will be addressed in the next section. As we can see from the empirical results older workers do tend to show less motivation to participate in training, and the next part of this section will review the research surrounding the factors leading to this lower motivation to participate in training among older workers.

Self-efficacy

Success in training for older trainees may be negatively affected by their own estimates of their ability to learn. In fact, Fossum, Arvey, Paradise, and Robbins (1986), using an expectancy theory perspective, suggested that older employees may not expend the effort to learn new skills and abilities unless they hold the positive expectation that skills mastery is attainable. In support of the expectancy model, Rosen, Williams, and Foltman (1965) found that older workers were most unlikely to volunteer for training programs because they had little confidence in their learning ability. Maurer et al. (2003) suggested that chronological age (the number of years old), and not relative age (perceptions of how old the person is relative to his/her work group), had significant relationships with career variables: a positive relationship with job involvement and a negative relationship with perceived need for development.

Self-efficacy has been widely studied in the topic of older workers' motivation to learn. Lower motivation to learn may be derived from lower self-efficacy among older workers. It is possible that older employees

have a lower sense of self-efficacy regarding self-development than younger employees (Lent and Hackett, 1987). Maurer (2001) developed a theoretical model exploring an underlying recognized factor that may contribute to older workers' lower desire to participate in learning and development activities compared to younger workers: a decline in self-efficacy for career-relevant learning and skill development with age. The model proposed four age-related effects – fewer mastery experiences, fewer positive vicarious experiences, reduced social support for development, presence of psychological variables such as anxiety and health – as the antecedents of lower self-efficacy and therefore lower participation in career-relevant learning and development. Maurer et al. (2003) further developed this model, and proposed that employees who are oriented toward employee development are those who have participated in development activities before, perceive themselves as possessing the qualities needed for learning, have social support for development at work and outside of work, are job involved, have insight into their career, and who believe in the need for development and in their ability to develop skills and receive intrinsic benefits from participating. Along the same line, it was found that age was negatively related to training and development willingness for the high-entity employees (Van Vianen, Dalhoeven, and De Pater, 2011), those who hold beliefs about the fixedness or malleability of personal characteristics (Dweck, 2000). The authors reason that it is because those older employees whose entity beliefs negatively impact their expectations of training success through their negative effect on self-efficacy.

Colquitt, LePine, and Noe's (2000) meta-analysis of training motivation suggested that age was linked to motivation to learn ($r = -.13$), as older trainees demonstrated lower motivation, learning, and post training self-efficacy. This suggests that trainers may have to take precautions to ensure that older trainees can succeed during the training program. This is especially critical as training content or methods use new technologies, such as web-based instruction or virtual reality, with which older workers may be less comfortable. These results pose a challenge to future training practitioners, given that two trends in today's organizations are the increasing age of the workforce and the increasing introduction of new technologies (Howard, 1995).

Return on investment

From the neoclassical economists' point of view, older employees do not seek training on their own because they are concerned about the loss of wages and believe there is too little time in which to benefit from their investment. In addition, they recognize that ageism in the external market may further reduce the potential returns from any new skills (Simpson et al., 2002). Older employees are less willing to engage in self-development because they have a shorter work horizon in which to recoup their investment (McEnrue, 1989).

In contrast to the neoclassical economist perspective, Sterns (1986) has proposed a life-span career development model that addresses the dynamic environment in which human capital investments decisions are made. He discussed how major economic and technological changes can generate new attitudes and behaviors with regard to human capital investment among successive cohorts of older workers. Facing obsolescence and job insecurity, growing numbers of older workers may be compelled to seek to retool. Thus, even if previous generations of older workers did not invest in their human capital, contemporary pressures could lead the present generation to do so. It seems that one of the primary motivations for older workers to enroll in adult education is productivity enhancement, especially through focused occupational skills development.

Indeed, rates of training participation among older workers have been rising dramatically in recent years. Elman (1998) notes that the enrolment of individuals aged 40 years and above in higher education grew by 235% between 1970 and 1993. The largest growth area in adult education for older adults has been vocational training and other work-related education formats, typically of short duration. While little direct evidence currently exists to suggest that older workers are training more than younger workers, Simpson et al.'s (2002) analysis of a national sample confirmed that individuals 40 and over were more likely than younger individuals to participate in specific types of work-related education like on-the-job computer training. They were even more likely to enroll in formal credentialing programs for purposes of job or career advancement than those younger than 40. In contrast, younger workers were more likely to enroll in core courses like ESL and basic skills to improve their employability. Further, when only labor force participants are included in the sample, the overall incidence of training is higher for older workers than for younger workers.

From the discussion above, we can see that rates of training participation among older workers have been increasing. The next part of this section will review the research supporting the ideas that older workers are still actively participating in training. Factors that prompt older workers to participate in training will also be discussed.

New technologies

Older workers' increasing training participation rate could be attributed to the introduction of new technologies, which have repeatedly elicited widespread changes in the makeup of student populations, educational delivery systems, and curriculum content within the United States. Most recently, the technological revolution has coincided with the rapid expansion of new educational delivery systems that have probably contributed to reducing the opportunity costs older workers face when retooling. Often incorporating non-traditional scheduling approaches, an expansive adult education system allows growing numbers of adults to enroll in classes and courses in their non-work hours. Further, adult education providers often incorporate non-traditional pedagogical approaches that tend to appeal to older learners (Sterns, 1986; Sterns and Doverspike, 1989).

Job security

Another reason that prompts older workers to participate in training is to maintain job security. For example, Sterns (1986) discussed how profound economic or technological change can generate new attitudes and behavior among older workers toward training. In his view, because older workers are more vulnerable to obsolescence when new technologies are being rapidly introduced, the number of them seeking retraining rises commensurately. Additionally, older workers are often targeted during the downsizing and restructuring which has occurred since 1980 (Farr, Tesluk, and Klein, 1998).

Organizational commitment

McEnrue's (1989) research reported that younger employees and those who express a high level of organizational commitment were more willing to engage in self-development in order to prepare themselves for higher levels of organizational responsibility than were other employees with equivalent managerial career aspirations.

In sum, although there are some factors leading to lower motivation to learn, such as lower self-efficacy and perceived lower return on educational investment that may reduce older workers' participation in training, nowadays many external factors such as new technologies and job security have prompted older workers to actively participate in training.

Are employers and peers less willing to train older workers than younger workers?

Organizations which create a discouraging job climate and offer few prospects for advancement to older workers are effectively reducing the likelihood that older workers will maintain and develop their skills (Sterns and Miklos, 1995). Prior literature has also outlined how social, behavioral, and organizational processes may operate to reduce older workers' access to successful experiences for developing and improving their career-relevant skills, thus reducing mastery experiences they may possess (Maurer, 2001; Salthouse and Maurer, 1996; Maurer and Tarulli, 1996). Unfortunately, the fact is that corporations do spend less on the development of older workers (Armstrong-Stassen and Lee, 2009).

Employers often deprive older workers of training opportunities (Rosen and Jerdee, 1976b). For example, Simon (1996) asserts that many older workers are being denied the opportunity to improve their skills, citing that 55–64 year-olds are only a third as likely as 35–44-year-olds to receive training in the workplace, according to a study by the US Department of Labor. Capowski (1994) reports that a study by AARP found that only three out of ten companies included older adults in their training programs. Studies have repeatedly indicated that older employees received less on-the-job training (Booth, 1993; Frazis et al., 1998). Recent results from the Boston College National Study of Business Strategy and Work Workforce Development (Center on Aging and Workplace Flexibility at Boston College, 2007) found that about 26% of employers reported that they increased training and cross-training efforts to a large extent for younger workers than for older workers. However, a recent study (Charness and Fox, 2010) using a sample of employees in IT firms did not show age as a significant predictor or experiencing formal training. The authors concluded that it may be due to differences between the IT industry and other industries.

In addition to formal training programs, researchers have found that older workers are less likely to receive career counseling from supervisors (Cleveland and Shore, 1992). Kram and Isabella (1985) suggest that older workers may not form peer relationships that would lead to psychological support. Maurer (2001) reviewed literature that suggested that older workers might receive less support and encouragement from supervisors, co-workers, and other people at work for engaging in learning and development activities. In addition to a lack of support at work, to the extent that family, friends, or others outside of work do not encourage older workers' participation in development, the non-work social support might also have a negative relationship with age. Maurer et al.'s (2003) research further indicated that *chronological age* had a negative relationship with non-work support, whereas *perceived relative age* had a negative relationship with work support. Perhaps being relatively older at work is a key concern with respect to learning and development rather than one's absolute, chronological age. However, outside of work, the relative age of an employee's workgroup is not a salient factor in determining the enthusiasm or support one's friends and family may lend toward development and learning. The results also suggest that attention in the workplace to employees' relative ages (and not just chronological age) should be a concern when addressing possible age bias or discrimination in development (Maurer and Rafuse, 2001).

There are so many overwhelming negative stereotypes toward older workers' training performance and motivation to learn. When Forte and Hansvick (1999) surveyed employers' perceptions about their employees learning ability, the results indicated that overall, older workers were rated lower on learning and development ability. Interestingly, this study did show evidence of in-group bias among younger employers toward older workers. Employers who were 50 or over themselves rated workers of similar age as being more desirable on all attributes. Thus, older employers viewed older workers as more able in learning and development than did younger employers.

As Sterns and Doverspike (1989) suggested, the negative relationship between age and learning may be due to both self-perceptions and managers' perceptions. Specifically, as employees age, managers may perceive that the employees' ability and training motivation decreases. Also, employees' fear of failure

may increase as they age, preventing older employees from seeking training opportunities. It has also been reported that age was negatively related to participation in training and development programs. For example, Cleveland and Shore (1992) found that age was negatively related to both self-reported and managers' evaluations of participation in on-the-job training. Certainly, it is not only employer attitudes toward retraining older workers that have hindered substantial progress; rather, workers themselves contribute through fear of competition from younger workers and doubts about their general abilities (Elias et al., 1987).

TRAINING OLDER WORKERS: SOME RECOMMENDATIONS FOR THE FUTURE

Age awareness training

Although the Age Discrimination in Employment Act of 1967 in the USA, like similar legislation in Europe and elsewhere, aims to reduce through legislated standards the stereotypes or even the age discrimination among employers and peers toward older workers, the better way forward is to conduct age awareness training for both employers and employees. Cleveland, Shore, and Murphy (1997) wrote that 'Many of the problems and challenges faced by older workers are likely to be the result of others' reactions to and beliefs regarding the individual's age rather than a result of age per se'. However, in a study of 400 US organizations, only 25% reported that they were educating managers about ways to utilize older employees (AARP, 2000). For employers who believe that investment in training older workers provides a poor return should understand that the turnover of older worker is low, and training a younger worker may also prepare them to leave for a competitor, so what matters most is whether employees have the ability and willingness to learn, regardless of age (Gray and McGregor, 2003). Thus, age awareness training would be an emergent need for organizations. Future research can investigate if age awareness training substantially changes the stereotypes of employers, peers, and older workers themselves in organizations.

Age tailored training

Many of the age-related stereotypes that have germinated in the workplace over the past several decades are a result of myths fostered by misinformation and failed experiments (Elliot, 1995). An example of a failed experiment is the 1973–1978 government project to retrain 2,500 air traffic controllers, whose average age was 45. The program cost over $100 million, and yielded a success rate of only 7%, based on the number of controllers who found second careers. The air traffic controllers responded poorly not because they were too old to learn, but rather because the classes were designed for participants in their 20s, not experienced 40-year old males (Carnevale and Stones, 1994). This example not only points out the possible research bias when comparing the training performance of older and younger workers but also most importantly points out the importance of tailoring training delivery methods or strategies to older workers.

Several researchers (Allen and Hart, 1998) have pointed out that even when training opportunities are available to older employees, there is a need to tailor the training design and methods to allow for the learning styles and experience of older employees. Industrial psychologists argue that many aspects of the training program need to be modified to account for the unique needs of older learners (Glass, 1994). Researchers have highlighted the need for studies of training methods appropriate to older adult learners and have noted that specific successes in training programs (especially in terms of self-efficacy) are necessary to promote motivation to engage in further retraining as it becomes necessary (Sterns, 1986).

Accordingly, training models that account for different training outcomes have been developed. For example, the industrial gerontology model suggests that five factors must be considered when designing training programs for older learners (Sterns and Doverspike, 1989). They are motivation, structure, familiarity, organization, and time. In general, these factors refer to issues such as: (1) whether the learner perceives the training content and materials as relevant; (2) whether sufficient time is provided to complete the training successfully; (3) whether the information is presented in a logical difficulty-graded sequence, i.e., from simple to complex; (4) whether the opportunity to master all training tasks is provided; (5) whether the training builds on current knowledge base; and (6) whether memory building instruction precedes contents instruction (Sterns and Doverspike, 1989). Additionally, Simpson (2005) proposed that allowing ample discussion time during the training and less required reading material are both favored training strategies. Trainers are encouraged to take such actions as (Goldstein and Goldstein, 1990; Sterns, 1986; Sterns and Doverspike, 1989): motivate the trainee to overcome apprehension, organize materials to facilitate recall, and vary the amount and distribution of time to accommodate individual needs.

The empirical research has focused primarily on the usefulness of the training methods in reducing the gap between older and younger adult learners' training performance (Belbin and Belbin, 1972; Sterns and Doverspike, 1989). Anecdotal evidence from the learning research literature suggests that experiential learning and self-pacing are especially helpful for older learners (Belbin, 1970). Generally, workers learn at different paces, through different methods, and by varied levels of motivation and enthusiasm. The variability in learning is especially evident among older workers, but older adult workers can be motivated to take on new challenges and master new skills with proper training methodologies (Ford and Orel, 2005).

Older workers learn best when they can learn at their own pace, when they are allowed to learn with their age peers, and when the anxieties associated with learning something new are addressed (Hogarth and Barth, 1991; Knowles, 1987). Anxiety among older workers can be reduced by providing training and education far in advance of when new skills are needed, providing a supportive and encouraging learning environment, allowing age peers to learn together, and offering additional learning opportunities for those who desire them (Knowles, 1987). Studies using self-paced methods have generally shown that the experience led to significant improvements in performance (Hoyer, 1985). Because much of learning depends on building on prior knowledge, older adult workers may not have the storage and/or organizational capacities to acquire the new knowledge. Employers will be more successful in training older adult workers if older adults' long-term memories are tapped or are related to prior experiences (Merriam and Caffarella, 1999). Callahan et al.'s (2003) meta-analysis explored the effects of three instructional methods (lecture, modeling, and active participation) and four instructional factors (materials, feedback, pacing, and group size) on older learners' observed training performance. The results revealed that all three instructional methods, and two instructional factors, self-pacing and group size, explain the unique variance in observed training performance. Self-pacing explained the greatest proportion of the observed variance.

Another line of research also indicated that older employees do better when they are trained separately from younger workers (Knowles, 1987). This approach is not always economically feasible, but there is some evidence that it overcomes the frustrations and distractions that older employees feel when they realize that younger students master tasks and material at a faster pace (Charness et al., 1992).

Previous studies of computer-based training have consistently shown that differences in how information is presented can have an effect on the training (Mayer, 2001; Wallen and Mulloy, 2005; Wallen, Plass and Brunken, 2005). Research into instructional techniques to overcome working memory deficits has resulted in a number of instructional prescriptions described in cognitive load theory (Sweller, Chandler, Tierney, and Cooper, 1990). These include avoiding split attention, where a learner's attention has to switch between two or more sources of information at once, such as with a figure and a distant legend, and delivering information to both the visual and verbal processing systems in order to avoid overloading working memory (Tindall-Ford, Chandler, and Sweller, 1997).

Gist et al.'s (1988) research indicated that regardless of which training methods (interactive tutorials and video modeling) were adopted in computer software training, older trainees showed significantly lower performance than younger trainees even though they controlled for previous computer experience. Video modeling is assumed to be more beneficial for older workers than interactive tutorials because it provides a coherent reference, which can facilitate the recall of individual procedures necessary to achieve the desired end state. Observations of mastery may clarify expectations of necessary actions and provide vicarious feedback and reinforcement; however, the research results reported no differences between these two training methods. Older trainees still performed more poorly than younger counterparts regardless of the training method used. The authors suggested it is probably because these two training methods may not have allowed older trainees to compensate with other strengths because of time restrictions.

Wallen and Mulloy's (2006) research suggested that computer-based training for safety with pictures and audio narration may be beneficial for workers over 45 years of age; however, their sample is composed of electronics manufacturing plant workers with little or no post-high school education. This brings up the question of generalizability – whether the results can be replicated if the sample were to be composed of professionals with higher education level. However, for employers dealing with low-education populations, pictures and audio narration will most likely improve performance.

Other than the format of training, researchers also found that older and younger workers differ in terms of content of training. While younger workers prefer to learn more theoretical and general knowledge, older workers prefer more practical and job-oriented knowledge (Vanmullem and Hondeghem, 2007).

In sum, age-tailored training methods are useful for older workers to enhance their training performance. As long as age-tailored training methods are designed to compensate for the physical and cognitive changes of older workers, they are generally beneficial.

DISCUSSION

'Old dogs can't learn new tricks' is probably the best description of the general public's stereotypes regarding the training performance of older workers. This review attempts to investigate the current research regarding the training and learning issues of older workers to clarify the misconceptions relating to older workers because workforce around the world is aging and continued learning for older workers in organizations is a critical issue for any organization who wishes to gain a sustained competitive advantage. After reviewing the current literature, I conclude that older workers can learn as well as younger workers as long as the training methods are tailored to compensate for the physical and cognitive changes that come with age. Older workers actively participate in training these days. They are also self-motivated to learn and participate in training as long as they overcome their learning anxiety and receive support from their peers and employers. Thus, organizations should keep on making investments in training and development for older workers just as extensively as they train and develop younger workers.

Although there are plenty of studies on this topic, there are many facets that the past research has neglected and which warrant further research. Some methodology deficits among current research also need improvements to better address the problems.

First, research has suggested that greater variation among older workers exists; however, current research tends to use age groups to study the differences between younger and older workers. Further research should take care to more thoroughly examine and account for the interrelationships and performance variability within older groups in training and in basic general abilities and motives.

Second, as mentioned in the beginning of this review, there has been considerable disagreement among researchers as to what constitutes an 'older worker'. According to Ashbaugh and Fay (1987), a variety of mostly arbitrary methods have been used to define the threshold age. Perhaps careful attention in future research can be given to the operationalization of the term 'older worker'.

Third, most of the empirical studies in this field are experimental in nature, but in the real business world, there may be other complicated factors out of researcher control which may yield different results from experimental studies. Thus, there is a need to conduct more field studies to examine the real-world training and learning issues of older workers.

Fourth, although research has suggested that there is greater variation among older workers with regard to their training performance; however, no researcher has paid attention to the training performance of older workers in a specific industry or occupation. While generally, older workers take more time to learn the training contents, it may not be the case for older workers among some occupations. For example, faculty members in academia accumulate their research experiences and learning abilities over time; therefore, their training performance may not decline with age. In short, there is a need to further disclose how occupations of older workers moderate the relationships between age and training performance.

Fifth, personality and learning goal orientation have been proven to have impact on motivation to learn and subsequent involvement in development activities. For example, Colquitt and Simmering (1998) indicated that conscientiousness and learning orientation are positively related to motivation to learn. In addition, Major, Turner, and Fletcher (2006) reported that proactive personality, extraversion, and openness are also positively related to motivation to learn. However, these constructs have not been studied in the literature surrounding the training of older workers. Workers' age might be an antecedent variable that contributes to the different motivations to learn and subsequent involvement in development activities because of different personality and goal orientation.

Last but not least, there is sparse research that investigates the question, 'Do older workers gain through participation in training?' Although current field studies have found that the productivity pre and post training is in order (Simpson, 2005), it would be interesting to longitudinally examine how participation in training impacts older workers' promotion, salary increase, working conditions, and so on. Additionally, research on the training performance of older workers tends to evaluate only at learning and behavior levels, but seldom evaluates at reaction level. Although reaction may not be related to learning and behavior, positive reaction toward the training experience may increase older workers' motivation to participate in future training. Therefore, there is also a need to evaluate older trainees' reaction level.

In conclusion, the aging workforce poses challenges to every organization especially in industrialized countries. Keeping older workers as vital members of their organizations is a critical issue. Based on this review, I believe that training could be an important vehicle to enhance the performance of older workers. This study contributes to the literature by providing a thorough survey of current research on training and learning issues

of older workers, proposing managerial implications on this issue, and pointing out current research gaps deserving further research. It also sheds light on the importance of clarifying misconceptions regarding training and learning issues of older workers.

REFERENCES

AARP. (2000) *American Business and Older Employees*, Washington, DC: Author.

Abraham, J. D., and Hansson, R. O. (1995) Successful aging at work: An applied study of selection, optimization and compensation through impression management, *Journal of Gerontology*, 50B(2): 94–103.

Allen, J. M., and Hart, M. (1998) Training older workers: Implications for HRD/HPT professionals, *Performance Improvement Quarterly*, 11(4): 91–102.

Andrisani, P., and Daymont, T. (1987) Age changes in productivity and earnings among managers and professionals, in S. H. Sandell (Ed.), *The Problem isn't Age: Work and Older Americans*. New York: Praeger. pp. 52–70.

Armstrong-Stassen, M., and Lee, S. H. (2009) The effect of relational age on older Canadian employees' perceptions of human resource practices and sense of worth to their organization, *International Journal of Human Resource Management,* 20(8): 1753–1769.

Armstrong-Stassen, M., and Ursel, N. D. (2009) Perceived organizational support, career satisfaction, and the retention of older workers, *Journal of Occupational and Organizational Psychology*, 82(1): 201–220.

Ashbaugh, D. L., and Fay, C. H. (1987) The threshold for aging in the workplace, *Research on Aging*, 9(3): 417–427.

Australian Bureau of Statistics [ABS]. (2007) *Australian Social Trends, 2007*. Retrieved September 26, 2007, from: http://www.abs.gov.au/AUSSTATS/abs@.nsf/Latestproducts/0CBA37179F1B71BACA25732C00207901?opendocument#2%20OECD%202006%2C%20'Improving%20Inc

Backman, L., Small, B., and Wahlin, A. (2001) Aging and memory: Cognitive and biological perspectives, in J. E. Birren and K. W. Schaie (Eds.), *Handbook of the Psychology of Aging* (5th ed.). San Diego, CA: Academic Press. pp. 349–377.

Baracat, B., and Marquie, J. C. (1994) Training middle-aged for new computerized technologies: A pilot study using TDS in a real-life word-processing learning situation, in J. Snel and R. Cremer (Eds.),

Work and Aging: A European Perspective. Amsterdam: Taylor and Francis. pp. 197–211.

Barr, R. A., and Giambra, L. M. (1990) Age-related decrement in auditory selective attention, *Psychology and Aging*, 5(4): 597–599.

Beatty, P. T., and Visser, R. M. S. (2005) Introduction, in R. M. S. Visser and P. T. Beatty (Eds.), *Thriving on an Aging Workforce: Strategies for Organizational and Systematic Change.* Malabar, FL: Krieger Publishing Company. pp.3–9.

Belbin, E. (1970) The discovery method in training older workers, in H. L. Sheppard (Ed.), *Toward an Industrial Gerontology.* Cambridge MA: Schenkman. pp. 56–60.

Belbin, E., and Belbin, R. (1972) *Problems in Adult Retraining.* London, England: Heinemann.

Birdi, K., Allan, C., and Warr, P. (1997) Correlates and perceived outcomes of 4 types of employee development activity, *Journal of Applied Psychology*, 82: 845–857.

Booth, A. L. (1993) Private sector training and graduate earnings, *The Review of Economics and Statistics*, 75:164–170.

Botwinick, J. (1984) *Aging and Behavior* (3rd ed.). New York: Springer Publishing.

Bureau of Labor Statistics [BLS]. (2010) *Civilian Labor Force by Sex, Age, Race, and Ethnicity.* Retrieved January 23, 2012, from: http://www.bls.gov/EMP/EP_TABLE_304.htm

Callahan, J. S., Kiker, D. S., and Cross, T. (2003) Does method matter? A meta-analysis of the effects of training method on older learner training performance, *Journal of Management*, 29: 663–680.

Capowski, G. (1994) Ageism: The new diversity issue, *Management Review*, 83: 10–15.

Carnevale, A. P., and Stones, S. C. (1994) Developing the new competitive workforce, in J. A. Auerbach and J. C. Welsh (Eds.), *Aging and Competition: Rebuilding the US Workforce.* Washington, DC: The National Council on the Aging, Inc., and the National Planning Association. pp. 94–144.

Center on Aging and Work Workplace Flexibility, Boston College. (2007) *Age Bias and Employment Discrimination.* Issue Brief7. Boston: Author.

Charness, N., Fox, M. C. (2010) Formal training, older workers, and the IT industry, in J. A. McMullin and V. W. Marshall (Eds.), *Aging and Working in the New Economy: Changing Career Structures in Small IT Firms.* Cheltenham, UK: Edward Elgar Publishing Limited. pp.143–162.

Charness, N., Kelly, C. L., Bosman, E. A., and Mottram, M. (2001) Word-processing training and retraining: Effects of adult age, experience, and interface, *Psychology and Aging*, 16: 110–127.

Charness, N., Schumann, C. E., and Boritz, G. M. (1992) Training older adults in work processing: Effects of age, training technique, and computer anxiety, *International Journal of Technology and Aging*, 5: 79–106.

Cleveland, J., and Shore, L. (1992) Self-and supervisory perspectives on age and work attitudes and performance, *Journal of Applied Psychology*, 77: 469–484.

Cleveland, J., Shore, L., and Murphy, K. (1997) Person and context oriented perceptual age measures: Additional evidence of distinctiveness and usefulness, *Journal of Organizational Behavior*, 18: 239–251.

Colquitt, J. A., and Simmering, M. J. (1998) Conscientiousness, goal orientation, and motivation to learn during the learning process: A longitudinal study, *Journal of Applied Psychology*, 83: 654–665.

Colquitt, J. A., and LePine, J. A., and Noe, R. A. (2000) Toward an integrative theory of training motivation: A meta-analytic path analysis of 20 years of research, *Journal of Applied Psychology*, 85: 678–707.

Costello, C. (1997) *Training older workers for the future, changing work in America series.* Cambridge, MA: Radcliffe Public Policy Institute.

Delgoulet, C., and Marquie, J. C. (2002) Age differences in learning maintenance skills: A field study, *Experimental Aging Research*, 28(1): 25–37.

Dweck, C.S. (2000) *Self-theories: Their role in motivation, personality, and development.* Lillington, NC: Psychology Press.

Dywan, J., and Murphy, W. E. (1996) Aging and inhibitory control in text processing, *Psychology and Aging*, 11(2): 199–206.

Elias, P. K., Elias, M. F., Robbins, M. A., and Gage, P. (1987) Acquisition of word-processing skills by younger, middle-age, and older adults, *Psychology and Aging*, 2(4): 340–348.

Elliott, J. R. (1995) Human resource management's role in the future aging of the workforce, *Review of Public Personnel Administration*, 15(1): 5–17.

Elman, C. (1998) Adult education: Bringing in a sociological perspective, *Research on Aging*, 20(4): 379–388.

Farr, J. L., Tesluk, P. E., and Klein, S. R. (1998) Organizational structure of the workplace and the older worker, in K. W. Schaie and C. Schooler (Eds.), *Impact of work on older adults.* New York: Springer. pp. 143–185.

Ford, R., and Orel, N. (2005) Older adult learners in the workforce, *Journal of Career Development*, 32(1): 139–152.

Forte, C.S., and Hansvick, C. L. (1999) Applicant age as a subjective employability factor: A study of workers over and under age fifty, *Journal of Employment Counseling*, 36(1): 24–34.

Fossum, J. A., Arvey, R. D., Paradise, C. A., and Robbins, N. E. (1986) Modeling the skills obsolescence process: A psychological/economic integration, *Academy of Management Review*, 11(2): 362–274.

Frazis, H., Gittleman, M., and Joyce, M. (1998) *Determinants of Training: An Analysis Using Both Employer and Employee Characteristics*. Washington, DC: Bureau of Labor Statistics. Retrieved April 15, 2003, from http://www.bls.gov/ore/pdf/ec980010.pdf.

Gist, M., Rosen, B., and Schwoerer, C. (1998) The influence of training method and trainee age on the acquisition of computer skills, *Personnel Psychology*, 41(2): 255–265.

Glass, J. C. (1994) Factors affecting learning in older adults, *Educational Gerontology*, 22(4): 359–372.

Goldstein, I. L., and Goldstein, H. W. (1990) Training as an approach for organizations to the challenges of human resource issues in the year 2000, *Journal of Organizational Change Management*, 3(1): 30–43.

Gornick, M. E. (2005) A proactive approach to retaining 'wisdom workers', *Benefits and Compensation Digest*, 42(3): 18–23.

Gray, J. H., Boyce, C. A., Hall, R. J., and McDaniel, M. A. (1996) Age differences in training: Less pre-training mastery of less learning? Poster presented at the 11th annual conference of the Society for Industrial and Organizational Psychology, San Diego, CA.

Gray, L., and McGregor, J. (2003) Human resource development and older workers: Stereotypes in New Zealand, *Asia Pacific Journal of Human Resources*, 41(3): 338–353.

Hartley, D., and Biddle, E. A. (2002) Will risks to older workers change in the 21st century, *Human and Ecological Risk Assessment*, 7(7): 1885–1894.

Hasher, L., and Zacks, R. T. (1998) Working memory, comprehension, and aging: A review and new view, in G. H. Bower (Ed.), *Vol. 22, The Psychology of Learning and Motivation*. San Diego, CA: Academic Press. pp. 193–225.

Hogarth, T., and Barth, M. C. (1991) Costs and benefits of hiring older workers: A case study of B and Q, *International Journal of Manpower*, 12(8): 5–17.

Howard, A. (1995) *The Changing Nature of Work*. San Francisco, CA: Jossey-Bass.

Hoyer, W. J. (1985) Aging and the development of expert cognition, in T. M. Shlecter and M. P. Toglia (Eds.), *New Directions in Cognitive Science*. Norwood, NJ: Ablex. pp. 69–87.

Jones, B. D., and Bayen, U. J. (1998) Teaching older adults to use computers: Recommendations based on

cognitive aging research, *Educational Gerontology*, 24(7): 675–689.

Kirasic, K. C., Allen, G. L., Dobson, S. H., and Binder, K. S. (1996) Aging, cognitive resources, and declarative learning, *Psychology and Aging*, 11(4): 658–670.

Knowles, M. (1987) Adult learning, in R. Craig (Ed.), *Training and Development Handbook*. New York: McGraw-Hill. pp. 168–179.

Knowles, M. (1973) *The adult learner: A neglected species*. Houston: Gulf.

Kram, K., and Isabella, L. (1985) Mentoring alternatives: The role of peer relationships in career development, *Academy of Management Journal*, 28(1): 10–132.

Krenn, M., and Oehlke, P. (2001) *Integration of the Aging Workforce*. Retrieved September 26, 2007, from: http://ec.europa.eu/employment_social/labor_law/docs/wointegrationagingworkforce_en.pdf

Kubeck, J. E., Delp, N. D., Haslett, T. K., and McDaniel, M. A. (1996) Does job-related training performance decline with age?, *Psychology and Aging*, 11(1): 92–107.

Laguna, K., and Babcock, R. L. (1997) Computer anxiety in young and older adults: Implications for human-computer interactions in older populations, *Computers in Human Behavior*, 13(3): 317–326.

Lent, R., and Hackett, G. (1987) Career self-efficacy: Empirical status and future directions, *Journal of Vocational Behavior*, 30(3): 347–382.

Lynch, L. (1992) Private sector training and the earnings of young workers, *American Economic Review*, 82(1): 299–312.

Major, D. A., Turner, J. E., and Fletcher, T. D. (2006) Linking proactive personality and the big five to motivation to learn and development activity, *Journal of Applied Psychology*, 91(4): 927–935.

Maurer, T. J. (2001) Career-relevant learning and development, worker age, and beliefs about self-efficacy for development, *Journal of Management*, 27(1): 123–140.

Maurer, T. J., and Rafuse, N. (2001) Learning not litigating: Managing employee development and avoiding claims of age discrimination, *Academy of Management Executive*, 15(4): 110–121.

Maurer, T. J., and Tarulli, B. (1996) Acceptance of peer/upward performance appraisal system: Role of work context factors and beliefs about managers' development capability, *Human Resource Management Journal*, 35(2): 217–241.

Maurer, T. J., Weiss, E. M., and Barbeite, F. G. (2003) A model of involvement in work-related learning and development activity: The effects of individual, situational, motivational, and age variables, *Journal of Applied Psychology*, 88(4): 707–724.

Maurer, T. J., Wrenn, K. A., and Weiss, E. M. (2001) Toward understanding and managing stereotypical beliefs about older workers' ability and desire for learning and development, in: G. R. Ferris and J. J. Martocchio (Eds.), *Research in Personnel and Human Resources Management* (Vol. 22, pp.253–285). Oxford, England: Elsevier Science Ltd.

Mayer, R. E. (2001) *Multimedia Learning*. Cambridge: University Press.

McEnrue, M. P. (1989) Self-development as a career management strategy, *Journal of Vocational Behavior*, 34(1): 57–68.

Merriam, S., and Caffarella, R. (1999) *Learning in Adulthood*. San Francisco: Jossey-Bass.

Morse, C. K. (1993) Does variability increase with age? An archival study of cognitive measures, *Psychology and Aging*, 8(2): 156–164.

Mueller, J. H. (1992) Anxiety and performance, in A. P. Smith and D. M. Jones (Eds.), *Vol. 3, Handbook of Human Performance*. London: Academic Press. pp. 127–160.

Myers, C., and Conner, M. (1992) Age differences in skill acquisition and transfer in an implicit learning paradigm, *Applied Cognitive Psychology*, 6(5): 429–442.

Perry, J. S., and Varney, T. L. (1978) College student's attitudes toward workers' competence and age, *Psychological Reports*, 42(3): 1319–1322.

Rebok, G., and Offerman, L. (1983) Behavioral competencies of older college students: A self-efficacy approach, *The Gerontologist*, 23(4): 428–432.

Reed, K., Doty, D. H., and May, D. R. (2005) The impact of aging on self-efficacy and computer skills acquisition, *Journal of Managerial Issues*, 17(2): 212–228.

Rix, S. E. (1996) Investing in the future: What role for older worker training?, in W. H. Crown (Ed.), *Handbook on Employment and the Elderly*. Westport, CT: Greenwoods Press. pp. 304–323.

Rosen, B., and Jerdee, J. H. (1976a) The nature of job-related age stereotypes, *Journal of Applied Psychology*, 61(2): 180–183.

Rosen, B., and Jerdee, J. H. (1976b) The influence of age stereotypes on managerial decisions, *Journal of Applied Psychology*, 61(4): 428–432.

Rosen, N., Williams, L., and Foltman, F. (1965) Motivational constraints in an industrial retraining program, *Personnel Psychology*, 18(1): 65–79.

Royalty, A. B. (1996) The effects of job turnover on the training of men and women, *Industrial and Labor Relations Review*, 49(3): 506–521.

Salthouse, T. A. (1989) Aging and skilled performance, in A. M. Colley and J. R. Beech (Eds.), *Acquisition and Performance of Cognitive Skills*. Chichester: Wiley. pp. 248–264.

Salthouse, T. A., and Maurer, T. J. (1996) Aging, job performance, and career development, in J. Birren and K. Schaie (Eds.), *Handbook of the Psychology of Aging* (4th ed). San Diego, CA: Academic Press. pp. 353–364.

Simon, R. (1996) Too damn old, *Money*, 25: 118–126.

Simpson, P. A. (2005) Academic perspectives on training older workers, in R. M. S. Visser and P. T. Beatty (Eds.), *Thriving on an Aging Workforce: Strategies for Organizational and Systematic Change*. Malabar, FL: Krieger Publishing Company. pp.62–69.

Simpson, P. A., Greller, M. M., and Stroh, L. K. (2002) Variations in human capital investment activity by age, *Journal of Vocational Behavior*, 61(1): 109–138.

Sparrow, P. R., and Davies, D. R. (1988) Effects of age, tenure, training, and job complexity on technical performance, *Psychology and Aging*, 3(3): 307–314.

Spirduso, W., and MacRae, P. (1990) Motor performance and aging, in J. Birren and K. Schaie (Eds.), *Handbook of Psychology and Aging* . San Diego, CA: Academic Press. pp. 184–200.

Stagner, R. (1985) Aging in industry, in: J. Birren and W. Schaie (Eds.), *Handbook of Psychology of Aging* (2nd ed.). New York: Van Nostrand Reinhold Co. pp. 789–817.

Sterns, H. L. (1986) Training and retraining adult and older adult workers, in J. E. Birren, P. K. Robbinsons, and J. E. Livingston (Eds.), *Age, Health and Employment*. Englewood Cliffs, NJ: Prentice-Hall. pp. 93–113.

Sterns, H. L., and Doverspike, D. (1989) Aging and the retraining and learning process in organizations, in. I. Goldstein and R. Katzel (Eds.), *Training and Development in Work Organizations*. San Francisco, CA: Jossey-Bass. pp. 229–332.

Sterns, H. L., and Gray, J. H. (1999) Work, leisure, and retirement, in J. Cavanaugh and S. K. Whitbourne (Eds.), *Gerontology: An Interdisciplinary Perspective*. New York: Oxford University Press. pp. 355–380.

Sterns, H. L., and Miklos, S. M. (1995) The aging worker in a changing environment: Organizational and individual issues, *Journal of Vocational Behavior*, 47(3): 248–268.

Straka, J. W. (1992) The demand for older workers: The neglected side of a labor market, *Studies in Income Distribution*, No. 15. Washington DC: US Department of Health and Human Services.

Sweller, J., Chandler, P., Tierney, P., and Cooper, M. (1990) Cognitive load as a factor in the structuring of technical material, *Journal of Experimental Psychology: General*, 119(2): 176–192.

Tindall-Ford, S., Chandler, P., and Sweller, J. (1997) When two sensory modes are better than one, *Journal of Experimental Psychology: Applied*, 3(4): 257–287.

United Nations (2007) *World Economic and Social Survey 2007: Development in an Ageing World*, United Nations, New York, NY.

Van Gerven, P. W. M., Pass, F. G. W. C., and Schmidt, H. G. (2000) Cognitive load theory and the acquisition of complex cognitive skills in the elderly: Towards an integrative framework, *Educational Gerontology*, 26(6): 503–521.

Vance, D. E., Heaton, K., Fazeli, P. L., Ackerman, M. L. (2010) Aging, speed of processing training, and everyday functioning: Implications for practice and research, *Activities, Adaptations and Aging*, 34(4): 276–291.

Vanmullem, K., and Hondeghem, A. (2007) Training the older worker. Paper presented at the 5th International Conference of the Dutch HRM Network. Tilburg University, The Netherlands.

Van Vianen, A. E. M., Dalhoeven, B. A. G. W., and De Pater, I. E. (2011) Aging and training and development willingness: Employee and supervisor mindset', *Journal of Organizational Behavior*, 32, 226-247.

Waldman, D. A., and Avolio, B. J. (1986) A meta-analysis of age differences in job performance, *Journal of Applied Psychology*, 71: 33–38.

Wallen, E. S. and Mulloy, K. B. (2005) Computer based safety training: An investigation of methods, *Occupational and Environmental Medicine*, 62(4): 257–262.

Wallen, E. S. and Mulloy, K. B. (2006) Computer-based training for safety: comparing methods with older and younger workers, *Journal of Safety Research*, 37(5): 461–467.

Wallen, E. S., Plass, J. L., and Brunken, R. (2005) The function of annotations in the comprehension of scientific texts: Cognitive load effects and the impact of verbal ability, *Educational Technology Research and Development*, 53(3): 59–72.

Warr, P. B. (1994) Age and employment, in: H. C. Triandis and M. D. Dunnette (Eds), *Handbook of Industrial and Organizational Psychology*. Palo Alto, CA: Consulting Psychologists Press. pp. 485–550.

Warr, P., and Bunce, D. (1995) Trainee characteristics and the outcomes of open learning, *Personnel Psychology*, 48(2): 347–375.

Warr, P., Allan, C., and Birdi, K. (1999) Predicting three levels of training outcomes, *Journal of Occupational and Organizational Psychology*, 72(3): 351–375.

17

Older Workers in the Professions: Learning Challenges and Strategies

Tara Fenwick

INTRODUCTION

Policy focus on older workers (50+ years of age) has steadily increased in many countries concerned about retaining these workers in the paid labour force – more specifically, retaining skilled and satisfied older workers (EU 2007, HRDC 2000, HRSDC 2013, OECD 2006, UK 2006). These policies are often linked to concerns for increased ratios of aging citizens to active workers, projections of a general critical shortage in skilled labour, and evidence of workplace ageism and exclusion. Studies have shown, for example, that older workers experience devaluing of their knowledge, stereotyping, subtle barriers to learning opportunities, and pressure to present themselves as younger and technologically savvy (Ainsworth 2006, Carroll 2007). Policy measures have been directed to address these issues, argues Weller (2007), in four main domains: removing regulatory structures that may discourage older workers' participation in employment, highlighting their work skills and other positive

contributions, encouraging participation through 'moral' injunctions to serve the labour market, and penalizing employers that discriminate.

Older workers' *learning* has also been identified as an important potential lever to counter perceived declining skill relevance of older workers. In Canada, for example, policy has focused on encouraging older workers' greater access to and participation in learning opportunities (HRDC 2000, HRSDC 2013). This focus is premised on assumptions that older workers engage less than younger workers in skill development, and generally do not participate in work learning as much as would be desirable to increase their employability and retain them in the labour market.

However, only limited evidence has been produced yet to examine the actual nature of older workers' engagement in learning. These studies indicate that the story is more complex than simply increasing older workers' access to learning. First, it appears that older workers may have unique attitudes to learning and perhaps even distinct approaches and processes for work learning (Canning 2011, Tikkanen and Nyhan 2006). Second, many have argued that these workers' learning cannot be simply understood in human capital terms as increasing individuals' acquisition of skills, but must be linked to workplace culture and its embedded learning opportunities (Fuller and Unwin 2005), and analysed in the context of capitalist relations that produce and value particular kinds of knowledge and work (Moore 2009, Roberts 2006, Porcellato et al. 2010). In general, Tikkanen and Nyhan (2006) conclude that older workers' learning is poorly understood, contributing to its low recognition and support in work organizations.

A further issue is that the few available studies have concentrated on non-professionals such as workers in hospitality or trades. If we turn to professionals and professional learning, much literature has accumulated to examine the learning of early career professionals, but little attention has focused on *older* professionals' learning. Even if we acknowledge the problematic category of 'older workers' (Roberts 2006), the fact remains that policy and related programmes are continuing to target this group for rehabilitation. Among professional groups, where continuous work learning has been emphasized as an important dynamic in late capitalism's global economy to supply flexible, multi-skilled and entrepreneurial knowledge workers), the case of older workers throws up additional questions. How do these older *professionals* conceptualize their work knowledge and learning in the face of increased demands for continuous learning? In what specific ways, and to what extent, do older professionals participate in learning?

These are the questions addressed in this chapter. The discussion centres upon research conducted in Canada to examine the professional learning of older Certified Management Accountants (CMAs).[1] Like other professionals in the financial sector, this group may be particularly pressured by changing financial regulations and industry

restructuring in 'new capitalism' (Sennett 2006) to maintain a high level of skill and skill adaptability. The chapter proceeds in four sections, beginning with a more detailed discussion of age and learning in the workplace. The second section describes the methods and population of the study, and the third presents findings showing older professionals' distinct approaches to and conceptions of learning. The concluding section argues that far from withdrawing from learning, these older professionals are particularly focused in what, when and how they engage. While few position themselves as critical or resistant to the intensified learning demands towards adding organizational value, many of these workers seem strategic and self-protective in their compliance. In fact most are astute in employing diverse strategies and resources in knowledge development, according to the knowledge orientation they adopt in their practice. These understandings may suggest ways to more effectively recognize and support older professionals' learning in organizations and professional associations.

CONCEPTIONS OF OLDER WORKERS' LEARNING AND PROFESSIONAL LEARNING

The category and definition of 'older worker' is troublesome, as Roberts (2006) has argued, partly because it makes little sense to abstract one age group from the intergenerational mix of work and knowledge activity to study in isolation. However, given the current policy emphases on older workers, the category is useful to retain if workplace research is to contribute to these policy debates. For purposes of this discussion, an 'older worker' is defined simply as 50+ years of age, following the delineation adopted in Europe and Canada (EU 2007, HRDC 2000). In studies examining issues pertaining to older workers, three inter-related issues have been raised: ageism, perceptions of older workers' insufficient competency; and lower participation in learning.

Some studies have focused on ageism in the workplace. Their evidence has raised concerns that age-related discrimination and discourses of 'decline' and obsolescence have generated negative stereotypes and ultimately, devaluing of aging workers by colleagues and employers, constructing them as 'problems' taking up jobs and resources (Ainsworth 2006, Carroll 2007). This ageism may function in very subtle ways, to the point of invisibility for many workers including those 50+. Or, it may only materialize clearly at the point of recruitment and selection, as Weller (2007) argues, where most of the 33 interviewees in her study claimed to have experienced age discrimination in some form in their search for employment. It also is likely the case that age is viewed differently in different vocational sectors, or different organizational settings. Ainsworth (2006) shows, for instance, that older workers are perceived as more acceptable in some professions such as law than in others such as the high tech industry. But stated views and everyday practices are, of course, not necessarily consistent. A body of research has accumulated revealing that even in cases where organizational rhetoric praises traits such as reliability, personal maturity, stability and punctuality that are assumed to characterize older workers, in practice what are valued and rewarded are the flexible dynamism and technological competence associated with younger workers (Riach 2007, McVittie et al. 2003).

Older workers' learning has become a particular policy focus through a perception that their qualifications become obsolescent or devalued in their current employment, and inadequate to permit entry to new employment (Porcellato et al. (2010). There is also some evidence of older workers' underparticipation in learning opportunities (Pillay et al. 2003). This may partly be their own choice not to participate due for example to low self confidence and negative self perceptions (Porcellato 2006: 493) and partly to lack of provision. Billett and van Woerkom (2008: 336) claim that 'the evidence consistently suggests that across Europe, employers are far more likely to spend funds on training the young and well-educated, rather than older workers'. Concern over inequitable training provisions have sparked further policy response. In Canada for instance, where this study was conducted, the national Human Resources and Skills Development department launched a major Targeted (training) Initiative for Older Workers to help retain or re-integrate older workers into the workforce (HRSDC 2007).

Such concerns must be understood within broader discourses demanding continuous learning in the workplace, where learning is represented often uncritically as a requirement for all workers in a fast-changing technologized knowledge economy emphasizing innovation, entrepreneurism and resilience (Organisation for Economic Co-operation and Development 1996). Notions of workers' learning and skill development framed in the rational assumptions of human capital accumulation often fail to account for the non-linear, participative processes that are now widely understood to characterize workers' learning (*inter alia*, Billett 2002, Bratton et al. 2003, Hager 2004, Hodkinson et al. 2008). Work-related learning has been demonstrated in many contemporary studies to be interwoven with individuals' identities and desires as well as the social relations and cultural-historical dynamics of particular communities, discourses and activities (Evans et al. 2006, Rainbird et al. 2004). In terms of older workers' learning, policy rhetoric still expresses concerns at their need, for instance, to acquire technological skills and capacity to adapt to changing workplaces (Pillay et al. 2003).

But there is more to this story. Older workers' learning is not often very well understood and therefore not always appropriately supported – indeed, as Weller (2007) showed, older workers say they encounter direct barriers to learning opportunities. One European study of 27 small-medium enterprises in England, Finland and Norway (Tikkanen and Nyhan 2006) found that while both older and younger workers are challenged by the same changes in working life, technology and workplace structures, older workers' learning is not acknowledged and developed to the extent of younger workers. In Canada, researchers examined the extent to which collective agreements in each province responded to the call for retraining older workers to meet new information technology demands imposed by organizations. They found that training opportunities and resources for older workers varied greatly by sector and specific organization (Fourzly and Gervais, 2002). Older workers were more often called upon to mentor younger workers than to participate in learning opportunities themselves. The study called for more awareness of older workers' learning needs, greater recognition and valuing of their strengths, and more inclusive support of their lifelong learning including targeted initiatives and promotion of intergenerational learning in the workplace.

In comparing companies in the UK, Fuller and Unwin (2005) found that older workers' attitudes to learning and uptake of opportunities for meaningful workplace learning depended very much on the way that these opportunities were embedded, supported and managed within a wider culture of workforce development. Among older hospitality workers in particular, Canning (2011) found that their learning is best supported and their contributions to the organization maximized by *valuing* their experience and emphasizing team building. That is, instead of emphasizing older workers' acquisition of new skills, organizations should focus on utilizing the skills that older workers have already developed, within arrangements of collaborative practice and opportunities for informal mentoring. However, older workers' participation in learning also appears to depend on their own beliefs about knowledge. Pillay et al. (2003), in studies of hospital administrative/security staff and transport workers, concluded that more older workers held 'low level' conceptions of learning, viewing work as a routine job and learning as acquiring skills to survive – beliefs which the researchers noted were inconsistent with a workplace

culture of knowledge generation and critical reflection. Billett and van Woerkom (2008) examined similar phenomena of older workers' 'personal epistemologies' among six health care workers in a psychiatric clinic, but differentiated them according to their performance ratings as high or low. While both groups engaged in critical reflection for learning, Billett and van Woerkom observed that the 'low-regarded' workers focused their learning more on simply maintaining their practice rather than upon goals valued by managers – goals echoing knowledge economy discourses of innovation, continuous knowledge development and so forth.

The results are certainly mixed, and suggest that older workers' different engagements in learning are mutually related to vocational cultures, the nature of work activity/knowledge, and broader discourses establishing what knowledge counts most. Overall, researchers have raised a collective call for nuanced and differentiated research to understand how older workers themselves understand and approach learning, understood as embedded within particular work practices, knowledge traditions and environments.

Turning to professional groups, the issue of older workers' learning has not yet begun to attract much attention. Professionals' learning is particularly interesting given the rapidly changing knowledges and professionalisms reported in a growing body of research (*inter alia*, Evetts 2009, Guile 2010, Nerland and Jensen 2010). Individuals are pressured to become more flexible and entrepreneurial to adapt to radical shifts in public demands, decline in professional authority and discretion, and sharp drops in institutional resources (Evetts 2003). External accountability requirements and managerial regulation of professionals' autonomy have increased alongside proliferating new knowledge resources and technologies. Emphasis on professionals' continuous lifelong learning is growing, and increasingly audited through assessment of professionals' annual participation in learning activities to meet a minimum standard (Fenwick 2009). Stronach et al.

(2002) show how public service professionals juggle these different discourses simultaneously: the 'economies of performance' and
the 'ecologies of practice', in everyday work
that reflects multiple performances of identity and professionalism. In general, Evetts
(2009) argues that professionalism is shifting
more to an organizational orientation and
away from an occupational professional alle-
giance. That is, professional practices and
outputs are increasingly determined more by
organizational demands and measures and
less by the professional disciplines and community. Expectations for inter-professional
collaboration have increased, demanding
new knowledge through 'co-production'
work (Lee and Dunston 2009), and new competencies in 'relational agency' (Edwards
2007) to build common knowledge across
what Nerland and Jensen (2010) refer to as
professionals' 'epistemic communities'. In
fact Nerland (2010) argues that *knowledge*
dynamics need to be foregrounded in professional practice in terms of knowledge
resources, ties and strategies. These forces
and their consequent tensions affect all professionals, but perhaps particularly those
older professionals who may be expected to
lead and mentor others through such changes,
as well as to adapt to difficult new demands
without the same developmental support
and understanding extended to their younger
colleagues.

STUDY METHODS AND POPULATION

The study, conducted in 2008–2009 in
Alberta Canada, focused on older (50+ years)
professional Certified Management Accountants (CMAs). The CMA group seemed
particularly appropriate for a study of professional learning for four main reasons.
First, CMAs are continually subject to massive changes presumably requiring constant
learning: national regulations in tax structures, international financial regulations,
and new IT systems. They also appear to

experience relatively high occupational
mobility, with job changes across diverse
sectors ranging from heavy construction or
oil and gas to government or retail, and
across diverse roles ranging from financial
systems analysis to senior management, with
many changes demanding new specialist
expertise. Second, more often than not,
CMAs do not work with other CMAs: many
firms or organization units would hire only
one CMA as Controller. Therefore, common
models of professional learning in a 'community of practice', or organization-based
mentorship and training do not necessarily
apply easily to CMAs.

A surprisingly large number of 117 older
CMAs volunteered for the interviews, and
we selected 60 (32 women and 28 men) to
represent a range of experiences in participants' years of experience and current
employment (sector, organizational size and
type). Two-thirds of the sample were aged
50–54, fifteen were 55–59, and five were
60–65. One-third worked in large businesses
(engineering, law, construction, insurance,
forestry), one-sixth in different multi-national
oil and gas companies, and one-sixth in government departments (municipal, provincial
and federal). Of the remainder, six individuals were instructors in post-secondary
institutions, five worked in not-for-profit
organizations, two in large banks, five were
independent consultants, and two were
unemployed. Interviews explored the individual's meanings, practices, values and
motives in their work-related learning, how
these have changed over time, particular
challenges or opportunities in learning
experienced as an older worker, and desired
supports for learning. What struck us in
particular was the confident, strategic positions that these older professionals took up
in relation to learning pressures and continuous change. What follows is an overview of
these positionings: first in terms of an
entitlement to control one's learning, and
secondly in terms of adopting a particular
orientation to knowledge and knowledge
development.

'I'M IN CONTROL': LEARNING AS FOCUSING AND MANAGING KNOWLEDGE

In contrast to a strong theme in the literature, most of these older professionals recalled relatively little age-related discrimination. In further contrast, most indicated enthusiastic and wide-ranging participation in work-related learning. Professional learning was commonly portrayed as a fundamental responsibility, even a pleasure, and an important part of their organizational roles. All indicated that they drew from wide-ranging knowledge resources, most of which were informal (unplanned and rooted in everyday activity). They readily identified moments and events as 'learning' activities that are not often recognized as such by workers: hallway conversations, surfing the web, solving problems, meeting informally with colleagues, and so forth. Only five interviewees referred to continuing professional development sessions offered by the CMA association as helpful: others described the content as too general or basic for their needs, using methods they didn't find useful. Interviewees were quite clear, for instance, about whether or not they learned effectively through 'network' gatherings. Most had developed strategies and confidence to access less evident knowledge sources. One had created his own knowledge network, another had sought out webinars hosted by different financial agencies, and several were sufficiently confident to contact knowledge elites directly:

If I need information, I go to the experts on the subject. So, take carbon capture and storage for instance. Go to the expert to find out, you know, where can we capture this stuff and, you know, where can, where could we possibly store it? Who is going to build the pipeline and how do we go about doing that?

Above all, focus was valued, often described in terms of a late career stage.

Your time becomes more precious. You're more aware of where you want to spend your time. I think that you're less interested in career development and growth. You really want to just target in on the things that you're interested in. (male VP of finance and administration, insurance, 52)

Some chose a specialist knowledge focus, such as in international auditing which required developing new competence, as a way to remain competitive and employable. Others spoke of focusing as being about learning to negotiate, and to avoid being overwhelmed by the increasing onslaught of information.

One of the problems that I actually struggle with is how much we have coming at us, so to try to sort that out as to what is important and what isn't. It's just impossible to take it all in. And so part of my learning now is learning how to figure out what I actually need and to pay attention to that and let the rest go. (woman senior manager, international chartered accounting firm, 60)

As this senior manager notes, one eventually learns to accept that keeping up with everything is impossible and that it is okay to be selective. There were also some references to age-related weariness influencing individuals' tendency to limit and focus their participation in learning activities: '*when you come home, you're tired*' (male financial supervisor for multi-national oil and gas firm, 58).

Overall, it became clear that advanced CMAs – which described most of the interviewees – felt, or expected to feel, personal control over how, when, and for what purposes they engaged in learning. They also expected to use knowledge resources and strategies that they believed worked best for their own needs at specific times.

I'm choosing to learn, whereas 10 years ago others chose. This is what I do for a living and these are the areas that I need to improve to better do what I'm doing. I'm actually learning more than when I was working years ago … because what I'm choosing to learn is related to what I'm doing, it's more specific. Right now I'm more in control. (male, controller of small tool business, 50)

This expectation of exercising control of their learning is perhaps obvious given the 'controller' positions that so many occupied. But beyond the influence of professional role, these older professionals seemed particularly strategic and deliberate in focusing their endeavors to develop knowledge. Most positioned themselves confidently as knowers: expert on some things and weak in others, and concerned with mastering only what they themselves had identified to be immediately important:

> I'm totally out of touch with accounting ... sophisticated modeling is definitely something I'm not learning. I'm not quite sure if I have the inclination and the energy to even learn that stuff. But that is an area that I'm kind of I'm weak in ... [what's important to me is] to keep abreast with what is happening out there, for instance on the climate change front. Like, so I need to know how the Europeans are thinking about it. How the Japanese and Australians are thinking. How the Americans are thinking and this is where the reading becomes critical, right? (male, senior business adviser, large oil and gas corporation, 58)

This became most evident when interviewees described the annual external assessments of their learning conducted by the CMA Association. All but three of the 60 expressed strong resentment about being treated as 'learners'.

> The constant logging learning activities is onerous I've got enough paperwork and files. That's the last thing I'm going to think about before I go home at night. It takes away from what you assume is something that is part of your professional obligation anyhow. (male, chief accountant, pulp mill, 56)

> They treat you like a school kid a bit. I suppose that's an old guy thing. I don't like being treated like a school kid. (man, manager large chemical firm, 59)

> Here I am and I'm advancing and people respect me and they really want me to do their work and yet I still have to prove that I'm learning. It seems kind of weird. (man, systems analyst, international concrete manufacturer, 57)

These statements are reminiscent of Boud and Solomon's (2003) contention that workers dislike the 'learner' label because of its incompatibility with their identities as 'competent workers'. However particularly here, these older professionals positioned themselves as knowers worthy of respect. They expected to be trusted to assess and develop their own knowledge.

LEARNING TO POSITION ONESELF TO PROFESSIONAL LEARNING

Looking more closely at this broad theme of older professionals positioning themselves as knowers with control over their learning strategies and focus, some distinctions appeared in terms of their actual orientations to knowledge. That is, individuals' overall direction and specific foci for knowledge development appeared to be oriented in different ways, and some similarities began to emerge across these orientations. These orientations were not clearly linked to any specific sectors of work, or specific forms of professional practices or roles. Instead, they seemed to reflect diverse deliberate ways to position oneself in late career amidst the onslaught of professional change and information. Four orientations were identified, which we called consolidating, outreaching, re-directing, and disengaging. Like all categorizations, these four orientations are fallible: the boundaries must be understood to be blurred and overlapping at best, and the categories indicative rather than definitive.

Consolidating

One orientation to learning reflected among these older professionals could be described as a 'consolidating' approach. This orientation reflected a desire to deepen and focus what one already knew, rather than seeking new information or developing new specialisms.

> All I need to do is keep myself aware of changes in the areas that are relevant to my clients. So instead of continually increasing and adding new knowledge and skills as I would have done and did do 15 years, 20 years ago now I'm simply broadening the knowledge base that's relevant to me at this point. (woman independent accounting practice, 52)

Individuals that reflected more of a consolidating orientation seemed to be particularly strategic, choosing knowledge according to what they needed at that particular time to consolidate their expertise. More than any other orientation they described themselves as 'focused', or as 'being choosey'. One woman, a 52-year-old government administrator who had been a practicing CMA over 21 years and four job changes, reframed her focus in professional learning as being more about 'practicing what I've learned over the years'. She talked about consolidating and deepening her existing knowledge base, 'honing the quality', instead of attempting to learn new knowledge. Some described a careful parsimonious approach, 'learning according to what the project needs' or 'just learning what's needed to keep up'. There were references to the need to focus selectively, given the overwhelming demands and information.

One of the problems that I actually struggle with is how much we have coming at us, so to try to sort that out as to what is important and what isn't. It's just impossible to take it all in. And so part of my learning now is learning how to figure out what I actually need and to pay attention to that and let the rest go. (woman senior manager for international chartered accounting firm, 60)

Outreaching

A second learning orientation, in some ways representing an opposite movement to consolidating, was what could be characterized as 'outreaching'. Older CMAs whose learning descriptions reflected an outreaching or divergent orientation described themselves in terms of 'stretching', 'insatiable' for new knowledge, and 'learning what's of interest to me'. For example, one woman Chief Financial Officer for a large health not-for-profit organization, 50 years of age, described a wide variety of learning pursuits as tied in with her own attitude of energy, 'following what's interesting, what I feel like doing ... I'm not dictated by what's needed for my career'. Another, particularly enthusiastic, example was a 56-year-old man who had worked for the federal taxation

office for 28 years and was planning to retire in two years and open an accounting consulting practice. He had recently begun a postgraduate degree in business, but was also undertaking other courses in computer-assisted auditing for personal interest. He went on to list other passionate interests that he pursued through learning activities in Chinese, yachting and photography.

Two individuals who were currently unemployed also described their orientation to learning in terms of seeking challenge and 'stretching'. One, a 58-year-old woman described herself with 'an insatiable appetite to learn', but feeling that sometimes she was 'unable to pull together knowledge'. The other, a 56-year-old who had been made redundant from a large bank and actively seeking work, was in the meantime enjoying seeking ad-hoc learning opportunities through volunteering on different boards, contracting with health care, and attending arts lectures. Beyond these two individuals who were not tied to any particular organization at the time of interviewing, the others who reflected this diverging inclination said they chose learning endeavors according to what questions interested them most. In some cases this was related to the job, and in others to their broader lives. As a 52-year-old sales manager said, 'learning is not about what will help me at work, but is it interesting and relevant to my life now – is it about the bigger me'.

Overall, an 'outreaching' orientation does not appear to be particularly linked with employment status or success, role, access to resources and networks, or even proximity to retirement. In fact, the motivating theme voiced by many interviewees who we associated with outreaching was similar to those who performed a more consolidating orientation to knowledge: a commitment and the confidence as an older professional to follow one's own interests in knowledge development.

Re-positioning

A third learning orientation suggested a decision to re-direct or re-position one's knowledge development in a new focus. Sometimes this was related to a new job, or a decision to reframe one's job – not just another career transition involving new learning, but a major re-directing of one's energies and professional identity. One 54-year-old man who had left his position as director of finance due to company restructuring, for example, said that he was now deliberately re-positioning himself by learning cost accounting for specific implementations. Another had, at 59, decided to become the ERP (enterprise resource planning) expert at his chemical firm: he explained that he had watched this area grow in importance, and finally had decided to learn all he could about it as his final contribution to the company. He also was clearly re-positioning himself as a knower within the firm, as someone with valuable and recognizable knowledge to offer.

In direct contrast to literature expressing concern about older workers' capacity or willingness to learn in and for such major adjustments, these professionals expressed enthusiasm for the knowledge development processes required in re-positioning. One woman, 62, who left a job as systems analyst in manufacturing after 15 years to become controller for an insurance firm, describing this as a 'big change in scope of responsibility and nature of activity, explains this willingness:

> [T]he learning is easier now than in previous job shifts. Before it was a struggle to find out how to do it, who I had to talk to, who I had to get authorization from. Now it's a lot easier – because, my age, you know, the confidence in what I'm doing and the maturity from my age.

The increased ease and desire for learning as an older professional is attributed not only to personal confidence and 'contentment' with one's own decisions and positions as a knower, but also to the increased learning opportunities that some felt they enjoyed in later career stages.

> I've reached a level that I'm comfortable at. I'm content. And that changes your perspective on a

> lot of things. But my intensity and my desire and need to learn has increased over the past five years compared to 10–15 yrs ago. It's because the job that I have, there is more to it, responsibility and scope. If there is something I need to learn I want to learn it. It's a question of an opportunity to learn. (male, senior bank manager, 59)

About one-third of this group talked explicitly about re-positioning themselves to mentor the knowledge development of younger professionals: '*ending my career doing something really, really good. Really positive and to help someone, you know, really help them to be successful*'. One explained this as a general re-positioning away from self-interest to promoting others:

> You're progressing in your career and moving upwards and want to have the sharpest best skills to move ahead, show you're better than others, and continue to be promoted. Then you reach a certain stage of a career where it becomes less self-focused and a progression to mentoring others. This starts to drive areas you're more interested in, which tend to be more around leadership and management capability – that's what I can help others in my organization with rather than the technical skills. (male, corporate secretary multi-national oil and gas company, 57)

Whether re-directing their knowledge development focus to their own new job and new area of expertise, or to developing other, younger professionals' knowledge, these older professionals appear to do so deliberately, strategically and enthusiastically. More than a simple transition, this orientation seems to reflect changes that shift one's professional learning in fundamentally new directions. As one woman explained, '*Re-positioning is about re-positioning your own knowledge identity*'.

Disengaging

A much smaller percentage of the interviewees reflected an orientation to knowledge development that was more about distancing than re-engaging in learning. Here, this orientation has been termed 'disengaging', but this should not be taken to indicate resistance or any sort of disengagement from good professional practice or from knowledge practices in particular. More accurately, these older professionals described themselves variously as 'slowing down', 'phasing myself out', or as 'giving the new guys the training'. This position was most often expressed in relation to impending retirement:

Of course I'm gearing up, I don't have that many years, so you know you get this kind of ender's disease where you're going to go pretty quick, so – how much do you want to invest in a project? I don't really want to learn this new model and these new skills. (woman, academic in a business faculty, 61)

Besides a personal decline in developing new professional knowledge, there was also a sense of wasted organizational resources.

Would you send me and spend 5 to $7,000, when I only got two to three years to be here? when the guy two doors over is more likely going to be the chief accountant and maybe you'd be bringing him up to speed.... What I'm more interested in learning is, do I have enough to retire on and what do I need to do to retire? (male chief accountant, pulp mill, 59)

Clearly, too, at least some older professionals were turning to focus more on knowledge related to their lives post-employment. However, some indicated a sense of having learned as much as they could with no real desire to develop any further knowledge, at least, not in terms of their professional work. One man, 63, a controller at an engineering firm, described his learning as having '*slowed down, I've already covered most of what's on offer*'. Another man, 61, controller at a large construction firm said that although he had no interest in retiring, that there also was '*not much more I can learn to do the job better – life has stabilized*'. One man explained that '*fifteen years ago I was more accepting and gung-ho [about learning] ... I don't see anything I need to develop at this stage*'. There is in these statements a suggestion of a learning trajectory, one that was more active at

some period in the past, but which has come to rest with the contentment of one's practice and position as a knower.

While interviewees who expressed a 'disengaging' orientation to professional learning and knowledge development were mostly in their late 50s or early-mid 60s, it must be recalled that other professionals in this age group expressed very different orientations of increased engagement, either in consolidating, outreaching, or re-positioning their knowledge. Nonetheless, it seems natural that at least some individuals were conscious of shifting interests as they enacted a final stage of a professional career, preparing for what came next.

CONCLUSIONS

Amidst the increasing concerns about retention and development of older workers, particularly through increasing what has been perceived to be their declining participation in continuous learning, research has shown that older workers are a complex group that cannot be universalized with such assumptions. We focused specifically on professionals, asking: How do these older accounting professionals conceptualize their work knowledge and learning in the face of increased demands for continuous learning? In what specific ways, and to what extent, do older professionals participate in learning? We found, first, that these older professionals engaged intensively and eclectically in developing knowledge through wide-ranging resources and strategies, in some cases more intensively than they recalled doing so in their earlier career periods. Second, these older professionals were particularly focused and strategic in *how* they engaged with knowledge. Most also resisted being viewed and assessed as 'learners', particularly evident in the almost unanimous resentment of the 'school kid' requirement to submit annual records of their 'professional learning activities'. They expected to decide for themselves what knowledge to develop and how. They expressed a sense of position and capacity as knowers, understanding their own priorities according to the demands of particular professional situations and roles, and deliberately selecting knowledge strategies accordingly. Again and again they referred to finding freedom, as older professionals, from learning driven by others' decisions of what knowledge was most valuable – whether in relation to managers' goals, accreditation requirements, professional development courses, or just the general onslaught of change and new information.

However it is useful to note that the kinds of knowledge they spoke about was, with very few exceptions, all related to improvement of professional practices. That is, almost all examples of learning offered by these older professionals focused on job performance rather than on critical questioning of factors compelling particular job performances or privileging particular knowledges. Clearly their narratives revealed many of the dynamics dominating literature about changing professionalisms and conditions of practice: the shift to organizational accountabilities with increased audit and managerialism (Evetts 2009), the co-production and interprofessional work arrangements (Lee and Dunston 2009), and the intensified workload and pace of change. However, most interviewees seemed comfortably accustomed to manouevring in and around these structures to balance what Stronach et al. (2002) called the conflicting discourses of 'ecologies of practice' with 'economies of performance'. That is, in each new situation whether a job change or new regulatory protocol, most figured out the activities and level of challenge that suited them most, then arranged ways to learn what they needed to engage these effectively. While some mentioned the relentless pace of change and the deluge of information, and incidentally the need for self-protective strategies of focusing and selecting what they engaged with, none registered critical concern about this change other than a few mentions of being 'tired'. In fact, many of their own knowledge development strategies were for adapting to continuous organizational restructuring, new

jobs and new procedures. Yet they didn't simply continue to drift through different knowledges according to demands of market and organization: they adopted orientations like 'consolidating' and 're-positioning' through which they created a stance, an anchor for themselves, almost a self-protective way of retaining recognizable value without being forced to continually 'shapeshift' to adapt to new work orders (Gee et al. 1996). In total there seemed to be, among these older professional workers, little critical challenge to the larger systems and forces in which they they worked, and in fact they appeared to accept the demand for their personal resilience. While almost all resented the drive for learning exerted by their professional association, this resentment never appeared to be directed at the pace or structure of their work organizations themselves.

Overall, these older professionals appeared to determine for themselves, and to defend, particular positions as knowers. This discussion highlighted four orientations to knowledge development that emerged in their descriptions of themselves as knowers and their knowledge-seeking endeavors. These four orientations of consolidating, outreaching, re-positioning, and disengaging are intended to suggest broad and overlapping tendencies, not discrete categories or a comprehensive typology. More accurately, they can be taken to suggest identifiable differences across older professionals in how they position and direct their learning, while demonstrating a strong general commitment to and interest in learning. Only a small percentage reflect the sorts of disengagement from continuous professional learning that have been envisioned in a general policy concern about older workers' participation. This finding alone raises interesting questions about how little we may understand older professionals' approaches to and participation in learning.

Most prescriptions for older workers and learning begin and end with recommendations for more learning opportunities to be provided. This study suggests that rather different approaches might be more helpful. First, employers and the professional association perhaps should be concerned less with provision of learning/training and more with explicit recognition and valuing of mature professionals' knowledge, their views of professional knowledge, and their approaches to learning. Second, processes for assessment of learning may focus less on listing quantities of personal learning activities and more on engaging older professionals in explaining their current areas of interest, the resources/activities that they find most useful, or the ways they are fostering knowledge development in their organizations. Third, employers and professional associations might take time to understand older professionals' unique orientation to knowledge development, and their reasons for this orientation. Some may desire new challenges, others to deepen what they already know, some more explicit opportunities to share knowledge with colleagues, and others to focus on learning for a new, post-employment sphere of living.

Finally, given the disparity between this study's findings and previous research indicating older workers' lower participation in learning (Pillay et al. 2003, Porcellato 2006), there clearly is need for greater precision in conceptualizing the category of 'older worker'. Perhaps important distinctions accrue to professionally trained knowledge workers, or to practitioners in the financial sector, or to professionals experiencing high rates of change in regulations or job change. It is also possible that older professionals' engagements in learning vary regionally, culturally and historically: the findings of this study of management accountants trained in the 1970s and 1980s practicing in oil-rich western Canada just prior to the global financial crisis may be very different from studies based in parts of Europe at the present historic moment. Further comparative research on different locations, disciplines and work arrangements of older workers and older professional workers, in context of changing regulations, expectations and conditions of

practice, may be very useful in the general development of this body of research.

This study has established that at least some groups of older professionals take professional learning very seriously, on their own terms. They position themselves in diverse ways as knowers and are strategic and focused in accessing learning strategies related to these particular knowledge orientations, which may range from consolidating to outreaching, or from re-positioning to disengaging. Policy development might consider a dual foci: first, promoting employers' and professional associations' recognition and valuing of older professionals' distinctive and contextually effective knowledge strategies; and second, promoting wider understanding and response to older professionals' adoption of particular knowledge orientations. While these may not on the surface appear to be consistent with fashionable notions of continuous innovation, they may offer a more realistic insight into how people actually engage knowledge and position themselves as knowers in mature career stages.

ACKNOWLEDGMENTS

This chapter is based on articles published in *Vocations and Learning* (Fenwick 2012a) and *Human Relations* (Fenwick 2012b).

NOTE

1 The two-year study 'Informal learning and the Older Professional Worker: Learning Practices, Challenges and Supports' conducted 2008–2009 in Alberta was funded by the Canada Council for Learning/CCA. Sixty individuals 50+ were interviewed and 270 were surveyed. Full details of the study and methods are available in Fenwick (2012a) and Fenwick (2012b).

REFERENCES

Ainsworth, S. (2006) 'Constructing older workers: Cultural meanings of age and work', in M. Hearn and G. Michelson (eds.), *Rethinking Work: Time,*

Space and Discourse (pp. 308–328). Port Melbourne, Victoria: Cambridge University Press.

Billett, S. (2002) 'Critiquing workplace learning discourses: Participation and continuity at work', *Studies in the Education of Adults*, 34 (1): 56–67.

Billett, S, and van Woerkom, M. (2008). Personal epistemologies and older workers. *International Journal of Lifelong Education*, 27 (3): 333–348.

Boud, D., and Solomon, N. (2003) '"I don't think I am a learner": acts of naming learners at work', *Journal of Workplace Learning*, 15 (7/8): 326–331.

Bratton, J., Mills, J.H., Pyrch, T., and Sawchuk, P. (2003) *Workplace Learning: A Critical Introduction*. Aurora, ON: Garamond Press.

Canning, R. (2011). Older workers in the hospitality industry: Valuing experience and informal learning. International Journal of Lifelong Education 30 (5), 667–679.

Carroll, T. (2007) 'Curious conceptions: Learning to be old', *Studies in Continuing Education*, 29 (1): 71–84.

CMA (2000) *Certified Management Accountants Regulation Part 1 Division 3, Section 15(a),(i).* Continuous Professional Learning and Development Policy. Available at: http://www.cma-alberta.com/8/4/8/5/index1.shtml

Edwards, A. (2007) 'Relational agency in professional practice: A CHAT analysis', *International Journal of Human Activity Theory*, 1 (1): 1–17.

EU (2007) *EQUAL Life Competence 50+ Project.* European Commission: Employment Social Affairs and Equal Opportunities News. Available at: http://ec.europa.eu/employment_social/equal/news/200707-got_en.cfm

Evans, Karen, Unwin, Lorna, Rainbird, Helen, and Hodkinson, Phil. (2006) *Improving Workplace Learning*. London: Taylor & Francis.

Evetts, J. (2003) 'The sociological analysis of professionalism: occupational changes in the modern world', *International Sociology*, 18: 395–415.

Evetts, J. (2009) 'New professionalism and new public management: Changes, continuities and consequences', *Comparative Sociology*, 8: 247–66.

Fenwick, T. (2009) 'Making to measure? Reconsidering assessment in professional continuing education', *Studies in Continuing Education*, 31 (3): 229–244.

Fenwick, T. (2012a) 'Learning among older professional workers: knowledge strategies and knowledge orientations', *Vocations and Learning*, 5(3): 203–23.

Fenwick, T. (2012b) 'Older professional workers and continuous learning in new capitalism', *Human Relations*, 65(8): 1001–20.

Fourzly, M. and Gervais, M. (2002) 'Collective agreements and older workers in Canada', *Human Resources Development Canada*, Ottawa, Ontario. Retrieved on May 14, 2009 from: http://www.rhdsc.gc.ca/en/lp/spila/wlb/caowc/04overview.shtml

Fuller, A. and Unwin, L. (2005) 'Older and wiser? Workplace learning from the perspective of experienced employees', *International Journal of Lifelong Education*, 24(1): 21–39.

Guile, David. (2010) *The Learning Challenge of the Knowledge Economy*. Rotterdam: Sense Publishers.

Hager, P. (2004) 'Lifelong learning in the workplace? Challenges and issues', *Journal of Workplace Learning*, 16 (1/2): 22–33.

Hodkinson, P., Biesta, G., and James, D. (2008) 'Understanding learning culturally: Overcoming the dualism between individual and social learning', *Vocations and Learning*, 1 (1): 27–47.

HRDC (Human Resources Development Canada) (2000) *Older worker adjustment programs: lessons learned,* HRDC, Ottawa, ON Available at: http://www11.hrdc-drhc.gc.ca/pls/edd/v_report.a?p_site=EDD&sub=OWAP

HRSDC (2013) Funding: Employment assistance for older workers. Ottawa, ON: Human Resources & Social Development Canada. Available at http://www.hrsdc.gc.ca/eng/jobs/older_workers/index.shtml [accessed 25 April 2013].

HRSDC (2011). Canada's aging workforce: A National Conference on Maximizing Employment Opportunities for Mature Workers. Public Policy Forum. Ottawa, ON: Human Resources & Social Development Canada. Available at ppforum.com/sites/default/files/canadas_aging_workforce_eng_report.pdf

Lee, A. and Dunston, R. (2009) 'Reconceptualising practice as co-production', in J. Higgs, D. Fish, I. Goulter, S. Loftus and J. Reid (eds), *Education for Future Practice*. Netherlands: Sense Publishers.

McVittie, C., McKinlay, A., and Widdicombe, S. (2003) 'Committed to (un)equal opportunities? "New ageism" and the older worker', *British Journal of Social Psychology*, 42: 595–612.

Moore, S (2009). "No matter what I did I would still end up in the same position" : Age as a factor defining older women's experience of labour market participation. *Work, Employment & Society* 23 (4): 655-71.

Nerland, M. (2010) 'Transnational discourses of knowledge and learning in professional work', *Studies in Philosophy of Education*, 29: 183–195.

Nerland, M. and Jensen, K. (2010) 'Objectual practice and learning in professional work', in S. Billett (ed.), *Learning through Practice: Models, Traditions, Orientations and Approaches*. Netherlands: Springer.

Organization for Economic Co-operation and Development (2006) *Live Longer, Work Harder – Ageing and Employment Policies*. Paris: OECD.

Pillay, H., Boulton Lewis, G., Willis, L., and Lankshear, C. (2003) 'Conceptions of work and learning at work: Impressions from older workers', *Studies in Continuing Education*, 25 (1): 95–111.

Porcellato, L., Carmichael, F., Hulme, C., Ingham, B., and Prashar, A. (2010) 'Giving older workers a voice: Constraints on the employment of older people in the north west of England', *Work, Employment and Society* 24 (1): 85–103.

Rainbird, Helen, Fuller, Alison, and Munro, A. (eds) (2004) *Workplace Learning in Context*. London: Taylor & Francis Group.

Riach, K. (2007) '"Othering" older worker identity in recruitment', *Human Relations*, 60 (11): 1701–1726.

Roberts, I. (2006) 'Taking age out of the workplace: Putting older workers back in?', *Work, Employment and Society*, 20 (1): 67–86.

Sennett, Richard. (2006) *The Culture of New Capitalism*. Yale University Press.

Stronach, I., Corbin, B., McNamara, O. Stark, S., and Warne, T. (2002) 'Towards an uncertain politics of professionalism: Teacher and nurse identities in flux', *Journal of Education Policy*, 17 (1): 109–138.

Tikkanen, T. and Nyhan, B. (2006) *Promoting Lifelong Learning for Older Workers – An International Overview*. Stavanger, Norway: European Centre for the Development of Vocational Training.

UK (2006) *The Employment Equality (Age) Regulations 2006*, Statutory Instrument 2006, No.1031, London: HMSO.

Weller, S.A. (2007) 'Discrimination, labour markets and the labour market prospects of older workers: What can a legal case teach us?' *Work, Employment & Society*, 21 (3): 417–37.

18

Quality of Work, Wellbeing, and Retirement

Johannes Siegrist and Morten Wahrendorf

Demographic aging is now expanding beyond economically advanced societies affecting also rapidly developing countries. In these former societies the aging process has led to remarkable demographic changes during the second half of the 20th century. Older people in general are in better health than two or three generations ago. Most convincing evidence of a process of healthier aging comes from demographic analyses demonstrating that human senescence, i.e. the period of the last few years of one's lifespan when severe functional loss can no longer be compensated has been postponed by about a decade (Vaupel, 2010). The fact that many older men and women reach their 'third' age in good health and continue to be free from severe disorder or disability for often up to 20 additional years has profound consequences for societies and their economy. It creates pressures for societies to adapt their labour, social and health policies to an extended lifespan and to modify established concepts of the life course. Importantly,

an extension of the period of regular employment beyond the traditional age of retirement requires that stakeholders undertake substantial investments into continued training of the workforce and into the provision of good quality of work and employment.

In this chapter, we first briefly describe main changes in the nature of work and employment that occurred during the past few decades. We then discuss health-adverse and health-promoting aspects of modern work environments, with particular emphasis on their impact on health and wellbeing of older workers, including risks of disability pensions and retirement behaviour. We also consider the potential impact of quality of work on socially productive activities after retirement, such as volunteering. In this main section a substantial body of empirical evidence is presented. A final section addresses practical implications of these new scientific finings and discusses options and limitations at the level of national and international policies.

CHANGES IN THE NATURE OF WORK AND EMPLOYMENT

Several substantial changes in the nature of employment and work occurred during the past century which exerted direct or indirect effects on aging working populations. First, we witness a large expansion of the service sector of employment, a sector that is mainly composed by academic professions, skilled white collar employees and low skilled service workers. Growing needs of education, health care and other welfare services have contributed – and continue to contribute – to this process. In general, the nature of work in service occupations and professions is less dangerous and less noxious than is the case in traditional areas of industrial production. As a consequence, the work ability and health of the older workforce in the service sector is in better shape compared to the one of older workers in the production sector (see below). Similarly, better health is observed among those parts of the industrial workforce whose job conditions were improved due to technical progress, in particular automation and implementation of new information technologies.

A further far-reaching change concerns an unprecedented flexibility of employment arrangements and contracts. Part-time working arrangements, non-permanent contracts, temporary work, job mobility, job instability and insecurity, flexible work hours including shift work, and growing interference between working life and family or private life are most visible manifestations of this change. While flexibility of work and employment to a certain extent may contribute to the maintenance of work ability among older employees it nevertheless can have adverse consequences on their health and wellbeing, most obviously in times of increased competition and work intensification.

Increased competition and work intensification are often explained as consequences of economic globalization, a process of expansion of free market principles in conjunction with technological innovations from economically advanced societies to rapidly developing countries. This process has initiated large flows of transnational capital, trade and labour force. While economic globalization is often perceived as enhancing gross national product and increasing national employment rates (particularly so in rapidly developing countries) its adverse consequences are less strongly emphasized. Yet, given growing competition and pressure a general intensification of work has been reported, especially so among the workforce of economically advanced societies (Eurostat, 2010). This intensification often goes along with an increase in job instability and insecurity, due to threat of job loss or redundancy, downsizing, outsourcing, and the privatization of public services (Landsbergis, 2003). Another consequence of economic globalization concerns the segmentation of the labour market and a related increase in income inequality. On the one hand, there is a well-trained, skilled and flexible workforce with fair promotion prospects and adequate earnings. On the other hand, large parts of the workforce suffer from precarious employment, low wages, exposure to hazards, low safety at work, and involuntary early retirement. At the same time, welfare state policies and trade union activities are weakened, thus augmenting the burden of stressful work amongst the most vulnerable and deprived groups of national workforces. It is obvious that these developments affect older workers even more so than younger ones (Landsbergis, 2003; Schnall et al., 2009).

HEALTHY AND UNHEALTHY WORK IN AN AGING WORKFORCE

These changes in the nature of work and employment have important consequences for working people's health and wellbeing. On the one hand, good and safe work can contribute to the maintenance and even promotion of health and wellbeing. On the other hand, poor quality of work and employment may have adverse effects on health. These adverse effects go beyond traditional occupational diseases. In fact, work makes a greater contribution to diseases and ill health not thought of as 'occupational'. In addition to physical, biological and chemical hazards work-time related factors with impact on mental and physical health (e.g. shift work, long work hours) and adverse psychosocial work environments are increasingly affecting workers' health and wellbeing. The following paragraphs provide a condensed overview of evidence documenting the burden of work-related ill health, with particular emphasis on older workers in economically advanced societies. In addition, we discuss the afflictions of job loss and long-term unemployment among older parts of the workforce.

Physically strenuous work

A representative source of the prevalence of unhealthy physical working conditions in modern societies, the European-wide panel survey on working conditions, indicates that, during the last ten years, every sixth worker in Europe was exposed to toxic substances at the workplace, and almost one third was exposed to noise at work, at least intermittently. Moreover, 24% reported exposure to vibrations, 45% were working in painful, tiring positions, and more than half were confined to repetitive hand or arm movements, mainly due to computer work (Eurostat, 2010; Parent-Thirion et al., 2007). These exposures are unequally distributed across different groups of the workforce, especially so according to level of skill and training. Thus, low-skilled workers are often exposed to physically strenuous work and, subsequently, are at elevated risk of occupational injuries and accidents. These groups include construction workers, agricultural workers, transport workers, or miners (Arndt et al., 2005). Moreover, unhealthy or restricted posture at work, repetitive movements and heavy lifting are more prevalent amongst lower status workers, and these conditions increase the risk of musculoskeletal disorders (Bernard, 1997). Workers exposed to these physically

stressful conditions are less likely to be able to work until retirement age (Parent-Thirion et al., 2007), and their risk of premature retirement due to disability is increased by 50 to 100% compared to unexposed workers (Blekesaune and Solem, 2005). Even amongst those who are able to stay at work the risk of long spells of sickness absence is substantially increased if their job requires repetitive heavy lifting or restricted posture (Hoogendorn et al., 2002). In addition to unhealthy posture at work, sedentary work was shown to be a risk factor of reduced health, with particular importance for cardiovascular disease (Olsen and Kristensen, 1991).

Physical, ergonomic, and chemical hazards at work are often combined with an adverse psychosocial work environment, thus multiplying health risks amongst exposed people. Few studies have documented the long-term health effects of such cumulative exposures in any detail (Devereux et al., 2002; Dragano, 2007).

Shift work and overtime work

Concerning work-time related health risks shift work must be considered the most important single stressor. Shift work is frequent in the production sector and in some service occupations and professions. Overall, in the European Union (EU-27), its prevalence is 17% (Eurostat, 2010). A strong social gradient of shift work is obvious. 26% of low skilled manual workers, compared to 12% of skilled manual workers, report regular shift work. Although the majority of shift workers is younger than 45 years, at least 10% of working people aged 55 to 65 are shift workers.

Results of studies exploring adverse health effects suggest that shift workers have an increased risk of cardiovascular disease compared to daytime workers (for a review see Härmä, 2006). Similarly, an increased risk of developing a metabolic syndrome was observed amongst Belgian shift workers (de Bacquer et al., 2009). Reported health effects are contingent on duration of shift work, with marked increases after more than 10 years of continued exposure (Steenland, 2000). Additional investigations demonstrate an elevated risk of accidents, particularly amongst evening and night shift workers (Bambra et al., 2008). In addition, night shifts are particularly relevant as a potential source of work accidents, cardiovascular and gastro-intestinal problems, and eventually cancer (Swerdlow, 2003). Combined effects of shift work and chronic psychosocial stress at work were observed for coronary heart disease and for poor mental health (Bøggild et al., 2001; Peter et al., 1999).

Overtime work, irregular work, and periods of commitment to extensive work hours define additional potential health risks. Within European countries about every tenth male worker reported to work regularly more than 60 hours per week (Parent-Thirion et al., 2007). For specific service occupations and professions it has become increasingly difficult to clearly distinguish between work and non-work periods in their daily life, in particular for those performing on-call jobs, freelancers, and several groups holding 'modern', less formalised atypical jobs.

Several investigations demonstrate health-adverse effects of overtime work. Evidence of an association between long working hours and poor health exists for several outcomes, including cardiovascular disease, diabetes, disability pension, and subjectively reported physical health (for a review see van der Hulst, 2003). In an 11-year longitudinal study amongst Finnish workers atherosclerotic plaque growth in the carotid was proportional to number of days worked per week and to annual work hours (Krause et al., 2009). Finally, the risk of coronary heart disease was increased by about 70 % amongst British civil servants who worked overtime for a period of about 10 years, compared to those working normal hours (Kivimäki et al., 2011).

Health-adverse psychosocial work environments

Psychosocial risks contributing to the experience of stressful work are widely recognized as major challenges to current occupational health. As explained, economic globalization induces work intensification amongst many occupational groups, often in combination with threats to job security, promotion prospects and fair pay. Being repeatedly challenged or overtaxed by demands, losing control over one's own tasks, being treated unfairly, and suffering from threats to one's legitimate rewards at work are major conditions that evoke recurrent stressful experience with adverse long-term effects on physical and mental health. To identify these conditions that are often embedded in complex and variable work environments a theoretical model is needed. While several such models were developed (Cartwright and Cooper, 2009), few concepts only were repeatedly tested with rigorous study designs, such as prospective cohort studies. Amongst these, three models have received special attention in international research, the demand–control (or job strain) model, the effort–reward imbalance model, and the model of organizational injustice.

The demand–control (or job strain) model identifies stressful work in terms of job task profiles defined by high psychological demands and a low degree of control or decision latitude (Karasek and Theorell, 1990). Stressful experience resulting from this exposure is due to limited experience of personal control and self efficacy in combination with continued high work pressure. 'Effort–reward imbalance' was developed as a complementary model with a primary focus on the work contract and the principle of social reciprocity lying at its core (Siegrist, 1996). Rewards received in return to efforts spent at work include money, esteem, and career opportunities (promotion, job security). The model asserts that lack of reciprocity (high effort in combination with low reward) occurs frequently and generates strong negative emotions and psychobiological stress responses with adverse long-term effects on health. More recently, the concept of organizational justice was introduced, proposing adverse health effects of three aspects of injustice (distributive, i.e. perceived fairness of the distribution of valued resources; procedural, i.e. perceived fairness of decision making; international, i.e. perceived fairness of being treated by superiors and colleagues) (Elovainio et al., 2002; Greenberg, 2010).

Several systematic reviews summarize the current state of the art in this rapidly expanding field of occupational health research (Eller et al., 2009; Greenberg, 2010; Kivimäki et al., 2006; Leka and Jain, 2010; Nieuwenhuijsen et al., 2010; Schnall et al., 2009; Stansfeld and Candy, 2006; Tsutsumi and Kawakami, 2004). A majority of prospective observational cohort studies tested these work stress models with regard to cardiovascular diseases and poor mental health (mainly depression), given their significant contribution to the worldwide burden of disease (for detailed review Siegrist et al., 2011). Concerning cardiovascular disease, a majority of at least 30 reports derived from prospective studies document elevated odds ratios of fatal or non-fatal cardiovascular events amongst those reporting job strain, effort–reward imbalance or organizational injustice. Overall, risks are about twice as high amongst those suffering from psychosocial stress at work compared to those who are free from stress at work. Effects are stronger in men than in women, but several studies observed that effects are more pronounced in middle-aged than older working populations. Similar associations are observed in case of re-infarction after survived first coronary heart disease.

In addition an adverse psychosocial work environment is associated with several cardiovascular risk factors, in particular metabolic syndrome (Chandola et al., 2006), type 2 diabetes (Kumari et al., 2004), hypertension (Schnall et al., 2009), and health-adverse behaviours (Siegrist and Rödel, 2006). With respect to mental health, major results from prospective investigations confirm elevated risks of depression amongst employees with work related stress in terms of these models, and odds ratios vary between 1.5 and 3.6, depending on measures, gender and occupational group under study (Bonde, 2008; Nieuwenhuijsen et al., 2010). Other health outcomes significantly related to job strain, effort–reward imbalance, or organizational injustice concern reduced physical and mental functioning (Stansfeld et al., 1998), and musculo-skeletal disorders (Rugulies and Krause, 2008). We can conclude from these findings that psychosocial work environments that offer control, autonomy and options of experiencing self-efficacy, while challenging, but not overtaxing working people, are health-protective and contribute to healthy aging. Similarly, experiencing equitable material and non-material rewards for efforts spent at work contributes to health and wellbeing by strengthening feelings of self worth and appreciation. Fair procedures within organizations, a high level of trust and social support further contribute to these favourable effects. By developing good working and employment conditions along these principles within and beyond organizations and enterprises a remarkable part of the burden of work stress-related physical and mental disorders could eventually be avoided, and a larger proportion of the aging workforce could reach retirement age in good health. Before discussing policy implications of this conclusion, the long-term effects of work stress on retirement behaviour and participation in productive activities after labour market exit deserve attention.

PRODUCTIVE ACTIVITIES IN A LIFE-COURSE PERSPECTIVE

To understand health in later life, 'life course' is the dominant perspective of sociological and epidemiological research on aging as it helps elucidating the interplay of social forces and individual characteristics that over time shapes older people's life and exerts long-term influences on health in older ages. With the advent of a 'third age' the traditional view of three main stages of the life course has been challenged. This new phase of the life course includes people with an age range from about 55 to about 80 years where a substantial proportion of men and women are still in good health and free from physical dependency. Yet, this phase lacks a clear societal definition in terms of social roles and social status, legitimized expectations, norms and values. Under these conditions, retirement no longer marks the definite end of productive activity, but at the same time a mismatch or 'structural lag' becomes evident between established societal regulations (e.g. legal retirement age) and the potential agency and productivity of older people. While most middle-aged people experience a secure sense of social identity by maintaining core social roles (such as the work role, family roles or civic roles), social identity during the third age becomes more fragmented and insecure, often in combination with reduced social networks and reduced opportunities of being employed or earning some type of income.

Quality of life in early old age and a related structure of opportunities largely depend on the trajectory of previous life stages. Different models of accumulation and compensation of resources and adversities over the life course were proposed to account for differences in quality of life, health and functioning later on (Bengtson et al., 2008; Kuh and Ben Shlomo, 2004). Among those, the 'cumulative inequality theory' (Ferrero and Shippee, 2009) seems to cover particularly well the available empirical evidence as it focuses on the socioeconomic transmission of resources and deficiencies across generations and across the previous life span.

A substantial body of research conducted in economically advanced societies demonstrates a social gradient of quality of life, morbidity and mortality in early old age across the whole of a society, leaving those in lower socioeconomic positions at higher risk (Marmot and Wilkinson, 2006; Huisman et al., 2004). In addition to higher mortality and higher morbidity from chronic diseases, socially less privileged older people suffer more often from disability and incidental mobility problems (McMunn et al., 2006) as

well as from reduced quality of life (Blane et al., 2007; von dem Knesebeck et al., 2007). Integrating conditions of individual life-courses into the analysis contributes to a better explanation of these variations. For instance, in a British study, occupational grade assessed at midlife strongly predicted level of functioning some 29 years later (Breeze et al., 2001).

Therefore, while substantial social inequalities in health and wellbeing persist into third age in modern societies, it is important to explore potential long-term effects on health of conditions operating during earlier stages of the life course, such as midlife working conditions. Studying long-term effects of working conditions on health is also instrumental in explaining continued participation in the labour market and other kinds of productive activities in older ages (e.g. voluntary work). This is due to the fact that good health and functioning are important preconditions of investments into these activities. In addition to health-promoting or health-adverse working conditions, opportunities of remaining socially productive after retirement are becoming more important since they may compensate to some extent people's loss of positive socio-emotional experiences related to their job, such as self-efficacy, esteem, and belonging. As will be demonstrated below, such socially productive activities contribute to health and wellbeing in later life. Therefore, as these opportunities are unequally distributed across society, they contribute to the persistence of social gradients of health and disease in older ages.

Along these lines, we provide a short overview of existing evidence of long-term effects of midlife working conditions on retirement behaviour and on participation in productive activities after labour market exit, with a particular focus on effects of psychosocial working conditions.

Work stress and retirement

Occupational research has shown that physical and chemical exposures at work increase the risk of early retirement (Dasinger et al., 2000; Krause et al., 1997; MacKenzie et al., 1998). Yet, given the more recent changes of the labour market the health effects of an adverse psychosocial work environment (as defined by the theoretical models of work stress described above) became more prominent. This fact is reflected, among others, in a substantial rise of mental disorders as the principal cause of granting workers with a disability pension in several European countries (Üstün et al., 2004). Several investigations document an association of psychosocial stress at work with early retirement, in particular in case of low control at work (Blekesaune and Solem, 2005), long working hours (Krause et al., 1997), high effort-reward imbalance (Dragano, 2007), and low job satisfaction (Mein et al., 2000). In line with these findings, Kubicek et al. (Kubicek et al., 2010) found in an American study that low job satisfaction predicts early retirement for both men and for women (see also Lund and Villadsen, 2005).

Further support comes from studies using retirement intention rather than factual retirement as an outcome, where low job control (Elovainio et al., 2005; Harkonmäki et al., 2006), psychologically demanding jobs (Forma, 2009), or conflicts between work and family (Harkonmäki et al., 2006; Raymo and Sweeney, 2006) were associated with employees' intention of premature retirement. Poor quality of work in terms of effort-reward imbalance was associated with retirement intentions in a large comparative European study, the Survey of Health Aging and Retirement in Europe (SHARE) including some 30000 individuals aged 50 years and over (Siegrist et al., 2006; Siegrist and Wahrendorf, 2009). In SHARE, employed participants were asked whether or not they intended to retire as early as possible if they were given the opportunity. Two remarkable findings became apparent. First, there was a north–south European difference with higher proportions of workers intending to leave early in southern European countries compared to proportions of workers in northern

European countries. Second, a strong negative correlation with quality of work was observed across the 15 countries: lower quality of work in terms of high effort in combination with low reward or in terms of low control at work was associated with a higher prevalence of intended early retirement.

Based on newly available information from SHARE, these findings were replicated, using an indicator of factual retirement behaviour rather than retirement intention as an outcome criterion (Siegrist and Wahrendorf, 2011). More specifically, the prevalence of being employed at the age of 60 was studied according to the experienced quality of work among retired respondents aged 60 or older. Figure 18.1 summarizes the results across 13 European countries.

In almost all countries the proportion of retired people who were still employed by the age of 60 was always lower among those who experienced low control or low reward at work compared to those with good quality of work in terms of these dimensions. Given the existing social gradient of work stress, with a higher prevalence in lower social positions (Bosma et al., 1998; Brunner et al., 2004), this highlights the importance of work stress in explaining associations between social position and retirement.

One may conclude from these findings that retirement is experienced as a relief from the burden of work amongst those who were exposed to poor working conditions. One of the first longitudinal studies disentangling the effects on health and wellbeing attributable to aging from the effects of retirement behaviour, the French GAZEL study, demonstrated that around the year of retirement, irrespective of people's age, the prevalence of reduced self-perceived health was sharply reduced, corresponding to a level of self-perceived health experienced 8 to 10 years earlier (Westerlund et al., 2009). This retirement-related health improvement suggests that quality of work and employment strongly affects perceived health, and thus might contribute to people's motivation to depart from their job as early as they can.

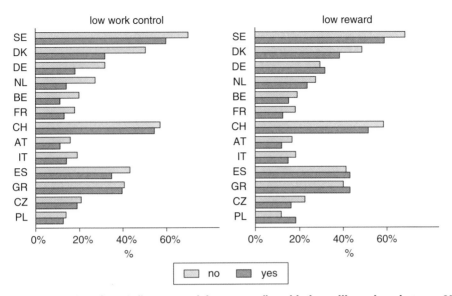

Figure 18.1 Quality of work (low control, low reward) and being still employed at age 60: Results from the SHARE Study (*n* = 14,307 men and women from 13 European countries)

Note: Based on weighted data (SHARELIFE, Release 1.0). Country abbreviations: Sweden (SE), Denmark (DK), Germany (DE), Netherlands (NL), Belgium (BE), France (FR), Switzerland (CH), Austria (AT), Italy (IT), Spain (ES), Greece (GR), Czech Republic (CZ), Poland (PL)

To summarize: Quality of work is a strong predictor of the risk of forced early retirement (due to disability pension), of intended and factual early retirement, and of health functioning after labour market exit. Poor quality of work and its adverse effects on health are more frequent amongst employed people with lower socioeconomic status, thus contributing to the persistence of health inequalities in older ages. So far, it is less well known to what extent quality of work additionally affects the opportunities, capabilities and motivations of retired people to participate in other types of social productivity, most importantly voluntary work. This important aspect of quality of life in early old age is discussed in the next section.

Work stress and participation in productive activities after retirement

Promoting participation in productive activities after retirement is an important policy challenge for advanced societies. Not only

society as a whole might profit from increased investments in productive activities, such as volunteering or providing informal help, but also older people themselves, since participating in such activities was shown to improve health and wellbeing (Bath and Deeg, 2005; Mendes de Leon et al., 2005). Favourable effects on wellbeing are in part due to the recurrent experience of goal-directed agency, self efficacy, appreciation and reward. This quality of experience elicits strong positive emotions and motivations that may promote health via psychobiological pathways (Ryff and Singer, 2009). Moreover, socially productive activities, whether informal or formal, are of particular importance for the preservation of social identity in early old age as this stage of life lacks an unambiguous, consensual social definition in terms of providing legitimate social roles.

The prevalence of volunteering and informal help varies widely between and within societies. It is of interest to note that the prevalence – at least in Europe – is higher in countries with a well developed welfare regime and a tradition of civic society, compared to the prevalence in liberal welfare states or in southern European countries with family-centred support systems (Erlinghagen and Hank, 2006). Within countries, age, gender and socioeconomic status are relevant determinants of activities, with higher rates among younger people, among women and among those with higher education and income (Hank, 2010).

In this context we ask whether quality of work acts as a further determinant of the probability of engaging in socially productive activity after retirement. The SHARE study mentioned provides an opportunity of answering this question. When entering five variables of experienced poor quality of work into a multivariate regression model (high physical demands, high psychological demands, low work control, low reward, and low social support) all variables except low psychological demands reduced the probability of participating in volunteering after retirement to a significant extent. These effects were not altered by adjusting for age, gender, education, self perceived health and functional limitations, and they persisted in addition to the effects of high occupational position and high number of job changes (which both were positively related to participation) (Wahrendorf and Siegrist, 2011). Although restricted to the European countries included in the SHARE study, these findings emphasize that people who experienced poor working conditions in midlife are less likely to engage in socially productive activities, such as volunteering, after labour market exit and, thus, may be deprived of the favourable effects on wellbeing attributed to these activities.

POLICY IMPLICATIONS

Improving quality of work and employment and, by doing so, increasing opportunities of health and wellbeing in an aging workforce is a target that can be tackled at several levels. International and national regulations and policies provide a fundamental umbrella of more specific organizational (e.g. company-level) interventions. At the macro-level, national budget and tax policies are recommended that allow the maintenance and further development of active labour market policies. In this process, improved monitoring and risk management systems with regard to occupational health hazards are instrumental. The same holds true for innovative regulations and successful policy models of increasing work ability and health amongst older workers. Priorities of national regulations that aim at promoting healthy work throughout work life careers concern the protection of workers from job instability and redundancy, the control of long work hours, shift work and exposure to hazardous chemical, physical and psychosocial exposures, and the provision of comprehensive occupational health and safety services that also meet prevention and rehabilitation needs of occupational risk groups. Particular emphasis should be put on workers with low level of skill, migrant workers, and other marginal groups within the labour market (e.g. those employed in precarious work, temporary or irregular work, those working in risky jobs, such as transport workers, construction workers, employees in emergency services). By improving their employment and working conditions a sizeable reduction of the social gradient of health and wellbeing is expected to occur.

At the level of single organizations, companies or branches at least the following policy recommendations can be proposed in view of currently available scientific evidence: (1) Increasing the flexibility of work-time arrangements, including broader opportunities for part-time work and continued training; (2) Securing fair pension and retirement arrangements in relation to both lifetime contributions to the labour market and major shocks (long-term unemployment, forced early retirement, disability pension); (3) Implementing measures of organizational and personnel development that are instrumental in increasing control at work and in providing fair rewards in return for effort expended; these measures concern separate organizations as well as larger bodies of branches, stakeholder associations, trade unions or even national and transnational legislation. This latter recommendation could be further specified by pointing to models of good practice that are already available in several countries (Siegrist et al., 2011). Measures include the reorganization of division of work, with the aim of developing more complete job task profiles (job enlargement, job enrichment, for example) and more adequate promotion prospects (including job security, more flexible forms of remuneration and non-monetary gratifications, enhanced leadership training and the development of a culture of trust, fairness, and transparency at organizational level). These measures could be tailored further towards specific age groups, particularly middle-aged and early old-aged groups, in order to maintain their health and work ability, and to enhance their motivation to stay at work.

Less-elaborate policy measures concern the realm of informal work after retirement. In this regard the opportunity structure of informal work, specifically volunteering, should be developed in a pro-active manner. This includes the creation of new social roles in the context of an emerging civil society, the liberalization of legal restrictions including tax allowance, and a change of societal attitudes and views of aging in the life course. Again, lower socioeconomic groups should become a primary target group, as they are largely excluded from socially productive activities after labour market exit and their beneficial effects. In addition to widening the opportunity structure of informal work quality issues of such activities should be addressed. In line with what was observed in paid work, informal work roles should provide some option of experiencing reward, appreciation, autonomy, and self-efficacy, even if material compensation is limited.

In conclusion, quality of work in formal and informal social roles is an important determinant of health and wellbeing in later life. Poor quality of work is more prevalent among socially less privileged population groups, and this unequal exposure contributes to the persistence of a social gradient of health and wellbeing into old age. Recent scientific progress has identified promising entry points of interventions at the macro-, meso-, and micro-structural level of policy measures. It is now the main challenge to reduce the gap between scientific knowledge and the implementation of policies that contribute to health and wellbeing in aging societies.

REFERENCES

Arndt, V., Rothenbacher, D., Daniel. U., et al. (2005) Construction work and risk of occupational disability: a ten year follow up of 14,474 male workers. *International Journal of Epidemiology* 62: 559–566.

Bambra, C., Whitehead, M., Sowden, A., et al. (2008) Shifting schedules; the health effects of reorganizing shift work. *American Journal of Preventive Medicine* 34 (5): 427–434.

Bath, P.A. and Deeg, D. (2005) Social engagement and health outcomes among older people: Introduction to a special section. *European Journal of Ageing* 2: 24–30.

Bengtson, V.L., Silverstein, M., Putney, N.P., et al. (eds) (2008) *Handbook of Theories of Aging*. New York: Springer.

Bernard, B.P. (ed.) (1997) *Musculoskeletal Disorders and Workplace Factors. A Critical review of Epidemiological Evidence for Work-Related Musculoskeletal Disorders of the Neck, Upper Extremity, and Low Back.* Columbia: National Institute for Occupational Safety and Health. (http://www.cdc.gov/niosh/97-141pd.html).

Blane, D., Netuveli, G. and Bartley, M. (2007) Does quality of life at older ages vary with socio-economic position? *Sociology* 41: 717–726.

Blekesaune, M. and Solem, P.E. (2005) Working conditions and early retirement. A prospective study of retirement behaviour. *Research on Aging* 7: 3–30.

Bøggild, H., Burr, H., Tüchsen, F. et al. (2001) Work environment of Danish shift and day workers. *Scandinavian Journal of Work Environment and Health* 27(2): 97–105.

Bonde, J.P.E. (2008) Psychosocial factors at work and risk of depression: a systematic review of the epidemiological evidence. *Occupational and Environmental Medicine* 65: 438–445.

Bosma, H., Peter, R., Siegrist, J., et al. (1998) Two alternative job stress models and the risk of coronary heart disease. *American.Journal of Public Health* 88: 68–74.

Breeze, E., Fletcher, A.E., Leon, D.A., et al. (2001) Do socioeconomic disadvantages persist into old age? Self-reported morbidity in a 29-year follow-up of the Whitehall Study. *American Journal of Public Health* 91: 277–283.

Brunner, E.J., Kivimäki, M., Siegrist, J., et al. (2004) Is the effect of work stress on cardiovascular mortality confounded by socioeconomic factors in the Valmet study? *Journal of Epidemiology and Community Health* 58: 1019–1020.

Cartwright, S. and Cooper, C.L. (eds) (2009) *The Oxford handbook of organizational well-being.* Oxford University Press, Oxford.

Chandola, T., Brunner, E. and Marmot, M. (2006) Chronic stress at work and the metabolic syndrome: prospective study, *British Medical Journal* 332: 521–525.

Dasinger, L.K., Krause, N., Deegan, L.J., et al.(2000) Physical workplace factors and return to work after compensated low back injury: A disability phase-specific analysis. *Journal of Occupational and Environmental Medicine* 42, 323–333.

De Bacquer, D., van Risseghem, M., Clays, E., et al. (2009) Rotating shift work and the metabolic syndrome: a prospective study. *International Journal of Epidemiology* 38 (3): 848–854.

Devereux, J.J., Vlachonikolis, I.G. and Buckle, P.W. (2002) Epidemiological study to investigate potential interaction between physical and psychosocial factors at work that may increase the risk of symptoms of musculoskeletal disorder of the neck and upper limb. *Occupational and Environmental Medicine* 59: 269–277.

Dragano, N. (2007) *Arbeit, Stress und krankheitsbedingte Frührenten. Zusammenhänge aus theoretischer und empirischer Sicht.* Wiesbaden:VS Verlag.

Eller, N.H., Netterstrøm, B., Gyntelberg, F., et al. (2009) Work-related psychosocial factors and the development of ischemic heart disease. *Cardiology in Review* 17: 83–97.

Elovainio, M., Forma, P., Kivimäki, M., et al. (2005). Job demands and job control as correlates of early retirement thoughts in Finnish social and health care employees. *Work and Stress* 19: 84–92.

Elovainio, M., Kivimäki, M. and Vahtera, J. (2002) Organizational justice: Evidence of a new psychosocial predictor of health. *American Journal of Public Health* 92: 105–108.

Erlinghagen, M. and Hank, K. (2006) The participation of older Europeans in volunteer work. *Ageing and Society* 26:567–584.

Eurostat (2010) *Europe in figures – Eurostat yearbook.* Brussels.

Ferrero, K.F. and Shippee, T.P. (2009) Aging and cumulative inequality: how does inequality get under the skin? *The Gerontologist* 49 (3): 333–343.

Forma, P. (2009) Work, family and intentions to withdraw from the workplace. *International Journal of Social Welfare* 18: 183–192.

Greenberg, J. (2010) Organizational injustice as an occupational health risk. *The Academy of Management Annals* 4: 205–243.

Hank, K. (2010) Societal Determinants of Productive Aging: A Multilevel Analysis Across 11 European Countries. *European Sociological Review* 27 (4): 526–541.

Harkonmäki, K., Rahkonen, O., Martikainen, P., et al. (2006). Associations of SF-36 mental health functioning and work and family related factors with intentions to retire early among employees. *Occupational and Environmental Medicine*, 63, 558–563.

Härmä, M. (2006) Workhours in relation to work stress, recovery and health. *Scandinavian Journal of Work and Environmental Health* 32: 502–514.

Hoogendoorn, W.E., Bongers, P., de Vet H.C.W., et al. (2002) High physical work load and low job satisfaction increase the risk of sickness absence due to low back pain: results of a prospective cohort study. *Occupational and Environmental Medicine* 59: 323–328.

Huisman, M., Kunst, A.E., Andersen, O., et al. (2004) Socioeconomic inequalities in mortality among elderly people in 11 European populations. *Journal of Epidemiology and Community Health* 58: 468–475.

Karasek, R.A. and Theorell, T. (1990) *Healthy Work.* New York: Basic Books.

Kivimäki, M., Batty, G.D., Hamer, M., et al. (2011) Using additional information on working hours to predict coronary heart disease: a cohort study. *Annals of Internal Medicine* 154 (7): 457–463.

Kivimäki, M., Virtanen, M., Elovainio, M., et al. (2006). Work stress in the etiology of coronary heart disease – a meta-analysis. *Scandinavian Journal of Work and Environmantal Health* 32: 431–442.

Krause, N., Brand, R.J., Kauhanen, J., et al. (2009) Work time and 11-year progression of carotid atherosclerosis in middle-aged Finnish men. *Preventing Chronic Disease* 6: 1–20.

Krause, N., Lynch, J., Kaplan, G.A., et al. (1997) Predictors of disability retirement. *Scandinavian Journal of Work, Environment and Health.* 23: 403–413.

Kubicek, B., Korunka, C., Hoonakker, P. et al. (2010) Work and family characteristics as predictors of early retirement in married men and women. *Research on Aging* 32: 467–498.

Kuh, D. and Ben-Shlomo, Y. (2004) *A Life Course Approach to Chronic Disease Epidemiology: Tracing the Origins of Ill-health from Early to Adult Life.* Oxford: Oxford University Press.

Kumari, M., Head, J. and Marmot, M. (2004) Prospective study of social and other risk factors for incidence of type II diabetes in Whitehall 2 study. *Annals of Internal Medicine* 164: 1873–1880.

Landsbergis, P. (2003) The changing organization of work and the safety and health of working people: a commentary. *Journal of Occupational and Environmental Medicine* 45: 61–72.

Leka, S. and Jain, A. (2010) *Health impact of psychosocial hazards at work: an overview.* Geneva:WHO.

Lund, T. and Villadsen, E. (2005) Who retires early and why? Determinants of early retirement pension among Danish employees 57–62 years. *European Journal of Ageing* 2: 275–280.

MacKenzie ,E.J., Morris, J., Jurkovich, G.J., et al. (1998). Return to work following injury: The role of economic, social, and job- related factors. *American Journal of Public Health* 88: 1630–1637.

McMunn, A., Breeze, E., Goodman, A., et al. (2006) Social determinants of health in older age. In: Marmot, M. and Wilkinson, R.G. (eds) *Social Determinants of Health.* Oxford: Oxford University Press, 267–298.

Marmot, M. and Wilkinson, R.G. (eds) (2006) *Social determinants of health.* Oxford: Oxford University Press.

Mein, G., Martikainen, P., Stansfeld, S.A., et al. (2000) Predictors of early retirement in British civil servants. *Age & Ageing.* 29: 529–536.

Mendes de Leon, C.F., Glass, T.A. and Berkman, L.F. (2003) Social engagement and disability in a community population of older adults: The new haven EPESE. *American Journal of Epidemiology* 157: 633–642.

Nieuwenhuijsen, K., Bruinvels, D. and Frings-Dresen, M. (2010) Psychosocial work environment and stress-related disorders, a systematic review. *Occupational Medicine* 60: 277–286.

Olsen, O. and Kristensen, T.S. (1991) Impact of work environment on cardiovascular diseases in Denmark. *Journal of Epidemiology and Community Health* 45: 4–10.

Parent-Thirion, A., Macias, E.F., Hurley, J., et al. (2007) *Fourth European working conditions survey.* Luxemburg: Office for Official Publications of the European Communities.

Peter, R., Alfredson, L., Knutsson, A., et al. (1999) Does a stressful psychosocial work environment mediate the effects of shift work on cardiovascular risk factors in men? *Scandinavian Journal of Work and Environmental Health* 25: 376–381.

Raymo, J.M. and Sweeney, M.M. (2006) Work-family conflict and retirement preferences. *Journals of Gerontology – Series B Psychological Sciences and Social Sciences* 61: S161–S169.

Rugulies, R. and Krause, N. (2008) Effort-reward imbalance and incidence of low back and neck injuries in San Francisco transit operators. *Occupational and Environmental Medicine* 65: 525–533.

Ryff, C.D. and Singer, B. (2009) Understanding aging: Key components and their integration. In: Bengtson, V.L., Silverstein ,M., Putney, N.P. and Gans, D. (eds) *Handbook of Theories of Aging.* New York: Springer, 117–144.

Schnall, .P., Dobson, M. and Rosskam, E. (eds) (2009) *Unhealthy Work: Causes, consequences, cures.* New York: Baywood.

Siegrist, .J (1996) Adverse health effects of high-effort/low-reward conditions. *Journal of Occupational Health Psychology* 1: 27–41.

Siegrist, J. and Rödel, A. (2006) Work stress and health risk behaviour. *Scandinavian Journal of Work and Environmental Health* 32: 473–481.

Siegrist, J. and Wahrendorf, M. (2009) Quality of work, health, and retirement. *The Lancet* 374: 1872–1873.

Siegrist, J. and Wahrendorf, M. (2011) Quality of work, health and early retirement: European comparisons. In: Schroeder M, Hank K and Börsch-Supan A (eds) *The Individual and the Welfare State – Life Histories in Europe.* Berlin: Springer, 169–177.

Siegrist, J., Wahrendorf, M., Von dem Knesebeck, O., et al. (2006) Quality of work, well-being, and intended early retirement of older employees – baseline results from the SHARE Study. *European Journal of Public Health* 17:62–68.

Siegrist, J., Rosskam, E., Leka, S., et al. (2011)*Review of Social Determinants of Health and the Health Divide in the WHO-European Region: Employment and Working Conditions including Occupation, Unemployment and Migrant Workers.* Copenhagen: World Health Organization (unpublished report).

Stansfeld, S.A., Bosma, H., Hemingway, H., et al. (1998) Psychosocial work characteristics and social support as predictors of SF-36 functioning: the Whitehall II Study. *Psychosomatic Medicine* 60: 247–255.

Stansfeld, S. and Candy, B. (2006) Psychosocial work environment and mental health – a meta-analytic review. *Scandinavian Journal of Work and Environ Health* 32: 443–462.

Steenland, K. (2000) Shift work, long hours, and cardiovascular disease: A review. *Occupational Medicine* 15: 7–17.

Swerdlow, A. (2003) *Shift work and breast cancer: a critical review of the epidemiological evidence.* Research Report 132. London: Health and Safety Executive.

Tsutsumi, A. and Kawakami, N. (2004) A review of empirical studies on the model of effort-reward imbalance at work: reducing occupational stress by implementing a new theory. *Social Science & Medicine* 59, 2335–2359.

Üstün, T.B., Ayuso-Mateos, J.L., Chatterji, S., et al. (2004) Global burden of depressive disorders in the year 2000. *British Journal of Psychiatry* 184: 386–392.

Van der Hulst, M. (2003) Long work hours and health. *Scandinavian Journal of Work and Environmental Health* 29 (3): 171–188.

Vaupel, J.W. (2010) Biodemography of human aging. *Nature* 464: 536–542.

Von dem Knesebeck, O., Wahrendorf, M., Hyde, M., et al. (2007) Socio-economic position and quality of life among older people in 10 European countries: Results of the SHARE study. *Ageing and Society* 27(2): 269–284.

Wahrendorf, M. and Siegrist, J. (2011) Working conditions in mid-life and participation in voluntary work after labour market exit. In: Schröder, M., Hank, K. and Börsch-Supan, A. (eds) *The Individual and the Welfare State – Life Histories in Europe.* Berlin: Springer, 179–188.

Westerlund, H., Kivimäki, M., Singh-Manoux, A., et al. (2009) Self-rated health before and after retirement in France (GAZEL): a cohort study. *The Lancet* 374: 1889–1896.

PART 4

Living in an Aging Society

19

Working Caregivers in the 'Sandwiched Generation'

Margaret B. Neal, Leslie B. Hammer, Ayala Malach Pines[†], Todd E. Bodner and Melissa L. Cannon

Many in today's workforce face the responsibilities of not only maintaining their job but also managing family responsibilities. Moreover, some workers are caring for family members at both ends of the life course: children and elders. These employees comprise the 'sandwich' or 'sandwiched' generation (Chassin, Macy, Seo, Presson, & Sherman, 2010; Durity, 1991; Fernandez, 1990; Grundy & Henretta, 2006; Keene & Prokos, 2007; Miller, 1981; Neal & Hammer, 2007; Nichols & Junk, 1997; Pines, Neal, Hammer & Icekson, 2011; Rosenthal, Martin-Matthews, & Matthews, 1996; Spillman & Pezzin, 2000). The sandwiched generation is metaphor for a unique and understudied group whose members are 'sandwiched' between meeting the needs of their dependent children and their dependent elders and, often, their jobs.

Interest in work and family issues has been traced to the work of Engels in 1844 (Wilensky, 1960). To date, most work–family research has focused on individuals who are combining work with their nuclear family responsibilities (e.g., spouse or partner, children); considerably less attention has been given to couples (Barnett, 1998; Hammer, Allen, & Grigsby, 1997; Rosenthal et al., 1996), despite the growing presence of such couples in the workforce (Zedeck, 1992). As Neal and Hammer (2007, p. 6) noted, 'Studying both members of the couple contributes to improved understanding of the family system and the ways in which it affects the work system and vice versa.' Even less attention in the work–family research literature (although not in the gerontological literature) has been paid to employees who are caring informally for aging parents and other elders or adults with disabilities, with less still to working couples who simultaneously provide care both for children and for aging parents (Neal & Hammer, 2007). Much can be learned from these couples with respect to how they are managing their multiple role responsibilities as spouses, parents, caregivers to aging parents, and workers. In this chapter, we provide an overview of the prevalence of working, sandwiched individuals, trends contributing to the phenomenon of working, and being sandwiched.

THE PREVALENCE OF WORKING, SANDWICHED INDIVIDUALS

Prevalence estimates of individuals in the sandwiched generation vary greatly depending on a number of factors. These include the country under study, the population (e.g., all adults, only women, only individuals between certain ages, only employees, only caregivers to elders), the age criterion for 'elder' (e.g., 50, 60, 65 years), the elder's relationship to the individual (e.g., parent, in-law, grandparent, aunt or uncle, spouse, or even friend or neighbor), the operational definition of what constitutes 'elder care,' and the age criterion for the participant, the age of the child, or the operational definition of 'child care' (see Neal & Hammer, 2007, for an extensive discussion of this issue). For example, some studies have used a narrow definition of elder care, including only the provision of the most intensive forms of care, such as nursing care or hands-on assistance with personal activities of daily living (ADLs) (e.g., help with dressing, bathing, toileting, eating; Stone, Cafferata, & Sangl, 1987) versus a broader definition to include, as well, the provision of instrumental care such as transportation, help with finances, emotional support, and making arrangements for care (instrumental activities of daily living, or IADLs) (Neal & Hammer, 2007). Similarly, some studies have focused broadly on participants' elder care responsibilities, including the care of elderly neighbors and friends as well as relatives, while others have focused on 'parent care,' or the care of aging parents, stepparents or parents-in-law (Neal & Hammer, 2007; Sahibzada, Hammer, Neal, & Kuang, 2005).

Some studies have derived their prevalence rates for the sandwiched generation using caregivers only between certain ages. For example, Nichols and Junk (1997) focused on individuals between the ages of 40 and 65 years. Survey responses were received from 1,466 randomly sampled individuals between these ages in four states, and the findings revealed that 15 percent of the respondents had responsibility both for aging parents and financially dependent children (no age of the children was specified). Alternatively, an AARP study (2001) categorized *all* individuals between the ages of 45 and 55 as being in 'the sandwich generation,' based solely on their age, regardless of any type of caregiving responsibilities or work status. Among the individuals in that age group, the study found that more than 20 percent were providing care to their parents or other older adults. No data were provided on what percentage was engaged in paid work. A National Alliance for Caregiving and AARP study (2009) estimated that among adults of all ages, regardless of work status, between 5.4 and 5.6 percent were caregivers of both adults and children.

Some studies have derived their estimates on the basis of samples composed only of employees (see Gorey, Rice, & Brice, 1992, and Wagner & Neal, 1994, for reviews). Neal, Chapman, Ingersoll-Dayton, and Emlen (1993) found, in their study of employees of 33 organizations, that 9 percent of employees had both child-care and elder-care responsibilities. Durity (1991) reported that a survey of IBM's workforce found 11 percent of employees were caring both for elders and for children in 1991, compared to just 6 percent only five years earlier, in 1986. Durity noted that estimates of sandwiched employees have varied from 6 percent to 40 percent, depending on the demographic characteristics (e.g., age, gender, marital status) of the workforces studied. In a more recent study, Keene and Prokos (2007) used three distinct literatures to examine social trends and test their hypotheses, one of which was that the proportion of workers who are sandwiched and engaged in multi-generational caregiving increased from 1992 to 2002. Their hypothesis was confirmed: They found that the percentage of working, sandwiched caregivers increased from 2.3 percent in 1992 to 6.5 percent in 2002. Moreover, the proportion of workers who *anticipated* that they would become sandwiched caregivers increased dramatically in this timeframe, from 4.5 percent in 1992 to 14.8 percent in 2002.

Using a set of fairly restrictive criteria to estimate how many US households were composed of working, sandwiched couples, Neal and Hammer (2007) conducted a telephone survey which revealed that between 9 and 13 percent of American households with a telephone and with one or more persons aged 30 to 60 were composed of dual-earner couples caring for children and aging parents. The criteria stipulated that: (a) the household contained a couple who had been living together for at least one year; (b) both members of the couple were working (one at least 20 hours per week, the other 35 hours or more per week); (c) together, one or both members of the couple were providing a minimum of three hours per week of care to an aging parent, stepparent, or parent-in-law; and (d) at least one child aged 18 or under lived in the household a minimum of three days per week. A final criterion was that the couple had an annual gross household income of $40,000 or higher (stipulated due to the special interest of the study's funder in middle- and upper-income couples).[1]

Using a similar methodology and definition (except for the final criterion), a national, representative sample of Israelis ($N = 1,303$ households)[2] was interviewed by phone to identify sandwiched-generation couples. The telephone calls identified 148 such couples (11.4 percent) (Pines et al., 2011).

As can be seen from the preceding review of existing estimates, prevalence rates of sandwiched-generation caregivers are heavily dependent on how this group is identified and defined. Rates, therefore, are highly inconsistent across studies.

TRENDS CONTRIBUTING TO THE PHENOMENON OF WORKING AND BEING SANDWICHED

Several social and demographic trends have contributed to the phenomenon of working, sandwiched-generation individuals in the United States and elsewhere. These include delayed childbearing (Casper & Bianchi, 2002); decreases in family size (and thus fewer adult children to care for aging parents); changes in family composition, including increases in multi-generational households (AARP, 2001); the aging of the American population; the aging of the American workforce; an increasing number of women (the traditional caregivers) in the workforce; and rising health care costs and the resulting increased pressure on families to provide care (Moen, Robison, & Fields, 1994; Neal & Wagner, 2002; Wagner, 2000). These trends, as well as growing evidence of the dynamic interplay between work and family demands and the effects on individuals' health and well-being (e.g., decreased mental health, increased stress, and strain both on and off the job; Hammer, Cullen, Neal, Sinclair, & Shafiro, 2005), as well as on organizations' bottom lines in the form of absenteeism, turnover, and overall market performance (Neal et al., 1993; Eby, Casper, Lockwood, Bordeaux, & Brinley,2005) are fueling interest in individuals who are working and caring for children and elders (Neal & Hammer, 2007).

For example, in 2009 women comprised about 59 percent of the US workforce, compared to about 43 percent in 1970 (US Department of Labor, 2011). A comparison of selected countries done by the US Department of Labor's Bureau of Labor Statistics (BLS) (2011) revealed that Canada had the highest rate of women in the workforce (62.6 percent), followed by Sweden (60.6 percent), the Netherlands (60.0 percent), the US (59.2 percent), the United Kingdom (56.8 percent), Germany (52.1 percent), Japan (48.2 percent), and Italy (38.2 percent).

An important labor force-related trend is the aging of the workforce. Between 1977 and 2007 in the US, the employment of workers aged 65 years and older increased 101 percent, compared to only 59 percent for all workers aged 16 years and older. The number of employed men aged 65 years and older increased 75 percent, but employment of women aged 65 years and older grew almost twice as much, by 147 percent. The group with the most dramatic increase comprised employed people aged 75 years and older: although the number is relatively small (0.8 percent of those employed in 2007), this group increased 172 percent between 1977 and 2007 (US Department of Labor, 2008). This graying of the US workforce is expected to continue, with Bureau of Labor Statistics data projecting an overall increase in the labor force of 8.5 percent during the period 2006–2016, but with large increases in the older age groups and declines in the younger. The number of workers aged 16–24 years is projected to decline during the period, and while the number of workers age 25–54 years will rise slightly, workers aged 55–64 years are expected to climb by 36.5 percent, and workers aged 65 years and older are projected to increase by more than 80 percent, accounting for 6.1 percent of the total labor force by 2016 (US Department of Labor, 2008).

Another workforce trend affecting caregiving is globalization. Globalization has caused an increase in workforce mobility, with large numbers of individuals seeking employment overseas. This phenomenon, along with increased longevity globally, has spawned caregiving across national borders, resulting in 'care drain' as workers leave elderly parents in need of care in their home countries (Dhar, 2011).

Married-couple family households comprised 50 percent of all households in 2011, compared to 51 percent of all households in 2006 and 53 percent in 2000 (US Census Bureau, 2012). This downward trend in married couples is consistent with the increase in single-parent households found by a 2008 study by the Families and Work Institute that was updated in 2011 (Galinsky, Aumann, & Bond, 2011). A trend in the opposite direction is the increase in multi-generational family households. Multi-generational family households are defined as those households with two or more generations of adults and also the 'skipped generations,' e.g., grandparents and grandchildren (who may be adults) without

the parental generation (Pew Research Center, 2010). Using data from the Pew Research Center's telephone survey of 2,696 adults in the US, including 1,332 respondents 65 years of age or older, the US Decennial Census data from 1900 to 2000, and the US Census Bureau American Community Surveys (ACS) from 2006 through 2008, the Pew Research Center (2010) reported that in 2008, 16 percent of the US population was living in multi-generational households, compared to 12 percent of the population in 1980. This is a reversal of a trend that had peaked in 1940, when 25 percent of Americans were living in such households. Explanations for the growth in this population since 1980 include demographic and cultural shifts, such as the rising number of immigrants in the US and the rising median age of adults getting married for the first time, as well as high unemployment and increased foreclosures, which led people of multiple generations in the same family to move in together (Pew Research Center, 2010). Nonetheless, as discussed below, it is important to note that although some sandwiched-generation caregivers do live with the aging parents or other adult relatives for whom they are providing care, those who do not are still considered to be caregivers by the vast majority of studies, as they provide instrumental or personal care such as help with household chores, making arrangements for assistance, emotional support, help with bathing, etc.

WHO ARE WORKING, SANDWICHED COUPLES?

Based on the research by Neal and Hammer (2007), the typical working, sandwiched couple in the US is composed of a 44-year old man and 42-year old woman who have been married about 18 years. The husband works 49 hours per week, and the wife works 38 hours per week. They have two children aged 18 or younger living in the household. Each member of the couple helps two aging parents, stepparents, or parents-in-law (mostly they help with instrumental activities of daily living (IADLs)), and each spends the equivalent of about one workday each week on parent care. Their median household income in 1997 was $62,500.

Cullen, Hammer, Neal, and Sinclair (2009) expanded upon this work and developed a typology of dual-earner couples caring for children and aging parents using cluster analysis. They identified three distinct profiles of these couples: a high child-care demands group, a high parent-care demands group, and a high work demands group. Interestingly, a group of individuals with both high child-care and high parent-care demands did not emerge; the authors stated that one interpretation of this finding was that 'something has to give,' consistent with the limited resources perspective of Goode's (1960) scarcity hypothesis. Having very high demands in one role may preclude having very high demands in another role. For example, perhaps couples with high child-care demands might have been characterized by high parent-care demands at one time but due to their aging parents' declining health, those couples may have had to obtain more external resources to assist them with managing their parent-care demands. Interestingly, differences in work-to-family conflict were found across the three groups but not differences in family-to-work conflict. Specifically, women with high child-care demands and women with high parent-care demands reported significantly more work-to-family conflict than women in the high work demands group. The results for men were the opposite, with men having high work demands reporting significantly more work-to-family conflict than men with high child-care demands. Cullen et al. (2009) explained that these gender differences likely occurred due to within-couple differences in hours worked per week, with men working more hours than the women in the high work demands group and more hours than the men in the other two groups and women in all three groups working approximately the same number of hours.

OUTCOMES OF COMBINING WORK AND CARE

Specifically with respect to employees caring for *elderly* family members, a number of studies have been conducted. A recent report by AARP's Public Policy Institute (Feinberg, Reinhard, Houser, & Choula, 2011) compiled the most current data available and estimated that in the US in 2009, of a total population of 307 million, about 42.1 million family caregivers (13.7 percent of the population) provided care specifically to an adult with limitations in daily activities at any given point in time, and about 61.6 million (20 percent of the US population) had provided care at some time during the year. They estimated the economic value of these caregivers' unpaid contributions at $450 billion in 2009, up from an estimated $375 billion in 2007. The estimated $450 billion is more than the total amount of Medicaid spending in 2009 ($361 billion), including federal and state contributions for health care and long-term services and supports. No data were reported on multi-generational caregivers or working caregivers.

Another recent study of employees caring for elders, *Working Caregivers and Employer Health Care Costs* (MetLife, 2010), was a collaboration between the MetLife Mature Market Institute, the National Alliance for Caregiving, and the University of Pittsburgh and was intended to address remaining questions regarding the direct relationship between caregiving, health status and health costs. Data for the study were derived from a case study analysis of anonymous aggregated responses to health risk assessment questionnaires completed by 17,097 US employees of a large multinational manufacturing firm headquartered in the northeast US. About 12 percent of the employees reported caring for an older person. Employees were not asked about other caregiving responsibilities, such as for caring for children; thus, no data on sandwiched-generation employees are available.

The majority of caregivers in the study (MetLife, 2010) were male (61 percent), and about half of them were aged 50 years or older. Two-thirds of the caregivers (67 percent) were married, and caregivers were divided evenly between blue- and white-collar workers. The study's findings indicated that caregiving employees reported poorer health and more chronic diseases than non-caregivers. Additionally, there was an 8 percent differential in increased health care costs between caregiving and non-caregiving employees, resulting in a potential additional cost of $13.4 billion per year to US employers. Employees caring for elders were significantly more likely to report depression, diabetes, hypertension or pulmonary disease, and female caregiving employees reported more stress at home than non-caregivers in every age group. Younger female caregivers appeared to be most frequently affected by stress at home. Caregiving resulted in more negative influences of personal life on work (i.e., family-to-work conflict). In addition, caring for elders was associated with greater health risk behaviors, including smoking, which was especially higher among younger male caregivers and white-collar caregivers relative to non-caregivers, and higher levels of alcohol use were reported among blue-collar caregivers compared to non-caregivers. Employed caregivers also reported greater difficulty in taking care of their own health or participating in preventive health screenings compared to non-caregivers. Those with elder-care responsibilities were more likely to miss days of work as well as to incur excess medical care costs. Finally, compared to younger non-caregivers (ages 18 to 39 years), younger caregivers reported significantly higher rates of cholesterol, hypertension, chronic obstructive pulmonary disease (COPD), depression, kidney disease, and heart disease, which will lead to increased health care costs as these workers age.

As noted earlier, Neal and Hammer (2007) conducted a national longitudinal study of working, sandwiched couples in the US that included two mailed surveys, one year apart, to determine how these couples were managing their multiple work and family roles. The findings revealed important mean differences in outcomes of being 'sandwiched' at the time of the first survey: Work-to-family conflict was higher than family-to-work conflict, and working, sandwiched men, and women even more so, were at greater risk for depression than the general population. Likewise, work-to-family positive spillover and family-to-work positive spillover were higher for men and women than were work–family conflict outcomes, with levels of family-to-work positive spillover being consistently higher than those of work-to-family positive spillover. Thus, women appeared to be more susceptible than men to both the positive and negative influences of family on work.

With respect to the effects of role demands, or objective role characteristics, Neal and Hammer (2007) found that:

1 Child-care role characteristics (i.e., number of children and having a special-needs child) did not affect work–family fit or well-being outcomes and only minimally affected work outcomes.
2 Parent-care role characteristics (i.e., number of parents/in-laws helping and number of ADLs helping the parent(s) with) were important in predicting well-being and work outcomes, with providing parent care being beneficial for one's well-being but detrimental for one's work. For example, husbands and wives who were helping a greater number of parents reported lower depression; for wives, this was also related to greater life satisfaction. At the same time, the more ADLs husbands and wives reported helping with, the higher their reports of absence and the greater their reports of poor work performance. Wives helping with more ADLs also reported making a greater number of accommodations at work. (These findings are especially salient in light of the increasing number of older workers and the growing percentage with parent-care responsibilities.) (p. 209)
3 Objective work role characteristics (i.e., number of hours worked per week and degree of flexibility in work schedule) significantly affected work–family fit and work outcomes. Specifically, working more hours per week was associated with higher levels of work-to-family conflict for both husbands and wives and with more family-to-work conflicts for wives, and with more reports

of poor work performance for husbands (but also greater life satisfaction for husbands). Flexibility in work schedules was related to lower work-to-family conflict but higher levels of family-to-work conflict for husbands and to higher levels of absence for both husbands and wives. It is clear, then, that these objective work characteristics had mixed effects. (p. 209)

4   Subjective role quality (i.e., spousal, child care, and job role quality) was a significant predictor of work–family fit, well-being, and work outcomes after the objective role characteristics had been taken into account. Role quality in the work and spousal roles was especially important in predicting these outcomes. Spousal role quality generally was related to improved work–family fit and well-being but was not related to work outcomes. Child-care role quality had minimal effects on work–family fit, well-being, and work outcomes, and parent-care role quality was not related to work–family fit and only minimally related to well-being and work outcomes. Job role quality was positively related to improved work–family fit, well-being, and work outcomes, with the most significant effects on improved job satisfaction and decreased absenteeism. (pp. 209–210)

COPING STRATEGIES USED BY WORKING COUPLES IN THE SANDWICHED GENERATION

Based on several theoretical frameworks (Amatea & Fong-Beyette, 1987; Folkman & Lazarus, 1980; Menaghan, 1983) and empirical data from their national study of dual-earner couples in the sandwiched generation, Neal and Hammer (2007) identified work–family coping strategies centered on increasing resources and decreasing demands, and doing so behaviorally, emotionally, and cognitively. Behavioral coping strategies that involved social withdrawal (behaviorally decreasing demands) were related to negative work and family outcomes, while emotional coping strategies that were centered on seeking emotional support (emotionally increasing resources) were beneficial, as were cognitive coping strategies focused on conscious attempts to prioritize tasks (cognitively decreasing demands). There were gender differences in

the strategies used, with wives more likely than husbands to use negative coping strategies involving decreasing social involvement, and husbands more likely to use positive coping strategies involving prioritizing. Wives also were more likely than husbands to make work accommodations, such as taking time off from work, foregoing promotions. The types of coping strategies used had more effects on work–family fit and well-being than on the work outcomes. Furthermore, these relationships were found to hold over time: one year later for these same individuals, coping strategies that increased emotional resources and coping strategies that involved prioritization had beneficial effects on well-being, while coping strategies that involved social withdrawal had negative effects on well-being (Neal & Hammer, 2010).

'CROSSOVER' OF STRESS, STRAIN AND RESOURCES FROM ONE SPOUSE TO THE OTHER

Consistent with the findings of earlier studies of the crossover effects (e.g., Bakker, Demerouti, & Schaufeli, 2005; Westman, 2001; 2006; Westman & Etzion, 1995), Neal and Hammer (2007) and Pines et al. (2011) also found evidence that one member of the couple's work–family experiences influenced the work–family experiences of his or her spouse. Because of the importance of subjective role quality that had been revealed in their previous analyses, Neal and Hammer conducted regression analyses to examine the crossover effects of one spouse's subjective role quality (i.e., spousal, child-care, parent-care, and job role quality) (after controlling for personal characteristics and objective role characteristics) on the partner's work and family outcomes. Several significant crossover relationships emerged:

- Higher spousal role quality reported by husbands was related to lower levels of work-to-family conflict and higher levels of overall role performance reported by their wives.

- Higher levels of spousal role quality and parent-care role quality among wives were related to higher levels of family-to-work positive spillover reported by their husbands.
- Higher spousal role quality among wives was positively related to their husbands' overall role performance.
- Higher child-care role quality among husbands was related to more work accommodations made in the past year by wives.
- Higher child-care role quality among wives was significantly related to lower levels of poor work performance reported by husbands.

In sum, spousal role quality generally had stronger crossover effects than child-care or parent-care role quality, and no crossover effects of job role quality were found.

Neal and Hammer (2007) also examined whether crossover effects occurred with respect to the types of coping strategies used. They found that husbands' use of emotional coping strategies had beneficial effects on wives' work–family fit and well-being outcomes.

Pines et al. (2011) also found crossover effects between spouses. In particular, husbands' job burnout was exacerbated by the stressors their wives experienced at work and was reduced by the rewards their wives experienced in their marriage. For wives, the level of couple burnout they experienced was compounded by their husbands' job stressors and reduced by their husbands' job rewards.

THE USE AND EFFECTS OF WORKPLACE SUPPORTS

Workplace supports, or family-friendly practices, have been implemented by organizations in an attempt to help employees manage their work and family responsibilities. These supports include both formal and informal means of support within organizations. Neal and Hammer (2007) examined the use and effects of 13 workplace supports, including policies (e.g., flexible work arrangements), services (e.g., resource and referral information about dependent-care

options), and benefits (e.g., child- or elder-care subsidies) (Neal et al., 1993). They found that the supports used most frequently were family health insurance, personal time off/paid leave, flexible work hours, and unpaid leave (paid leave was preferred, when available). The least-used supports were those specifically related to family-care needs (e.g., on-site child care, resource and referral for child and elder care, pre-tax dollars set aside to pay for elder care), generally because these were largely unavailable. Consistent with previous research, Neal and Hammer (2007) also found gender differences in the use of workplace supports, with wives being more likely to make use of these supports than husbands.

To examine the effects of using supports, Neal and Hammer (2007) created two composite measures of workplace supports, placing the 13 supports into one or the other of the two categories most examined in prior research, alternative work arrangements and dependent-care supports. They found that using workplace supports positively affected well-being, but at the same time, use of workplace supports was related to higher levels of work–family conflict, possibly because the utilization of supports allowed couples to reallocate or take on more family and work-related responsibilities than would have been possible otherwise.

Using workplace supports also was associated with poorer work outcomes such as increased absences and poorer work performance, suggesting that using supports alone is not sufficient to minimize absence from work due to dependent care responsibilities. It may be that those who use such supports are those who are having the greatest difficulty managing work and family, and/or the supports provided increase employees' awareness of community services that may require taking time off in order to connect with services that are available only during the work day.

Sahibzada, Hammer, Neal and Kuang (2005) found that availability of workplace supports was a significant positive predictor of job satisfaction when work–family culture is not supportive. They also found, however, that overall job satisfaction was higher when work–family culture was supportive. Their results clearly supported the importance of distinguishing the effects of family-friendly culture from actual availability of supports and suggested that organizations that provide workplace supports may see even more significant employee and overall organizational gains if they place greater emphasis on increasing the organization's perceived family friendliness.

Chen, Hedrick, and Young (2010) evaluated a federal and state-funded Family Caregiver Support Program (FCSP) and explored what types of caregiver support services were associated with what caregiver outcomes. Information on 164 caregivers' use of 11 different types of support services was obtained, and users and nonusers were compared. The findings revealed that using consulting and education services was associated with reduced subjective burden and using financial support services was associated with more beneficial caregiver appraisal, such as improved feelings of mastery.

As these findings illustrate, it is important to note that simply having caregiving responsibilities does not necessarily lead to negative outcomes. For example, a study by AARP (2001) reported that 70 percent of Americans aged 45 to 55 years had aging parents or parents-in-law as well as children under the age of 21 years, but 70 percent of those reported that they felt comfortable handing their family responsibilities, feeling 'squeezed' but not 'stressed' (Keene & Prokos, 2007, p. 371). Keene and Prokos (2007, p. 371), also cited Hochschild (1997) as having posited that 'lacking substantial organizational changes in family life, employees actually enjoy the format of paid work as well as the system of rewards and feelings of accomplishment in comparison to their family responsibilities.'

An unexpected finding by Keene and Prokos (2007), given the many US studies showing employee preferences for shorter work hours, was that workers who expected to be sandwiched were less likely to want to reduce their workweek hours than others. Keene and Prokos argued that this finding supports Hochschild's (1997) argument. They also noted that perhaps these workers were anticipating needing to reduce their work hours in the future and thus wanting to earn as much now as possible. Alternatively, they suggested that these workers might not have fully considered the financial or time demand-related implications of that care, and advised, 'As the number of workers who are actively sandwiched continues to grow, researchers should consider the work hour preferences of these future sandwiched workers because this cohort appears to have different preferences than those who are currently sandwiched' (Keene & Prokos, 2007, p. 382).

OUTCOMES REPORTED IN RECENT STUDIES IN COUNTRIES OUTSIDE THE US

Relatively little research has been conducted with 'sandwiched-generation' couples outside of the US, and even less research has compared working, sandwiched couples from different countries. One exception is an exploratory study by Pines, Hammer, and Neal (2009) that compared 40 Israeli 'sandwiched-generation' couples living on a kibbutz (a collective community in Israel traditionally based on agriculture), 80 Israeli couples living in small towns and 75 American men and women. All participants completed a self-report questionnaire (in Hebrew for the Israelis and in English for the Americans) that included measures of social support, work–family conflict and burnout.

Both cross-cultural and cross-gender differences were found. In particular, Israelis reported greater satisfaction from both their work and their families than Americans. Americans reported higher work-to-family conflict than Israelis, and Israelis reported higher family-to-work conflict than Americans. When asked about the support they received from their partners, family, colleagues and superiors for problems at home and work, Israelis reported receiving higher levels of support from their spouses with both home- and work-related problems than Americans, and Israeli kibbutz members reported receiving more help than Israeli city dwellers. Among both groups of Israelis and the Americans, men reported greater satisfaction from work than women, and men reported receiving higher levels of support from their spouses than did women with regard to both work and family problems. Spousal support and support from one's supervisor at work with both home- and work-related problems were negatively correlated with burnout. This study enabled comparison of various theoretical explanations for gender and cultural differences and highlighted the importance of social support at work and at home and the need to identify ways of increasing the support available to working, sandwiched couples (Pines, Hammer & Neal, 2009; Pines, Hasan, Hammer & Neal, 2010).

Pines, Neal, Hammer, and Ickeson (2011) used existential theory as a framework to explore the levels of, and relationship between, job and couple burnout in this same sample of sandwiched-generation couples in Israel and a comparison sample in the US. They found that job burnout was higher than couple burnout, that wives were more burned out than husbands, and that Americans were more burned out than Israelis. Job-related stressors and rewards as well as parent-care stressors predicted job burnout, and marital stressors and rewards predicted couple burnout. In addition, multiple regressions and Actor–Partner Interdependence Model (APIM) analyses (Kenny, 1996) documented crossover effects, and focus groups with the Israeli couples suggested that sandwiched couples were facing existential issues brought about by reaching middle age and facing their parents' deterioration.

Grundy and Henretta (2006) conducted a comparative analysis of data from national surveys in the US and UK to investigate women aged 55–69 years who were caregivers to their descendent and ascendant relatives.

Citing Murphy and Grundy (2003), Grundy and Henretta (2006) pointed out that demographic modeling suggests that the number of women in Britain ages 60 to 69 years whose mothers are still living will continue to increase until those born during the 1970s reach that age; as a result, considerable attention has been paid to the concept of the 'sandwich generation' caregivers. Grundy and Henretta also noted that current research on three-generation families has focused mostly on women in late middle age because of their greater likelihood of experiencing simultaneous responsibilities of caring for elderly parents and children. In the French literature, these women have been termed the 'pivot generation' on whom family relationships turn (Grundy & Henretta, 2006, p. 709).

Grundy and Henretta (2006) were particularly interested in learning whether demands from adult children and elderly parents compete, or whether there is a positive association between helping parents and helping children (the solidarity hypothesis). To examine this issue, they analyzed data from comparable nationally-representative British and American surveys, specifically the British data from the Retirement and Retirement Plans Survey (RS) of 1988 and the American data from the fourth wave of the Health and Retirement Study (HRS) in 1998. The analysis revealed that among married women in Great Britain and among married and unmarried women in the US, all in the 'sandwiched part' of three generations, those who helped one generation were more likely than those who did not to help the other generation. In other words, among American women and married British middle-generation women, helping children was positively associated with helping a parent and vice versa. The researchers noted that this finding is counter to previous research (e.g., Wong, Capoferro, & Soldo, 1999), which has found a high prevalence of assisting only children, possibly because the norms governing normative obligations toward parents are less clearly defined than the norms governing parental responsibility toward children (Grundy & Henretta, 2006).

Künemund (2006) analyzed data from the second wave of the German Aging Survey and found that while being sandwiched (described as a 'generational constellation') is very common, simultaneous *care* activities for both older and younger family members are relatively rare, especially in combination with labor force participation. In addition, the analyses found that being sandwiched was not necessarily associated with a specific burden as far as it could be measured with psychological scales such as life satisfaction. Künemund agreed that the competing demands from work and family, especially with respect to elder care, may induce a heavy burden but suggested that rather than merely being an additional burden, younger family members may also be a source of help in providing care for the elderly. He concluded that 'the metaphor of the sandwich generation is not a very useful description, and the connotation of a specific overburden due to the existence of both older and younger generations has to be rejected' (p. 24). Similarly, other research has found that aging parents not only receive help from their adult children but also provide assistance (Ingersoll-Dayton, Neal, & Hammer, 2001).

CHANGE OVER TIME IN ROLE RESPONSIBILITIES AND OUTCOMES FOR WORKING, SANDWICHED COUPLES

Neal and Hammer (2007) examined the changes in role demands and role quality that occurred in the year between the two mailed surveys and also the changes that occurred in key characteristics of the roles of spouse, parent to dependent children (the child-care role), caregiver to aging parent (the parent-care role), and worker. Of special interest was how those changes affected such outcomes as work–family fit, well-being, and work-related outcomes (e.g., job satisfaction, overall absence). In particular, they

examined *which* role changes, objective role demands or subjective role quality, were the strongest predictors of changes in outcomes over time.

In the one year between the two mailed surveys, Neal and Hammer (2007) found that some couples' work and family lives changed dramatically. For example, after one year, a few couples no longer held one or more roles, with some couples no longer having children aged 18 years or younger living with them, no longer providing parent care, no longer being together as a couple, and/or no longer having both members working. Others had less drastic reductions in demands, including now having fewer children aged 18 years or younger living in the household, having fewer children in the household with special needs, caring for fewer aging parents, helping parents with fewer ADLS, working fewer hours, and/or having more flexibility in their work schedules to deal with family-related demands. Overall, however, role demands generally either stayed the same or, in some cases, decreased over time. When there were increases in role demands, these tended to be related to increased negative outcomes, while increases in role quality resulted in increases in positive outcomes, and changes in role quality had a greater effect than did changes in objective role demands. With respect to the changes that occurred in the outcomes, at the time of the second survey compared to the first, both husbands and wives had lower levels of work-to-family and family-to-work conflict, wives had lower levels of depression, and husbands were using fewer work accommodations. In sum, these findings indicated the salience of role quality in predicting work and family outcomes and thus have important implications for practice, policy, and research.

A 10-year follow-up study of the caregivers in the original Neal and Hammer study was conducted in conjunction with the comparative study of working, sandwiched couples in Israel noted earlier (i.e., Pines, Hammer, & Neal, 2009). Of particular interest were two

Table 19.1   Changes by role after 10 years

Change in marital status	Wives (%) (N = 125)	Husbands (%) (N = 108)
No longer married	3.2	–
Currently married	95.2	100
Did not indicate	1.6	–
Change in child-care status		
No longer had children ≤ 18	72	78.7
Currently had children ≤ 18	27.2	19.4
Did not indicate	0.8	1.9
Change in parent-care status		
No longer cared for parent	31.2	50.9
Currently cared for parent	68.8	48.1
Did not indicate	–	0.9
Change in work status		
No longer working	18.4	15.7
Currently working	79.2	83.3
Did not indicate	2.4	0.9

questions: (a) What changes had occurred in the roles held by the US working, sandwiched-generation couples after 10 years (i.e., spouse, caregiver to dependent children, caregiver to aging parent(s), and worker)? and (b) What effects did those role changes over time have on individuals' work–family fit, health and well-being, and work outcomes, as well as on the quality of their other roles?

In the original study, 338 couples (676 individuals), including those with annual household incomes lower than $40,000, from across the US completed a mailed survey. Ten years later an attempt was made to re-contact all participants in the first survey and ask that they again complete a mailed survey. A total of 233 individuals (34.5 percent), specifically 125 wives (37 percent) and 108 husbands (32 percent), participated.

As shown in Table 19.1, many changes in the roles occupied had occurred over the 10 years. The majority, two-thirds or more, of the participants, all of whom had been working, married or partnered, and caring both for children and for aging parents in the original study, no longer had children aged 18 years

or younger living in the household. One-third to one-half of the participants were no longer caring for an aging parent, and just under one-fifth were no longer working. A few of the participants were no longer married.

Table 19.2 depicts the most common role combinations after 10 years. The numbers and percentages differ across husbands and wives because in some couples, both members did not complete this wave of data collection. The sample sizes differ between the two tables because to be included in Table 19.2, respondents had to have answered all four role occupation-related questions. As Table 19.2 shows, only about 12 percent of the men and 19 percent of the women who responded continued to hold all four roles, that is, were still working, married/partnered, with a child aged 18 years or younger living with them, and caring for one or more parents at least three hours a week. Overall, then, the working couples who were sandwiched 10 years earlier were much less sandwiched. For the majority, their children had grown up and left home; parent care, however, was more enduring. The most frequent role combination was 'working, married, and caring for a parent' (34 percent of women and 35 percent of men).

To determine the effects of these role changes, multiple regression analyses were conducted. After controlling for the Time 1

Table 19.2   Role combinations after 10 years

Roles held	Wives (%) (N = 121)	Husbands (%) (N = 104)
Working, married, child ≤ 18, and caring for a parent	19.1	11.5
Working, married, and caring for a parent (no child ≤ 18)	33.9	34.6
Working and married (No child ≤ 18 and not caring for a parent)	18.2	32.7
Married and caring for a parent (Not working, no child ≤ 18)	13.2	9.6
All other combinations	15.6	11.6

level of the outcome variable, the findings were as follows. Compared to 10 years earlier:

Effects of role changes on work–family fit

- Wives no longer caring for parents had lower work-to-family conflict.
- Wives no longer caring for parents tended to have higher family-to-work positive spillover ($p = .052$).
- Wives no longer caring for children had lower family-to-work positive spillover.

Effects on health and well-being

- Wives no longer caring for children had lower negative affect.
- Wives no longer married rated themselves more highly in caring for themselves.
- Wives no longer caring for parents rated themselves more highly in caring for themselves.
- Husbands no longer caring for children rated themselves more highly in caring for themselves.

Effects on role quality and performance

- Wives no longer caring for parents had higher job role quality.
- Wives no longer caring for children had higher spousal role quality.
- Wives no longer caring for children rated themselves more highly in performance as a spouse.
- Wives no longer married rated themselves more highly in performance as a parent.
- Husbands no longer caring for children tended to have higher spousal role quality ($p = .058$).

The impact of these role changes (losses) was greater for wives than for husbands. In general, the impact was positive, with the exception of couples who divorced, and wives who no longer had minor children had a lower level of positive family-to-work spillover. For most couples who are working and sandwiched, the message may be that, with time, 'This, too, shall pass.' These analyses demonstrated that after 10 years, the couples' relationship generally improved with the loss of caregiving roles, husbands and wives felt that they were doing a better job of caring for themselves, and wives reported better performance at work and as parents.

THE IMPLICATIONS FOR WORKING, SANDWICHED EMPLOYEES AND THEIR ORGANIZATIONS, POLICY MAKERS AND SERVICE PROVIDERS

Although the bulk of work–family research has focused on the stress and negative effects of holding multiple work and family roles, Neal and Hammer (2007) found higher levels of positive work–family spillover than of conflict between work and family. These results highlight the importance of not overlooking the positive aspects of multiple roles. Family practitioners and managers alike should be aware of the positive spillover that can occur between work and family and attempt to help employees recognize and maximize that positive spillover.

Similarly, Neal and Hammer's (2007) findings concerning the effects of subjective role quality, over and above the objective demands of the various roles, on employees' work and family outcomes suggest the need for practitioners to assist employees in improving their family relationships and perceptions of their family roles and for employers to attempt to enhance employees' job role quality.

The crossover effects found by Neal and Hammer (2007) testify to the importance of considering both members of the couple in work–family research. Collecting data from both members of working, sandwiched couples provides the ability to examine the effects of one spouse's behaviors and perceptions on the other's outcomes. That such effects were found have implications for organizations, service providers, and individuals alike.

Neal and Hammer's (2007) findings suggest several specific things that *employers* can do to help employees who have multi-generational caregiving responsibilities. Minimizing long work hours and increasing employees' sense of control on their jobs (thereby enhancing job role quality) will likely improve employees' work outcomes. Providing flexibility in the place, hours, and time of work will help as well. Similarly, providing and increasing awareness and utilization of workplace supports will be beneficial. Also, since an organization's work–family culture may influence an individual's decision to use a support, and use of workplace supports can lead to better employee health and well-being, ultimately reducing employer health care costs and benefitting organizations' bottom lines, organizations can work toward creating an atmosphere, or culture, that is more family friendly. One way to improve the family-friendliness of organizations is through developing and implementing supervisory training programs focused around being sensitive to employees' work and family responsibilities (Hammer, Kossek, Anger, Bodner, & Zimmerman, 2011).

Regularly publicizing the supports available to employees is another action that organizations can take to enable the maximum number of employees to use the necessary supports. Since Neal and Hammer (2007) and others (e.g., Rosin & Korabik, 2002) have shown that women are more likely than men to use workplace supports, and that men are experiencing more work–family conflict than previously (Galinsky et al., 2011), providing special help to men, as well as marketing available supports to particularly to male employees, may be especially beneficial.

Even though Neal and Hammer (2007) found that as utilization of supports increased, so did work–family conflict and negative work outcomes, they argued that this is not a reason for employers to abstain from providing workplace supports, since employee well-being, especially for men, increased as well. It very well could be the case that as work–family conflict increased, utilization of workplace supports also increased to help men and women better manage their multiple work and family demands. Additionally, these findings highlight the complexity of the work and family system as it may also be the case that when given the opportunity to relieve work–family stress through the use of family-friendly workplace supports, employees (women in particular) may feel that they are able to take on even more family-care responsibility, leading to increased life satisfaction but also increased work–family conflict.

The longitudinal analyses presented here, along with the findings from Neal and Hammer (2007) and Cullen et al. (2009), suggest that there are different developmental stages in caregiving, wherein the demands associated with the various roles (caregiver to children, aging parents, spouse, worker) can be expected to change over time with employees making tradeoffs as they move through these different stages. These findings point to the need for organizations to recognize that they are likely to have employees dealing with multiple caregiving demands and that the demands associated with caregiving are likely to vary considerably, both among employees and over time, necessitating a range of workplace supports (e.g., flexible work arrangements, referral services).

Similarly, the findings by Pines and colleagues (2011) point to the need to consider cultural variations among working, sandwiched individuals. Other findings in the same study indicate the role that social support groups can play in reducing both job burnout and couple burnout. Managers are encouraged to conduct a needs assessment of current employees before implementing family supports, with periodic reassessments conducted to ensure that the supports offered are continuing to meet employees' needs.

It is important to note that the use of supports may not be as important in influencing working, sandwiched individuals' work–family conflict and work outcomes as is the work–family culture in the organizations in which these individuals are employed. The follow-up analyses that Neal and Hammer (2007) conducted provided some support for this idea and suggested that improving the family-friendliness of organizations may prove useful.

This would include creating a culture in which work–family issues are understood and where managers at all levels, from the top to the first-line supervisors, are socialized to be sensitive and supportive of employees' work and family responsibilities. Also, as organizations develop workplace supports, they should consider the increasingly diverse and changing nature of employees' family roles over times (Sahibzada et al., 2005).

Family care practitioners such as counselors, social workers, family therapists, psychiatrists, and employee assistance professionals can assist working, sandwiched individuals by helping them to identify and use positive coping strategies (i.e., prioritizing tasks, seeking emotional and tangible support, maintaining significant social relationships, especially with one's spouse). Also, by being aware of the greater risk of depression, particularly for women, family practitioners can implement strategies for prevention, such as the provision of information and resources, and may be able to diagnose and intervene earlier in cases of depression. Family practitioners can also help working caregivers identify ways in which the individuals for whom they are providing care, children and aging parents alike, can give, as well as receive, assistance. Assisting working caregivers to find ways to enhance the quality of their various roles, particularly the quality of their spousal role, will be beneficial for employees and their spouses, alike. Helping couples to improve their communication techniques and counseling them with respect to effective strategies to use in managing their work and family responsibilities may help to enhance spousal role quality. Aiding couples in understanding how each member's behaviors and attitudes affect the other's experiences will be beneficial as well. Finally, because many sandwiched individuals are working during the weekdays, it will be beneficial for practitioners to be available during at least some evening and weekend hours.

Individuals themselves who are working, caring for children, and caring for aging parents or other elders should strive to increase their resources, such as through seeking emotional and tangible support and through prioritizing, and decrease the demands they face as a way of coping with their multiple work and family responsibilities. They should be cautioned against using coping strategies that involve social withdrawal, however, such as reducing social contacts when overwhelmed with work and family, as the use of such strategies is actually related to negative well-being and work outcomes. Working, sandwiched individuals should be encouraged to nurture their supportive relationships. Because positive coping strategies and role quality sometimes 'cross over' and affect one's spouse's outcomes, couples are urged to seek emotional and tangible support to improve not only their own work and family outcomes, but also those of their spouse.

Finally, in the US, *public policy* changes are needed. As Neal and Hammer (2007) noted, public support for family care in the US lags far behind that available in all other industrialized countries and even many developing countries. In particular, although the provision of leave to care for family members is mandated by federal, and in some cases, state law, this leave tends to be *unpaid* and thus is not frequently used. Similarly, health care coverage is not universal, contributing to huge out-of-pocket expenses for medical care for families. Also, few supports are available related to elder care, and quality, affordable child care is lacking. Neal and Hammer argued for implementing changes to correct these public policy deficiencies in the US

FUTURE RESEARCH

As revealed in the longitudinal analyses presented here, caregiving responsibilities are developmental in nature and change over time. Additional longitudinal research is needed to more completely understand these changes and their implications for individuals, couples, and organizations. Interview, focus group and observational data, as opposed to only survey data, would contribute to deeper understanding, as well. Using a systems framework by gathering data from the children and the aging parents, as well as the working caregivers themselves, would further enhance this understanding.

Additional research also is needed concerning the best means for organizations to improve their work–family culture and the relative importance of work–family culture versus formal workplace supports in influencing work–family fit, well-being and work outcomes.

Because of variations in the definitions of caregiving that have been used and the groups identified for study, precise estimates of the number of people who are engaged in paid work while caring for dependent children and aging parents have proven elusive in the US. Also, there has been relatively little research in other countries concerning the prevalence of working while being sandwiched. Only limited cross-cultural research has been conducted. The Pines et al. (2011) study identified both cross-cultural similarities as well as differences (such as the lower burnout among the Israeli couples) and highlighted the interesting role that reaching middle age seemed to play. More such research is needed to identify similarities as well as divergences in the types of caregiving responsibilities of working, sandwiched individuals in different countries, the perceptions and effects of caregiving, the variations in the supports provided and the use and effects of those supports. Such cross-cultural comparative research would be beneficial not only for more fully understanding cultural variations in caregiving but also for identifying best practices.

NOTES

1   Funding for this study was provided by the Alfred P. Sloan Foundation, Grant # 96-10-20, to M. B. Neal and L. B. Hammer.

2   Funding for this study was provided in part by the US–Israel Binational Science Foundation, Grant #2006213, to A. M. Pines, L. B. Hammer, and M. B. Neal.

REFERENCES

AARP. (2001). *In the middle: A report on multicultural boomers coping with family and aging issues.* Washington, D.C.: AARP. Retrieved from http://assets.aarp.org/rgcenter/il/in_the_middle.pdf

Amatea, E. S., & Fong-Beyette, M. L. (1987). Through a different lens: Examining professional women's interrole coping by focus and mode. *Sex Roles, 17,* 237–252.

Bakker, A. B., Demerouti, E., & Schaufeli, W. B. (2005). The crossover of burnout and work engagement among working couples. *Human Relations, 58,* 661–89.

Barnett, R. (1998). Toward a review and reconceptualization of the work/family literature. *Genetic, Social, and General Psychology Monographs, 124,* 125–183.

Casper, L. M., & Bianchi, S. M. (2002). *Continuity and change in the American family.* Thousand Oaks, CA: Sage.

Chassin, L., Macy, J. T., Seo, D.C., Presson, C. C., & Sherman, S. J. (2010). The association between membership in the sandwich generation and health behaviors: A longitudinal study. *Journal of Applied Developmental Psychology, 31*(1), 38–46.

Chen, Y. M., Hedrick, S. C., & Young, H. M. (2010). A pilot evaluation of the Family Caregiver Support Program. *Evaluation and Program Planning, 33,* 113–119. Retrieved from: http://www.ncbi.nlm.nih.gov/pubmed/19729198

Cullen, J. C., Hammer, L. B., Neal, M. B., & Sinclair, R. R. (2009). Development of a typology of dual-earner couples caring for children and aging parents. *Journal of Family Issues, 30,* 458–483. doi: 10.1177/0192513X08326003

Dhar, V. E. (2011). Transnational caregiving: Part 1, caring for family relations across nations. *Care Management Journals, 12*(2), 60–71.

Durity, A. (1991). The sandwich generation feels the squeeze. *Management Review, 80*(12), 38–41.

Eby, L.T., Casper, W.J., Lockwood, A., Bordeaux, C., & Brinley, A. (2005). Work and family research in IO/OB: Content analysis and review of the literature (1980–2002). *Journal of Vocational Behaviour, 66,* 124–197.

Feinberg, L., Reinhard, S., Houser, A., & Choula, R. (2011, July). Valuing the invaluable: 2011 update. The economic value of family caregiving in 2009. Washington, DC: AARP. Retrieved from: http://assets.aarp.org/rgcenter/ppi/ltc/fs229-ltc.pdf

Fernandez, J.P. (1990). *The politics and reality of family care in corporate America.* Lexington, MA: Heath.

Folkman, S., & Lazarus, R. S. (1980). An analysis of coping in a middle-aged community sample. *Journal of Health and Social Behavior, 21*, 219–239.

Galinsky, E., Aumann, K., & Bond, J. T. (2011, August). Times are changing: Gender and generation at work and at home. Families and Work Institute 2008 National Study of the Changing Workforce. Retrieved from: http://familiesandwork.org/site/research/reports/Times_Are_Changing.pdf

Goode, W. (1960). A theory of strain. *American Sociological Review, 25*, 483–496.

Gorey, K.M., Rice, R.W., & Brice, G.C. (1992). The prevalence of elder care responsibilities among the work force population: Response bias among a group of cross-sectional surveys. *Research on Aging, 14*, 399–418.

Grundy, E., & Henretta, J. C. (2006). Between elderly parents and adult children: a new look at the intergenerational care provided by the 'sandwich generation. *Ageing and Society, 26*, 707–722. doi:10.1017/S0144686X06004934.

Hammer, L., Allen, E., & Grigsby, T. (1997). Work–family conflict in dual-earner couples: Within-individual and crossover effects of work and family. *Journal of Vocational Behavior, 50*, 185–203.

Hammer, L.B., Cullen, J.C., Neal, M.B., Sinclair, R.R., & Shafiro, M. (2005). The longitudinal effects of work–family conflict and positive spillover on experiences of depressive symptoms among dual-earner couples. *Journal of Occupational Health Psychology, 10*, 138–154.

Hammer, L. B., Kossek, E. E., Anger, W. K., Bodner, T., & Zimmerman, K. (2011). Clarifying work–family intervention processes: The roles of work–family conflict and family supportive supervisor behaviors. *Journal of Applied Psychology, 96*, 134–150.

Hochschild, A. (1997). *The Time Bind: When Work Becomes Home And Home Becomes Work*. New York: Henry Holtand Company

Ingersoll-Dayton, B., Neal, M. B., & Hammer, L. B. (2001). Aging parents helping adult children: The experience of the sandwiched generation. *Family Relations, 50*, 262–271. Blackwell Publishing Ltd. Retrieved from: http://www.jstor.org/stable/585878

Keene, J. R., & Prokos, A. H. (2007). The sandwiched generation: Multiple caregiving responsibilities and the mismatch between actual and preferred work hours. *Sociological Spectrum, 27*, 365–387.

Kenny, D. A. (1996). Models of non-independence in dyadic research. *Journal of Social and Personal Relationships 13*, 279–94.

Künemund, H. (2006). Changing welfare states and the 'sandwich generation': Increasing burden for the next generation? *International Journal of Ageing and Later Life, 1*(2), 11–30. Retrieved from: http://www.ncbi.nlm.nih.gov/pubmed/20210842

Menaghan, E. G. (1983). Marital stress and family transitions: A panel analysis. *Journal of Marriage and the Family, 45*, 371–386.

MetLife Mature Market Institute. (2010). *The MetLife study of working caregivers and employer health care costs: New insights and innovations for reducing health care costs for employers*. New York, NY: MetLife. Retrieved from: http://www.metlife.com/assets/cao/mmi/publications/studies/2010/mmi-working-caregivers-employers-health-care-costs.pdf

Miller, D.A. (1981). The 'sandwich' generation: Adult children of the aging. *Social Work, 26*, 419–423.

Moen, P., Robison, J. & Fields, V. (1994). Women's work and caregiving roles: A life course approach. *Journal of Gerontology: Social Sciences, 49*, S176–S186.

Murphy, M. and Grundy, E. 2003. Mothers with living children and children with living mothers: the role of fertility and mortality in the period 1911–50. *Population Trends, 112*, 36–45.

National Alliance for Caregiving in collaboration with AARP. (2009). Caregiving in the US 2009. Report from a study funded by the MetLife Foundation. Retrieved from: http://www.caregiving.org/data/Caregiving_in_the_US_2009_full_report.pdf

Neal, M.B., Chapman, N.J., Ingersoll-Dayton, B., & Emlen, A.C. (1993). *Balancing work and caregiving for children, adults, and elders*. Newbury Park, CA: Sage.

Neal, M. B., & Hammer, L. B. (2007). *Working couples caring for children and aging parents: Effects on work and well-being*. Mahwah, NJ: Lawrence Erlbaum.

Neal, M. B., & Hammer, L. B. (2010). Dual-earner couples in the sandwiched generation: Effects of coping strategies over time. *The Psychologist-Manager Journal, 12*, 205–234.

Neal, M.B., & Wagner, D.L. (2002). Working caregivers: Issues, challenges and opportunities for the aging network. An issue brief commissioned by the US Administration on Aging National Family Caregiver Support Program. Retrieved from: http://www.vickivogt.caregiverslibrary.org/Portals/0/Working%20Caregivers%20-%20Issues%20for%20the%20Aging%20Network%20Fin-Neal-Wagner.pdf

Nichols, L. S. & Junk, V. W. (1997). The sandwich generation: Dependency, proximity, and task assistance needs of parents. *Journal of Family and Economic Issues, 18*(3), 299–326.

Pew Research Center. (2010). *The return of the multi-generational family household*. Washington, D.C.: Pew Research Center's Social & Demographic Trends Project. Retrieved from: http://www.pewsocialtrends.org/files/2010/10/752-multi-generational-families.pdf

Pines, A. M., Hammer, L., & Neal, M. (2009). 'Sandwiched generation' couples: A cross-cultural, cross-gender comparison. *Pratiques Psychologiques*, *15*, 225–237.

Pines, A. M., Hasan, Y., Hammer, L. & Neal, M. (2010). Working couples of the 'Sandwiched Generation' in Israel. In V. Muhlbauer & L. Kulik (Eds.) *Working Families in the Job market in Israel: Social, Economic and Legal Aspects* (pp. 277–305). Tel-Aviv: Peles (Hebrew).

Pines, A. M., Neal, M. B., Hammer, L. B., & Icekson, T. (2011). Job burnout and couple burnout in dual-earner couples in the sandwiched generation. *Social Psychology Quarterly*, *74*, 361–386.

Rosenthal, C. J., Martin-Matthews, A. & Matthews, S. H. (1996). Caught in the middle? Occupancy in multiple roles and help to parents in a national probability sample of Canadian adults. *Journal of Gerontology: Social Sciences*, *51B*, S274–S283.

Rosin, H. M., & Korabik, K. (2002). Do family-friendly policies fulfill their promise? An investigation of their impact on work–family conflict and work and personal outcomes. In D. L. Nelson & R. J. Burke (Eds.), *Gender, work stress, and health* (pp. 211–226). Washington, DC: American Psychological Association.

Sahibzada, K., Hammer, L.B., Neal, M.B., & Kuang, D.C. (2005). The moderating effects of work–family role combinations and work–family organizational culture on the relationship between family-friendly workplace supports and job satisfaction. *Journal of Family Issues*, *26*, 820–839. doi:10.1177/0192513X05277546

Spillman, B. C., & Pezzin, L. E. (2000). Potential and active family caregivers: Changing networks and the 'sandwich generation.' *The Milbank Quarterly*, *78*, 347–374. Retrieved from: http://www.jstor.org/stable/3350598

Stone, R., Cafferata, G. L., & Sangl, J. (1987). Caregivers of the frail elderly: A national profile. *The Gerontologist*, *27*, 616–626.

US Census Bureau. (2012). Statistical Abstract of the United States: 2012, Table 59. Households, Families, Subfamilies, and Married Couples: 1980 to 2011. Retrieved from: http://www.census.gov/compendia/statab/2012/tables/12s0059.pdf

US Department of Labor, Bureau of Labor Statistics. (2008, July). Spotlight on statistics: Older workers. Retrieved from: http://www.bls.gov/spotlight/2008/older_workers/

US Department of Labor, Bureau of Labor Statistics. (2011, March). Women at work. Retrieved from: http://www.bls.gov/spotlight/2011/women/

Wagner, D.L. (2000). The development and future of workplace eldercare. In *Dimensions of family caregiving: A look into the future.* Westport, CT: MetLife Mature Market Institute.

Wagner, D.L., & Neal, M.B. (1994).Caregiving and work: Consequences, correlates, and workplace responses. *Educational Gerontology*, *20*, 645–663.

Westman, M. (2001). A model of stress crossover. *Human Relations*, *54*, 557–91.

Westman, M. (2006). Crossover of stress and strain. In F. Jones, R. J. Burke & M. Westman (Eds.), *Work-Life Balance: A Psychological Perspective* (pp. 164–84). New York: Psychological Press.

Westman, M., & Etzion, D. (1995). Crossover of stress, strain and resources from one spouse to another.' *Journal of Organizational Behavior*, *16*, 169–81.

Wilensky, H.L. (1960). Work, careers, and social integration. *International Social Science Journal*, *12*, 543–560.

Wong, R., Capoferro, C., & Soldo, B.J. (1999). Financial assistance from middle-aged couples to parents and children: Racial-ethnic differences. *The Journals of Gerontology: Psychological and Social Sciences*, *54*, S145–53.

Zedeck, S. (1992). Introduction: Exploring the domain of work and family concerns. In S. Zedeck (Ed.), *Work, families, and organizations* (pp. 1–32). San Francisco: Jossey-Bass.

20

The Social Connections of Older Europeans

Martin Kohli and Harald Künemund

INTRODUCTION[1]

Social connections operate at different levels. There are connections between individuals and society at large, for example, feelings of attachment to and participation in communities and nation-states. There are connections within organizations, from firms, unions, parties or churches to clubs, associations or self-organized initiatives. And there are connections at the interpersonal level: communications among family members, friends, neighbours or colleagues – face-to-face, by phone, mail or e-mail or in virtual social networks on the internet – and the exchanges of services and support that go along with them.

As societies age, increasing numbers and proportions of older people may be in need of such support. On the other hand, the elderly may also become a resource for others. The social connections of older people – among themselves, with other age groups, within organizations and with society at large – are thus increasingly important for personal well-being as well as for social cohesion.

The conceptualization of social connectedness has changed over time. While the emphasis was originally on activities and their social contexts – on the roles still available to the elderly (Rosow, 1974), and on the properties of the social fields in which they participate (Kohli et al., 1993) – recent years have seen a shift away from such a focus on roles and activities toward more network-oriented constructs (Cornwell et al., 2008, 2009; Kohli et al., 2009). The network approach positions itself against both the Parsonian emphasis on the normative integration of society and the atomizing emphasis of much of survey research. The more recent survey work on intergenerational relationships and exchanges also goes beyond treating the respondents as atomized individuals, and thus incorporates (some of) the network dimensions (Kohli, 1999; Künemund and Hollstein, 2000).

Social networks have been shown to buffer the effects of negative life events such as spousal bereavement (Ferraro, 1984; Li, 2007), to reduce mortality (Moen et al.,

1989; Musick et al., 2004; Litwin and Shio-vitz-Ezra, 2006), or to serve as a financial protection mechanism (Lyberaki and Tinios, 2005; Wall et al., 2001). Social networks are thus crucial for well-being in old age. They mediate a range of activities and support, such as participation in volunteering and societal affairs, emotional support, practical help with everyday activities, and personal care in situations of dependency. Beyond personal well-being, support is also important in economic terms (such as for the prevention or delay of costly institutional placement) as well as in sociological terms (for the social inclusiveness and moral cohesion of societies). By this, social networks also contribute to a reduction in public expenditure (European Commission, 2006; Johnson et al., 2007). Social connections are thus a key issue for policies that address aging at both the individual and the societal level.

A third approach that has recently gained currency is that of social capital, a term that is used to refer to both activities and networks: to 'the way in which people participate in their society and the forms of social bonding that take place' (Pichler and Wallace, 2007: 423). This approach has raised a great deal of interest in sociology and political science (Putnam, 2000) as well as in economics (Glaeser et al., 2002).

The three approaches (*activity, network* and *social capital*) are often treated as mutually exclusive alternatives. In our view, this is not compelling. The concept of 'activity' has to do with the opportunities and demands for individuals to be socially productive, while the concept of 'network' focuses on the social relationships that accompany such opportunities and demands. The concept of 'social capital' implies that activities and networks yield certain profits or dividends from which individuals can draw, such as contacts and information that facilitate access to a better position in the labour market or help in situations of need.

In this chapter, we will discuss some of these issues. We will start with a brief theoretical account (section 2), then discuss social

connections in the family (section 3) and in productive activities of the elderly (section 4) before examining the relationship between these interpersonal ties and the welfare state, especially the question of crowding out versus 'crowding in' (section 5). Finally, we draw up a list of the most pressing issues for future research (section 6).

SOCIAL CONNECTEDNESS: THE CENTRAL THREAD IN SOCIAL GERONTOLOGY AND THE SOCIOLOGY OF AGING

Maintaining social connectedness through the transitions of later life (fraught with the potential for isolation) is an important prerequisite for 'successful aging' (see Rowe and Kahn, 1998; Kohli et al., 2009; Sirven and Debrand, 2008). Before going into the current empirical record on the social connections of the elderly, it may be useful to briefly review how the theoretical ideas have evolved. That the elderly are at risk of social isolation has been one of the founding ideas of modern aging research. The explanations for this risk and its evaluation in terms of positive or negative outcomes have changed over time, however. The early activity theories proposed that taking on new roles and relationships is crucial for successful adaptation to retirement (Cavan et al., 1949) and that satisfaction with life is higher when older people are able to maintain their social roles (Havighurst and Albrecht 1953). Social norms and their respective age boundaries were seen as a major reason for decreasing activities and shrinking social networks in old age. Burgess (1960) spoke of aging as a 'roleless role', and thus a life phase in which individuals were at risk of losing their social connectedness. Many authors asserted this to be a consequence of societal modernization, with its devaluation of the productive capacities of the elderly and its dissolution of family solidarity beyond the nuclear household (Cowgill and Holmes, 1972).

As an alternative perspective, Cumming and Henry (1961) proposed the disengagement theory of aging. They shared the view that as people approach old age, they gradually withdraw from social roles and relations. However, they held this 'disengagement' to be a functionally necessary process of the individual retreating from society and the society releasing its hold on the individual – necessary in order to minimise the disruption caused by the individual's eventual physical decline and death.

Other theoretical accounts for the changes in social relations in old age were developed by viewing old age as a stigma, as in the labelling approach (Ward 1977), or as a subculture (Rose 1962) with age-homogeneous relationships, by drawing attention to the shrinking resources of older people as a consequence of having little to offer in exchange processes (Dowd 1975), or as a result of the welfare state that constitutes 'structured dependency' (Townsend 1981).

More recent approaches have focused on preferences, motives and routines that develop earlier in life, so that a life course perspective is required (e.g., Heckhausen et al., 2010). This applies also to the establishment of social networks as 'convoys of support' across the life course (Kahn and Antonucci, 1980). Here, the decreasing network size with age is partly explained by the increasing probability of a death of parents, partners, siblings and friends. The theory of socioemotional selectivity (Carstensen, 1991) highlights changes in individual time perspective as the future lifespan shrinks: People carefully choose with whom to spend their remaining lifetime, and drop less important relations. This explanation has been used to explain the reduction of volunteer activity in old age as well (Hendricks and Cutler, 2004).

CONNECTIONS IN FAMILIES

While most studies concur that network size decreases with age (e.g., Wagner and Wolf, 2001), this does not mean social isolation.

There is some evidence that relationship quality increases with age (Luong et al., 2011). With regard to family integration, the literature today concludes that family bonds usually remain strong throughout adulthood and old age. They are not restricted to nuclear and couple households but go much beyond, especially in terms of connections among adult family generations (whether co-residing or not). This has been shown in detailed country studies including France (Attias-Donfut, 1995), Germany (Kohli, 1999) and the US (Bengtson, 2001), and increasingly also in comparative studies based on data sets such as the *Survey of Health, Aging and Retirement in Europe* (*SHARE*) (e.g., Attias-Donfut et al., 2005; Albertini et al., 2007; Kalmjin and Saraceno, 2008; Kohli et al., 2010) or the *Kinship and Social Security* project (*KASS*) (Heady and Kohli, 2010).

Intergenerational family connections are important for three pervasive crises of contemporary developed societies (Kohli et al., 2010). The first is the proliferation of life course risks due to the retrenchment of welfare states and the loss of stability of work and family careers (e.g., unemployment, divorce). Can intergenerational family support compensate for the retreat of the welfare state and act as an informal insurance for life course risks? The second crisis is that of fertility. Can intergenerational support from parents to their adult children help the latter in their parenting (e.g., through financial support or grandparenting), and thus promote the reconciliation of parenthood and employment? The third crisis is that of dependency in very old age. Can the family help bear the burden of eldercare?

Moreover, families are an important source of generational integration. Contemporary societies are highly age-graded and age-segregated, and thus present a risk of intergenerational conflict and warfare. Families create emotional and material linkages and help to equalize the disparities between generations (Kohli, 1999).

These intergenerational bonds may even become more important for well-being over the life course than nuclear family ties (Bengtson, 2001). They range across different dimensions that have been conceptualized as dimensions of intergenerational 'solidarity': affective, associational, consensual, functional, normative and structural (Szydlik, 2000; Bengtson, 2001).

'Structural solidarity' refers to the physical availability of other family members, in other words, their residential closeness. While new media facilitate communication across space, geographical proximity is still a prerequisite for many types of support. Co-residence among adult family generations has decreased massively over the last century.[2] Today, among the Europeans above the age of 80 who have at least one living child, only 17 percent live together with a child in the same household (Kohli et al., 2008; Hank, 2007).[3] However, by extending the boundaries of 'togetherness' the situation turns out to be very different. If one includes parents and children living not only in the same household but also in the same house – a pattern that is common above all in Germany and Austria – the proportion rises from 17 to 32 percent. By including the neighbourhood (less than 1 km away), the proportion rises to 53 percent. 84 percent have a child living within 25 km.

These European means hide considerable differences between Scandinavia, Central and Western Continental countries, and those of the Mediterranean. The latter are often grouped together as 'strong family countries', and contrasted with the 'weak family countries' of the centre and north of Europe and of North America (Reher, 1998). The strength or weakness refers to cultural patterns of family loyalties, allegiances, and authority but also to demographic patterns of co-residence with adult children and older family members and to organizing support for the latter. The 'strong family countries' have had high fertility in the past but today, paradoxically, are those with the lowest fertility – a state of affairs that is directly linked to the strength of their family tradition. This trend has mostly not yet directly affected the elderly of today and of the near future. For them, the pattern remains one of comparatively high marriage rates and low rates of childlessness. But they are affected in an indirect way, through the decreasing prevalence of marriage and childbearing among their children.

The Mediterranean countries are characterized by very late (and increasing) ages of leaving the parental home among adult children. This is often interpreted solely as an effect of opportunity structures (employment and housing markets), but the variation among countries may also be explained by a cultural tendency towards closer intergenerational ties. While we are not able at this point to differentiate between those who have never left the parental home and those who have moved back later or have had their parents moving closer, the overall proportions are striking. In Denmark and Sweden, 8 and 10 percent of all *SHARE* respondents live with an adult child in the same household, in the 'centre' countries this amounts to between 15 and 22 percent, but in the South to between 37 and 43 percent. Moving beyond the boundaries of the household yields a similar picture. For those below 60, the different ages of leaving the parental home show up clearly. Among the 50–59 year old Mediterraneans, around three fifths still have an adult child living at home with them, while among the Scandinavians, this amounts to less than one fourth. For the oldest age group, the proportions are smaller but the differences between countries even heavier: only 2 percent of the oldest Swedes and 3 percent of Danes live with an adult child, compared to 22 percent of Italians and 32 percent of Spaniards.

But as shown above, living in separate households does not imply that today's elderly have been left alone by their children. Unlike their own parents or grandparents, they are no longer forced by economic necessity to co-reside, and cultural traditions may also be losing their compulsory character. The preference today (at least outside the Mediterranean countries) seems to be for 'intimacy at a (small) distance' – small enough so that relations of exchange and support may function easily across the boundaries of the separate households. This may have resulted in even better generational relationships (Künemund and Rein, 1999). Findings on the frequency of contact, emotional closeness and the exchange of support confirm this view (Kohli et al., 2005). Adult generations in families – even in countries with comparatively weaker family traditions and larger geographical distances – remain closely linked. Contact with the most contacted child is daily for 42 and 45 percent in Denmark and Sweden, respectively, and for between 47 and 55 percent in the countries of continental Western Europe; the Mediterranean countries stand out, with between 84 and 86 percent. In all countries, 70 percent or more have contact at least several times a week; in the Mediterranean countries, this amounts to 95 percent or more. There are those who have no contact at all with their living child or children, but in no country they comprise more than one percent. In the older age groups contact is less frequent – but even among those over 80 years of age between three-fifths (in Switzerland) and more than nine-tenths (in Mediterranean countries) are in contact with a child daily or several times a week. A recent study of longitudinal cohort data in the Netherlands between 1992 and 2002 confirms the view that support exchange and contact have held their own: 'Macrostructural changes have had less destructive influence on parent–child relationships than we initially thought' (van der Pas et al., 2007: 271).

It is obvious that geographic mobility increases in line with labour market flexibility. But to date, it is less well known whether at least one of the children (most likely the youngest; see Konrad et al., 2002) stays within close distance to their parents, or whether 'trailing' parents relocate to move closer to one of their children (Attias-Donfut and Renaut, 1994). Such 'trailing' has its price. Current findings suggest that elderly persons in need of help will try to keep living

as independently as possible in order not to 'burden' their children (Lewinter, 2003), but will turn to their next of kin when this is no longer possible. Providing the elderly with sufficient resources to live on their own so that they can age in place is therefore one of the main policy goals here (OECD Health Project, 2005).

Adult children and their elderly parents thus live close to each other (although seldomly in the same household). Furthermore, they feel close to each other emotionally, have frequent contact with each other, and mutually support each other with several types of help. It is especially this last dimension – in Bengtson's terms, 'functional solidarity' – that has become the focus of attention in recent years. There is now consistent evidence that financial transfers and social support among adult family members are (still) frequent and substantial. They occur mostly in the generational lineage, and – in what has come as a surprise to many, public commentators and academics alike – their net flow is mostly downward, from parents to children (Kohli et al., 2010). They thus serve as an important reminder that the elderly contribute to the well-being of younger age groups.

SHARE data shows that the downward direction is indeed a general pattern, both for *inter vivos* financial transfers and for social support (cf. Albertini et al., 2007, for more detailed results). Resource transfers from parents to children are much more frequent and usually also more intense than those from children to parents. In the ten European countries considered here, more than 21 percent of the respondents have given financial transfers to, and only slightly more than 2 percent have received financial transfers from their children in the previous twelve months. For social support, if looking after grandchildren – which can be critical for young mothers' labour force participation and thus for their ability to combine parenthood and gainful work – is included, the downward direction of help is reaffirmed: almost 37 percent of elderly parents with at least one child outside the household have given to their offspring; among those with at least one grandchild, this percentage increases to 46 percent. The average intensity of the help provided by parents to their children is also higher than the opposite flow: 952 hours of social support per year given versus 530 hours received, and €4698 of financial transfers given versus €1768 received.

The story varies to some extent with age. It is often assumed that children receive financial and social support when their parents are still young and give it back when their parents become old and frail. *SHARE*'s age range of 50 years or more comprises several distinct life phases. Patterns of intergenerational transfers reflect these different situations. While in the youngest group (50–59 years) only 7 percent of respondents receive social support, among those aged 70–79 years this proportion increases to 20 percent, and among the oldest ones (aged 80 or more), to 42 percent. Social support given decreases from 11 percent among those up to 59 years to 7 percent among the 70–79 and 3 percent among the oldest group, and when looking after grandchildren is included (and thus only grandparents are considered), from 63 percent (50–59) to 36 (70–79) and 12 percent (80+). In the latter perspective, therefore, up to those aged 70–79 giving support remains more frequent than receiving it. With financial transfers, there is a net downward flow for all age groups, even though it is less marked among the older ones. Regarding the balance between receiving and giving in monetary value, where time transfers are calculated by an assumed wage rate the results are similar (Kohli et al., 2010; see also Litwin et al., 2008). The age groups from 50–79 are net givers in financial as well as social terms. For those above age 80, the balance of financial transfers remains positive (except for Greece and Spain) while that of social support becomes negative. Financial transfers *inter vivos* are moreover complemented by bequests. *Inter vivos* transfers often go to children in need ('altruism'),

while bequests are distributed equally among all children. The SHARE results thus do not support the assumption of a reversal of the direction of support among the young old. They show that there is a net downward flow of resources from parents to their adult offspring across all countries up to about age 80, and even past that age for financial resources.

How the close ties should be evaluated is controversial, however. Intergenerational relationships in the family are inherently ambivalent (Pillemer and Lüscher, 2004); the balance between solidarity and autonomy has to be continually negotiated among the participants, and under contemporary conditions of individualization this is no easy matter. Close relationships need not be an unmitigated blessing; they can also be a source of conflict, anxiety and frustration (Birditt et al., 2009). The family itself may generate conflicts (such as over inheritance). Network obligations may become burdensome, as in the case of sustained family care for dependent elderly parents, which may restrict caretakers' own life plans. However, open intergenerational conflicts occur in only a small minority of families (Szydlik, 2002)[4] and are less often present in older age groups than in younger ones (Akiyama et al., 2003).

Another issue is partnership disruption. While many studies confirm the view that current family changes pose a risk for the support potential available to future cohorts of elderly people (Pezzin et al., 2008), some evidence indicates that the increase in divorce has not resulted in less support in old age (Glaser et al., 2008). A key for understanding these partly counter-intuitive results may be the interplay between family changes and increasing resources of individuals (education, health, wealth, social connections) and society (welfare state spending, availability of community and market-based services) These resources help to improve intergenerational relationships and to make family support less burdensome (Künemund, 2008).

PRODUCTIVE POTENTIALS AND ACTIVITIES BEYOND THE FAMILY

The traditional view of population aging promotes the idea of the elderly as (only or mainly) a burden on society (in terms of both income and care needs). Much of the discourse on the new challenges posed by aging populations to contemporary welfare systems is based on the assumption that greater longevity implies a higher financial demand for pensions and a higher care demand from families and public services – at a time when the proportion of 'producers' (those in the labour force and those able to give care) is shrinking. The extent to which these, often catastrophic, predictions will become reality depends on several factors, among them (i) how people will be aging: in other words, the extent to which the increasing life expectancy will be accompanied by an improvement in the health of the elderly population (compression of morbidity); (ii) when people will move into retirement, and thus no longer have earnings that cover their financial needs, (iii) what social connections will be available for supporting the elderly, and (iv) the extent to which elderly people will themselves remain productive in their social networks.

The fourth factor addresses the opposite of the traditional view of the elderly as receivers of support from the younger generations, and thus as a *social problem* to be solved, by conceiving of them as supporters of others, and thus as a *social resource*. This view is supported by the data on family exchanges presented above, and has also been gaining ground in the domain of activities outside the family (Herzog et al., 1989; Coleman, 1995; Künemund, 1999; Erlinghagen and Hank, 2008). We should of course not fall into the trap of an exaggerated gerontological optimism by claiming that old age is only about productivity and not also about dependency and need for care. But until recently, the latter aspect has been unduly exaggerated at the expense of the former.

Withdrawal from the labour force may be expected to result in fewer social connections, as far as interactions with work colleagues are concerned. But the transition to retirement is not paralleled by withdrawal from social participation in general. The term 'productive aging' is sometimes used to refer to continued labour force participation, but this is overly restrictive; it should rather be used to point out that activity and social engagement of any kind play a major role in old age as well – a fact that is often neglected in the discourse of intergenerational equity. Several attempts have been made to estimate the value of productive activities in economic terms (Herzog et al., 1989; Herzog and Morgan, 1992; Coleman, 1995; Künemund, 1999). The results obviously differ according to how productive activity is defined.

Economic perspectives generally focus on remunerated activities or those producing valued goods and services that would otherwise have to be purchased in the market – for the most part, paid work and some dimensions of household production, sometimes including care work. Sociological perspectives add not only the latter but informal help of all types, volunteerism and other activities (to the extent that they are of value to others). A broader definition may also take into account activities that help to maintain the ability of an individual to be productive (further education, for example). Finally, psychological perspectives include activities that help to maintain the emotional and motivational preconditions for productivity, for example, the successful adaptation to age-related losses (Staudinger, 1996; O'Reilly and Caro, 1994 provide an excellent overview of definitions of productivity). In this perspective, individual well-being also becomes a productive resource. According to the definition chosen for analysis, either only a minority of older people or nearly all of them are productive (and those who are not can hardly be held responsible for their 'unproductivity' – in most cases we would expect that it is not a voluntary decision to be unproductive in psychological terms).

Using a sociological definition, we find that older people are productive to a remarkable degree. Our data from the 1996 German Aging Survey showed that older people were seldomly active on the labour market (3 percent of the 70–85 year-olds), but 16 percent were active in childcare, 8 percent in personal care, 7 percent in voluntary activities, and 18 percent in informal help within the last three months. Taken together, 39 percent of this age group were 'productive' in a way that produces valued goods and services (Künemund, 1999). Furthermore, 39 percent supported their children and grandchildren by substantial intergenerational material transfers (Kohli et al., 2000). The total number of hours of productive activity solely in volunteerism, childcare and personal care in the population aged 60 to 85 was nearly 3.5 billion hours of (usually unpaid) production of valued goods and services a year. The monetary value of these activities – calculated by the mean net hourly wage rate of workers in the non-profit sector –amounted to about 21 percent of the public pensions in Germany (Künemund, 1999). In 2008, labour market participation and volunteering have increased, while childcare activities have decreased in response to the sharp drop in East German birth rates after unification. Thus, the general conclusion is that older people are contributing to society in economically highly relevant dimensions.

Studies in other countries, such as the US, have come up with roughly similar numbers. More than one-third of Americans aged 65 or over reported voluntary activities, more than 50 percent informal help (Herzog et al., 1996: 327). Coleman (1995) estimated the value of productive activities – care and volunteerism – to be almost 2 percent of US GDP in 1990.

Demand structures play a major role with respect to age-group differences in these activities. Childcare becomes less relevant in old age because the grandchildren have by then reached an age at which they no longer need care. Many aggregate group differences in levels of childcare – such as the difference

between East and West Germany – mainly reflect the difference in the existence of children. Personal care, on the other hand, declines with age mainly because fewer parents are left. For voluntary activities, demographic opportunity structures are less important. The decrease of volunteerism with advancing age – to the extent that it really represents an age rather than a cohort process – may result from self-initiated disengagement on the part of the elderly; our findings suggest, however, that the organizations of this sector have also implemented some informal age limits (Kohli and Künemund, 1996).

International comparisons show that even the definitions of 'voluntary activity' and 'informal help' differ among countries – and so do the opportunities, necessities and constraints for such activities. The numbers are therefore not strictly comparable. They do show, however, that older people are not merely passive recipients of pensions and welfare. In addition to the economic value of their activities, the elderly also contribute productively to society in many different ways – not least in terms of social integration and cohesion. The psychological aspects include benefits in terms of self-efficacy and life satisfaction, which in turn are related to health and longevity.

The positive impact of networks of productive activities would show up even more strongly if reliable and comparable data were available on new forms of engagement and volunteering beyond formal organizations (such as social movements, self-help groups or self-organized learning networks).

By any definition, however, such productive activities comprise, for most people, only a small part of everyday life in retirement – and a large share of older people are not involved at all. Despite the substantial productivity outlined so far, much of life in retirement seems to be oriented towards leisure and consumption. But even here, social connections may play an important and hitherto neglected role. While many of these consumptive activities may be solitary, others are embedded in regular and stable network structures, where meeting for purposes of sociability ('bowling together') may create potentials for more sustained support when it is needed (Putnam, 2000; Brauer, 2005). To date, reliable knowledge about these types of social integration into private (mostly non-kin) networks is extremely rare. In the German Aging Survey, about 40 percent of the 40- to 85 year-olds were regularly involved in at least one such setting (Künemund, 2001). Further research is needed to identify, and possibly strengthen the potentials of these informal social networks. The latter may, in turn, become productive in a wider sense – for instance, in rural communities where formal community services and supports are increasingly lacking.

SOCIAL CONNECTIONS AND THE WELFARE STATE: CROWDING OUT OR CROWDING IN?

Will the social connections of older people still be able to perform? The threats for their effectiveness come first of all from the current demographic shifts. Increasing generational co-longevity and decreasing numbers of siblings and children combine to create 'beanpole families'. Increasing proportions of singles, both among the elderly and among their children, reduce the supply of carers. Increasing rates of divorce and remarriage produce 'blended families'. As a consequence, we may predict a higher potential for parental support and transfers to each adult child, but smaller and less reliable support networks for the elderly. Other societal changes are also relevant. Cultural individualization results in a diminished sense of obligation towards other family generations and more legitimacy of personal choice.

There is a potential dilemma between care and paid employment both at the individual and at the societal level (Keck, 2012). Johnson and Lo Sasso (2000) examined whether the rising labour-force participation rates of married women interfere with care-giving for frail elderly parents. Their results based

on the US *Health and Retirement Study* (*HRS*) indicate that time spent helping parents substantially reduces the labour supply of both women and men. This is especially acute for those in the position of the 'sandwich generation' (Künemund, 2006; Fingerman et al., 2011) – those with a double obligation of care for dependent parents and children. A 'hard' sandwich position – having to care for both dependent generations while simultaneously being in the labour force – is rare. In Germany in 2002, only three percent of the women aged 40 to 44, eight percent of those aged 45 to 49, and three percent of those aged 50 to 54 cared for an elderly family member while having children at home or caring for grandchildren and simultaneously participating in the labour force at least one hour per month (Künemund, 2006). But these low numbers may already be partly the result of a withdrawal from the labour force due to family care obligations.[5] With the rising labour force participation of women and the extension of working life through a later retirement age, the potential time crunch is likely to become harsher. The mid-lifers and young elderly will be faced with the choice between foregoing care and reducing or abandoning employment – even at the expense of the heavy penalties for early exit from the labour force in terms of pension levels that are now being instituted in many European countries. At the societal level, the dilemma is between increasing the labour-force participation of those beyond 55 (an important policy goal of national and EU agendas) and increasing the demand for public care services and institutions. The dilemma also applies to grandparenting. While grandparents may be willing to give substantial amounts of time to the task of caring for their grandchildren – thus allowing their daughters or daughters-in-law to combine parenthood and engagement in the labour force – this may interfere with their own employment.

This creates a need for new arrangements between employment and care – not only for young parents, but for the younger old as well, for example, through the availability of part-time work and leaves or sabbaticals (Keck, 2012). Family care work also needs to be supported by public policy, both in terms of financial subsidies (which will remain much less costly than publicly funded institutional care) and in terms of services to help the helpers. Another principle for public policy is that it needs to be conceptualized as generational policy, being aware that provisions (or their withdrawal) for one generation affect the welfare of all other generations.

A crucial issue here is the mode of articulation between private and public provision of services and resources. In the conventional story of modernization, the emergence of the nuclear family and that of the public old-age security system were seen as parallel and mutually reinforcing processes. The basic assumption was that the development of the welfare state would crowd out the private support within families. The historical shift of responsibility from the family to public social security – with respect to income (from children and savings to pension systems) or care (from the family to the state or community) – may thus have resulted in a general decline of private intergenerational solidarity ('crowding out'; Künemund and Rein, 1999). Recent evidence, however, points to the opposite conclusion: Welfare state provisions, far from crowding out family support, enable the family, in turn, to provide new intergenerational support and transfers (Kohli, 1999; Künemund and Rein, 1999; Lowenstein and Ogg, 2003). For example, when the elderly have sufficient financial resources from state pensions, there is less need for their kin to provide monetary support. Thus, monetary transfers from children to their elderly parents may indeed be crowded out (Reil-Held, 2006). But parents' increasing resources allow them to be not only better able to buy missing services on the market, but also in a better position to initiate an exchange with their children, and by this, to receive more support from them. They can accept help offered to them more easily as they have something to reciprocate;

the quality of the parent–child relationship is improved when there is no need to financially support the aged parents and when public services support the relationship; and some children may offer help in expectation of later transfers. When these public services increase, the family may be expected to provide more of other services, such as emotional support. The overall outcome of this process of substitution is probably more, not less, family solidarity. In these terms, the available empirical findings do not support the crowding-out hypothesis, and partly support the reverse: that the relationship between the state and the family is a process of 'crowding in': Generous welfare systems give resources to the family that help to increase rather than undermine its own solidarity among its members.

The evidence on intergenerational family transfers allows us to conclude that public retirement pension arrangements support not only the elderly themselves, but through them, also their descendants, which improves the quality of intergenerational relations within the family. The current reductions in pension spending could therefore result in less family solidarity. To date, several studies have confirmed this view (Attias-Donfut, 2000; Lund, 2002; Knijn, 2004; Motel-Klingebiel et al., 2005; Armi et al., 2008; Kalmijn and Saraceno, 2008). Nevertheless, these findings are often overlooked in the debate on generational equity (see Kohli, 2006); the idea that the welfare state crowds out the family is still prominent among politicians and the broader public.

Regarding friendship, privately organized groups, and social activities in associations – ranging from active involvement and volunteering to long-term membership – the same argument of 'crowding in' may apply. When the elderly have sufficient resources of their own, they are not forced by necessity to rely on their families. Instead, their resources enable them to stay involved in reciprocal giving and receiving, to initiate an exchange, and also to participate in volunteering activities (Oorschot and Arts, 2005).

WHAT REMAINS TO BE DONE?

As the preceding sections have shown, the basic patterns of family connections in old age and of the exchanges within them have by now been well established. The same is true for some of the productive activities outside the family. In order for policy to be adequately targeted, however, more specific research will need to address a number of substantive issues that have been neglected so far:

- the role of *wider kinship ties* (for example, the demographic potential and relevance in case of need of siblings or in-laws);
- the needs of *special groups* (the childless or divorced, for example) and the availability of compensatory ties;
- the extent and effect of *gender differences* in social connections and exchange activities (the incidence of caring men, for example, or the effects of caring on the couple's division of formal and informal work);
- the incidence, strength and reliability of *informal sociability and solidarity* in situations of need;
- the extent and consequences of *regional disparities* (urban–rural differences in aging and service provision, for example);
- the impact of *ethnic or religious disparities* (with respect to family ties;, for example)[6]
- the way in which *socio-economic disparities* affect formal and informal networks;[7] and
- the functioning of *kin and non-kin ties of elderly migrants* (both for those having migrated earlier and those migrating after retirement.

The last issue merits special attention. Immigrants in most European countries are younger than the native populations, and this may explain the fact that research has been late to address elderly migrants. But immigrant populations now age rapidly and present new challenges for policies of aging. There is some evidence that the patterns of exchange in the family ties of immigrants differ systematically from those of natives (Baykara-Krumme, 2008). Networks of immigrants often remain transnational and may function as channels of remittances from host to home societies. Another important phenomenon that gives rise to specific transnational links is the migration of retirees from Northern and Western Europe to the Mediterranean countries in search of better living conditions ('amenity migration', King et al., 2000; Braun and Arsene, 2009).

There is, moreover, a range of more systematic problems to be addressed:

- *The comparative dimension:* Europe can be considered a 'laboratory' for assessing the impact of structures, cultures and institutions (Kohli, 2004). There is a well-developed research literature on welfare states and family regimes, but few studies have focused on social connections. Comparisons are needed among European societies, but also with the other advanced societies in North America and East Asia that face similar challenges of population aging.
- *The life-course dimension:* A key question here is how social connections are differentially important and provide different benefits in different periods of the life course. On the one hand, networks may be less important for the elderly because there is no longer a need for them in processes of job search or partner search (which has been the focus of much of early social network analysis). On the other hand, they may become more critical because the elderly are no longer integrated into the formal organizations of the workplace and have higher needs of security and support. There is some research on the life-course changes of network size and composition (e.g., Wagner and Wolf, 2001). But more systematic analyses of network patterns and network salience over the life course are required to overcome the narrow focus on specific periods such as older age (or adolescence or early adulthood, for that matter).
- *The longitudinal dimension:* While cross-sectional associations between the patterns of social connections and their antecedents and consequences can yield more or less plausible interpretations, reliable knowledge about trends (age-period-cohort matrix) and about causal processes presupposes longitudinal data. A number of single-country longitudinal surveys (especially the large household panels) are available for this purpose, while comparative panel databases – such as *SHARE* – are still in their infancy. Changes over time in network composition and in the support and exchange relations of elderly people need to be described and analysed in greater depth (Peek et al., 1997).

- *Integration of substantive research on the social connections of the elderly with the formal approaches of general network analysis*: Network analysis is a burgeoning field that has spawned its own theoretical and methodological approaches as well as a broad research literature. The lack of articulation between general network analysis and the analysis of the social connections of the elderly is an obvious knowledge gap.
- *Trends in technology:* This chapter has not gone into how new information technologies facilitate social interaction, or into social networks in terms of 'web 2.0' internet communities. The current elderly are not yet much affected by developments such as computer-mediated friendships, chatting or discussion groups; the 'digital divide' is not least a cohort divide. But it is obvious that these new technologies will in many ways alter our social relations, including those of the coming cohorts of elderly people. These trends are important not only from an individual point of view, but also with respect to interfaces between formal and informal support (healthcare systems, service providers etc.). Serious research in this new field is still rare and should be expanded.

NOTES

1 Parts of this chapter are based on our contribution to the European Science Foundation Forward Looks Project *Ageing, Health and Pensions in Europe* directed by Arthur van Soest and Lans Bovenberg (Kohli and Künemund, 2010). We are grateful to the editors, reviewers and conference participants of this project for their many valuable suggestions.
2 There have been some countervailing trends recently for young adults: The median age of exit from the parental home in Southern Europe has in fact increased during the last two decades (Billari and Liefbroer, 2010).
3 These and the subsequent findings are based on the second wave of the *Survey of Health, Ageing and Retirement in Europe (SHARE)*, with data collected in 2006 in fourteen countries (Sweden, Denmark, Germany, the Netherlands, Belgium, France, Switzerland, Austria, Poland, Czech Republic, Spain, Italy, Greece and Israel).
4 Among the respondents in the German Aging Survey (1996) – the German population aged 40–85 – 11 percent said they were in conflict with a close person in an intergenerational family relation (Szydlik, 2002).
5 Note that the numbers reported in the literature diverge hugely. Between one and 80 percent of the population have been identified as sandwiched adults. The divergence is a consequence of different concepts, operationalizations and samples (Künemund, 2006). In Germany,

more than 80 percent of the men and women aged 40 to 44 have at least one relative of both younger and older generations, but most of the parents of these sandwiched adults are not in actual need of personal care, nor are most of their children. Furthermore, many studies do not find a negative relationship to well-being (e.g, Spitze et al., 1994). There is already a tradition of calling the metaphor of the sandwich generation a modern myth (e.g., Loomis and Booth, 1995). There can be no doubt, however, that the competing demands from work and family – especially with regard to caring for disabled family members – take a heavy toll on some women.
6 See Litwin's typological approach to the comparison of ethnic groups in Israel (Litwin, 2004).
7 Findings so far tend to show that upper classes have higher levels of formal social capital, especially through associational networks, while informal contacts are not so clearly stratified by class (Pichler and Wallace, 2009).

REFERENCES

Akiyama, H., T.C. Antonucci, K. Takahashi and E.S. Langfahl (2003) 'Negative Interactions in Close Relationships across the Life Span', *Journal of Gerontology* 58B, P70–P79.

Albertini, M., M. Kohli and C. Vogel (2007) 'Intergenerational Transfers of Time and Money in European Families: Common Patterns – Different Regimes?' *Journal of European Social Policy* 17, 319–334.

Armi, F., E. Guilley and C.J. Lalive d'Epinay (2008) 'The Interface between Formal and Informal Support in Advanced Old Age: A Ten-year Study', *International Journal of Ageing and Later Life* 3 (1), 5–19.

Attias-Donfut, C. (1995) 'Le double circuit des transmissions' in C. Attias-Donfut (ed.) *Les solidarités entre générations. Vieillesse, familles, État.* (Paris: Nathan), 41–81.

Attias-Donfut, C. (2000) 'Familialer Austausch und soziale Sicherung' in M. Kohli and M. Szydlik (eds) *Generationen in Familie und Gesellschaft.* (Opladen: Leske + Budrich), 222–237.

Attias-Donfut, C. and S. Renaut (1994) 'Vieillir avec ses enfants - Corésidence de toujours et recohabitation', *Communications* 59, 29–53.

Attias-Donfut, C., J. Ogg and F.-C. Wolff (2005) 'European Patterns of Intergenerational Financial and Time Transfers', *European Journal of Ageing* 2, 161–173.

Baykara-Krumme, H. (2008) *Immigrant Families in Germany: Intergenerational Solidarity in Later Life* (Berlin: Weißensee).

Bengtson, V.L. (2001) 'Beyond the Nuclear Family: The Increasing Importance of Multigenerational Bonds', *Journal of Marriage and Family* 63, 1–16.

Billari, F.C. and A.C. Liefbroer (2010) 'Towards a New Pattern of Transition to Adulthood?', *Advances in Life Course Research* 15, 59–75.

Birditt, K.S., L.M. Miller, K.L. Fingerman and E.S. Lefkowitz. (2009) 'Tensions in the Parent and Adult Child Relationship: Links to Solidarity and Ambivalence', *Psychology and Aging* 24, 287–295.

Brauer, K. (2005) *Bowling Together: Clan, Clique, Community und die Strukturprinzipien des Sozialkapitals* (Wiesbaden: VS Verlag für Sozialwissenschaften).

Braun, M. and C. Arsene (2009) 'The Demographics of Movers and Stayers in the European Union' in E. Recchi and A. Favell (eds) *Pioneers of European Integration: Citizenship and Mobility in the EU* (Cheltenham: Edward Elgar), 26–51.

Burgess, E.W. (1960) 'Aging in Western Culture' in E.W. Burgess (ed.) *Aging in Western Societies* (Chicago: University of Chicago Press), 3–28.

Carstensen, L.L. (1991) 'Socioemotional Selectivity Theory: Social Activity in Life-span Context', *Annual Review of Gerontology and Geriatrics* 11, 195–217.

Cavan, R. S., E.W. Burgess, R.J. Havighurst and H. Goldhamer (1949) *Personal Adjustment in Old Age* (Chicago: Social Science Research Associates).

Coleman, K.A. (1995) 'The Value of Productive Activities of Older Americans' in S. A. Bass (ed.) *Older and Active: How Americans over 55 are Contributing to Society* (New Haven: Yale University Press), 169–203.

Cornwell, B., E.O. Laumann and P.L. Schumm (2008) 'The Social Connectedness of Older Adults: A National Profile', *American Sociological Review* 73, 185–203.

Cornwell, B., L.P. Schumm, E.O. Laumann and J. Graber (2009) 'Social Networks in the NSHAP Study: Rationale, Measurement, and Preliminary Findings', *Journal of Gerontology: Social Sciences,* 64B (Supplement 1), i47–i55.

Cowgill, D.O. and L.D. Holmes (eds) (1972) *Aging and Modernization* (New York: Appleton-Century-Crofts).

Cumming, E. and W.E. Henry (1961) *Growing Old: The Process of Disengagement* (New York: Basic Books).

Dowd, J:J. (1975) 'Aging as Exchange: A Preface to Theory', *Journal of Gerontology* 30, 584–593.

Erlinghagen, M. and K. Hank (eds) (2008) *Produktives Altern und informelle Arbeit in modernen Gesellschaften. Theoretische Perspektiven und empirische Befunde* (Wiesbaden: VS Verlag für Sozialwissenschaft).

European Commission (2006) *The Impact of Ageing on Public Expenditure: Projections for the EU-25 Member States on Pensions, Healthcare, Long-term Care, Education and Unemployment Transfers (2004–50). Report Prepared by the Economic Policy Committee and the European Commission (DG ECFIN).* (Brussels: European Communities).

Ferraro, K.F. (1984) 'Widowhood and Social Participation in Later Life: Isolation or Compensation?' *Research on Aging* 6, 451–568.

Fingerman, K.L., L.M. Pitzer, W. Chan, K.S. Birditt, M.M. Franks and S. Zarit (2011) 'Who Gets What and Why: Help Middle-aged Adults Provide to Parents and Grown Children', *Journal of Gerontology: Social Sciences* 66B, 87–98.

Glaeser, E.L., D. Laibson and B. Sacerdote (2002) 'An Economic Approach to Social Capital', *Economic Journal* 112, 437–458.

Glaser, K., C. Tomassini and R. Stuchbury (2008) 'Differences over Time in the Relationship between Partnership Disruptions and Support in Early Old Age in Britain', *Journal of Gerontology* 63B, S359–S368.

Hank, K. (2007) 'Proximity and Contacts between Older Parents and their Children: A European Comparison', *Journal of Marriage and Family* 69, 157–173.

Havighurst, R.J. and R. Albrecht (1953) *Older People* (New York: Longmans Green).

Heady, P. and M. Kohli (eds.) (2010) *Family, Kinship and State in Contemporary Europe, Vol. 3: Perspectives on Theory and Policy* (Frankfurt/M: Campus).

Heckhausen, J., C. Wrosch and R. Schulz (2010) 'A Motivational Theory of Life-span Development', *Psychological Review* 117, 32–60.

Hendricks, J. and S.J. Cutler (2004) 'Volunteerism and Socioemotional Selectivity in Later Life', *Journal of Gerontology* 59B, S251–S257.

Herzog, R.A. and J.N. Morgan (1992) 'Age and Gender Differences in the Value of Productive Activities. Four Different Approaches', *Research on Aging* 14, 169–198.

Herzog, R.A., R.L. Kahn, J.N. Morgan, J.S. Jackson and T.C. Antonucci (1989) 'Age Differences in Productive Activities', *Journal of Gerontology* 44, S129–138.

Herzog, A.R., M.M. Franks, H.R. Markus and D. Holmberg (1996) 'Productive activities and agency in older age' in M.M. Baltes and L. Montada (eds) *Produktives Leben im Alter.* (Frankfurt/M.: Campus), 323–343.

Johnson, R.W. and A.T. Lo Sasso (2000) *The Trade-off between Hours of Paid Employment and Time Assistance to Elderly Parents at Midlife* (Washington: The Urban Institute) (Ms.).

Johnson, R.W., D. Toohey and J.M. Wiener (2007) *Meeting the Long-term Care Needs of the Baby Boomers: How Changing Families Will Affect Paid Helpers and Institutions* (Washington: The Urban Institute) (Ms.).

Kahn, R.L. and T.C. Antonucci (1980) 'Convoys over the Life Course: Attachment, Roles, and Social Support' in P.B. Baltes and O.G. Brim (eds) *Life-span Development and Behavior* (New York: Academic Press), 383–405.

Kalmijn, M. and C. Saraceno (2008) 'A Comparative Perspective on Intergenerational Support: Responsiveness to Parental Needs in Individualistic and Familialistic Countries', *European Societies* 10, 479–508.

Keck, W. (2012) *Die Vereinbarkeit von häuslicher Pflege und Beruf* (Bern: Huber).

King, R., T. Warnes and A. Williams (2000) *Sunset Lives* (Oxford: Berg).

Knijn, T. (2004) 'Family Solidarity and Social Solidarity: Substitutes or Complements?' in T. Knijn and A. Komter (eds) *Solidarity between the Sexes and the Generations* (Cheltenham: Edward Elgar), 18–33.

Kohli, M. (1999) 'Private and Public Transfers between Generations: Linking the Family and the State', *European Societies* 1, 81–104.

Kohli, M. (2004) 'Intergenerational Transfers and Inheritance: A Comparative View' in M. Silverstein (ed.) *Intergenerational Relations across Time and Place* (*Annual Review of Gerontology and Geriatrics*, vol. 24). (New York: Springer), 266–289.

Kohli, M. (2006) 'Aging and Justice' in R. Binstock and L. George (eds) *Handbook of Aging and the Social Sciences, 6th ed.* (San Diego: Elsevier), 456–478.

Kohli, M., M. Albertini and H. Künemund (2010) 'Linkages among Adult Family Generations: Evidence from Comparative Survey Research' in P. Heady and M. Kohli (eds) *Family, Kinship and State in Contemporary Europe. vol. 3: Perspectives on Theory and Policy* (Frankfurt/M: Campus), 195–220.

Kohli, M. and H. Künemund (1996) *Nachberufliche Tätigkeitsfelder – Konzepte, Forschungslage, Empirie* (Stuttgart: Kohlhammer).

Kohli, M. and H. Künemund (2010) 'Social Networks' in L. Bovenberg, A. Van Soest, and A. Zaidi (eds) *Ageing, Health and Pensions in Europe: An Economic and Social Policy Perspective* (Basingstoke: Palgrave Macmillan),141–167.

Kohli, M., H.-J. Freter, M. Langehennig, S. Roth, G. Simoneit and S. Tregel (1993) *Engagement im Ruhestand. Rentner zwischen Erwerb, Ehrenamt und Hobby.* (Opladen: Leske + Budrich).

Kohli, M., K. Hank and H. Künemund (2009) 'The Social Connectedness of Older Europeans: Patterns, Dynamics and Contexts', *Journal of European Social Policy* 19, 327–240.

Kohli, M., H. Künemund and J. Lüdicke (2005) 'Family structure, proximity and contact' in A. Börsch-Supan et al. (eds) *Health, Ageing and Retirement in Europe.*

First Rresults from SHARE (Mannheim: Mannheim Research Institute for the Economics of Aging),164–170, 207–231.

Kohli, M., H. Künemund, A. Motel and M. Szydlik (2000) 'Families Apart? Intergenerational Transfers in East and West Germany' in S. Arber and C. Attias-Donfut (eds) *The Myth of Generational Conflict: Family and State in Ageing Societies* (London: Routledge), 88–99.

Kohli, M., H. Künemund and C. Vogel (2008) 'Shrinking Families? Marital Status, Childlessness, and Intergenerational Relationships' in A. Börsch-Supan et al. (eds) *Health, Ageing and Retirement in Europe (2004–2007) Starting the Longitudinal Dimension* (Mannheim: Mannheim Research Institute for the Economics of Aging), 164–171.

Konrad, K.A., H. Künemund, K.E. Lommerud and J.R. Robledo (2002) 'Geography of the Family', *American Economic Review* 92, 981–998.

Künemund, H. (1999) 'Entpflichtung und Produktivität des Alters', *WSI-Mitteilungen* 52, 26–31.

Künemund, H. (2001) *Gesellschaftliche Partizipation und Engagement in der zweiten Lebenshälfte. Empirische Befunde zu Tätigkeitsformen im Alter und Prognosen ihrer zukünftigen Entwicklung* (Berlin: Weißensee Verlag).

Künemund, H. (2006) 'Changing Welfare States and the "Sandwich Generation" – Increasing Burden for the Next Generation?' *International Journal of Ageing and Later Life* 1, 11–30.

Künemund, H. (2008) 'Intergenerational Relations within the Family and the State' in C. Saraceno (ed.) *Families, Ageing and Social Policy: Intergenerational Solidarity in European Welfare States* (Cheltenham: Edward Elgar), 105–122.

Künemund, H. and B. Hollstein (2000) 'Soziale Beziehungen und Unter-stützungsnetzwerke. in M. Kohli and H. Künemund (eds) *Die zweite Lebenshälfte – Gesellschaftliche Lage und Partizipation im Spiegel des Alters-Survey* (Opladen: Leske + Budrich), 212–276.

Künemund, H. and M. Rein (1999) 'There is More to Receiving than Needing: Theoretical Arguments and Empirical Explorations of Crowding in and Crowding out', *Ageing and Society* 19, 93–121.

Lewinter, M. (2003), 'Reciprocities in Caregiving Relationships in Danish Elder Care', *Journal of Aging Studies* 17, 357–377.

Li, Y. (2007) 'Recovering from Spousal Bereavement in Later Life: Does Volunteer Participation Play a Role?' *Journal of Gerontology* 62B, S257–S266.

Litwin, H. (2004) 'Social Networks, Ethnicity and Public Home-care Utilisation', *Ageing and Society* 24–921–939.

Litwin, H. and S. Shiovitz-Ezra (2006) 'Network Type and Mortality Risk in Later Life', *The Gerontologist* 46, 735–743.

Litwin, H., C. Vogel, H. Künemund and M. Kohli (2008) 'The Balance of Intergenerational Exchange: Correlates of Net Transfers in Germany and Israel', *European Journal of Ageing* 5, 92–102.

Loomis, L.S. and A. Booth (1995) 'Multigenerational Caregiving and Well-being: The Myth of the Beleaguered Sandwich Generation', *Journal of Family Issues* 16, 131–148.

Lowenstein, A. and J. Ogg (eds) (2003) *OASIS – Old Age and Autonomy: The Role of Service Systems and Intergenerational Family Solidarity*, final report. Haifa (Ms.).

Lund, F. (2002) 'Crowding in Care, Security and Micro-enterprise Formation: Revisiting the Role of the State in Poverty Reduction and in Development', *Journal of International Development* 14, 681–694.

Luong, G., S.T. Charles and K.L. Fingerman (2011) 'Better with Age: Social Relationships Across Adulthood', *Journal of Social & Personal Relationships* 28, 9–23.

Lyberaki, A. and P. Tinios (2005) 'Poverty and Social Exclusion: A New Approach to an Old Issue'. in A. Börsch-Supan et al. (eds) *Health, Ageing and Retirement in Europe: First Results from the Survey of Health, Ageing and Retirement in Europe* (Mannheim: MEA), 302–309.

Moen, P., D. Dempster-McClain and R.M. Williams (1989) 'Social Integration and Longevity: An Event History Analysis of Women's Roles and Resilience', *American Sociological Review* 54, 635–647.

Motel-Klingebiel, A., C. Tesch-Römer and H.-J. von Kondratowitz (2005) 'Welfare States Do Not Crowd out the Family: Evidence for Mixed Responsibility from Comparative Analyses', *Ageing and Society* 25, 863–882.

Musick, M.A., J.S. House and D.R. Williams (2004) 'Attendance at Religious Services and Mortality in a National Sample', *Journal of Health and Social Behavior* 45, 198–213.

OECD Health Project (2005) *Long-term Care for Older People* (Paris: OECD).

Oorschot, W. and W. Arts (2005) The Social Capital of European Welfare States: The Crowding out Hypothesis Revisited, *Journal of European Social Policy* 15, 5–26.

O'Reilly, P. and F.G. Caro (1994) 'Productive Aging: An Overview of the Literature', *Journal of Aging and Social Policy* 3 (6), 39–71.

Peek, C.W., B.A. Zsembik and R.T. Coward (1997) 'The Changing Caregiving Networks of Older Adults', *Research on Aging* 19, 333–361.

Pezzin, L.E., R.A. Pollak and B.S. Schone (2008) 'Parental Marital Disruption, Family Type, and Transfers to Disabled Elderly Parents', *Journal of Gerontology* 63B, S349–S358.

Pichler, F. and C. Wallace (2007) 'Patterns of Formal and Informal Social Capital in Europe', *European Sociological Review* 23, 423–435.

Pichler, F. and C. Wallace (2009) 'Social Capital and Social Class in Europe: The Role of Social Networks in Stratification', *European Sociological Review* 25, 319–332.

Pillemer, K. and K. Lüscher (eds) (2004) *Intergenerational Ambivalences: New Perspectives on Parent-child Relations in Later Life* (Boston: Elsevier).

Putnam, R.D. (2000) *Bowling Alone: The Collapse and Revival of American Community* (New York: Simon and Schuster).

Reher, D. S. (1998) 'Family Ties in Western Europe: Persistent Contrasts', *Population and Development Review* 24, 203–234.

Reil-Held, A. (2006) Crowding Out or Crowding In? Public and Private Transfers in Germany', *European Journal of Population* 22, 263–280.

Rose, A.M. (1962) 'The Subculture of the Aging: A Topic for Sociological Research', *The Gerontologist* 2: 123–127.

Rosow, I. (1974) *Socialization to Old Age.* (Berkeley: University of California Press).

Rowe, J.W. and R.L. Kahn (1998) *Successful Aging* (New York: Pantheon).

Sirven, N. and T. Debrand (2008) *Promoting Social Participation for Healthy Ageing. A Counterfactual Analysis from SHARE*. Paris: IRDES working paper 7.

Spitze, G., J.R. Logan, G. Joseph and E. Lee (1994) 'Middle Generation Roles and the Well-being of Men and Women', *Journal of Gerontology* 49, S107–S116.

Staudinger, U.M. (1996) 'Psychologische Produktivität und Selbstentfaltung im Alter' in M.M. Baltes and L. Montada (eds) *Produktives Leben im Alter*. (Frankfurt/M.: Campus), 344–373.

Szydlik, M. (2000) *Lebenslange Solidarität? Generationenbeziehungen zwischen erwachsenen Kindern und Eltern* (Opladen: Leske + Budrich).

Szydlik, M. (2002) 'Wenn sich Generationen auseinanderleben', *Zeitschrift für Soziologie der Erziehung und Sozialisation* 22, 362–373.

Townsend, P. (1981) 'The Structured Dependency of the Elderly: A Creation of Social Policy in the Twentieth Century', *Ageing and Society* 1, 5–28.

van der Pas, S., T. van Tilburg and K. Knipscheer (2007) 'Changes in Contact and Support within Intergenerational Relationships in the Netherlands: A

Cohort and Time-sequential Perspective' in T. Owens and J.J. Suitor (eds) *Advances in Life Course Research: Interpersonal Relations Across the Life Course (vol 12)* (London: Elsevier), 243–274.

Wagner, M. and C. Wolf (2001) 'Altern, Familie und soziales Netzwerk', *Zeitschrift für Erziehungswissens chaft* 4, 529–554.

Wall, K., S. Aboim, V. Cunha and P. Vasconcelos (2001) 'Families and Informal Support Networks in Portugal: The Reproduction of Inequality', *Journal of European Social Policy* 11, 213–33.

Ward, R.A.(1977) 'The Impact of Subjective Age and Stigma on Older Persons', *Journal of Gerontology* 32, 227–232.

21

Engaging Elders in Community and Society

Stina Johansson

INTRODUCTION

In this chapter I will address contradictory perspectives related to old people and their engagement in the community. Some perspectives take their point of departure in the idea of the individual steadily developing their abilities, with the aim being to live in later life as an active and equal citizen. Close to it is the ideal of life-long learning. Similarly, this perspective can include the ideal of an aging community in which people's networks are organically linked and create a social capital. Such perspectives are mostly found within social gerontology, psychology, social psychology and pedagogy. For one reason or another some people are, during shorter or longer periods of their lives, excluded from such a self-realization. This brings us into perspectives that focus on people who, during their lives, become marginalized. Poverty, health problems, disability and the need for social care can be reasons for non-participation or exclusion. Disciplines like sociology, social policy, economics,

social work, geriatrics or social medicine focus on such causes. Sometimes on the surface those contradictory perspectives can intersect, for example when active engagement is directed towards marginalized people. Such processes could be found in research performed within social work, pedagogy, psychology or social medicine.

POLICIES RATHER THAN THEORIES DEFINE THE RESEARCH AREA

All disciplines normally change in focus and scope over time, because of scientific achievements or changes in social policies. I will demonstrate that the expectations of old people's active participation, both in society and in their private lives, has increased. People are nowadays expected to take responsibility for their own health and well-being. Old people are also expected to participate in a thriving economy, sometimes referred to as the 'silver economy' (*silverekonomi*), making them effective consumers. Increased expectations can be both encouraging and marginalizing.

To make a clear distinction between a scientific conceptualization and a concept formed by a political ideology is not easy. My first example intends to show how the view of the elderly and their abilities has changed, thanks to research taken from the field of sexology. The transformation has been one of the elderly being viewed as a homogeneous group with quite low expectations towards viewing the elderly as a heterogeneous group with high demands directed towards them. The low expectations were embedded in the elderly as well as in others in the community. In a study by Zetterberg (1969), the expectation of sexual activity among old people was low. Zetterberg limited the interviewees to people under 62, in an imagination that people above that age weren't sexually active. In a later study (Lewin 1998), knowledge about sexual activity among elderly people had increased and the selection of interviewees was extended to people below 74. A replication of the study is planned but still there is no decision about the selection criteria.

As a result of increased expectations the market creates new opportunities, but also stressful situations, for people who want to take full advantage. My analysis discusses such changes in terms of the dilemmas that arise.

Expectations on people to engage with their own aging and in societal formations have influenced professional attitudes. For example, two relevant concepts, *reciprocity* and *dependency* are not only *theory-impregnated* but also *policy-impregnated*. A Swedish example within the field of social care could give an idea of what could happen with a concept over time.

Material on the micro level collected in the NETWORK study from the end of 1980s and early1990s (Anderson and Johansson 1989) found that many elderly care recipients were not themselves active in negotiations about how much help they should receive. A husband, Sven, helps his wife, Anna:

Interviewer:	Who took the initiative to [get] your public help?
Husband:	I did. It was not so easy because I do not think she had let anybody into the house.
Interviewer:	So you contacted home care services?
Husband:	Yes I think so. I do not remember so well. You know in the beginning the same person came and it was easy then. Also the neighbor had such help, and she could learn to know the care workers. It went easier so…

As I see it, Sven negotiates for Anna and the social services gradually adapt to her needs at that time, yet aware of her desire to keep control over their house. The staff accepted her attitude and gave her the chance to actively keep control over her home.

In a later study of old people's coping in everyday life Dunér and Nordström (2005) found three types of care recipients: those who took an active part in the negotiation, those who took an adaptive part and those who were passive in the negotiation. The latter were described as persons '*No longer having the strength to manage their everyday lives, such elderly people have given up the control over their lives*'. The conclusion the authors make is that those elderly *who give up control see no chance of doing anything autonomous about their situation*.

By the time of their first conversation, the choice was between *caring* or *nursing*, in which the care provided related to the relation between the care recipient and the care provider/s. The care recipient was seen as a part of a social context and her or his dependency on that setting was understood and respected. The relationship between the parties was easily negotiated. With the policy shift from a caring perspective to a *service* perspective, the needs assessment also shifted, from focus on the *relationship* between service provider and recipient to focus on the *individual citizen*. The people who did not have the capacity to take an active part in the negotiation were at risk of being directed towards standardized programs not suited to them.

Another shift refers to the view of the active citizen. Volunteering was traditionally an activity chosen because it was valued meaningful for the volunteer. Now such activities may have become a way to supplement public welfare, and is partly a publicly organized (M. Johansson 2008) *welfare need*. The term was coined by Laslett (1991), who suggested volunteering as a welfare *need* and suggests the support of older volunteers, who should be offered meaningful activities. Activities mentioned were in the cultural sector and bound, perhaps, to more urban lifestyles. The transformation from an individual need into a societal may change the motive and the motivation for volunteering.

This chapter will contextualize active aging where healthy and wealthy persons are involved, not only on their participation in unpaid activities, but also on the role of the active older person as taxpayer and costumer.

MATERIAL

My intention is to give a broad picture of research in different disciplines about elder engagement, supplemented by some in depth presentations from my own research over 25 years. I will stress the relational aspects and return to the early work of Kari Wærness (1984), who makes an analysis of the concept of caring. Her analysis provides a deeper understanding of why care is different to services. *Reciprocity*, which is a necessity in a caring perspective, is not necessarily implied in service relations. With a deeper understanding of reciprocity and dependency we can better understand many of the activities where elders are engaged.

By re-using examples from the already introduced NETWORK-study (Anderson and Johansson 1991) and contrasting the findings with more recent knowledge I will clarify how attitudes and norms have changed since that material was collected in the late 1980s and the early 1990s. By studying communication in networks at different times we can reach a deeper understanding of changed patterns for relations within families and relations between the individual, the family

and the community. People with extensive care needs participated in a study performed in three Swedish municipalities. The municipalities chosen provided different examples of how social services and informal social networks influence the everyday situation for the care recipient.[1] Further material, the GERDA-study, was collected almost 20 years later. This was a survey of people aged 65 and 75 in the Ostrobothnia Region, and the county of Västerbotten, Sweden conducted in 2005 (the total number of participants was 4927) (Johansson 2006). A replication of the GERDA-study was performed in 2010. A survey of people aged 65, 70, 75 and 80, and in the same regions as the 2005 study (the number of participants was 10208). A third set of material was collected in an Australian-Swedish project called the SOCIAL CAPITAL-study, which aimed to compare the generation of social capital in the two countries through volunteering (Leonard and Johansson 2008; Johansson, Leonard and Noonan 2012). All three projects focused on rural areas, bringing a dimension of diversity between rural and urban areas into the discussion.

DEMOGRAPHY AND ENGAGEMENT

With longer life expectancy and a decrease in numbers of births there follows an age structure with a higher proportion of old people. In 2010 18 percent of the Swedish population was 65 and over while 12 percent were 10 or younger.

Demography and social security

When Sweden in 1913 decided on introducing retirement pensions the age of retirement was set at 67. The argument was that the life expectancy at that time was 69 for those who had reached 67, and that the pension should cover the two remaining years. At that time 32 percent of the population was under 15, 7.1 percent were between 65 and 80, and 1.8 percent were 80+. The proportion of elderly people (65+ and 70+) was at that time higher than in other European countries. Today life expectancy in Sweden is calculated at 83.2 years for new-born girls and 79,1 years for new born boys. The age of retirement is flexible and set between 61 and 67. This means that if you retire early you can be alive another 20 years, many of those years in a healthy condition. A discussion about rising the retirement age is underway.

Since the introduction of pensions in 1913 almost one generation has been added to our lives. A four-generation family is today a quite common phenomenon, as are centenarians. The period between wage-work and dependency of help or healthcare has for a short period in modern societies been looked upon as a period of 'free time'. Expectations have been built on a period of life when people can satisfy some of their earlier repressed wishes. When two years of freedom increased to 20 maybe this expectation on later life has merely to be looked upon as illusory, given a lack of resources to fund pensions. From this perspective elderly people are often looked upon as a burden (c.f. Almberg et.al. 1997). This is not the whole truth. As I will show in this chapter the elderly can also be looked upon as a resource.

One way to stay engaged in community and society is to participate in paid labor up in old ages. People who remain as wage workers will be rewarded with a higher pension. The Swedish legislation raised the right to job retention to 67 years of age. In an international perspective, the Swedish employment rate after the age of 65 is high. Of 11 countries investigated only Denmark and Switzerland show activity on about the same level (SOU 2010: 85).

People's movements

In Sweden the most significant role for voluntary organisations has since long been the strengthening of democracy and citizenship. One traditional role of such organisations has been to influence government. Older people would be some of the most active members of the large organizations associated with the peoples' movements, and in Sweden with its 9 million residents there are five established general pensioner's organizations: *Pensionärernas riksorganisation* (Swedish National Pensioners' Organization) PRO, with 404,800 members, established 1942. www.pro.se; *Sveriges Pensionärsförbund* (The Swedish Pensioner's Association) SPF, with 262,000 members, established 1932, www.spfpension. se; *Sveriges Pensionärers Riksförbund* SPRF, 35,000 members, established 1937 (www. sprf.se); *Riksförbundet Pensionärsgemenskap* 30,000 members, established 1974, ecumenical (www.rpg.org.se); As a fifth one *Svenska Kommunalpensionärers Riksförbund* (SKPF) could be mentioned, 150 000 members, trade union related (www.skpf.org). The organizations act as pressure groups with interests in pensions, elderly care, consumer's issues etc. They also organize cultural activities for their members. Volunteering has become important.

The membership in Swedish voluntary organizations has changed in its character so also it´s dependency from the public sector. M. Johansson (2008) presents the new form of hybrid organizations that have stronger links to local organizations – like the eldercare cooperatives described above - than to people's movements. The transformation may lead to that individual motive for volunteering changes.

Eldercare cooperatives – linking micro to macro

At the end of the last decade, a network of NGOs together with the Swedish Ministry of Enterprise, Energy and Communications started a rural campaign 'All Sweden shall live'. The depopulation of the Swedish countryside formed the setting for this campaign. The sparsely populated areas in the northern inland regions in particular faced a lack of jobs and service facilities. The ones who moved away were mostly young people. The villagers felt abandoned by the authorities. The aim of the campaign was to mobilize the people in the rural districts and to change the attitudes of the general public and the decision makers. Last but not least, the objective was to improve national rural policies (http://www.helasverige.se/kansli/in-english/our-history/).

The focus was on mobilizing local people, changing the attitudes of the public and decision-makers and improving national rural policies. Village Action Groups were formed to deal with local matters using community development principles. As part of this campaign, at least eight villages started eldercare cooperatives. For a more detailed description, see Johansson, Leonard and Noonan (2012).

In Figure 21.1 you can see the demographic structure in one typical sparsely populated municipality, Strömsund, the small city chosen to represent the rural areas in the northern part of Sweden. We find a concentration of residents partly with middle-aged wage earners, sometimes characterized as old employees, and partly in what we should

call young olds. Bengtsson (2010) argues that young and middle-aged wage earners have different relations to the welfare structure because their capacity as consumers increases with age (ibid.: 2). Middle-aged wage earners participate actively in the welfare economy both as producers and as consumers. Thanks to them both public services and private activities can keep running. With that in mind, the population structure is at present favorable in Strömsund, but within a few years the situation might be different. Those middle-aged wage-earners will have retired and the proportion of participants in labor will be decreased. Strong norms may indicate to residents that if the municipality is to survive all citizens must mobilize and take an active part in the process. In Strömsund, the first cooperative for elderly care was founded in May 1990 by four women, the intention being to not only work with elderly people but also to create opportunities for the survival of the village. As an

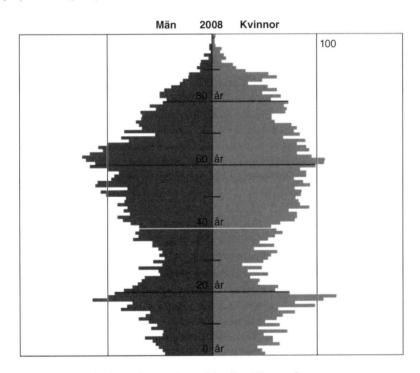

Män   2008   Kvinnor

ⁱ**Figure 21.1   Demography in Strömsund municipality. Men and women**

Source: http://www.h.scb.se/kommunfakta/pyramider/index.asp

i Thanks to Fredrik Snellman who has provided the tables from the GERDA-study.

individual initiative which generated followers, it could be used for theoretical reflection
for a deeper understanding of the process.

The demographic structure illustrates (see
Figure 21.1) that the initiative for the survival strategy and the responsibility for its
implementation in fact comes from the relatively old people in the community. From a
social capital perspective, the integration of
people of different ages is important, and in
this community a role for pensioners was
created.

The eldercare facility was a hub for the village. The elderly care recipients played an
important role as consumers of services.
Although many of the cooperatives obtained
financial support from the Swedish state or the
EU to start up, all were now dependent on the
favour of the municipal governments that distributed the funding for elderly care hostels by
purchasing accommodation. Sometimes the
strategies of the municipalities to deploy their
budget through standardized facilities could
be unfavourable to the cooperatives (Turunen
and Maruzars 2010) as well as the minimum
requirements of trained personnel (Johansson,
Leonard and Noonan 2012). All the eldercare
cooperatives had facilities for non-residents,
such as lunches for school, a library, TV with
a large screen display for watching football or
as a cinema, thus strengthening the networks
with the community.

Another way that strong networks and
trust was built was by encouraging neighbours to contribute gifts, such as elk meat or
cloud berries, or by helping, for instance with
clearing away snow. From a social care perspective the integration of care with a variety
of social practices is vital. Some cooperatives formally incorporated volunteering into
their functioning, both to reduce costs and to
encourage social interaction from the village.
People's contribution generates social capital
through the creation of networks with strong
and trustful social bonds.

Also important for creating social capital
was the cooperative structure. Most are based
on joint ownership with the villagers and
future residents of the facility, who have

bought shares to raise funds for the cooperative. In one village, everybody bought a
share. As managers, the villagers could also
incorporate other services that provided an
income stream, created job opportunities,
and that would not otherwise have been possible in a small village. From a caring perspective the trustful personal relation is
important. This community development
function is also a key strategy in the 'All
Sweden shall live' campaign.

Despite the pressures of finance and
national standards, the cooperatives grow
stronger by learning from one another. One
of the longest running cooperatives advises
others not to depend on one income source
but to cooperate with many different partners. Their experiences are also being transmitted globally. One of the cooperatives is
often visited by foreign experts (for instance,
from. Ireland, Iceland, Finland and China)
and has developed the model of 'A House of
Activities for All', which promotes the
importance of activities for all generations,
not only for old people.

THIRD AGE, SOCIAL NETWORKS AND SOCIAL CAPITAL

To describe the consequences of increased
life expectancy the concept of 'third age' has
been used. The problematic concept has been
defined from different perspectives. Thelin
(2010) found three main definitions: First,
third age could be the phase of life which
starts with retirement from wage work and
ends with the dependency of informal and/or
formal help and services. Second, it could be
a homogeneous group dealing with achievement and personal fulfillment. Third, it could
be what we call active aging, engaging
healthy and wealthy persons. George (2011:
248) adds that authors concerned with the
concept of third age might disagree with
what they view as defining the life-style.
Some authors focus on the unpaid productive
activities performed by persons between paid
work and health problems and dependency of

health care, other authors focused on leisure and self-actualization, while a third group of authors focus on consumerism. Marginalization or exclusion – which I think is a dilemma – does not form a theme in the discussion about third age.

When third agers appear in relation to work it is as a resource for society. That sometimes this norm could be stressful is something often missed. Unpaid activities, which have been delivered voluntarily, might now turn into something more enforced due to demography and economy.

When third agers appear in relation to the market their role as consumers is underlined. The medical industry has delivered solutions for how to cope with higher demands with new products to meet expectations of a longer and healthier life (Tiefer 2004). A growing market is the industry of wellness, with companies producing health food, wellness through training, massage, naprapathy or other alternative treatment methods. Enterprises concerned with wellness production are mostly established in big cities, but in rural areas it is a growing part of entrepreneurship (Lönnbring 2010: 111).

Not all third-agers have the same capabilities to engage in productive activities and do not then experience the same benefit. In the literature the risk for exploitation is mentioned (Carr and Hendricks 2011; Johansson, Leonard and Noonan 2012). Carr and Hendricks (2011) question whether the language of productive aging itself is promoting potentially unrealistic expectations of what people should do in later life.

In the description of the cooperative two concepts were introduced: social networks and social capital. Both of them are often used in relation to health and volunteering. Sometimes the concepts overlap and sometimes they are defined as being distinct. In research literature social capital has a positive relation to democracy, well-being, physical and mental health, quality of life, crime reduction and economic growth (Putnam 1993; Hyyppä and Mäki 2001a, 2001b), and it is also how it can be used in relation to

elders engagement in society. Social capital describes how society accumulates resources from individuals who engage in activities that benefit the greater society (Carr and Hendricks 2011). Social capital then refers to more or less dense interlocking networks of relationships between individuals and groups with positive effects on engagement and democratic development (Portes 1998, Putnam 1993, Woolcock 1998). People engage with others through a variety of lateral associations which must be voluntary and equal (for an overview see Onyx and Bullen, 2000).

If we accept the simplest definition, social capital has to do with what can be generated in social networks. It is then important to ask: a value for whom? When caring is linked to social capital it is generally assumed that the nature of the relationship is that social capital is a resource that can be used for care work. When there is inadequate funding of aged care services by the public sector then social capital may be seen as a substitute for economic and human capital. Caring therefore is seen as a drain on capital, whether it be economic or social capital. However, this does not have to be the case. Johansson, Leonard and Noonan (2012) show in the SOCIAL CAPITAL-study that aged care services, if thoughtfully designed, can not only consume social capital, but also generate it.

MUTUAL AID

Informal care-giving remains the backbone of care provision in Europe and for many dependent older people it is their preferred care option. People belonging to the third age, sometimes called the 'sandwich generation' (Norris 1988), often balance caring relations between both younger and older generations. They often help their children, grandchildren and other relatives as well as other people in the same generation. They often help people with severe care needs on a regular basis.

Johansson and Fahlström (1993) analysed material from eight caring women who experienced stress in the caring situation. They all helped a relative with severe care needs. The relative received extensive assistance from the public care services. It was not the work load itself that influenced how stressed the women felt, it was rather the conditions of everyday life, their autonomy, and the rewards of the care situation. It became clear that the feeling of 'being recognized' in the situation, either by the care receiver or by the home help staff, was clearly negatively related to feelings of stress. We also found that some of these eight women described a kind of stress that was not mentioned in the literature, what we have called existential stress, caused by pondering about the meaning of what one does and whether it is right or wrong.

Theodor and his helping network

Theodor´s problem is a form of circular disorder that has led to a series of amputations of legs and arms. To begin with, his need of care was not so extensive, but as far as his arms and legs have been amputated he now needs help with almost everything. Theodor did not want any help from the public home care services. He arranged an informal care network with his family and relatives. His wife Kristin was central. She had to leave her employment. After some time caring for her husband made her stressed and she wanted to go back to her earlier employment. After some crisis in the family, their daughter then became the main carer. When the daughter could not cope any more a grandchild took on a role, half-time employed by the municipality. The granddaughter seems to be satisfied. For her it is natural that caring for a family member in something which should be arranged for within the family. Yet Kristin, Theodor's wife, preferred help from public home help services. The extensive support network around Theodor is presented in Figure 21.2.

This example from the 1990s (Johansson and Fahlström 1993) shows that family caring is not always unproblematic. Stress among informal family carers is often mentioned in literature (Johansson and Åhlfeldt 1996, Sand 2000). Eva F. Kittay et.al. (2005) argues that it is quite reasonable that public funds are used to build a supporting structure that includes supervision and education, which involves volunteers and caring family members.

The Swedish government has in recent years worked on the supposition that the

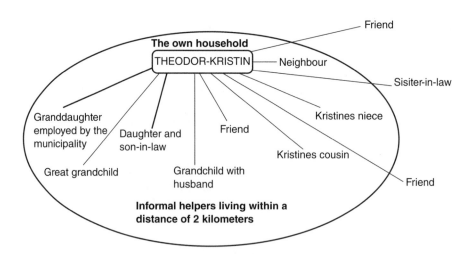

Figure 21.2   A network of informal helpers around a care recipient living in a rural area

healthy elderly will contribute to the care of their peers in need of support. Some municipalities provide financial compensation for family members who provide help and care. In certain cases family members can be employed by the municipality and in other cases the person in need of assistance can obtain a family caregiver grant to pay a family member for the work carried out (L Johansson et.al. 2011). Cash benefits for family care do not give full compensation.

WHO VOLUNTEER?

It might be assumed that the full employment policy (work-line) allows less time for wage-workers to participate in informal care or to volunteer in an organization on a regular basis. However, there is no evidence to support this. In the following I will describe how the multiple dimensions of volunteering appear, both contextually as in urban and rural areas and individually with different patterns of involvement for women and men and also for healthy persons compared to persons in poor health conditions.

Jegermalm and Jeppson-Grassman (2009, 2010) present data from an interview study undertaken with a representative sample of Swedes aged 18–84 about their volunteering. The response rate was 70 percent. They found that among old people (60+), informal contributions as well as formal volunteering are quite common between the ages of 60–74.

A greater age follows a decrease in contributions. In the GERDA study, using the same volunteering questions as the Australian Bureau of Statistics Survey (ABS 2000), we found the same pattern as in the Jegermalm and Jeppson-Grassman study: that volunteering decreases with higher age. Persons aged 65 and 75 in the counties of Västerbotten, Sweden and Ostrobothnia, Finland, were – among other things – asked if they contribute in voluntary work either for an organization or if they volunteer outside of a formal organization. In both Sweden and Australia older people make a considerable contribution to their communities through their engagement in voluntary work. The volunteering rate for people aged 65 and 75 years was about 30 percent for the Swedish county sample (GERDA).

Survey of rural Sweden

In Sweden there are 20 sparsely populated municipalities.[2] It is unsurprising that people in those municipalities have started cooperatives in which elderly care is organized with both employed staff and volunteers. Berglund and her research team (2005) found that in small communities where public care is either absent or insufficient, a reciprocal exchange between friends or extended families develops. Social movements and special interest organizations have acted as a driving force in the fight for equal treatment and political equality (Berglund et.al. 2005: 270).

Table 21.1   Percent of males and females aged 65 and 75 living in urban and rural areas who volunteered 2005 and 2010 in Västerbotten and Ostrobothnia (*N* in formal org. = 7384, *N* in households = 6293)

Forms of volunteering	Urban area (municipality more than 50 000 inhabitants)			Rural area (municipality less than 50 000 inhabitants)		
	Total	Males	Females	Total	Males	Females
Formal organization	29.7	32.3	27.4	40.7	40.9	40.5
Help in own household	17.1	22.0	12.7	22.3	26.5	18.8
Help in another household	31.8	31.2	32.5	32.3	35.8	29.4

Source: The GERDA-material.

The rate of volunteering was as shown in Table 21.1 higher in rural than in urban areas. More in-depth analysis of the GERDA-material revealed that the smaller the municipality of residence, the more voluntary work was reported. For example the self-reported voluntary work in the largest and the fastest growing city was 24 percent while in the smallest municipalities self-reported engagement in voluntary work for an organization was 39 percent. Also, 38–42 percent of respondents in small communities reported that they performed informal voluntary work. Similarly it is 38 percent for the Australian non-metropolitan population (ABS 2000).

Probably, the demographic structure is one reason for that. Society has to adapt to rising life expectancy through local services, the use of modern assistive devices and the general welfare does not reach the periphery.

A focus on gender

In literature it is often shown that volunteering displays a gender divide. Early feminists such as Gilligan (1982) and Noddings (1984) have stressed women's communicative and caring skills. Swedish researchers also convey that belief. The role model is a well educated person – not economically privileged – mostly an elderly woman who participates in many different activities (SOU 1999: 84, 150). Later feminists criticized those findings for being essentialist and built on measures that belittle communications skills into submissiveness and dependency (Buss 1990). In an Australian study (Onyx and Bullen 2000) where questions about attitudes (value of self), trust/ perceived safety, participation in the local community, reciprocity, personal empowerment, diversity/openness, relations within the workplace, attitudes to government, and demographic information were asked, no gender differences were revealed on the total score, subscales and individual items. Only in the smaller Networking Study significant differences were found in the Family and Friends subscale.[3] Leonard and Onyx (2007) argue

that if there are differences between men and women, such differences are likely to be qualitative and subtle, and perhaps dependent on the context in which they occur.

In our early NETWORK-study the living conditions in the early 1990s were found to be of importance for the interplay between formal and informal care. In cases where the care giver lived with the care recipient the public services provided were adjusted to the family situation. But there was a gender dimension in the balance between formal and informal help received. A woman supported by her husband or her son received more formal help than a man supported by his wife or daughter. Women were expected to help more. Men caring for somebody also received more informal help from relatives and neighbors compared to women providing the same amount of help. (Johansson and Åhlfeldt 1993) With a more gender equal society those differences might disappear. They can also show up in new patterns (Andersson 2007).

Jegermalm and Jeppson-Grassman (2009, 2010) found a more complicated pattern. In their study men dominated among the formal volunteers while women dominated among the informal contributors. The GERDA-study presents a regional picture of men and women participating equally in formal volunteering, while informal volunteering was more common among men. Men also more frequently helped a person living in another household. In the 2010-study there was an increase in volunteering compared to 2005 (see Table 21.2). When controlling for place of residence we found that men and women participate in voluntary work equally in urban areas, but that men participate more than women in rural areas (see Table 21.1). One interpretation of the findings in the GERDA-material could then be that gender roles under such circumstances are renegotiated.

When controlling for age, in the data collection from the 2005 GERDA-study, it was more common that 65 year olds participated than 75 year olds, except when caring for a

Table 21.2   Forms of volunteering in Västerbotten and Ostrobothnia 2005 and 2010. Percent volunteers among men and women aged 65 and 75 (N = 7384)

Forms of volunteering	Young olds aged 65						Old olds aged 75					
	Total		Males		Females		Total		Males		Females	
	2005	2010	2005	2010	2005	2010	2005	2010	2005	2010	2005	2010
Formal organization	31.6	35.9	33.6	39.5	29.9	32.4	30.0	40.3	28.8	42.6	30.9	38.5
Help in own household	17.7	14.5	21.8	19.3	14.1	9.8	27.2	21.9	32.0	27.5	23.5	17.1
Help in another household	36.3	41.5	34.3	41.3	38.0	41.6	25.8	25.8	27.0	28.9	24.8	23.1

Source: The GERDA-material.

person within their own household, in which the elderly frequently performed such work. We also found a change between 2005 and 2010. In the 2010 data collection both men and women, regardless of age, had increased their volunteering in formal organizations, while helping someone in their own household had decreased. Also, men's assisting somebody in another household had increased while women 75+ reported providing less of such help.

The magnitude of volunteerism among men is in a way remarkable, as we are used to findings that doing unpaid work is, if not a female undertaking, at least an undertaking in which men and women participate equally. The GERDA-material shows that men volunteered more than did women (see Table 21.1). I suggest four possible explanations:

1 The result shows the importance of context analysis. My guess is that the peripheral situation, with the unbalanced demographic structure that follows, will create an environment for renegotiation of the gender roles.
2 Everyday life tasks are difficult to describe and we are not used to reflect on what and how we perform certain tasks. Men can better than previously supposed describe their efforts as the situation is new for them.
3 According to Berleen (2004) elderly Swedish men have better health than elderly women.
4 Men are more ready to perform these tasks as it is a new experience whereas women are dissatisfied with such work (c.f. Ghazanfareeon Karlsson et.al. 2007).

A focus on health

In the political discussion the relation between health and volunteering has two sides. Primarily the healthy elderly should take responsibility for their own healthy aging.

Jegermalm and Jeppson-Grassman (2009, 2010) found that people who volunteer in formal organizations estimated their health as good. This was also the case for people in the group who informally contributed by helping next of kin, even if the proportion of self estimated health was slightly lower in their group. People contributing both informally and in formal organizations, the 'superhelpers', were the healthiest. Jegermalm and Jeppson-Grassman argue that it is important for social policy planners to recognize these groups of older people and better understand the dynamics of their unpaid work in order to ascertain whether they might need support as providers and to enhance their well-being. There is a risk their generosity could be exploited.

In the GERDA-study (see Table 21.3) we found the same pattern for those volunteering in formal organizations while the pattern was the opposite for people assisting people in the own household. Those 1584 (of 4927) people still in wage-work volunteered more for an organization than non wage-working people. Further, 37.8 percent of the wage-working women did volunteer work for an organization, compared to 33.1 percent of the already retired;

Table 21.3 Percent of males and females with good or poor health respectively who volunteer 2005 and 2010 aged 65 and 75 in Västerbotten and Ostrobothnia (N = 7384)

Forms of volunteering	Excellent/good health			Fair/poor health		
	Total	Males	Females	Total	Males	Females
Formal organization	38.6	39.7	37.5	28.3	29.3	27.6
Help in own household	18.0	22.6	13.5	21.8	26.4	18.5
Help in another household	35.5	36.0	34.9	26.1	27.3	25.3

Source: The GERDA-material.

40.2 percent of the wage-working men volunteered compared to 35.4 percent of the retired. One possible explanation is that those who still wage-work are healthier than their retired counterparts. Another explanation could be that the activity level is constant during the life-span. Active citizens participate constantly in public relations. With regard to helping a person in their own household the pattern was different. A higher proportion of retired people than wage-working people helped somebody in their own household.

MOTIVES FOR ENGAGEMENT

I want to return to the conversation from the beginning of the chapter, where Anna's need of services and care in the example from 1990 was negotiated in the context of her social network and family situation, in a good example of a trustful situation without pressure.

The GERDA-findings are that most people volunteer because it gives them positive experiences. They become personally satisfied, and feel good helping others. They use knowledge they have got earlier in life and they are satisfied by social contacts.

The most common answer (Table 21.4) among both men and women is that it gives them personal satisfaction and that they want to help others. More men than women say that it gives them personal satisfaction. Men also refer more often than women to membership of an organisation as a positive reason, while women more often than men

Table 21.4 Motives for volunteering. The GERDA-study 2005 (N = 1471)

Motives	Percent
It gives me personal satisfaction	24
I want to help others	19
I can use my knowledge	18
It gives me social contacts	17
It works activating	14
It is a project within the family	14
I want to be useful	12
I am a member	11
Nothing special	11
Religious conviction	9
I learn new things	7
Obliged to	2

refer to religious conviction. Women also mention social reasons for their engagement. More in-depth analysis shows that reasons for doing voluntary work differ between cities and sparsely populated areas.

In the SOCIAL CAPITAL-study, Johansson, Leonard and Noonan (2012) argue that pressure to care may be a barrier to the requirement that social capital is generated by voluntary activity. Because social capital requires trust, activities generated by emotional manipulation, or the perception that there is no alternative, are problematic.

The voluntary center (Frivilligcentral)

Bergström (2005) interviewed five volunteers – all retired – at a Swedish Centre for voluntary work (Frivilligcentral), which was founded in 1999 and is conducted in cooperation with Red Cross and some pensioners' associations. The target is to conduct 'friendships services'(väntjänst) among lonely and isolated people, to create and offer a better quality of life. The activities are built on voluntary contributions with some subsidies from the municipality and county council, and are complementary to public services.

The Centre has a phone time on restricted hours as it is staffed by volunteers. Callers are relatives, professionals or the person in need of help. The Centre offers personal visits, accompaniment to the health center or hospital, dentist, to the hair dresser etc. They can also offer help with reading, gymnastics and singing groups at the service centre. Professionals distribute the assignments.

The motivation for doing voluntary work with elders was the focus of the study. Some of the answers included:

- 'I want something to do. A retired person not engaged in others will feel confined. You lose contact with circumstances'.
- 'Some are clever in reading. I am not. Needlework takes time and I have what I need. Of course you miss many other pleasant activities as a volunteer so I choose to care for my old relatives all the time'.
- I think it is important to have a mission to fulfill. To feel needed. I don't know what to do if not engaged in this. I reflected on that when I retired; that I should experience time as too slowly moving. How should I while away the time? I have never regretted my choice. I feel happy with my situation. I get so much back.
- 'To volunteer has always been a natural part of my life. I want to make an effort for others. It gives me so much. If there was not a Voluntary Centre I should search for something else. The voluntariness is important and makes the contribution less demanding'.
- 'I know that there are many lonely people, old people. If you then can contribute a little… you will get old one day. Maybe it is a little egoistic…'
- 'And the pleasure. I can see that she recovers when I come. You make a good deed if you may call it so, and old people can give you much through talking about old days. I have got many good friends, if I may call them so'.

- 'Sometimes I realize that it takes all the day. I consider that I could go down town for shopping and nothing should happen. It is of a great value to feel that you have done something'.
- 'I feel it is stimulating, to be outdoors and to recognize what happens. If you don't engage yourself you will feel empty'.

The caring circle (Noddings, 1984) has widened from the family circle towards the community. In the study from the Voluntary Centre (Bergström 2005), the volunteers mentioned such positives as 'possibilities to learn more through education and study visits', 'the response is so rewarding', 'the joy and happiness', 'the possibilities to get new friends', 'one becomes extrovert', 'the appreciation', 'the belonging to a group'.

THE AGING FRIENDLY COMMUNITY

In the beginning of the chapter I introduced the idea of an ideal aging community as a context in which people's networks are organically linked and in which old people are looked upon as resources and capable to create social capital. In the chapter I have presented a more complex picture of participation in networks and NGOs where demography, place, gender and individual health matter. Old people represent a heterogeneous group. Different individuals have different capacities for engagement.

As shown in the chapter much has been changed in Sweden during the period that passed between the NETWORK-study and the GERDA-study. The public services are more restrictive with their assistance. People´s movements have reduced their ambitions to influence the central government and strengthened their commitment to local contexts. Some areas have been opened even for older people to engage in. Old people have become healthier, work more and retire later in life so they might be willing to fill up the gaps provided the conditions will be reasonable. How can we use our knowledge related to demography, place, gender and health to understand more about what happens in the heterogeneous group called "the elderly"?

Recall Sven and his wife Anna, the rural couple who participated in a network-focussed negotiation with public authorities. Such negotiation has become rarer in present Swedish elderly care. In literature we can locate a need for some filter between the frail elderly person and the care manager when caring is negotiated. For Theodor's family members the demands of the care situation became increasingly in conflict with the demands of their life situation, which explained, in part, the different degrees of feelings of stress that the daughters and sons, siblings and husband/wife described. There were different expectations of help, the 'psychological demands' varied among the groups, and there was variation regarding how well the care of a family member could be fitted into the demands of their overall life situation. Once again we encountered difficulties in articulating the choices that had to be made in everyday situations. 'I had no choice' was a common response.

Researchers agree on that at least some frail old people need more protection than public services offer. Sometimes families in the NETWORK-study couldn't supplement care that public services provided. Johansson et.al. (2012) argue that when the public authorities are relying on the social capital of the citizens, it seems reasonable that they should identify and support models that replenish the assistance. Fagerström et.al. (2011) reported from the GERDA-study that weak trust in family and friends or neighbours and decreased functional ability seem to be associated with a subjective feeling of insecurity. The recommendation is then to strengthen their opportunities to build social networks, such as discussion groups and group activities from whom they could gain strength.

Subsidies to support active engagement in society after retirement are devised on a macro level, of what is best from a societal perspective. There is a major concern that governments' interest in social capital is solely about saving money on service provision. In this chapter I have focused on efforts from below to adapt local communities to their needs for survival. Whatever models are developed, there is a need to link together micro and macro provision to harness the resources of wider society to support both individuals and communities. It is then important to adapt to local variations as well as differences in individual capacities.

In this chapter I have argued that the pressure to engage has increased. The combined effect of aging populations and a decrease in governments' ability to fund services have created a climate that can both build and disassemble social capital. To build social capital it is important to keep voluntary and unpaid activities meaningful and stimulating for those who engage in them. Some scholars raise a warning finger:

> But the stronger the norms that emphasize volunteering as a hallmark for the Third Age, the more that adults who are unable to do so will be marginalized. They will be seen by others as failing to meet social expectations and, to the extent that they internalize these norms, will view themselves as failures. (George 2011: 250)

There may be a need for more volunteering. However, it needs to be supported and given public recognition. Volunteering in the context of cooperatives can be structured to further build social capital while still contributing to the financial viability of that organisation. Because the volunteers in the SOCIAL CAPITAL-study would be members of the cooperative, they would contribute to the management and decision-making and voluntary activities could be designed so as not to be burdensome to the volunteer. Such cooperative still need support from their municipalities. Also Jegermalm and Jeppson-Grassman suggest a better understanding and support to prevent exploitation of peoples generosity.

Research from a social planning perspective indicates that there are differences in building and participating in social networks. Granovetter (1973, 1982) suggested three types of social networks: strong, weak and absent. In social planning research weak networks have been highlighted, while weak ties create a sense of security and social embeddedness. This is knowledge that social planners have embraced and which made it possible for them to plan for social contacts to be facilitated. Henning and Svensson (2010) found a big difference between how people build and use networks in urban and rural areas respectively. They found that in rural areas there was a need for stable contacts including help and care, while in urban areas the networks provided a resource that could respond to demands placed upon them. After this re-use of earlier collected data material we can conclude that social planners also could add gender and health to their list of variables to be highlighted.

When Laslett (1991) wrote about volunteering as a welfare need he probably meant that engaging in meaningful publicly organized activities would help the elderly to stay healthy, and not that activities must be related to their own mortality. A top-down change in attitude would depart from the view of volunteering as a meaningful activity to a view in which it is seen as something needed to maintain the quality of welfare services. Finally, it is important to keep the need for reciprocity in mind and bear in mind support groups, professionals, and ordinary citizens. We are all dependent on each other and it is important not to exploit people.

NOTES

1   The care recipient, the main informal care provider chosen by the recipient and the main formal caregiver were all interviewed between one and three times dependent on the continued existence of the networks over the time period.
2   *Sparsely populated municipalities*, defined as municipalities where less than 70 percent of the population lives in urban areas and less than eight inhabitants per square kilometre. http://www.skl.se/kommuner_och_landsting/om_kommuner/kommungruppsindelning
3   Multidimensional Scale of Perceived Social Support (Zimet, Dahlem, Zimet & Farley 1988)

REFERENCES

ABS (2000) *Voluntary Work, Australia* (Cat No. 4441.0). Canberra, Australian Bureau of Statistics.

Almberg, B., M. Grafström & B. Winblad (1997) Caring for a demented elderly person – burden and burnout among caregiving relatives. *Journal of Advanced Nursing*, 25 (1), 109–16.

Anderson Bo & Stina Johansson (1989) Om sociala nätverk och hälsa. (On social networks and health). *Socialmedicinsk tidskrift* 5–6, 223–229.

Anderson Bo, Stina Johansson (1991) On Collective Actions in Social Networks: Should We Expect People to Join Health Support Networks? In: *Forvitring eller fornyelse? De nordiske velferdsstater mot år 2000*. (Weathering or renewal? The Nordic welfare states towards 2000). INAS report 91:8. Oslo: Norway.

Andersson Katarina (2007) *Omsorg under förhandling* (Care under negotiation). Diss. Department of Social Work, Umeå University.

Bengtsson, Tommy (ed.) (2010) Population and Ageing – A threat to the Welfare State – The Case of Sweden. Heidelberg: Springer-Verlag. p 2.

Berglund, Anna-Karin, Susanne Johansson & Irene Molina (eds.) (2005) *Med periferien i sentrum* (With focus on the periphery). Alta: Norut NIBR Finnmark.

Bergström Helen (2005) Frivilligarbete – varför då? En studie om motiv och drivkrafter inom det frivilliga sociala arbetet. (Why volunteer? A study in motives and incentives in voluntary work). Master thesis. Department of social work. Umeå University.

Berleen, Göran (2004) *A Healther Elderly Population – Sweden*. Stockholm; National Institute of Public Health in Sweden.

Buss, David. M. (1990) Unmitigated agency and unmitigated communion: an analysis of negative components of masculinity and femininity. *Sex Roles*, 22, 9/10, 555–568.

Carr, Dawn C. & Jon Hendicks (2011) Relevance of social capital and lifestyle for the third age. In Dawn C. Carr & Kathrin Comp (eds.) *Gerontology in The Era of the Third Age*. New York: Springer Publishing Company, pp 207–223.

Dunér, Anna & Monica Nordström (2005) Intentions and strategies among elderly people: Coping in everyday life. *Journal of Aging Studies*, 19, 4, 437–451.

Fagerström, Lisbeth, Yngve Gustavsson, Gunborg Jakobsson, Stina Johansson & Pirkko Vartiainen (2011) Sense of security among people aged 65 and 75: external and inner sources. *Journal of Advanced Nursing*, 67, 6, 1305–1316.

George, Linda K. (2011) Afterword: The third age: fact or fiction – and does it matter? In Dawn C. Carr & Kathrin Comp (eds.) *Gerontology in The Era of the Third Age*. New York: Springer Publishing Company, pp. 245–260.

GERDA (GErontological Regional Database and Resource Center) [online] http://www.umu.se/forskning/forskningsprojekt/forskningsdatabasen/visa-projekt/?code=579&currentView=base&doSearch=true&scbCode=0&searchString=GERDA

Gilligan, Carol (1982) *In a Different Voice*. Boston: Harvard University Press.

Granovetter, M. (1973) The strength of the weak ties. *American Journal of Sociology*, 78, 1360–1380.

Granovetter, M. (1982) The strength of the weak ties. A network theory revisited. In P.V. Marsden & N. Lin (eds.) *Social Structure and Network Analysis*. London: Sage Publications.

Henning, C. & L.A. Svensson (2010) Mötesplatser för äldre – en viktig aspekt i samhällsplaneringen. (Meeting points for elders – an important aspect in community planning. In K. Gynnerstedt & M. Wolmesjö. *Tredje åldern* (Third age). Malmö: Gleerups.

Hyyppä, Markku T. & Juhani Mäki (2001a) Individual level relationships between social capital and self-rated health in bilingual community. *Preventive Medicine*, 32, 148–155.

Hyyppä, Markku T. & Juhani Mäki (2001b) Why do Swedish-speaking Finns have a longer active life? An area for social capital research. *Health Promotion International*, 16, 55–64.

Jegermalm, Magnus & Eva Jeppson-Grassman (2009) Caregiving and volunteering among older people in Sweden – prevalence and profiles. *Journal of Aging and Social Policy*, 21(4), 352–73.

Jegermalm, Magnus & Eva Jeppson-Grassman (2010) Äldres engagemang i civilsamhället: roller och profiler. (Elders engagement in civil society: roles and profiles). In K. Gynnerstedt & Maria Wolmesjö (eds.) *Tredje åldern*. (Third age). Malmö: Gleerups.

Johansson Mairon (2008) *Gamla och nya frivillighetsformer*. (Old and new forms of voluntarism). University of Växjö.

Johansson Lennarth, H. Long & M. Parker (2011) Informal Caregiving for Elders in Sweden: An Analysis of Current Policy Developments. *Journal of Aging and Social Policy*, 23:4, 335–353.

Johansson, Stina (2006) GERDA. Gerontological Regional Database and Resource Centre. 18th Nordic Congress of Gerontology. 29–31.5.2006. Conference Publications, Posters 109. Jyväskylä, Finland.

Johansson, Stina & Johan Åhlfeldt (1993) Do public services influence patterns of informal care? Informal networks and public home care in three Swedish municipalities. *Scandinavian Journal of Social Welfare*, 2, 69–79.

Johansson, Stina & Johan Åhlfeldt (1996) Stress experienced by informal caregivers. On conflicting demands in every-day life. *Scandinavian Journal of Social Welfare*, 5, 83–96.

Johansson, Stina & Gunilla Fahlström (1993): I nöd och lust. En studie av kvinnor som vårdar en närstående. *Vård i Norden*, 2, 16–23.

Johansson, Stina, Rosemary Leonard and Kerrie Noonan (2012) Caring and the generation of social capital: Two models for a positive relationship. *International Journal of Social Welfare*, 21, 44–52.

Karlsson, S.G., S Johansson, A Gerdner, K. Borell (2007) Caring while living apart. *Journal of Gerontological Social Work*. 49, 4, 3–27.

Kittay, E. F., Jennings, B. & Wasunna, A. A. (2005) Dependency, Difference and the Global Ethic of Long-Term Care. *The Journal of Political Philosophy*. 13, 4, 443–469.

Laslett, Peter (1991) *A Fresh Map of Life. The Emergence of the Third Age*. Cambridge MA: Harvard University Press.

Leonard, Rosemary & Stina Johansson (2008) Policy and practices to the active engagement of older people in the community: A comparison of Sweden and Australia. *International Journal of Social Welfare*, 17, 37–45.

Leonard, Rosemary & Jenny Onyx (2007) *Social Capital and Community Building. Spinning Straw into Gold*. London; Janus Publishing Company Ltd.

Lewin, Bo (1998) Studiens genomförande. In Bo Lewin (ed.) *Sex i Sverige: Om sexuallivet i Sverige 1996*. Stockholm: Folkhälsoinstitutet, pp. 27–55.

Lönnbring, Gunilla (2010) En bransch med fokus på hälsa, må-bra och hela människan. (A bransch with a holistic focus on health, well-being). In Forsberg Gunnel & Gerd Lindgren (eds.) *Nätverk och skuggstrukturer i regionalpolitiken* (Network and overshadowing structures in the regional policy). Karlstad: Karlstad University Press.

Noddings, Nel (1984) *Caring. A Feminine Approach to Ethics and Moral Education*. Berkeley and Los Angeles: University of California Press.

Norris. Jane (1988) *Daughters of the Elderly*. Bloomington and Indianapolis: Indiana University Press.

Onyx, Jenny & P. Bullen (2000) Measuring social capital in five communities. *Journal of Applied Behavioral Science*, 36 (1), 23–42.

Portes, A. (1998) Social capital: Its origins and applications in modern sociology. *Annual Review of Sociology*, 24, 1–24.

Putnam, Robert D. (1993) *Making democracy work: Civic traditions in modern Italy*. Princeton NY: Princeton University Press.

Sand, Ann-Britt M. (2000) *Ansvar, kärlek och försörjning*. (Responsibility, Love and Maintenance. Om Employed Relative Carers in Sweden). PhD Dissertation, University of Gothenburg.

SOU (1999: 84). Civilsamhället (Civil Society). Governmental investigation. Stockholm.

SOU (2010: 85). *Vem arbetar efter 65 års ålder? En statistisk analys. En rapport från sociala rådet*. Stockholm.

Thelin, Angelika (2010). Tredje åldern – ett mångtydigt och problematiskt begrepp. (Third age – a problematic and multi-dimensional concept). In Gynnerstedt K. and M. Wolmesjö (eds.) *Tredje åldern. Sociala aspekter och medborgarskap*. (Third Age. Social Aspects and Citizenship). Malmö: Gleerups.

Tiefer, Leonore (2004). *Sex is Not a Natural Act*. Oxford: Westview.

Turunen Päivi & Marika Marusarz (2010). Alternativ omsorg i glesbygd. (Alternative care in rural areas). In Johansson s. (ed.) *Omsorg och mångfald*. (Care and diversity). Malmö: Gleerups.

Waerness, Kari (1984). The rationality of caring. *Economic and Industrial Democracy*, 5, 185.

Woolcock, M. (1998) Social capital and economic development: Toward a theoretical synthesis and policy framework. *Theory and Society*, 27, 151–208.

Zetterberg, Hans L. (1969). Om sexuallivet i Sverige. Utredningen rörande sexual- och samlevnadsfrågor i undervisnings- och upplysningsarbetet (USSU). *SOU 1969:2*. Stockholm.

Zimet, G.D., N.W. Dahlem, S,G. Zimet & G.K. Farley (1988). The multidimensional scale of perceived social support. *Journal of Personality Assessment*, 52, 30–41.

22

Learning in Later Life

Franz Kolland and Anna Wanka

Spurred by globalization, socio-demographic changes, skill-biased technological advancements, and the emergence of a knowledge society, learning in later life is becoming increasingly important. Socio-demographic changes have resulted in a rapidly growing number of elderly with new needs and expectations. Longer life expectancy and social changes have led to the disappearance of traditional roles, like that of the (male) bread-winner and employment roles in general. However, under favourable conditions, changed roles also provide the individual with continuity and the opportunity for development, facilitating 'freedom later in life'. Older people become agents of their own fate. They are able to develop and use their capabilities for action in the wider world (Field, 2005).

Education is no longer an asset only achieved in youth that remains of constant value during a stable employment and unbroken career followed by a long period of retirement (Allmendinger et al., 2011). Education should be integrated into all stages of life in order to ensure longevity in modern societies is not a burden but rather a social dividend.

Lifelong learning is important for social productivity in old age, whether in professional, voluntary work, or care-taking contexts. Social productivity is greater when old age is regarded a separate and active phase of life (Kohli 2009), not merely a period of recreation and rest. As a different stage of life, old age is defined by its own challenges; statutory age limits and social benefits. Aging is increasingly seen in terms of opportunities and activities in this phase of life.

In addition, we live in a knowledge based society where education determines the opportunities of its members. Education throughout all stages of life is one of the most important issues of the twenty first century. Long periods of education significantly influence different areas of life, such as general lifestyle, involvement in politics or value orientation. The importance of education for social status has diminished. Nonetheless, its significance in terms of cultural participation has increased.

Education has become a central requirement for social development, and the resulting societal changes in turn shape the education system. Ever faster social and technological developments, exponentially growing scientific insights and information have contributed significantly to a commonly accepted concept of lifelong learning. In this sense, lifelong learning is mainly understood as vocational education and training in spite of some general rhetoric about the non-economic, personal and social benefits (Withnall, 2010). Lifelong and life-wide learning are not only important for improving human capital, education and learning are also important for their social benefits and for their critical potential reflecting the shortfalls and erroneous trends of modern market economies. The critical dimension of education is also empowering and strengthens individual and their social skills.

This chapter will focus on learning processes in later life from a sociological perspective. Initially, the chapter presents theoretical concepts of learning and education in later life and distinguishes between different forms of learning processes. Aging has emerged as a separate stage of life. This distinct stage of life is further differentiated between third and fourth age – what does that mean for learning in old age? Are inequalities in learning increasing or decreasing over the life course, and which concepts can we use to address them? Subsequently, it outlines the ideal of the autonomous learner and its implications for the institutional context of learning in old age are outlined, focusing on adult education measures such as the Universities of Third Age and the Elderhostel Movement that have shaped the culture of aging. Participation rates and factors facilitating differences in participation presented, emphasizing the significance of learning motivation. The chapter concludes with the positive and negative personal and societal effects of educational participation in later life.

EDUCATION AND LEARNING: THEORETICAL CONCEPTS

Theoretical concepts are used differently in the various contexts of late life education academic discourse. Definitions range from education in advanced age to lifelong learning and continuing education in later life. From an interdisciplinary perspective, lifelong learning in old age is on the one hand, an area pertaining to gerontology and life course research and on the other hand, a sub-discipline of adult education. Furthermore, it is related to sociology, social work, psychology, geriatrics, theology and political sciences.

What is the definition of lifelong and lifewide learning in later life? What is the significance of learning in formal and non-formal contexts and what are the links between firstly learning and competence and secondly, learning and skills?

Answering these questions requires educational concepts that transcend discussions of qualifications. We learn and consider many things that have no professional relevance. We are motivated to learn not only for the prestige or use value of qualifications, but also due to our intrinsic motivation. We learn something because we are interested in it, because it assists us with daily activities and because it helps us contribute to society. In this sense, education is possible in any phase of life.

The concept of lifelong education was first used in 1929 by Basil Yeaxlee, who described education as an aspect of daily life. Our modern culture and society is subject to more rapid changes than in earlier periods, which increase the necessity for continuous education. New experiences that encourage education are a result of our highly technological working environments, structural changes in our cities, the shifting relationship between the sexes and changing recreational habits. The notion of learning is changing visibly in how terms such as 'incomplete' and 'ongoing' are becoming more and more relevant.

Since the 1970s, a distinction has been made between 'formal learning', 'non-formal learning' and 'informal learning'. In this sense, planned, organized and socially recognized learning (in the context of government-funded education institutions) is referred to as 'formal learning'. The results of formal learning are characterized and classified based on the International Standard Classification of Education (ISCED) standard, developed initially by UNESCO and now widely accepted. Here, six levels of formal learning and academic education are distinguished. They range from pre-school to university education. Conversely, 'Non-formal learning' includes all forms of systematic, organized learning outside of formal learning settings. Informal learning refers to the lifelong practice of processing experiences and learning skills in everyday life, as well as in a professional and recreational context.

Since the 1990s, there has also been a shift in emphasis from the provision of (institutionalized) formal and non-formal learning to informal and autonomous learning (Jarvis, 1995: 60). As Billet points out, 'Learning is something that humans do continuously and across our lives: we are all and have to be lifelong learners' (Billett, 2010: 401–402). Informal learning over the life course is a crucial precondition for coping with everyday challenges and primarily directed by the individual's capacities and interests (Ibid.: 402). It is not necessarily dependent upon others and, as such, a personal rather than an institutionalized process.

Theories of situated learning thus postulate that learning is always situated in everyday activities, contexts and cultures (Lave, 1988). Learners become involved in 'communities of practice', social situations in which the knowledge they acquire is normally used, in the way of 'legitimate peripheral participation' (Lave & Wenger, 1990). Because informal, situated learning helps people to better solve situational requirements. It is more activity-based and therefore especially relevant for quality of life at an advanced age. However, situated learning does not necessarily have to be, and is often not, intentional (Lave 1988). Thus, when using the concept of informal learning a problem of definition revolves around the question where learning begins and where it ends. Consequently, Billett (2010) argues that it is nonsense to analyse why individuals

may or may not learn in terms of age gender and class because 'everybody learns all the time' (Billett, 2010: 409). Unfortunately, this approach is rather unsatisfying for empirical social research. Bereiter and Scardamalia (1989) therefore offer the concept of 'intentional learning' as an alternative.

Intentional learning goes beyond the notions of active or self-regulated learning. It is characterized by the presence of a personal learning agenda (Scardamalia & Bereiter 2006: 104). It refers to processes that feature learning as a goal and not just an incidental outcome (Bereiter & Scardamalia 1989: 363). Intentional learning is not limited to formal or non-formal learning. It emphasizes the divide between intrinsically and extrinsically motivated learning by differentiating into 'learning as problem solving' (the goals itself being to learn) and 'learning through problem solving' – both of which can, but do not have to be, intrinsically motivated and self-regulated. Thus, intentional learning is essential for understanding who is or will be a 'lifelong learner' (Bereiter & Scardamalia, 1989: 365–66).

Complementary to the differentiation between formal, non-formal and informal learning, a sharper distinction between learning and education has to be made. Education is defined by its public character (Jarvis, 1995: 60). It is the institutionalized attempt to direct the individual's (learning) interests towards certain social or economic concerns, like lifelong employability in aging societies (Billett, 2010: 405, 407). This distinction is especially important for the analysis of learning in later life, as participation in education, but not learning declines with age.

Education is a societal process whereas learning is a personal process. Learning is basically independent from others. Yet, the social situation in which it is embedded also shapes learning. Jarvis (1987) states that every social situation is potentially stimulating learning processes – some of them reflective, some of them not. Differentiating between practical and academic, that is, abstract, intelligence, several studies have come to the conclusion that practical intelligence functions best in authentic (real life) situations (Pogson & Tennant, 2000: 27).

In conclusion, research about learning in later life has given more weight to participation in education focus more than on engagement in learning. The gap in the research leads us to posit that future studies should give informal forms of learning significantly more space than they do currently. One widespread attempt to present non-formal and informal learning in a standardized manner is the systematic documentation of skills that have been acquired in so-called competency portfolios. In recent years the OECD developed a programme that assesses the competencies of the adult population. The Programme for the International Assessment of Adult Competencies (PIAAC) aims at creating a strategy to address the supply and demand of competencies. The programme does a number of things: identifies and measures differences between individuals and countries in competencies believed to underlie both personal and societal success, assesses the impact of these competencies on social and economic outcomes at individual and aggregate levels and gauges the performance of education and training systems in generating required competencies (http://www.oecd.org/piaac).

Competency can be defined as both a precondition for learning and the result of learning processes. Competency constitutes the ability to act independently in a particular context, be it personal, professional or political. For issues relating to late-life learning it is important to make a clear distinction from formal qualifications. Regarding old age, the concept of competency is considered helpful because it relates to the individual, whereas qualification refers to objectively required criteria. Competency is associated with the individual and involves previous experiences. It denotes complex and modifiable behavioural patterns. Acquiring competency or skills does not refer to one-sided learning aspects but rather real life experiences, which may include informal learning.

To remain active in old age, five skills are essential and must be strengthened and expanded upon (Erpenbeck & Heyse, 1999: 157). First are cognitive skills, which refer to understanding and processing of contextual information. In practical terms, this means successfully operating new technologies (e.g. ticket vending machines). Second, social skills are relevant. They include all abilities that facilitate satisfying social relationships and that prompt sympathy. The third key skill is productive competency, which means dedication and persistence, both of which are the result of educational measures (e.g. memory training). The fourth area is self-competency: the ability and willingness to act independently and responsibly and to reflect on one's own and others' actions. People can learn to act in a reflective manner in organized learning processes. A fifth ability, which is particularly relevant during transitional periods in the second half of life, is orientation competency. It implies responding adequately to changes in the environment and orientating oneself with regard to time.

THE HETEROGENEITY OF OLD AGE AND ITS CONSEQUENCES FOR LEARNING IN LATER LIFE

Research on aging stimulates lifelong learning in old age by providing relevant research results related to learning abilities in old age, the learning processes over the life course and the context of educational processes. Results show that there is potential for learning in later life, but the exploitation of this potential varies because of the heterogeneity of older people.

Psycho-gerontological research is widely based on the assumption that human learning processes are characterized by plasticity, leaving room for development (Labouvie-Vief, 1985; Baltes & Lindenberger, 1988; Verhaeghen & Marcoen, 1996) over the entire lifespan. Analysing gains and losses, as well as the associated contents and proportions over the course of life, prompted the

Definitions

Lifelong learning in old age can be defined as personally and socially-motivated experience-based learning. It includes every targeted learning activity that serves to improve skills continuously, abilities and competencies. It can occur both in and outside of organized learning settings. It helps to acquire basic qualifications including digital and practical skills to handle daily tasks better. The objective is self-determination.

Education in later life can be defined as acquiring knowledge and new skills in a conscious and targeted manner. Many also use the term education to refer to the result of this process. Educational goals can be pursued over an extended period and may involve undertaking various activities such as academic studies, reading books, discussions and the acquisition of skills. Education is obtained in a targeted and meaningful way by dealing with social, societal, historical and cultural aspects of life. Education is a broader term than learning as it implies reflection and the ability to generate theories.

Geragogy is the pedagogy of the aging and elderly individual. It is related to gerontology and educational sciences and deals with aspects and processes associated with aging and daily life. It is an academic discipline that investigates learning in old age and the application of research data from geriatrics and social gerontology to the daily life of the elderly. Dörr (2006) defines geragogy as teaching and learning that prompts adaptations to the changes associated with aging: 'Geragogy could be defined as the teaching towards older people accommodating the normal physical, cognitive and psychological changes'.

Senior education refers to learning initiatives fashioned to the specific learning needs and motivations of old and no longer gainfully employed people. This implies target-group-specific adult education, where the target group is characterized by similar experiences, problems and abilities.

Educational gerontology comprises educational measures that focus on topics related to aging that occur over the entire course of life. It does not specifically address older people. Educational gerontology combines education for the elderly and intergenerational learning. Both learning in age-homogeneous groups and in groups of mixed ages are part of educational gerontology.

---

emergence of plasticity research out of cognitive research on aging. Plasticity research features the dual objective of identifying latent potential (plasticity) as well as limitations in old age.

What is significant for lifelong learning at an advanced age is the diversity within the older generations with regard to gender, socio-economic status (social class) and ethnicity. Labelling old age as a separate, and in many cases, active, period of life does not imply that people in this phase of life are a homogeneous social group. Rather, most theories assume a high degree of heterogeneity and diversity. Diversity is the result of an internal differentiation of age concerning education, gender and the increasing number of older migrants.

The internal differentiation stimulated Peter Laslett (1989) to distinguish between the third and fourth age. This categorization shows widely differing lifestyles and needs within the 'group' of older people. The elderly that constitute the third age generally have a high degree of mobility, fewer health problems and a higher level of education. They use educational measures to kick-start a new lifestyle after retirement. Geragogic interventions face entirely different requirements in light of socio-economic disadvantages and health problems associated with old age. The fourth age is characterized by frailty and increased physical and social vulnerability. Learning processes are more oriented towards issues related to the meaning of life and daily living.

Indeed, because 'the elderly' are such a heterogeneous group, the latent potential for, or plasticity of learning in older age, is not always fully implemented. Learning processes can be described as linear or consecutive, transformative or expansive. They are considered linear when we operate under the assumption that learning helps to acquire skills, and if these skills are attained gradually. The same processes are, however, transformative when they induce individual and social changes. These changes are wide reaching in contrast to learning processes that simply require adapting to altered circumstances and situations. For individual and social changes, reflective, critical and self-directed learning is essential. Expansive learning is self-directed in nature, and the subject expands his or her skills by way of learning. It is only expansive when the subject has specific reasons to engage in it. Practical interest is always necessary to prompt learning motivation. Fears, and coping with them, play a much-underestimated role in this context. Both the desire for public display and the willingness to overcome fears and expose oneself facilitate learning. Older learners must try to eliminate or overcome interferences. Older learners must exercise their cognitive skills and not accept forgetfulness as an inevitable fate. The individual must learn to manage his or her own way of learning. They need to know how to sort and code things, as well as be able to identify stimuli and cues that help to retrieve previously learned content. Learning potential can thus be realized within individually specified boundaries, if the learning individual is able to identify and use his or her own learning strategies, and partly his or her subconscious abilities.

One attempt to addressing the inequalities regarding learning in later life is the sociological life course approach (Mayer, 1990). It regards the life course of an individual as a sequence of activities and events in various domains and spheres of life. In this approach, life courses are rule-based, dynamic characteristics of the social structure that affect numerous individuals and determine the social positions they reach. Institutions influence life courses, intentionally or unintentionally. Additionally, individuals themselves decide their life course – partly through goal-oriented behaviour and partly as unintentional outcomes of their actions (Allmendinger et al., 2011). This perspective allows us to handle age, cohort, and period effects simultaneously. In particular, we are able to examine the timing and sequencing of lifelong (formal) learning, as well as social activities in other areas of life. From a life course perspective, it is possible to analyse the way adult education is embedded in the individual's life course. Research may focus on decision-making processes regarding participation in educational activities, including the importance of schooling and vocational training.

The life course approach is supported by empirical research that shows learning in later life is tied to lifelong practices of curiosity and continuous engagement in learning processes (Withnall, 2010). It is a habit integrated into one's biography. The acquisition of knowledge occurs not only as a lifelong process, but also as something integrated into life that can be conceptualized as life-integrated and life-integrating learning. For example, feminization and lower educational levels based on cohort differences have a substantial effect on lifelong learning in old age. We can characterize this situation as one of triple jeopardy. In addition to the disadvantages imposed by their gender and educational status, older women with fewer qualifications also experience the devaluation in status associated with old age. This marginalization not only calls for the development of learning programmes for disadvantaged target groups, but also for the consideration of aspects of social inclusion.

One gerontological concept that is aimed at social inclusion and clearly affects late life learning is that of 'active aging' (WHO, 2002) as proposed by the World Health Organization (WHO). Active aging refers to the process of optimizing people's opportunities.. A healthy lifestyle and socio-cultural participation can help achieve such optimisation. The term 'active' denotes lasting participation in social, economic, cultural, spiritual and civic life. Learning and educational processes are important conditions for older people's lasting participation in different areas of society. They are supposed to help people gain insights into their own social situation to foster active participation.

Empirical studies highlight the potential for activity over the course of aging as well as the necessity of initiating measures to achieve satisfaction in later life (cf. Rowe & Kahn, 1997). Individuals who participate in educational measures and are physically active tend to be healthier and exhibit a lower rate of morbidity.

However, the concept of active aging also has some weaknesses; one being that it cannot be separated from the discourse over the burden of old age and the issue of the *activating welfare state*. The concept of active aging helps to address individual resources and to reduce the necessity for social services. The activating welfare state aims to provide relief resources whilst specifically targeting the needs of the elderly. What does this mean? To enable active aging it is not enough to demand activity as a norm, but adequate opportunities have to be created to overcome various obstacles on the way to realising an active life. A second weakness is the realisation that *activity does not help one to stay young per se*, but that heavy physical and routine work can even facilitate premature aging. A third weakness is that activity is *primarily associated with the individual*, while the structures that hinder activity are ignored. The demand for activity is furthermore associated with new forms of discrimination. Reacting in a manner as was habitual for old people may lead to being stigmatized.

THE AUTONOMOUS LEARNER – A NEW IDEAL IN LATER LIFE?

The concept of active aging has also shaped the notion of learning in later life and the ideal mature learner. While in the 1960s, programmes focused on measures for the educationally disadvantaged, since the late 1990s, they have supported self-directed activity on the part of older people. The latter corresponds to the new didactic and methodological approaches pursued in adult and continuing education. The so-called new learning culture comprises all programmes that promote self-care, self-understanding and learning. As Klingovsky states, 'The goal is to maximize subjective potential and to optimize the self' (translated from Klingovsky, 2009: 142). In its normative approach, self-determination not only entails a can-do approach, but a clear should-do expectation. This expectation is: Pursue self-directed activity in old age, take care of yourself and take responsibility for your actions.

Increasingly, older people tend to re-define themselves, express their needs and rights but they also need to be more self-reliant. This ranges from planning their leisure activities in a self-directed manner, to strategies that promote independence, if care and assistance are required, through to an individually designed patient's provision for the final stage of life.

How can the objective of a self-determined subject be achieved, all the while maximizing the subjective potential of the older learner? Scholars have proposed various methodological approaches to this end, such as empowerment didactics (Arnold & Schüßler, 2003) or self-directed learning. Self-directed learning assumes that the human being grows in capacity (and need) to be self-directing as an essential component of maturing (Knowles, 1975).

Different theories consider the role of self-determination for engagement in learning processes. Bandura's (1997) concept of self-efficacy refers to the judgement of one's own capability of asserting control, which is strongly related to learning outcomes, even if the judgement is not true. Similarly, Deci and Ryan's (2004) self-determination theory revolves around the concept of autonomy: the perception of oneself as the source of one's own behaviour. Deci and Ryan explain, 'When autonomous, individuals experience their behaviour as an expression of the self (…) even when actions are influenced by outside sources, the actors concur with those influences, feeling both initiative and value with regard to them' (Deci & Ryan, 2004 : 8).

Two decades of empirical research has made the utility of using self-determination theory for the explanation of learning processes evident. It comprises four mini-theories – cognitive evaluation theory, organismic integration theory, causality orientations theory and basic needs theory – of which cognitive evaluation and organismic integration theory are of particular interest when looking at learning processes. Cognitive evaluation theory identifies autonomy supportive elements of social contexts and links them to different kinds of motivation. Organismic integration theory explains to which degree individuals experience autonomy while engaging in extrinsically motivated behaviours. It assumes that individuals initially internalize external regulations when they emanate from significant others. That means that individuals can be autonomously extrinsically motivated. Learning environments can thus support an intrinsic motivation (Deci & Ryan, 2004: 9ff).

Most theories dealing with the perception of one's own capability of control acknowledge that it changes across the lifespan. Heckhausen and Schulz (1998) offer a model for these changes, claiming that the judgement of self-efficacy is low in childhood, increasing until midlife, where it plateaus, and declining in old age (p. 53). In this sense, self-determination theories that consider life course approaches offer one explanation of the low rates of participation in education in later life.

Bubolz-Lutz (1999) argues that not all old people are able to act in a self-determined way, and self-directed learning remains restricted to an elite group of the population. Individuals with few qualifications perceive self-directed learning processes as an unreasonable demand (Kolland & Ahmadi, 2010). Further, openly defining goals signifies arbitrariness. Revision of the learning environment cannot be the main goal, but rather learning should be positioned as active engagement. Jack Mezirow (1985) points out the impossibility of freely choosing objectives unless all possible objectives are known. Constructivist learning theories that only are interested to envision a learning environment for autonomously learning subjects do ignore the restrictions embedded in social environments. So a critical reflection of these environments is necessary and are the basis for transformative learning. It is an orientation where the learners interpret and reinterpret their experiences with the aim not only to change attitudes and social behaviour but also transform them (Mezirow, 1991).

Learning as a process of self-determination favours certain groups of society who are more independent to begin with. Differences are thus stabilized, whereby individuals who are externally controlled in everyday life are automatically at a disadvantage (Meyer-Drawe, 2008). The reform-pedagogical approach of self-activity confirms this. This approach can also be considered a new form of social control. Control is no longer exerted from above or via classroom-based teaching, but it is rather perceived as self-control. Power is not exercised from the top to the bottom. The individual assumes responsibility and manages his or her own activities.

What does this increasing tendency towards self-control and self-management mean for public lifelong learning policy? Can it be assumed that the objective of a self-determined subject results in the withdrawal of public provision and funding of programmes for learning in later life? And if so, which actors substitute for the public sector?

THE DEVELOPMENT OF EDUCATION IN LATER LIFE

Learning options for the elderly developed and became institutionalized in the second half of the twentieth century. Several societal changes like longer life expectancy and a

shift of values have promoted this development. These led to the consideration of retirement as a distinct life stage with its own
peculiar characteristics and possibilities. At
the same time, a progressive educational
policy started which promoted education as a
citizen's right (Arnold & Costa, 1999).
Demographic and socio-political changes
also stimulated academic research concerning learning in later life. In 1978, Ronald H.
Sherron and D. Barry Lumsden published a
first comprehensive reader on educational
gerontology in the United States.

Amidst these societal changes, old age
education became a subject when universities began to admit older adults as students.
Additionally, autonomous institutions were
founded in Europe and the United States,
including some of the largest organizations
like the Open University, Universities of the
Third Age (U3A), Elderhostel or the Lifelong Learning Institutes (LLI). Moody
(2010) calls these organizations 'New Aging
Enterprises' – a term referring to the collective of organizations that 'show a way to
prosper in an aging society' and represent
aspects of positive aging (p.483). These
enterprises do not rely so much on governmental support, but individual agency and
intrinsic motivation of their participants.
They represent what the 'Third Way', as promoted by Giddens, could look like in an
aging policy of the twenty-first century
(ibid.). Here, we sketch the development of
the most influential initiatives in brief.

In the United States, the learning in later
life movement began in the 1960s with the
formation of a self-governing group of retired
public school teachers designing their own
schedule of course offerings under the name
of 'Institute for Retired Professionals' (IRP).
This idea spread and expanded as Institutes
for Learning in Retirement (ILRs) into
several host colleges. Another initiative,
Elderhostel, was founded in 1975 in New
Hampshire. The core concept was to invite
adults over the age of sixty to occupy empty
dorms at college campuses and participate in
courses held by staff faculty. The idea

expanded quickly into all (the-then) fifty
states. One problematic aspect of Elderhostel
was, however, that it required travelling and
overnight stays and did not take place in the
participants' communities. Thus, Elderhostel
and the ILRs decided to work together and in
1988 created the Elderhostel Institute Network (EIN) to assist colleges, universities
and local learners as an administrative base
in developing their own organisations or programmes. However, during the 1990s, ILRs
started dropping out of the Network, as they
were not willing or able to pay dues any-
more. In 2002, EIN dropped the dues and
became a 'virtual' organization providing
services from their website (Knowlton, 1980;
http://www.roadscholar.org). In recent years,
most of the ILRs changed their names to
Lifelong Learning Institutes (LLIs), as market surveys showed that young retirees would
prefer to join organizations that are not
labelled as being for retirees.

In Europe, one of the main initiatives for
learning in later life is the University of the
Third Age (U3A). These universities follow
different approaches: the French model
(UTA), the British model and hybrids of both.
The French model is rooted in the passing of
French legislation in 1968 that required universities to provide more community education. In 1973, the first UTA was founded
exclusively for persons over retirement age.
The UTA model was characterized by its
location within traditional university systems;
however, this feature seems to be on the
decrease, even in France. In contrast, the British model is entirely self-organized. The
central idea (especially promoted by Peter
Laslett) is that it is unnecessary to employ
(younger) teachers as retired people themselves have a huge base of knowledge and
should run classes and courses as volunteers
(Swindell, 2011: 50). Arnold and Costa
(1999) visualize these different approaches as
a spectrum ranging from intergenerational
study options to autonomous self-organized
models. In the first approach, the study programme is pre-shaped and adult learners can
choose the courses they want to take. In the

second approach, older people are both teachers and students, organizing activities of their own choice. Both approaches meet different needs, as the second approach requires more resources from its participants, which not all learners are willing or able to invest.

From the 1980s onwards, countries all over the world have adopted U3As.. The first adopters outside of Europe were Australia, New Zealand, China and Japan. In Australia and New Zealand, the British model began as a 'grassroots' movement with little or no support from established institutes or the government. In China, the Lifelong Learning movement also formed during the 1980s, after the Cultural Revolution. In contrast to the beginning of the Australian movement, the Chinese government has financed most U3As. Japanese society has put emphasis on the challenges of an aging society for quite some time. The Japanese Lifelong Learning movement has a long history with various providers including private companies, NGOs or government running colleges and universities. Most of the programmes, however, involved little participation and self-determination on the part of older learners. Japanese citizens founded the first U3A in 1985 following the British approach and offered an alternative to the traditional courses. The movement did not stop in the 1980s and there are still countries adopting the U3A idea. In the twenty-first century, the first U3As were formed in South Africa (2000), Nepal, Singapore (both 2006) and India (2007; for more information see Swindell 2011: 50ff).

Some researchers see the widespread development of Universities of the Third Age as a chance to give new roles to older people or for them to cultivate an interest staying involved in an information society. There are, however, studies highlighting the critical aspects of the late-life-learning movements. Marvin Formosa (2010) addresses four points in particular: positive ageism, third ageism, elitism and discrimination against both sexes (p. 202). Positive ageism refers to the vision that individuals can achieve 'positive' (e.g. healthy, active) aging through lifestyle modification,

thus making the individual responsible if they experience disadvantages in later life. This positive ageism is accompanied by what Formosa calls third ageism, addressing the issue that U3As make little effort to reach elderly people who do not participate because of physical and mental difficulties. Both attitudes lead to a learning culture that is elitist: U3As mainly attract the middle-classes. The elitist character might not have arisen by coincidence, but through what Bourdieu called social closure tactics or strategies of distinction, 'by members' pursuit of expressive lifestyles, eagerness to instruct themselves in the bourgeois ethos of freedom, close affinity with traditional intellectuals, and preference for expressive over instructional education' (Formosa, 2012: 121). The burdened term 'University' in the title, the choice of subjects and authoritarian didactics add to this elitist learning environment, leading to a withdrawal of the socially disadvantaged (Formosa, 2000).

Thus, researchers identify three main challenges for the development of education initiatives for later life. One challenge is to widen the participation of learning in later life. The Grundtvig Programme of the European Union or the Inquiry into the Future of Lifelong Learning (IFLL) in the UK promote to include socially disadvantaged groups like frail people, elderly with lower educational levels, former workers or older migrants. Secondly, there is a growing consciousness that it will be necessary to adapt to the needs of the baby boomer generation as the upcoming senior's cohort. The assumption is that the 'new retirees' increasingly demand an active role in creating their own leisure opportunities, and do not perceive themselves as 'old people' (Harrison & McGuire, 2008). Adaptations to serve this new clientele have been made, for example, by renaming the Institutes for Learning in Retirement as Lifelong Learning Institutes, or the more intergenerational programmes or the introduction of Elderhostel's sub-brand, 'Road Scholar' that is available without any age-restrictions at all. Scholars expect that the 'spectrum', from intergenerational study to autonomous self-organized models, will shift even more in favour of self-organized learning opportunities. A critical gerontological perspective could be useful here to replace the top-down didactics of schooling in favour of entering into a dialogue with the participants (Formosa, 2010). Another challenge is the adaptation to the processes of globalization, while at the same time considering the importance of locality for learning in later life. One response to meet this challenge is networking. Examples for this are The International Associations of the universities of the Third Age (IAUTA) formed in 1975 or the WorldU3A formed in 1997, which both aim to stimulate exchange among participants of UTA and U3A respectively (Swindell, 2011). At the same time, new initiatives try to 'go local' to better understand and reach out to the elderly and to strengthen the local identities, like the R3L-Initiative (Learning Regions) in Europe or the Aging in Place Initiative in the USA. The inclusion of information and communication technologies, which have been widely neglected by U3A curricula (Formosa 2010), might play a crucial role here. To face these challenges and keep the education initiatives for old age vivid and resilient, it is crucial for them to adopt a transformative, inclusive agenda, approaching different target groups and widening the programmes to participants with illness or from lower socio-economic backgrounds.

PARTICIPATION IN EDUCATION IN OLD AGE

In the wake of the movements portrayed above, many smaller initiatives have arisen, all offering possibilities for learning in later life. Lifelong Learning has also become part of the political agenda, and governments in many countries support or supply programmes for learning in later life. Apart from these issues of supply, the demand of older people for learning opportunities is of interest to any discussion of learning in later life.

Here, it is useful to distinguish between formal and non-formal learning environments. Formal learning environments are institutionalized and most often lead to recognized certificates, whereas non-formal learning is less certificate-oriented in the sense of degrees concerning the ISCED classification. We can measure engagement in formal and non-formal learning using participation rates. However, beyond pure participation rates in different population segments, information about informal learning that is, learning processes that are organized by the individuals themselves, is sparse. This is particularly true regarding the decisions that lead to these learning processes or their (cumulative) returns. One main reason is a methodological one. On the one hand, the operationalization is still underdeveloped – which activities should researchers label informal – and how could they measure these activities. Even if informal learning activities could be operationalized satisfactorily, unintentional learning could not be measured directly (e.g. by questionnaires). Nonetheless, we know that this form of learning is very important – not only in everyday activities, but also in the course of voluntary work and political involvement.

Gathering comparative statistical data is fraught with great difficulties even for formal and non-formal adult education. This is especially true of southern and developing countries, where enrolment data in non-governmental programmes is particularly rare. In a great number of these countries, many adults have not even completed primary schooling or have never been to school (estimates lie at 50% of the adult population in sub-Saharan Africa; and 53% in South and West Asia). For high-income countries, data about participation rates have been fairly robust since the mid-1990s. Despite the growing supply of formal and non-formal learning options for the elderly, the UNESCO *Global Report on Adult Learning and Education* (2010) shows that participation rates in education decrease with age in most countries. However, there are great differences even

Table 22.1 Participation in educational or training courses by individuals aged 50+ in the last month

	50–59 years (%)	60–69 years (%)	70+ years (%)	Country total (%)
Poland	2	1	–	1
Italy	3	2	1	2
Spain	4	3	1	3
Greece	5	3	2	3
Czech Republic	8	4	1	4
Austria	8	5	1	4
France	7	5	3	5
Germany	11	6	2	7
Netherlands	13	9	5	10
Denmark	15	9	3	10
Ireland	17	7	5	10
Belgium	15	12	5	11
Switzerland	25	17	7	17
Sweden	27	17	11	18
Total	**10**	**7**	**3**	**7**

Source: Survey of Health, Ageing and Retirement in Europe (SHARE) 2006, weighted, own calculations [C22Q1]

between high-income countries. The average participation rate in formal and non-formal education and training for people aged 55–64 years amounted to 40% in the USA (2004–2005) and 22% in the EU (2005–2006). Variations between countries with similar income levels suggest that other factors, like public policy, influence participation rates. With regard to Europe, Sweden has the highest participation rate with 60.7%, followed by Norway (41.2%), Finland (37.8%) and the United Kingdom (37%). Poland, Hungary and Greece, on the other hand, have participation rates below 10% (UNESCO 2010: 59ff). Table 22.1 provides an overview of the participation rates of people aged 50 and over in fourteen European countries.

The main questions are which conditions are responsible for the declining participation in education in old age and which factors can help to increase participation rates? Individual as well as institutionalized and cultural factors have to be considered. Cruikshank (2003) attributes low rates of participation to the fact that currently, available educational systems fail to encourage sufficiently the participation of all elderly. Cross (1981) differentiates between three kinds of barriers that cause inequalities in access and participation

in education: dispositional, institutional and situational barriers. Institutional barriers refer to provision, fees or formalized entry qualifications and exclude the poor and less educated. Related to these institutional barriers are situational barriers that arise mostly out of the family-life cycle and thus affect women more than men. Dispositional barriers refer to psychological factors, like perception of usefulness, self-perception or societal images of aging (UNESCO, 2010: 68f). Notions about aging that are associated with decline and dependence are examples of such dispositional factors that have a negative impact on learning. These types of barriers are inter-related: Older employees are, for example, less often encouraged (extrinsically motivated) to participate in continuing education programmes because management believes they are less likely to learn. Thus, they encounter and eventually adapt negative stereotypes and are less likely to be intrinsically motivated to learn.

Research suggests that dispositional barriers are most difficult to overcome in most countries and that targeted public intervention is of great importance for overcoming barriers and increase participation rates (UNESCO, 2010). This would also explain the high participation rates in the Nordic European countries. Unless public policy is decidedly equity-oriented, formal educational systems tend to reinforce social inequalities during all life stages (Bourdieu & Passeron, 1970; Shavit & Blossfeld, 1993; Rubenson, 2006; Rubenson & Desjardins, 2009). Thus, it is not a sufficient measure to make education available to all social groups in later life when it has not been so from an early age.

The personal learning biography is one of the most influential dispositional factors for learning in later life, and the process of 'cooling out' might be responsible for the low participation rates especially for the generations (and among them, women in particular) that had little or no learning opportunities in earlier life stages. The risk of failure makes it understandable why necessary steps towards education are often not taken. Formal learning processes, such as learning through instruction, provide feedback loops of failure alternating with processes of *cooling out* for many children, adolescents and adults (Clark, 1960). In academic and school-type settings, not only is attaining qualifications important but also the labelling process, which often occurs vertically. Pupils are categorized according to their marks and results in performance tests. Failure in this competition can result in instructors labelling learners as untalented, unintelligent, and afflicted by behavioural and learning problems. As a result, performance motivation and effort invested tend to diminish. Subsequently, learning motivation 'cools' out and leads to social disengagement. In this context, we also refer to a 'negative learning history'. Disengagement or distancing oneself from institutional learning is not a passive adaptation, but rather as an attempt to maintain some degree of personal identity. Underprivileged, uneducated groups of society adopt a habitus that is characterized by distance from institutionalized education. Less qualified seniors perceive educational institutions as 'closed shops', frequented by people that they do not associate with (Kolland, 1996). Such groups compensate for the lack

of human capital and qualifications with *social capital*, which is acquired over the course of life. These individuals modify their behaviour and adapt to changing conditions via exchange in the immediate networks. Vester (2004: 50) even argues that under-privileged individuals have special skills in which they triumph over members of other social groups. He states, 'The sensitivity for perceiving, communicating and dealing with social relationships, physical sensations, emotions and unexpected situations'.

FACTORS THAT FACILITATE EDUCATION IN OLD AGE – THE NEED FOR LEARNING AND LEARNING MOTIVATION

What is the goal of education in old age? After retirement, educational goals shift from the attainment of qualifications toward those with cultural orientation. Cultural orientation entails the finding of meaning, the development of rationality and a scientific approach and the ability to reflect and independently form an opinion. The aim is not to modify behaviour in an undirected manner, but rather to expand one's own horizon.

Staudinger and Heidemeier (2009) summarize three goals very well, as namely *developmental goals, the ability to participate* and *value creation*. The first goal refers to self-actualisation, while the second goal promotes social participation and the third goal supports productivity in old age, be it in a professional setting, at home or in the context of volunteering.

What constitutes learning in old age is practical knowledge and individual experiences that people acquire over the course of a lifetime. Educational gerontology and geragogy are concerned with daily challenges and life experiences in addition to academic knowledge. Learning in old age refers to changes that go along with retirement, health related changes, changes resulting from technological advancements and changing social relationships. All of these aspects constitute learning and education as a process that takes living conditions in old age into consideration and which generates new opportunities in life.

Aside from cognitive prerequisites and living conditions, a third aspect that defines education in old age is the learning individual. Peter Jarvis (2001) found four types of individual learning motivations. The first group he labelled as 'harmony seekers' with low interest in learning, motivated to feel safe and satisfied with the current situation. The second group are the 'sages'. They are learning from experience and have the feeling that there is much to learn. The third group, the 'doers' participate in social activities, are interested to be up-to-date, and are very active. Lastly, he describes 'anomics', the non-learners who never had the opportunity to learn.

Similar to Jarvis' typology Cyril Houle (1961) classified adult learners on the basis of qualitative empirical research into three orientations: (a) the goal-oriented, those who employ adult education as a means for achieving clear-cut goals; (b) the activity-oriented, those who utilize adult education as a means for satisfying social needs; and (c) the learning-oriented, those who seek knowledge for its own sake. Later, Roger Boshier transformed this qualitative based typology into a more complex instrument, the Education Participation Scale (EPS). The EPS consists of seven, six-item factors of motivational orientations (Boshier, 1971; Boshier & Collins, 1985).

Many motivational theories (e.g. Achievement Motivation Theories) focus on motives that are not specifically directed at learning, but at learning outcomes. These motivational theories therefore only consider goal-oriented learners. Those might be predominant among younger and working adults, but are they also among older learners? Moreover, talking about goal-orientation, do aspired learning outcomes and thus learning motives not change across the life course?

Howard Y. McClusky (1973) defines learning orientations for older learners as needs-based and distinguishes five needs in this context which educational measures must take into consideration: coping needs (1), including economic self-sufficiency and physical fitness by means of basic education; expressive needs (2), which refers to participation in activities that are intrinsically motivated; contributive needs (3) refers to social activities that are directed to others; education is acquired through social involvement; influence needs (4) are connected with the desire to be politically active and to acquire wisdom and lastly transcendence needs (5) which seek to transcend the frailty associated with old age.

Thus McClusky presented a holistic educational concept without – as outlined by Brian Findsen (2007) – reducing the elderly in their need for learning to the role of education consumers, but rather proposing an educational model which emphasizes the active and productive side of aging in the context of contributive and influence needs.

Despite the lack of a satisfactory theory, empirical findings provide insights into the motivation of older learners and the differences between younger and older adults' motivations to learn. In the US, Romaniuk and Romaniuk (1982) surveyed older adults who attended Elderhostel programmes in Virginia colleges and universities. They demonstrated that the two most important motives to attend Elderhostel were to learn something new and to become involved in a new experience.

Sommer and Künemund (1999) summarize eight motives of older participants in formal and non-formal education from various studies: to appropriate knowledge that could not be appropriated before due to lack of time or economic usability, meeting people, organizing the new leisure time, coping with identity crises, staying mentally fit, social inclusion and participation, sustaining purpose and gaining or sustaining independence.

What are the differences between younger and older adults' motivation to learn? Wlodkowski (2008) found three aspects that differentiate older adults' motivations to learn from those of children and younger adults: (a) older adults are more pragmatic learners, which means that they rate usefulness higher than intellectual value; (b) their motivation to learn relies on their accumulated experience, which influences what one regards as relevant or interesting; (c) they want to be successful learners – if they don't expect to be, they won't participate.

Analysis of SHARE data (2005–2006) reveal that the most frequently mentioned reason for participating in education in later life is by far to use skills or to keep fit, followed by social aspects, while younger people are more instrumentally motivated (e.g. to acquire skills, to get a better qualification).

Older adults are, however, not a homogeneous group either. There are differences in learning motivation not only between younger and older adults but also between the 'young old' and the 'old old' (between which the transitions are flowing). Recently retired persons often still connect learning to the acquisition of new skills whilst older people might concentrate their motivation on health or aging issues. When differentiating between third and fourth agers, cohorts must be considered too. Antikainen et al. (1996) have done so in an educational context by differentiating between four 'educational generations': those born up to 1935 with little formal education; those born from 1936 to 1945 that benefited from educational growth, but with persisting educational inequalities; those born from 1946 to 1965 during the 'Golden Age of Welfare' and those born after 1966. However, this classification does not reach far enough, as it only differentiates between formal educational generations and does not consider generational differences in informal learning. Consequently, the concept of learning in older age is used too narrowly, as it neither recognizes the importance of informal learning across the life course nor considers that non-educational experiences can shape learning motivation in later life.

The meaning of learning motivation makes it clear that learning opportunities do not automatically create participants who want to engage in them. Beyond that, people that do not engage in education do not necessarily perceive this as a lack (Coffield, 2000). Eurobarometer (European Commission, 2003) data shows that the desire to participate in training declines rapidly after the age

of 55. Half of the respondents aged 65 years and older state that nothing could ever encourage them to participate in education again. So talking about motives to learn, we must also talk about motives not to learn. Wittpoth (2011) raises the question whether, and in which situations, resignation from participation can be very rational, particularly for members of lower status groups. He postulates that participation in education is often extrinsically motivated, starting from compulsory education in early age and continuing through the working life, where it is often 'motivated' by social pressure and informal duties. Once retired, individuals are finally free to decide against participation in education. Additionally, there are many challenges in life that an educational course cannot help individuals to cope with adequately. Therefore, what are the benefits of learning in later life – why should people participate?

INDIVIDUAL EFFECTS OF EDUCATIONAL PARTICIPATION IN LATER LIFE

Education shapes competencies later in life, and competencies affect social and political engagement, subjective well-being, and health. According to a Dutch study on mortality rates among the elderly across eleven European countries (Huisman et al., 2004), there are considerable differences between males and females regarding mortality, depending on their level of education. The conclusion from this study is best described with British socio-epidemiologist, Michael Marmot's words: 'The higher the education, the longer people are likely to live, and the better their health is likely to be' (Marmot, 2004: 15).

What are the effects of educational participation in later life, and which causes can be empirically tested? The following research results focus on one main effect of education, but other factors like gender and social status also accompany them.

Medical research attests to the positive effects of continuous mental stimulation on health. Neurological research shows that mental exercises positively influence intellectual abilities by minimizing memory losses or even reversing them. Learning induces changes in the brain structure (Kotulak, 1997). And: Individuals who pursue education are more likely to avoid coronary diseases and high blood pressure because they tend to seek medical assistance sooner and more effectively prevent and treat ailments by self-diagnosis. Furthermore, older people who participate in learning processes recover better from diseases. They tend to be released sooner from hospitalized care into home care. However, researchers cannot neglect the fact that education acquired earlier in life has a much greater influence on health in old age than learning activities in old age. The health gap between individuals with high and low educational levels increases for certain health indicators like grip strength or functional health like limitations of general and instrumental activities of daily living, mobility limitations, depressive symptoms, numerical ability, and time orientation (Leopold & Engelhardt, 2011).

On average, learning capacity tends to diminish in later life compared to earlier stages of life (Kruse, 2008). However, even older people show clear learning effects in novel situations. Over the course of aging, a number of typical changes in performance are found which are partly structural. These changes include sensory limitations on the one hand, and an increased ability to solve complex problems on the other (Hardy, 2005). Changes in performance that occur with aging are overanalysed, if no other effects are observed that result from generational differences or changes in the labour market. These changes include intergenerational qualification-based differences. Older people often have a lower academic education to begin with.

Research on educational habits of older people shows that learning positively impacts satisfaction with life and health in general (Khaw, 1997). Education and a healthy lifestyle help an individual to stay fit. Respondents with a lower level of education tend to exercise less and suffer more often from obesity than their more highly educated peers (cf. Börsch-Supan et al., 2008).

Lifelong learning and education in later life ensure participation in social life. They counteract the risk of poverty and improve equal opportunities. In this respect, third-age learning can help challenge (negative) stereotypes and expectations regarding social class, gender and age (Withnall, 2010). There is a link between participation in education and involvement in social activities, as well as between learning and political engagement. Older people who participate in continuing education often take up voluntary work; they have more faith in political institutions and participate more often in petitions and political discussions (Kolland & Ahmadi, 2010). What is more, aging occurs in a social context, in a social network of friendships, (former) work relationships, neighbourly contacts and in interactions with family members. Educational participation enriches those who attend courses or attain knowledge. It also has 'spread effects', affecting the entire social context.

The cited (positive) effects of education on the quality of life can be seen as undifferentiated educational optimism, if reasons and limitations remain unconsidered. Why is it that mostly positive effects are pointed out? The educational optimism that results from presenting all the benefits of learning and education is supposed to counteract the deficit model of aging. In this sense, the empirical results fuel a normative reorientation. Thus, scientists adopt unproven assumptions adopted without too much questioning (Withnall, 2010) and neglect negative effects or drawbacks of learning. John Field (2009) emphasized some critical aspects of education in later life. He claims not just any type of education empowers older people, education in later life can evoke unpleasant and stressful experiences from people's earlier lives, and education can disrupt existing social networks. Stress and anxiety caused by participation in learning can then also

2

have a negative effect on the health of older learners (Alridge & Lavender, 2000).

When highlighting positive effects, it is important not to neglect educational differences and deficits that occur over the entire course of life and that become even more pronounced in the fourth age. If only one quarter of individuals aged seventy and above has access to new information technologies then this is not only a 'technical gap', but a double social discrimination. Certain skills are lacking that are relevant for social status, and this results in a withdrawal from the main project of our modern age, namely the knowledge society.

SOCIETAL EFFECTS OF EDUCATIONAL PARTICIPATION IN LATER LIFE – PRODUCTIVITY

This section highlights the value of learning activities to society. This refers to the link between learning activity and *productivity*. If we see productivity as creating value, productivity in later life would entail contributing to the economic, political and socio-cultural prosperity of society. The difficulty lies in distinguishing productive from non-productive activities. Much as not every achievement in life inspires interest due to its inherent productivity, productivity is also not necessarily a relevant aspect of individual and social activities. Nonetheless, expanding the concept of learning to 'productive activities' would have the advantage that activity would become 'valuable', for both society and the individual.

Prototypically, the continuity between work and retirement is successfully achieved whenever one reverts to 'holistic' activities associated with pre-industrial production stages, such as housework or gardening. Domestic work and gardening, repairs, arts & crafts, and all other 'do it yourself' activities appear to compensate for the losses of rational labour division and help to reclaim initiative, control, meaning and responsibility generally associated with the completion of an entire product. Hobbies seem to help in acquiring

self-determination, which the external control present in professional work hinders.

Self-actualization and self-determination are rarely the result of reproducing existing knowledge, or defensive learning. They rather develop from productive learning (Holzkamp, 1993), which is the expansion of an individual's abilities. Productive learning spurs the development of one's self-concept and worldview, producing a subjective quality of life (cf. Köster, 2005). Productive learning refers to self-directed learning, implying sensitivity for new and unusual stimuli, the ability to experience surprise, amazement and to marvel (Schäffter, 1989). It increases the capacity to perceive a novel context first as incongruent and to explore it later based on one's individual beliefs. Self-directed productivity does not imply self-assuredness, integrity/authenticity and self-sufficiency, but rather self-reflective sensitivity for unknown stimuli. It requires a learning culture based on stimulation, challenges, provocation and contrasting exploration. Stimulation is rarely confined to life experiences, but requires institutionalized and professional educational measures that provide sufficient contrast to the familiar to stimulate learning.

The ambiguity of the concept of productivity results from the danger that, outside the context of work, integration of seniors may depend on their benefit to society. It is a one sided-view to consider the elderly only as producers of marketable achievements. In our social system, they could be viewed as consumers of performance and as such, considered socially productive. Emphasizing the productivity of lifelong learning entails the risk that older people will be adjusted to the social order according to free market values and will fail to help marginalized groups. We must instead acknowledge that learning and education are never, at any age, neutral or inherently good (Formosa, 2010). Following Glendenning and Battersby (1990) we should always ask whose interests are being served and whose interests are being neglected by educational policy and provision in later life.

OUTLOOK

To encourage lifelong learning in later life, a new educational charter is necessary that focuses on a four-generation society. These four generations comprise individuals younger than 25, the group of 25–50-year olds, individuals aged 50–75 and people aged 75+ (Schuller, 2010). This educational charter should not be a legal contract but rather one based on a social agreement. It should envision the fair distribution of educational resources across all four ages. Furthermore, to realize this contract policy requires a flexible system of 'credits' that allows a high degree of permeability within the educational system. Policy makers must develop a coherent national framework. This contract should be thoroughly grounded in knowledge of demographic, economic and social conditions. If an educational system integrates all generations, this could lead to mutual advantages, because resources and opportunities would be more balanced. Learning in this context does not mean learning for professional reasons, but rather for personal and social development. People should see education in its generative function and not only as an activity that each generation pursues for itself.

An educational policy oriented towards the future that pursues the interests of senior citizens should address lifelong learning and create structures that ensure equal opportunities for senior citizens and unhindered access to high-quality and diverse learning opportunities. It should ensure access for all to education and learning in old age. It should take into account the diversity of aging and intergenerational learning. Furthermore, quality standards for senior educational initiatives need to be implemented and qualification opportunities must be established at different levels of senior education. Educational counselling and improved provision of information for older people in the post-professional phase must be provided. Learning opportunities must be offered in close proximity to the living environment. Continuing education measures in the domain of information and communication technologies need be introduced.

Considering the very limited systematic research on the learning needs and learning methods of older persons, the further development of the discipline of Educational gerontology should be stimulated. To accomplish this, some prerequisites are necessary, such as a trans-disciplinary and methodologically open direction. The goal should be an innovative, practical research approach that critically reflects upon the living conditions of the elderly and their educational patterns. Such a research programme would also highlight the connection between research and the political agenda. The future of an independent discipline depends on how successfully it responds, with adequate measures, to the growing educational interest of older people. One of the main difficulties for the future of geragogy is its distinction from adult education and gerontology. The social climate is favourable; however, the socio-political acceptance for geragogic action must be continuously claimed anew. In this sense, geragogy remains a risk and a continuous quest.

ACKNOWLEDGEMENT

This paper uses data from SHARE 2006. The SHARE data collection has been primarily funded by the European Commission through the 5th framework programme (project QLK6-CT-2001-00360 in the thematic programme Quality of Life), through the 6th framework programme (projects SHARE-I3, RII-CT- 2006-062193, COMPARE, CIT5-CT-2005-028857, and SHARE-LIFE, CIT4-CT-2006-028812) and through the 7th framework programme (SHARE-PREP, 211909 and SHARE-LEAP, 227822). Additional funding from the US National Institute on Aging (U01 AG09740-13S2, P01 AG005842, P01 AG08291, P30 AG12815, Y1-AG-4553-01 and OGHA 04-064, IAG BSR06-11, R21 AG025169) as well as from various national sources is gratefully acknowledged (see www.share-project.org for a full list of funding institutions).

REFERENCES

Allmendinger, Jutta; Kleinert, Corinna; Antoni, Manfred; Christoph, Bernhard (2011): Adult education and lifelong learning. *Zeitschrift für Erziehungswissenschaft*, 14/2: 283–299.

Alridge, Fiona; Lavender, Peter (2000): *The Impact of Learning on Health*. Leicester: NIACE.

Antikainen, Ari; Houtsonen, Jarmo; Kauppila, Juha; Huotelin, Hannu (1996): *Living in a Learning Society: Life histories, identities and education*. London: Falmer Press.

Arnold, Brunhilde; Costa, Jean F. (1999): A new vision of the third age for the individual and society as a result of learning possibilities for older adults. Continuing scientific education in Europe – a comparative study. http://www.lill-online.net/5.0/E/5.3/vision.html

Arnold, Rolf; Schüßler, Ingeborg (2003): *Ermöglichungsdidadktik –Erwachsenenpädagogische Grundlagen und Erfahrungen*. Hohengehren: Schneider Verlag.

Baltes, Paul B; Lindenberger, Ulman (1988): On the range of cognitive plasticity in old age as a function of experience: 15 years of intervention research. *Behaviour Research*, 19(3): 283–300.

Bandura, Albert (1997): *Self-Efficacy: The exercise of control*. New York: Freeman & Co.

Bereiter, Carl; Scardamalia, Marlene (1989): Intentional learning as a goal of instruction. In: Resnick, Lauren B. (Ed.): *Knowing, Learning and Instruction. Hillsdale*: Routledge. pp. 361–392.

Billett, Stephen (2010): The perils of confusing lifelong learning with lifelong education. *International Journal of Lifelong Education*, 29(4): 401–413.

Börsch-Supan, Axel; Brugiavini, Agar; Jürges, Hendrik; Kapteyn, A.; Mackenbach, Johan; Siegrist, Johannes; Weber, Guglielmo (2008): *Health, Ageing and Retirement in Europe (2004–2007). Starting the Longitudinal Dimension*. Mannheim: Mannheim Research Institute for the Economics of Aging (MEA).

Boshier, Roger (1971): Motivational orientation of adult education participants: A factor analytic exploration of Houle's typology. *Adult Education*, 21(2): 3–26.

Boshier, Roger; Collins, John B. (1985): The Houle typology after twenty-two years: A large scale empirical test. *Adult Education Quarterly*, 35(3): 113–130.

Bourdieu, Pierre; Passeron, Jean-Claude (1970): *La reproduction: Eléments pour une théorie du système d'enseignement*. Paris: Editions de Minuit.

Bubolz-Lutz, Elisabeth (1999): Autonomie statt Didaktik – Gegenthesen zum Infrastruktur-Ansatz. In: Bergold, Ralph; Knopf, Detlef; Mörchen, Anette (Eds.): *Altersbildung an der Schwelle des neuen Jahrhunderts*. Bonn: Deutsches Institut für Erwachsenenbildung. pp.67–64.

Clark, Burton (1960): The cooling out function in higher education. *American Journal of Sociology*, 65(6): 569–576.

Coffield, Frank (2000): *Differing Visions of a Learning Society: Research Findings Volume 1*. Bristol: The Policy Press.

Cross, K. Patricia (1981): *Adults as Learners: Increasing Participation and Facilitating Learning*. San Francisco: Jossey-Bass.

Cruikshank, Margaret (2003): *Learning to be Old: Gender, culture, and aging*. Lanham, MD: Rowman & Littlefield.

Deci, Edward L. and Ryan, Richard M. (Eds.) (2004): *Handbook of Self-determination Research*. Rochester, New York: University of Rochester Press.

Dörr, Karin (2006): *The Situation of Geragogic-Pedagogy for Senior Citizens in European Countries*. Cham: Volkshochschule im Lankreis Cham.

Erpenbeck, John; Heyse, Volker (1999): *Die Kompetenzbiographie. Strategien der Kompetenzentwicklung durch selbstorganisiertes Lernen und multimediale Kommunikation*. Münster: Waxmann.

European Commission (2003) *Eurobarometer 59.0*, January–March 2003, European Opinion Research Group, Brussels (Producer), Cologne: GESIS: ZA3903.

Field, John (2005): *Social Capital and Lifelong Learning*. Bristol: The Policy Press.

Field, John (2009): *Well-being and Happiness: Inquiry into the future for lifelong learning*. Leicester: National Institute of Adult Continuing Education.

Findsen, Brian (2007): Freirean philosophy and pedagogy in the adult education context: The case of older adults' learning. *Studies in Philosophy and Education*, 26: 545–559.

Formosa, Marvin (2000): 'Older adult education in a Maltese University of the Third Age: A critical perspective'. *Education and Ageing*, 15(3): 315–339.

Formosa, Marvin (2010): Universities of the Third Age: A rationale for transformative education in later life. *Journal of Transformative Education*, 8(3): 197–219.

Formosa, Marvin (2012): Education and older adults at the University of the Third Age. *Educational Gerontology*, 38(2): 114–126.

Glendenning, Frank; Battersby, David (1990): Why we need educational gerontology and education for older adults: a statement of first principles. In: Glendenning, Frank; Percy, Keith (Eds.): *Ageing, Education and Society: Readings in educational* gerontology. Keele, Staffordshire: Association for Educational Gerontology, pp.219–231.

Harrison, Marion B.; McGuire, Francis (2008): Starting a lifelong learning institute: A firsthand perspective. *Activities, Adaptation & Aging*, 32(2): 149–157.

Heckhausen, Jutta; Schulz, Richard (1998): Development regulation in adulthood: Selection and compensation via primary and secondary control. In: Dweck, Carol S.; Heckhausen, Jutta (Eds.): *Motivation and Regulation Across the Lifespan*. Cambridge: University Press.

Holzkamp, Klaus (1993): *Lernen. Subjektwissenschaftliche Grundlegung*. Frankfurt am Main: Campus.

Houle, Cyril O. (1961): *The Inquiring Mind: A Study of the Adult Who Continues to Learn*. Madison, WI: University of Wisconsin Press.

Huisman, M.; Kunst, A.E.; Andersen, O.; Bopp, M.; Borgan, J.-K.; Borrell, C.; Costa, G.; Deboosere, P.; Desplanques, G.; Donkin, A.; Gadeyne, S.; Minder, C.; Regidor, E.; Spadea, T.; Valkonen, T.; and Mackenbach, J.P. (2004) Socioeconomic inequalities in mortality among elderly people in 11 European populations. *Journal of Epidemiology and Community Health*, 58(6): 468–475.

Jarvis, Peter (1987): *Adult Learning in the Social Context*. London: Croom Helm.

Jarvis, Peter (1995): *Adult and Continuing Education*. London: Routledge.

Jarvis, Peter (2001): *Learning in Later Life*. London: Kogan Page.

Khaw, Kay-Tee (1997) Healthy ageing/, *British Medical Journal*, 315(7115): 1090–1096.

Klingovsky, Ulla (2009): *Schöne Neue Lernkultur: Transformationen der Macht in der Weiterbildung. Eine gouvernementalitätstheoretische Analyse*. Bielefeld: transcript Verlag.

Knowles, Malcolm S. (1975): *Self-Directed Learning: A Guide for Learners and Teachers*. New York: Association Press.

Knowlton, Martin P. (1980): The Elderhostel philosophy. *Innovative Higher Education*, 5(1): 65–70.

Kohli, Martin (2009): The world we forgot: A historical review of the life course. In: Walter R. Heinz, Johannes Huinik, Ansgar Weymann (eds), *The Life Course Reader: Individuals and societies across time*, Frankfurt, Campus-Verlag, 64–90.

Kolland, Franz (1996): *Kulturstile älterer Menschen*. Wien: Böhlau.

Kolland, Franz; Ahmadi, Pegah (2010): *Bildung und aktives Altern*. Bielefeld: Bertelsmann.

Köster, Dietmar (2005): Bildung im Alter …die Sicht der kritischen Sozialwissenschaften. In: Klie, Thomas; Buhl, Anke; Entzian, Hildegard; Hedtke-Becker,

Astrid; Wallrafen-Dreisow, Helmut (Eds.): *Die Zukunft der gesundheitlichen, sozialen und pflegerischen Versorgung älterer Menschen*. Frankfurt am Main: Marbuse Verlag. pp.96–109.

Kotulak, Ronald (1997): *Inside the Brain: Revolutionary Discoveries of How the Mind Works*. Kansas City: Andrews McMeel Publishing.

Kruse, Andreas (Hrsg.) (2008): *Weiterbildung in der zweiten Lebenshälfte*. Bielefeld: Bertelsmann.

Labouvie-Vief, Gisela (1985): Intelligence and cognition. In: Birren, James E.; Schaie, K. Warner (Eds.): *Handbook of the Psychology of Aging*. New York: Von Nostrand Reinhold. pp.500–530.

Laslett, Peter (1989): *A Fresh Map of Life*. London: Weidenfeld & Nicolson.

Lave, Jeanne (1988): *Cognition in Practice: Mind, mathematics, and culture in everyday life*. Cambridge: Cambridge University Press.

Lave, Jeanne; Wenger, Etienne (1990): *Situated Learning: Legitimate Peripheral Participation*. Cambridge: Cambridge University Press.

Leopold, Liliya; Engelhardt, Henriette (2011): Bildung und Gesundheitsungleichheit im Alter: Divergenz, Konvergenz oder Kontinuität? *Kölner Zeitschrift für Soziologie*, 63(2): 207–236.

Marmot, Michael (2004): *The Status Syndrome*. New York: Times Books.

Mayer, Karl Ulrich (ed.) (1990): *Lebensverläufe und sozialer Wandel*. In: *Kölner Zeitschrift für Soziologie und Sozialpsychologie*, Sonderheft 31, Opladen: Westdeutscher Verlag.

McClusky, Howard Y. (1973): Education and aging. In: A. Hendrickson (Ed.), *A Manual on Planning Educational Programs for Older Adults*. Tallahassee: Department of Adult Education, Florida State University.

Meyer-Drawe, Käte (2008): *Diskurse des Lernens*. München: Fink.

Mezirow, Jack (1985): A critical theory of self-directed learning. *New Directions for Continuing Education*, 25: 17–30.

Mezirow, Jack (1991): *Transformative Dimensions of Adult Learning*. San Francisco, CA: Jossey-Bass.

Moody, Harry R. (2010): The new aging enterprise. In: Dannefer, Dale; Phillipson, Chris (Eds.): *The SAGE Handbook of Social Gerontology*. Thousand Oaks, CA: SAGE Publications Ltd., pp. 483–494.

Pogson, Philip; Tennant, Mark (2000): Understanding adult learners. In: Foley, Griff (Ed.): *Understanding Adult Education and Training*. New South Wales: Allen & Unwin. pp.23–33.

Romaniuk, Jean Gasen; Romaniuk, Michael (1982) Participation motives of older adults in higher education: The Elderhostel experience. *The Gerontologist*, 22(4): 364–368.

Rowe, John W.; Kahn, Robert L. (1997): Successful aging. *The Gerontologist* 37(4): 433–440.

Rubenson, Kjell (2006): The Nordic model of lifelong learning. *Compare*, 36(3): 327–341.

Rubenson, Kjell; Desjardins, Richard (2009): The impact of welfare state regimes on barriers to participation in adult education. A bounded agency model. *Adult Education Quarterly*, 59(3): 187–207.

Scardamalia, Marlene; Bereiter, Carl (2006): Knowledge building: theory, pedagogy and technology. In: Sawyer, K (Ed.): *Cambridge Handbook of the Learning Sciences*. New York: Cambridge University Press. pp. 97–118.

Schäffter, Ortfried (1989): Produktivität. System-theoretische Rekonstruktionen aktiv gestaltender Umweltaneignung. In: Knopf, Detlef; Schäffter, Ortfried; Schmidt, Roland (Eds.): *Produktivität des Alters*. Berlin: Deutsches Zentrum für Altersfragen. p.257–325.

Schaie, K. Warner; Willis, Sherry L.; Caskie, Grace I.L. (2004): The Seattle Longitudinal Study: Relationship between personality and cognition. *Aging, Neuropsychology and Cognition*, 11(2–3): 304–234.

Schuller, Tom (2010): Learning through life: The implications for learning in later life of the NIACE inquiry. *International Journal of Education and Ageing*, 1(1): 41–52.

Shavit, Yossi; Blossfeld, Hans-Peter (1993): Persisting barriers: Changes in educational opportunities in thirteen Countries. In: Blossfeld, Hans-Peter; Shavit, Yossi (Eds.): *Persistent Inequality: Changing Educational Attainment in Thirteen Countries*. Boulder: Westview Press.

Sherron, Ronald H.; Lumsdon, D. Barry (1978): *Introduction to Educational Gerontology*. Washington: Hemisphere Pub Corp.

Sommer, Caroline; Kuenemund, Harald (1999): *Bildung im Alter. Eine Literaturanalyse. Forschungsgruppe Altern und Lebenslauf (FALL)*, Forschungsbericht 66.

Staudinger, Ursula M.; Heidemeier, Heike (Eds.) (2009): *Altern, Bildung und lebenslanges Lernen*. Stuttgart: Wissenschaftliche Verlagsgesellschaft.

Survey of Health, Ageing and Retirement in Europe (SHARE) (2006): Munich: Munich Center of the Economics of Ageing. http://www.share-project.org

Swindell, Rick (2011): Successful ageing and international approaches to later-life learning. In: Boulton-Lewis, Gillian M.; Tam, Maureen (Eds.): *Active Ageing, Active Learning: Issues and Challenges*. New York: Springer, p.35–66.

UNESCO (2010): *Global Report on Adult Learning and Education*. Hamburg: UNESCO Institute for Lifelong Learning.

Verhaeghen, Paul; Marcoen, Alfons (1996): On the mechanisms of plasticity in young and older adults after instruction in the method of loci: Evidence for an amplification model. *Psychology and Aging*, 11(1): 164–178.

Vester, Michael (2004) Die sozialen Milieus und die gebremste Bildungsexpansion. *Report*, 27(1): 15–34.

WHO (2002): *Aktiv Altern. Rahmenbedingungen und Vorschläge für politisches Handeln*. Vienna: BMSK.

Withnall, Alexandra (2010): *Improving Learning in Later Life*. New York: Routledge.

Wittpoth, Juergen (2011): Beteiligungsregulation in der Weiterbildung. In: Tippelt, Rudolf; von Hippel, Aiga (Eds.): *Handbuch Erwachsenenbildung/ Weiterbildung*. Wiesbaden: Verlag fuer Sozialwissenschaft, pp. 771–788.

Wldokowski, Raymond J. (2008): *Enhancing Adult Motivation to Learn: A comprehensive guide for teaching all adults*. New York: John Wiley & Sons.

Yeaxlee, Basil A. (1929): *Lifelong Education*. London: Cassell.

23

The Role of Social Networking Games in Maintaining Intergenerational Communications for Older Adults

Yunan Chen, Jing Wen and Bo Xie

INTRODUCTION

Population aging has become a salient issue in contemporary Chinese society (Lee, 2004). An important concern for any aging society is to maintain the health and well-being of older adults (Xie, 2008d, 2009). Studies have shown that family relationships play a critical role in maintaining individuals' psychological well-being and life satisfaction (Litwin and Shiovitz-Ezra, 2010; Lou, 2010; George, 2010; Phillips, Siu, Yeh and Cheng, 2008). Older adults have a strong desire to communicate more frequently with their children (Lindley, Harper and Sellen, 2009). However, evidence shows that Chinese adults receive relatively poor support from their adult children (Ng, 2002: 135). Many of these intergenerational communication challenges

are due to geographical distances (Ng, 2002: 135), time zone differences (Cao et al., 2010), and the busy schedules of the adult children (Tee, Brush and Inkpen, 2009).

In China, the family has always been, and is still, the predominant mode of support for aging parents (Tu and associates 1989). However, with the projected increase in the absolute number and proportion of older adults in China, the family-based support system is increasingly under strain. In addition, the traditional family structure has been undergoing rapid transformation as young adults migrate to other regions seeking better employment opportunities (Silverstein, Cong and Li, 2006; Glei et al 2005). Empirical evidence suggests that in contemporary Chinese society, filial piety may be eroding and the family may no longer be the primary

source of support for older Chinese parents
(Joseph and Philips, 1999; Ng, Philips and
Lee, 2002). Ongoing societal changes resulting from industrialization, capitalization,
and globalization challenge the conventional
family-based patterns that feature the co-
location of the aging parents and adult children
(Bian, 2002; Ikels, 1996; Perry and Selden,
2003; Price and Fang, 2002).

The recent popularity of online social networking games among older adults in China
suggests the potential of online game playing
as influential in older adults' daily lives.
Anecdotal data suggest that social networking games have become an activity for family members of different generations to do
together.[1] These new practices raise an interesting question: how might social network
game playing affect intergenerational family
relationships? In this study, we explore how
aging parents and their adult children play
QQ Farm, one of the most popular online
social networking games in China, and how
such game playing may affect their relationships.

RELATED WORK

Family relationships play a critical role in
supporting older adults' psychological well-
being, morale, and life satisfaction (Litwin
and Shiovitz-Ezra, 2010; Lou, 2010; George,
2010; Phillips, Siu, Yeh and Cheng, 2008).
Family relationships are especially important
for older Chinese adults, since family support is more effective than support from
friends in preventing psychological distress
(e.g., depression) (Chi and Chou, 2001).
Older Chinese parents living in three-generation households or with grandchildren in
skipped-generation households had better
psychological well-being than those living in
single-generation households (Silverstein,
Cong and Li, 2006).

Despite their desire for more family communication (Lindley, Harper and Sellen,
2008; Lindley, Harper and Sellen, 2009),
older Chinese adults receive limited informal

support from their adult children (Ng et al.,
2002). Geographic proximity is an important
determinant of the amount and types of support older adults receive from their adult
children: the shorter the geographical distance, the more support older adults receive.
In contrast, family members who live in different time zones face difficulties in finding
a convenient time to communicate (Cao,
2008). The busy schedules adult children
have and the lack of technology use among
older people make it challenging for family
members to communicate (Tee, Brush and
Inkpen, 2009).

Digital devices have the potential to alleviate these intergenerational communication
challenges (Romero et al., 2007; Tee, Brush
and Inkpen, 2009), particularly for family
members who live far away. For example,
the 'HomeNote' device was designed to promote remote, situated messaging within the
family (Sellen et al., 2006). The results highlight the role of digital messaging in enabling
subtle ways of requesting action, expressing
affection, and marking identity in the family
(Sellen et al., 2006).

Video- or camera-based technologies may
be the best technology for connecting family
members, since the use of video-mediated
communication can foster closeness between
the communicators (Kirk, Sellen and Cao
2010). One study (Ames et al., 2010) found
that video chat could be used to reinforce
family identity and values. *Digital Family
Portrait* displays iconic projections of older
adults' daily activities to family members living far away (Rowan and Mynatt, 2005).
Family Window (Judge and Neustaedter,
2010) uses an always-on video camera to
connect family members residing in two
households. These devices allow family
members to see each other's daily activities.
Similarly, devices such as SPARCS (Brush
et al., 2008) and Wayve (Lindley, Harper and
Sellen, 2010) also encourage information
and photo sharing among family members.
Although these image-based systems present
new opportunities for facilitating family
communication, sharing daily activities with

family members also raises privacy concerns (Judge and Neustaedter, 2010).

Recently, various game-based technologies have been used to support the health and well-being of older adults. One aspect of this approach is to encourage physical activity. For example, Age Invaders (Khoo et al., 2008), an interactive intergenerational social-physical game, allows older adults to play with children in the physical world. Unlike standard computer games, Age Invaders brings the game playing to a physical platform and requires physical movements instead of constraining the user being in front of a computer for hours. Similarly, Voida, Carpendale and Greenberg (2010) examined intergenerational gaming practices of four generations of console gamers and the roles gamers of different generations take when playing together in groups. Their analysis revealed a more flexible combination of roles in the computer-mediated interactions than the roles found in the physical world.

Intergenerational game playing can also take place across distance (Davis et al., 2008), indicating the potential role of games in mediating geographically distant family relationships. Interestingly, the majority of the current games still require family members to have available time to play together. In this sense, although the game might bridge the physical distance between remotely located family members, possible time constraints among family members can still exist.

QQ FARM: AN ONLINE SOCIAL NETWORKING GAME

We studied family game play on QQ Farm. QQ Farm is one of the most popular social networking games on Qzone, a major social networking site in mainland China. Both QQ Farm and QZone were developed and built by Tencent Inc. in 2009. On March 31, 2010, it was reported that there were 568.6 million active user accounts on all QQ service platforms.[2] QQ Farm is designed to encourage

Interact users from all age groups to play social games with friends in their social networks. Surprisingly, the popularity of QQ Farm has spread to many older adults who previously were not playing online games. Anecdotal cases of older adults engaged in or even addicted to playing QQ Farm have been reported as an interesting social phenomenon.[3] Unlike many other games that are played mainly among friends of similar ages, it is not unusual for QQ Farm to be played among older parents and their adult children on a daily basis. This study intends to examine the impact of playing QQ Farm on intergenerational family interactions to shed light on the role of social networking gaming in mediating family communication and relationships.

QQ Farm offers relatively simple and intuitive game features that can be easily adopted by various types of players. In the game, players act as farm owners and manage their own farms, cultivating, irrigating, and harvesting crops in one's own farm. In addition, players can also visit farms owned by their friends, where players can perform limited actions – some helpful, others mischievous. Helpful actions include weeding and irrigating, whereas mischievous actions include stealing the other players' mature crops. Beyond game playing itself, each player has access to a personal message board associated with his or her farm. The personal message board shows log information about one's farm, including both helpful and mischievous actions by other players. A player can see who visited his or her farm and when, and the actions of the other players. Players can also personalize their QQ Farm space by naming and decorating their own farms. These game features allow players to visit, help and connect with each other during the process of game playing.

METHODS

We conducted a nine-month ethnographic study from March to November 2010 to examine the potential influence of social network gaming on the communications and relationships between parents and their adult children. We studied sixteen pairs of parent–adult child ($N = 32$), each containing one older parent and one adult child. Participants were recruited through snowball techniques. The first two adult children were recruited from the university where the first and second authors are affiliated, and the rest of the participants were referred by people we studied earlier. Snowball sampling appears to be an appropriate method to study players in a social networking game since it allows us to reach QQ game players through people's social networks. Because the goal of the study was to examine intergenerational game play among adult children and their older parents, we did not include children under 18 in this study.

Among the sixteen pairs of participants, seven pairs lived in the same household, or in nearby neighborhoods where they could maintain face-to-face interactions frequently. The remaining nine pairs of participants lived in different regions, with all the parents living in China and their adult children living in the United States, Japan, Australia, or Denmark. In this paper we refer to them as the 'local' or 'remote' families, respectively. Studying the communication behaviors in both types of families allowed us to compare the impact of game playing on family members who do not have face-to-face interactions frequently to those who do.

The parents being studied were aged from 47 to 66 years old, with an average age of 58. (While this age group may not be perceived as 'old' in countries like the United States, it is nonetheless commonly perceived as 'old' in countries like China; for instance, the *Chinese Seniors Rights Protection Law* defines seniors as individuals age 60 or older; however, in some cases the mandatory retirement age can be as young as 50 or even below;[4] for a more detailed discussion on cultural differences in the perception of 'old' in Chinese and American cultures, see Xie, 2006, 2008a, 2008b, 2008c.) Six out of the sixteen parents were over 60 years old, and eleven were

retired by the time this study was conducted. The sixteen adult children aged from 18 to 42, with an average age of 28. At the time of the study, almost all adult children (15 out of 16) were working or attending college/graduate schools. All participants had more than six months of gaming experience and reached at least the 15th level according to the ranks designed in QQ Farm (0 is the lowest and 50 is the highest level in the current game system).

The sixteen pairs of participants fall into three conditions: the parent and the child both are current players (9 pairs); either the parent or the child is a player (4 pairs); neither the parent nor the child are players (3 pairs). The non-playing or partial-playing participants served as comparisons for us to examine the intergenerational communication patterns between the 'dual-play' pairs and those having one or more non-playing participants. It is worth noting that among the nine dual-play pairs, four pairs were local and the other five were remote families. The participants' basic characteristics are summarized in Table 23.1.

DATA COLLECTION

To better understand how game playing influences family communication, we first observed the online game behaviors of six dual-play family members. Semi-structured, open-ended interviews were conducted with all sixteen pairs of participants based on the insights drawn from the online observations. Using observations and interviews ensured that both the actual game play patterns and user attitudes were included in our data set. Human subject study approval was obtained prior to data collection. All participant names reported in this paper are pseudonyms.

Online observations were conducted at the beginning of the study to understand the basic gaming behaviors among the 'dual-play' pairs. Specifically, one researcher joined each participant's QQ Farm friend list and examined their game behaviors by

Table 23.1 Participant characteristics

Relation (R) pairs	Parents–children relationship	Age	Occupation	Playing status	Living Situation
R1	Father	59	Senior Official	Play	Remote
	Daughter	28	PHD Student	Play	
R2	Father	58	Retired	Play	Remote
	Daughter	29	Junior Engineer	Play	
R3	Father	64	Retired	Play	Local
	Daughter	39	Primary Teacher	Play	
R4	Father	66	Retired	Play	Local
	Daughter	37	University faculty	Play	
R5	Mother	64	Retired	Play	Remote
	Son	28	PHD Student	Play	
R6	Mother	60	University Staff	Play	Remote
	Son	29	PHD Student	Play	
R7	Mother	63	Retired	Play	Local
	Daughter	36	Account	Play	
R8	Mother	66	Retired	Play	Local
	Daughter	42	University faculty	Play	
R9	Father	64	Retired	Play	Remote
	Son	28	PHD Student	Play	
R10	Mother	54	Marketing Staff	Non-play	Remote
	Son	24	PHD Student	Non-play	
R11	Mother	47	Account	Non-play	Local
	Son	26	Undergraduate	Play	
R12	Mother	56	Retired	Non-play	Remote
	Son	26	Businessmen	Non-play	
R13	Mother	56	Retired	Non-play	Remote
	Daughter	26	PHD Student	Non-play	
R14	Mother	53	Retired	Play	Remote
	Daughter	26	Housewife	Non-play	
R15	Father	51	Deliveryman	Non-play	Local
	Son	18	Undergraduate	Play	
R16	Father	61	Retired	Play	Local
	Son	28	Manager	Non-play	

observing their game activities, which are publicly viewable to all friends in QQ Farm.

In the study, we first observed the game behaviors of six pairs of dual-play families daily, including four remote pairs and two local pairs over a period of two weeks. We observed the general game behaviors of participants, particularly their interactions with family members in the game space. Brief questions were probed through the instant messaging (IM) system associated with QQ Farm during the online observation sessions. In addition, we collected the game logs from the personal message board of each participant twice a day, once in the morning and once at night. These logs record participants' interactions with their online players in the game space. Log analysis helped us to understand how and when participants visit or play

with their family members. Next, we weekly followed the six pairs' gaming behaviors for three months. In this phase, our goal was to understand whether family members continued to play QQ Farm, and whether family communication was sustained between the older parent and the adult child over an extended period of time. This observation helped us to discern the potential long-term impact of game-mediated communication on intergenerational relationships.

We developed a semi-structured, open-ended interview guide based on the family play behaviors observed online. Specifically, observation data were discussed among authors to identify questions and issues to be addressed in the interviews. Family communication emerged as one important factor in family game play that deserved further investigation. In addition to the six pairs of dual-play participants reported above, the interview study was extended to three additional pairs of dual-play partici-pants, as well as seven single-play or non-playing pairs to provide comparisons. The interview questions centered on the follow-ing three topics:

- How participants played the QQ Farm game in general;
- How participants communicated with their family members in general; and
- How participants played the game with their family members.

At the participants' convenience, interviews were conducted by telephone or in-person. When telephone or in-person interviews were impossible, we interviewed participants using the IM associated with QQ Farm. Of the thirty-two participants, twenty-three of them were interviewed via the telephone, five were interviewed in person, and the remaining four were interviewed through IM. Each interview lasted from 30 to 60 minutes in length and was audio-recorded. Interview and observational data were first transcribed into Chinese, and then translated into English for further analysis.

DATA ANALYSIS

Data analysis for this study was guided by grounded theory (Glaser and Strauss, 1967; Strauss and Corbin, 1998) that emphasizes the co-evolution of data and theory by conducting data collection and analysis simultaneously. Following the constant comparative method (Glaser and Strauss, 1967) after the online observations, the immediate first step was to write a short descriptive summary to record general impressions about the family interac-tion in the game space. After each individual interview was conducted, audio data were transcribed into text as promptly as possible.

Four pairs of interview transcripts were randomly selected from the sixteen pairs of interviewees for the initial round of data analysis. Sample data were analyzed using the techniques of microanalysis or 'detailed line-by-line analysis' (Strauss and Corbin, 1998, p. 57) by three researchers independently. First, open coding was conducted by each researcher to identify salient concepts and their properties (i.e., characteristics) and dimensions (i.e., 'the range along which general properties of a cat-egory varies, giving specification to a cate-gory and variation to the theory') (Strauss and Corbin, 1998, p. 101). Gaming as a communi-cation medium to mediate intergenerational family communication quickly emerged from this initial round of analysis. Once this core category was identified, axial coding was then conducted to systematically explore the prop-erties and dimensions of this core category. This led to the formation of the subcategories (i.e., the three themes of game-based commu-nications). The themes produced by each researcher were compared, discussed and revised through a series of iterations until agreements were reached among all research-ers. Results of the microanalysis of the sample interviews were used to guide the next stage of coding, during which one researcher coded the remaining data using the developed cod-ing scheme. This second stage of the analysis generated similar concepts and themes to those identified in the initial coding stage, demonstrating dependability of the findings.

Meanwhile, quantitative data (i.e., log data about participants' use of the game) were entered into SPSS for descriptive statistical analyses. For each sample of the six pairs' log data, we summed all log messages, and then calculated the frequency and percentage of the interactive messages belonging to par-ents and his/her children by taking their vir-tual names in QQ Farm as the input variable.

KEY FINDINGS

Through comparing the dual-play, single-play, and non-play pairs, we find that QQ Farm has become a main channel for dual-play family members to stay connected. Our observations

Figure 23.1   Playing QQ Farm: left, a participant (son) playing game while studying; right, two parents discussing the game together

Table 23.2   Game use patterns of the six observed dual-play pairs

Relation pairs	Parents–children relationship	Age	Game ranks (Levels)	Time of logins per day	Playing Time (minutes) per day	Total number of interaction messages over the 2-week period
R1	Father	59	38	6	30	93
	Daughter	28	18	6	25	
R4	Father	63	34	1	5	37
	Daughter	34	19	5	15	
R5	Mother	63	22	3	10	47
	Son	28	15	5	20	
R6	Mother	60	41	6	30	49
	Son	29	39	4	15	
R8	Mother	65	26	6	30	35
	Daughter	36	24	5	10	
R9	Father	63	19	2	5	58
	Son	28	15	5	20	

of the 'dual-play' pairs suggest these participants constantly interact with their family members in the game space (Figure 23.1).

Analysis of the QQ Farm log data shows that eight percent of all the overall game interactions (319 out of 4132 messages) occurred between the pairs of study participants (i.e., a parent and an adult child). Overall, each pair of family members contacted each other an average of 53 times during the two-week period. Table 23.2 shows the game rank, logins and playing time of the six observed dual-play pairs.

Interestingly, for many of the dual-play families, communication through the game space is more preferable than other forms of communication, such as the telephone and face-to-face interactions. Family members

prefer to have some daily interaction, but do not need to have daily verbal conversations. *Xu*, a retired high school teacher, explained why the QQ game became a better way for him to stay connected with his adult daughter.

R2-father: It is almost impossible to have daily communications with my daughter, since she lives very far away from me. Now I have to [communicate with her] through QQ Farm. In the game, we don't really need to 'talk', but I know what she's doing... this provides a very good way to connect us. Sometimes it is even better than phone conversations, because we don't always have new things to talk about on the phone, especially when we already talked [lately]. Then it's actually better to meet on the Internet [in QQ Farm], leave a message, send an emotion icon and 'steal' in the farm. These stealing and harvesting are a way to relax.

In comparison, the non-play or single-play pairs often experience a sense of disconnection when talking about their relationships with their family members. Maintaining effective intergenerational communication is not an easy task, even when family members live in the same household or can meet regularly. *Zhao*, a mother living in the city of Wuhan, complained about how difficult it was to stay connected with her son who worked abroad.

> R12-Mother: I usually contact my son on the Internet (via Instant Messaging). We don't talk if he is not online. We usually only have contacts once, or twice a week. Sometime we don't even talk for an entire week. If I don't hear from him for too long, I just give him a call. And if he did not answer, I would be very worried... that's why I feel the telephone and the Internet (IM) aren't good enough for me to communicate with my son, but I have no other choice.

Zhao feels finding 'common time' is a major challenge for her to communicate with her son. Also, the lack of common conversational topics hinders intergenerational communication. *Chen*, a father with a college age son who studies in the same city and goes back home every weekend, still thinks of intergenerational communication as a difficult task.

> R15-Father: I don't have much communication with my son, in fact, quite rare... The only time we could talk is during lunchtime. After that, he goes back to play on his computer. We just don't have more time to talk. This happens everyday... I tried to communicate more with him or to find other more effective ways to talk to him, but it's very difficult... He spends lots of time on his computer. Other than playing games, he also chats with his friends and studies on his computer. I am not sure what he was doing exactly, 'cause I don't know much about computers and games.

This suggests that there is no time for this father to talk to his son, even when they spend every weekend together at home. Living in the same household doesn't guarantee communication time between the son and the father. The 18-year-old son spends most of his time in front of the computer. Both the 'computer time' that occupies the younger person and the lack of the older person's computer skills limit the opportunities for them to communicate.

GAME-BASED COMMUNICATION: THREE KEY FUNCTIONS

In this section, we detail how QQ game was used as a new communication medium to connect intergenerational family members. Specifically, the game appeared to have three key functions: (1) as an 'I am safe and well' message board; (2) helping family members to express care and stay connected; and (3) providing relaxing conversation topics for intergenerational family members.

A key purpose for communication among family members, especially those who live far away, is to know whether one is safe and well. As our participants *Lee* and *Jean* expressed in their interviews, they may not need to talk to their family members regularly, but they want to know whether their family members are safe. For most dual-play families, QQ Farm has turned into an *'I'm safe and well'* message board for them to stay connected. In the shared game space, family members get to know each other's online activities without having to talk or write directly to each other. This is especially useful for older generations, since they often desire to know their adult children's situations, while their children may be busy with their own life activities and don't have much time to communicate with their parents.

Lee, a father who lives in Wuhan, China, told us how through game playing, he is able to keep track of whether or not his daughter is safe in the United States.

> R1-father: If my daughter didn't call or chat online with us for a week, we would worry whether she ran into any difficulties in her life. But I don't actually need my daughter to leave any message to me [on Internet]. As long as I see she keeps stealing crops (in QQ Farm), I would feel very relived because I know she is safe.

Similarly, QQ Farm also serves as a platform for parents to know whether remote family members are safe during natural disasters. For geographically distributed families, verbal communication is sometimes not easy due to both distance and time difference. For these families, seeing each other's online activities would suggest they were not affected by a natural disaster.

> R9-father: When some disasters happened in the United States, like a flood, fire or earthquake, if I saw him [his son] played in the QQ Farm, I'd know his was safe.

Many parents feel that playing QQ game is a sign indicating their family members are safe and well, particularly when other forms of communication do not frequently occur. As one father explained to us:

> R1-father: Since my daughter is playing QQ game frequently, that means she is in a very good mood now. I think she should be happy over there [in the United States].

During family game playing, even if no word is exchanged, the behaviors in the game can still indicate the safe status of a loved one. The game activities thus help family members to not worry, even when they don't have more direct daily communication, such as on the phone or in face-to-face conversations.

Similarly, playing QQ Farm also offered adult children a way of knowing their parents' situation. As mentioned above, often times, adult children's busy work and life obligations leave them little time for their parents, and sometimes they worry whether their parents will feel lonely. To these adult children, playing a game is a good way to engage their parents in some fun and healthy activities.

> R7-daughter: My mom is retired and stays at home now. She has lots of free time. But we are too busy at work to be with her. When she plays this game, I know she is safe and happy.

In this case, R7-daughter works at a local bank and lives in the same city, but not the same household as her mother. Due to her busy work schedule, she is only able to visit her parents on the weekends. Knowing her mother is playing the game during the day assures her that her mother is not lonely. Further, the lightweight QQ Farm game is regarded as healthy by many participants, and thus they don't mind their loved ones playing it.

Participants of our study perceive their virtual activities in QQ Farm as a way to show *care and love* to their parents/adult children. As a result, playing together is often associated with the feelings of 'happy,' 'not lonely,' and 'comforting.' *Peng*, a mother, talked about how 'stealing crops', an originally mischievous action, would cheer her up during her busy days or when she was traveling alone.

> R6-mother: When I saw my children stealing crops from my farm, I even felt happy… It makes me very happy when they took care of my farm. It feels like I am not alone; I feel energetic there and it ties our family together. No matter wherever I travel, I feel my children are always with me.

In QQ Farm, when mature crops are stolen by others, the owner no longer gains experience points from growing it. However, different from common gaming competitors, the mother in our study does not care much about her game playing scores. Instead, she deems the 'stealing' action as a way to connect with her children who live abroad. Adult children also seem to play the game with their parents with the sense of being with them when they are not around.

> R9-son: I can't live with my parents since I am studying abroad now. I think this game has some effects [on the family relationship]. There aren't that many games for you to play with your parents. Playing games online makes me feel like I am with them at home. It makes my parents feel happy and also gives me a sense of comforting.

Beyond playing together, the helpful activities designed in QQ Farm, such as weeding and irrigating are even more appreciated by parents. Many parents are proud that their children are helping them in the game space (by doing, for instance, weeding for them). For instance, *Zhang*, a mother of four, checks her QQ farm daily to see who had helped her.

> R5-mother: I check the messages in my farm everyday. I know they [her adult children] helped me to take care of my farm; they cultivated grass and removed weeds for me... Through these little things I know how much they care about us, which made me very happy... it's just fun to play with my family, no matter daughter, son or daughter in law, we all play together.

These quotes suggest that, although care is not explicitly expressed through verbal or written communication, care and love are exchanged through game playing. Without calling each other and saying how much they love each other, care is represented through actions in the game. Thus, game playing is fun for parents because they can entertain themselves during their free time, and also because it is a platform for them to be with their adult children and observe what their children do for them everyday.

Interestingly, the ability of game playing in transiting care among family members also encouraged many parents to learn and use technologies. As one participant told us:

> R8-mother: I am really happy when I play this game... You know, when they [her two daughters] left for work, only their father and I are at home, and we have to wait till dinner time to see them. After that they will be busy mentoring their own kids' coursework. So there left only us again. But when I am on the computer, I can play and communicate with them more.

Many parents are fully aware of how busy their adult children might be, and they have learned computer game playing as a way to connect with their children, since their adult children are often in front of computers everyday. In this way, the desire for getting care from adult children has fostered technology adoption among these older adults.

GAME PLAYING PROMOTES MORE RELAXED FAMILY COMMUNICATIONS

Game playing is perceived as a 'fun and relaxing' conversational topic that encourages common interests between the aging parents and the adult children. The lack of common interests between the two generations often hinders effective family communication. As showed in Chen's case earlier, even when family members are co-residing in the same household, communication can be lacking. At home, his son spends most of his time in front of the computer. For Chen, not engaging much in computer activity prevents him from talking to his son, both through the computer and beyond; on the one hand, *Chen* was not able to spend much time with his son since his son was mostly in front of the computer; and on the other hand, this also suggests that there is an interest gap between the two generations. This lack of common interests leads to topic deprivation and affects face-to-face communication as well. In comparison, in the 'dual-play' families, game playing enhanced their daily interactions, strengthened family ties, and enriched the mutual shaping of online and offline communications by creating relaxed family communication topics and fostering shared common interests between the two generations.

The difficulties adult children have in communicating with their aging parents are bounded by traditional Chinese culture and values, whereas parents tend to talk about 'serious' or 'heavy' topics. *Yang*, a son who lives close to his parents' home and maintains routine face-to-face communications with his parents, found online game playing beneficial to their already frequent family communication.

> R16-son: Sometimes I watch how they [parents] play at home, like how they harvest crops. We talk and laugh together in doing so. I also told them some tips on how to play this game better. Sharing game playing experiences just improved our family communication and it's very enjoyable for us. In general, Chinese parents are always concerned

with their children's lives, such as their jobs, their relationships, how they get along with their wives or girl friends, etc. That's what our parents always talk to us about when we were growing up. QQ Farm brought in fun and easy topics for us. The issues they talked to us previously were all about lecturing us about how to live better. Adult children sometimes may feel they are over-controlled and thus not interested in those topics.

The easiness and relaxation brought by game playing are also applauded by the older generation, since talking about games provides them with new opportunities to interact with their children.

R1-father: Sometimes we only discuss very serious issues. This [the game] transformed our conversations into more relaxed ones, such as whether you go online today, whether you plan to steal my vegetables, etc. These are very easy and fun topics for us.

Conventionally, the topics that the older generation prefers to talk about with their children tend to be serious ones (e.g., those related to work, marriage). In contrast, playing and discussing games helps to convert the previously 'serious' family conversations into 'fun' and 'relaxing' ones. Interestingly, the game is rarely a separate conversation, but often facilitates other family talks.

R4-daughter: Ever since we played this game together, we have more common conversational topics. We sometimes discuss the skills, and tips in playing the games. But I would never call them just to talk about the game.

The conversations about the game may not replace other serious conversations. Instead, it supplements other family conversations, and may provide a sense of fun during serious talks.

DISCUSSION

The findings of this study suggest that QQ Farm game playing provides an important new communication channel through which family members can stay connected,

enriching existing family communication. While parents still expect to hear from or see their adult children regularly, and to discuss serious family matters face-to-face or over the phone, game playing adds onto existing family communication a sense of continuous updates, fun and relaxing topics that other communication channels may not be able to provide as easily.

In this section, we discuss three unique aspects of game-based communication that are crucial for mediating intergenerational family interactions: *communication topics, communication roles* and *communication styles.*

Communication roles

For families who live far away or co-reside, the basic communication goal is to know each other's daily routines. For the older generation who might have retired and have more free time on a daily basis, getting to know their adult children's daily routines is one important part of their daily lives. Nevertheless, family communication is often limited by time and distance barriers. With a busy life and work activities, adult children may not be able to find time to report their daily activities or have frequent visits with their parents. Consequently, parents often feel a sense of disconnectedness and loneliness.

Different from phone calls, Instant Messaging or face-to-face contacts that occur once or twice a week, updates from the online game space can be constant and continuous. The updates that parents receive in the game space are generated naturally through game playing, and serve as a message board for them to connect with their children. This continuous updating and awareness raising changes the dynamics associated with the previous reporting-and-receiving style of family communication. Family activities are no longer reported to each other at the same time, but rather are observed and checked in at the shared space in a non-time sensitive way. This new communication medium overcomes time and distance barriers that parents and their adult children often experience. In this way, adult children are no longer expected to report their daily activities to their parents everyday and the parents do not need to wait to hear what is going on in their children's lives. Activities are documented and stored online as it occurs and can be reviewed whenever the parents have time.

This change from 'reporting and receiving' to 'documenting and reviewing' in the participants' family communication process is preferred and has become part of their new daily communication routine. For intergenerational family members who have distinct life styles, updating whether they are safe and well every single day may seem tedious and finding the common time to do so may also be challenging. In the game space, no one intentionally sends 'safe and well' messages, but such information is documented in the shared family space, and is checked either synchronously or asynchronously. While this documenting and reviewing mechanism may not be suitable for communicating urgent or other complicated family matters, it may be ideal to enhance awareness of each other's daily activities.

Communication styles

Compared with other types of communications, game-mediated communication is more implicit and less intrusive (e.g., it keeps the balance of delivering the 'safe and well' messages without revealing every detail of daily activities). As described in the Key Findings section, game activities are considered reflections of their family members' real life activities by the participants and thus could help parents to infer what their adult children are doing in real life. Parents often use the game space as a 'monitoring' or 'tracking' device to help them to stay aware of their children's activities. In their mind, playing a game could imply that their children are safe and happy. Monitoring game activities provides continuous connection between parents and adult children and sheds away the possible

worries that parents may have. Nevertheless, game activities can only represent minimal activities that occur in real life. They cannot reveal details of adult children's daily routines. Communication content mediated through games is less intrusive. It helps to keep the balance of showing 'I'm safe and well' messages on the one hand, while not revealing every detail of daily activities on the other. In this sense, social network game playing may be a good way to take advantage of the benefits associated with the technology while avoiding potential concerns for privacy that have been reported in prior research (e.g., Judge and Neustaedter, 2010).

In addition to being less intrusive, the 'caring and loving' messages expressed through game playing provide family members with a new way to implicitly communicate with each other. In Chinese culture, critical emotional ties that connect family members, such as love and care, are rarely expressed explicitly in daily communication (Chen and Silverstein, 2000). This emotional expression may become even more challenging when adult children and their parents live in different households, since the traditional ways of showing love and care, such as cleaning the house, buying gifts and having dinner together (Schwarz et al., 2010), cannot be as easily carried out on a daily basis. QQ Farm serves as a lightweight communication medium, which could implicitly deliver love and care to family members while avoiding the potential awkwardness of saying 'I care about you' directly.

Communication topics

The lack of common conversational topics is a major challenge for effective intergenerational communication. Parents interviewed in the study repeatedly expressed their frustrations in not being able to communicate with their adult children, even when the two generations co-reside in the same household. Being too 'serious' is often used by the younger generation to describe the conversations occurring between them and their parents. As it is shown in our study, discussing serious topics often leads to a sense of being over-controlled among the younger generation and adds stress to their lives. As a result, adult children often avoid engaging in 'serious' conversations with their parents.

In line with prior research showing the use of computers creating a new 'common language' between parents and their child (Xie, 2006), in the present study, game playing also helps parents to better understand what their adult children are doing on the computer. This common online gaming experience is then transformed into shared interests that stimulate conversations in the physical world, e.g., during family gatherings and interactions. Different from the 'serious' or 'heavy' topics that Chinese parents tend to talk about with their adult children, game playing is considered a more 'relaxed and fun' topic to talk about with their parents. Thus, the game playing experience transcends the online space and enhances family communication in the offline world. Consequently, family members may communicate via the computer and share game playing tips with each other or discuss what happened in the game space in person or over the phone. These game playing-related topics enrich the more 'serious' conversations and may eventually make adult children less resistant to communicate with their parents. This finding on the mutual shaping of online and offline relationships is in line with that reported in the prior research of older Chinese internet users (Xie, 2007, 2008a).

LIMITATIONS OF THE STUDY

This study has some limitations. Although most of the parents who participated in this study qualify as older adults according to the Chinese standards, a few of them were only in their early 50s or late 40s, making it challenging to compare the findings with Western studies of older parent–adult child

relationships. Also, this study only investigated current game play behaviors between family members. More insights could be obtained in studying the process of transitioning from non-play to game-play. Studying such a transition could help us better understand how game play may influence the frequency and content of existing family communication behaviors.

CONCLUSION

Maintaining intergenerational communication is not an easy task. Various factors such as time and distance between adult children and their parents, a lack of common conversational topics and differing values all hinder effective communication. In our study, the online game serves as a new medium to mediate and foster intergenerational family communication, both online and offline. Different from other forms of communication that often require simultaneous engagement, game-based communication can be performed asynchronously and less intrusively; messages can be conveyed in a more implicit manner, and do not require much time commitment by family members. While game-based communication may not replace other forms of family communication, it nonetheless enriches other forms of family communication through continuous game updates and interactions. For older parents, getting in touch with their adult children, and receiving caring and loving messages are crucial for their health and well-being.

ACKNOWLEDGEMENT

An earlier version of this paper was published in the *Journal of Community Informatics* (http://ci-journal.net/index.php/ciej/article/view/802). We thank the *Journal of Community Informatics* for granting us permission to publish a revised and extended version in the Handbook.

NOTES

1   *A report of QQ farm from Chinese website NetEase (163. com)*, available at: http://tech.163.com/10/0730/11/6CR9G68A00094IL6.html
2   Posted by Steven Chow on November 25, 2010; Tencent Inc. QQ: http://www.china-online-marketing.com/news/china-tech-companies/portal-website/tencent-inc-qq/
3   http://web.pcgames.com.cn/qqnc/xinwen/
4   The Chinese Seniors Rights Protection Law http://www.chinalawinfo.com/chyzl/detail.asp?id=202andcid=47

REFERENCES

Ames, M., Go, J., Kaye, J. and Spasojevic, M. (2010) 'Making Love in the Network Closet: The Benefits and Work of Family Videochat'. Proceedings of the 2010 ACM Conference on Computer Supported Cooperative Work, CSCW 2010' Savannah, Georgia, USA: 145–154.

Bian, Y. (2002) 'Chinese social stratification and social mobility', *Annual Review of Sociology*, 28: 91–116.

Brush, A. J. B., Inkpen, K. M. and K. Tee, K. (2008) 'SPARCS: Exploring Sharing Suggestions to Enhance Family Connectedness', Paper presented at the Conference on Computer Supported Cooperative Work. San Diego, CA, USA: 629–638.

Cao, X., Sellen, A., Brush, A. J. B., Kirk, D., Edge, D. and Ding, X. (2010) 'Understanding Family Communication across Time Zones', Paper presented at the Conference on Computer Supported Cooperative Work, Savannah, Georgia, USA.

Chen, X. and Silverstein, M. (2000) 'Intergenerational social support and the psychological well-being of older parents in China', *Research on Aging*, 22(1): 43–65.

Chi, I., & Chou, K.-L. (2001). Social support and depression among elderly Chinese people in Hong Kong. *International Journal of Aging and Human Development, 52*(3), 231-252.

Davis, H., Vetere, F., Francis, P., Gibbs, M., and Howard, S (2008). '"I wish we could get together": Exploring intergenerational play across a distance via a "magic xox"', *Journal of Intergenerational Relationships*, 6(2): 191–210.

George, L. (2010) 'Still happy after all these years: research frontiers on subjective well-being in later life', *The Journals of Gerontology*, Series B, 65(3): 331–339.

Glaser, B. G., and Strauss, A. L. (1967). *The Discovery of Grounded Theory: Strategies for Qualitative Research*. Chicago: Aldine.

Glei, D., Landau, D., Goldman, N., Chuang, L.-Y., Rodriguez, G. and Weinstein, M. (2005) 'Participating in social activities helps preserve cognitive function: an analysis of a longitudinal, population-based study of the elderly', *International Journal of Epidemiology*, 34(4): 864–71.

Ikels, C. (1996) *The Return of the God of Wealth: The Transition to a Market Economy in Urban China*. Stanford, California: Stanford University Press.

Joseph, A. E. and Phillips, D. R. (1999) 'Ageing in rural China: Impacts of increasing diversity in family and community resources', *Journal of Cross-Cultural Gerontology*, 14(2): 153–168.

Judge, T. K. and Neustaedter, C. (2010) 'Sharing Conversation and Sharing life: Video Conferencing in the Home', paper presented at the SIGCHI Conference on Human Factors in Computing Systems. Atlanta, Georgia, USA: 655–658.

Judge, T. K., Neustaedter, C. and Kurtz, A. F. (2010) 'The Family Window: The Design and Evaluation of a Domestic Media Space' , paper presented at the SIGCHI Conference on Human Factors in Computing Systems. Atlanta, GA, USA.

Khoo, E. T., Cheok, A. D., Nguyen, T. H. D. and Pan, Z. (2008) 'Age invaders: social and physical intergenerational mixed reality family entertainment', *Virtual Reality* 12(1): 3–16.

Kirk, D., Sellen, A. and Cao, X. (2010) 'Home Video Communication: Mediating "Closeness"', paper presented at the Conference on Computer Supported Cooperative Work, Savannah, Georgia, USA.

Lee, L. (2004). The current state of public health in China. *Annual Review of Public Health*, 25: 327–339.

Lindley, S., Harper, R. and Sellen, A. (2008) 'Designing for Elders: Exploring the Complexity of Relationships in Later Life', paper presented at the the 22nd BCS conference on Human Computer Interaction, Liverpool, United Kingdom.

Lindley, S., Harper, R. and Sellen, A. (2009) 'Desiring to be in Touch in a Changing Communications Landscape: Attitudes of Older Adults', Paper presented at the 27th international conference on Human Factors in Computing Systems Boston, MA, USA.

Lindley, S. E., Harper, R and Sellen, A. (2010) 'Designing a Technological Playground: A Field Study of the Emergence of Play in Household Messaging', paper presented at the SIGCHI Conference on Human Factors in Computing Systems, Atlanta, GA, USA.

Litwin, H. and Shiovitz-Ezra, S. (2010) 'Social network type and subjective well-being in a national sample of older adults', *The Gerontologist*, 51(3): 379–388.

Lou, V. (2010) 'Life satisfaction of older adults in Hong Kong: The role of social support from grandchildren', *Social Indicators Research*, 95(3): 377–391.

Ng, A. C. Y., Phillips, D. R., and Lee, W. K.-M. (2002) 'Persistence and challenges to filial piety and informal support of older persons in a modern Chinese society: A case study in Tuen Mun, Hong Kong', *Journal of Aging Studies*, 16(2): 135–153.

Ng, S. H. (2002) 'Will families support their elders? Answers from across cultures', in T. D. Nelson (Ed.), *Ageism: Stereotyping and Prejudice against Older Persons,* Cambridge, Massachusetts: The MIT Press. pp. 295–309.

Perry, E. J. and Selden, M. (Eds.) (2003) *Chinese Society, Change, Conflict and Resistance* (2nd ed.). London and New York: RoutledgeCurzon.

Phillips, D., Siu, O., Yeh, A. and Cheng, K. (2008) 'Informal social support and older persons' psychological well-being in Hong Kong', *Journal of Cross-Cultural Gerontology*, 23(1): 39–55.

Price, R. H. and Fang, L. (2002) 'Unemployed Chinese workers: the survivors, the worried young and the discouraged old', *International Journal of Human Resource Management*, 13(3): 416–430.

Romero, N., Markopoulos, P., van Baren, J, de Ruyter, B., IJsselsteijn, W. and Farshchian, B. (2007) 'Connecting the family with awareness systems', *Personal and Ubiquitous Computing*, 11(4): 299–312.

Rowan, J. and Mynatt, E. D. (2005) 'Digital Family Portrait Field Trial: Support for Aging in Place', paper presented at the SIGCHI Conference on Human Factors in Computing Systems. Portland, Oregon, USA, 521–530.

Silverstein, M., Cong, Z. and Li, S. (2006) Intergenerational transfers and living arrangements of older people in rural China: Consequences for psychological well-being. *J Gerontol B Psychol Sci Soc Sci*, 61 (5): S256–S266.

Schwarz, B., Albert, I., Trommsdorff, G., Zheng, G., Shi, S. and Nelwan, P.R. (2010) 'Intergenerational support and life satisfaction: A comparison of Chinese, Indonesian, and German elderly mothers', *In Journal of Cross-Cultural Psychology*, 41(5–6): 706–722.

Sellen, A., Harper, R., Eardley, R., Izadi, S., Regan, T., Taylor, A. and Wood, K. (2006) 'HomeNote: Supporting Situated Messaging in the Home', paper presented at the 20th conference on Computer Supported Cooperative Work. Banff, Alberta, Canada: 383–392.

Strauss, A. L. and Corbin, J. (1998) *Basics of Qualitative Research: Techniques and Procedures for Developing Grounded Theory* (2nd ed.). Thousand Oaks, CA: Sage.

Tee, K., Brush, K.A. and Inkpen, K. (2009) 'Exploring communication and sharing between extended families', *International Journal of Human-Computer Studies*, 67(2): 128–138.

Tu, E. J.-C., Liang, J., & Li, S. (1989). Mortality decline and Chinese family structure: Implications for old age support. *Journal of Gerontology: Social Sciences, 44*(4), 157–168.

Voida, A., Carpendale, S. and Greenberg, S. (2010) 'The Individual and the Group in Console Gaming' paper presented at the Conference on Computer Supported Cooperative Work. ACM, New York.

Xie, B. (2006) 'Perceptions of computer learning among older Americans and older Chinese', *First Monday*, 11(10), accessed at: http://firstmonday. org/htbin/cgiwrap/bin/ojs/index.php/fm/article/ view/1408/1326

Xie, B. (2007) 'Using the Internet for offline relationship formation', *Social Science Computer Review*, 25(3), 396–404.

Xie, B. (2008a) 'The mutual shaping of online and offline social relationships', *Information Research*, 13(3): paper350. http://informationr.net/ir/13-3/ paper350.html.

Xie, B. (2008b) 'Multimodal computer-mediated communication and social support among older Chinese', *Journal of Computer-Mediated Communication*, 13(3): 728–750.

Xie, B. (2008c) 'Civic engagement among older Chinese Internet users', *Journal of Applied Gerontology*, 27(4): 424–445.

Xie, B. (2008d) 'Older adults, health information, and the Internet', *Interactions*, 15(4): 44–46.

Xie, B. (2009) 'Older adults' health information wants in the Internet age: Implications for patient-provider relationships', *Journal of Health Communication*, 14(6): 510–524.

24

Making a Case for the Existence of Generational Stereotypes: A Literature Review and Exploratory Study

Elissa L. Perry, Apivat Hanvongse and Danut A. Casoinic

Although sociologists have been interested in generational issues and differences at the national and societal levels for decades (Mannheim, 1952), only over the last two decades have scholars shown an increasing interest in the implications of generational differences for managing people at work (Parry & Urwin, 2010). Increased attention to generational issues in the workplace may be due, in part, to the fact that members of several generations now work alongside one another as a consequence of the global aging of societies, and older workers postponing retirement (Adler & Hilber, 2009; Shore, Chung-Herrera, Dean, Holcombe Ehrhart, Jung, Randel & Singh, 2009). As a result, practitioners are increasingly heralding the importance of generational differences in the workplace

and the need to understand how to manage these differences (Armour, 2005; Chao, 2005; Francis-Smith, 2004; Howe & Strauss, 1991, 1993, 2000; Tulgan, 1995, 2009).

While generational differences allow workers to learn from one another and contribute to a better quality of work, they can also lead to conflicts related to *perceived* and *actual* differences in work ethics, views on authority, and differences in values regarding change (SHRM, 2004). Moreover, practitioners and academics suggest that generational differences may have implications for a variety of organizational and management functions including recruitment (Charrier, 2000), training and development (Berl, 2006; Tulgan, 1995), career development (McDonald & Hite,

2008), reward systems, work arrangements (Carlson, 2004; Filipczak, 1994), and workplace conflicts (Losyk, 1997; Tulgan, 1995).

Academic research has tended to focus on actual differences between generations with little attention paid to perceived differences. The practitioner literature suggests that generational perceptions and stereotypes may help us understand generational differences and conflict in the workplace, but provides limited empirical evidence that this is the case (Appelbaum, Serena & Shapiro, 2005). While *actual* differences are important, so too are *perceived* differences based on stereotypes. Stereotypes are important because they can influence organizational decision-makers' perceptions and judgments and therefore have consequences for employees' work related outcomes (Fiske, Bersoff, Borgida, Deaux, & Heilman, 1991; Kulik & Bainbridge, 2006). Moreover, stereotypes can also affect the attitudes and behaviors of those to whom these stereotypes might apply. Stereotype threat, the fear of being judged and treated according to negative stereotypes about members of an individual's group, can have negative effects on employees' feelings, behaviors, and work performance (Roberson & Kulik, 2007). Therefore, it is important to determine whether there is any empirical basis for generational stereotypes and if so, what types of information they provide beyond that derived from age stereotypes.

The purpose of the current study was to determine whether individuals possess generational stereotypes. While a significant body of research has studied age stereotypes (Posthuma & Campion, 2009), to date, limited empirical research has examined whether there is evidence for the existence of generational stereotypes that are distinct from age stereotypes. Although there is some variation in the exact definition and birth year ranges used to describe different generations, they are generally grouped into four distinct cohorts: Veterans, Baby Boomers, Generation-X, and Generation-Y/Millennials (Parry & Urwin, 2010). This chapter focuses on stereotypes related to the latter three generations because

these generations are the most active in the workforce today.

LITERATURE REVIEW

Generations

A 'generation' can be defined as a group of individuals who share 'birth years, age, location, and significant life events at critical development stages' (Kupperschmidt, 2000, p. 6). Mannheim (1952) emphasized that individuals are not members of the same generation simply by sharing the same birthday, but they must share 'an identity of responses, a certain affinity in the way in which all move with and are formed by their common experiences' (p. 306). Following Mannheim (1952), sociologists have theorized that people of the same generation form a shared memory of significant national or international events that shapes their future attitudes, preferences, and behaviors. Moreover, this collective memory is maintained throughout the lifespan of a generation (Eyerman & Turner, 1998; Schuman & Scott, 1989). Sociologists make a distinction between the terms generations and cohorts. A cohort is often used as a proxy for generational categories and refers to generations by their cut-off birth date (Parry & Urwin, 2010). We focus on three cohorts identified in previous research and theory (Parry & Urwin, 2010; SHRM, 2004): Baby Boomers (1943–1960), Generation-Xers (1961–1981), and Generation-Y/Millennials (1982–present).

Most academic research studying generations in the workplace has focused on measuring *actual* differences in individuals' *self-reported* values, preferences, attitudes and behaviors as they pertain to the workplace (e.g., Parry & Urwin, 2010; Twenge, 2010). This research typically categorizes participants into mutually exclusive generational categories based on their birth year and then explores generational differences via self-report surveys. There is mixed evidence for the existence of generational effects. For example, studies consistently find that Generation-Y/Millennials believe that work is less central to their lives (Twenge, 2010). However, while Cennamo and Gardner (2008) found that younger generations (Generation-Y/Millennial) valued freedom-related factors at work more than Baby Boomers, Jurkiewicz (2000) found that Baby Boomers ranked 'freedom from pressures to conform' higher than younger generations (Generation-X) (p. 63). Although actual differences between the generations have been explored, there has been relatively little attention paid to perceived differences in the traits and characteristics of different generational cohorts.

Perceived differences refer to how different generational members are perceived to differ regardless of their actual characteristics. A good deal of the practitioner literature seems to suggest that members of different generational cohorts have *actual* as well as *perceived* differences in workplace characteristics, values, expectations, attitudes, and behaviors (Erickson, 2009; Perelman, 2007; Watt, 2010). Some practitioners suggest that perceived differences between generations are the result of stereotypes (Lindgren, 1998; Perry, 2000; Stein & Berardinelli, 2009; Wolfson, 1999). Practitioners often seem to blur the distinction between actual generational characteristics and generational stereotypes and there is little empirical basis for their claims regarding the latter. Lyons, Duxbury, and Higgins (2007) suggested that 'despite the popularity of this topic, there has been relatively little academic work either to confirm or refute popular stereotypes' related to Baby Boomers, Generation-X, and Generation-Y (p. 339).

The case for generational stereotypes

Stereotypes are cognitive structures that are comprised of associations between attributes (e.g., personality traits, physical characteristics) and social categories (e.g., Asian

Americans) (Perry, 1994). Stereotypes have been documented to influence a variety of organizational decisions including selection decisions (Perry, 1994), performance evaluations (Deaux, 1985; Deaux & Kite, 1993), and promotions (Fiske et al., 1991). They also have been found, in certain contexts, to decrease performance, and increase anxiety among those to whom stereotypes apply (Roberson & Kulik, 2007). Stereotypes are associated with members of different social categories including: women (Heilman, 1983; Fiske et al., 1991), older workers (Perry, 1994), and African-Americans (Roberson, Deitsch, Brief & Block, 2003). Understanding stereotypes and how they operate is important because their use can lead to bias, discrimination, and poor workplace decisions (e.g., Fiske et al., 1991) as well as have negative effects on employee feelings and behaviors (Roberson & Kulik, 2007). Furthermore, the impact of documented *actual* differences between different generations may be limited until we have a fuller understanding of the extent to which these differences are *perceived* accurately. Organizations may fall short of harnessing the positive effects of workplace diversity when they neglect how stereotypes may influence perceptions of different social groups.

While our knowledge of age stereotypes is fairly extensive (Posthuma & Campion, 2009), we found little empirical research documenting the existence and content of generational stereotypes. Much of the practitioner literature seems to refer to age and generational stereotypes as interchangeable concepts (Appelbaum et al., 2005; Goodger, 2008; Lindgren, 1998; Perry, 2000). For example, Appelbaum et al., (2005) conducted a study to dispel stereotypes about Generation-X and Baby Boomers. However, the authors focused on age-related myths identified in a previous publication by Paul and Townsend (1993). The authors asked Baby Boomer and Generation-X respondents about their perceptions of *older* and *younger* workers confounding respondents' perceptions of generational compared to age differences (Appelbaum et al., 2005).

We found several empirical studies that provide some but limited evidence of generational stereotypes, in part, because none of these studies intentionally sought to measure generational stereotypes (Gursoy, Maier, & Chi, 2008; Jovic, Wallace, & Lemaire, 2006; SHRM, 2004). As a result, it is unclear whether participant perceptions in these studies are based on actual observations, feelings/attitudes, or stereotypes.

The empirical work that has been conducted to this point is limited in several ways. First, some of these studies asked participants to provide their perceptions of generations along a narrow set of dimensions. For example, Gursoy et al. (2008) asked respondents specifically about 'feelings toward younger and older managers' and coworkers' *work styles* (p. 451). In order to get a fuller and more accurate picture of generational stereotypes, it is important to allow respondents to comment on the full range of content they have about any given generational cohort.

Second, some of these studies sampled respondents employed in a single profession (physician) or industry (hospitality) (Jovic et al., 2006; Gursoy et al., 2008). As a result, the extent to which generational perceptions identified in these studies are generalizable is unclear.

Third, age and generational perceptions may have been unintentionally confounded in some of these studies. For example, a SHRM (2004) report provided respondents with a generational label as well as birth years associated with it. Therefore, it is difficult to know with certainty whether respondents used the generational label or age as derived from the birth years provided or both to make their judgments.

Fourth, respondents in these studies were often asked to make implicit comparisons between 'older' and 'younger' generations, thus inviting comparisons across generations (e.g., Gursoy et al., 2008; Jovic et al., 2006; SHRM, 2004). For example, in the SHRM study, respondents were asked to make trait ratings for four generational cohorts which were listed consecutively (SHRM, 2004, p. 20). This could have encouraged respondents to make comparisons across generations and served to make differences and similarities between generational cohorts particularly salient. A different picture of stereotype content may emerge if respondents are asked to provide their perceptions of each cohort independently.

Fifth, the instructions used in the studies that we identified did not measure, nor were they generally intended to measure, generational stereotypes per se. Study instructions used in these studies did not specifically ask respondents to provide their socially shared perceptions (i.e., stereotypes) about different generations, regardless of the respondents' own endorsement of these perceptions. Thus, this research provides only indirect evidence that people perceive generational cohorts differently. Moreover, these few studies do not paint a unified and coherent picture of the different generations, perhaps due to the conceptual and methodological factors we identified. Research is needed that: employs a sample with work experience across multiple industries and professions; allows for respondent-generated traits on a wide range of generational characteristics; does not ask respondents to directly compare generations; does not confound people's perceptions of generations and age; and specifically instructs participants to reflect on their socially shared perceptions regardless of the favorability of these perceptions and whether the respondent personally endorses them.

The current research

The purpose of our own study was to determine whether people have generational stereotypes and, if so, what the content of these stereotypes is. First, we reviewed the practitioner literature to see how members of different generations (e.g., Baby Boomers, Generation-X, and Generation-Y/Millennials) are described. Second, we examined the academic literature to see if there is an empirical basis for the claims of the existence of generational stereotypes made in the practitioner literature. Third, we conducted an exploratory study measuring generational stereotypes in the workplace using a sample of graduate students. We compared characteristics/themes generated from our exploratory study and claims of generational stereotypes identified in the practitioner and academic literatures. In addition, we compared the content of generational stereotypes with that of age stereotypes, based on the age stereotype literature. Our aim was to determine whether a case could be made for the existence of generational stereotypes that are different from what we understand age stereotypes to be.

PRACTITIONER AND ACADEMIC LITERATURE REVIEW METHODOLOGY

We conducted a search of practitioner and academic articles that focused on the topic of generations in the workplace from 1995–2011 to see how and whether generational stereotypes were discussed. Each identified article was coded for stereotypical themes.

Practitioner articles sample

We conducted a search of the practitioner literature to determine how different generations (Baby Boomer, Generation-X, and Generation-Y/Millennial) are described. We searched several databases including: ProQuest (Multiple databases); EBSCO (Business Source Complete, Academic Search Complete); and OVID (PsycINFO). We limited our search from 1995 to 2011. While the term 'Generation X' was popularized in the early 1990s (Coupland, 1991; Strauss & Howe, 1991), discussion of generations within the context of employment really began with the publication of Bruce Tulgan's 'Managing Generation X' (1st Edition, 1995). We conducted multiple searches using various combinations of search terms: Generation-X/Gen-X/Xers; Generation-Y/Gen-Y/

Yers (or Millennial); Baby Boomer (Boomer); Generational difference; Generational gap; Workplace; Stereotype (Perception). We limited our search to the following publication types: magazines; trade publications; newspapers; periodicals; and market reports. We excluded all scholarly journal articles.

In addition, we searched the references of the articles we identified in our searches and included articles that seemed particularly relevant to the topic of generational perceptions. We focused our attention on articles that categorized generations into cohorts such as Baby Boomer, Generation-X, and Generation-Y/Millennials. We excluded articles that mentioned family generation (e.g., parents, grandparents) or immigrant generations (e.g., first-, or second-generation Chinese). We eliminated publications that simply reviewed previous research or authors' statements. We further limited our search to those articles that explicitly discussed generational characteristics in the workplace. Applying these criteria yielded a total sample of $N = 64$ codeable practitioner articles. These references are indicated with an asterisk in the reference section.

Method

One of the authors read and conducted the initial coding of each of the 64 articles. A second author read and conducted the initial coding for a subset of these 64 articles ($N = 26$). For each article that the authors read, they listed all of the characteristics used to describe each of the three generational cohorts. The articles were often unclear about whether the generational characteristics identified were perceived or actual trait differences (sometimes within the same article) (e.g., Kronenberg, 1997; Wolfson, 1999). An attempt was made to retain the exact wording used to describe each generation by the authors. The current study authors/coders reviewed and discussed the subset of articles until 100% agreement in their coding was achieved. A given characteristic was listed only once from each article. This allowed us to calculate the percentage of articles that mentioned a particular trait for a given generation; providing a sense of which characteristics are most typically associated with a particular generational cohort.

Once all unique characteristics from each article were listed by generational cohort, both authors were engaged in the second part of the coding process; independently clustering similar items into category themes for each generational cohort. For example, 'nose to the grindstone' and 'hardworking go-getters' were clustered together under the theme 'Hardworking' for Baby Boomers. An online dictionary and thesaurus (www.dictionary. com, www.meriam-webster.com, www.thesaurus.com) were used to determine whether items were similar enough to be clustered into the same category (e.g., 'independent' and 'individualistic' were clustered together) or distinct enough to warrant being placed in separate categories (e.g., 'self-centered' and 'self-gratification' were not clustered together). Items that were generated by only one article and which could not be placed into a larger category were eliminated. We used a roughly 10% cut off rule, retaining category themes only if 10% or more of our sample of articles mentioned it. Therefore, each identified category theme was mentioned by at least six articles, suggesting some level of convergence around the content of generational stereotypes. Other researchers have used a similar cut off in their studies (see Esses, Haddock, & Zanna, 1993; Marin, 1984; Niemann, Jennings, Rozelle, & Sullivan, 1994; Spencer-Rodgers, 2001). These authors retained traits if 10% of participants in their study endorsed them.

We focused our coding on traditional stereotypic content: attitudes, traits, values and attributes (Hamilton & Trolier, 1986). We eliminated items that seemed more situationally and less dispositionally relevant (e.g., 'lacks job security' was eliminated). Moreover, items that were factual in nature and revealed little about generational *perceptions* were also eliminated (e.g., Baby Boomers listed as 'retiring soon'). Category theme titles were based on words or phrases generated

most frequently within the category and/or those most representative of the category.

The two coders reviewed the category theme titles and the items they included for each cohort. An effort was made to use the same terms to name the cluster themes that emerged across the generational cohorts. Where there were discrepancies regarding item placement, the coders discussed the coding until 100% agreement was reached. At that point, a third author reviewed the items and clusters. Discrepancies were discussed until all coders were in 100% agreement about the clustering of items.

Results

Table 24.1 lists the themes discussed for each cohort across the 64 practitioner articles. Themes are listed from the most to the least frequently mentioned. Eight themes described Baby Boomers. The top five most frequently mentioned themes in descending order were: hardworking; has company loyalty; (not) technology savvy; resistant to change, and optimistic. There were 21 themes used to describe Generation-X and the top five most frequently mentioned in descending order were: values work/life balance; independent; technology savvy; values learning and development opportunities; and does (not) have company loyalty. There were 21 themes used to describe Generation-Y/Millennials and the top five most frequently mentioned in descending order were: technology savvy; expects regular feedback; multi-tasker; needs attention and praise; and arrogant/confident. We used a series of Venn diagrams to determine the extent of overlap in the themes used to describe each generation.

Figure 24.1 shows that, interestingly, there were no themes common to all three cohorts. However, there appeared to be some overlap between themes used to describe Generation-X and Generation-Y/Millennials. There were 6 themes common to Generation-X and Generation-Y/Millennials out of the total 43 unique practitioner article themes generated across cohorts (14%). These included: technology savvy; values work/life balance;

Table 24.1   Frequency of generational themes identified in the practitioner literature

Baby Boomer		Generation-X		Generation-Y	
Theme	n(%)	Theme	n(%)	Theme	n(%)
1 Hardworking	23(36%)	1 Values work/life balance	24(38%)	1 Technology savvy	24(38%)
2 Has company loyalty	9(14%)	2 Independent	20(31%)	2 Expects regular feedback	15(23%)
3 (not) Technology savvy	8(13%)	3 Technology savvy	18(28%)	3 Multi-tasker	14(22%)
4 Resistant to change	8(13%)	4 Values learning and development opportunities	17(27%)	4 Needs attention and praise	12(19%)
5 Optimistic	7(11%)	5 (not) Has company loyalty	16(25%)	5 Arrogant/Confident	12(19%)
6 Prefers face-to-face communication	7(11%)	6 Lazy	15(23%)	6 Seeks mentorship	12(19%)
7 Values monetary rewards of their job	7(11%)	7 Prefers work flexibility	15(23%)	7 Team oriented	11(17%)
8 Competitive	6(9%)	8 Prefers self-management	14(22%)	8 Prefers work flexibility	11(17%)
		9 Cynical	13(20%)	9 Wants to make an impact at work	10(16%)
		10 Distrust institutions	11(17%)	10 Prefers a fun workplace	10(16%)
		11 Values challenging work	11(17%)	11 Likes to use technology to communicate	9(14%)
		12 (not) Appreciates job security	10(16%)	12 Values work/life balance	9(14%)
		13 Expects regular feedback	10(16%)	13 Wants respect	9(14%)
		14 Skeptical	7(11%)	14 Values meaningful work	8(13%)
		15 Casual	7(11%)	15 Impatient	8(13%)
		16 Pragmatic	7(11%)	16 (not) Has company loyalty	8(13%)
		17 Well educated	7(11%)	17 Entitled	7(11%)
		18 Hardworking	6(9%)	18 Values job advancement opportunities	7(11%)
		19 Values diversity	6(9%)	19 Values learning and development opportunities	6(9%)
		20 Entrepreneurial	6(9%)	20 Want recognition for their work	6(9%)
		21 (not) Believes in paying their dues at work	6(9%)	21 Rebellious	6(9%)

n = number of articles mentioning a given theme
% = n / 64 total practitioner articles

prefers work flexibility; expects regular feedback; values learning and development opportunities; and does (not) have company loyalty. There was 1 common theme between Baby Boomers and Generation-X out of the total 43 unique practitioner article themes generated (2%); hardworking. Baby Boomers and Generation-Y/Millennials workers did not share any common themes based on the practitioner articles we reviewed.

Figure 24.1 also indicates that there were 7 themes (7/43 total unique themes = 16%) that were unique to Baby Boomers, 14 themes (14/43 total unique themes = 33%) unique to Generation X, and 15 themes (15/43 total unique themes = 35%) unique to Generation Y/Millennials. Overall, the practitioner literature suggests there are more perceived differences than similarities between the three generations.

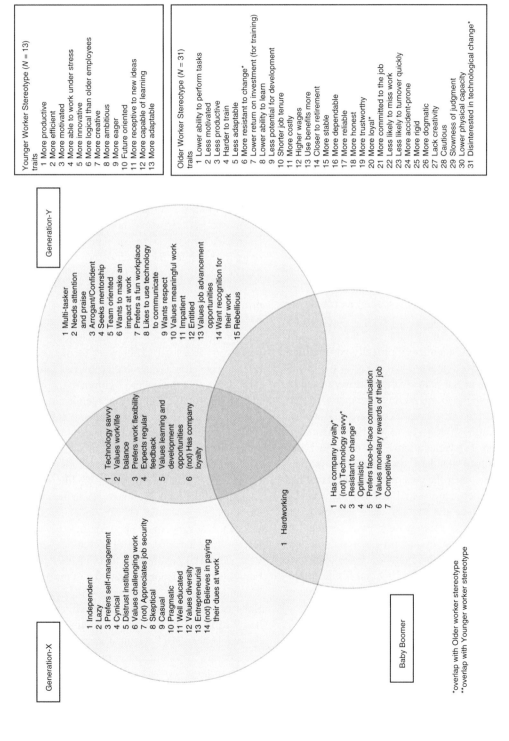

Younger Worker Stereotype (N = 13)
traits
1 More productive
2 More efficient
3 More motivated
4 More able to work under stress
5 More innovative
6 More logical than older employees
7 More creative
8 More ambitious
9 More eager
10 Future oriented
11 More receptive to new ideas
12 More capable of learning
13 More adaptable

Older Worker Stereotype (N = 31)
traits
1 Lower ability to perform tasks
2 Less motivated
3 Less productive
4 Harder to train
5 Less adaptable
6 More resistant to change*
7 Lower return on investment (for training)
8 Lower ability to learn
9 Less potential for development
10 Shorter job tenure
11 More costly
12 Higher wages
13 Use benefits more
14 Closer to retirement
15 More stable
16 More dependable
17 More reliable
18 More honest
19 More trustworthy
20 More loyal*
21 More committed to the job
22 Less likely to miss work
23 Less likely to turnover quickly
24 More accident-prone
25 More rigid
26 More dogmatic
27 Lack creativity
28 Cautious
29 Slowness of judgment
30 Lower physical capacity
31 Disinterested in technological change*

Generation-Y

1 Multi-tasker
2 Needs attention and praise
3 Arrogant/Confident
4 Seeks mentorship
5 Team oriented
6 Wants to make an impact at work
7 Prefers a fun workplace
8 Likes to use technology to communicate
9 Wants respect
10 Values meaningful work
11 Impatient
12 Entitled
13 Values job advancement opportunities
14 Want recognition for their work
15 Rebellious

1 Technology savvy
2 Values work/life balance
3 Prefers work flexibility
4 Expects regular feedback
5 Values learning and development opportunities
6 (not) Has company loyalty

1 Hardworking

Generation-X

1 Independent
2 Lazy
3 Prefers self-management
4 Cynical
5 Distrust institutions
6 Values challenging work
7 (not) Appreciates job security
8 Skeptical
9 Casual
10 Pragmatic
11 Well educated
12 Values diversity
13 Entrepreneurial
14 (not) Believes in paying their dues at work

Baby Boomer

1 Has company loyalty*
2 (not) Technology savvy**
3 Resistant to change*
4 Optimistic
5 Prefers face-to-face communication
6 Values monetary rewards of their job
7 Competitive

*overlap with Older worker stereotype
**overlap with Younger worker stereotype

Figure 24.1   Practitioner literature themes (N = 43 unique themes)

Academic articles sample

We obtained the sample of academic articles through a process similar to that described in the practitioner sample section. The only difference was that we limited our search to 'scholarly journals' (peer reviewed) rather than practitioner-oriented publications. We did this by selecting the 'scholarly journals' (peer reviewed) option in our online searches. Further, we focused on articles where empirical data was actually collected. This process yielded $N = 37$ empirical, peer reviewed articles (these references are indicated with two asterisks in the reference section).

Method

The process for extracting themes from the academic literature differed slightly from that used for the practitioner articles. When extracting themes from an empirical study, we only coded themes for which a given article found significant results. We did so because we aimed to identify empirically-based differences across generational cohorts. We identified the actual items/words that were used by the authors to measure generational differences. If an article made comparisons between generational cohorts (e.g., Baby Boomers greater than Generation-X on 'high pay based on industry standard'), we placed that particular item under the generational cohort that had the higher score (i.e., Baby Boomers in this case). Once the themes were extracted, the process of clustering items was identical to that described in the previous section (see practitioner articles method). Once again, we used an approximately 10% cutoff rule, retaining category themes only if 10% or more of our sample of articles ($N = 3$) mentioned it.

Results

Table 24.2 lists the themes discussed for each cohort across the 37 academic articles. Themes are listed from the most to the least frequently mentioned in the academic literature. There were eight themes generated for Baby Boomers and the top five most frequently mentioned, in descending order, were: values monetary rewards of their job; values honest leaders; values learning and development opportunities; believes in lifetime employment; and values loyalty. There were 11 themes identified for Generation-X and the top five most frequently mentioned, in descending order, were: values job advancement opportunities; values work/life balance; values learning and development opportunities; values monetary rewards of their job; and values leisure time. There were 12 themes generated for Generation-Y/Millennials and the top five most frequently mentioned, in descending order, were: values job advancement opportunities; values friendship at work; prefers supportive leaders; values honest leaders; and ambitious. We used a series of Venn diagrams in order to determine the extent of overlap in the themes used to describe each generation.

The empirical research has tended to focus primarily on actual differences in values between generational cohorts unlike the practitioner literature which has tended to focus on perceived *or* actual differences (sometimes referring to them interchangeably). Figure 24.2 shows that there were 2 common themes out of the total 23 unique academic article themes generated across generational cohorts (9%) that were shared by all three generations: values learning and development opportunities; and values monetary rewards of their job. Generation-X and Generation-Y/Millennial shared 4 of the total 23 unique academic article themes generated (17%): independent; values job advancement opportunities; values learning and development opportunities; and values monetary rewards of their job. Generation-X and Baby Boomers shared 2 of the total 23 unique themes generated (9%). Finally, Baby Boomers and Generation-Y/Millennials had 4 of the total 23 unique academic article themes generated (17%) in common: values learning and development opportunities; values monetary rewards of their job; values freedom at work; and values honest leaders.

Figure 24.2 also shows there were four themes unique to Baby Boomers (4/23 total unique themes = 17%), seven themes

Table 24.2 Frequency of generational themes identified in the academic literature

Baby Boomer		Generation-X		Generation-Y	
Theme	n(%)	Theme	n(%)	Theme	n(%)
1 Values monetary rewards of their job	4(11%)	1 Values job advancement opportunities	6(17%)	1 Values job advancement opportunities	6(17%)
2 Values honest leaders	4(11%)	2 Values work/life balance	6(17%)	2 Values friendship at work	6(17%)
3 Values learning and development opportunities	4(11%)	3 Values learning and development opportunities	6(17%)	3 Prefers supportive leaders	5(14%)
4 Believes in lifetime employment	4(11%)	4 Values monetary rewards of their job	5(14%)	4 Values honest leaders	4(11%)
5 Values loyalty	4(11%)	5 Values leisure time	5(14%)	5 Ambitious	4(11%)
6 Values freedom at work	3(8%)	6 Wants to make an impact at work	5(14%)	6 Values freedom at work	4(11%)
7 Has a strong work identity	3(8%)	7 Independent	3(8%)	7 Values monetary rewards of their job	4(11%)
8 Values job status	3(8%)	8 (not) Committed to the job	3(8%)	8 Independent	3(8%)
		9 (not) Believes in lifetime employment	3(8%)	9 Appreciates job security	3(8%)
		10 Values challenging work	3(8%)	10 Achievement oriented	3(8%)
		11 Values honesty	3(8%)	11 Values learning and development opportunities	3(8%)
				12 Values self-respect	3(8%)

n = number of articles mentioning a given theme
% = n / 37 total empirical articles

unique to Generation-X (7/23 total unique themes = 30%), and six themes unique to Generation-Y/Millennial (6/23 total unique themes = 26%). While there is a higher percentage of overlap between the generational cohorts here compared to the practitioner literature, the academic literature also suggests that the generational cohorts have unique dimensions.

GENERATIONAL STEREOTYPES: AN EXPLORATORY STUDY

Method

In order to more fully understand the content of generational stereotypes, we conducted an exploratory study. Our study used a methodology that allowed respondents to comment on the full range of their generational stereotype content. We tried not to confound age and generation, in part, by purposefully not associating birth ranges with generational cohort labels. Unlike previous research, we used a student sample that had employment experience across a number of professions and industries. Moreover, we asked respondents about each generation individually rather than asking them to make direct comparisons, the latter of which may have made certain traits and features more salient. Finally, we used instructions that we believed would more directly measure stereotypes by asking participants to identify socially shared perceptions that they may or

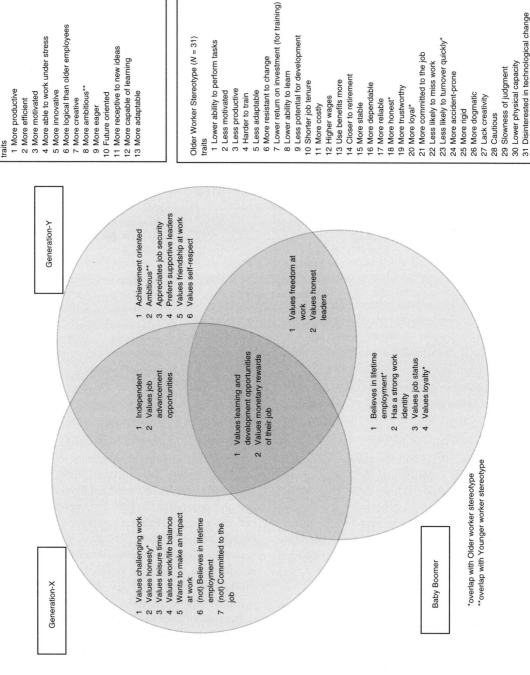

Younger Worker Stereotype (N = 13)
traits

1 More productive
2 More efficient
3 More motivated
4 More able to work under stress
5 More innovative
6 More logical than older employees
7 More creative
8 More ambitious**
9 More eager
10 Future oriented
11 More receptive to new ideas
12 More capable of learning
13 More adaptable

Older Worker Stereotype (N = 31)
traits

1 Lower ability to perform tasks
2 Less motivated
3 Less productive
4 Harder to train
5 Less adaptable
6 More resistant to change
7 Lower return on investment (for training)
8 Lower ability to learn
9 Less potential for development
10 Shorter job tenure
11 More costly
12 Higher wages
13 Use benefits more
14 Closer to retirement
15 More stable
16 More dependable
17 More reliable
18 More honest*
19 More trustworthy
20 More loyal*
21 More committed to the job
22 Less likely to miss work
23 Less likely to turnover quickly*
24 More accident-prone
25 More rigid
26 More dogmatic
27 Lack creativity
28 Cautious
29 Slowness of judgment
30 Lower physical capacity
31 Disinterested in technological change

Generation-Y

Generation-X

Baby Boomer

1 Achievement oriented
2 Ambitious**
3 Appreciates job security
4 Prefers supportive leaders
5 Values friendship at work
6 Values self-respect

1 Values freedom at work
2 Values honest leaders

1 Independent
2 Values job advancement opportunities

1 Values learning and development opportunities
2 Values monetary rewards of their job

1 Believes in lifetime employment*
2 Has a strong work identity
3 Values job status
4 Values loyalty*

1 Values challenging work
2 Values honesty*
3 Values leisure time
4 Values work/life balance
5 Wants to make an impact at work
6 (not) Believes in lifetime employment
7 (not) Committed to the job

*overlap with Older worker stereotype
**overlap with Younger worker stereotype

may not personally endorse and which could be accurate or inaccurate.

Sample

Instructors in a variety of graduate level courses were contacted and asked if their students could participate in the current study. Extra credit for participation in the study was left to the discretion of the course instructor. With permission from the instructors, researchers visited the classrooms to describe the study. Participants were told that the study was about perceptions in the workplace. Students were given the opportunity to participate or leave the classroom.

Subjects in this study were N = 58 graduate students from a large northeastern university (72% female, 26% males, 2% unidentified). The racial/ethnic composition of the sample was: 52% White; 17% Asians; 12% African-American; 9% Hispanic American; and 9% identified as other. The average age was 28 years (*SD* = 6.62). Our sample identified themselves as members of one of three generations: Baby Boomer (3%); Generation-X (24%); Generation-Y (52%); Baby Boomer/Generation-X (2%); Generation-X/Generation-Y (3%); and 16% that did not identify or did not know. The average length of full-time work experience was 6 years (*SD* = 7.06).

Procedure

Students who chose to participate in the study were given a packet containing the stimulus materials. The first page described the study and asked for their consent to participate. Responses were anonymous and participants were asked to generate a unique code only to allow us to ensure that a given person did not participate in our study more than once. Next, participants were told that they would be completing a 'word generation' exercise. The instructions were as follows:

'Form an image of a typical **Baby Boomer worker**. You have *2 minutes* to write down all of the things you typically think about, hear about, or read about the **Baby Boomer worker**. Include anything that is typically associated with the **Baby Boomer worker** regardless of whether it is favorable or unfavorable or whether you personally believe it to be true.'

Given that we were attempting to measure participants' knowledge rather than their endorsement of stereotypes, we did not require respondents to 'personally believe' in the traits they listed (Devine, 1989). These instructions were repeated on separate pages for each of three generational cohorts (Baby Boomer, Generation-X, and Generation-Y). Similar methods have been used by other researchers to measure other types of stereotypes (e.g., Jacobs, Kulik, & Fichman, 1993; Kulik, 1989; Perry, 1994). The order in which the generational cohorts were presented was counterbalanced to prevent order effects.

Subjects were given two minutes to list everything that came to mind for each generational cohort. This allowed us to identify particularly salient aspects of respondents' stereotypes. After two minutes, participants were told to turn the page, read the instructions, and write everything that came to mind about the second generational cohort. This continued until participants generated characteristics for each of the three generational cohorts. On the last page, participants provided demographic information and then returned their packets to the researcher.

Analyses

The process we used to create category themes in this exploratory study was the same that we used for the practitioner and academic literatures (see previous methods sections). The same approximately 10% cutoff rule was employed, resulting in a minimum of five participants listing an item for each category theme (approximately 10% of *N* = 58).

Categories with fewer than five items were eliminated as they were not generated by a sufficient number of participants to suggest that the theme was socially shared.

Table 24.3 lists the most frequently generated themes for each cohort. There were 17 themes generated for Baby Boomers and the top five most frequently mentioned, in descending order, were: hardworking; (not) technology savvy; old; traditional; and has company loyalty. There were 17 themes generated for Generation-X and the top five most frequently mentioned, in descending order, were: technologically savvy; creative; ambitious; hardworking; and self-centered. There were 24 themes generated for Generation-Y and the top five most frequently mentioned, in descending order, were: technologically savvy; creative; young; likes to use technology to communicate; and (not) committed to the job. We used a series of Venn diagrams in order to illustrate the extent of overlap in the themes used to describe each generation.

Figure 24.3 shows that 2 out of the total 42 unique exploratory study themes generated across cohorts were shared by all three generational cohorts (5%): hardworking, and values monetary rewards of their job. There were 2 themes shared between Baby Boomers and Generation-X and Baby Boomers and Generation-Y out of the total 42 unique exploratory study themes generated (5%): hardworking; and values monetary rewards of their job. There were 14 themes shared between Generation-X and Generation-Y out of the total 42 unique exploratory study themes generated (33%). Finally, Figure 24.3 shows there were 15 themes unique to Baby Boomers (15/42 total unique themes = 36%), three themes unique to Generation-X (3/42 total unique themes = 7%) and 10 themes unique to Generation-Y (10/42 total unique themes = 24%). This analysis suggests that Generation-X and Generation-Y stereotypes are not that clearly differentiated. Moreover, Generation-X appears to be less distinct (i.e., has fewer unique themes) than Generation-Y.

However, the Baby Boomer stereotype is clearly differentiated from the Generation-X and Generation-Y stereotypes.

Analyses of each cohort across sources

Next, we compared how each generational cohort was described across the academic and practitioner literatures and in our exploratory study to determine if one consistent image of each cohort could be abstracted across these sources. In order make these comparisons, two coders went through a process of calibrating themes across sources (practitioner literature, academic literature, and exploratory study). In other words, we attempted to ensure that we used one common word or phrase where different words and phrases were used across sources to describe synonymous concepts. For example, instead of using both 'less comfortable with technology' from one source and '(not) technology savvy' from another source, we used '(not) technology savvy' to capture this common theme. This allowed us to determine how each cohort (Baby Boomers, Generation-X, and Generation-Y/Millennial) was described across the different sources of data (practitioner literature, academic literature, and our exploratory study) and whether a consistent image of each cohort emerged.

For Baby Boomers, the only theme that was common across all three sources was that they value monetary rewards of their job (see Figure 24.4). There was more overlap between the practitioner literature and our exploratory study (five themes) than between the practitioner and academic literatures (one theme), or between our exploratory study and the academic literature (two themes). This pattern makes some sense as the academic literature has tended to focus on actual work values and attitudes whereas the practitioner literature and our exploratory study focused on a broader range of perceived traits and characteristics. Five themes from our exploratory study out of a total of 20

Table 24.3   Frequency of generational themes identified in the exploratory study

Baby Boomer		Generation-X		Generation-Y	
Theme	n(%)	Theme	n(%)	Theme	n(%)
1 Hardworking	32(55%)	1 Technologically savvy	23(40%)	1 Technologically savvy	37(64%)
2 (not) Technology savvy	20(34%)	2 Creative	17(29%)	2 Creative	17(29%)
3 Old	19(33%)	3 Ambitious	13(22%)	3 Young	15(26%)
4 Traditional	19(33%)	4 Hardworking	11(19%)	4 Likes to use technology to communicate	15(26%)
5 Has company loyalty	18(31%)	5 Self-centered	9(16%)	5 (not) Committed to the job	13(22%)
6 Rigid	15(26%)	6 Lazy	8(14%)	6 Flexible	13(22%)
7 Family oriented	12(21%)	7 Young	8(14%)	7 Lazy	12(21%)
8 Believes in lifetime employment	10(17%)	8 Values monetary rewards of their jobs	7(12%)	8 Entitled	11(19%)
9 Resistant to change	8(14%)	9 Values work/life balance	7(12%)	9 Socially responsible	10(17%)
10 Values monetary rewards of their job	8(14%)	10 Rebellious	6(10%)	10 Globally aware	9(16%)
11 People oriented	7(12%)	11 Flexible	6(10%)	11 Self-centered	8(14%)
12 Prefers organizational hierarchy	6(10%)	12 Well educated	5(9%)	12 Has a short attention span	8(14%)
13 Career Driven	6(10%)	13 Active	5(9%)	13 Independent	7(12%)
14 Dependable	6(10%)	14 Motivated	5(9%)	14 Values monetary rewards of their job	7(12%)
15 Achievement oriented	5(9%)	15 (not) Has company loyalty	5(9%)	15 Hardworking	6(10%)
16 Has had to make sacrifices	5(9%)	16 Socially responsible	5(9%)	16 Collaborative	6(10%)
17 Slow	5(9%)	17 Globally aware	5(9%)	17 Motivated by non-monetary rewards	6(10%)
				18 Well educated	6(10%)
				19 Multi-tasker	6(10%)
				20 Ambitious	6(10%)
				21 Rebellious	6(10%)
				22 Values work/life balance	5(9%)
				23 Wants instant gratification	5(9%)
				24 (not) Dependable	5(9%)

n = number of students mentioning a given theme
% = n / 58 total students

Figure 24.3 Exploratory study themes (N = 42 unique themes)

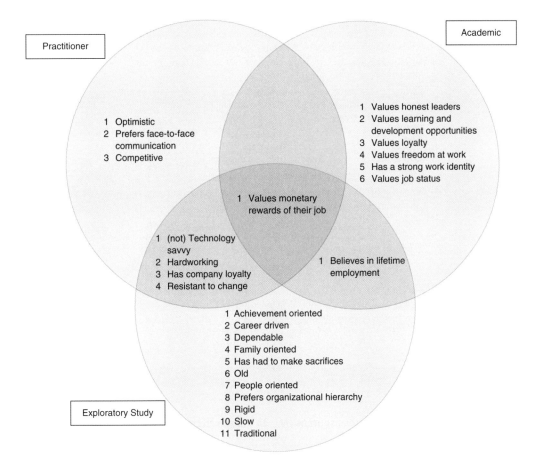

Figure 24.4   Baby Boomer themes across sources (*N* = 26 unique themes)

unique Baby Boomer themes identified across our exploratory study and the practitioner literature (25%) were shared. This suggests that there is some, but limited empirical support for the generational stereotypes that the practitioner literature asserts exist.

For Generation-X, the only theme consistent across the three sources was 'values work/life balance' (see Figure 24.5). Comparing areas of overlap across sources, there was more overlap between the practitioner literature and our exploratory study (six themes) than between the practitioner and academic literatures (four themes), or between our exploratory study and the academic literature (two themes). Six themes from our exploratory study out of a total of

32 unique Generation-X themes generated across our exploratory study and the practitioner literature (19%) were shared (see Figure 24.5). Again, we suggest that greater overlap between our exploratory study and the practitioner literature is a function of a more similar focus relative to the focus of the academic literature. Further, while there is some empirical support for practitioners' claims, such support is far from complete. It is noteworthy that the practitioner literature has much to say about Generation-X workers (i.e., a relatively large number of themes were identified for this generation). This might be in part because the first practitioner book to make a case for paying attention to generations in the workplace, focused primarily on Generation-X (Tulgan, 1995).

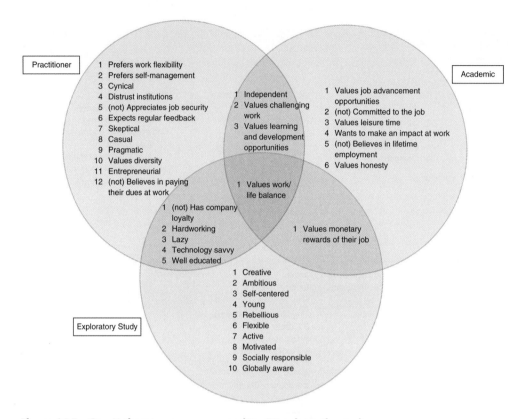

Figure 24.5   Gen-X themes across sources (*N* = 38 unique themes)

Finally, for Generation-Y/Millennial, there was no common theme that emerged across the three sources (see Figure 24.6). Furthermore, similar to the Generation-X and Baby Boomer analyses, there was more overlap between the practitioner literature and our exploratory study (six themes) than between our exploratory study and the academic literature (three themes), or between the practitioner and academic literatures (two themes). Six themes from our exploratory study out of the 39 total unique Generation-Y/Millennial themes generated across our exploratory study and the practitioner literature (15%) were shared. The limited overlap between the practitioner literature and our exploratory study suggests limited empirical support for practitioners' claims about generational stereotypes and a relatively unclear picture of the Generation-Y/Millennial cohort as a result of the limited convergence across the two sources.

Generational versus age stereotypes

To understand whether the generational cohorts share overlapping themes with age stereotypes, we compared each cohort as depicted in each source of data with older and younger worker age stereotypes (see Figures 24.1–24.3). Specifically, we looked at the number of themes that each cohort shared with age stereotypes (i.e., older workers with Baby Boomers; younger workers with Generation-X and Generation-Y/Millennials). We based our age stereotypes on a recent meta-analysis (Posthuma & Campion, 2009) and other key articles that have measured age stereotypes (Rosen & Jerdee, 1976a; Rosen & Jerdee, 1976b).

Posthuma and Campion's (2009) recent meta-analytic review spanning 117 publications (i.e., research articles and books)

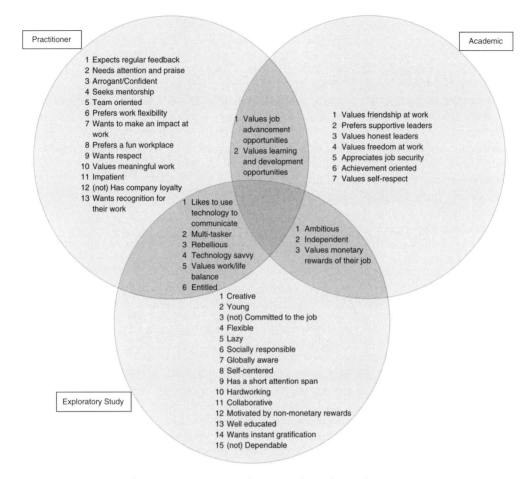

Practitioner

1 Expects regular feedback
2 Needs attention and praise
3 Arrogant/Confident
4 Seeks mentorship
5 Team oriented
6 Prefers work flexibility
7 Wants to make an impact at
   work
8 Prefers a fun workplace
9 Wants respect
10 Values meaningful work
11 Impatient
12 (not) Has company loyalty
13 Wants recognition for
    their work

Academic

1 Values friendship at work
2 Prefers supportive leaders
3 Values honest leaders
4 Values freedom at work
5 Appreciates job security
6 Achievement oriented
7 Values self-respect

1 Values job
  advancement
  opportunities
2 Values learning
  and development
  opportunities

1 Likes to use
  technology to
  communicate
2 Multi-tasker
3 Rebellious
4 Technology savvy
5 Values work/life
  balance
6 Entitled

1 Ambitious
2 Independent
3 Values monetary
  rewards of their job

Exploratory Study

1 Creative
2 Young
3 (not) Committed to the job
4 Flexible
5 Lazy
6 Socially responsible
7 Globally aware
8 Self-centered
9 Has a short attention span
10 Hardworking
11 Collaborative
12 Motivated by non-monetary rewards
13 Well educated
14 Wants instant gratification
15 (not) Dependable

Figure 24.6   Gen-Y themes across sources (*N* = 46 unique themes)

focused on age stereotypes at work. The most prevalent stereotypes of older employees in the workplace noted in this meta-analysis were: poor performance; resistant to change; lower learning ability; shorter job tenure; more costly for organizations; and more dependable. Some other common older worker stereotypes include: less productive; harder to train; lack creativity; lower physical capacity; disinterested in technological change; higher wages; cautious; more reliable; and more loyal (see Figures 24.1–24.3 for additional age stereotypes) (Brooke, 2003; Finkelstein & Burke, 1998; Finkelstein, Higgins, & Clancy, 2000; Greller & Simpson, 1999; Hedge, Borman, &

Lammlein, 2006; Isaksson & Johansson, 2000; Kulik, Perry, & Bourhis, 2000; Paul & Townsend, 1993; Ringenbach & Jacobs, 1994; Rosen & Jerdee, 1976b; 1977; Taylor & Walker, 1994). While Posthuma and Campion's (2009) meta-analytic review found less evidence for younger worker than older worker stereotypes, other sources suggest that younger worker stereotypes tend to be more positive including perceptions of them as: more productive; more efficient; more motivated; more innovative; better able to work under stress; more creative and more logical (Rosen & Jerdee, 1976a).

The practitioner literature indicates some areas of overlap between Baby Boomer and

Older worker stereotypes (see Figure 24.1) with 3 out of 8 Baby Boomer themes (38%) overlapping with the Older worker age stereotype: has company loyalty; (not) technology savvy; resistant to change. The academic literature also suggests some overlap between the Baby Boomer and Older worker stereotypes (see Figure 24.2) with 2 out of 8 Baby Boomer themes (25%) overlapping with the Older worker stereotype: believes in lifetime employment; and values loyalty. Finally, our exploratory study suggests some overlap between the Baby Boomer worker and Older worker stereotypes (see Figure 24.3). Seven out of 17 Baby Boomer themes (41%) overlapped with the Older worker stereotype: believes in lifetime employment; dependable; has company loyalty; resistant to change; rigid; slow; and (not) technology savvy. These analyses indicate some, but a less than 50%, overlap between the Baby Boomer and the Older worker stereotypes across sources.

Within the practitioner literature, none of the 21 Generation-X themes (0%) overlap with the Younger worker stereotype. The academic literature indicates no overlap between Generation-X and the Younger worker stereotype. However, 1 out of 11 Generation-X themes (9%) overlaps with the Older worker stereotype: values honesty (see Figure 24.2). Our exploratory study found that 4 out of 17 Generation-X themes (24%) overlap with the Younger worker stereotype: motivated; ambitious; creative; and flexible (see Figure 24.3). Therefore, there is some, but limited overlap between the Younger worker and Generation-X worker stereotypes.

Finally, there appears to be no overlap between Generation-Y themes and the Younger worker stereotype within the practitioner literature. The academic literature suggests only 1 out of 12 Generation-Y/Millennial themes (8%) overlap with the Younger worker stereotype: ambitious (see Figure 24.2). Our exploratory study findings indicate that 3 out of 24 themes (13%) overlap between Generation-Y/Millennials and the Younger worker stereotype: ambitious; creative; and flexible (see Figure 24.3).

These analyses suggest that there is some, but limited overlap between Generation-X and Generation-Y/Millennial stereotypes and the Younger worker stereotype. There is greater overlap between the Older worker and Baby Boomer worker stereotypes; particularly in our exploratory study. Yet, even here, the overlap is less than 50% suggesting that generational stereotypes overlap with, but are *distinct* from age stereotypes.

DISCUSSION

We conducted this research to determine whether there is evidence for the existence of generational stereotypes. From our analyses, it appears that generational stereotypes do exist. First, we assessed how differentiated perceptions of each of the three generations were within each of three sources of data (practitioner literature, academic literature, and our exploratory study). Generational stereotypes were most differentiated in the practitioner literature, while the academic literature generally suggested a higher percentage of similarities between the generational cohorts in terms of their work values and attitudes. On the other hand, Generation-X and Generation-Y/Millennial stereotypes were the least clearly distinguishable in our exploratory study. However, in our study, respondents clearly distinguished between Baby Boomer and Generation-Y/Millennial and Generation-X stereotypes.

Second, we sought to determine whether a clear image of each cohort emerged across the three sources of data (practitioner literature, academic literature, and exploratory study). Out of the three sources of data, the academic literature appears to have the least in common with the other two sources (the practitioner literature and our exploratory study). This appears to be a function of the academic literature's narrow focus on actual generational work values and attitudes. Focusing on the practitioner literature and on our study (both of which considered perceptions), the common themes used to describe Baby Boomers were: hardworking; has company loyalty;

(not) technology savvy; resistant to change; and values monetary rewards of their job. Generation-X themes that emerged from our exploratory study and the practitioner literature were: lazy; technology savvy; values work/life balance; (not) has company loyalty; hardworking; and well educated. Generation-Y/Millennial workers were commonly described in our exploratory study and in the practitioner literature as: technology savvy; likes to use technology to communicate; multi-tasker; rebellious; values work/life balance; and entitled.

The Venn diagrams also revealed that while there was some overlap in the themes discussed in the practitioner literature and our exploratory study, for each generational cohort, the overlap was not particularly large (ranging from 15% to 25%). Moreover, the overlap between the practitioner and academic literatures was far from complete. This suggests that practitioners are endorsing generational stereotypes for which there is little empirical support. As a result, we currently have a somewhat limited understanding of generational stereotypes.

Third, we assessed the extent to which generational stereotypes are distinct from age stereotypes. Across the different sources, there appears to be more overlap between Baby Boomer themes and the Older worker stereotype than between Generation-X or Generation-Y/Millennials and the Younger worker stereotype (see Figures 24.1–24.3). Nevertheless, there are significant areas of difference between the Baby Boomer and Older worker stereotypes. Baby Boomers are not associated with the traits typically attributed to Older workers such as: lower ability to perform tasks; less productive; less motivated; and lower return on investment (for training). To the contrary, Baby Boomers are regarded as having a strong work identity, being career driven, achievement oriented, hardworking and competitive. These traits are hardly consistent with images of an older worker past his/her prime.

Perceptions of Generation-X appear to be even more distinct from what is traditionally thought of as a Younger worker. The Younger worker stereotype tends to be mostly positive in nature (e.g., more productive, more receptive to new ideas, more eager). However, the Generation-X stereotype includes both positive as well as negative traits (e.g., lazy, self-centered). Moreover, Generation-X members are perceived as more worldly (e.g., globally aware, socially responsible) and as having more balanced work needs (e.g., values work/life balance) relative to Younger workers.

Generation-Y/Millennial workers are also perceptually differentiated from the Younger worker stereotype. While the Younger worker stereotype focuses on ability to do work in general and an openness to learning, the Generation-Y/Millennial worker stereotype seems to emphasize: technology (e.g., technology savvy, likes to use technology to communicate), impatience (e.g., has short attention span, wants instant gratification), as well as some negative traits (e.g., entitled, arrogant). Overall, our analyses suggest some overlap between age and generational stereotypes, but also some important differences.

Research and practical implications

Our results suggest two clear directions for future research. First, additional studies are needed to better clarify the traits and characteristics that are most closely associated with each generational cohort. Our analyses suggest that the academic studies conducted to this point have too narrowly focused on actual work values and attitudes of different generations. Academics need to broaden their focus to explicitly look at generational stereotypes. Our exploratory study provides some preliminary evidence for the existence of generational stereotypes, but more research is clearly needed. Moreover, aspects of generational stereotypes discussed in the practitioner literature must be empirically verified. Further, additional research is needed to more clearly delineate the differences between the content of generational compared to age stereotypes.

Second, while it is important to understand the content of generational stereotypes more fully, future research is also necessary to begin to understand the implications of using these stereotypes for employment related decisions and outcomes as well as for employees' attitudes and behaviors. For example, our findings indicate that there are differences between generational and age stereotypes. Would an individual who is described as a 60 year old experience different work outcomes if he or she was instead described as a Baby Boomer? Future research should explore whether the activation of these two different stereotypes can result in different employment related outcomes for the same individual. Research could also explore stereotype threat among workers who self-identify as older workers (and who are typically perceived in less positive terms with respect to performance related traits) compared to Baby Boomers (who are typically perceived in relatively more positive terms on these traits).

Further, there are practical implications of this research. Our exploratory study suggests that while there is some overlap between Baby Boomer and Older worker stereotypes, there are also meaningful differences. While the overlap between Baby Boomer and Older worker stereotypes consists of both positive (e.g., dependable, has company loyalty) and negative characteristics (e.g., resistant to change, rigid, slow, and (not) technology savvy), the unique aspects of Baby Boomer stereotypes are generally positive in nature (e.g., competitive, achievement oriented, career driven, people and family oriented). Our study results suggest that it may be fruitful for older workers to encourage perceptions of themselves as Baby Boomers. While older workers are seen as less productive and motivated, Baby Boomers are perceived as competitive and achievement oriented. Consequently, managing one's impression of himself or herself (e.g., describing oneself as a Baby Boomer) could positively influence a variety of employment outcomes (e.g., selection, performance appraisals, promotions).

It is not obvious whether similar potential gains exist for younger workers who could encourage perceptions of themselves as Generation-X or Generation-Y/Millennials. In fact, it may be more advantageous for younger workers to distance themselves from the Gen-X and Gen-Y/Millennial labels which tend to be associated with more negative traits and characteristics than the relatively more positive Younger worker stereotype. However, some aspects of Generation-X or Generation-Y/Millennial stereotypes (e.g., perceptions as technologically savvy) may be particularly helpful for younger people in certain jobs and industries (e.g., high tech industry).

Our study also suggests that the potentially negative feelings, behaviors, and work outcomes that older workers experience in the workplace may be improved by encouraging them to assume an alternative identity (i.e., Baby Boomer) that may have more positive implications for their self-perceptions. Researchers have studied ways in which individuals self-stereotype and have provided ways to mitigate some of the negative effects of certain stereotypes (Levy, 1996; Roberson & Kulik, 2007; Shih, Pittinsky, & Ambady, 1999). Our research suggests that one potentially fruitful strategy may be to encourage individuals of a particular age to think of themselves as Baby Boomers rather than older workers. To the extent that individuals self-identify as Baby Boomers (e.g., hardworking, competitive), stereotypes about older workers' lower performance capabilities may become less relevant and consequently stereotype threat less likely (Roberson & Kulik, 2007).

Limitations

This research is not without limitations. First, the average age of the participants in our exploratory study was 28 years old. Moreover, 52% of our respondents identified themselves as members of Generation-Y/Millennial compared to 24% who identified as Generation X, and 4% as Baby Boomers.

Our relatively young sample may have had more knowledge about their own generation, which could have influenced the content of their generational stereotypes. Consistent with this, respondents in our exploratory study used more traits to describe Generation-Y than Baby Boomer or Generation-X workers. Thus, it is unclear how generalizable the stereotype content of our student sample is. Future research should employ a broader range of participants in terms of age and generational identity. In this way we could assess the role of perceivers' age and generational identity in stereotype content. The authors are currently collecting data for a follow-up study with a more age-diverse sample.

The academic and practitioner literatures relevant to the topic of generations are vast. We used a variety of relevant search terms and focused on articles that were most relevant to our topic. However, it is possible that our search, although quite thorough, overlooked some relevant articles. Consequently, our conclusions are based on the sample of articles that we identified and analyzed.

A survey of the practitioner and empirical literatures suggests that the concept of generations is 'comparative' in nature; that is, a given generation is often described and measured relative to another generation (e.g., Generation-X may be 'technologically savvy' compared to Baby Boomers, but deficient compared to Generation-Y/Millennials). In our study we intentionally asked participants to report their stereotypes of each of three generations without explicit reference to (direct comparison with) other generations. While we may have accurately captured the content of each generational stereotype, this approach may have made it more difficult to clearly determine the edges of these potentially fuzzy, overlapping stereotypes. Future research that asks respondents to make direct comparisons between generations may focus attention on certain content and highlight differences between cohort stereotypes, resulting in a slightly different picture of stereotype content than observed here. Additional

research employing different methods to measure generational stereotypes is therefore important for obtaining a more comprehensive picture of these stereotypes.

CONCLUSIONS

This chapter contributes to the literature in a variety of ways. First, we provided some empirical evidence for the existence of generational stereotypes. Second, we underscored that while there is some empirical support for generational stereotypes endorsed in the practitioner literature, more research is needed. Third, the actual generational differences studied by academics are narrow in focus and consequently do not greatly overlap with the findings that emerged in our exploratory study. Fourth, we delineated differences between generational and age stereotypes. While there appears to be some overlap between the Baby Boomer and Older worker stereotypes, and Younger worker and Generation-X and Generation-Y/Millennial stereotypes, there is also evidence that generational stereotypes are unique and qualitatively different from age stereotypes. Additional research is necessary to more closely examine the content and implications of generational stereotypes in the workplace.

REFERENCES[1]

*Practitioner articles (n = 64); **Empirical articles (n = 37)

Adler, G., & Hilber, D. (2009). Industry hiring patterns of older workers. *Research on Aging*, *31*: 69–88.

*Alexander, D., & Alexander, B. (2005). Generations in the workplace: Are you prepared? *The Catalyst*, *34*(3): 3–4.

*Allen, P. (2004, September). Welcoming Y. *Benefits Canada*, *28*(9): 51–53.

*Andersen, M. L., & Taylor, H. F. (2006). *Sociology: Understanding a Diverse Society* (4th Ed). Belmont, CA: Thomson Wadsworth.

*Anonymous. (2002a, March). How to better meet the needs of your firm's Gen-Xers. *Law Office Management & Administration Report*, pp. 3–6.

*Anonymous. (2002b, May). Gen-X staff: What they want ... and how to manage it. *Accounting Office Management & Administration Report*, p. 4.

*Anonymous. (2009a, May 7). Metlife mature market institute: New employee engagement study defines how employers can harness the power of a multi-generational workforce. *Women's Health Weekly*, p. 411.

*Anonymous. (2009b, November 16). Different generations, same objectives: Boomers, Gen-X and Gen-Y want the same things at work. *Canada News Wire*. Ottawa, Ontario.

*Anonymous. (2010a, September/October). The Boomer–Millennial workplace: How to defuse the tension. *Nonprofit World, 28*(5): p. 24.

*Anonymous. (2010b). Generations work it out. *The Corporate Citizen, 4*: p. 3.

*Anonymous. (2010c, November 2). Lose the Gen-Y stereotypes, new survey shows Gen-Y employees prefer traditional approach to work environment, pay and dressing for success. *Canada News Wire*. Ottawa, Ontario.

Appelbaum, S.H., Serena, M., & Shapiro, B.T. (2005). Generation 'X' and the Boomers: An analysis of realities and myths. *Management Research News, 28*(1): 1–33.

Armour, S. (2005, November 6). Generation Y: They've arrived at work with a new attitude. *USA Today*. Retrieved from: http://www.usatoday.com/money/workplace/2005-11-06-gen-y_x.htm?POE=click-refer

**Arsenault, P. M. (2004). Validating generational differences: A legitimate diversity and leadership issue. *Leadership & Organization Development Journal, 25*(2): 124–141.

Berl, P. (2006, March/April). Crossing the generational divide. *Exchange*, pp. 73–76.

*Bernstein, L., Alexander, D., & Alexander, B. (2008). Generations: Harnessing the potential of the multigenerational workforce. *The Catalyst, 37*(3):17–23.

**Beutell, N., & Wittig-Berman, U. (2008). Work-family conflict and work-family synergy for generation X, baby boomers, and matures: Generational differences, predictors, and satisfaction outcomes. *Journal of Managerial Psychology, 23*(5): 507–523.

*Bisch, D. (2007, June). Dusting off the gold watch. *Benefits Canada, 31*(6): p. 5.

*Booth, F. (1999, March 22). Back to the basics: Generation-X needs to connect to people, not just computers. *Nation's Restaurant News, 33*(12): p. 30.

**Bova, B., & Kroth, M. (1999). Closing the gap: The mentoring of Generation X. *Journal of Adult Education, 27*(1): 7–17.

**Bova, B., & Kroth, M. (2001). Workplace learning and Generation X. *Journal of Workplace Learning, 13*(2):57–65.

Brooke, L. (2003). Human resource costs and benefits of maintaining a mature-aged workforce. *International Journal of Manpower, 24*(3): 260–283.

**Busch, P., Venkitachalam, K., & Richards, D. (2008). Generational difference in soft knowledge situations: Status, need for recognition, workplace commitment and idealism. *Knowledge and Process Management, 15*(1): 45–58.

*Business/Technology Editors. (1999, August 16). Workplace survey results defy generational stereotypes: Unveils surprising similarities and divisions across age groups. *Business Wire*, p. 1.

Carlson, H. (2004, August). Changing of the guard. *The School Administrator*, pp. 36–39.

**Cennamo, L., & Gardner, D. (2008). Generational differences in work values, outcomes and person-organisation values fit. *Journal of Managerial Psychology, 23*(8): 891–906.

*Chao, L. (2005, November 29). What Gen-Xers need to be happy at work. *The Wall Street Journal*, p. B6.

Charrier, K. (2000, December). Marketing strategies for attracting and retaining Generation X police officers. *The Police Chief, 67*(12): 45–51.

**Chen, P., & Choi, Y. (2008). Generational differences in work values: A study of hospitality management. *International Journal of Contemporary Hospitality Management, 20*(6): 595–615.

Coupland, D. (1991). *Generation X: Tales for an accelerated culture*. New York: St. Martin's Press.

**D'Amato, A., & Herzfeldt, R. (2008). Learning orientation, organizational commitment and talent retention across generations: A study of European managers. *Journal of Managerial Psychology, 23*(8): 929–953.

**Davis, J. B., Pawlowski, S. D., & Houston, A. (2006). Work commitments of Baby Boomers and Gen-xers in the IT profession: Generational differences or myth? *Journal of Computer Information Systems, 46*(3): 43–49.

Deaux, K. (1985). Sex and gender. *Annual Review of Psychology, 36*: 49–81.

Deaux, K., & Kite, M.E. (1993). Gender stereotypes. In F. L. Denmark & M. A. Paludi (Eds.), *Psychology of Women: A Handbook of Issues and Theories* (pp. 107–139). Westport, CT: Greenwood Press.

**De Hauw, S., & De Vos, A. (2010). Millennials' career perspective and psychological contract expectations: Does the recession lead to lowered expectations? *Journal of Business Psychology, 25*: 293–302.

Devine, P. G. (1989). Stereotypes and prejudice: Their automatic and controlled components. *Journal of Personality and Social Psychology, 56*(1): 5–18.

**Dries, N., Pepermans, R., & De Kerpel, E. (2008). Exploring four generations' beliefs about career: Is 'satisfied' the new 'successful'? *Journal of Managerial Psychology, 23*(8): 907–928.

**Dulin, L. (2008). Leadership preferences of a Generation Y cohort: A mixed-methods investigation. *Journal of Leadership Studies, 2*(1): 43–59.

*Dwan, S. (2004, February). From one generation to the next. *NZ Business, 18*(1): 40.

**Egri, C., & Ralston, D. (2004). Generation cohorts and personal values: A comparison of China and the United States. *Organization Science, 15*(2): 210–220.

**Eisner, S. P. (2005). Managing Generation Y. *SAM Advanced Management Journal, 70*(4): 4–15.

*Elmore, L. (2010, June). Generation gaps. *Women in Business, 62*(2): 8–11.

*Erbe, B. (2003, July 4). Generational gyrations. *Tribune,* Welland, Ontario, p. A6.

*Erickson, T. (2009, February). Gen-Y in the workforce. *Harvard Business Review, 87*(2): 43–49.

**Eskilson, A., & Wiley, M. G. (1999). Solving for the X: Aspirations and expectations of college students. *Journal of Youth and Adolescence, 28*(1): 51–70.

Esses, V., Haddock, G., & Zanna, M.P. (1993). Values, stereotypes, and emotions as determinants of intergroup attitudes. In D.M. Mackie & D.L. Hamilton (Eds.), *Affect, Cognition, and Stereotyping: Interactive Processes in Group Perceptions* (pp. 137–166). San Diego: Academic Press.

Eyerman, R., & Turner, B. (1998). Outline of a theory of generations. *European Journal of Social Theory, 1*: 91–106.

Filipczak, B. (1994). It's just a job: Generation X at work. *Training, 31*: 21–27.

Finkelstein, L. M., & Burke, M.J. (1998). Age stereotyping at work: The role of rater and contextual factors on evaluations of job applicants. *Journal of General Psychology, 125*: 317–345.

Finkelstein, L. M., Higgins, K. D., & Clancy, M. (2000). Justifications for ratings of old and young job applicants: An exploratory content analysis. *Experimental Aging Research, 26*: 263–283.

*Fisher, A. (2009, May 25). When Gen-X runs the show. *Time, 173*(20): 48–49.

Fiske, S. T., Bersoff, D. N., Borgida, E., Deaux, K., & Heilman, M. E. (1991). Social science research on trial: Use of sex stereotyping research in Price Waterhouse v. Hopkins. *American Psychologist, 46*(10): 1049–1060.

*Fox, A. (2011, May). Mixing it up. *HR Magazine, 56*(5): 22–28.

*Francis-Smith, J. (2004, August 26). Surviving and thriving in the multigenerational workplace. *The Journal Record, 1.* Retrieved from: http://www.journalrecord.com/2004/08/26/surviving-and-thriving-in-the-multigenerational-workplace.

*Furlong, K. (2010, May 15). Are you really NextGen? *Library Journal, 135*(9): 48–49.

*Gage, A. (1999, November 6). All ages adapting to changing workplace, experts discover. *Calgary Herald,* Calgary, Alberta, p. W14.

*Gatewood, D. (1995, February 5). Careers workplace X: A new generation of workers is redefining the way things are done. Sidebar: Xers Have Less Luck Finding Employment. *Newsday,* 01. Long Island, NY.

**Gibson, J. W., Greenwood, R. A., & Murphy, Jr., E. F. (2009). Generational differences in the workplace: Personal values, behaviors, and popular beliefs. *Journal of Diversity Management, 4*(3): 1–7.

*Gilburg, D. (2008, February 1). They're Gen-Y and you're not. *CIO Insight,* p. 40–43.

*Goodger, K. (2008, August 2). Working for the business. *The Nelson Mail,* p. 11.

Greller, M. M., & Simpson, P. (1999). In search of late career: A review of contemporary social science research applicable to the understanding of late career. *Human Resource Management Review, 9*: 307–347.

*Groves, M. (1996, March 25). Managing in the next millennium; Q & A; Gen-Xer offers advice for baby boom managers; forget the stereotypes, but remember that this group is independent and has a different style of communicating. *Los Angeles Times,* p. 4. Los Angeles, California.

**Gursoy, D., Maier, T. A., & Chi, C. G. (2008). Generational differences: An examination of work values and generational gaps in the hospitality workforce. *International Journal of Hospitality Management, 27*: 448–458.

*Haeberle, K., Herzberg, J., & Hobbs, T. (2009, October). Leading the multigenerational work force. *Healthcare Executive, 24*(5): 62–67.

Hamilton, D. L., & Trolier, T. K. (1986). Stereotypes and stereotyping: An overview of the cognitive approach. In J. F. Dovidio & S. L. Gaertner (Eds.), *Prejudice, Discrimination, and Racism* (pp. 127–163). San Diego, CA: Academic Press.

*Harris Interactive. (2006, July 24). Higher stress costing job satisfaction in U.S. companies: 2006 survey reveals generational differences, employment issues and productivity perceptions. *Business Wire,* p. 1.

*Hart, K. (2007, April 14). Generations in the workplace: Finding common ground. Retrieved from: www.mlo-online.com.

*Hays, S. (1999, November). Gen-X and the art of the reward. *Workforce, 78*: 44–47.

Hedge, J. W., Borman, W. C., & Lammlein, S. E. (2006). The Aging Workforce: Realities, Myths and Implications for Organizations. Washington, DC: American Psychological Association.

Heilman, M.E. (1983). Sex bias in work settings: The lack-of-fit model. In B. Staw and L. Cummings (Eds.), *Research in Organizational Behavior (Vol. 5)*, (pp. 269–298). Greenwich, CT: JAI.

**Hess, N., & Jepsen, D. M. (2009). Career stage and generational differences in psychological contracts. *Career Development International, 14*(3): 261–283.

Howe, N., & Strauss, W. (1991). *Generations: The History of America's Future, 1584 to 2069*. New York, NY: Harper Perennial.

Howe, N., & Strauss, W. (1993). *13th Gen: Abort, Retry, Ignore, Fail?* New York, NY: Vintage Books.

Howe, N., & Strauss, W. (2000). *Millennials rising: The Next Great Generation*. New York, NY: Vintage Books.

Isaksson, K. & Johansson, G. (2000). Adaptation to continued work and early retirement following downsizing: Long-term effects and gender differences. *Journal of Occupational and Organizational Psychology, 73* (2): 241–256.

Jacobs, S. L., Kulik, C. T., & Fichman, M. (1993). Category-based and feature-based processes in job impressions. *Journal of Applied Social Psychology,* 23: 1226–1248.

*Johnson, A. (2011, April). From the mouth of Ys. *Chartered Accountants Journal, 90*(3): 28–29.

**Jovic, E., Wallace, J., & Lemaire, J. (2006). The generation and gender shifts in medicine: An exploratory survey of internal medicine physicians. *BMC Health Services Research, 6*(55): 1–10.

**Jurkiewicz, C. (2000). Generation X and the public employee. *Public Personnel Management, 29*(1): 55–74.

**Jurkiewicz, C., & Brown, R. (1998). GenXers vs Boomers vs Matures: Generational comparisons of public employee motivation. *Review of Public Personnel Administration, 18*: 18–37.

*Katzanek, J. (2008, June 15). Study dashes stereotypes about 'Millennials' in the workplace. *McClatchy – Tribune Business News*. Washington.

*Klie, S. (2008, May 19). Handling the 'alien invasion.' *Canadian HR Reporter, 21*(10): 8–9.

*Kronenberg, G. (1997, February 24). Why Gen-Xers become Ex-ers; Baby Boomer managers often struggle to handle younger employees. Those who succeed will have found a key to the future. *Los Angeles Times*, p. 14. Los Angeles, California.

Kulik, C. T. (1989). The effects of job categorization on judgments of the motivating potential of jobs. *Administrative Sciences Quarterly,* 34: 69–90.

Kulik, C. T., & Bainbridge, H. T. J. (2006). Psychological Perspectives on Workplace Diversity. In A. M. Konrad, P. Prasad, & J. K. Pringle (Eds.), *Handbook of Workplace Diversity* (pp. 25–52). Thousand Oaks, CA: Sage.

Kulik, C. T., Perry, E. L., & Bourhis, A. C. (2000). Ironic evaluation processes: Effects of thought suppression on evaluations of older applicants. *Journal of Organizational Behavior, 21*: 689–711.

*Kunde, D. (1995, July 16). Generation X network group prospering. *The Salt Lake Tribune*, Salt Lake City, Utah, p. F3.

Kupperschmidt, B. (2000). Multigenerational employees: Strategies for effective management. *Health Care Manager, 19*: 65–76.

**Lamm, E., & Meeks, M. (2009). Workplace fun: The moderating effects of generational differences. *Employee Relations, 31*(6): 613–631.

Levy, B. R. (1996). Improving memory in old age through implicit self-stereotyping. *Journal of Personality and Social Psychology, 71*(6): 1092–1107.

*Leyes, M. (2010, April). Talkin' 'bout my generation. *Advisor Today, 105*(4): 34–38.

*Lindgren, A. (1998, October 5). Countering stereotypes: Generation-Xers need own special job-search plan. *The Gazette*, Montréal, Québec, p. C14.

*Lines, D. (2011, January). The Generation Y effect on L&D. *Training Journal*, pp. 40–43.

Losyk, B. (1997). How to manage an X'er. *The Futurist, 31*, p. 43.

Lyons, S., Duxbury, L., & Higgins, C. (2007). An empirical assessment of generational differences in basic human values. *Psychological Reports, 101*: 339–352.

*Madore, J. T. (1995, August 21). Generation X wants more than fun out of life employers must spend more time determining what motivates the younger set. *Buffalo News*, Buffalo, NY, p. D7.

*Main, B. (1999, February). Valued employees strive to please. *ID, 35*(2): 66–67.

Mannheim, K. (1952). The problem of generations. In P. Kecskemeti (Ed.), *Essays on the Sociology of Knowledge* (pp. 276–322). London: Routledge & Kegan Paul.

Marin, G. (1984). Stereotyping Hispanics: The differential effect of research method, label, and degree of contact. *International Journal of Intercultural Relations*, 8: 17–27.

**Martin, N., & Prince, D. (2008). Factoring for X: An empirical study of generation X's materialistic attributes. *Journal of Management & Marketing Research*, *1*: 47–55.

*Maynard, R. (1996, November 1). A less-stressed work force. *Nation's Business*, *84*(11): 50–51.

*McDonald, J. (2008, October 26). Treat them right and Generation Y workers are workplace assets. *McClatchy – Tribune Business News*. Washington.

**McDonald, K. S., & Hite, L. M. (2008). The next generation of career success: Implications for HRD. *Advances in Developing Human Resources*, *10*(1): 86–103.

**Montana, P., & Petit, F. (2008). Motivating Generation X and Y on the job and preparing Z. *Global Journal of Business Research*, *2*(2): 139–148.

**Murphy, Jr., E. F., Gibson, J. W., & Greenwood, R. A. (2010). Analyzing generational values among managers and non-managers for sustainable organizational effectiveness. *SAM Advanced Management Journal*, *75*(1): 33–35.

*Neville, A. (2008, July). Generation next: Strategies for recruiting younger workers. *Power*, *152*(7): 32–39.

**Ng, E. S., Schweitzer, L., & Lyons, S. T. (2010). New generation, great expectations: A field study of the millennial generation. *Journal of Business Psychology*, 25: 281–292.

Niemann, Y., Jennings, L., Rozelle, R., & Sullivan, E. (1994). Use of free responses and cluster analysis to determine stereotypes of eight groups. *Personality and Social Psychology Bulletin*, 20: 379–390.

**Noble, S., & Schewe, C. (2003). Cohort segmentation: An exploration of its validity. *Journal of Business Research*, *56*(12): 979–987.

*O'Brien, M. (2008, September 23). Misunderstood Millennials. *LRP Publications*. Retrieved from: http://www.hreonline.com/HRE/story.jsp?storyId=128339936

*Ott, B., Blacksmith, N., & Royal, K. (2008, March 13). What generation gap? Job seekers from different generations often look for the same things from prospective employers, according to recent Gallup research. *Gallup Management Journal Online*, pp. 1–4.

Parry, E., & Urwin, P. (2010). Generational differences in work values: A review of theory and evidence. *International Journal of Management Reviews*, *13*(1): 79–96.

Paul, R. J. & Townsend, J. B. (1993). Managing the older worker – Don't just rinse away the gray. *Academy of Management Executive*, 7: 67–74.

*Perelman, D. (2007, October 19). The generation gap challenges IT managers; making the generational mix work means changing a workplace's culture, a prolonged but necessary process. *CIO Insight*, 86.

*Perry, A. (2000, July 30). Seniority in the workplace is on the way. *The San Diego Union – Tribune*, p. I1. San Diego, CA.

Perry, E. (1994). A prototype matching approach to understanding the role of applicant gender and age in the evaluation of job applicants. *Journal of Applied Social Psychology*, *24*(16): 1433–1473.

*Pooley, E. (2005, June 6). Kids these days... *Canadian Business*, *78*(12): 67–68.

Posthuma, R. A., & Campion, M. A. (2009). Age stereotypes in the workplace: Common stereotypes, moderators, and future research directions. *Journal of Management*, *35*(1): 158–188.

**Riesenwitz, T. H., & Iyer, R. (2009). Differences in Generation X and Generation Y: Implications for the organization and marketers. *Marketing Management Journal*, *19*(2): 91–103.

Ringenbach, K. L., & Jacobs, R. R. (1994). Development of age stereotypes in the workplace scale. Paper presented at the Society for Industrial and Organizational Psychology, Annual Meeting, Nashville, TN.

Roberson, L., Deitsch, E. A., Brief, A. P., & Block, C. J. (2003). Stereotype threat and feedback seeking in the workplace. *Journal of Vocational Behavior*, *62*(1): 176–188.

Roberson, L., & Kulik, C. T. (2007). Stereotype threat at work. *Academy of Management Perspectives*, *21*(2): 24–40.

*Rock, C. U. (2010). Gen Y has arrived. *Family Business*, *21*(3), p. 6.

**Rodriguez, R. O., Green, M. T., & James Ree, M. (2003). Leading generation X: Do the old rules apply? *The Journal of Leadership and Organizational Studies*, *9*(4): 67–75.

Rosen, B., & Jerdee, T. H. (1976a). The influence of age stereotypes on managerial decisions. *Journal of Applied Psychology*, 62: 428–432.

Rosen, B., & Jerdee, T. H. (1976b). The nature of job-related age stereotypes. *Journal of Applied Psychology*, 62: 180–183.

Rosen, B., & Jerdee, T. H. (1977). Too old or not too old? *Harvard Business Review*, 55: 97–106.

*Roy, J. G. (2008, December). Ten tips for retaining the next generation. *Utility Automation & Engineering T&D*, *13*(12): 8–11.

*Sacks, D. (2006, February). Scenes from the culture clash. *Fast Company*, 102: 72–77.

*Sandler, S. F. (2000). Is the Boomer/Gen-X war over? *HR Focus*, *77*(5): 1–13.

*Saunderson, R. (2009, February). Is it really so hard to reward and recognize a multi-generational workforce? *Employee Benefit Plan Review*, pp. 6–7.

Schuman, H., & Scott, J. (1989). Generations and collective memories. *American Sociological Review*, 54: 359–381.

**Sessa, V., Kabacoff, R. I., Deal, J. J., & Brown, H. (2007). Generational differences in leader values and leadership behaviors. *The Psychologist-Manager Journal*, 10(1): 47–74.

Shih, M., Pittinsky, T. L., & Ambady, N. (1999). Stereotype susceptibility: Identity salience and shifts in quantitative performance. *Psychological Science*, 10(1): 80–83.

Shore, L. M., Chung-Herrera, B. G., Dean, M. A., Holcombe Ehrhart, K., Jung, D. I., Randel, A. E., & Singh, G. (2009). Diversity in organizations: Where are we now and where are we going? *Human Resource Management Review*, 19: 117–133.

*Society for Human Resource Management (SHRM) (2004, August), 2004 Generational Differences Survey Report. *SHRM*, Report No. 04-0432: 1–29.

**Smola, K. W., & Sutton, C. D. (2002). Generational differences: Revisiting generational work values for the new millennium. *Journal of Organizational Behavior*, 23: 363–382.

Spencer-Rodgers, J. (2001). Consensual and individual stereotypic beliefs about international students among American host nationals. *International Journal of Intercultural Relations*, 25(6): 639–657.

*Spinks, N. (2005, November). Talking about my generation. *Canadian Healthcare Manager*, 12(7): 11–13.

*Stafford, D. (2002, April 18). *The Kansas City Star, Mo., Workplace Column*. Knight Ridder/Tribune Business News, Washington, p. 1.

*Stein, P. M., & Berardinelli, E. (2009, April). Bridging the gaps among the generations. *Fire Engineering*, 162(4): 169–176.

Strauss, W., & Howe, N. (1991). *Generations: The history of America's future, 1584 to 2069*. New York: Morrow.

**Sullivan, S. E., Forret, M. L., & Carraher, S. M. (2009). Using the kaleidoscope career model to examine generational differences in work attitudes. *Career Development International*, 14(3): 284–302.

Taylor, P. E. & Walker, A. (1994). The ageing workforce: Employers' attitudes towards older people. *Work, Employment & Society*, 8(4): 569–591.

*Thielfoldt, D., & Scheef, D. (2004, August). Generation X and the Millennials: What you need to know about mentoring the new generations. *Law Practice Today*. Retrieved from: http://apps.americanbar.org/lpm/lpt/articles/mgt08044.html

*Trunk, P. (2010, March). The new workforce will job-hop. And that's good. *HVACR Distribution Business*, pp. 20–22.

**Tung, K., Huang, I., Chen, S., & Shih, C. (2005). Mining the Generation Xers' job attitudes by artificial neural network and decision tree – empirical evidence in Taiwan. *Expert Systems With Applications*, 29(4): 783–794.

Tulgan, B. (1995). Managing Generation X: How to Bring Out the Best in Young Talent. New York, NY: W.W. Norton & Company.

Tulgan, B. (2009). *Not Everyone Gets a Trophy: How to Manage Generation Y*. San Francisco, CA: Jossey-Bass.

Twenge, J. M. (2010). A review of the empirical evidence on generational differences in work attitudes. *Journal of Business & Psychology*, 25: 201–210.

**Twenge, J. M., Campbell, S. M., Hoffman, B. J., & Lance, C. E. (2010). Generational differences in work values: Leisure and extrinsic values increasing, social and intrinsic values decreasing. *Journal of Management*, 36(5): 1117–1142.

*Watt, D. (2010, March). Different generations, same objectives. *CA Magazine*, 143(2), p. 1.

*Wendover, R. (2009, February). Meet your new boss … a Gen Xer! *Compensation & Benefits for Law Offices*, 9(2): 1–15.

**Westerman, J. W., & Yamamura, J. H. (2007). Generational preferences for work environment fit: Effects on employee outcomes. *Career Development International*, 12(2): 150–161.

*Wolfson, B. J. (1999, August 7). Work and play a healthy mix. *The Ottawa Citizen*, Ottawa, Ontario, p. K4.

**Wong, M., Gardiner, E., Lang, W., & Coulon, L. (2008). Generational differences in personality and motivation: Do they exist and what are the implications for the workplace? *Journal of Managerial Psychology*, 23(8): 878–890.

PART 5

Developing Public Policy

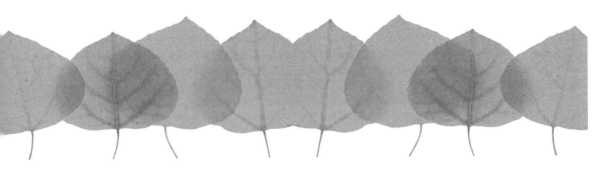

25

Reconstructing Work and Retirement: Labour Market Trends and Policy Issues

Chris Phillipson

INTRODUCTION

The social organisation of work and retirement has undergone radical transformation over the past four decades. In the 1960s a broad consensus appeared to have been reached – at least in the case of industrial countries – of the value of developing retirement as a distinct stage in the life course. This was linked with an evolving infrastructure of support – notably through public old-age insurance systems and occupational pensions – which seemed to provide the basis for challenging many of the insecurities traditionally associated with later life. However, within a short (in historical terms) space of time the basis of retirement was progressively challenged: de-stabilised at first through the rapid expansion of early retirement or 'early exit' (see below), and subsequently fears about an excess of older people over younger workers (fuelled by the arrival into retirement of the cohort of post-war baby boomers).

Exploring the complex tie between aging, work and retirement is the primary concern of this chapter.[1] All three elements emerged out of the chain reaction set off by industrialisation, with the growth of population and the gradual standardisation of entry and exit from the workplace. And the links between them have continued to develop in different ways, notably with shifting boundaries between work on the one side and retirement on the other. Arising from this, the chapter has four main aims: first, to review the relationship between aging, work and retirement, and current influences affecting the relationship between all three; second, to assess changes in the institution of retirement and comparative trends in labour force participation; third, to assess policy options for extending working life and strengthening the position of older people in the workplace; finally, to consider likely research agendas for future studies involving older workers.

AGING, WORK AND RETIREMENT

Changing work and retirement

The institutions and relationships associated with work and retirement have been central to shaping many aspects of aging and the individual's movement through the life course. Work plays an important role influencing financial resources as well as (for many) creating the basis of a secure identity for later life. But retirement – as it emerged through the 20th century – has become increasingly important as well, with the creation of new life styles and interests for a period which may occupy up to one-third of an individual's life. The relationship between the two is, however, complex, with retirement invariably being placed in a subordinate role when considered beside the importance of work as an economic necessity and (in some interpretations) social and moral obligation.

The shifting relationship between work and retirement can be traced in terms of three main phases over the period since the 1950s: first, the emergence of retirement in the 1950s and 1960s; second, the expansion of early retirement and unemployment in the 1970s and 1980s; third, the 'individualisation' of retirement along with pressures to extend working life from the 1990s onwards.

The first phase occurred in the two decades following the ending of the Second World War. A key element concerned the way in which, in most capitalist societies, growing old was transformed by the social and economic institutions associated with the welfare state and mandatory retirement. Both were instrumental in shaping the dominant discourse around which old age and its associated images and identities were framed (Phillipson, 2013). The idea of 'retirement' was an essential part of the narrative driving the reconstruction of aging. In the 1950s and 1960s, retirement at age 60 (in the case of women) and 65 (in the case of men) became

widely established. Indeed: 'By the late 1960s it was accepted that the *normal* period of full-time employment would cease for *most* of the population at these ages' (Harper and Thane, 1989: 59). Retirement thus became an important economic and social institution regulating the passage from paid employment through to the final stages of the life course (Kohli and Rein, 1991).

This movement of people out of the workplace – at a point marked by the drawing of a publicly-provided old age pension – was further reinforced by the availability of occupational pensions for (in most cases) men from middle class and a limited number of skilled working-class occupations. In the UK, the growth in membership of private sector schemes (along with the steady expansion of the public sector) had been substantial during the period of economic boom in the 1950s and 1960s. The total number of occupational scheme members increased from 8.0 million in 1956 (around one-third of the work force) to 12.2 million in 1967 (almost one-half of the workforce) (Hannah, 1986), a development which – along with support from state pensions – provided the financial basis for the emergence of retirement.

In the case of the UK, the pattern set in the 1950s and 1960s was for most men to remain in work up until age 64 but for a minority staying on for varying lengths of time after their 65th birthday: in 1961, 91 per cent of men aged 60–64 were in paid employment or looking for work, this dropping to 25 per cent for those 65 plus (Lackzo and Phillipson, 1991). From a sociological perspective two important features emerge in the 1960s and the early 1970s regarding the move from work to retirement. First, leaving employment came to be viewed as part of a 'mass transition', with associated 'rites of passage' (Crawford, 1971). Linked with this was a discussion about the value of retirement as a 'distinctive' phase in life, together with the importance of 'preparation for retirement' (Help the Aged, 1979; Phillipson, 1981) and the case for developing a 'third age' built around securing 'personal achievements' separate from those associated with work (Laslett, 1989). Kohli and Rein (1991: 21) summarised this development as follows:

> By the 1960s, retirement for men had become a normal feature of the life course, a taken-for-granted part of one's biography. The modern tripartition of the life course into a period of preparation, one of 'active' work life and one of retirement had become firmly established. Old age had become synonymous with the period of retirement: a life-phase structurally set apart from the 'active' work life and with a relatively uniform beginning defined by the retirement age limit as set by the public old-age pension system. With the increasing labour force participation of women, they too have increasingly been incorporated into this life course regime.

This pattern lasted for a relatively short period of time before being undermined by rising levels of unemployment and redundancies, beginning in the 1960s but accelerating through the 1970s (Dex and Phillipson, 1986). The context here was the decline affecting major industrial sectors across Europe (e.g. steel, mining and shipbuilding), coupled with a global economic crisis (Armstrong et al., 1984), both of these creating mass unemployment and pressures for earlier retirement (McGoldrick and Cooper, 1989; Laczko and Phillipson, 1991). Given a large cohort of younger workers (a result of the early-1960s baby boom), older workers were targeted as a key group to remove from employment. Early retirement came to be viewed as a 'bloodless' way of coping with structural unemployment (Kohli and Rein, 1991) and the need to create jobs for younger workers.

The speed of change was considerable: in 1971, 83 per cent of men 60–64 in the UK were in employment, compared with 19 per cent of those 65 plus; in 1981 the figures had declined to 69 per cent and 10 per cent; and by 1991 to 54 per cent and 10 per cent (Laczko and Phillipson, 1991). Put another way, while in 1950 the average age of exit from employment (for men) was 67.2 years, with a life expectancy of 10.8 years after leaving work, by 2004 life expectancy at age of exit from work had nearly doubled to 20.1 years.

(Pensions Commission, 2004; see further below).

Arising from these trends, a new phase in the relationship between work and retirement was established in the 1970s and 1980s, with researchers drawing a distinction between 'retirement' on the one side and 'early exit' on the other: the former referring to entry into a publicly-provided old-age pension scheme; the latter early withdrawal from paid employment supported through unemployment, disability or associated benefits. Rather than employment ceasing after a set number of years, at a fixed chronological age, there was now a measure of ambiguity about the ending of work and the beginning of retirement. Kohli and Rein (1991: 21) argued that the transition from work to retirement was 'less a matter of following a well-institutionalized and largely self-evident normative schedule, and … more a matter of personal timing'. At the same time, 'counter-transitions' – people moving into or back to what came to be termed as 'bridge jobs' (e.g. part-time or self-employment) became increasingly common.

Walker (2006) suggests that the expansion of early retirement and early exit had three main consequences: first, reconstructing old age from a simple age-related status with a single entry point into a much broader category stretching from around age 50 until death; second, devaluing the role of older people in the labour market and exacerbating age discrimination (see, also, McEwan, 1990); third, creating a view of older people as an economic 'burden' with the potential to undermine intergenerational solidarity (OECD, 1988). At the same time, it is also the case that the 'public image' of retirement began to change in the 1970s and 1980s, with a shift towards 'viewing it as an eagerly anticipated escape from the routine of work to the discretion of leisure' (Hardy, 2011: 215). Arguments emerged suggesting that the extended period of retirement associated with 'early exit' from work could lead to more expansive lifestyles, an approach associated with the idea of a 'third age' of personal development and liberation (Costa, 1998;

Laslett, 1989). Gilleard and Higgs (2000: 34) took the view that:

> In Britain, as in many other countries, increasing number of people aged 55 and over are choosing to retire. The break between ages 64 and 65 for men and 59 and 60 for women, has become a less distinct transition within what amounts to a continuum of 'ages at retirement' ... What evidence there is suggests that a combination of state benefits and occupational private pensions have enabled more people to withdraw themselves from the market, rather than continuing to sell their labour and mortgage their lifetime. (see also Scales and Scase, 2001)

The emphasis on supporting the institution of retirement – a significant theme in social policies during the 1970s and 1980s – was ultimately overtaken by a new set of concerns which started to emerge in the late-1980s but which developed on a much larger scale in the 1990s and 2000s. Finding solutions to the economic and social pressures arising from aging populations came to dominate the policy agenda, with delaying retirement and extending working life emerging as an attractive option (Vickerstaff, 2010). 'Living longer' meant, according to the OECD (2006), that we should also 'work longer': a theme which had already been pursued in labour market strategies through the 1990s but which became even more popular in the 2000s. This aspect is reviewed in the next section of this chapter.

Extending working life and individualising retirement

The 1990s and early-2000s brought a significant change to debates around work and retirement. On the one side, came increasing pressure on individuals to remain in some form of work for as long as possible; on the other side, a decline in the institutional supports associated with the welfare state, with greater emphasis placed on the responsibility of individuals for managing their own retirement. Following the move out of economic recession in the mid-1990s, the pattern of early exit from work went into reverse with

increases in economic activity for men and (much more pronounced) women in their 50s and 60s. Governments became increasingly concerned about the economic consequences of aging populations and the associated costs of pensions and care services (e.g. OECD, 2006). Delaying retirement became a central policy theme, with a shift from promoting early exit/early retirement to identifying pathways into work or helping people to remain at work, combating age discrimination, and encouraging self-employment (Phillipson, 2009a).

In the UK the Pensions Commission (2004: 38) identified improvements in employment in the 1990s among those 50-State Pension Age (SPA) as the result of four main effects:

- *Demand side factors* such as the absence of major macroeconomic shocks comparable to the 1970s/1980s, this producing fewer redundancies and the possibility of re-entry into the labour market once unemployed.
- *Supply side factors* such as changes in pensions with the move from *'defined benefit'* (DB) to *'defined contribution'* (DC) schemes – retirement behaviour in the latter tending towards later retirement given the context of a fall in equity markets and a reduction in annuities, and reduced opportunities for early retirement on grounds of 'ill-health'.[2]
- Pressures arising from the substantial deficits which had developed in many company pension funds.
- Closure or restriction of pathways into early retirement (for example changes in eligibility tests for disability benefits; initiatives to encourage disability beneficiaries back into the workplace).

The resulting trends can be illustrated by reviewing labour participation rates for selected OECD countries for the period 1983 to 2011 (see Tables 25.1 and 25.2). The first half of this period – the mid-1980s – was characterised by the promotion of early exit and early retirement for older workers. The second half of the period – from the mid-1990s – sees attempts by governments to reverse this trend with increased emphasis placed on extending working life. For all the

Table 25.1   Labour force participation rates among men aged 55–64: selected countries

	1983 %	1995 %	1983–1995 %	2001 %	2011 %	1995–2011 %	1983–2011 %
Australia	62.0	60.9	−1.1	60.0	71.6	+10.7	+9.6
Finland	54.1	41.6	−12.5	51.2	61.4	+19.8	+7.3
France	53.6	41.5	−12.1	43.8	47.1	+5.6	−6.5
Germany	63.1	52.7	−10.4	52.2	71.7	+19.0	+8.6
Netherlands	54.1	41.4	−12.7	51.4	68.6	+27.2	+14.5
Portugal	70.4	61.9	−8.5	63.3	61.6	−0.3	−8.8
Spain	71.5	54.9	−16.6	61.4	63.7	+8.8	−7.5
UK	70.0	62.4	−7.6	64.4	68.6	+6.2	−1.4

Source: OECD Economic Outlook (various years)

Table 25.2   Labour force participation rates among women aged 55–64: selected countries

	1983 %	1995 %	1983–95 %	2001 %	2011 %	1995–2011 %	1983–2011 %
Australia	20.5	28.6	+8.1	36.9	55.0	+26.4	+35.0
Finland	47.4	42.9	−4.5	49.5	60.5	+17.6	+13.1
France	32.7	30.9	−1.8	34.1	41.8	+10.9	+9.1
Germany	26.3	28.1	+1.8	33.6	56.7	+28.6	+30.4
Netherlands	13.4	18.6	+5.2	28.3	48.4	+29.8	+35.0
Portugal	33.7	34.5	+4.6	41.5	46.5	+12.0	+12.8
Spain	20.3	19.9	−0.4	23.6	41.7	+22.8	+21.4
UK	36.1	40.8	+4.7	44.0	51.0	+10.2	+14.9

Source: Employment Outlook (various years)

selected countries (with one exception), there were substantial declines in male labour force participation among those 55–64 over the period 1983–1995, with rates starting to fall to around or even below 50 per cent (the trends for France and the Netherlands are especially striking in this regard). Women in contrast show modest gains in employment in some countries, albeit from a very low base (notably so in Germany and the Netherlands) and reflecting in particular the expansion of part-time work in service-related employment.

The period from the mid-1990s to the end of the 2000s demonstrates a contrasting picture. Men show mostly gains in participation, although these are uneven with substantial increases in Finland and the Netherlands but more modest gains elsewhere and virtually no change in the case of Portugal. In the case of women, there are substantial gains in labour force participation – especially in the case of Australia, Germany and the Netherlands. For men, though, the contrast between 1983 and 2011 is instructive: gains there may have been in the period of economic growth during the 1990s up until 2008 but rates in 2011 were still below those in 1983 for a number of countries. Thus despite considerable efforts in countries such as the UK to extol the virtues of older workers, the evidence would suggest significant barriers and rigidities within the labour market limiting their employment (Macnicol, 2006; see further below).

Economic recession in western economies has itself exerted an important influence on the employment of people from mid-life onwards. Arguments about extending working life still have the upper hand, spurred on by pressures to reduce public expenditure and concerns about the impact of the boomer generation (Willetts, 2010; Vickerstaff et al., 2010). And the reality in many countries – with the introduction of later pension ages – is that many workers now face the need to work well into their 60s and for some even later. Against this, older workers have almost certainly experienced an increase in discriminatory pressures during the economic recession following the 2007 financial crisis. In the US, workers aged 45 years and older form a disproportionate share of the long-term unemployed, albeit with a lower unemployment rate compared with younger workers (Ekerdt, 2010). In the UK, the evidence is that once out of employment, those 50 and over find it harder to get back into work in comparison with younger people. The proportion of unemployed 50–64 year olds unemployed for more than a year rose from 33.2 per cent to 44.5 per cent over the period 2008–2012. Older workers also saw the biggest increase in redundancies over this period (Cory, 2012).

Changing patterns of work and retirement from the mid-1990s have been reinforced by a transformation in social policies towards older workers. Walker (2006; see also Phillipson, 2013) summarises this in terms of the 'individualization of risk and welfare', with individuals and families 'taking responsibility for risks that were previously collectivized' (Walker, 2006: 66). Stiglitz (2003) argued that risks had been turned into a 'way of life' through a combination of changes in the labour market (with the erosion of jobs for life) and reliance on private pension arrangements – these subject to the volatility of the global stock market (Blackburn, 2006). And Vickerstaff and Cox (2005: 91) concluded from their interviews with retired and older workers that: 'it is possible to identify a pattern of individualisation in contrast to its opposite of a mass transition into retirement,

collectively understood and embedded in formal, institutionalised arrangements'.

Over the next decade there is likely to be a mix of pressures to extend working life on the one hand, but with 'exclusionary forces' on the other – especially from employers facing pressures to reduce costs in the workplace. And the impact of large-scale unemployment in high- as well as low-income countries may create severe restrictions on the opportunities available to older employees. Such challenges are reinforced by the various transitions affecting people moving from work to retirement, a theme explored in the next section of this chapter.

WORKFORCE AGING: NEW TRANSITIONS AND CHALLENGES

Mid-life and later life transitions

Pressure to adapt to an aging workforce – through policies such as extending working life – are complicated by the range of influences affecting older workers and their position in the labour market. These include, first, the impact of the type of transitions made between work and retirement; second, pressures arising from health changes in later life; and, third, changes in the workplace. In terms of the first of these, all of the 50 plus age group are affected by the evolution of the more complex transitions associated with what may be termed a 'post-industrial' life course. Here, the evidence suggests that the apparent stability of work-retirement transitions in the 1950s and 1960s (limited in any event to men in secure occupations), was almost certainly a brief interlude in what has always been an unsettled period of the life course. What came to be seen as the norm in this period was the idea of a 'crisp' transition from employment to retirement at a standard (for example 60 or 65) age. Increasingly, however, departure from work is 'blurred' rather than 'crisp' and may involve a number of moves in and out of paid work (Phillipson, 2002).

The new transitions from work are reflected in the rise of 'bridging employment' (e.g. part-time work, self-employment) increasingly common for women and men in their 50s and 60s in the UK and the US. Cahill et al.'s (2006: 523) research using data from the US Health and Retirement Study found that the majority of older Americans leaving full-time career employment (about 60 per cent of those leaving a full-time career job after 50 and about 53 per cent of those leaving after the age of 55) moved first to a bridge job rather than directly out of the labour force. Analysis of the British Household Panel Survey (BHPS), examining job movements among men in their 50s, indicated around one in five had spells of part-time, bridging forms of employment (Phillipson, 2002).

On the one hand, such movements might, from one perspective, be taken as illustrative of the emergence of greater choice for individuals in re-shaping the ending of their work careers. Many workers, however, will move into 'bridge employment' out of 'financial necessity' and often into contingent or 'non-core' areas of the workforce (Cahill et al., 2006). Cahill et al. (2006: 523) comment here that:

> Bridge jobs can provide older [workers] with the opportunity to stay active and productive, to experience a different line of work, and to earn income ... For others, however, especially those at the lower end of the socio-economic scale, bridge jobs may reflect financial necessity – an unfortunate and undesirable finale during the twilight of their work career.

Ekerdt (2010: 75), writing from a US perspective, makes the point that the characterisation of bridge jobs has important theoretical and ideological implications. He puts forward the following questions:

> Are older workers strategic, driven by values and goals, and able to control their conditions of work and the course of their late careers? Or, are they buffeted by structural changes at work that threaten their plans for an orderly and secure retirement? ... There is an oft-quoted finding from surveys of older workers that 70% or 80% of respondents ... plan to work to some extent in retirement ... These expectations are wishful and unlikely to be fulfilled, but it is interesting to consider in what proportion they are founded on an upbeat agentic view of one's labor market chances versus a resolution to soldier on due to financial necessity.

Health transitions

The ability to manage health conditions in order to continue in paid employment has always been important for both the individuals whose health is compromised and the organisation trying to retain older workers (Vickerstaff et al., 2013). Poor health and disability have been identified in a range of studies as important factors 'pushing' people out of employment, although this may not be described as 'retirement', and may not be recognised at the time as a permanent move (most of those leaving work between 50 and age 64 move into unemployment or onto disability benefits). Cappellari et al.'s (2005) analysis of British Labour Force Survey (LFS) data found 45 per cent of men aged 50–65 and 41 per cent of women aged 50–60, had experienced a health problem for 12 months or longer.

The association between poor health and early retirement has been examined in a range of quantitative (e.g. Humphrey et al., 2003; McNair et al., 2004; Cappellari et al., 2005) and qualitative (Barnes et al., 2002; Barnes e al., 2004) studies in the UK. Humphrey et al. (2003) examined factors behind labour market participation and withdrawal among those aged 50–69. Among those respondents who had taken early retirement, 49 per cent gave ill-health as one of the reasons, with 53 per cent of men and 44 per cent of women. The lower a person's retirement age, the more likely it was that they would have left because of an illness or disability of some kind; they were also less likely to have an income from a personal pension.

Many countries (including the UK) are now moving towards a pension age of 68 or thereabouts, yet few have thought about how to manage the high prevalence of disability affecting people in their 60s (Vickerstaff et al., 2013). The Marmot Review (2010: 12) in the UK showed that more than three-quarters of the population do not have disability-free life expectancy as far as the age of 68. The Review concluded that: 'If society wishes to have a healthy population, working until age 68 years, it is essential to take action to both raise the general level of health and flatten [health inequalities between different groups]'.

Workplace transitions

Ekerdt (2010: 74) poses the question: 'has the labour market become more welcoming to older workers, accommodating them in ways that could sustain an expansion in employment in later life?' The evidence here would suggest only a limited response by employers to assist those wishing to extend their working life. Sennett (2006) suggests that the collapse of the work-based bureaucracies associated with what he terms 'social capitalism' has fostered a rise in 'precarious' and 'insecure' employment. Levels of workplace insecurity were high even before the economic recession following the 2007 credit crunch: data from the 2004 Survey of Health, Aging and Retirement in Europe (SHARE) indicates workers 50 plus ranking their job security as poor varying from 18 per cent in Sweden to 34 per cent in the Netherlands, with a median value of 23 per cent (Hank and Erlinghagen, 2009). Green (2005) reviewed a number of large data sets which indicated significant declines in job satisfaction over the course of the 1990s.

The programme of research on *Transitions to Retirement* conducted by the Joseph Rowntree Foundation (e.g. Barnes et al., 2002; Arthur, 2003) found that many people leaving work early disliked their jobs because they felt they were not leading anywhere, and felt undervalued by employers. Siegrist et al.'s (2007) survey of ten European countries found that poor quality of work was significantly associated with early retirement. In the UK survey by Humphrey et al. (2003), 31 per

cent of men gave a work-related reason for their early retirement; 37 per cent in the case of women. Eleven per cent of men and 16 per cent of women reported that their work had become too 'physically demanding'; 8 per cent of both that it had become too stressful. Such findings are reflected in the extent of 'underemployment' or 'semi-employment' affecting a substantial group of older workers – around one-fifth of men in their fifties according to one estimate for the United States (Sennett, 2006).

All of the above findings raise important issues for policy goals aimed at extending working life. Moreover, additional problems associated with this policy are important to highlight. From a social class perspective, policies to increase pension ages raise a number of concerns. They appear to take as self-evident the desirability of working additional years, this viewed as acceptable given increased life expectancy and necessary as a means of reducing the cost of pensions. But such measures may be seen as especially unfair on working class groups whose lower life expectancy means that they will draw their pension for a significantly shorter period in comparison with those from professional and managerial groups. A further concern is that increasing numbers of workers will be forced to remain in employment despite major health problems, with many experiencing downward mobility through a move into low-paid, part-time working. In reality, many workers may find higher state pension ages an unfair exchange between guaranteed retirement benefits on the one side, and insecure employment on the other (see Ghilarducci, 2004, for evidence from the US on this point). Of course, good quality part-time working (or so-called 'bridge employment') may be one option, and opportunities for this may be greater in the context of a fluid and open labour market (Ekerdt, 2010). But, equally, part-time work is often poorly paid with limited opportunities for training and skill development. Developing policies that can address poor quality work environments must be an essential part of any realistic strategy for extending working life as well as helping to improve the experience of people entering retirement.

OCCUPATIONAL AND SOCIAL POLICIES FOR NEW LIFE COURSE TRANSITIONS

Achieving greater security for older workers, faced with a range of transitions, will require initiatives in a number of areas, with particular emphasis around: first, promoting occupational health; second, extending the scope of flexible employment; third, supporting education and training. Each of these will now be reviewed.

Developing health interventions and improving the quality of work

As discussed previously in this chapter, research has confirmed the importance of ill-health and disability as factors which can lead to premature withdrawal from the workplace. This is especially the case for men and women in routine or manual employment, with one-third of men in their 50s in the UK reporting a long-standing limiting illness. By comparison, similar rates for men from professional and managerial backgrounds are not reached until they are aged over 75: what Yeandle (2005: 2) refers to as a '20 year "illness gap"'. The significance of this needs greater recognition in respect of a preventative approach to health issues at work. Awareness of the importance of this area is longstanding, both in the British context (e.g. Health Education Authority, 1994), and elsewhere in Europe – notably the Finnish Older Workers' Programme (1998–2002).

Hirsch (2003: 13–14) makes the case for re-focusing attention not so much on matching workers to jobs but on 'matching jobs to workers'. He highlights that the fact that:

In some European countries, most notably Finland, efforts to integrate older people into employment have aimed to combine an improvement in occupational health with changes in the workplace. Finland's Programme on Aging Workers (1998–2002) was aimed at improving attitudes to older workers and services available to them, as well as their preparedness for employment … This high-profile campaign has made Finnish employers aware of the need for greater flexibility in the way they structure work, both in terms of assigning occupational roles and in making flexible working hours available in cases where these are needed.

Phillipson et al. (2013: 277) argue that the first stage in developing effective interventions must be to address the still limited understanding about the impact of health problems within the workplace. They note that: 'Lack of detailed information is still leading to off-the-shelf interventions focusing on single issues rather than the combination of conditions affecting people in middle and older age'. In short, it remains the case that extending working life will prove difficult unless more general steps are taken to improve both the quality of work and the management of physical and mental health conditions within the workplace. Research, as noted above, highlights job insecurity, limited support for working carers, and poor quality employment as factors precipitating departure from work. Further research is needed to identify specific policies aimed at improving quality of life in the workplace and their possible benefits for extending working life. More information is also required about the problems facing specific groups – in particular those from routine and manual work occupations; those involved in informal care; and those with mental health problems (see, further, Vickerstaff et al., 2013).

Extending the scope of flexible employment

Despite interest and attention to promoting flexible pathways from work to retirement, the evidence at present suggest these remain narrow in scope and limited to particular groups of workers and specific occupations. The lack of progress must be a concern given the extensive debate around encouraging gradual forms of retirement. Platman (2004: 3) makes the point that:

> Policy-makers and campaigning groups have been advocating a more flexible approach to later careers for many years. In 1980, the International Labour Organisation recommended that its member states introduce measures which ensured a gradual transition from work to retirement, by adopting voluntary, flexible ages for retirement and pension eligibility ... Since then, flexible employment as a solution to 'the problem' of older workers has surfaced with increasing regularity in a broad range of international policy briefings, research reports, academic texts and good practice guides.

Loretto et al. (2005) have highlighted some of the difficulties in this area, notably around problems of providing good quality flexible employment and resolving difficulties presented by tax and occupational pension rules. Currently, the implications of the research evidence to date is that: (a) very few workers get access to high quality flexible employment, and (b) that options in this area remain limited. Loretto et al. (2005: 153) note that: 'The majority of older workers currently work standard full-time patterns of work; with the exception of part-time work there is little evidence of other forms of flexible working such as temporary work or term-time working.'

Implementing flexible working raises a number of difficulties for older workers and employers. Platman (2004) makes the point that flexibility may have perverse consequences. Extended breaks from the labour market can create problems unless supported by work-related training and refresher courses. The issue of low pay is also a key concern for those 'stepping down' from full-time to part-time work. Flexibility for older workers is already a feature of labour force management with adjustment of working hours, and earlier, gradual or delayed retirement. The difficulty is that this type of flexibility is often 'externally directed' rather than something that individuals are able to determine and control for themselves.

The policy issue therefore involves, first, ensuring that significant numbers of older workers are not excluded from the benefits of flexible employment; and, second, ensuring that this does not lead to a lowering of status and reduced economic benefits within the workplace. The type of initiatives that might support such a policy could include:

- Those designed to create great choice and flexibility about moves in and out of work (such as career breaks and time credit systems), with the possibility of spreading paid work more evenly across the life course (see further Phillipson, 2002).
- Those tailored to the needs of specific groups (e.g. those with mental health problems, those balancing work with care responsibilities) (see further Irvine, 2013; Vickerstaff et al., 2009).
- Those which enhance the capacity of older workers as a group – through training, improvements to the work environment, lifelong learning, the development of anti-discrimination policies.
- Those which encourage support towards the end of working life, with the promotion of gradual retirement and preparation for retirement.

Supporting education and training

Building on the above arguments, improving the position of older workers will also require new initiatives in the area of education and training. However, the evidence suggests that older workers continue to lose out on access to support in this area. Humphrey et al. (2003), in research from the UK, found that while most employees received some encouragement to learn more job-related skills, this tended to tail-off after 50–54. Thus among men, 58 per cent had received a 'great deal' or a 'fair amount' of encouragement, this compared with 41 per cent for those 60–64 and 35 per cent for those 65–69. Among women, the equivalent figures for the 50–54 and 60–64 age groups were 63 per cent and 40 per cent.

Lissenburgh and Smeaton's (2003) analysis of LFS data confirmed the link between increased age and declining access to training. Logistic regression models used in their study suggested that men and women in part-time and temporary employment were especially disadvantaged in respect of training. Humphreys et al. (2003) also found that the level of encouragement to undertake training varied between full-and part-time employees. In their survey one-third of part-time employees were offered no encouragement to learn more job-related skills, compared with one-quarter of full-time employees. Carmichael and Ercolani (2012: 2), analysing European Labour Force Survey data, find that across the 15 member states prior to the 2004 enlargement: 'not only are older people less likely to be involved in any kind of training, they are also less likely to participate in training that is work-related or undertaken during working hours. The duration of training they do is also likely to be shorter.'

Developing new training initiatives targeted at older workers will require recognition of the different kinds of support likely to be required. For example, among those in their late-40s to mid-50s, demand for job training and professional courses is likely to increase, since many in this age group will have a substantial number of working years to complete before eligibility for a pension. Many in this age group will have been part of the expansion of higher and further education from the 1970s onwards and may view lifelong learning as an essential part of continued employment. Among those in their late-50s and 60s, the need for new skills may be an essential requirement if meaningful employment is to be secured. Mayhew and Rijkers (2004: 2), in a review for the OECD, stress the importance of 'continuous learning during the whole of working life as a means of reducing the dangers of labour market disadvantage in later years'. Policies for change will need to focus on the following areas:

- first, developing entitlements for 'third age learning';
- second, re-assessing methodologies and techniques for training older workers;
- third, expanding provision for those in non-standard forms of employment;
- fourth, developing the involvement of higher and further education.

The first of the above was addressed by Schuller and Watson (2009) as part of the *Inquiry into the Future of Lifelong Learning.* In their recommendations for change they set out a four-stage model to encourage learning across the life course, recognising different periods of development in the years up to 25, 25–50, 50–74 and 75 plus. They suggest that what has been termed the 'Third Age' (50–74) should be viewed as a central period for encouraging enhanced training and education opportunities, based upon a more even distribution of work across the life course. This would be buttressed by: (a) a fairer allocation of educational resources (public, private and employer-based) to meet the needs of third and fourth age (those aged 75 plus) groups; (b) a legal entitlement of free access to learning to acquire basic skills (e.g. in literacy and numeracy); (c) a 'good practice' entitlement to learning leave as an occupational benefit; (d) specific 'transition entitlements' e.g. for people on their 50th birthday, to 'signal the continuing potential for learning of those moving into the third age' (Schuller and Watson, 2009: 133).

The second area raises issues about developing more effective training programmes targeted at older adults. The research evidence reviewed above suggests that employer (or line manager) 'discouragement' partly explains decreasing participation in training. Yet it is also clear that this not a complete explanation for the problem. In particular, workers themselves may consider – after a certain age or stage in their career – that further training is unnecessary. Or, as is also possible, they may feel that the type of training and learning they are likely to receive is inappropriate given their level of skill and experience. Czaja and Sharit (2009: 266) make the point that although many existing training techniques are effective for older adults, we lack an adequate research database to 'determine whether some training techniques are consistently differentially beneficial to older workers'. On the other hand, literature from work-based psychological studies has demonstrated the benefits as well as limitations of particular approaches to training involving older workers. Tsang (2009: 289), for example, cites a number of studies which demonstrate how relatively small amounts of training can reverse cognitive decline and assist the retention of newly acquired skills. Conversely, the limitations of training benefits are also noted, these including reduced magnitude of learning and slower learning rates. Given the emergence of a more diverse aging workforce, attention to new ways of delivering work-based training would seem an urgent requirement. One suggestion here would be to encourage a single organisation to lead research and policy initiatives linking trades unions, business organisations and government around the theme of training for an aging workforce. This would require dedicated funding and staffing but could be the responsibility of a non-governmental organisation (NGO) specialising in the employment field.

The third area concerns the need to encourage training programmes specifically targeted at those in part-time and flexible forms of employment, and with those older workers who are self-employed. The issues here have been summarised by Czaja and Sharit (2009: 259) as follows:

> ... as the number of workers in non-standard work arrangements ... continues to increase, one important issue confronting workers will be access to traditional workplace benefits such as training. [Such] workers will be less likely to receive structured company-sponsored training and the responsibility of continuous learning and job training will fall to a greater extent on the individual. It is not yet clear how to best develop and disseminate training programs to promote lifelong learning for these 'non-traditional' workers. This issue is especially pertinent for older workers, given that they are less likely to be provided with access to training and development programmes in traditional work environments where company-sponsored training is available.

There are no immediate solutions to the problems facing part-time and related groups of workers. On the one side, studies already cited (e.g. those by Lissenburgh and Smeaton,

2003; Humphrey et al., 2003) highlight inequalities between full- and part-time workers in respect of access to training. Such difficulties are unlikely to have changed – they have probably worsened – in the period since the research was published. On the other side, opportunities from providers such as community and further education colleges have been steadily reduced, with the major focus now placed on preparing younger people for entry into the labour market. Some options for consideration here might include: first, adoption of Schuller and Watson's (2009) plan for legal and transitional entitlements (mentioned earlier), a proposal highly relevant to those entering non-standard and flexible forms of employment; second, more imaginative use of computer-based training or 'e-learning' to assist those working from home or those juggling work and caregiving responsibilities (Czaja and Sharit, 2009); third, specific obligations placed upon employers to expand training and learning as a pre-condition for creating non-standard forms of employment.

The final area for discussion concerns encouraging closer involvement from higher and further education in responding to the needs of older workers, with the development of new programmes or the adaptation of existing courses. Older students have always had an important presence in university adult education classes, with those over 50 comprising the majority of participants. They also form a significant group studying for part-time degrees and programmes related to continuing professional development (Phillipson, 2010; Phillipson and Ogg, 2010). The number of older learners moving into higher education will almost certainly increase given broader demographic and social changes. Key factors are likely to include, first, the demand for vocational and non-vocational courses coming from 'first wave' baby boomers (those born in the late-1940s and early-1950s), a larger proportion of whom – in comparison with earlier cohorts – have degrees and related qualifications; second, the need for new qualifications among those changing careers in mid and later working life. Reflecting this development, three pathways might be followed by higher education institutions to support older workers:

- *educational and personal development programmes*: these would build upon existing work in adult and continuing education, but would identify new types of courses and markets among a diverse and segmented post-50s market.
- *employment-related programmes*: these might support the policy objective of extending working life, although the extent of employer demand may be fragile in the context of high levels of unemployment. The development of courses supporting people moving from full-time paid employment to various forms of self-employment may, however, remain a source of growth among higher education institutions (HEIs).
- *social inclusion programmes*: substantial numbers of older people – in current as well as succeeding cohorts – remain educationally and socially disadvantaged. HEIs, with partners such as local authorities, further education colleges and the major national charities, should focus on a 'widening participation' agenda that covers all age groups and not just younger adults.

CONCLUSION: BUILDING NEW RESEARCH AGENDAS

Changing patterns of work and retirement raise major questions for social and public policy in the twenty-first century. A key issue concerns how to handle the legacy of the 20th century – namely the institutionalisation of retirement as a major part of the life course. The acceptance of early retirement in the 1970s and 1980s accelerated the growth of post-work lifestyles, consolidated by the cohort of 'first wave' baby boomers. Both aspects are now in collision with the drive to delay retirement and put in place later pension ages. Such policies must themselves be considered as conditional upon major improvements to the quality of work, early intervention to support people with long-term health conditions, and a radical overhaul of the current system of education and training. The danger is that without these people will

be increasingly caught between insecure work on the one side and an increasingly insecure retirement on the other.

The issues identified in the chapter indicate the basis for a new research agenda around the theme of older workers and transitions from work to retirement. Identifying links between attitudes to work and expectations and experiences about retirement has become an important issue for sociological research. This area has always been significant for social gerontology but demographic and economic changes have placed issues affecting older workers a key issue for social science in general. The reasons for this include: first, the impact of the boomer cohort and the tension between relatively high expectations about retirement but anxieties about the adequacy of retirement income; second, the importance of the extended working life agenda for employers and employees; third, pressures within the workplace associated with job insecurity and work-related stress; fourth, the increasing diversity of older workers, notably in respect of gender and ethnicity.

A number of important research issues arise from the changing landscape of work and retirement. The most important of these include: How will older workers reconcile pressures to remain in the workplace with continuing aspirations to develop new life styles in retirement? How will the work environment need to change to support individuals with responsibilities beyond paid employment, or those with long-term health conditions, or those interested in moving to new types of work? How will the training and education system respond to the needs of an aging workforce? To what extent will an extended working life reproduce, modify or accentuate inequalities accumulated through the life course? What is the range of transitions through middle and late life likely to emerge with new and more diverse cohorts of older people? These and many other questions highlight the extent to which the interaction between aging, work and society touches key issues of concern for the range of disciplines within social science. Strengthening the contribution of social science to research and policy on older workers will be a vital task for researchers and policy-makers in the years ahead.

NOTES

1   Some of the arguments in this paper were originally developed in Phillipson (2011); see also Phillipson and Smith (2005). Taylor (2010) provides a wide-ranging comparative review of work and retirement trends.
2   Defined contribution schemes favour later retirement ages where there is a fall in equity markets and a reduction in the value of annuities (see, further, Phillipson, 2009b).

REFERENCES

Armstrong, P., Glyn, A. and Harrison, J (1984) *Capitalism since 1945*. London: Fontana Books.

Arthur, S. (2003) *Money, Choice and Control*. Bristol/York: Policy Press/Joseph Rowntree Foundation.

Barnes, H., Parry, J. and Lakey, J. (2002) *Forging a New Future: The experiences and expectations of people leaving paid work over 50*. Bristol: Policy Press/Joseph Rowntree Foundation.

Barnes, H., Parry, J. and Taylor, R. (2004) *Working after State Pension Age: Qualitative Research Report*. Research Report No. 208. London: Department of Work and Pensions.

Blackburn, R. (2006) *Age Shock: How finance is failing us*. London: Verso.

Cahill, K., Giandrea, M. and Quinn, J. (2006) 'Retirement patterns from career employment'. *The Gerontologist*, 46: 514–23

Cappellari, L., Dorsett, R. and Haile, G. (2005) *Labour Market Transitions among the Over-50s*. London: Department of Work and Pensions.

Carmichael, F. and Ercolani, M. (2012) 'Age-training gaps in the European Union'. *Ageing and Society*, available on CJO 2012 doi: 10.1017/S014468X12000852. Accessed August 12 2012

Cory, G. (2012) *Unfinished Business: Barriers and opportunities for older workers*. London: Resolution Foundation.

Costa, D. (1998) *The Evolution of Retirement*. Chicago, IL: Chicago University Press.

Crawford, M. (1971) 'Retirement and Disengagement'. *Human Relations*, 24: 217–36.

Czaja, S. and Sharit, J. (2009) *Aging and Work: Issues and implications in a changing landscape*. Baltimore: Johns Hopkins.

Dex, S. and Phillipson, C. (1986) 'Social Policy and the Older Worker'. In Phillipson, C. and Walker, A. *Ageing and Social Policy*. Aldershot: Gower., pp. 45-60.

Ekerdt, D. (2010) 'Frontiers of research on work and retirement'. *Journal of Gerontology: Social Sciences*, 65B(1): 69–80.

Ford, G. (2005) 'Am I Still Needed: Guidance and Learning for Older Adults'. Summary of Report in Hirsch, D. (ed.) *Sustaining Working Lives: A Framework for Policy and Practice*. York: Joseph Rowntree Foundation.

Ghilarducci, T. (2004) *The Political Economy of 'Pro-Work' Retirement Policies and Responsible Accumulation*. University of Notre Dame, Indiana. Available online at: www.havenscenter.org/real_utopias/2004documents/Ghilarducci%paper.pdf Accessed July 6th 2012

Gilleard, C. and Higgs, P. (2000) *Cultures of Ageing*. London: Prentice Hall.

Green, F. (2005) *Understanding Trends in Job Satisfaction: Final Report*. Report to the Economic and Social Research Council. Swindon: ESRC.

Hank, K. and Erlinghagen, M. (2009) *Perceptions of Job Security in Europe's Ageing Workforce*. MEA Discussion Paper (176–09) Mannheim: University of Mannheim.

Hannah, L. (1986) *Inventing Retirement*. Cambridge: Cambridge University Press.

Hardy, M. (2011) 'Rethinking retirement'. In Settersten, R and Angel, J. (eds) *Handbook of Sociology of Aging*. New York: Springer, pp. 213–228.

Harper, S. and Thane, P. (1989) 'The consolidation of old age as a phase of life, 1945–1965'. In Jeffreys, M. (ed.) *Growing Old in the Twentieth Century*. London: Routledge, pp. 43–61.

Health Education Authority (HEA) (1994) *Investing in Older People at Work*. London: HEA.

Help the Aged (1979) *Time of Your Life: A handbook for retirement*. London: Help the Aged.

Hirsch, D. (2003) *Crossroads after 50: Improving choices in work and retirements*. York: Joseph Rowntree Foundation.

Humphrey, A., Costigan, A., Pickering, K. , Stratford, N. and Barnes, M. (2003) *Factors Affecting the Labour Market: Participation of older workers*. London: Department of Work and Pensions.

Irvine, A. (2013) 'Common mental health problems and work'. In Vickerstaff, S., Phillipson, C. and Wilkie, R. (eds) *Work Health and Well-Being: The challenges of managing health at work*. Bristol: Policy Press, pp. 39–58.

Kohli, M. and Rein, M (1991) 'The changing balance of work and retirement'. In Kohli, M., Rein, M.,

Guillemard, A.-M. and van Gunstern, H. (1991) *Time for Retirement: Comparative studies of early exits from the labour force.* Cambridge: Cambridge University Press, pp. 1–35.

Laczko, F. and Phillipson, C (1991) *Changing Work and Retirement.* Milton Keynes: Open University Press.

Laslett, P. (1989) *A Fresh Map of Life.* London: Weidenfeld and Nicolson.

Lissenburgh, S. and Smeaton, D. (2003) *Employment Transitions of Older Workers: The role of flexible employment in maintaining labour market participation and promotion of job quality.* Bristol/York: Policy Press/Joseph Rowntree Foundation.

Lorretto, W., Vickerstaff, S. and White, P. (2005) 'Flexible work and older workers'. In Loretto, W., Vickerstaff, S. and White, P. (eds) *The Future for Older Workers.* Bristol: Policy Press, pp. 139–160.

McEwan, E. (ed.) (1990) *Age: The Unrecognised Discrimination.* London: Age Concern England.

McGoldrick, A. and Cooper, C. (1989) *Early Retirement.* Aldershot: Gower.

McNair, S., Flynn, M., Owen, L., Humphreys, C. and Woodfield, S. (2004) *Changing Work in Later Life: A study of job transitions,* University of Surrey: Centre for Research into the Older Workforce.

Macnicol, J. (2006) *Age Discrimination: An Historical and Contemporary Analysis.* Cambridge: Cambridge University Press.

Marmot, M. (2010) *The Marmot Review: Fair society, healthy Lives.* London: Strategic Review of Health Inequalities.

Mayhew, K. and Rijkers, B. (2004) 'How to improve the human capital of older workers, or the sad tale of the magic bullet'. Paper prepared for the joint EC OECD seminar on Human Capital and Labour Market Performance, held in Brussels on 8 December 2004.

Organisation of Economic Co-operation and Development (1988) *Reforming Public Pensions.* Paris: OECD.

Organisation of Economic Co-operation and Development (2006) *Live Longer, Work Longer.* Paris: OECD.

Pensions Commission (2004) *Pensions: Challenges and Choices. The First Report of the Pensions Commission.* London: The Stationery Office (TSO).

Phillipson, C. (1981) 'Pre-retirement education: The British and American experience'. *Ageing and Society,* 1: 392–414.

Phillipson, C. (2002) *Transitions from Work to Retirement: Developing a new social contract.* Bristol/York: The Policy Press/Joseph Rowntree Foundation.

Phillipson, C. (2009a) 'Changing life course transitions: implications for work and lifelong learning'. In Chiva,

A. and Manthorpe, J. (eds) *Older Workers in Europe.* Maidenhead: Open University Press, pp. 110–126.

Phillipson, C. (2009b) 'Pensions in crisis: Aging and inequality in a global age'. In Rogne, L., Estes, C., Grossman, B., Hollister, B and Solway, E. (eds) *Social Insurance and Social Justice.* New York: Springer Publishing Company, pp. 319–340.

Phillipson, C. (2010) 'Active ageing and universities: engaging older learners'. *International Journal of Education and Ageing,* 1 (1): 9–23.

Phillipson, C. (2011) 'Extending Working Life and Re-defining Retirement: Problems and Challenges for Social Policy'. In Ennals, R and Salomon, R. (eds) *Older Workers in a Sustainable Society.* Frankfurt am Main: Peter Lang. pp. 245–252.

Phillipson, C. (2013) *Ageing.* Cambridge: Polity Press.

Phillipson, C. and Ogg, J (2010) *Active Ageing and Universities: Engaging older learners.* London: Universities UK.

Phillipson, C. and Smith, A. (2005) *Extending Working Life: A review of the research literature.* London: Department of Work and Pensions, Research Report No. 299.

Platman, K. (2004) 'Flexible employment in later life: public policy panaceas in the search for mechanisms to extend working lives', *Social Policy and Society,* 3 (2): 181–188.

Scales, J. and Scase, R. (2001) *Fit at Fifty.* Swindon: Economic and Social Research Council.

Schuller, T. and Watson, D. (2009) *Learning through Life.* Leicester: NIACE.

Siegrist, J. , Wahrendorf, M., von dem Knesebeck, O., Jürges, H., A, Börsch-Supan (2007) 'Quality of work, well-being and intended early retirement of older workers'. *European Journal of Public Health,* 17 (1): 62–68.

Sennett, R. (2006) *The Culture of the New Capitalism.* New Haven, CT: Yale University Press.

Stiglitz, J. (2003) *The Roaring Nineties.* London: Penguin Books.

Taylor, P. (2010) 'Cross-national trends in work and retirement'. In Dannefer, D. and Phillipson, C. (eds) *The Sage Handbook of Social Gerontology.* London: Sage, pp. 540–550.

Tsang, T. (2009) 'Age and performance measures of knowledge-based work: a cognitive perspective', in Czaja, S.J. and Sharit, J. (eds) *Aging and Work: Issues and implications in a changing landscape.* Baltimore, NJ: The John Hopkins University Press, pp. 279–306

Vickerstaff, S. (2010) 'Older workers: The "unavoidable obligation" of extending our working lives?' *Sociology Compass,* 4: 869–879.

Vickerstaff, S. and Cox, J. (2005) Retirement and risk: the individualisation of retirement and experiences? *The Sociological Review*, 53: 77–95.

Vickerstaff, S., Loretto, W., Milne, A., Alder, E. and Billings, J. and White, P. (2009) *Employer Support for Carers*. Research Report 597. London: Department of Work and Pensions.

Vickerstaff, S., Phillipson, C. and Wilkie, R. (eds) (2013) *Work Health and Well-Being: The challenges of managing health at work*. Bristol: Policy Press.

Walker, A. (2006) 'Reexamining the political economy of ageing: understanding the structure/agency tension'. In Baars, J., Dannefer, D., Phillipson, C. and Walker, A. (eds) *Aging, Globalization and Inequality*. New York, Amityville: Baywood, pp. 59–80.

Willetts, D. (2010) *The Pinch*. London: Atlantic Books.

Yeandle, S. (2005) 'Older workers and work–life balance'. In Hirsch, D. (ed) *Sustaining Working Lives: A framework for policy and practice*. York: Joseph Rowntree Foundation.

26

Policies for Older Adult Learning: The Case of the European Union

Marvin Formosa

INTRODUCTION

Older adult learning has gained an ever-present presence in international and national policies on lifelong learning. An increasing preoccupation with the crises in fiscal competitiveness and political integration has elevated lifelong learning in later life as a key tactic in improving economic development and social cohesion. Older adult learning is presently regarded as a necessary lubricant for a smooth transition to an upcoming scenario where the number of older adults will outnumber children, a state of affairs that will have deep socio-economic impacts on post-industrial societies. The European Union (EU) is no exception. Continuous learning through life deemed as a comprehensive strategy to meet the requirements for a Single European Market as well as address the repercussions of increasing structural unemployment. In view of the aging of European society – due to falling birth rates, shrinking family sizes, fewer numbers of young people in the labour market, and increasing life expectancies – recent EU directives on lifelong learning advised formal and non-formal learning providers of education to plan and implement further educational opportunities for older adults (EC, 2006a, 2007). Indeed, the EU considers late-life learning as a positive investment on the basis that not only it engenders positive returns of economic growth, but also improves the quality of life and social development of older persons. This chapter presents a critical analysis of that interface between older adult learning and lifelong learning in a EU context. It includes four parts. Whilst the first introduces the key dynamics of older adult learning, the second focuses on EU policy on lifelong and late-life learning. The third part provides a constructive critique of EU policy on older adult learning by uncovering a range of social, economic, and ageist biases. The final part forwards proposes a future agenda for late-life learning policy for the EU.

OLDER ADULT LEARNING

Older adult learning refers to the process in which older adults, 'individually and in association with others, engage in direct encounter and then purposefully reflect upon, validate, transform, give personal meaning to and seek to integrate their ways of knowing' (Mercken, 2010: 9). As is expected, older adult learning takes place in formal, non-formal, and informal avenues. Older adults constitute a minority in formal education. For instance, a study on higher education in the United Kingdom (UK) found that during the 2008–2009 academic year only some 4,000 first-year students (0.7 percent of total) aged 50-plus were enrolled in undergraduate and postgraduate courses (Phillipson and Ogg, 2010). This age-group was, however, better represented with respect to part-time study, comprising 15 and 10 percent of part-time undergraduates and postgraduates (respectively) which, in numerical terms, totalled up to 62,000 students (ibid.). On the other hand, non-formal learning avenues have always been highly successful in attracting older adults. The past three decades saw a steep proliferation of third-age learning programs catering exclusively to the interests of older adults such as Universities of the Third Age, Elderhostels, Lifelong Learning Institutes, and University Programs for Older People (Findsen and Formosa, 2011). In Europe, trade union education, liberal education, folk high schools, as well as universities and non-formal study circles are amongst various types of learning open to third agers. In North America, practice in older adult education has transformed itself from operating in a social service framework to an entrepreneurial one and part of the so-called 'silver industry'. However, one also finds various examples of late-life learning programs in low-income countries (ibid.). The appeal of non-formal learning lies in the opportunity to engage in serious learning projects, socialize with peers, and engaging in physical and cognitive activities, but without any pressures of accreditation and assessment whatsoever. Similarly, older persons are also extensively involved in informal modes of learning – in a variety of contexts ranging from the family, religious institutions, mass media, the workplace, volunteering, and various community-based initiatives – as well as through the creative use of museums, theatres, libraries, online surfing, and travel (Findsen, 2005).

Comparative data on participation rates are sporadic, and the few that exist tend to be 'unreliable' and 'not comparable' as they include different definitions of 'non-formal' and 'informal' learning (Percy and Frank, 2011). It is lamentable that most educational statistics – including those issued by Eurostat – take the age of 65 as a cut-off point. Yet, a review of the literature elicits three persistent findings – namely, a lower percentage of elder learners compared to younger peers, a sharp decline of participation as people reached their seventh decade, and that typical learners are middle-class women so that the working classes, older men, and elders from rural communities and ethnic minorities are highly underrepresented. A recent survey conducted in the UK concluded that 'the older people are, the less likely they are to participate in learning', with participation declining especially 'for those aged 55 and over, such as that only 33 per cent of adults aged 55–64, 23 per cent of adults aged 65–74 and 14 per cent of those aged 75 and over regard themselves as learners' (Aldridge and Tuckett, 2010: 19). Various propositions have been put forward to explain why participation declines with age. Whilst there will always be some older persons who are not interested in taking part in learning activities, the consensus is that potential participants face four types of barriers which become more intense with increasing chronological ages. These include situational barriers (obstacles relating to the unique circumstances of later life), institutional barriers (unintended barriers erected by learning organizations that exclude subaltern elders), informational barriers (failure of agencies to communicate what learning are available), and psychosocial barriers (attitudinal beliefs and perceptions that inhibit a person's participation) barriers (Findsen, 2005).

For many years, older adults have been stereotyped as participating in more expressive than instrumental forms of learning. This developed out of the assumption that in retirement people prefer to devote time to personal development tasks as opposed to learning vocational skills associated with the labour market. Yet, whilst the interest of older adults to engage in expressive learning programs can never be overstated, this narrow and binary approach to describe educational participation in later life is obsolete nowadays. Whilst in the UK information and communication technology has taken over from the humanities as the most popular subject, with more than half the learners over 65 claiming 'computer skills' as their main subject of study (Aldridge and Tuckett, 2010), a Canadian survey found older learners to be highly goal-oriented so that participation in technological learning programs ranked highest amongst respondents (Sloane-Seale and Kops, 2004). Another study, specifically geared towards older adults from economically deprived areas of Glasgow (Findsen and McCullough, 2008), also provides firm evidence that older people are greatly motivated to study a wide range of instrumental forms of curriculum. It is also noteworthy that in OECD (Organization for Economic Co-operation and Development) countries some 25 percent of older workers (55+) were found to have participated in training programs, although in some countries – such as Japan (51 percent) – participation rates were even higher (OECD, 2004). This shift reflects wider and important changes in aging transitions. Whilst many older adults continue to pursue learning for pleasure purposes, an increasing number are engaging in learning to enhance or change their careers, to fulfil lifelong ambitions, and seize the opportunities that they were denied earlier in life. Retirement is no longer a passive stage of the life course where incumbents reach out to learning simply to age actively and successfully. Rather, it should be acknowledged that older people are active and useful citizens who seek out learning opportunities that aid them to continue living their lives as productively as possible.

A key debate in older adult learning is concerned not with 'whether we can or cannot teach or retrain an older adult' but 'to what end?' and 'why?'. Late-life learning is commended for aiding adults adjust to the transformations that accompany 'old age' such as decreasing physical strength and health, the retirement transition, reduced income, death of spouse, and changing social and civic obligations (Rowe and Kahn, 1999). However, Glendenning and Battersby (1990) posited a more radical agenda and bestow late-life learning the task of achieving the 'liberation of elders' – that is, empowering older persons with the advocacy skills necessary to counter-act the social and financial disadvantages brought on by neo-liberal politics of aging. From a humanistic point of view, learning is perceived as a 'personal quest', a necessary activity if older adults are to achieve the potential within them (Percy, 1990). This rationale prioritizes 'process' over 'content' by stressing that the role of an educator 'is to facilitate the process of learning for the learner rather than persuade him [sic] to social action or to be dissatisfied if a certain political awareness is not achieved' (ibid.: 237). Finally, transcendence rationales argue that learning must not let adults forget that they are old and are to enable them 'to know themselves as a whole, as they really are, in the light of finitude and at the horizon of death' (Moody, 1990: 37). Learning thus arises as an opportunity to explore goals that younger peers are too busy to pursue such as developing a reflective mode of thinking and contemplating the meaning of life. Although these rationales include various valid arguments, it is also possible they miss the point. Industrial societies have now reached a 'late' phase of modernity, wherein people's lives are characterized by 'instability' and 'risk' – economic, political, and social – and hence, personal and social disorientation. In Bauman's words,

Society is being transformed by the passage from the 'solid' to the 'liquid' phases of modernity, in which all social forms melt faster than new ones can be cast. They are not given enough time to solidify, and cannot serve as the frame of reference for human actions and long-term life-strategies because their allegedly short life-expectation undermines efforts to develop a strategy that would require the consistent fulfilment of a life-project. (Bauman, 2005a: 303)

In the contemporary life-world, aging has become increasingly marked by a blurring of what appeared previously to be the typical behavior associated with this stage. Whilst in the past the aging self was based on occupational biographies and incumbents' relationship to the welfare state, presently 'the old have moved into a new "zone of indeterminacy" [so that] growing old is itself becoming a more social, reflexive and managed process, notably in the relationship between the individual, the state and a range of public as well as private services' (Phillipson and Powell, 2004: 21, 22). Yet, the aforementioned rationales persist in operating within 'grand narrative' frameworks which embed older adult learning in strict, and therefore, limiting ideological constraints. Overcoming such a lacuna necessitates the shifting of 'the debate away from the policy maker and practitioner perspectives on *education* towards *learning* [to] ensure that the voices of older learners themselves, hitherto largely ignored, can emerge' (Withnall, 2006: 30 – italics in original). Indeed, what is needed is 'a more comprehensive analysis of all the various dimensions and features of the nature, aims and purposes of policies for realizing a lifelong approach to learning for all' (Aspin and Chapman, 2000: 16). Following Withnall (2010 : 116), this warrants that late-life learning brings the 'need for economic progress and social inclusiveness in tandem with recognition of individual desires for personal development and growth as people age'. A key attraction of this vision is that it enables the possibility of granting priority to both the process and content of older adult learning, depending on whether the goal is personal or

social transformation (ibid.). Indeed, policies should offer a range of tangible benefits – at individual, community and societal levels – by spreading out to all facets of later life, and recognizing that learning takes place in a variety of everyday contexts ranging from formal classrooms, self-directed learning, voluntary organizations, residential and nursing homes, to intergenerational settings. As Withnall (ibid.) underlines, it is only so that policies on late-life learning will succeed in becoming embedded in an 'operational belt' (strategies) guided by an 'ideological core' (values). It is against such ontological and epistemological backdrops that the EU directives on older adult learning will be examined and discussed.

EU POLICY AND OLDER ADULT LEARNING

In recent years it has become virtually impossible to locate a policy document issued by the European Commission (EC) that makes no reference to lifelong learning. Of course, it is erroneous to think that lifelong learning emerged onto the EU policy scene with the suddenness of a new fashion. The idea was widely touted in the late 1960s, and even experienced a degree of political flavour early 1970s. Indeed, any discussion on the EU's take on lifelong learning will be amiss if it overlooks the fundamental role of the intergovernmental bodies of UNESCO (United Nations Educational, Social and Cultural Organization) and OECD in the genealogical development of lifelong learning. In particular, the UNESCO report *Learning to Be* (Faure et al., 1972), as a public statement on the principles of lifelong education, was crucial in fostering a global debate. Herein, education was postulated to 'last the whole life for *all* individuals and not just be tacked on to school or university for a privileged or specialized few' (Field, 2000 : 6 – italics in original), and hence, serve to 'initiate an optimistic phase of international education policy and reform, and also as the beginning of the debate over lifelong education' (Knoll, original emphasis, quoted in Field, 2000: 6). On the other hand, OECD's rationale was embedded in terms of human capital thinking, albeit laced with a few dashes of social democracy. In *Recurrent Education: A Strategy for Lifelong Education*, the OECD (1973) stressed the need of high quality pre-school and compulsory education if lifelong learning is to have effective meaning for the population as a whole, the necessity of school curricula to lay the foundations for lifelong learning, the vital roles of qualifications and technology to open lifelong learning opportunities, the necessity of a dialogue on the financial aspect of lifelong learning (especially the prospect of paid educational leave), and an urgent focus on how demographic trends (such as the rising number of older workers) will impact lifelong learning patterns.

The EU responded to such an international debate by commissioning its own policy enquiry. A 1974 communication on education in the European Community put forward the concept of 'education permanente' – that is, 'planned learning from cradle to grave' where 'the Community's specific responsibilities within this strategy should include promotion of foreign languages, staff and student exchanges between schools and universities … through each individual's working life' (Field, 1998: 30). Yet, the limited power of the EC over member states' educational policy meant that during the 1980s there were no unique developments regarding this matter. It was only after the concept of lifelong learning constituted one of the cornerstones of Jacques Delors' white paper on competitiveness and economic growth that it became possible to distinguish the EU's thinking from that of other agencies:

> Preparation for life in tomorrow's world cannot be satisfied by a once-and-for-all acquisition of knowledge and know-how … All measures must therefore must therefore necessarily be based on the concept of developing, generalizing, and systematizing lifelong learning and continuing training. (CEC, 1994: 16, 136)

The Commission subsequently declared 1996 to be the European Year of Lifelong Learning and published a series of directives that left no doubt as to the lynchpin status of the concept in EU socio-economic and political policy. This 'fixation' with lifelong learning reflects two key facets of the EU's modus operandi – namely, economic competitiveness and citizenship. On one hand, the EU shares the dominant global concern with regard to the strategic importance of lifelong learning 'in meeting the challenges of globalization and the emergence of knowledge economies, promoting the competitiveness of national economies, creating jobs and reducing unemployment, and securing the social inclusion of groups at risk of exclusion' (Hake, 2006: 37). Indeed, lifelong learning has been adopted as the basis of the EU's education and training strategy to achieve the Lisbon objective – namely, making the continent 'the most competitive and dynamic knowledge-based economy in the world, capable of sustainable economic growth with more and better jobs and greater social cohesion' by 2010 (EC, 2000a: 3). On the other hand, the EU believes that lifelong learning holds the potential to unite the member states of this diverse continent into a coherent whole. Although the initial countries in the union were wealthy capitalist countries from Western Europe with a great deal of common and overlapping history, the EU now incorporates countries from both the Eastern Bloc and Southern Europe that have a very differentiated history and are less economically advanced. It was emphasized that

> Lifelong learning will facilitate an enhancement of citizenship through the sharing of common values, and the development of a sense of belonging to a common social and economic area. It must encourage a broader-based understanding of citizenship, founded on active solidarity and on mutual understanding of the cultural diversities that constitute Europe's originality and richness. (EC, 1997: 4)

Following the millennium, the EC published the *Memorandum on Lifelong Learning*

(2000b) and *Making a European Area of Lifelong Learning a Reality* (2001: 33) where lifelong learning was defined as 'all learning activities undertaken throughout life with the aim of improving knowledge, skills and competences within a personal, civic, social and/ or employment related perspective'. In June 2002, the European Council of Heads of State and Governments adopted a *Resolution on Lifelong Learning*, as the guiding principle for the reform of education and training in the member states, and which argued that lifelong learning is an 'indispensable means for promoting social cohesion, active citizenship, personal and professional fulfilment, adaptability and employability' (CEC, 2002: 1). Furthermore, it was underlined that lifelong learning 'should enable all persons to acquire the necessary knowledge to take part as active citizens in the knowledge society and the labour market' (ibid.).

Older persons were a late entry in policy documents, as it was only in 2006 – some eleven years after the first policy document – that late-life learning was first mentioned. This was during a time when the EU was expressing serious reservations as to whether member states were making adequate progress towards the targets of economic growth and job creation established in Lisbon, and was also preoccupied by the decreasing average age at which older persons exited from the labour force into retirement (EC, 2006b). Arguing that the participation of older workers in the workforce is vital to the development of socially inclusive economies and the reduction of the risk of social exclusion among the older population, the EU issued directives calling for active employment policies to discourage older workers from leaving the workforce and the development incentives to stay in work (CEC, 2004). Although the key argument consisted in that lifelong learning and access to training must provide older workers with the necessary skills to adapt to changes on the employment market, with the EU encouraging member states to use the European Social Fund to develop active labour market policies (ibid.),

the subsequent documents *Adult Learning: It is never too late to learn* (2006a) and *Action Plan on Adult Learning* (2007) attempted at developing a more holistic approach to older adult learning. Stressing that the growing numbers of retirees in Europe should be regarded as a potential source of educators and trainers for adult learning, the former posited two objectives for lifelong learning as far as older adults are concerned:

> [1] to ensure a longer working life, there is a need for up-skilling and increasing lifelong learning opportunities for older workers. It is widely acknowledged that in order to keep older workers employable, investment is needed throughout the life cycle and should be supported by government, professional bodies and sectors ... [2] an expansion of learning provision for retired people is needed (including for instance increasing participation of mature students in higher education) ... Learning should be an integral part of this new phase in their lives ... the Commission invited universities to 'be more open to providing courses for students at a later stage of their life cycle'. Such provisions will have a vital role in keeping, retired people in touch with their social environment. (EC, 2006a: 8–9)

The *Action Plan on Adult Learning* (EC, 2007) reiterated the assumption that in a knowledge-based and aging society access to lifelong learning is a condition for both economic growth and social cohesion. However, although it calls upon member states to ensure sufficient investment in the education of older people, it is disappointing that the document does not address the issue of late-life learning in any specific detail. As the following excerpt shows, the directive seeks to locate one solution for all vulnerable citizens:

> This Action Plan focuses on those who are disadvantaged because of their low literacy levels, inadequate work skills and/or skills for successful integration into society ... these could include migrants, older people, women or persons with a disability. It starts from the premise that the need for a high quality and accessible adult learning system is no longer a point of discussion, given the challenges Europe has to meet in the coming years: [i] to reduce labour shortages due to demographic changes by raising skill levels in the workforce generally and by upgrading low-skilled

workers ... [ii] to address the problem of the persistent high number of early school leavers (nearly 7 million in 2006) ... [iii] to reduce the persistent problem of poverty and social exclusion among marginalised groups ... [iv] to increase the integration of migrants in society and labour market ... [and v] to increase participation in lifelong learning and particularly to address the fact that participation decreases after the age of 34. (EC, 2007: 3)

In an attempt to link policy with practice, as well as aiding member states reach the directives' objectives, the EU coordinates the Grundtvig program which provides funding for projects on lifelong learning. Priority 6 in the Grundtvig guide pledges financial resources to learning programs related to teaching and learning in later life, and 'intergenerational and family learning' (EC, 2010). More specifically, funding is promised to programs engaging in '[i] transferring knowledge, methods and good practice for senior citizen education, [ii] equipping senior citizens with the skills that they need in order to cope with change and remain active in society, [iii] strengthening the contribution of older people to the learning of others, and [iv]. innovative approaches to intergenerational and family learning' (ibid.: 29–30). Over the last ten years, the Grundtvig program has supported many projects aimed at promoting active aging and solidarity between generations. The breadth of funded projects is impressive as a recent mapping exercise conducted by Soulsby (2010) identified some 200 initiatives covering a range of learning activities, but mostly, e-learning, intergenerational learning, and older volunteering. The implementation of Grundtvig projects resulted in a number of clear benefits such as recognizing that older adults are valuable human capital, that in the context of population aging lifelong learning is a necessity rather than a luxury, and that both computer and intergenerational learning offer a great potential for active aging. Another benefit includes the mobilization of national senior organizations to involve themselves in policy for late-life learning – hence, 'a

change from a "top-down" to a "bottom-up" approach to policy-making' (Klercq, 2010: 105). Moreover, instead of waiting for policy makers to become aware of issues around education for older adults, funded programs 'prompted initiatives and actions which would put pressure on the policy makers at national and local level to acknowledge the magnitude of the human capital represented by older adults' (ibid.).

BEYOND RHETORIC: CRITICAL ISSUES IN EU POLICIES ON OLDER ADULT LEARNING

The above section confirms how older adult learning has taken on a much higher profile in recent years, as the EU attempted to present a broad and inclusive solution to the challenges arising from the aging of European nations. The key argument, as we have seen, is that the proliferation of learning opportunities for older adults within the wider context of lifelong learning promises to help people adjust to aging-related transitions as well as unravel the idiosyncrasies brought about by an aging workforce. At the same time, however, a critical lens uncovers robust biases in the EU's road-map for late-life learning. The following three sub-sections seek to go beyond the rhetoric of EU policy to highlight its difficulties in establishing truly democratic and transformative practices in older adult learning.

Beyond the rhetoric of activity theory

EU policy and funding priorities laud late-life learning for its potential to aid older adults remaining active and find new roles following the end of work and independence of children. This is a valid argument as many research studies have substantiated how late-life learning helped him/her to adjust, and at times overcome, the physical, social, and psychological challenges brought on by the onset of later life. However, such a rationale has its own limitations. One key lacuna consists of its support of an ideological construction of later life where – to paraphrase Mills (1959) – 'public issues' are projected as 'private troubles'. It is unjust to expect older persons to solve the contemporary problems associated with retirement when such issues surfaced only as the result of wider and structural predicaments.

A general disinterest to participate in learning activities on behalf of non-typical learners – that is, working class, men, those living in rural areas, and elders from ethnic minorities – does not suffice as a complete justification for their invisibility in learning programs. For instance, one study on working-class participants' access to and experience of learning programs found interviewees to be highly motivated to acquire new knowledge (Findsen and McCullough, 2008). It is thus more plausible that certain features of the way elder-learning programs are organized are somehow acting as a barrier to the enrolment of working-class elders whose life situation tends to be characterized by 'at-risk-of-poverty' lifestyles (Formosa, 2009). The low percentage of older men signals strongly that opportunities for late-life education are not attractive to them. Primarily, third-age learning activities are promoted in avenues – such as health programs on the broadcasting media or through leaflets at health centres – where most of the clients are women. Secondly, late-life learning tends to be feminized, with Williamson (2000: 63) concluding that 'in Universities of the Third Age, for example, not only is the membership mostly female, but so are management committees'. As Scott and Wenger (1995) stated, older men tend not to want to become involved with old people's organizations they perceive to be dominated by women. Thirdly, courses tend to reflect the interests of the dominant female membership. Although no comparative studies on curricula in late-life learning are available, it is noteworthy that Golding and colleagues (2007: 7) note how in Australia 'adult and community education tends to be underpinned by feminist pedagogies and practice that tends not to encourage or welcome working class masculinities and pedagogies'.

One's residential location is also an important variable to consider as only a very limited number of learning programs tend to be available in 'rural' areas – that is, farms, towns, and small cities located outside urban or metropolitan areas. Research finds that living in rural areas arises as a strong barrier to participation in late-life learners since residents find it difficult to travel to metropolitan areas (Mott, 2008). Whilst many rural elders (especially women) neither own a driving license nor a car, public transport tends to be limited in rural areas. The absence of outreach work on behalf of formal and non-formal education providers means that rural elders are generally left out in the cold, with state subsidies and volunteering activities being disproportionally biased in favour to those living in metropolitan areas. Of course, there have been a number of projects which addressed successfully the problems experienced by older learners in rural communities. For instance, the Department of Continuing Education at Lancaster University operated an innovative *Learning from Home* program that enabled groups of adults, many of whom were older people living in rural areas, to engage in learning through telephone conferencing (Withnall, 2010). Another success story is *Stories of Our Age* – coordinated by the Workers Educational Association Northern Ireland and Age Northern Ireland – and which was aimed at older people living rurally to give them the opportunity of having their voices heard on issues affecting them as they grew older, and to offer them the chance to develop some new skills using digital technology (WEANI, 2011).

Beyond the rhetoric of productive aging

Another positive aspect of EU policy is a strong commitment to portray aging in a positive light, and especially, highlight the potential of an aging population. In this sense, it provides a welcome respite from traditional policies on social and health care which support the stereotypes of frail elders, and the view of older persons as dependent members of our population. Learning is treated as a key strategy in bringing unprecedented levels of 'productive aging' – which refers to any activity 'that contributes to producing goods and services or develops the capacity to produce them' (Caro et al., 1993: 6). Such activities 'are socially valued in the sense that, if one individual or group did not perform them, there would be a demand for them to be performed by another individual or group' (Bass and Caro, 2001: 37). The EU's position is admirable as it affirms a cultural ideal, one promoting the idea that older adults can be productive, and hence, counteracting the stereotypes of older adult as 'greedy geezers'.

The problem, however, is that such an commendable rationale is not embedded in a wide range of possible productive lifestyles – ranging from volunteering, informal care, to independent living – but solely in the sphere of paid employment. The assumption is that economic status has the most profound impact on the older adult's ability to experience a meaningful and productive aging experience. Albeit the goals of lifelong learning as premised by the EU also include inclusion, active citizenship, and personal development, nevertheless, the discourse linking learning and later life is biased towards the economic realm. Human experience is surrendered to the controls of the market, so that any notion of meaning detached from 'work' and not defined according to capitalist logic, simply disappears (Estes and Mahakian, 2001). This stance is not surprising considering that from the very beginning the EU (2001) posits the need to expand lifelong education and learning in terms of the competitive advantage that is increasingly dependent on investment in human capital, and on knowledge and competences becoming a powerful engine for economic growth. As Bauman (2005b: 121) states, the task of achieving a 'more inclusive, tolerant, and democratic' society marked by 'greater participation, higher reported well-being and lower criminality'

seems like an afterthought in the EU's documents on lifelong learning, as some kind of natural consequence of a full labour market.

Unfortunately, human capital theory is a key driving point in the EU's vision on lifelong and later learning, as it is assumed that there will be economic payoffs if a society broadens access and opportunities for lifelong learning. Indeed, it is the 'future worker-citizen' rather than the 'democratic-citizen who is the prime asset of the social investment state', so that one locates a strong interdependence between citizenship and employability (Lister, 2003: 433). The position promulgated in EU policy for late-life learning is unashamedly economic, where the solution to the 'aging' problem is put as simply finding a way for older people to be economically useful. Yet, it is noteworthy that there is hardly any evidence to support the usefulness of a strong human capital theory for older persons (Cole, 2000). The increase of opportunities for late-life learning does not result in a surge of older persons going back into either full- or part-time employment, but only a rise in pensioners becoming increasingly active in community and civic engagement affairs. The EU's extensive drive to improve the e-learning skills of older is also problematic. The dominant emphasis towards e-learning that weaves through Grundtvig-funded projects in late-life learning is, ultimately, nothing more than a response to 'skills crisis' in information and communication technology that characterizes older cohorts in European society. As Borg and Mayo (2005) pointed out, the net result of this European hysteria around ICT skills is an increase in public financing of private needs in an area of human resources that is crucial to latter-day capitalism so that private and public interests and concerns are slowly becoming one. Borg and Mayo (ibid.) concluded that 'the memorandum's messages ought to be read against an economic backdrop characterized by a market oriented definition of social viability'.

Beyond the rhetoric of third age learning

Another limitation of EU policy and Grundtvig funding priorities constitutes their celebration and promotion of third age learning, ultimately at the expense of older and more defenceless people – namely, those in the fourth age. The 'third age' refers to a specific socio-demographic trend within population aging. It alludes to how the combination of increased longevity and a number of other social factors – ranging from earlier retirement, improving health status, establishment of the welfare institutions of retirement and pensions schemes, to more positive values and beliefs towards older persons – have opened up what could be loosely termed as a new phase in life, in which significant numbers of older persons spend a considerable amount of time in relative active years following exit from work. The third age thus denotes the emergence of a period of time separating the working years on one hand, and frailty and death on the other (Laslett, 1989). In Weiss and Bass's (2002: 3) words, the third age is described as a 'life phase in which there is no longer employment and child-raising to commandeer time, and before morbidity enters to limit activity and mortality brings everything to a close'. On the other hand, the fourth age refers to 'the age of frailty, dependency and being in need of care' (MacKinlay, 2006: 12). Indeed, even at a relatively young age, many older adults experience complications from strokes, diabetes, and neurological diseases. Suffice to say that as much as 17 and 23 percent of men and women aged over 65 in the EU experience some level of physical dependence (ECFIN, 2006). The range of cognitive limitations experienced in later life is also substantial with, for instance, 9.95 million older adults suffering from some form of dementia in Europe, a figure that should reach approximately 18.65 million by the year 2050 (Alzheimer Disease International, 2010). Indeed, some 8 percent of persons aged over 65 in the EU resided in long-term care settings in 2004 (ECFIN, 2006).

The rationale underpinning fourth age learning is that dependent older adults still hold varied cognitive needs and interests which can be met through learning opportunities. Aldridge (2009) reports on the UK context which includes programs such as the *Music for Life* program consisting of regular weekly activities including quizzes, puzzles, and games and discussions, and *The Signatures Project* which engages older migrants in an eight-week project to assist them in developing their written signatures and learning to print their names. Other literature documents the potential of reminiscence to aid older persons remember forgotten proficiencies and even develop new skills. Housden (2007), for instance, forwards many examples of learning projects in nursing homes which use learners' personal memories as a resource in learning, and where residents have gone on to develop skills in forming and sustaining relationships, oral and written communication, as well as engaging in arts, crafts and literacy. Fourth age learning has also been developed with homebound elders, with most programs providing distance learning through radio, television, and especially, online information and communication technology (Gagliardi et al., 2008). Programs providing learning opportunities to older persons at different stages of dementia have also registered varying degrees of success in improving learners' levels of social and emotional intelligence (ibid.). However, and notwithstanding this rich vein of literature, EU policy on late-life learning overlooks how rising life expectancies warrants new learning needs and interests amongst the oldest and most frail sectors of the older population. It is assumed that only 'healthy' older adults are capable of engaging in learning initiatives, and no call is made for governments to reach those persons who due to various physical and/or cognitive challenges are precluded from participating in lifelong learning. Indeed, there seems to be no place for frail elders and carers in EU policy on lifelong learning, and as far as the available literature indicates, no Gruntvig-funded project has yet focused exclusively on the fourth age.

FUTURE DEVELOPMENTS

The EU must work toward ensuring that access to learning throughout the life course is perceived as a human right, while strongly guaranteeing that adequate learning opportunities in later life becomes a central objective in its policies. There is no doubt that as the time that people in a relatively healthy and independent later life increases, there warrants a public policy which looks at late-life learning beyond just a resource for employment and extending working life. The following broad priorities emerge from the results and discussion reviewed in this chapter.

EU policy on older adult learning is characterized by an unwarranted optimism as far as participation is concerned when it is clear that opportunities to learn are not evenly distributed. Rationales for late-life learning remain incomplete unless they are framed in terms of a discussion of appropriate provision on behalf of the state for both active and excluded elders. This is because irrespective of older persons' interests and yearning for learning opportunities, structural circumstances continue to impact greatly on the extent of participation in older adult learning. For instance, the Grundtvig program is biased by an urge to showcase the potential of the well educated, healthy, and affluent seniors, whilst overlooking the increasing dependency ratios and that as much as 19 percent of persons aged 65 and above in the EU (a total of 16 million) experience at-the-risk-of-poverty lifestyles (Zaidi, 2010). As Parent (2010: 88) emphasized, it is important that Grundtvig 'respond[s] more effectively to the very diverse and evolving needs of older people and the challenges that to many of them posed by financial constraints, social exclusion, lack of basic skills, digital illiteracy, and discrimination'. Whilst ensuring that the freedom of those who choose not to be included is not taken away, policy has the obligation to facilitate the inclusion of persons who, shackled by structural inequalities, are unable to participate in elder-learning. This warrants the drawing of inclusive strategies

that overcome class-, ethnic-, and gender-specific barriers that hinder the realization of a more democratic version of elder-learning practice. Achieving a lifelong learning for all necessitates a widening participation agenda where policy-makers and providers 'think out of the box' to attract older adults who could or would not usually participate in traditional organized provision. This objective will be facilitated if the EU mandates local authorities and voluntary agencies a clearer role in the coordination and lead development of elder learning. Moreover, policies on older adult learning cannot overlook how learning in later life occurs through informal networks. Policy frameworks should advocate those learning aids that facilitate and even initiate informal learning. Hence, There is a need for a structure within which older adults gain insight into themselves as learners. Older adults must be aided to learn how they learn, examine multiple ways to learn, and look for ways to plan their future learning more effectively. In practice, this necessitates elder clubs in libraries, and age-friendly functional literacy and e-learning support.

The EU vision on late-life learning never escapes the greater project to render Europe more competitive in the face of fierce competition from the transitional and multinational corporations' ability to reap the advantages of economies of scale through expansion of international capital mobility. However, aiding older people to remain in paid work represents only one goal amongst others for late-life learning, with other possible objectives being recognizing the diversity of older persons, challenging stereotypes of aging, maximizing social inclusion, maintaining personal independence, and retaining a sense of purpose and meaning. In addition to employment-related programs that support older people moving from full-time employment to various forms of work, higher education must also provide 'personal development' programs which identify new types of courses and markets among a diverse and segmented post-50s market, and 'health and social care' programs orientated to professionals working with older people that vary from foundation degrees through to modules for continuing professional development (Phillipson and Ogg, 2010). So that the integration of older persons in the labour market becomes a real possibility, policies must break down barriers to labour market entry with active and preventive measures such as job search assistance, guidance and training (Formosa, 2012). Late-life learning should be supplemented by holistic approaches to the needs and wishes of older workers with respect to motivation, and income and social protection issues (ibid.). It is hoped that in the foreseeable future EU policy on late-life learning embraces a broader perspective of citizenship, one that includes both political and social rights. However, this goal will certainly not be achieved by any type of learning environment and I join other critical educators (e.g. Findsen, 2007) in stressing the importance of educators and learners to embrace a transformative rationale that enables them to imagine and work together towards the realization of a social world that is governed by life-centred values rather than the ideology of the market. Late-life learning has huge potential to expand the opportunities for 'civic engagement' for those older persons who wish to partake in volunteerism as is generally expected from older generations. Policies on older adult learning should lead learners towards higher rates of political activism, a type of activity that despite being central to citizenship has been delegitimized and is absent from the official policy agenda (Formosa, 2011).

At the same time, EU policy on late-life learning should not overlook the learning needs and interest of frail elders living in the community whose mobility, sight, and/or hearing impairments restricts their mobility. The goal of such programs can range from empowerment to retaining a degree of autonomy, as well as enabling homebound elders to engage in pleasurable and relaxing activities. One possible strategy is to provide adequate transport facilities to and back from the learning centre. This is feasible if providers pool their resources and provide disability vehicle-careers that are multiseated. Other possible strategies include enabling homebound elders to participate in learning environments through e-learning strategies or having the learning sessions taking place in learners' homes. Despite widespread scepticism towards the provision of online learning towards homebound elders, participants display great enthusiasm for such programs (Swindell et al., 2011). It is important that homebound elders are provided with the opportunity to engage in self-directed learning through the availability of informative radio/television programmes, mobile libraries, and intergenerational activities such as grandchild-adoption initiatives. The special needs of some elders are also to be given attention. For example, whilst partially sighted elders require publications to be issued in 'clear print', large print and 'raised diagrams', it is also necessary that information is presented in Braille tactile codes and speech-reading computer software. Learning opportunities is also to be made available to informal carers where curricula may range from assertiveness, welfare benefits, self-protection, to social/cultural outings. Of course, providers must also provide respite care while the learning program is taking place, for which funds may be derived from Grundtvig programs. Moreover, there is no doubt that an educational system that spends some 18 years, and substantial financial capital, to prepare citizens for the world of work, but simply a couple of afternoons (if lucky) to leave it, is clearly biased against older persons. Society has an obligation toward its citizens to provide them with learning initiatives that help them plan for their third and fourth ages. However, a really democratic pre-retirement education is not simply instruction about the formalities surrounding pensions, the drawing of wills, and health. It is one which also includes a discussion of psychological and social strategies that lead older adults to improve their quality of life.

It follows that, for lifelong learning to be really 'lifelong', learning opportunities should also be provided to occupants of residential and nursing homes. Although the link between learning and good health is a slippery one and may never be unequivocally resolved, older people who continue to engage in cognitively stimulating activities have been found to be in a better position to adopt strategies assisting them to augment their well-being and independence (Findsen and Formosa, 2011). This warrants that EU policy mandates learning opportunities to be made central to daily life in long-term care settings. As an emergent body of literature strongly demonstrates, the quality of learning participation, processes and outcomes in fourth-age learning is impressive and exceeds all expectations (Housden, 2007; Aldridge, 2009). For example, residential and nursing homes are to provide arts and crafts centres with paid teaching staff, as well as employ an activity and leisure manager who facilitates or runs clubs, discussion groups, reading societies, social/cultural outings, as well as in-house magazine. Residents are to be encouraged to engage in life-history project where they record their past, the present, and most importantly, the future in terms of unfulfilled ambitions, dreams, and aspirations, which they can present to their relatives, friends, and case workers. Interest-groups ranging from choirs, horticulture therapy, reflexology, keep fit, and sports activities, must also be encouraged. Residents experiencing confusion and dementia, together with their carers, are to be engaged in reminiscence activities which focus on the personal manner one experiences and remembers events, and hence, re-living the experiences that are personal in a way that is vivid and engaging. Through such interpersonal relationships residents will have the opportunity to keep on learning that their personhood is still valued, that they are valued, and that they still have some power over their own lives. Following Jarvis (2001), it is beneficial if there was one person in each long-term care setting who is a specialist in helping create and facilitate learning environments. This position need not necessarily be a separate occupation, but could be a 'specialism learning' by any one from the caring professionals who could be sponsored to read for a post-secondary or tertiary qualification in social gerontology or adult education. Only so will long-term settings be successful in drawing together the seemingly disparate but ultimately overlapping acts of 'learning' and 'caring'.

CONCLUSION

This critical overview of EU policy and opportunities relating to older adult education argues that the current dominant vision is based more on rhetoric than grounded attempts to establish wider and more democratic practices in elder-learning. While there is no doubt that the EU policy documents and action plans dealing with some aspect of late-life learning are well-intentioned, ultimately they function as nothing more than empty rhetoric that conceal neo-liberal values. As Bauman (2005b: 126 – italics in original) underlines, 'it is not only the *technical skills* that need to be continually refreshed, not only the job-focused education that needs to be lifelong' but 'the same is required, and with greater urgency, by education in *citizenship*'. Whilst the EU's rationale for older adult learning is characterized by a sense of urgency to keep up the rapid 'technological process', no exigency is located 'when it comes to catching up with the impetuous stream of political developments and the fast changing rules of the political game' (ibid.). For instance, despite the EU's dedication of the year 2010 to the combat of social exclusion and poverty, there is still very little research, policy or educational practice relating to vulnerable older persons. Of course, the road towards a successful EU policy and action plan on lifelong and late-life learning is not without obstacles. The hegemonic grip of Third Way politics (Giddens, 1998), which celebrate the human capital model of development and individuated lifestyles, has led to an almost absence of philosophical reflection on the empowering potential of late-life learning. On a more practical level, one must also admit that public resources may be seriously limited. Such lacunae may be overturned if policy makers shift their focus away from formal 'economistic' avenues of education to informal 'humanistic' contexts of learning – ranging from libraries to social dancing to volunteering – which are so popular with older persons. Here, it is noteworthy to point out Hiemstra's (1976) long-standing finding that the marginalisation of subaltern groups in late-life learning relates to non-participation from education rather than learning per se. Indeed, future EU directives on (older) adult learners would do well to heed his advice that 'educators must learn to remove institutional barriers and recognize that self-directed, independent learning is going on – outside of institutional structures' (ibid.: 337). Such a policy vision, together with accompanying action plans, has immense potential to construct a more holistic approach to late-life learning, one that is sensitive both to the heterogeneous character of older cohorts as well as the diverse meanings that the act of learning has for different persons. In this respect, there is no better way to end this critical commentary than to leave the final word to Withnall (2008: 3) who stressed how lifelong learning policy needs 'a better understanding of the ways in which older people learn, whether and how they differ from those used by younger people and if so, how their learning could be enhanced' on the basis that such a policy direction would bring a more 'inclusive society where all forms of learning are valued, older people are held in higher esteem for the contribution they make, and learning for everyone is truly acknowledged as a desirable lifelong process'.

ACKNOWLEDGEMENT

An earlier version of this paper was presented at the conference on *Intergenerational Solidarity and Older Adults Education in the Community* organized by the European Network on Education and Learning of Older Adults in Ljubljana, Slovenia, 19–21 September 2012

REFERENCES

Aldridge, F. (2009) *Enhancing Informal Adult Learning for Adult Learning in Care Settings: Interim Report and Consultation Document*. Leicester: NIACE.

Aldridge, F. and Tucket, A. (2010) *A Change for the Better: The NIACE Survey on Adult Participation in Learning 2010*. Leicester: NIACE.

Alzheimer Disease International, (2010) *World Alzheimer Report 2010*. Available at: http://www.alz.co.uk/research/files/WorldAlzheimerReport2010.pdf (Accessed 12 May 2011).

Aspin, D.N. and Chapman, J.D. (2000) 'Lifelong learning: Concepts and conceptions', *International Journal of Lifelong Education*, 19(1): 2–19.

Bass, S.A. and Caro, F.G. (2001) 'Productive aging: A conceptual framework', in C. Morrow-Howell, J. Hinterlomng, and M. Sherraden, (eds.), *Productive Aging: Concepts and Challenges*. Baltimore, MA: The John Hopkins University Press. pp. 37–78.

Bauman, Z. (2005a) 'Education in liquid modernity', *Review of Education, Pedagogy, and Cultural Studies*, 27(4): 303–317.

Bauman, Z. (2005b) *Liquid Life*. Cambridge: Polity Press.

Borg, C. and Mayo, P. (2005) 'The EU Memorandum on lifelong learning: Old Wine in new bottles?', *Globalization, Societies and Education*, 3(2): 257–278.

Caro, F.G., Bass, S.A. and Chen, Y.P. (1993) 'Introduction: Achieving a productive aging society', in S.A. Bass, F.G. Caro and Y.P. Chen (eds.), *Achieving a Productive Society*. Westport, CT: Auburn House. pp. 1–15.

Cole, M. (2000) 'The issue of age in The Learning Age: A critical review of lifelong learning in the United Kingdom under New Labour', *Education and Ageing*, 5(3): 437–53.

Commission of the European Communities (CEC), (1994) *Competitiveness, Employment, Growth*. Luxembourg: Office for Official Publications.

Commission of the European Communities (CEC), (2002) *Council Resolution of 27 June 2002 on Lifelong Learning* (2002 C 163/1). Official Journal C 163/1 2002: 1–3.

Commission of the European Communities (CEC), (2004) *Education and Training 2010: The Success of* the Lisbon Strategy Hinges on Urgent Reforms. Luxembourg: Office for Official Publications.

Economic Policy Committee and European Commission (ECFIN), (2006) The Impact of Ageing on Public Expenditure. European Economy, Special Reports No 1, 2006.

Estes, C.L. and Mahakian, J.L. (2001) 'The political economy of productive aging', in N. Morrow, J. Hinterlong and M. Sherraden (eds.), Productive Aging: Concepts and Challenges. Baltimore, MA: Johns Hopkins University Press. pp. 197–213.

European Commission (1997) Towards a Europe of Knowledge. COM (1997) 563 final. Brussels: European Commission.

European Commission (2000a) Presidency Conclusions – Lisbon European Council, 23 and 24 March 2000. Available at: http://www.consilium.europa.eu/ ueDocs/cms_Data/docs/pressData/en/ec/00100-1. en0.htm, 8.11.2006 (Accessed 1 October 2011).

European Commission (2000b) A Memorandum on Lifelong Learning. SEC (2000) 1832. Brussels: European Commission.

European Commission (2001) Making a European Area of Lifelong Learning a Reality. Brussels: European Commission.

European Commission (2006a) Adult learning: It is never too late to learn. COM (2006) 614 final. Brussels: European Commission.

European Commission (2006b) The Demographic Future of Europe – From Challenge to Opportunity. COM (2006) 571 final. Brussels: European Commission.

European Commission (2007) Action Plan of Adult Learning: It is always a good time to learn. COM (2007) 558 final. Brussels: European Commission.

European Commission (2010) Grundtvig. Available at: http://eacea.ec.europa.eu/llp/events/infodays_2010/ pdf_1pp/4_2_grundtvig_en.pdf (Accessed 12 January 2011).

Faure, E., Herrera, F., Kaddowa, A., Lopes, H., Petrovsky, A., Rahnema, M. and Ward, F. (1972) Learning to Be: The World of Education Today and Tomorrow. Paris: UNESCO/Harrap.

Field, J. (1998) European Dimensions: Education, Training and the European Union. London: Jessica Kingsley.

Field, J. (2000) 'Lifelong education', International Journal of Lifelong Education, 20(1/2): 3–15.

Findsen, B. (2005) Learning Later. Malabar. FL: Krieger Publishing Co.

Findsen, B. (2007) 'Freirean philosophy and pedagogy in the adult education context: The case of older adults' learning', Studies in Philosophy and Education, 25(6): 545–59.

Findsen, B. and Formosa, M. (2011) Lifelong Learning in Later Life: A Handbook on Older Adult Learning. Amsterdam: Sense.

Findsen, B. and McCullough, S. (2008) Older Adults' Engagement with Further and Higher Education in West of Scotland. Glasgow: Department of Adult and Continuing Education.

Formosa, M. (2009) Class Dynamics in Later Life: Older Persons, Class Idenity and Class Action. Hamburg: Lit Verlag.

Formosa, M. (2011) 'Universities of the Third Age: A rationale for transformative education in later life', Journal of Transformative Education, 8(3): 197–219.

Formosa, M. (2012) 'Education for older adults in Malta: Current trends and future visions', International Review of Education, 58(2): 271–292.

Gagliardi, C., Mazzarini, G., Papa, R., Giula, C. and Marcellini, J. (2008) 'Designing a learning program to link and disabled people to computers', Educational Gerontology, 34(1): 15–29.

Giddens, A. (1998) The Third Way: The Renewal of Social Democracy. Cambridge: Polity Press.

Glendenning, F. and Battersby, D. (1990) 'Why we need educational gerontology and education for older adults: A statement of first principles', in F. Glendenning and K. Percy (eds.), Ageing, Education and Society: Readings in Educational Gerontology. Keele, Staffordshire: Association for Educational Gerontology. pp. 219–231.

Golding, B., Foley, A. and Brown, M. (2007) Shedding some new light on gender: Evidence about informal learning preferences from Australian men's sheds in community contexts. Paperto SCUTREA Conference, 3–5 July 2007, The Queen's University of Belfast, Ireland.

Hake, B. (2006) 'Lifelong learning in Europe from a life course perspective: Progress, problems and challenges in ageing European societies', in A. Dwojak-Matras and E., Kurantowicz (eds.), Strategies of Lifelong Learning: Access and Implementation in Practice. Wroclaw, Poland: Wydawnictwo Naukowe. pp. 37–48.

Hiemstra, R. (1976) The older adults learning projects. Educational Gerontology, 1(4): 331–341.

Housden, S. (2007) Reminiscence and Lifelong Learning. Leicester : NIACE.

Jarvis, P. (2001) Learning in Later Life: An Introduction for Educators and Carers. London: Kogan Page.

Klercq, J. (2010) 'The EU Grundtvig Programme: Its contribution to later life learning and active citizens for older adults', International Journal of Education and Ageing, 2(1): 101–106.

Laslett, P. (1989) *A Fresh Map of Life: The Emergence of the Third Age*. London: Weidenfeld and Nicholson.

Lister, R. (2003) 'Investing in the citizen-workers of the future: Transformations in citizenship and the state under New Labour', *Social Policy and Administration*, 37(5): 427–443.

MacKinlay, E. (2006) *Spiritual Growth and Care in the Fourth Age of Life*. London: Jessica Kingsley.

Mercken, C. (2010) *Education in an Ageing Society*. Sittard: Drukkerij.

Mills, C.W. (1959) *The Sociological Imagination*. London: Oxford University Press.

Moody, H.R. (1990) 'Education and the life cycle', in R.H. Sherron and B. Lumsden (eds.), *Introduction to Educational Gerontology*. Washington, DC: Hemisphere. pp. 23–39.

Mott, V.W. (2008) 'Rural education for older adults', *New Directions for Adult and Continuing Education*, 117: 47–57.

OECD (1973) *Recurrent Education: A Strategy for Lifelong Learning*. Paris: OECD.

OECD (2004) *Ageing and Employment Policies: Japan*. Paris: OECD. Available at: http://www1.oecd.org/publications/e-book/8104051E.pdf. (Accessed 13 May 2010).

Parent, A.-S. (2010) 'Active ageing and the EU Grundtvig Programme', *International Journal of Education and Ageing*, 1(1): 87–92.

Percy, K. (1990) 'The future of educational gerontology: A second statement of first principles', in F. Glendenning and K. Percy (eds.), *Ageing, Education and Society: Readings in educational gerontology* (pp. 24–46). Keele, Staffordshire: Association for Educational Gerontology.

Percy, K. and Frank, F. (2011) 'Senior learners and the university: Aims, learning and "research" in the third age', in S. Jackson (ed.), *Innovations in Lifelong Learning: Critical Perspectives on Diversity, Participation, and Vocational Learning*. New York: Routledge. pp. 126–141.

Phillipson, C. and Ogg, J. (2010) *Active Ageing and Universities: Engaging Older Learners*. London: Universities UK.

Phillipson, C. and Powell, J.L. (2004) 'Risk, social welfare and old age', in E. Tulle (ed.), *Old age and agency*. New York: Nova Science Publishers. pp. 17–26.

Rowe, J. and Kahn, R. (1999) *Successful Aging*. New York: Random House.

Scott, A. and Wenger, G.C. (1995) 'Gender and social support networks in later life', in S. Arber and J. Ginn (eds.), *Connecting Gender and Ageing: A Sociological Approach*. Buckingham: Open University Press. pp. 158–172.

Sloane-Seale, A. and Kops, B. (2004) 'Creative retirement: Survey of older persons' educational interests and motivations', *Canadian Journal of Continuing University Education*, 30(2) : 73–89.

Soulsby, J. (2010) 'Editorial essay: Learning in later life – Projects, conferences, and examples of practice in Europe', *International Journal of Education and Ageing*, 2(1): 77–85.

Swindell, R., Grimbeek, P. and Heffernan, J. (2011) 'U3A Online and successful aging: A smart way to help bridge the grey digital divide', in J. Soar, R.F. Swindell and P. Tsang (eds.), *Intelligent Technologies for Bridging the Grey Digital Divide*. New York: Information Science Reference. pp. 122–140.

Weiss, R.S. and Bass, S.A. (2002) 'Introduction', in R.S. Weiss and S.A. Bass (eds.), *Challenges of the Third Age: Meaning and Purpose in Later Life*. New York: Oxford University Press. pp. 3–12.

Williamson, A. (2000) 'Gender differences in older adults' participation in learning', *Educational Gerontology*, 26(1): 49–66.

Withnall, A. (2006) 'Exploring influences on later life learning', *International Journal of Lifelong Learning*, 25(1): 29–49.

Withnall, A. (2008) 'Lifelong learning and older persons: Choices and experiences', *Teaching and Learning Research Briefing*, 58: 1–4.

Withnall, A. (2010) *Improving Learning in Later Life*. London: Routledge.

Workers Educational Association Northern Ireland and Age Northern Ireland (WEANI), (2011) *Stories of Our Age*. Available at: http://www.wea-ni.com/current-news-stories/stories-of-our-age (Accessed 20 September 2011).

Zaidi, A. (2010) *Poverty Risks for Older People in EU Countries – An update*. Policy brief January (11) 2010. Austria, Vienna: European Centre for Social Policy and Research.

27

Optimizing the Long Future of Aging: Beyond Involvement to Engagement

Jacquelyn Boone James, Marcie Pitt-Catsouphes, Jennifer Kane Coplon, and Betty Eckhaus Cohen

It is widely recognized that the experience of aging is not what it used to be both in the US and abroad. Although new expectations for active and healthy aging have begun to emerge, many older adults feel that they are not sure what it means to be older in the 21st century. Not that long ago, disengagement was considered both normative and adaptive (Cumming, 2000; Cumming et al., 1960), and later life was characterized as a time of 'rolelessness' (Burgess, 1960). Today there are questions about what roles older adults should assume. Asset paradigms for aging suggest that older adults can (and perhaps should be expected to) contribute in meaningful ways to society – either through work, volunteer activities, providing care to family members or friends, or participating in education or training. However, while it may be important for older adults to 'stay busy and active,' there is limited understanding about the impact that involvement in activities can have on older adults.

In this chapter, we first set the stage and consider indicators which suggest that the experience of aging is different today; for purposes of this paper, our focus is largely in the US. Then, we explore the important difference between involvement and engagement in roles which add value to the greater good. We focus on the different dimensions of engagement (absorption, dedication, and vigor), considering why being enlivened can be so important for older adults. Data from the 'Life & Times in an Aging Society' study are presented which indicate that involvement without engagement can pose risk to older adults' well-being.

SHIFTING SANDS: THE EXPERIENCE OF AGING YESTERDAY, TODAY, AND TOMORROW

Today's older adults often observe:

> 'My retirement years are not like my grandmother's … or even my mothers.'

> 'I have the energy and passion to do something meaningful with this stage of my life, but I feel like I am "making it up" because I see so few role models.'

> 'Somehow, I expected that I would hit the age of eligibility for social security and I would mysteriously become a frail elder. But here I am, a senior citizen who is looking for the next thing.'

While many people glibly observe that aging today is not what it used to be, it is important to grapple with the characteristics of these changes because they can either open up opportunities or constrain the choices in front of today's older adults. Although there is evidence to support some of the assertions that aging today is different, we need to wave a flag of caution about broad generalizations which lead to inaccurate conclusions that today's 60 is like yesterday's 40. Not exactly … and, not in all ways.

The physical experience of aging

As many have observed, life expectancy continued to increase throughout the 20th and into the 21st century. Even during the last sixty years (when we witnessed the production of many miracle drugs including immunizations that prevent some diseases and antibiotics that cure others), life expectancy increased over 10 years, from an average of 68.9 years in 1950 to 79.2 years in 2009 (Jacobsen et al., 2011). Those who reach 65 today can expect to live for another 18.5 years. White women continue to live the longest, on average, and White adults who are age 65 live about 1.5 years more than African-Americans (Centers for Disease Control and Prevention, 2010; Federal Interagency Forum on Aging-Related Statistics, 2010).

The compelling question is how healthy are these extra years. In some ways, today's older adults are healthier. For example, surveys have found that, in 2007–2009, higher percentages of adults 45–64 reported that their health was 'good/excellent' compared to 25 years earlier (50.1% in 1982–88). Among adults aged 65 and older, 75% rated their health as good, very good, or excellent in the 2007–2009 time period. And, rates of functional limitations have decreased. However, rates of several chronic diseases including diabetes and respiratory diseases have increased (Federal Interagency Forum on Aging-Related Statistics, 2010). Of course medications can help some people to manage their chronic diseases so that the symptoms are reduced.

Health is a gatekeeper which affects if and how older adults become involved in a range of activities. Poor health is one reason people leave the labor force earlier than expected. Surveys have found that one-third to one-half of those who retire early report that health problems, chronic illness or disability was the reason (Dalirazar, 2007; Helman et al., 2008).

> *Observation 1*: It is true that people (in general) are living longer and that, in many ways, a majority is healthier than their counterparts were 50 years ago. These changes have paved the way for the emergence of a period of life during the so-called retirement years when they might experience the vigor and capacities associated with 'the third age' (before the onset of frailty) (James and Wink, 2007). However, it remains true that the incidence of some health problems increase with age.

Family caregiving

It is more likely that today's older adults are providing care to a parent or spouse than was true even twenty years ago. According to AARP, there was a nine percentage point increase in the number of Boomers who have been/are responsible for the care an elderly parent in 2004 compared to 1998 (AARP, 2004).

It is possible that we are also witnessing some changes with regard to the caregiving relationships between older adults and their grandchildren. A survey conducted by the Pew Research Center found that 39% of those 65 and older with grandchildren provided help with child care in the previous year (Livingston and Parker, 2010). Of those grandparents who live in the same home as their grandchildren, 42% report having responsibility for those grandchildren (US Census Bureau, 2005). Unfortunately, historical comparisons are difficult to make due to data limitations.

Observation 2: Given the aging of the population (in general), it is anticipated that there will be increased need for and expectations that those older adults who are healthy will contribute to their families' responsibilities for dependent care (either elder care, care of adults with disabilities, or care for grandchildren).

Living situations

There have been interesting changes to the life stage experiences of today's older adults. In 2009, more than half (54.9%) of the non-institutionalized people aged 65+ in the US lived with their spouses. However, older men are still more likely than women to be married (Federal Interagency Forum on Aging-Related Statistics, 2010).

In 2009, approximately one-third (30.1% or 11.4 million people; 38.8%/8.3 million women and 18.7%/3.0 million men) of all non-institutionalized older adults age 65+ lived alone. However, due to the increases in male longevity, there has been a decrease in the percentage of older women (age 65–75) who are widows, from 44% in 1960 to 24% in 2010 (Jacobsen et al., 2011).

The increase in the number of multi-generational families has also contributed to a decrease in the numbers of older adults who are living alone. Consider, for example, that just 12% of the US population was in a multi-generational family with at least two adult generations in 1980. By 2008, this had increased to 16% of the US population (Pew Research Center, 2010). The 2011 Profile of Older Americans published by the Administration on Aging indicated that approximately 716,000 grandparents age 65 or

older maintained households where grandchildren were present (that is, the grandparents were the heads of households) and another 942,000 were living in parent-maintained households (where their adult children were the heads of households) where grandchildren were present (Administration on Aging, 2010).

Observation 3: Today's older adults may be re-writing the scripts of what it means to be a parent of an adult child and what it means to be a grandparent. Two factors – the increased health and vitality experienced by many older adults and the emergence of new forms of caregiving supports that are available to some older adults (such as continuing care communities) – may make it more likely that older adults will actively re-construct the responsibilities they assume for family caregiving (possibly in partnership with health care professionals).

Education

The educational attainment of today's older adults is impressive. Several reports show that a greater proportion of older adults have graduated from high school (among those aged 65+, 24% in 1965 compared to 77% in 2008) and attained a college degree (among those aged 55–74, an increase from 9% to 27%) than was true in previous generations of older adults. Women have made particular gains, with 24% attaining a college degree in 2004, compared to 10% in 1984 (Federal Interagency Forum on Aging-Related Statistics, 2010; Iams et al., 2008; Mermin et al., 2008).

Although it is difficult to compare the findings of surveys which gather data about older adults' participation in formal education and training programs, recent reports show that a small proportion of older (1.4% of those aged 40+) are enrolled in public or private institutions of higher education (OECD, 2009). That said, projections are that educational upgrading by older adults (ages 40–64) in the US is occurring, with approximately 1 million projected to earn bachelor's degrees and 1.2 million master's degrees between 2008–2018 (Public Policy Institute of California, 2011). Among college-going adults aged 50+, half of them attend community colleges (Lakin et al., 2008).

> *Observation 4*: Education has been woven into the lives of many of today's older adults. As education and training providers design innovative programs that might fit with the needs of this demographic in the market, we anticipate that it will become more commonplace for older adults to take their places in seats next to younger adults enrolled in education programs. Community-based programs, such as those offered by community colleges as well as universities responsive to their localities, may be well-positioned to engage the interest of older adults in life-long learning.

The civic-mindedness of today's older adults

Significant attention has been focused on the passion expressed by today's older adults about making a difference. Surveys have found that there are many reasons why older adults volunteer, including feeling a sense of responsibility to help others, having the opportunity to make life more satisfying, wanting to help their own communities, wanting to contribute to a social issue or problem, and wanting to remain active (see, for example, AARP, 2003).

There are three primary ways that older adults can express these passions: (1) seeking paid work in the social sector; (2) volunteering; and (3) charitable giving. For the purposes of this chapter, we focus on unpaid work (volunteering).

It is difficult to compare patterns of volunteering over time because studies have adopted different ways to gauge volunteer efforts (For example, metrics for volunteering can be: the number of different types of volunteer associations with which a person is affiliated; the number of hours during a specified time period a person has volunteered; the frequency of volunteering; etc.). While it is complicated to interpret historical trends, it appears that older adults of today may be volunteering more compared to those in the past but, on average, they may volunteer for fewer hours (Williams et al., 2010).

One survey found that 29% of those between the ages of 46–64 volunteered in 2010 compared with 28.6% between the ages of 29–45, and 21.4% of those aged 28 or younger (Corporation for National and Community Service, 2006, 2011). However, the BLS reports that, in 2009, people between the ages of 35–54 were the most likely to volunteer (Bureau of Labor Statistics, 2010).

> *Observation 5*: It appears that many older adults may be poised for paid/unpaid purpose work. The primary question is whether institutions in our civil society are willing to re-design volunteer opportunities to take full advantage of the desire that many older adults have to 'give back' as well as the skills that they have to doing so.

Paid employment

One of the most visible changes in the experience of aging in America has been the new patterns of labor force participation among older adults. In 2000, the labor force participation rate of adults age 55+ was 32.4%; a decade later, in 2010, it had risen significantly, to 40.2%. BLS projections indicate that it will reach 43.0% in 2020 (Toossi, 2012).

The findings of surveys suggest that today's older adults expect to remain in the labor force during their so-called retirement years (Banerjee, 2011; First Command, 2011; Helman et al., 2011). While economic necessity is a factor in this decision, many older adults may feel that paid work offers them opportunities to continue as a productive member of society. In fact, according to one recent survey, one in five working Americans state that they do not plan to retire (Sun-Life Financial, 2011).

> *Observation 6*: Paid work has been a salient feature of the adult lives of today's older adults. The rise of the dual earner household as the normative coupled household for Baby Boomers meant that the structure and demands of work have affected both men and women. It should not be surprising that a majority of today's older adults might expect to incorporate paid work

(whether as a part- or full-time employee or as someone who is self-employed, possibly working as a consultant) into their retirement years before experiencing the frailties of later life (Brown et al., 2010).

Thus, there are strong indications that the experience of aging is different today than it was for the parent and grandparents of the Baby Boomers. The added years of vitality and health lavished upon adults in later life today have ushered in a new stage of life. While it has many names – 'third age' (James and Wink, 2007; Laslett, 1991); 'third chapter' (Lawrence-Lightfoot, 2009); 'active wisdom' (Bateson, 2010); 'middlescence' (Dychtwald, 2005); Act IV (Carstensen, 2009); 'encore adulthood' (Freedman, 2011)' and 'midcourse' (Moen, 2006) – none appear to have taken hold. Recently, we have referred to this new life stage as the X Revolution (James et al., 2012). Nevertheless, most agree that there is a new time of life following the most active work and parenting years, and before the demise that inevitably comes to all of us, that represents an opportunity for new roles and responsibilities. As Freedman points out, the period opening up in the 'bonus decades beyond midlife marks an extraordinary coming together of experience, perspective, motivation, capacity, and the time to do something with it all. Or, put differently, it is a time when many have insights about what matters, a special impetus to act on this wisdom, and the ability to do so' (2011: 98). To wit, older adults of today may engineer a very different later life than did previous cohorts.

Given the emerging trends related to aging, it is likely that today's older Americans will need to be trailblazers … but that could put them in a vulnerable position for two principal reasons. First, the normative experiences and expectations connected to aging are in flux. As a result, some people may experience some sense anxiety because they do not know what they 'should' do. Secondly, although new experiential and cultural norms are emerging, most of the institutional structures, policies and programs reflect the experience of aging in the past but not the present (for many) and probably not the future (for most).

Rowe and Kahn (1998) suggest that staying engaged with life is one of the critical factors that affect success in older adulthood. This idea of staying engaged has been interpreted broadly as an injunction to maintain an active lifestyle, or one form or another of the 'busy ethic' (Ekerdt, 1986; see also Katz, 2000; Moody, 1988). The 'productive aging' paradigm recommends active involvement in so-called productive roles, activities that contribute to the economy, whether paid or unpaid (Morrow-Howell, 2010). We argue that such injunctions help to move the field away from the old ideas of disengagement and rolelessness, but that activity for activity's sake is unlikely to facilitate well-being to the extent that experiences that have psychological meaning will.

It must be said too that so-called 'successful' and 'productive' aging paradigms can be taken too far. As Gilleard and Higgs (2008) suggest, an over-emphasis on health and wellness or hyperactivity becomes a form of 'non-agedness that further reinforces the undesirability and fear of old age' (Wink and James, 2013: 81). The ability to accept limitations is crucial to well being – the fact that one cannot work as much, run as fast, and do as many activities in a day. The old context is still with us; we will inevitably leave this earth. Aging is most surely a process that involves some level of self-acceptance, along with a sense of humor. Yet, life has meaning no matter what is going on. Engagement is still possible. It helps to be healthy and well, but there are plenty of examples of frail elders' generous acts and continued role involvements. As we will see, when these acts flow out of deep investment of the self, such involvements in turn enhance the well-being of the role enactors. Staying busy for just the sake of it may be counterproductive and contribute to ill health.

ACTIVE INVOLVEMENT, BUT IN WHAT?

There are many activities and role involvements among the roster of possibilities for which older adults might get involved including travel, hobbies, playing golf and other games, playing musical instruments, gardening, and watching TV. For the most part, such activities all fall under the rubric of leisure and are considered part and parcel of the rewards of later life for those who can afford them. In fact, 'the principal activity of old age has become identified as leisure' (Uhlenberg, 1992: 460). In addition, there are social roles in which the majority of older adults are involved including that of grandparent, parent, spouse and friend, all valuable, important, and satisfying involvements. Activity theorists have long recognized that both leisure and social role activities are beneficial for both physical and mental health in later life (Lemmon et al., 1972; Reitzes et al., 1995).

In this chapter, however, along with our emphasis on expanding options for later life role activity, we focus on less typical roles that might be considered 'generative' in the sense that they have the potential to be both useful to society and personally gratifying. In addition, we focus on role theory. Roles, by definition are prescriptive; they define behavior. They come with obligations. 'Role consists of the expected behavior considered appropriate to any set of rights and duties' (Rosow, 1976: 462). Throughout life roles shift and change, but in later life, role obligations are perceived as receding. Even the word 'retirement' suggests as much.

Given the relative lack of norms for later life roles, especially in light of increased longevity, it is not surprising to find that role theory has been largely applied to young and middle adult roles, most especially in the lives of parents of young children, who are seen as adding the role of parent to that of worker. Although not focused on later life, some of these theoretical perspectives do provide insight about possible new roles for older adults. For instance, while there is some debate about the optimal number of roles that adults can assume with too many putting the adult at risk for role strain, (e.g., Goode, 1960), there is evidence that many adults benefit from simultaneously holding multiple roles (e.g., role enhancement theory, Gove and Geerken, 1977). Seldom, however, are older adult roles the focus of inquiry in discussions of multiple roles. In one exception, Adelmann (1994) examined the relationships between older adult involvement in eight roles and well-being, and in keeping with earlier work, found support for the role enhancement hypothesis. Unfortunately, this study, heuristic in many ways, but like previous studies, lacked any examination of the quality of the roles.

Options to become more engaged in diverse roles present new choices. What are the new 'role buckets'? During the past few decades, there has been increased attention paid to generative roles, or so-called 'productive aging roles' (Morrow-Howell, et al., 2001). These include activities and role-involvements that serve both the self and some social good such as paid work, volunteering, caregiving, and continued learning. Continued learning, for example, allows older adults to be fully prepared citizens for active involvement in their communities. Although there are many exemplars of active older adults among television advertisements, *AARP Magazine* covers, and *Today Show* centenarians, it is clear that there are many older adults who are not involved in paid employment, care giving, volunteer and/or educational roles, than might be if they perceived more options. In one study, for example, among older adults who were uninvolved in either employment or volunteer work, 70% indicated that their main retirement activity was watching television (Kaskie et al., 2008). As can be seen in Figure 27.1, most older adults are not involved in these particular generative roles.

Some retirees, who appear to be uninvolved, report that there are few opportunities in their locales for either volunteering or

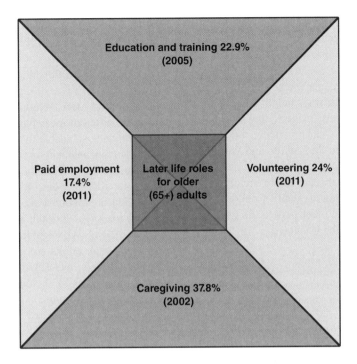

Figure 27.1 Involvement of older adults (65+) in productive aging roles

Notes:

1 Paid employment is defined as the percentage of the civilian non-institutional population that is working or looking for work.

2 Volunteering is defined as those persons who did unpaid (except for expenses) volunteer activities for an organization. The time period covers September 2010 through September 2011.

3 Education and training includes part-time degree programs, work-related courses, personal interest courses, and other activities. Categories are not mutually exclusive.

4 Other activities include: basic skills training, apprenticeships, and English as a Second Language (ESL) courses.

5 Caregiving is defined as the share of older adults providing care to relatives. Relatives include children, grandchildren, great grandchildren, parents or in-law, and spouses. Care provided to grandchildren or great grandchildren consists of 100 or more hours over the past two years. Parents living with minor children are assumed to be providing care. Care to spouses refers to the previous month, with the exception of deceased spouses, in which case care refers to the three months prior to death.

Sources:

1 US Bureau of Labor Statistics (2011) *Employment and Earnings* (January).

2 US Bureau of Labor Statistics (2012) *Volunteering in the United States*, 2011 (February). Volunteers are defined as persons who did unpaid work (except for expenses) through or for an organization.

3 US Department of Education (2007) *The Condition of Education, 2007* (Table 10.2, p. 133)

4 Johnson, R.W. and Schaner, S.G. (2005) 'Many older Americans engage in caregiving activities', *Urban Institute* (pp. 2–3). Caregiving is defined as the share of older adults providing care to relatives.

paid work (Kaskie et al., 2008). There is some question about the extent to which opportunities for engagement are as readily available for less well-educated individuals (Csikszentmihalyi, 1988; Morrow-Howell, 2010). However, several of our participants from one less-resourced community within the city revealed an array of generative involvements. One was a volunteer at the community center where we held the group. Another ran a 'chair exercise program' for the very old. Another volunteered as a reader in an inner-city elementary school. In the words of one, 'We were always taught … back from the time we were teenagers, that we had to "give back,"… it's like practicing etiquette…' [you learn how to do it early, and you don't stop just because you get older.] There are social and political needs in our society today, many of which would benefit from the skills and experience of older people. As one journalist writing in the US noted:

> Beyond working as greeters in Wal-Marts – or the better option of embarking on new careers based on unfulfilled lifelong interests – older Americans could help address many pressing national needs, such as looming teacher shortages, caregiving for the very elderly, mentoring the young and providing support for charitable and nonprofit organizations. Many also could be hired part-time for their experience, to train and impart knowledge to younger workers. (Yarrow, 2009)

IS 'JUST STAY ACTIVE' GOOD ADVICE?

Many forward-thinking gerontologists, in sync with and contributing to this changing context of aging, have worked to swing the pendulum toward a discussion of 'well-being' in later life and away from an overwhelming focus on the process of aging as inevitable decline, disease-oriented, and determined predominantly by genes – 'ill-being' (Ryff, 1989). While many prominent thinkers have contributed to these efforts, starting with, for example, the World Health Organization (WHO, 1948, cited in Ryff, 1989) and others (Jahoda, 1958) one of the most well-known concepts from recent years is that of 'successful aging', popularized by Rowe and Kahn (1998). This theory along with other positive aging approaches suggests that staying engaged with life is a major dimension of healthy aging.

WHAT DOES IT MEAN TO BE *ENGAGED* IN LATER LIFE?

In this chapter, we differentiate being *involved* (participating) in a role or set of activities and being *engaged* (deep investment of the self). Given the different meanings of engagement, it is quite understandable that most of the literature on engagement uses the two terms interchangeably, especially when thinking about later life activities. We learn then that older adults are involved in a variety of activities and roles (Katz, 2000; Litwin and Shiovitz-Ezra, 2006). We might learn how much or how often older adults are involved in those activities or role sets (Fischer et al., 1991; Kaskie et al., 2008). Seldom do we learn about the quality of those experiences or how deeply engaged or invested role enactors are.

We know that older adults appear to be more interested in the 'satisfaction of emotionally meaningful goals, which entails far more than simply feeling good' (Carstensen et al., 2000: 645). Critics of the successful and the productive aging paradigms suggest that life is meaningful regardless of health or ability to contribute to the economy (Estes and Mahakian, 2001; Wong, 1989). As Wong says, 'Life is worth living when there are dreams to be fulfilled, tasks to be accomplished, and new joys to be experienced' (1989: 521). Japanese centenarians refer to such commitments as *ikigai*, a reason to get up in the morning, or the practice of maintaining a purpose-filled life (Buettner, 2008). Similarly, Ryff and Singer assert that engaged living is purpose-driven (2008). Katz suggests that older adults want to be active in 'ways that open up … life to new possibilities' (2000: 145). Importantly, as Ryff et al. note, 'Human well-being is ultimately an issue of engagement in living, involving expression of a broad range of human potentialities: intellectual, social, emotional, and physical' (1998: 2). Taking up new roles opens doors of new possibilities and meaning (e.g., becoming a grandparent; getting involved in volunteer and civic activities, starting a retirement job).

Some theorists have studied the manifestations of engagement with paid work as a single focus. Kahn viewed work engagement as the 'harnessing of organizational member's selves to his or her work role; in engagement, people employ and express themselves physically, cognitively, and emotionally during role performances' (1990: 694). Kahn then, distinguished *engagement* (active investment of the self) from *involvement* (just going through the motions). Since then, work engagement or employee engagement has become a buzz word, and a matter of great concern to employers, most of whom want employees who are deeply engaged, not just involved, in their work (James et al., 2011). To be engaged at work is to have an energetic and affective connection with one's role as an employee (Kahn, 1990; Pitt-Catsouphes and Matz-Costa, 2009; Saks, 2006; Schaufeli et al., 2002). Importantly, Schaufeli & Bakker, following both Kahn (1990) and Csikszentmihalyi (1988), developed a measure of work engagement that was deemed to assess a state of mind characterized by 'dedication, absorption, and vigor' (Schaufeli & Bakker, 2003: 702).

These authors suggest that 'dedication' means being strongly invested in the work and experiencing a sense of significance, enthusiasm, inspiration, pride, and challenge. Absorption refers to being happily engrossed in one's work, such that time passes quickly; when fully absorbed, for example, one might have difficulties detaching from the activity. Vigor, the third factor in this model of work engagement, is manifesting high levels of energy and mental resilience, perhaps 'zest,' (following Russell, 1930), the willingness to invest effort in one's work, and to persist even in the face of difficulties.

It should be noted that all of these theories of engagement involve some level of challenge, a confrontation of difficulties, even struggle along the way. Ryff and Singer for example say that 'happiness is not always an easy pursuit, but a struggle … positive health is ultimately about engagement in living;

difficult experience, pain, and struggle are inevitably parts of such engagement … The negative may even contribute to the attainment of deeply felt life purpose and richly experienced relationship with others' (2008: 10). Csikszentmihalyi (1988) says that people will go to great lengths of suffering to achieve the feeling of 'flow'. Persistence in the face of difficulties is also an element of both Kahn's (1990) and Schaufeli's et al. (2002) ideas about engagement. The opposite of engagement then might be ennui, boredom, lacking a reason to live, or feeling that one's life does not matter, which indeed might follow from 'rolenessness.'

As we have pointed out, there are many different perspectives on the meaning of engagement, and with those perspectives, different ways of assessing it. Only the measures of work engagement, however, assess engagement in relation to a particular role. Thus, we have drawn heavily from measures of work engagement (Schaufeli et al., 2002) to assess engagement with other later life roles including volunteer, caregiving, and educational and training activities (James et al., 2012). Although both our measure and our ideas about engagement continue to evolve, and are based on our understanding of multiple other perspectives on it, our current working definition of engagement with a role is:

> … an enthusiastic, affective connection with a role that both motivates individuals to invest their valuable resources in it, and simultaneously energizes them. Engagement is characterized by a high degree of investment of personal energies (physical, cognitive, emotional) into a role, by an intense focus on the role activities to the point where other thoughts and distractions melt away, and by genuine enthusiasm and interest in the involvement. Highly engaged individuals feel enlivened and invigorated when participating and feel that they can persist in the face of difficulties. Disengagement is characterized by a lack of investment of personal energies (physical, cognitive, or emotional) into a role, being largely unfocused on the role activities to the point where one is almost always distracted or thinking about other things, and experiencing a complete lack of interest in the activities. Disengaged individuals

feel indifferent or bored by their participation in the role and tend to give up in the face of difficulties. (Matz-Costa, 2012, personal communication)

Thus, we view involvement in a role or set of activities and engagement as two very different things.

WHAT ARE THE CONSEQUENCES OF ENGAGEMENT?

Even with the various meanings of engagement, the different disciplines that embrace the term or that use it as an umbrella for other terms, and the different strategies used to measure it, it is not difficult to summarize across such an expanse of research. Broadly speaking, it is widely seen as a positive both at the individual and the organizational levels.

Ryff (1989), for example, who defines engagement as having purpose in life and quality connections to others, reports that engagement is associated with multiple indicators of both physical and mental health. Similarly, Csikszentmihalyi and his colleagues (see, for example, Csikszentmihalyi, 1988) find that flow is related to positive outcomes such as life satisfaction and successful coping, at least among younger people. Collins, Sarkisian and Winner (2009) extended this work to show that 'flow' also predicted well-being in older adults.

In the workplace, engagement with work is said to predict all manner of positive outcomes for employers and their employees. Research suggests, for example, that workers who are engaged tend to be less stressed and more satisfied with their personal lives; they also tend to use less health care, take fewer sick days, be more productive, and stay longer with their organizations than their less engaged counterparts (Gallup Organization, 2003, 2006). Although the research is somewhat mixed, there is some evidence that older workers are more engaged than are younger workers (James et al., 2011; Robinson et al., 2004).

It would seem that structured and meaningful activities are especially important for the well-being of older adults who are in the process of redefining, gaining and losing later life roles. Yet, what we know about engagement comes from global summaries of it (e.g., Rowe and Kahn, 1998) or confined to engagement with the work role (Schaufeli et al., 2002). Research within the productive aging paradigm has suggested many positive links on the basis of 'involvement' with the roles of work, volunteering, and caregiving, (for a review, see Morrow-Howell, 2010) but seldom examines links based on the quality of those involvements. To correct for some of these gaps in the literature, we conducted a study examining the relationship between engagement and four later life activities: paid work, volunteering, education and training, and caregiving.

Findings from the Life & Times in an Aging Society Study (James et al., 2012), based on a convenience sample of over 800 adults, ages 21–83, suggest that being *involved* in any one of the four roles of interest, but not particularly challenged by it, excited about it, or dedicated to it is worse for well-being than not being involved in the activity at all. Those who are highly engaged in any of the four roles report significantly greater well-being than those who are low in engagement. Importantly, the well-being gap between those whose level of engagement in an activity was low and those who were not involved in the activity at all was widest in the 65 and older age group, suggesting that the quality of one's experience of an activity may be most consequential for the well-being of individuals in later life. *Engagement*, then, is important for older adults' well-being.

Ryff and Singer suggest that we have yet to provide older adults with 'meaningful roles and opportunities for continued growth,' (2008: 27–28), another example of a structural lag (Riley et al., 1994). We believe a new focus on engagement is valuable in itself to better assess what people do and how that changes as they 'age' in roles, and also how these aspects are related to well-being.

WHAT ARE THE BARRIERS TO ENGAGEMENT IN GENERATIVE ROLES?

The way forward is not clear, however. There are both implicit and explicit barriers to engagement in these generative roles. Both individuals and social structures must change so that opportunities are easier to come by.

Work

As for opportunities to continue work, the rigid job structure so common today may make it difficult for older adults to either postpone retirement, or adjust the ratio of work to leisure (Christensen and Schneider, 2010). The types of jobs sought by older workers may not be as available as they would like (Heidkamp et al., 2010; Johnson and Park, 2011; Moen and Huang, 2010;). The recession has driven both employers and employees to rethink assumptions about 'ideal jobs,' careers, and employment opportunities for employees of all ages but particularly for older workers. Negative perceptions of the capabilities of older workers persist (James et al., in press).

Voluntarism

Similarly, volunteer activities that draw upon the skill and experience of older adults are still not readily available. Some of the same negative perceptions of older adults in the workplace limit their ability to engage in volunteer activities as well. According to a National Council on Aging report, there is little confidence in the leadership abilities of older adults; instead they are viewed as 'service providers … and not as leaders, project coordinators, advocates, or in other roles of directing efforts or shaping strategies' (2005: 13) Many older adults say that they simply have not found the opportunity they are looking for. Among those most interested in volunteering, 39% say that they have not found the right opportunity; 27% report that they have not found anything well-suited to their skills (VolunteerMatch, 2007: 19).

Another perception that limits older adult involvement with volunteer activities is that they can be most helpful to members of their own group. In the same report mentioned above, older adults are more likely to get volunteer assignments for groups that work with older adults than they were to find assignments working with children and youth. To the extent the older adults are interested in working with the young, the perception that they can be most helpful *only* to older people limits their opportunities for finding meaningful activities.

According to a recent report (sponsored by the National Council on Aging, 2005) surveying numerous organizations, few make it a priority to attract and retain older volunteers. This may be a staffing problem (no one to do the work) or a lack of desire, or downright ageism. Until more organizations recognize the expressed wish of older adults to volunteer (at least 50% do according to an AARP (2003) study), there will be more who are willing to volunteer than there will be assignments for them.

Caregiving

As for caregiving, there are barriers as well. There is a popular perception that most informal caregiving activities are performed by young to middle-aged adults. The perception is that the care of dependent children is primarily performed by young to middle-aged women and the care of dependent elderly is primarily performed by middle-aged offspring, especially daughters and daughters-in-law. As noted above, however, a substantial number of adults aged 55+ provide care to their parents and in-laws, frail spouses, children, and grandchildren (Johnson and Schaner, 2005). The obstacle then, in relation to older adults' involvement in caregiving role, is the lack of recognition of the enormity of their money-saving contributions to care in our society.

Education and training

Although the situation is changing there are many barriers to engagement with educational activities. Colleges and universities are still largely youth-oriented (Lakin et al., 2008). There is a widely held perception that older adults cannot learn, or retool for a new job (Hedge et al., 2006). Older adults themselves may steer clear of educational and training activities for fear of their own ability to keep up (Golub et al., 2002).

If older adults of today are to forge new paths in later life, attention to such constraints is one of the challenges of our time. There are, however, a growing number of organizations and groups working to overcome such barriers. For the last seven years, we and our colleagues have conducted research examining the needs of older workers and employer responses to those needs, especially the importance of workplace flexibility (Christensen and Schneider, 2010; James et al., 2010; Smyer and Pitt-Catsouphes, 2007; Van Dalen et al., 2010). There are also non-profit organizations in the US such as Civic Ventures that support older adults in their efforts to find 'encore careers' or participate in civic activities (Freedman, 1999, 2007, 2011). A recent report from the National Governors Association (Hoffman and Andrew, 2010) describes various initiatives being implemented at the state level to promote engagement of older adults. For example, many states allow retired educators as well as health care professionals to return to the public sector without penalizing retirement plans. In Arizona, the Civilian Volunteer program uses volunteers throughout the agency to assist officers and civilian personnel. In regard to caregiving, many new approaches are being implemented to provide support, training and services to family caregivers, including, for example, the participant-directed model of care, in which family caregivers can be integrated into the care plan for patients receiving care funded through Medicaid and state programs (Feinberg et al., 2011). Early adopters such as these lead the way and encourage others to catch up. Eventually, new norms are established.

EMBRACING THE NEW CONTEXT OF AGING

Being older in today's society is not what it used to be. It is therefore an exciting time for older adults who continue to have life and limb well into the conventional retirement ages. These individuals are increasingly aware as they age that they are healthier, living longer than their parents, and desirous of engaging in activities that make a difference in society and enrich their own personal lives.

Older adults are welcoming new roles and opportunities, not the shedding of these. With more flexible time, there are possibilities for participating in multiple roles. While focusing on the social good, they are also able to attend to their own needs. They want to be available to others, especially family and volunteering, but they also desire time for personal pursuits. They often express a wish to stay in the workforce, yet they also look forward to having time for other valued activities.

Now that we envision longer lives, there are many more options available that were unforeseen when we thought life was short. Seniors, just like their younger counterparts, want to be involved in activities that matter and make a difference, not just keeping busy without purpose or direction. When people participate fully in their roles and activities, society also tends to benefit. When these older adults work, volunteer, provide care, and learn, they are assets to their communities.

Successful and productive aging paradigms are changing. Older adults are in transition from the order and structure provided by prescribed prior roles (including work) and new pursuits not yet socially valued or even personally well defined. Yet, the new opportunities for healthy aging are limitless (e.g., college education, live-in-place communities, and Peace Corps programs for seniors). Generative acts and continuing role involvement are alerting society to prepare new institutional pathways and social structures that embrace these dedicated and vigorous older adults.

FUTURE DIRECTIONS

It has been said that engagement is just the latest 'buzz word' (Wefald and Downey, 2009). Although we disagree with this assessment, it is clear that more work is needed to clarify the definition and theory of engagement. While the literature on work engagement is quite extensive, the measurement of engagement as investment of the self has seldom been expanded to roles other than paid employment. Moreover, there appears to be some confusion over the extent to which engagement is a state (that can be modified) or a trait (that is stable over time). Longitudinal data are needed to shed light on this latter issue.

Longitudinal data are also needed to establish causal relationships between engagement and well-being. Most research, including ours, examining links between engagement and well-being is correlational. Perhaps happy and healthy older adults engage in meaningful pursuits rather than our contention that engagement in such pursuits enhances well-being. Longitudinal research is needed to better understand both the antecedents and consequences of engagement in later life and the extent to which engagement in different roles changes over time.

As we have mentioned, our sample for our study of engagement was highly educated. Research is needed that identifies pathways to engagement for marginalized groups such as lower income adults, racial and ethnic minorities, and rural older citizens.

Finally, we used a measure of work engagement that we revised and applied to volunteer, caregiving and educational activities (James et al., 2012). While our measure exhibited acceptable psychometric properties, there is a need for further understanding

of the extent to which engagement is similar across the generative roles that we studied or whether there are subtle differences that require separate measures. Perhaps new measures are needed.

In sum, there is much work to be done to take advantage of the shifting sands that we are experiencing worldwide in terms of aging today. Factors that contribute to or inhibit the engagement of adults in the third age may help to expand options, provide new possibilities for health aging. In these ways, we can truly optimize the long future of aging.

REFERENCES

AARP (2003) *Multicultural Study 2003: Time and Money: An in-Depth Look at 45+ Volunteers and Donors.* Washington: AARP.

AARP (2004) *Baby Boomers Envision Retirement II, Key Findings: Survey of Baby Boomers' Expectations for Retirement.* Washington: AARP.

Adelmann, P.K. (1994) 'Multiple roles and psychological well-being in a national sample of older adults', *Journals of Gerontology*, 49(6): S277–S285.

Administration on Aging (2010) *A Profile of Older Americans – 2009.* Washington: US Department of Health and Human Services.

Banerjee, S. (2011) 'Retirement age expectations of older Americans between 2006 and 2010', *Employee Benefit Research Institute Notes*, 13(12): 2–12.

Bateson, M.C. (2010) *Composing a Further Life: The Age of Active Wisdom.* New York: Alfred A. Knopf.

Brown, M., Aumann, K., Pitt-Catsouphes, M., Galinsky, E. and Bond, J.T. (2010) *Working in Retirement: A 21st Century Phenomenon.* New York: Families and Work Institute.

Buettner, D. (2008) *The Blue Zone: Lessons for Living Longer from the People Who've Lived the Longest.* Washington: National Geographic.

Bureau of Labor Statistics (2010) *Volunteering in the United States, 2009.* Washington: United States Department of Labor.

Bureau of Labor Statistics. (2011). *Employment and earnings.* Washington, DC: United States Department of Labor

Bureau of Labor Statistics. (2012). *Volunteering in the United States, 2011.* Washington: United States Department of Labor

Burgess, E.W. (1960) *Aging in Western Societies.* Chicago: University of Chicago Press.

Carstensen, L.L. (2009) *A Long Bright Future: An Action Plan for a Lifetime of Happiness, Health, and Financial Security.* New York: Broadway Books.

Carstensen, L.L., Pasupathi, M., Mayr, U. and Nesselroade, J.R. (2000) 'Emotional experience in everyday life across the adult life span', *Journal of Personality and Social Psychology*, 79(4): 644–655.

Centers for Disease Control and Prevention (2010) 'QuickStats: Life Expectancy at Birth, by Race and Sex – United States, 1970–2007', *Morbidity and Mortality Weekly Report*, 59(36): 1185.

Christensen, K. and Schneider, B. (2010) *Workplace Flexibility: Realigning 20th-Century Jobs a for a 21st-Century Workforce.* New York: Cornell University Press.

Collins, A.L., Sarkisian, N. and Winner, E. (2009) 'Flow and happiness in later life: An investigation into the role of daily and weekly flow experiences', *Journal of Happiness Studies*, 10(6): 703–719.

Corporation for National and Community Service (2006) *Volunteer Growth in America: A Review of Trends since 1974.* Washington: Corporation for National and Community Service.

Corporation for National and Community Service (2011) *New Report: Americans Devote 8.1 Billion Hours to Volunteering in 2010.* Washington: Corporation for National and Community Service.

Csikszentmihalyi, M. (1988) 'The flow experience and human psychology', in M. Csikszentmihalyi and I.S. Csikszentmihalyi (eds.), *Optimal Experience: Studies of Flow in Consciousness.* New York: Cambridge University Press. pp. 15–35.

Cumming, E. (2000) 'Further thoughts on the theory of disengagement', in J.F. Gubrium and J.A. Holstein (eds.), *Aging and Everyday Life.* Malden, Mass.: Blackwell. pp. 25–39.

Cumming, E., Dean, L.R., Newell, D.S., and McCaffrey, I. (1960) 'Disengagement – a tentative theory of aging', *Sociometry*, 23(1): pp. 23–35.

Dalirazar, N. (2007) *Reasons People Do Not Work: 2004.* Washington, DC: U S Census Bureau.

Department of Education. (2007). *The condition of education, 2007. (table 10.2, p. 133).* Washington, DC: United States Department of Education.

Dychtwald, K. (2005) 'Ageless aging: The next era of retirement', *Futurist*, 39(4): 16–21.

Ekerdt, D.J. (1986) 'The busy ethic: Moral continuity between work and retirement', *The Gerontologist*, 26(3): 239–244.

Estes, C.L. and Mahakian, J.L. (2001) 'The political economy of productive aging', in N. Morrow-Howell, J. Hinterlong and M.W. Sherraden (eds.), *Productive Aging: Concepts and Challenges.* Baltimore, MD: Johns Hopkins University Press. pp. 197–213.

Federal Interagency Forum on Aging-Related Statistics (2010) *Older Americans 2010: Key Indicators of Well-being.* Washington: U S Government Printing Office.

Feinberg, L., Reinhard, S.C., Houser, A. and Choula, R. (2011) *Valuing the Invaluable: The Economic Value of Family Caregiving, 2011 Update – the Growing Contributions and Costs of Family Caregiving.* Washington: AARP Public Policy Institute.

First Command (2011) *Reinventing Retirement.* USA: First Command Financial Services.

Fischer, L.R., Mueller, D.P. and Cooper, P.W. (1991) 'Older volunteers: A discussion of the Minnesota Senior Study', *The Gerontologist*, 31(2): 183–194.

Freedman, M. (1999) *Prime Time: How Baby Boomers Will Revolutionize Retirement and Transform America.* New York: Public Affairs.

Freedman, M. (2007) *Encore: Finding Work that Matters in the Second Half of Life.* New York: PublicAffairs.

Freedman, M. (2011) *The Big Shift: Navigating the New Stage Beyond Midlife.* New York: PublicAffairs.

Gallup Organization (2003, June 12) 'Bringing work problems home', *Gallup Management Journal*, online edition.

Gallup Organization (2006, October 12) 'Gallup study: Engaged employees inspire company innovation', *Gallup Management Journal*, online edition.

Gilleard, C., & Higgs, P. (2008). Internet use and the digital divide in the English longitudinal study of ageing. *European Journal of Ageing*, 5(3), 233-239. doi:10.1007/s10433-008-0083-7

Golub, S.A., Filipowicz, A. and Langer, E.J. (2002) 'Acting your age', in T.D. Nelson (ed.), *Ageism: Stereotyping and Prejudice Against Older Persons.* Cambridge: MIT Press. pp. 277–294.

Goode, W.J. (1960) 'A theory of role strain', *American Sociological Review*, 25: 483–496.

Gove, W.R. and Geerken, M.R. (1977) 'The effect of children and employment on the mental health of married men and women', *Social Forces*, 56(1): 66–76.

Hedge, J.W., Borman, W.C. and Lammlein, S.E. (2006) *The Aging Workforce: Realities, Myths, and Implications for Organizations.* Washington: American Psychological Association.

Heidkamp, M., Corre, N., & Van Horn, C. (2010). *The new unemployables: Older job seekers struggle to find work during the great recession – comparing the job search, financial, and emotional experiences of older and younger unemployed americans.* Chestnut Hill, MA: Sloan Center on Aging & Work at Boston College. Retrieved from http://www.bc.edu/content/dam/files/research_sites/agingandwork/pdf/publications/IB25_NewUnemployed.pdf

Helman, R., Copeland, C. and VanDerhei, J. (2008) *The 2008 Retirement Confidence Survey: Americans Much More Worried about Retirement, Health Costs a Big Concern*. Washington: Employee Benefit Research Institute.

Helman, R., Copeland, C., & VanDerhei, J. (2011). *The 2011 retirement confidence survey: Confidence drops to record lows, reflecting "the new normal".* (Issue Brief No. 355). Washington, DC: Employee Benefit Research Institute. Retrieved from http://www.ebri.org/pdf/briefspdf/EBRI_03-2011_No355_RCS-2011.pdf

Hoffman, L. and Andrew, E. (2010) *Maximizing the Potential of Older Adults: Benefits to State Economies and Individual Well-being*. Washington: NGA Center for Best Practices.

Iams, H.M., Phillips, J.R.W., Robinson, K., Deang, L. and Dushi, I. (2008) 'Cohort changes in the retirement resources of older women', *Social Security Bulletin*, 68(4): 1–13.

Jacobsen, L.A., Kent, M., Lee, M. and Mather, M. (2011) *America's Aging Population*. Washington: Population Reference Bureau.

Jahoda, M. (1958) *Current Concepts of Positive Mental Health*. New York: Basic Books.

James, J.B. and Wink, P. (2007) *The Crown of Life: Dynamics of the Early Postretirement Period*. New York: Springer.

James, J. B., Besen, E., Matz-Costa, C., & Pitt-Catsouphes, M. (2010). *Engaged as we age: The end of retirement as we know it*. (Issue Brief No. 24). Chestnut Hill, MA: Sloan Center on Aging and Work at Boston College. Retrieved from http://www.bc.edu/content/dam/files/research_sites/agingandwork/pdf/publications/IB24_EngagedAsWeAge.pdf

James, J.B., Besen, E., Matz-Costa, C. and Pitt-Catsouphes, M. (2012) *Just do it?... Maybe Not! Insights on Activity in Later Life from the Life & Times in an Aging Society Study*. Chestnut Hill, MA: Sloan Center on Aging & Work at Boston College.

James, J.B., McKechnie, S. and Swanberg, J. (2011) 'Predicting employee engagement in an age-diverse retail workforce', *Journal of Organizational Behavior*, 32(2): 173–196.

James, J. B., McKechnie, S. P., Swanberg, J. E., & Besen, E. (in press). Exploring the workplace impact of intentional and unintentional age discrimination. *Journal of Managerial Psychology*.

Johnson, R.W. and Park, J.S. (2011) *Can Unemployed Older Workers Find Work?* Washington: Urban Institute.

Johnson, R.W. and Schaner, S.G. (2005) *Value of Unpaid Activities by Older Americans Tops $160 Billion Per Year*. Washington, DC: Urban Institute.

Kahn, W.A. (1990) 'Psychological conditions of personal engagement and disengagement at work', *Academy of Management Journal*, 33(4): 692–724.

Kaskie, B., Imhof, S., Cavanaugh, J. and Culp, K. (2008) 'Civic engagement as a retirement role for aging Americans', *Gerontologist*, 48(3): 368–377.

Katz, S. (2000) 'Busy bodies: activity, aging, and the management of everyday life', *Journal of Aging Studies*, 14(2): 135–152.

Lakin, M.B., Mullane, L. and Robinson, S.P. (2008) *Mapping New Directions: Higher Education for Older Adults*. Washington: American Council on Education.

Laslett, P. (1991) *A Fresh Map of Life: The Emergence of the Third Age*. Cambridge: Harvard University Press.

Lawrence-Lightfoot, S. (2009) *The Third Chapter: Passion, Risk, and Adventure in the 25 Years After 50*. New York: Farrar, Straus and Giroux.

Lemmon, B.W., Bengtson, V.L. and Peterson, J.A. (1972) 'An exploration of the activity theory of again: Activity types and life satisfaction among in-movers to a retirement community', *Journal of Gerontology*, 27(4): 511–523.

Litwin, H. and Shiovitz-Ezra, S. (2006) 'The association between activity and wellbeing in later life: What really matters?', *Ageing & Society*, 26(2): 225–242.

Livingston, G. and Parker, K. (2010) *Since the Start of the Great Recession, More Children Raised by Grandparents*. Washington: Pew Research Center.

Matz-Costa, C. (2012) Personal communication.

Mermin, G.B.T., Johnson, R.W. and Toder, E. (2008) *Will Employers Want Aging Boomers?* Washington: Urban Institute.

Moen, P. (2006) 'Midcourse: Navigating retirement and a new life stage', in J.T. Mortimer and M.J. Shanahan (eds.), *Handbook of the Life Course*. New York: Plenum. pp. 269–294.

Moen, P. and Huang, Q. (2010) 'Customizing careers by opting out or shifting jobs: Dual-earners seeking life-course "fit"', in K. Christensen and B. Schneider (eds.), *Workplace Flexibility: Realigning 20th-Century Jobs for a 21st-Century Workforce*. Ithaca, NY: Cornell University Press. pp. 73–94.

Moody, H.R. (1988) 'The contradictions of an aging society: From zero sum to productive society', in R. Morris and S.A. Bass (eds.), *Retirement reconsidered: economic and social roles for older people*. New York: Springer. pp.15–34.

Morrow-Howell, N. (2010) 'Volunteering in later life: Research frontiers', *The Journals of Gerontology Series B: Psychological Sciences and Social Sciences*, 65B(4): 461–469.

Morrow-Howell, N., Hinterlong, J. E., Sherraden, M. W., & Rozario, P. (2001). Setting a research agenda on productivity in later life. In N. Morrow-Howell, J. E. Hinterlong & M. W. Sherraden (Eds.), *Productive aging: Concepts and challenges*. Baltimore, Md: Johns Hopkins University Press. pp. 285–312.

National Council on Aging (2005) *Respect Ability Web Survey Executive Summary*. Washington: National Council on Aging.

OECD (2009) 'Who participates in education?' in OECD Directorate for Education, *Education at a Glance 2009: OECD Indicators*. Paris: Organisation for Economic Co-operation and Development. pp. 277–291.

Pew Research Center (2010) *The Return of the Multi-Generational Family Household*. Washington: Pew Charitable Trusts.

Pitt-Catsouphes, M. and Matz-Costa, C. (2009) *Engaging the 21st Century Multi-Generational Workforce: Findings from the Age & Generations Study*. Chestnut Hill, MA: Sloan Center on Aging & Work at Boston College.

Public Policy Institute of California (2011) *An Assessment of Labor Force Projections through 2018: Will Workers have the Education Needed for the Available Jobs?* Washington: AARP.

Reitzes, D.C., Mutran, E.J. and Verrill, L.A. (1995) 'Activities and self-esteem: continuing the development of activity theory', *Research on Aging*, 17(3): 260–277.

Riley, M.W., Kahn, R.L., Foner, A. and Mack, K. (1994) *Age and Structural Lag: Society's Failure to Provide Meaningful Opportunities in Work, Family, and Leisure*. Oxford: John Wiley.

Robinson, D., Perryman, S. and Hayday, S. (2004) *The Drivers of Employee Engagement*. Sussex, UK: Institute for Employment Studies.

Rosow, I. (1976) 'Status and role change through the life span', in R.H. Binstock and E. Shanas (eds.), *Handbook of Aging and the Social Sciences*. New York: Van Nostrand Reinhold. pp. 457–482.

Rowe, J.W. and Kahn, R.L. (1998) *Successful Aging*. New York: Pantheon/Random House.

Russell, B. (1930) *The Conquest of Happiness*. New York: The Book League of America.

Ryff, C.D. (1989) 'Happiness is everything, or is it? Explorations on the meaning of psychological well-being', *Journal of Personality and Social Psychology*, 57(6): 1069–1081.

Ryff, C.D. and Singer, B.H. (2008) 'Know thyself and become what you are: a eudaimonic approach to psychological well-being', *Journal of Happiness Studies*, 9(1): 13–39. doi:10.1007/s10902-006-9019-0

Ryff, C.D., Singer, B., Love, G.D. and Essex, M.J. (1998) 'Resilience in adulthood and later life: Defining features and dynamic processes', in J. Lomranz (ed.), *Handbook of Aging and Mental Health: An Integrative Approach*. New York: Plenum Press. pp. 69–96.

Saks, A. M. (2006). Antecedents and consequences of employee engagement. *Journal of Managerial Psychology*, 21(7), 600-619. doi:10.1108/02683940610690169

Schaufeli, W.B. and Bakker, A.B. (2003) *Test Manual for the Utrecht Work Engagement Scale*.

Schaufeli, W.B., Salanova, M., González-Romá, V. and Bakker, A.B. (2002) 'The measurement of engagement and burnout: A two sample confirmatory factor analytic approach', *Journal of Happiness Studies*, 3(1): 71–92.

Smyer, M.A. and Pitt-Catsouphes, M. (2007) 'The meanings of work for older workers', *Generations*, 31(1): 23–30.

Sun-Life Financial (2011) *Sun Life Financial US Unretirement Index – Fall 2011: Americans' Trust in Retirement Reaches a Tipping Point*. US: Sun-Life Financial.

Toossi, M. (2012) 'Labor force projections to 2020: a more slowly growing workforce', *Monthly Labor Review*, 135(1): 43–49.

US Census Bureau (2005) *Statistical Abstract of the United States: 2004–2005. Population. (Section 1, Tables 31, p. 35)*. Washington: US Census Bureau.

Uhlenberg, P. (1992) 'Population aging and social policy', *Annual Review of Sociology*, 18: 449–474.

Van Dalen, H.P., Henkens, K. and Schippers, J. (2010) 'How do employers cope with an ageing workforce? Views from employers and employees', *Demographic Research*, 23(32): 1015–1036.

VolunteerMatch (2007) *Great Expectations: Boomers and the Future of Volunteering*. San Francisco: VolunteerMatch.

Wefald, A.J. and Downey, R.G. (2009) 'Job engagement in organizations: Fad, fashion, or folderol?', *Journal of Organizational Behavior*, 30(1): 141–145.

Williams, A., Fries, J., Koppen, J. and Prisuta, R. (2010) *Connecting and Giving: A Report on How Mid-Life and Older Americans Spend their Time, Make Connections and Build Communities*. Washington: AARP Knowledge Management.

Wink, P. and James, J.B. (2013) 'The Life Course Perspective on Life in the Post-Retirement Period', in M. Wang (ed.), *The Oxford Handbook of Retirement*. New York: Oxford University Press. pp. 59–72.

Wong, P.T. (1989) 'Personal meaning and successful aging', *Canadian Psychology/Psychologie Canadienne*, 30(3): 516–525.

Yarrow, A.L. (2009, November 3) *The New 'Awkward Age'*. Baltimore, MD: *Baltimore Sun*.

28

The Measurement of Multiple Dimensions of Subjective Well-being in Later Life

Bram Vanhoutte

INTRODUCTION: WHY MEASURE WELL-BEING?

In the last decades, well-being has received increasing attention from both social scientists and government officials. On an international level, the OECD has included subjective measures in its statistics since the declaration of Istanbul in 2007. Similarly the EU Commission and Eurostat have launched initiatives to capture subjective components of well-being. These developments on the international level have incited national and regional initiatives, among which the most influential are the 2009 French Commission on the Measurement of Economic Performance and Social Progress, headed by Joseph Stiglitz, Amartya Sen and Jean-Paul Fitoussi, and the more recent effort of the UK Office for National Statistics to Measure Well-Being (Beaumont, 2011).

The fairly recent policy interest in measuring subjective well-being is based on a longer tradition of academic research into quality of life (Nussbaum & Sen, 1993) and positive

psychology (Seligman & Csikszentmihalyi, 2000), aimed at extending the focus of research in the behavioural sciences from problematic behaviour to positive qualities, from repairing and healing to enhancing the ability of individuals to maintain a good life (Seligman & Csikszentmihalyi, 2000). In an aging society, it can be said that measuring subjective well-being and enhancing a good later life are even more important.

In this chapter an overview of the existing approaches to examine subjective well-being in later life is given. The focus is on subjective measures of well-being, but I acknowledge that different approaches such as objective lists of conditions from which well-being emerges (Nussbaum & Sen, 1993) or preference satisfaction (Dolan & Peasgood, 2008) also have their merits. Both theoretical background and methodological issues of the measures are addressed. An important division in measuring instruments is made on the basis of different philosophical backgrounds of what well-being actually entails (Ryan &

Deci, 2001). Is subjective well-being mainly about being happy, or are there other things than pleasure and pain, such as self-actualisation, that influence one's level of contentment? Both approaches to well-being, classified as respectively hedonic and eudaimonic well-being, are a first point of attention. A second point of interest is the structure of measurement instruments of well-being when applied to the English Longitudinal Study of Aging (ELSA). A third point is to empirically investigate how many dimensions of well-being are ideally discerned.

DIFFERENT APPROACHES TO MEASURING SUBJECTIVE WELL-BEING

In everyday life subjective well-being (SWB) is probed for by the straightforward question 'How are you?', but accurate and reliable assessment of well-being is at the base of a quite complex and substantial debate. Subjective well-being is often used in conjunction with physical health, and is commonly used as a concept for psychological health. Secondly, it is seen as the subjective counterpart of objective indicators for quality of life, and involves an individual judgement. A third point which defines subjective well-being is that, just like its counterparts madness and illness, it is at least partly a social construct. What well-being entails therefore depends not only on the psychological outlook one has on life, but equally on the position in society and the society one lives in. This makes any enquiry into the nature of well-being a meeting ground between philosophical theory and empirical measurement (Sumner, 1999).

Hedonic well-being

The hedonic view on well-being assumes that through maximizing pleasurable experiences, and minimizing suffering, the highest levels of well-being can be achieved. This emphasis

on pleasure and stimulation entails not only bodily or physical pleasures, but allows any pursuit of goals or valued outcomes to lead to happiness. Both cognitive and affective aspects of well-being can be identified within this approach (Diener, 1984). A high level of well-being in the hedonic approach consists of a high life satisfaction, the presence of positive affect and the absence of negative affect (Figure 28.1) (Diener, 1984). Well-being resides within the individual (Campbell, Converse, & Rodgers, 1976), and therefore does not include reference to objective realities of life, such as health, income, social relations or functioning.

The affective aspect of hedonic well-being consists of moods and emotions, both positive and negative. Positive and negative affect each form a separate domain, and are not just opposites (Watson, Clark, & Tellegen, 1988). Positive affect (PA) is a state wherein an individual feels enthusiastic, active and alert. High PA means high energy, full concentration and pleasurable engagement, while low PA encompasses sadness and lethargy. Negative affect generally captures subjective distress and unpleasurable mood states, such as anger, disgust, guilt, fear and nervousness. Low negative affect (NA) on the other hand encompasses calmness and serenity. Both positive and negative affect are usually measured by letting the respondent assess the prevalence of a number of emotional states in the last month (Watson et al., 1988). The affective approach to well-being can be traced back to the first enquiries on psychological well-being and quality of life (Bradburn, 1969).

The affective aspect of well-being brings measurement very close to assessing mental health. Therefore it is not surprising that depressive symptoms are sometimes used as a measure of NA (Demakakos, McMunn, & Steptoe, 2010). Depression is traditionally assessed by the Centre for Epidemiological Studies Depression (CES-D) scale (Radloff, 1977), which has been shown to be accurate and valid among the older population as well as at younger ages (Lewinsohn, Seeley,

Roberts, & Allen, 1997). A second measure for mental health, the 12 item version of the General Health Questionnaire (GHQ) (Goldberg, 1988) can be seen in the light of affective measures of SWB as well. The GHQ-12 is a widely used screening tool for psychiatric disturbance, and has shown to have good psychometric properties and reliability for older people (Cheung, 2002).

In relation to later life, affective aspects of well-being have been studied quite intensively. On the level of measurement, it has been illustrated that the PANAS scale (Watson et al., 1988) has good psychometric and scale properties among the old, and yields information that is comparable to other age groups (Crawford & Henry, 2004; Kercher, 1992; Kunzmann, Little, & Smith, 2000). In regard to differences in mean levels of affect, it is an established fact that NA decreases over the lifespan, albeit the rate of decline is slower in old age, and may reverse in old-old age, while results for PA are not unequivocal (Charles, Reynolds, & Gatz, 2001; Crawford & Henry, 2004; Kunzmann, 2008; Kunzmann et al., 2000; Ready et al., 2011). From investigations into the facets of emotions, there is some evidence that although PA and NA are valid and separate factors, the structure of the interrelations among emotions in older adults differs from younger adults (Ready et al., 2011). Specifically sadness and depressive feelings seem to be more interrelated with anxiety. In connection to that, some studies report more somatic symptoms than emotional moods of depression by older adults (King & Markus, 2000), leading to the challenged idea that depression manifests itself in a different way for older adults, a phenomenon called later life depression (Alexopoulos, 2005; Lebowitz et al., 1997). As depression is not a monolithic disease, but an emotional disorder accompanied by physiological symptoms, it is difficult to distinguish it from conditions in later life that trigger similar symptoms, such as chronic illness or cognitive impairment as the result of dementia or Alzheimer's disease (Lebowitz et al., 1997). In addressing this issue, it is helpful to make a distinction between major depression, which is less prevalent among the elderly (2%), and minor depression (15%), which is more common, and closely interrelated with stressful life events in later life and vascular risk factors (Beekman & Deeg, 1995; Van den Berg et al., 2001). While the CES-D scale and GHQ are robust instruments to measure major depression in later life, they are less accurate in picking up minor depression (Papassotiropoulos, Heun, & Maier, 1999; Watson & Pignone, 2003).

The cognitive component of hedonic well-being, often referred to as life satisfaction, is a judgemental process in which individuals asses the quality of their life based on their own set of criteria (Pavot & Diener, 1993). As such, it differs from domain specific evaluations of satisfaction (Campbell, Converse, & Rodgers, 1976) in that an idiosyncratic set of standards is taken into account, which allows comparing satisfaction with life over groups of people with different aspirations in life. The Satisfaction With Life Scale (SWLS) (Diener, Emmons, Larsen, & Griffin, 1985; Pavot & Diener, 1993) consists of 5 items to be rated on a response scale ranging from 1 (strongly disagree) to 7 (strongly agree), inviting respondents to make a global evaluation of their life. It was also explicitly tested on older respondents (Diener et al., 1985). From a methodological perspective, it is surprising that all the items are worded in a positive way, because this way the scale could suffer from extreme response and acquiescence bias. Often at least one item is worded in a negative sense, to avoid respondents answering without really thinking about the question asked.

Perceptions about the self and one's own life tend to be too positive and optimistic (Kahneman & Thaler, 2006; Taylor & Brown, 1988), so that hedonic well-being ultimately depends on how high or low one sets his goals. This judgemental relativity is seen as a major problem in assessing the validity across the population for hedonic cognitive measures, as even a slave can be happy. Similarly, adaptation plays a main role in the

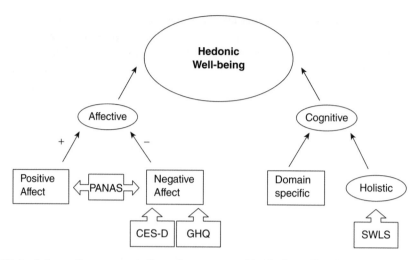

Figure 28.1　Schematic representation of measures of hedonic well-being

cognitive process of accepting the circumstances as they are and moving to a normal level of well-being (see further). A second severe criticism on well-being as maximizing pleasure, is that negative events have an important role in providing insight about one-self, or growing as a person (Ryff & Singer, 1998). Positive psychology itself is deeply rooted in investigating which type of persons are resilient to negative conditions (Seligman & Csikszentmihalyi, 2000).

Eudaimonic well-being

A second, and in practice largely complementary (Waterman, 1993), approach starts from a different concept of well-being. A good life is not just about pleasure and happiness, but involves developing one-self and realizing one's potential (Ryff & Keyes, 1995). Eudaimonic well-being reflects positive functioning and personal expressiveness. Positive functioning, or psychological well-being, reflects the need for self-actualisation in Maslow's (1968) need hierarchy. Similarly, positive functioning can be seen from the perspective of developmental psychology, as personality changes articulate well-being as trajectories of continued growth across the life cycle (Erikson, 1959).

As the concept of positive functioning is rooted in different approaches, several different measurement instruments can be found. Ryan and Deci (2000) conceptualize it in their self-determination theory and see autonomy, competence and relatedness as three basic necessities for personal growth, integrity and well-being. By looking at six distinct aspects of actualisation (autonomy, personal growth, self-acceptance, life purpose, mastery and positive relatedness), Ryff & Keyes (1995) measure psychological well-being, which they see separate from subjective well-being.

In the framework of studies on later life, a measure specifically targeted at older populations has been developed (Hyde, Wiggins, Higgs, & Blane, 2003). Four constructs, namely Control, Autonomy, Self-realization and Pleasure (CASP) together can be seen as an accurate measure of positive functioning, and subjective quality of life in later life. An explicit aim of this measure from it's conception was to distinguish quality of life from it's drivers, such as health (Hyde et al., 2003). Therefore it is quite surprising to see explicit references to the respondents' age and health on the item level, in items such as 'My age prevents me from doing the things I would like to' and 'My health stops me from

Table 28.1 Overview of dimensions of eudaimonic well-being

PWB (Ryff & Keyes, 1995)	SDT (Ryan & Deci, 2000)	CASP 19 (Hyde et al. 2003)
Autonomy	Autonomy	Autonomy
Personal growth	Competence	Self-realisation
Self-acceptance		
Life purpose		
Environmental mastery		Control
Positive relatedness	Relatedness	
		Pleasure

doing the things I want to do'. Theoretically this is unsound because it contaminates the measure with aspects of health status. From a methodological point of view, a confirmatory factor analysis by the developers of the measure has equally shown that the error term of the item referring to health correlates with some other items in the scale, and that the scale shows better properties in a reduced form with 12 items (Wiggins, Netuveli, Hyde, Higgs, & Blane, 2008). A second point of importance concerns the domain of Pleasure, which could be seen more as a hedonic than a eudaimonic form of well-being. When looking at different measures of well-being at the same time, this should be kept in mind.

Comparing the dimensionality of different conceptualisations of eudaimonic well-being it becomes clear that in large lines they rely on very similar concepts and sub-dimensions (see Table 28.1). All three approaches depart from the idea that human flourishing depends on the satisfaction of certain psychological needs. Autonomy is a need that is present explicitly in psychological well-being (PWB), self-determination theory (SDT) and CASP. Both control in CASP, and environmental mastery in PWB can be seen as a closely related concept, relating to autonomy. The second key aspect of eudaimonic well-being is developing one-self, and is captured as personal growth in PWB, as competence in SDT and self-realisation in CASP. The largest difference between the three approaches is that both PWB and SDT do not see pleasure, or any other aspect of

Diener's hedonic concepts as an explicit psychological need (Diener, Sapyta, & Suh, 1998; Ryff & Singer, 1998), while CASP does. While Ryff & Singer (1998) downplay the importance of hedonic well-being altogether, Ryan & Deci (2001) see it as a consequence of the fulfilment of needs, that goes hand in hand with eudaimonic well-being. Secondly, relatedness, or having warm and positive social relations, is seen as an essential need for psychological well-being, while it is not explicitly defined in the CASP scale.

Retrospective, experienced and reconstructed well-being

A second form of measurement diversity reflects theoretical and methodological considerations on the nature of changes in well-being. Is well-being a relatively stable stock product, affected little by fluctuations over time and life-events, or can it better be characterized as a flow, volatile and changeable? In later life, the evolution of well-being over time is specifically interesting, as old age is often characterized as a period in life where health risks and social losses occur within a short time-span.

One way to look at well-being is to see it as experienced utility in the classical economical sense. Probing for someone's level of well-being as a stock, by using self-reporting in surveys, can be prone to errors because of effects of social desirability, judgement and memory, which have been illustrated extensively in the case of hedonic well-being

(Kahneman & Thaler, 2006). Nevertheless, both hedonic and eudaimonic self-reported well-being have shown to be grounded in reality, as they are closely associated to the attribution of positive personality traits by both acquaintances and clinicians, and cheerful, socially skilled behaviour (Kahneman & Krueger, 2006; Nave, Sherman, & Funder, 2008).

To emphasize the flow of hedonic well-being, alternative methods of collecting information have been set up. One influential but time-consuming approach is experience sampling (Csikszentmihalyi, 1990), where people report their moods and emotions on the spot in everyday life, by describing the activity they are doing and the pleasure achieved from it when a timer beeps, which happens several times during a day. In a recent effort to make this information easier to acquire, the day reconstruction method, where the respondent reconstructs his previous day episode by episode and then assigns moods to each period, has shown to be a reliable equivalent (Kahneman, Krueger, Schkade, Schwarz, & Stone, 2004).

A last influential approach to changes in well-being focuses on the impact of positive and negative effects of life events and changes in conditions. The main argument is that there is a form of adaptation, or treadmill effect, meaning that well-being levels adapt to both positive and negative events and emotions, so that there is no actual evolution in the long term (Brickman & Campbell, 1971; Diener, Lucas, & Scollon, 2006). Although there initially was substantive evidence for the treadmill effect when looking at hedonic measures of well-being (Brickman, Coates, & Janoff-Bulman, 1978), some substantial revisions to the treadmill argument have been suggested (Diener et al., 2006). A first domain of concern is set point theory, or the idea that there is a fixed level of well-being that one departs or returns from when experiencing an event. These points are multidimensional, meaning that they can differ for affective and cognitive aspects of well-being. Set points also are not neutral, but instead tend to be positive (Diener & Diener, 1996), and vary considerably among

individuals, due to inborn personality based influences (Diener, Suh, & Lucas, 1999). Secondly, while the treadmill argument implies that people eventually adapt the both good and bad circumstances, it has been illustrated that change does happen on the long term, for example when faced with unemployment (Lucas, Clark, Georgellis, & Diener, 2004), or loss of a partner (Lucas, Clark, Georgellis, & Diener, 2003). The extent to which adaptation occurs is heavily dependent on the individual as well, and coping and personality characteristics seem to play an important role. It has to be kept in mind that the bulk of the research on this topic has examined hedonic well-being. Nonetheless, also when it comes to eudaimonic well-being processes of adaptation can be thought of, especially when looking at self-realisation (Waterman, 2007). The experience of flow (Csikszentmihalyi, 1990), when the challenge posed and the skill of an individual are balanced, could become quite rare as a person is becoming more experienced and hence more skilled, leading to an eudaimonic treadmill. Waterman (2007) argues that the opposite is actually the case, since eudaimonic well-being is the result of striving more than the actual outcome, and new fields for self-realisation are in practice endless.

In this analysis we will limit ourselves to the traditional retrospective, self-reported, measurements of hedonic and eudaimonic well-being, but it is clear that alternative measures are possible and available.

ASSESSING MEASUREMENT

It is beyond the scope of this chapter to examine all possible aspects of the measurement of well-being. In this analysis we limit ourselves to a more conceptual question on the nature of well-being: Can well-being be seen as a single dimension or not? To what extent do different scales reflect different aspects of well-being? In a first step the ideal structure for several aspects of subjective well-being, reflected in different scales is investigated. While some scales were specifically designed for an older population (CASP), others are scales (SWLS,

CES-D, GHQ) usually applied to a general population sample. Therefore it is important to look at the structure of these scales specifically for an older population, and to investigate if they function in the same way as they do in the general population. In a second step, a second-order model of well-being is constructed, to see how the different sub-dimensions relate to each other. Can we really distinguish two main dimensions, a eudaimonic and a hedonic form of well-being, or is a different conceptual framework more suited when looking at well-being in later life? A last important note is that while it focuses on problems associated with measurement, it does not insinuate that analyses based on 'bad' versions of a scale are flawed. Measurement models are very useful in testing the latent structure behind a scale, but usually using a refined scale does not alter substantive conclusions based on robust analysis.

Data and methods

These questions will be investigated using the self-completion part of the first three waves (collected in respectively 2002, 2004 and 2006) of ELSA (Marmot et al., 2011).[1] Different waves are used, because although not all instruments are present in the first or second wave, they have larger sample sizes (respectively 10253 and 8780) and as such allow for greater variability in the data. The third wave (using both core sample members and the refreshment sample, in total 8598 respondents) is used to assess the interrelations between all available scales. The exact item wording and answering categories used can be found in the appendix to this chapter.

The structure of the scales is often examined using factor analysis. Two main forms of factor analysis can be distinguished: exploratory factor analysis (EFA) and confirmatory factor analysis (CFA). EFA is more data-driven, and is often used in scale development, when there is little underlying theory on how items should load on a factor, or how many factors are present. CFA is used to test and confirm theoretical hypotheses on scale structure, as is the case in this chapter.

Examining scale structure consists of making the best configuration of items and factors based on substantive theory. A good scale structure in the first place consists of high factor loadings across the items that define it. A second, connected issue is the number of factors, or sub-dimensions that exist in a scale. In EFA, the data provides the number of dimensions asked and it's up to the researcher to determine the criterion for cut-off. The extensive use of EFA has been criticized, as it assumes that variables are measured perfectly, without any form of measurement error, so that all observed variance is true score variance (Brown, 2006). Secondly, a false number of factors can surface if method effects are not taken into account (Brown, 2003; Chen, Rendina-gobioff, & Dedrick, 2010; DiStefano & Motl, 2009; Hankins, 2008; Van de Velde, Bracke, Levecque, & Meuleman, 2010; Wood, Taylor, & Joseph, 2010). One possible method effect is that items posed in a negative manner can provoke different answers of a respondent, not due to the substantive matter but rather to the fact that the item is worded negatively (Marsh, 1996). Asking someone 'how often are you unhappy' is not simply the inverse of 'how often are you happy'. To account for this with CFA, one can either specify a separate and uncorrelated method factor, on which negatively worded items load, or allow error correlations between negatively worded items in the scales.

Usually maximum likelihood estimation (MLE) is used to estimate CFA models, but although this method is more precise in parameter estimation, it's limited to estimating two or three factors. A different estimator, weighted least squares means and variances adjusted (WLSMV), is computationally more efficient and gives equally reliable estimates as MLE (Beaducel & Herzberg, 2006). A positive aspect of this method is that since it does not assume normality of the distribution over the different answering categories, it can handle categorical or binary data. A drawback is that the chi-square based statistics cannot be directly compared between nested models, as is the case with MLE.

To determine which model fits better, a number of test statistics are available. The tests most widely used are the Root Mean Square Error of Approximation (RMSEA) (lower than .8 for decent fit and lower than .06 for good fit), the Comparative Fit Index (CFI) (higher than .95 for good fit) and Tucker Lewis Index (TLI) (higher than .95 for good fit) (Hu & Bentler, 1999). Similarly the size of factor loadings will be taken into account, because the use as a sum scale requires all items to load equally good (more than .60) on the latent constructs. A low factor loading means that in practice the item does not contribute a great deal to the latent measure.

Identifying factor structures

CASP

The CASP scale, a measure of quality of life in later life, in its original form has 19 items, but revised forms of 12 items (Wiggins et al., 2008) and 15 items (Vanhoutte, 2012) have been proposed for use. CASP is present in the self-completion questionnaire in its 19 item form in waves 1 to 5 of ELSA. Since often the individual items are not mentioned when the scale is used, and the psychometric tests on the original scale are referred to, it is relevant to investigate the structure of the latent concept in all versions of the scale. In the original study that tested the qualities of the CASP scale, a four dimensional structure was proposed for the 19 item scale, and a three dimensional structure was proposed for both the 12 and 15 item version (Vanhoutte, 2012; Wiggins et al., 2008).

In our analysis the dimensionality of the CASP scale is investigated, next to the usefulness of accounting for negative item wording. Understanding the differences between the structure of the models is key to grasping how confirmatory factor analysis is used to test theoretical models, therefore a schematic representation of the models is shown in Figures 28.2–28.6. The 19 item CASP-scale is used to illustrate the possible model configurations. The baseline model (Figure 28.2) assumes all

items load onto the same factor. Each item is associated with an item-specific error term, which represents the variation that is not accounted for by the latent factor, in this case the CASP scale. To account for the possible measurement bias introduced by negative item wording, two possible specifications are used interchangeably in the literature. A first option is to allow correlations between the error terms of the items that are phrased negatively (Figure 28.3). A second, more restricting option is to specify a latent 'method' factor onto which these items load, next to their loading onto the substantive factor (Figure 28.4). If less than three items are phrased negatively, only error correlations are possible since a factor needs at least three items to be identified. As the dimensionality of CASP is also a point of interest, different models are specified to see which solution gives us the best factor model. A division between eudaimonic and hedonic aspects of well-being can be expected following the literature, so a two factor solution, isolating pleasure from control, autonomy, and self-actualisation, should also be tested (Figure 28.5). The best fitting model for CASP in other studies (Vanhoutte, 2012; Wiggins et al., 2008), distinguishing three dimensions, is also specified (Figure 28.6). Multidimensional models can equally be specified with a method factor or error correlations. Table 28.2 illustrates the results for these different configurations of the 15 item version of the CASP scale.

Table 28.2   Fit statistics for CFA of 15 item CASP scale in ELSA wave 1

	RMSEA	CFI	TLI
One factor (Quality of life)	.097	.928	.916
With error correlations	.087	.942	.932
Two factors (Pleasure/Control, Autonomy & Self-actualisation)	.089	.940	.929
With error correlations	.078	.954	.945
Three factors (Pleasure/Control & Autonomy/Self-actualisation)	.080	.952	.943
With error correlations	.072	.961	.953

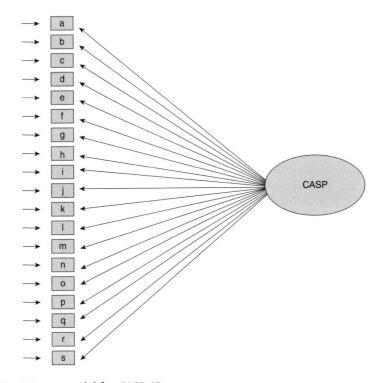

Figure 28.2   1 Factor model for CASP 19

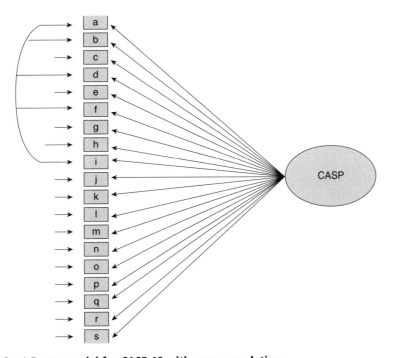

Figure 28.3   1 Factor model for CASP 19 with error correlations

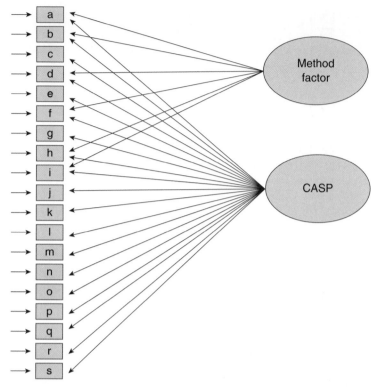

Figure 28.4   1 Factor model for CASP 19 with method factor for negatively worded items

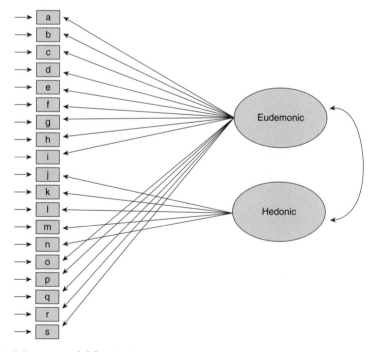

Figure 28.5   2 Factor model for CASP 19

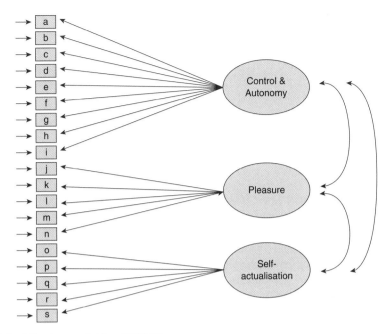

Figure 28.6   3 Factor model for CASP 19

In the best fitting solution, with three factors, each dimension is measured by 5 items, and error correlations are allowed between negatively phrased items. It is also clear that the negative item wording has an effect on the model, and as such should be taken into account.

CES-D

The original CES-D scale (Radloff, 1977) comprises 20 items, but shorter versions are frequently used and have shown not to lose a lot of information (Kohout, Berkman, Evans, & Cornoni-Huntley, 1993). In ELSA an 8 item version is used. When looking at the CES-D scale in its extended form with EFA, four sub-dimensions surface: positive affect, depressed affect, somatic complaints and interpersonal problems (Kohout et al., 1993; Radloff, 1977; Ross & Mirowsky, 1984). In the 8 item version only two subscales surface, one that captures mood symptoms and one that refers to somatic aspects of depression (Van de Velde et al., 2010; Wallace et al., 2000). The scale can be seen as a single scale, since internal consistency is high, and correlations between the

Table 28.3   Fit statistics for CFA of 8 item CES-D scale in ELSA wave 1

	RMSEA	CFI	TLI
1 factor (Depressive Symptoms)	.075	.964	.958
With error correlations	.066	.978	.958
2 factors (Somatic/Mood Symptoms)	.054	.986	.978
With error correlations	.035	.994	.991

sub-dimensions are higher than .90 in the general population (Van de Velde et al., 2010). In this analysis we will look at the two factor solution, since theoretically depression in later life is explicitly linked to its somatic component. Testing the scale in a CFA framework, it has also been established that the CES-D scale represents a continuum rather than forming separate factors for positively and negatively worded items, if correlations between negatively worded items are allowed (Wood et al., 2010).

All fit statistics, both for one or two factors, are acceptable (see Table 28.3). It is clear that allowing error correlations between negatively worded items significantly improves the models. The two factor model has a better fit, and there is a correlation of .82 between both factors, which is still high, but substantially lower than the .90 reported in the general population. The data clearly favour the most complex model, with two factors and error correlations between the negatively worded items, but even a simple one factor model has an acceptable fit, illustrating the robust reliability of the shortened CES-D scale.

General health questionnaire (GHQ)

The GHQ is a 12 item scale, intended as a general screening instrument for psychiatric morbidity (Goldberg & Williams, 1988). Most researchers examining the factor structure have focused on the number of sub-dimensions. While a large part of the scientific work has been highlighting the plausibility of a two or three factor structure (anxiety, social dysfunction and loss of confidence) instead of the original one factor (Graetz, 1991; Shevlin & Adamson, 2005), recently the inclusion of method effects of negative wording has shown this multidimensionality to be a measurement artefact (Hankins, 2008). The two dimensional structure groups positive and negative items in separate dimensions, just like the three

Table 28.4 Fit statistics for CFA of 12 item GHQ scale in ELSA wave 1

	RMSEA	CFI	TLI
1 factor (mental health)	.143	.913	.894
With error correlations	.072	.984	.973
With method factor	.087	.972	.961
2 factors (positive/negative items of mental health)	.085	.970	.963
3 factors (anxiety/social dysfunction /loss of confidence)	.076	.977	.970

dimensional model (anxiety, social dysfunction and loss of confidence) (Graetz, 1991).

Our test on a representative sample of community dwelling people aged 50 or older seems to confirm these findings, showing a robust one factor solution (see Table 28.4). Since there is a significant difference in fit between the specifications

with error correlations and the method factor, allowing the error correlations might be masking substantial aspects of the scale. Therefore the three dimensional model is preferred to allow for greater conceptual nuance.

Satisfaction with life scale (SWLS)

The satisfaction with life scale (Diener et al., 1985) is commonly seen as a one dimensional scale for global life satisfaction, comprising 5 items (Pavot & Diener, 1993), but sometimes even only a single item is used (Morrison, Tay, & Diener, 2011). Some find a two factor structure for the SWLS (McDonald, 1999; Wu & Yao, 2006), with the last two items of the scale, which refer more to past experiences, having a different importance for the total score both in later life compared to younger people, and in different cultures compared to the US, where the scale has been most extensively tested (Hultell & Petter Gustavsson, 2008; Oishi, 2006; Pons, Atienza, Balaguer, & García-Merita, 2000). These two factors are very closely related in most studies (correlation around .90). Since all items are worded in the same sense, a method factor is not necessary. Since the scale was only included from ELSA wave 2 onwards, we tested the models on wave 2.

Both the one factor and two factor model do not seem to fit very well according to the RMSEA, but have a very good fit according to the CFI (see Table 28.5). The two factor model fits marginally better, but the correlation between both factors is very high (.938). It is a quite surprising finding

Table 28.5 Fit statistics for CFA of 5 item SWLS scale in ELSA wave 2

	RMSEA	CFI	TLI
1 factor (Life satisfaction)	0.135	0.995	0.989
2 factor (Past/Present life satisfaction)	0.121	0.997	0.991
With error correlation between a and c	0.073	0.999	0.997

that one of the most used scales to measure subjective well-being does not fit particularly well for older respondents in England. Modification indices indicate that being satisfied with life (item c) is more closely related to evaluating one's life as ideal (item a), and less to perceiving one's life conditions as ideal. We allow this correlation, and keep in mind that conditions seem to be less important for life satisfaction among the elderly in the UK.

Well-being measures combined: a second order measure of well-being

Table 28.6 Overview of scales present in each wave of ELSA

	Wave 1	Wave 2	Wave 3	Wave 4	Wave 5
CES-D	X	X	X	X	X
GHQ12	X		X		X
SWLS		X	X	X	X
CASP	X	X	X	X	X

Now that we have an indication on the structure of separate aspects of well-being, it can be investigated to what extent these different aspects coincide. From the theory a number of specific hypotheses on the structure of well-being can be deducted. The most influential approach in well-being research, hedonic well-being, based on the work of Diener, assumes two components, an affective part, captured in our measurements by the CES-D and GHQ scales and a cognitive part, in our available data the SWLS (Diener, 1984; Diener et al., 1999; Pavot & Diener, 1993). An alternative approach states that well-being results not from happy mood or a good evaluation of one's life, but through attainment of life goals. This eudaimonic approach does not directly address it's relation with hedonic measures, but sees itself as a separate and conceptually different approach to measuring well-being. This raises the question if and to what extent both approaches are different from one another.

Two aspects of our available data complicate this undertaking. Firstly, not all scales are available in each wave of ELSA (Table 28.6). Therefore we will present the findings of the analysis on the most complete set of measures, in wave 3, in the text.[2] Secondly, each scale allows a different way of answering an item. The CES-D items are binary in nature, while both CASP and GHQ provide 5 response categories and the SWLS 7. Although the CASP and GHQ items have the same number of answering possibilities, their meaning differs as in CASP the frequency of something happening is asked for, while in GHQ the respondent is asked to compare the something with their 'usual' behaviour. This means that the highest correlations between sub-dimensions will logically occur within the same scale. It is nonetheless useful to look at the correlations between the sub-dimensions to investigate which aspects of well-being are less related. Correlations lower than .60 are considered weak, while correlations higher than .75 are considered strong.

The 10 factor model, specifying all subscales of all available measures of well-being, and error correlations between negatively worded items within each scale, has a good fit (Model 1 in Table 28.9). A first step in examining the interrelations of aspects of well-being is to examine the correlations in detail (Table 28.7). As expected, the highest correlations can be observed between subscales derived from a similar instrument. More relevant for the topic of this chapter, is that a number of concepts only are weakly related to each other. Satisfaction with life in general can be seen as only weakly related to most aspects of mental health, which is indicated by the moderate correlations with most subscales of the GHQ and CES-D. On the other hand satisfaction with life, especially in the present, is strongly related to self-actualisation. Anxiety is closely related to symptoms of a depressive mood, but less to self-actualisation and pleasure. Loss of confidence seems closely associated with low control and autonomy. Somatic symptoms of

Table 28.7   Overview of correlations between sub dimensions in wave 3 of ELSA (*n* = 8598)

	SWLS Present	SWLS Past	GHQ Anxiety	GHQ Social dysfunction	GHQ Loss of confidence	CES-D Somatic	CES-D Mood	CASP Control & Autonomy	CASP Self-Realisation
SWLS Past	0.926								
GHQ Anxiety	0.609	0.527							
GHQ Social dysfunction	0.579	0.454	0.715						
GHQ Loss of confidence	0.593	0.521	0.857	0.748					
CES-D Somatic	−0.508	−0.384	−0.664	−0.630	−0.617				
CES-D Mood	−0.628	−0.544	−0.766	−0.703	−0.674	0.834			
CASP Control &Autonomy	−0.730	−0.641	−0.666	−0.589	−0.717	0.640	0.656		
CASP Self-Realisation	0.779	0.753	0.546	0.617	0.607	−0.667	−0.639	−0.847	
CASP Pleasure	0.710	0.732	0.582	0.566	0.648	−0.512	−0.646	−0.790	0.886

depression are especially weakly related to satisfaction with past life, and only moderately with satisfaction with life in the present, or pleasure. In general depressed mood is slightly closer related to satisfaction with life and general mental health compared to somatic symptoms. Surprisingly the pleasure domain of CASP is not more strongly related to the hedonic measures in comparison with the domains control and autonomy and self-realisation. This could indicate that for most respondents, enjoyment is something else than mere satisfaction. Similarly, no measure of positive affect is available in the current ELSA dataset, so it could well be that pleasure is not that closely related to negative affect and satisfaction with life, but more with positive affect.[3] A second explanation is that the frequency of enjoyment asked for in CASP is more related to eudaimonic aspects of well-being than satisfaction with current or past life. A last explanation is that eudemonia, or fulfilling one's psychological needs, is enjoyable and as such should always be seen as partly hedonic.

In a next step a number of theoretically grounded second order factor models (Table 28.8) are tested. This allows to draw conclusions on the most adequate conceptual model to represent subjective well-being in later life.

A second order model essentially adds a latent factor measured by latent factors on top of the model. Theoretically this investigates to what extent the factors on the first level can be seen as representing a common part, or relate to a more abstract concept. What is specifically relevant for this chapter, is the configuration and dimensionality of the second order model. Is well-being in later life best captured by a single second order factor, where all sub-dimensions refer to the same latent concept, as in Model 2? Or is a split between eudaimonic and hedonic well-being (Model 3) more accommodating for our data? A second two dimensional structure could also be distilled from the literature, in the sense that eudaimonia is a part of hedonic cognitive well-being (Model 4). A three factor latent structure, which distinguishes a hedonic affective, hedonic cognitive and eudaimonic component of well-being, could be seen as a compromise between these two dimensional models, and therefore also between hedonic and eudaimonic conceptions of well-being (Model 5). A last possibility is that there is no real second order structure except the different scales used (Model 6).

An overview of the model fit of these different second order models is given in Table 28.9. Specifying a single second order factor

Table 28.8 Overview of second order structures

Model 1	Model 2	Model 3	Model 4	Model 5	Model 6
GHQ Anxiety					GHQ
GHQ Social dysfunction			Affective Well-being	Hedonic Affective Well-being	
GHQ Loss of confidence		Hedonic Well-being			
CES-D Somatic					CES-D
CES-D Mood	Subjective Wellbeing				
SWLS Present				Hedonic Cognitive Well-being	SWLS
SWLS Past					
CASP Control & Autonomy			Cognitive Well-being		
CASP Self-Realisation		Eudaimonic Well-being		Eudaimonic Well-being	CASP
CASP Pleasure					

Table 28.9 Fit statistics for second order CFA in wave 3 of ELSA

	RMSEA	CFI	TLI
Model 1	0.052	0.954	0.948
Model 2	0.074	0.903	0.896
Model 3	0.070	0.914	0.907
Model 4	0.058	0.940	0.935
Model 5[1]	0.053	0.950	0.946
Model 6	0.053	0.951	0.947

1 One cross loading had to be allowed in this model to avoid a negative covariance of self-realisation with cognitive hedonic well-being. The item 'I feel satisfied with the way my life has turned out' of the self-realisation domain was allowed to load on the hedonic cognitive latent second order factor. This is defendable since the nature of the item explicitly refers to satisfaction with life.

(Model 2) means reducing all these aspects of well-being to a single dimension. Although this model has an acceptable fit in terms of RMSEA, this seems less the case for the other fit indices. This means that a single well-being concept is defendable, but does not fully grasp the complexity of the subject at hand. Distinguishing hedonic from eudaimonic well-being (Model 3), does not greatly improve the fit. The division between hedonic and eudaimonic measures seems less substantial than expected. It has to be kept in mind that pleasure is seen as a eudaimonic measure in this context.[4] Distinguishing affective from cognitive aspects of well-being (Model 4) on the other hand, has a substantial impact on

the model fit, since this model approaches very good fit. The compromise between both two dimensional approaches (Model 5), specifying a dimension of hedonic cognitive, hedonic affective and eudaimonic well-being, fits our data very well, and adds conceptual nuance to subjective well-being. An extra factor for the two measurements of affective well-being (Model 6) does not really improve our model fit, so that we can confidently assume a three dimensional nature of well-being.

CONCLUSIONS

This chapter investigates the empirical measurement of well-being in later life, by examining a number of commonly used scales and looking at their interrelations. This examination is framed in the discussion on the difference between hedonic and eudaimonic well-being. The dominant approach, hedonic well-being, assumes that well-being emanates from pleasure and the avoidance of painful experiences, however these are defined by the individual. Measuring well-being in this framework tries to capture moods and emotions on one hand, in the form of positive and negative affect, and cognitive evaluations of one's life on the other hand (Diener, 1984). Eudaimonic well-being is not such a unified approach as hedonic well-being, and consists of several multidimensional approaches (Hyde et al., 2003; Ryan & Deci, 2000; Ryff & Keyes, 1995). What they have in common is that they assume well-being emerges as a result of the satisfaction of universal human psychological needs. While Ryan & Deci (2001) and Hyde et al. (2003) assume pleasure, or hedonic well-being, is one of those needs, Ryff & Keyes (1995) state that at best there is a weak relation between need fulfilment and pleasure.

To what extent do indicators of these different aspects of well-being, commonly developed by testing on either relatively small groups of students or in population wide large scale surveys, replicate their structure among adults aged 50 or older in England? Both instruments aimed at capturing negative affect, CES-D and GHQ, performed most in line with their expectations. While considering CES-D as a one dimensional instrument screening for depression is acceptable, a more fine grained approach to depression clearly distinguishes somatic aspects from emotional ones. The GHQ measure in a similar vein is acceptable as a one dimensional construct, but allows more nuance when looking at anxiety, social and confidence aspects of mental health separately. Satisfaction with life, the most commonly used measure for well-being, seems to perform relatively poorly. Not only can a distinction between satisfaction with the past or present be made, which was already noted by other researchers (Hultell & Petter Gustavsson, 2008; Oishi, 2006), in our sample satisfaction, more precisely seeing one's life as ideal, was less related with how one perceives one's life conditions. The CASP scale was used in a revised 15 item version, and a balanced three dimensional structure, consisting of control and autonomy, self-realisation and pleasure, was found to be most accurate to measure eudaimonic aspects of well-being.

The relations between these different facets of well-being were largely in line with our expectations. Present satisfaction with life was slightly closer related to measures of negative affect, control and autonomy and self-realisation than satisfaction with the past life. Both present and past satisfaction were more related

to aspects of human flourishing than to mental health and depression. Anxiety, social dysfunction, pleasure and both dimensions of satisfaction were more related to emotional symptoms of depression than somatic ones, while the associations were about the same for control and self-realisation. Surprisingly pleasure was not significantly closer related to both affective and evaluative aspects of hedonic well-being compared with other dimensions of the CASP scale. Looking at the second order structure of the scales, it is clear that the difference between hedonic and eudaimonic well-being had been exaggerated in the literature, and is smaller than the difference between affective and cognitive aspects of well-being. If a multidimensional concept of well-being is used, a threefold structure, distinguishing cognitive, affective and eudaimonic well-being is most informative.

What would help us answer the questions posed in this analysis better, or in other words what are the suggestions for further research? First of all, access and inclusion to more measures of well-being, such as positive affect and perhaps loneliness could broaden our understanding of how eudaimonic well-being relates to cognitive and affective aspects. In the case of loneliness this creates the question to which extent it should be seen as an aspect of well-being, and hence a basic psychological need, instead of a possible cause of low well-being, and hence a driver. Secondly, substantial analysis using multiple dimensions of subjective well-being can highlight how the mechanisms producing different forms of well-being differ. Up until now, most attention has been focused on cognitive measures of well-being, and as this chapter illustrated, this might not be the most reliable measure. A last suggestion in a similar vein, is to strengthen the theoretical work on how eudaimonic, affective and cognitive well-being are interrelated. While up until now most research efforts using both hedonic and eudaimonic aspects of well-being are rather partisan in nature, and try to contrast and compare the relative merits of each approach, the real way forward lies in capitalising on the inherent value of both approaches.

APPENDIX

SWLS (Diener, 1984)

a   In most ways my life is close to ideal
b   The conditions of my life are excellent
c   I am satisfied with my life
d   So far, I have gotten the important things I want in life
e   If I could live my life again, I would change almost nothing

Answering categories

1   Strongly agree
2   Agree
3   Slightly agree
4   Neither agree nor disagree
5   Slightly disagree
6   Disagree
7   Strongly disagree

CES-D (Radloff, 1977)

Now think about the past week and the feelings you have experienced. Please tell me if each of the following was true for you much of the time during the past week.

(Much of the time during past week),

a   You felt depressed?
b   You felt that everything you did was an effort?
c   Your sleep was restless
d   You were happy
e   You felt lonely
f   You enjoyed life
g   You felt sad
h   You could not get going

Answering categories

1   Yes
2   No

GHQ (Goldberg, 1988)

We should like to know how your health has been in general over the past few weeks. Have you recently…

a   been able to concentrate on whatever you're doing?

b   lost much sleep over worry?
c   felt you were playing a useful part in things?
d   felt capable of making decisions?
e   felt constantly under strain?
f   felt you couldn't overcome your difficulties?
g   been able to enjoy your normal day-to-day activities?
h   been able to face up to your problems?
i   been feeling unhappy and depressed?
j   been losing confidence in yourself?
k   been thinking of yourself as a worthless person?
l   been feeling reasonably happy, all things considered?

Answering categories

1   Better than usual
2   Same as usual
3   Less than usual
4   Much less than usual

Quality of life (CASP) (Hyde et al., 2003)

Here is a list of statements that people have used to describe their lives or how they feel. We would like to know how often, if at all, you think they apply to you.

Control

a   My age prevents me from doing the things I would like to.
b   I feel that what happens to me is out of control.
c   I feel free to plan things for the future.
d   I feel left out of things.

Autonomy

e   I can do the things that I want to do.
f   Family responsibilities prevent me from doing what I want to do.
g   I feel that I can please myself what I can do.
h   My health stops me from doing the things I want to do.
i   Shortage of money stops me from doing the things I want to do.

Pleasure

j   I look forward to each day.
k   I feel that my life has meaning.

l   I enjoy the things that I do.
m   I enjoy being in the company of others.
n   On balance, I look back on my life with a sense of happiness.

Self-realization

o   I feel full of energy these days.
p   I choose to do things that I have never done before.
q   I feel satisfied with the way my life has turned out.
r   I feel that life is full of opportunities.
s   I feel that the future looks good for me.

Answering categories

1   Often
2   Sometimes
3   Not often
4   Never

NOTES

1   The data were made available through the UK Data Archive (UKDA). ELSA was developed by a team of researchers based at the National Centre for Social Research, University College London and the Institute for Fiscal Studies. The data were collected by the National Centre for Social Research. The funding is provided by the National Institute of Aging in the United States, and a consortium of UK government departments co-ordinated by the Office for National Statistics. The developers and funders of ELSA and the Archive do not bear any responsibility for the analyses or interpretations presented here.
2   Preliminary analysis on waves 1 and 2 point to similar results.
3   Positive affect apparently is available for a subsample of ELSA respondents, who provided saliva samples, through ecological momentary assessments derived from their logbooks (Steptoe & Wardle, 2011). These data are not part of the current version of the ELSA dataset.
4   An alternative model with pleasure as a part of hedonic well-being did not converge, indicating a worse model specification.

REFERENCES

Alexopoulos, G. S. (2005). Depression in the elderly. *Lancet*, *365*(9475), 1961–70. doi:10.1016/S0140-6736(05)66665-2.

Beauducel, A., & Herzberg, P. Y. (2006). Structural Equation Modeling : A On the Performance of Maximum Likelihood Versus Means and Variance Adjusted Weighted Least Squares Estimation in CFA. *Structural Equation Modeling*, *13*(2), 186–203.

Beaumont, J. (2011). *Measuring National Well-being – Discussion paper on domains and measures*. London.

Beekman, A. T., & Deeg, D. J. (1995). Major and minor depression in later life: a study of prevalence and risk factors. *Journal of Affective Di*, 36, 65–75. doi:10.1111/j.1752-0606.2011.00243.x

Bradburn, N. M. (1969). *The Structure of Psychological Well-being*. Chicago: Aldine .

Brickman, P., & Campbell, D. T. (1971). Hedonic relativism and planning the good society. In M. H. Appley (Ed.), *Adaptation Level Theory A Symposium* (pp. 287–302). Academic Press.

Brickman, P., Coates, D., & Janoff-Bulman, R. (1978). Lottery winners and accident victims: is happiness relative? *Journal of Personality and Social Psychology*, *36*(8), 917–27.

Brown, T. A. (2003). Confirmatory factor analysis of the Penn State Worry Questionnaire: Multiple factors or method effects? *Behaviour Research and Therapy*, *41*(12), 1411–1426.

Brown, T. A. (2006). *Confirmatory Factor Analysis for Applied Research*. New York: The Guilford Press.

Campbell, A., Converse, P. E., & Rodgers, W. L. (1976). *The Quality of American Life: Perceptions, Evaluations, and Satisfactions.* (p. 583). New York: Russell Sage Foundation.

Charles, S. T., Reynolds, C. A., & Gatz, M. (2001). Age-related differences and change in positive and negative affect over 23 years. *Journal of Personality and Social Psychology*, *80*(1), 136.

Chen, Y., Rendina-gobioff, G., & Dedrick, R. F. (2010). Factorial invariance of a Chinese self-esteem scale for third and sixth grade students : Evaluating method effects associated with positively and negatively worded items. *International Journal of Educational and Psychological Assessment*, *6*(December), 21–35.

Cheung, Y. B. (2002). A confirmatory factor analysis of the 12-item General Health Questionnaire among older people. *International Journal of Geriatric Psychiatry*, *17*(8), 739–44. doi:10.1002/gps.693

Crawford, J. R., & Henry, J. D. (2004). The positive and negative affect schedule (PANAS): construct validity, measurement properties and normative data in a large non-clinical sample. *The British Journal of Clinical Psychology/the British Psychological Society*, *43*(Pt 3), 245–65. doi:10.1348/0144665031752934

Csikszentmihalyi, M. (1990). *Flow: The Psychology of Optimal Experience*. (H. Collins, Ed.) *Annals of Physics* (Vol. 54, p. 303). Harper & Row.

Demakakos, P., McMunn, A., & Steptoe, A. (2010). Well-being in older age: a multidimensional perspective . In J. Banks, C. Lessof, J. Nazroo, N. Rogers, M. Stafford, & A. Steptoe (Eds.), *Financial Circumstances, Health and Well-being of the Older Population in England. The 2008 English Longitudinal Study of Ageing*. (pp. 115–177). London: Institute for fiscal studies.

DiStefano, C., & Motl, R. W. (2009). Self-esteem and method effects associated with negatively worded items: investigating factorial invariance by sex. *Structural Equation Modeling: A Multidisciplinary Journal*, *16*(1), 134–146. doi:10.1080/10705510802565403

Diener, E. (1984). Subjective well-being. *Psychological Bulletin*, *95*(3), 542–575.

Diener, E., & Diener, C. (1996). Most people are happy. *Psychological Science*, *7*(3), 181–185.

Diener, E., Emmons, R., Larsen, R. J., & Griffin, S. (1985). Satisfaction with life scale. *Journal of Personality Assessment*, *49*(1), 71–75.

Diener, E., Sapyta, J. J., & Suh, E. (1998). Subjective well-being is essential to well-being. *Psychological Inquiry*, *9*(1), 33–37.

Diener, E., Suh, E., & Lucas, R. E. (1999). Subjective well-being: Three decades of progress. *Psychological Bulletin*, *125*(2), 276–302.

Diener, E., Lucas, R. E., & Scollon, C. N. (2006). Beyond the hedonic treadmill: revising the adaptation theory of well-being. *The American Psychologist*, *61*(4), 305–14. doi:10.1037/0003-066X.61.4.305

Dolan, P., & Peasgood, T. (2008). Measuring well-being for public policy : Preferences or experiences ? *Journal of Legal Studies*, *37*(2), 5–31.

Erikson, E. (1959). Identity and the life cycle. *Psychological Issues*, *1*(1), 18–164.

Goldberg, D. P. (1988). *A User's Guide to the GHQ*. Windsor.

Goldberg, D. P., & Williams, P. (1988). *A User's Guide to the General Health Questionnaire*. Basingstoke.

Graetz, B. (1991). Multidimensional properties of the General Health Questionnaire. *Social Psychiatry and Psychiatric Epidemiology*, *26*(3), 132–138.

Hankins, M. (2008). The reliability of the twelve-item general health questionnaire (GHQ-12) under realistic assumptions. *BMC Public Health*, *8*, 355. doi:10.1186/1471-2458-8-355

Hu, L., & Bentler, P. M. (1999). Cutoff criteria for fit indexes in covariance structure analysis: Conventional criteria versus new alternatives. *Structural Equation Modeling: A*, *6*(1), 1–55.

Hultell, D., & Petter Gustavsson, J. (2008). A psychometric evaluation of the Satisfaction with Life Scale in a Swedish nationwide sample of university students. *Personality and Individual Differences*, *44*(5), 1070–1079. doi:10.1016/j.paid.2007.10.030

Hyde, M., Wiggins, R. D., Higgs, P., & Blane, D. (2003). A measure of quality of life in early old age: the theory, development and properties of a needs satisfaction model (CASP-19). *Aging & Mental Health*, *7*(3), 186–94. doi:10.1080/1360786031000101157

Kahneman, D., & Krueger, A. B. (2006). Developments in the measurement of subjective well-being. *Journal of Economic Perspectives*, *20*(1), 3–24.

Kahneman, D., & Thaler, R. H. (2006). Utility maximization and experienced utility. *Journal of Economic Perspectives*, *20*(1), 221–234.

Kahneman, D., Krueger, A. B., Schkade, D. A., Schwarz, N., & Stone, A. A. (2004). A survey method for characterizing daily life experience: the day reconstruction method. (F. A. Huppert, B. Kaverne, & N. Baylis, Eds.) *Science*, *306*(5702), 1776–80. doi:10.1126/science.1103572

Kercher, K. (1992). Assessing subjective well-being in the old-old: The PANAS as a measure of orthogonal dimensions of positive and negative affect. *Research on Aging*, *14*(2), 131–168. doi:10.1177/0164027592142001

King, D. A., & Markus, H. E. (2000). Mood disorders in older adults. In S. K. Whitbourne (Ed.), *Psychopathology in Later Adulthood* (pp. 141–172). New York: Wiley.

Kohout, F. J., Berkman, L. F., Evans, D. A., & Cornoni-Huntley, J. (1993). Two Shorter Forms of the CES-D Depression Symptoms Index. *Journal of Aging and Health*, *5*(2), 179–193. doi:10.1177/089826439300500202

Kunzmann, U. (2008). Differential age trajectories of positive and negative affect: further evidence from the Berlin Aging Study. *The journals of gerontology. Series B, Psychological sciences and social sciences*, *63*(5), P261–70.

Kunzmann, U., Little, T. D., & Smith, J. (2000). Is age-related stability of subjective well-being a paradox? Cross-sectional and longitudinal evidence from the Berlin Aging Study. *Psychology and Aging*, *15*(3), 511–526. doi:10.1037//0882-7974.15.3.511

Lebowitz, B. D., Pearson, J. L., Schneider, L. S., Reynolds, C. F., Alexopoulos, G. S., Bruce, M. L., … Parmelee, P. (1997). Diagnosis and treatment of depression in late life. Consensus statement update. *Journal Of The American Medical Association*, *278*, 1186–1190.

Lewinsohn, P. M., Seeley, J. R., Roberts, R. E., & Allen, N. B. (1997). Center for Epidemiologic Studies

Depression Scale (CES-D) as a screening instrument for depression among community-residing older adults. *Psychology and Aging, 12*(2), 277–87.

Lucas, R. E., Clark, A. E., Georgellis, Y., & Diener, E. (2003). Reexamining adaptation and the set point model of happiness: Reactions to changes in marital status. *Journal of Personality and Social Psychology, 84*(3), 527–539. doi:10.1037/0022-3514.84.3.527

Marmot, M., Banks, J., Blundell, R., Erens, B., Lessof, C., Nazroo, J., & Huppert, F. A. (2011). English Longitudinal Study of Ageing: Wave 0 (1998,1999 and 2001) and Waves 1-4 (2002-2009). Colchester, Essex: UK Data Archive.

Marsh, H. W. (1996). Positive and negative global self-esteem: a substantively meaningful distinction or artifactors? *Journal of Personality and Social Psychology, 70*(4), 810–9.

Maslow, A. (1968). *Towards a psychology of being.* New York: Van Nostrand.

McDonald, R. P. (1999). *Test Theory: A unified treatment.* Mahwah, NJ: Lawrence Erlbaum.

Morrison, M., Tay, L., & Diener, E. (2011). Subjective well-being and national satisfaction: findings from a worldwide survey. *Psychological Science, 22*(2), 166–71. doi:10.1177/0956797610396224.

Nave, C. S., Sherman, R. A., & Funder, D. C. (2008). Beyond self-report in the study of hedonic and eudaimonic well-being: correlations with acquaintance reports, clinician judgments and directly observed social behavior. *Journal of Research in Personality, 42*(3), 643–659. doi:10.1016/j.jrp.2007.09.001

Nussbaum, M., & Sen, A. (1993). *The Quality of Life.* (M. C. Nussbaum & A. K. Sen, Eds.) *Development* (Vol. 1, p. xi, 453). Oxford University Press. doi:10.1093/0198287976.001.0001.

Oishi, S. (2006). The concept of life satisfaction across cultures: An IRT analysis. *Journal of Research in Personality, 40*(4), 411–423. doi:10.1016/j.jrp.2005.02.002

Papassotiropoulos, A., Heun, R., & Maier, W. (1999). The impact of dementia on the detection of depression in elderly subjects from the general population. *Psychological Medicine, 29*(1), 113–20.

Pavot, W., & Diener, E. (1993). Review of the satisfaction with life scale. *Psychological Assessment, 5*(2), 164.

Pons, D., Atienza, F. L., Balaguer, I., & García-Merita, M. L. (2000). Satisfaction with life scale: analysis of factorial invariance for adolescents and elderly persons. *Perceptual and Motor Skills, 91*(1), 62–8.

Radloff, L. S. (1977). The CES-D Scale: A self-report depression scale for research in the general population. *Applied Psychological Measurement, 1*(3), 285–401.

Ready, R. E., Vaidya, J. G., Watson, D., Latzman, R. D., Koffel, E. A., & Clark, L. A. (2011). Age-group differences in facets of positive and negative affect. *Aging & Mental Health, 15*(6), 784–95. doi:10.1080/13607863.2011.562184.

Ross, C. E., & Mirowsky, J. (1984). Components of depressed mood in married men and women. *American Journal of Epidemiology, 119*(6), 997–1004.

Ryan, R. M., & Deci, E. L. (2000). Self-determination theory and the facilitation of intrinsic motivation, social development, and well-being. *The American Psychologist, 55*(1), 68–78.

Ryan, R. M., & Deci, E. L. (2001). On happiness and human potentials: A review of research on hedonic and eudaimonic well-being. *Annual Review of Psychology, 52*(1), 141–166.

Ryff, C. D., & Keyes, C. L. M. (1995). The structure of psychological well-being revisited. *Journal of Personality and Social Psychology, 69*(4), 719–27.

Ryff, C. D., & Singer, B. H. (1998). The contours of positive human health. *Psychological Inquiry, 9*(1), 1–28.

Seligman, M. E. P., & Csikszentmihalyi, M. (2000). Positive psychology: An introduction. *American Psychologist, 55*(1), 5.

Shevlin, M., & Adamson, G. (2005). Alternative factor models and factorial invariance of the GHQ-12: a large sample analysis using confirmatory factor analysis. *Psychological Assessment, 17*(2), 231–6. doi:10.1037/1040-3590.17.2.231.

Steptoe, A., & Wardle, J. (2011). Positive affect measured using ecological momentary assessment and survival in older men and women. *Proceedings of the National Academy of Sciences, 108*(45), 18244–18248. doi:10.1073/pnas.1110892108

Sumner, L. (1999). *Welfare, Happiness, and Ethics.* Oxford: Oxford University Press.

Taylor, S. E., & Brown, J. D. (1988). Illusion and well-being: a social psychological perspective on mental health. *Psychological Bulletin, 103*(2), 193–210.

Van de Velde, S., Bracke, P., Levecque, K., & Meuleman, B. (2010). Gender differences in depression in 25 European countries after eliminating measurement bias in the CES-D 8. *Social Science Research, 39*(3), 396–404. doi:10.1016/j.ssresearch.2010.01.002

Van den Berg, M. D., Oldehinkel, A. J., Bouhuys, A. L., Brilman, E. I., Beekman, A. T., & Ormel, J. (2001). Depression in later life: three etiologically different subgroups. *Journal of Affective Disorders, 65*(1), 19–26.

Vanhoutte, B. (2012). Measuring subjective well-being in later life: a review. CCSR Working Paper 2012-06. Manchester, UK: CCSR, University of Manchester.

Wallace, R. B., Herzog, A. R., Ofstedal, M. B., Steffick, D., Fonda, S., & Langa, K. M. (2000). *Documentation of Affective Functioning Measures in the Health and Retirement Study*. Ann Arbor, MI.

Waterman, A. S. (1993). Two conceptions of happiness: Contrasts of personal expressiveness (eudaimonia) and hedonic enjoyment. *Journal of Personality and Social Psychology, 64*(4), 678–691.

Waterman, A. S. (2007). On the importance of distinguishing hedonia and eudaimonia when contemplating the hedonic treadmill. *The American Psychologist, 62*(6), 612–3. doi:10.1037/0003-066X62.6.612

Watson, D., Clark, L. A., & Tellegen, A. (1988). Development and validation of brief measures of positive and negative affect: the PANAS scales. *Journal of Personality and Social Psychology, 54*(6), 1063–70.

Watson, L. C., & Pignone, M. P. (2003). Screening accuracy for late-life depression in primary care: A systematic review. *Journal of Family Practice, 52*(12), 956–64.

Wiggins, R. D., Netuveli, G., Hyde, M., Higgs, P., & Blane, D. (2008). The evaluation of a self-enumerated scale of quality of life (CASP-19) in the context of research on ageing: a combination of exploratory and confirmatory approaches. *Social Indicators Research, 89*(1), 61–77. doi:10.1007/s11205-007-9220-5

Wood, A. M., Taylor, P. J., & Joseph, S. (2010). Does the CES-D measure a continuum from depression to happiness? Comparing substantive and artifactual models. *Psychiatry Research, 177*(1–2), 120–123. doi:10.1016/j.psychres.2010.02.003

Wu, C., & Yao, G. (2006). Analysis of factorial invariance across gender in the Taiwan version of the Satisfaction with Life Scale. *Personality and Individual Differences, 40*(6), 1259–1268. doi:10.1016/j.paid.2005.11.012

29

Legal Aspects of Age Discrimination

Malcolm Sargeant

INTRODUCTION

This chapter is concerned with some aspects of the regulation of age discrimination. Of interest really is the way that age discrimination is treated in comparison to other possible grounds of discrimination such as disability, race or sex. One of the arguments put forward here is that age is treated differently than other grounds because there are still an important amount of age-related practices that are considered legitimate. This chapter first considers the motivation for age discrimination legislation; then looks at the debate taken in the European Court of Justice as to whether equality in relation to age amounts to a fundamental principle of Community law; we then examine the legislation enacted in the EU and the USA as well as some of the issues that have arisen from litigation on the subject; finally we look at the exceptions contained in the UK legislation as an example of how differently age is treated when compared to other grounds.

THE REASON WHY

The answer to the question 'why do we have legislation on age discrimination?' is both interesting and important. If it is merely a reaction to an aging population then its treatment and justification might be different to a situation where it is introduced as a rights-based measure taken as a way of protecting individuals against unfair treatment. It might be acceptable, for example, to have many more exceptions to the principle of equality if the justification is a demographic one rather than a human rights one.

An example of this dual justification can be seen in the preamble to the EU Directive 2000/78/EC establishing a general framework for equal treatment in employment and occupation. This Directive provides for the principle of equal treatment (Article 1) in relation to age, disability, religion or belief and sexual orientation in employment. Recital 4 of the preamble refers to the 'right of all persons to equality before the law and protection against discrimination constitutes a universal right recognised by the Universal Declaration of Human Rights', as well as various other international declarations by the United Nations and the International Labour Organisation. Recital 6 also refers to the European Community Charter of the Fundamental Rights of Workers which 'recognises the importance of combating every form of discrimination, including the need to take appropriate action for the social and economic integration of elderly and disabled people'. Recital 25, however, then takes a perhaps pragmatic view when it states that:

> differences in treatment in connection with age may be justified under certain circumstances and therefore require specific provisions which may vary in accordance with the situation in Member States. It is therefore essential to distinguish between differences in treatment which are justified, in particular by legitimate employment policy, labour market and vocational training objectives, and discrimination which must be prohibited.

Thus, we have a situation where discrimination must be prohibited, but not when it interferes with labour market or employment policy. This contradiction is given prominence in Article 6 of the Directive which is headed 'Justification of differences of treatment on grounds of age'. Article 6 proposes three differences of treatment on the grounds of age that may be justifiable by 'a legitimate aim, including legitimate employment policy, labour market and vocational training objectives'. The first difference permits some positive action for specific groups including young people, older workers and those with caring responsibilities to encourage their integration into the workforce; the second allows for the fixing of minimum conditions or the giving of advantages linked to age, professional experience or seniority; the third allows a maximum recruitment age based on the training requirements of the post or the need for a reasonable period of employment before retirement. These exceptions seem to be in opposition to any principle of equality and suggest a contradiction between the equal-treatment justified approach and an approach justified on demographic grounds.

This wish to dilute the rights based approach with exceptions related to the needs of the labour market is manifested in the implementing legislation and in the decisions of the Courts. The United Kingdom (UK) Equality Act 2010, for example, has one part (Schedule 9 part 2) headed 'Exceptions relating to age'. These exceptions include retirement, people approaching retirement age, benefits linked to length of service, the national minimum wage and redundancy payments. Thus there appeared to be a willingness to compromise the principle of equality in favour of perhaps more pragmatic exceptions. Age discrimination in employment is to be specifically allowed to continue in certain circumstances in order to encourage the employment of older people and not to place an apparently too onerous a burden upon employers. A rights based approach might provide that people are entitled not to be discriminated against on the grounds of their chronological age and it might impose a stricter test for any potential exceptions. Given that there are manifestations of discrimination based upon age and that there continues to be a stereotyping of the relative abilities of different groups of workers based on age, one might conclude that there is a case for treating such discrimination in the same way as governments have tackled discrimination based upon gender and race.

Is age discrimination different, or to be treated differently, than some other forms of discrimination? The approach does appear to be different. There might be more opportunities to *differentiate* rather than *discriminate* between persons of different ages. The US Secretary of Labor commenting in 1965 (Eglit, 1999, and *The Older American Worker-Age Discrimination in Employment* (1965), report to the US Congress), prior to the introduction of the US Age Discrimination in Employment Act (ADEA), on the existence of age discrimination, stated that 'we find no significant evidence of … the kind of dislike or intolerance that sometimes exists in the case of race, color, religion, or national origin, and which is based on considerations entirely unrelated to ability to perform a job'. He did go on to say, however, that 'we do find substantial evidence of … discrimination based on unsupported general assumptions about the effect of age on ability … in hiring practices that take the form of specific age limits applied to older workers as a group'.

Age discrimination took place then (and still does of course), but it may not create the strong emotions that are sometimes created in consideration of some other forms of discrimination. Perhaps it is the lack of these strong feelings that allows the current approach to the subject to predominate.

AGE AS A FUNDAMENTAL PRINCIPLE

The view that age is treated differently to other grounds of discrimination can be illustrated by comments at the European Court of Justice. In *Palacios* the Advocate General (AG) stated:

> So far as non-discrimination on grounds of age, especially, is concerned, it should be borne in mind that that prohibition is of a specific nature in that age as a criterion is a point on a scale and that, therefore, age discrimination may be graduated. It is therefore a much more difficult task to determine the existence of discrimination on grounds of age than for example in the case of discrimination on grounds of sex, where the comparators involved are more clearly defined.

AG Geelhoed further stated in *Chacon Navas* (a disability discrimination case) that:

> the implementation of the prohibitions of discrimination of relevance here [disability and age] always requires that the legislature make painful, if not tragic, choices when weighing up the interests in question, such as the rights of disabled or older workers versus the flexible operation of the labour market or an increase in the participation level of older workers.

This issue of where age stood in relation to the other grounds of discrimination further

manifested itself in a debate about whether the principle of non-discrimination on the grounds of age was to be regarded as a general principle of Community law. The Court of Justice held, in *Mangold* v *Helm*, that this was so. This case concerned a German law which placed limits on the use of fixed-term contracts of employment. There needed to be an objective justification for the fixed-term contract and limits were imposed on the number of times it could be renewed and how long a person could stay on successive fixed-term contracts (in accordance with European Directive 1999/70 concerning the framework agreement on fixed-term work). These restrictions were removed for workers over a certain age. The age was reduced in stages until the exclusion applied to all those aged 52 years and older (by the First Law for the Provision of Modern Services on the Employment Market of 23 December 2002 – known as the 'Hartz Law'). The purpose of removing these restrictions was, of course, to try to make older workers more attractive to employers.

One of the ways that the Court of Justice appears to have faced up to the issues of a reference from the national court even though the transposition date had not passed, and to the possibility of a horizontal application of the Directive, was to consider the principle of equal treatment as being something beyond the Directive itself. The Court relied upon the third and fourth recitals in the preamble to the Directive to show that the principle derived from various international instruments and in the constitutional traditions of the Member States of the EU. Recital 3 concerns the aim of eliminating inequalities between men and women and Recital 4 refers to the Universal Declaration of Human Rights, the European Convention for the Protection of Human Rights and various other international agreements on this subject. It is these international agreements and the 'constitutional traditions' of Member States that are the source of the principle of equal treatment. The Directive does not of itself lay down the principle of equal treatment. It has the purpose of providing a framework for combating discrimination on the grounds of religion or belief, disability, age or sexual orientation. The Court then stated that 'the principle of non-discrimination on grounds of age must thus be regarded as a general principle of Community law' (para 75).

This statement caused some controversy, especially amongst the Advocate Generals who advise the Court on specific cases. In *Lindorfer*, AG Sharpston referred to the *Mangold* decision as 'identifying a hitherto unacknowledged fundamental principle of Community law' (para 57) and that this had caused concern in academic circles. The AG proposed that what the Court had actually intended to say was not that there was a specific pre-existing principle of non-discrimination on the grounds of age in Community law, but rather a general principle of equality which Directive 2000/78/EC had specifically applied to various grounds including age (para 58).

In *Bartsch*, Advocate General Sharpston continued the debate and considered the critical views of a colleague in Palacios:

In *Palacios de la Villa* AG Mazák offered an extended criticism of *Mangold*. He stated that a general principle of equality potentially implies a prohibition of discrimination on any grounds deemed unacceptable; however, it is quite a different matter to infer from the general principle of equality the existence of a prohibition of discrimination on a specific ground.

Despite the debate amongst the Advocate Generals, AG Sharpston pointed out that the Court had delivered judgments in a number of cases without reviewing or even mentioning the views of its Advocate Generals.

Subsequently, however, the subject of age as a principle of Community law was raised in the German case of *Kücükdeveci*. This questioned a national provision that provided for periods of notice to increase with length of service, but disregarded service before the age of 25. The Court referred to the *Mangold* judgment and again 'acknowledged the existence of a principle of non-discrimination on

grounds of age which must be regarded as a general principle of European Union law'. It also referred to Article 6(1) of the TFEU which provided that the Charter of Fundamental Rights is to have the same legal value as the Treaties and that Article 21(1) of the Charter provided for the prohibition of age discrimination. Directive 2000/78/EC gives expression to, but does not lay down, the principle of equal treatment and that 'the principle of non-discrimination on grounds of age is a general principle of European law in that it constitutes a specific application of the general principle of equal treatment'.

LEGISLATION IN THE EU AND THE USA

There are different approaches adopted by different states, although legislation concerning age discrimination in employment always seems to be the starting point. Below we consider some aspects of the legislation in Europe and the USA in order to illustrate some differences. Indeed the derivations of the legislation in the two are different. The USA adopted the ADEA in 1976, following on, and being part of, the civil rights legislation of the 1970s which also saw protection given on race and sex discrimination (Oppenheimer 2010). The EU legislation, on the other hand, is much more recent as the Framework Directive (2000/78/EC) was adopted in 2000. It appears to have been driven by the necessity to act with regard to the aging workforce and the desire to increase the numbers at work. One major difference, of course, is the fact that the US legislation is designed to assist older workers, whilst the EU legislation applies to all those at work. Under ADEA it would not be unlawful to discriminate in favour of a person in the protected class (those aged 40 plus) at the expense of a younger person. This would not be possible under the EU directive (unless there was justification). Both the US and the EU measures have significant weaknesses which perhaps put age discrimination lower in the hierarchy than other grounds such as race and sex. The ADEA has a small firm exclusion, has doubts about whether disparate impact is protected against and requires an intention to discriminate. Perhaps worst of all is the situation in mixed motive cases and the need to show that age was the most important, if not overriding factor in the employer's decision to discriminate. In the EU directive, there is the possibility of justifying exceptions if the aim is legitimate and the means proportionate, but Article 6 of the Directive permits a wide interpretation of the meaning of legitimate aim. In a sense both the pieces of legislation are similar in that they are really an inadequate response to the need for age discrimination protection.

THE EU FRAMEWORK DIRECTIVE

Directive 2000/78/EC establishing a general framework for equal treatment in employment and occupation only applies to 'employment and occupation' with regard to discrimination on the grounds of religion or belief, disability, age or sexual orientation. It was an important legislative step in dealing with age discrimination because it has been transposed into national legislation in all 27 Member States of the EU. The Framework Directive is, however, part of a fragmented approach to discrimination as it is essentially one of three directives making such discrimination unlawful. The other two being Directive 2000/43/EC implementing the principle of equal treatment between persons irrespective of racial or ethnic origin and Directive 2006/54/EC on the implementation of the principle of equal opportunities and equal treatment of men and women in matters of employment and occupation. This last directive is the latest in a line of equal treatment directives dealing with gender equality. These directives are inconsistent in their scope and do not impose a positive duty to end discrimination. The Directive also distinguishes between those aspects of age discrimination which are unjustifiable, and should therefore be made

unlawful, and those aspects which are justifiable, and should therefore be permitted. The main limitation in terms of the scope of Directive 2000/78/EC is that it is confined to employment and occupation. There is a proposal for a Directive extending this to areas outside employment law (COM(2008) 426) but it is likely to be some years (if ever) before this comes to fruition.

The purpose of the Directive is set out in Article 1 as being to lay down a general framework for combating discrimination and putting into effect the principle of equal treatment. The principle of equal treatment here means, according to Article 2, that there should be no direct or indirect discrimination on the grounds of age (the Directive also makes harassment and victimisation unlawful). There is no need for a comparator to actually exist. Article 2(a) refers to comparison with another who 'has been or would be treated in a comparable situation'. Thus it is possible to use a hypothetical comparator. Deciding who or which group is to be the hypothetical comparator may not be as straightforward as in gender or race cases. Indirect discrimination is taken to occur where an apparently neutral provision, criterion or practice would put persons having a particular age at a particular disadvantage with other persons, unless 'that provision, criterion or practice is objectively justified by a legitimate aim and the means of achieving that aim are appropriate and necessary' (Article 2.2(b)(i)). Thus it is possible to justify age discrimination if the purpose is 'legitimate', such as that contained in Article 6 (see below) and if the means of achieving that purpose are appropriate and necessary.

It is for the employer to justify the difference in treatment. In the case of *Mangold* the European Court of Justice considered a situation where German law allowed for the employer to conclude, without restriction, fixed-term contracts of employment with employees over the age of 52 years. The purpose of the German legislation was to encourage the vocational integration of unemployed workers. The Court agreed that such a purpose could be 'objectively and reasonably' justified. The question then was whether this legitimate objective was 'appropriate and necessary'. The problem was that the national legislation applied to all people over the age of 52 years and not just to those who were unemployed. The Court concluded:

> In so far as such legislation takes the age of the worker concerned as the only criterion for the application of a fixed-term contract of employment, when it has not shown that fixing an age threshold, as such, regardless of any other consideration linked to the structure of the labour market in question or the personal situation of the person concerned, is objectively necessary to the attainment of the objective pursued. Observance of the principle of proportionality requires every derogation from an individual right to reconcile, so far as is possible, the requirements of the principle of equal treatment with those of the aim pursued.

Thus the Court found that the measure did not meet the criteria of being 'appropriate and necessary'. The problem is that to help unemployed older workers, the measure took away employment protection for all older workers. There are also other examples where national rules have taken away employment rights from particular age groups in order to make them more attractive to employers (see below) and it is questionable whether these examples of 'justifiable' age discrimination do achieve the aim which the measures set out to achieve.

The Directive applies to both the public and the private sector and has a wide scope, albeit limited to the areas of employment and vocational guidance and training. In particular it applies to conditions for access to employment, self-employment or to occupation, including selection criteria and recruitment conditions; all types of activity and at all levels of the professional hierarchy, including promotion; access to all types and all levels of vocational guidance and vocational training, including practical work experience; employment and working conditions; pay and dismissals. Specifically excluded are payments of any kind made by state schemes, including social security or social protection schemes

and the armed forces, at the Member State's discretion. Thus the scope is quite wide, but it is still limited to the fields of employment and vocational training. Age discrimination has a more limited scope than the directives concerned with sex and race.

Article 6 of the Directive provides for specific exceptions to the principle of equal treatment. They must be 'objectively and reasonably justified by a legitimate aim, including legitimate employment policy, labour market and vocational training objectives'. In addition the means of achieving the aim must be 'appropriate and necessary'. There are then some specific examples of differences in treatment which could be justified. These differences include the setting of special conditions on access to employment and vocational training, employment and occupation (including dismissal and remuneration conditions) for young people, older workers and persons with caring responsibilities in order to promote their vocational integration or ensure their protection; the fixing of minimum conditions of age, professional experience or seniority of service for access to employment or to certain advantages linked to employment; the fixing of a minimum age for recruitment which takes into account the training period and the need for a reasonable period of work before the individual retires.

Article 7.1 provides that the principle of equal treatment will not stop Member States from maintaining or adopting specific measures to prevent or compensate for disadvantages linked to age. Positive action is different to positive discrimination. The limits for the latter have been drawn by the European Court of Justice in relation to other grounds of discrimination. This was tested in *Marschall*, where the complainant was a male comprehensive school teacher who had applied for promotion to a higher grade. He was told that an equally qualified female applicant would be given the position as there were fewer women than men in the more senior grade. The Court of Justice considered previous judgments (for example, Case C-450/93 *Kalanke* and Case C-312/86

Commission v *France*) which concluded that the Equal Treatment Directive did not permit national rules which enabled female applicants for a job to be given automatic priority. Article 2(4) of the Directive 2006/54/EC, however, provided that the Directive should be 'without prejudice to measures to promote equal opportunity for men and women' and the ECJ considered whether this could alter the outcome. It distinguished between those measures which were designed to remove the obstacles to women and those measures which were designed to grant them priority simply because they were women; the latter measures conflict with the Directive. There was a difference between measures concerned with the promotion of equal opportunity and measures imposing equal representation.

Positive action is a term that includes measures designed both to counter the effects of past discriminatory practices and to assist members of the protected group to compete on an equal basis with those not in the protected group. In relation to age where the whole working population is the protected group, positive action for one age group may result in negative effects for other age groups. Thus a decision to only recruit younger employees in the interest of long-term staff planning will have an effect on older applicants. This will not be a case of helping the protected group in contrast with those not in the protected group; it is a case of advantaging one part of the protected group against another part of the same group.

Implementation of the age aspects of the Framework Directive has presented a special challenge to some Member States as most did not have any existing general legislation concerning age discrimination. Cormack and Bell (2005) reported that there are two contrasting 'models or patterns' that have emerged in the way that Member States have faced up to these difficulties. One pattern or model has been to directly enact the provisions of the Directive, using the same or very similar words. This happened in Italy, Cyprus and Greece as well as Denmark, Austria,

Slovakia and Slovenia. The alternative model or pattern is to indulge in elaborate debate as to how the age aspects of the Directive might be fully integrated into national law. This debate tends to be difficult and complex as in Belgium, Germany, Netherlands and the United Kingdom.

THE AGE DISCRIMINATION IN EMPLOYMENT ACT

In the United States, there had been a history of legislation at State level to outlaw age discrimination in employment before the adoption of the Age Discrimination in Employment Act 1967 (the ADEA). Indeed, in 1965, there were 20 States that already had such legislation, including Colorado which had introduced such a law as far back as 1903. The majority of these laws outlawed discrimination against older workers (those between 40 and 65 years), although Colorado, Idaho, Louisiana, New Jersey and Oregon had either lower minimum ages or none at all. In 1964 also, the President, Lyndon B. Johnson issued an Executive Order (Order No 11141, February 12 1964) establishing a policy against age discrimination in employment by Federal contractors and sub-contractors. The Order provided that contractors and sub-contractors could not discriminate on the basis of age in hiring, promotion, termination or terms and conditions of employment. It also barred age limits in recruitment advertising.

The ADEA is only concerned with older workers, in contrast to the EU Directive which cover all ages of people at work. It applies to workers who are least 40 years of age (ADEA Section 12(a)). The Act also only applies to those employers who had at least 20 employees for 20 or more calendar weeks in the preceding year (ADEA Section 11(b)). The ADEA 'requires the employer to ignore an employee's age (absent a statutory exemption or defense); it does not specify further characteristics that an employer must ignore' (*Hazen Paper Co* v *Biggins*).

The Act itself has been amended on a number of occasions. This has, most notably, resulted in the removal of the upper age limit, firstly, for federal employees in 1978 and then for non-federal employees in 1986. The purpose of the ADEA is described in Section 2(b) as threefold: firstly, to promote employment of older persons based on their ability rather than age; secondly, to prohibit arbitrary age discrimination in employment; and, thirdly, to help employers and workers find ways of meeting problems arising from the impact of age on employment. The Act applies to labour organisations and employment agencies as well as to employers in general.

Section 4(a) states that it is unlawful for an employer–

(1) to fail or refuse to hire or to discharge any individual or otherwise discriminate against any individual with respect to his compensation, terms, conditions, or privileges of employment, because of such individual's age;

(2) to limit, segregate, or classify his employees in any way which would deprive or tend to deprive any individual of employment opportunities or otherwise adversely affect his status as an employee, because of such an individual's age;

(3) to reduce the wage rate of any employee in order to comply with this chapter.

Thus discrimination on the grounds of age is unlawful in hiring and firing; compensation, assignment, or classification of employees; transfer, promotion, layoff, or recall; job advertisements; recruitment; testing; use of company facilities; training and apprenticeship programs; fringe benefits; pay, retirement plans, and disability leave; or other terms and conditions of employment.[1]

There are, however, a number of exceptions, which include where 'the differentiation is based on reasonable factors other than age'; where there is a bona fide occupational qualification (BFOQ) reasonably necessary to the normal operation of the particular business; 'highly compensated people'. Similarly there is an exception to the retirement provisions of the higher paid. Section 12(c)(1)

states that 'nothing in this chapter shall be construed to prohibit compulsory retirement of any employee who has attained age of 65 years … and for 2 years prior has been a bona fide executive or in a high policy making position and can receive a pension of at least $44 000 per annum'.

An individual claiming unlawful age discrimination will need to show disparate treatment. Disparate treatment requires it to be shown that the employer intentionally treated an individual less favourably because of their age. The onus is first on the plaintiff to establish a prima facie case of discriminatory intent. The employer is then able to argue a permissible non-discriminatory justification, then leaving the plaintiff with the opportunity to argue that this non age-based justification is false. This no longer seems to apply in some situations making it much more difficult to bring age claims (see below – 'Supreme Court limits the effects of ADEA').

In *Woroski* v *Nashau Corporation* the Court accepted that a prima facie case had been indicated when two plaintiffs complained of age discrimination after losing their jobs in a 'reduction in force' exercise. The employers, however, were able to show a proper business motivation for large-scale downsizing and that there was a lack of evidence that the operation was 'infected by age bias'. In order to establish a prima facie case of age discrimination a plaintiff needed to show that they were in the protected age group; were qualified for the position; were adversely affected; and the discharge occurred under circumstances giving rise to an inference of age discrimination.

Disparate impact, on the other hand, would require an apparently neutral employment policy that in fact has an adverse impact on older workers, but cannot be justified by any sort of business necessity justification. Traditionally this had not been possible under ADEA, but in March 2005 the US Supreme Court handed down a judgment stating that age discrimination may be shown using the disparate impact approach (*Smith* v *City of Jackson, Mississipi*).

An employer may be permitted to take actions against an older worker for reasons other than age (Mitchell 2001), and it seems to be considered on a case-by-case basis. The employer, however, cannot rely on stereotypical images of a decline in abilities with age. In *Beith* v *Nitrogen Products Inc* an employer dismissed a 55-year-old employee because of back problems. He had been taken on as a temporary operator pending a physical examination. Mr Beith's examination revealed that he had some degenerative disc disease and some osteoarthritis. As a result it was recommended that he did not lift, regularly, weights over 20 lbs. On the basis of the report his employers decided that he was at high risk of being injured and claiming compensation. His employment was therefore terminated. The Court stated that 'Congress made it plain that the age statute was not meant to prohibit employment decisions based on factors that sometimes accompany advancing age, such as declining health or diminished vigor and competence'. There is an overlap between disability and age (Sargeant, 2005), but the Court dismissed Mr Beith's argument that because his back condition was an ordinary and natural consequence of aging, then, by inference, he was really dismissed because of his age. Because such back conditions are more common in older persons, it did not follow that a dismissal because of the back condition was an age-based decision.

There is also the opportunity for an employer to show that age is a bone fida occupational qualification (BFOQ) and that some members of an age-defined group cannot perform the job safely and efficiently and that they cannot be identified by any means other than age. One example is having a compulsory retirement age for airline pilots. In *Western Airlines Inc.* v *Criswell* the Airline had a policy of retiring its pilots at the age of 60 years The airline argued that the retirement age was a BFOQ 'reasonably necessary' to the safe operation of the airline, or the essence of the airline's business. There is a two-stage approach: firstly, the employer must establish that there is a potential for unacceptable risk to the employer or third parties that older workers are more likely to impose; and, secondly, the employer must prove that it is impracticable to perform individual evaluations that could identify which of these older workers pose that risk. The employer thus has two options: they can establish that there is an unacceptable risk associated with all employees over a certain age.

There is also an issue about the ability of complainants to show age discrimination when the employer has 'mixed-motives', i.e. when there are possibly a number of reasons for the employer's actions, one of which may be age. Indeed the Supreme Court has held that a plaintiff would need to show that age was the crucial issue, that age was a 'but-for' cause. In other words that the action would not have taken place but for the age issue, regardless of all the other factors that might have been involved (*Gross* v *FBL Financial Services*).

ISSUES IN AGE LITIGATION

In this part of the chapter we consider some of the issues raised by litigation, particularly at the European Court of Justice, and use them to illustrate the scope of the legislation needed to combat age discrimination.

Reduction in employment rights

Both younger workers and older workers share a problem in having higher levels of unemployment than other age groups. One way in which governments have tried to tackle this is by reducing the levels of employment protection compared to these other age groups, in order to make both younger workers and older workers more attractive to employers. It is not clear what sort of research has been done to show that this policy actually works, e.g. in the United Kingdom, workers below the age of 21 years are entitled to a lower national minimum wage (Sargeant 2010b). The somewhat contradictory justification for this was that it would encourage young people to stay in education, but also make them more attractive to employers. Despite this over 80 per cent of 18–21 year olds are paid at the adult rate, rather than the reduced rate for younger workers (National Minimum Wage: Low Pay Commission Report, 2007) and youth unemployment continues at high levels. The problem with such policies is that they apply a general rule to a whole age group, even though the majority of the age group will not benefit from the policy. This was illustrated with regard to older workers in the case of *Mangold* (see above) where all those aged 52 years and above had a reduction in protection from being employed continuously on fixed-term contracts, even though it was only a minority of the age group that had the problem of being unemployed and finding it difficult to obtain work.

An example of the application of the reduction of rights for young people occurred in the case of *Kücükdeveci*. This was a reference from the Landsarbeitsgericht, Düsseldorf. It concerned the German Law on Equal Treatment. Paragraph 622 of the German Civil Code is concerned with periods of notice which are related to the length of employment and it stated that in 'calculating the length of employment, periods prior to the completion of the employee's 25th year of age are not taken into account'. Ms Kücükdeveci joined Swedex when she was 18 years of age and was dismissed after ten years' service. The employer based the notice period, to which she was entitled, on that period of service after the age of 25. This gave her three years' service in all. She argued, not unreasonably, that she should be entitled to ten years' service for the calculation of her notice period. She claimed that the failure to do this amounted to age discrimination. There was a necessity to show that there was a legitimate aim and the measure was appropriate for achieving that aim, in accord with Article 6 of the Directive. The 'legitimate aim' was set out as being that 'young workers generally react more easily and more rapidly to the loss of their jobs and greater flexibility can be

demanded of them. A shorter notice period for younger workers also facilitates their recruitment by increasing the flexibility of personnel management' (Para 25 of the Judgment). The Court pointed out, however, that 'the legislation is not appropriate for achieving that aim, since it applies to all employees who joined the undertaking before the age of 25 whatever their age at the time of dismissal' (para 40). Thus it would affect someone with long service who could not be classified as a young person. The legislation also affected young people unequally; those who had little vocational training and started work earlier were at a disadvantage compared to those that started at a later age.

Retirement

Rules concerning mandatory retirement are examples of age discrimination. People are made to retire, whether they wish to or not, at a certain chronological age. In certain circumstances it may be possible to justify mandatory retirement as an appropriate and necessary means to a legitimate aim. There have been a number of cases concerning this at the European Court of Justice. One of the earliest was *Palacios de la Villa*. In 2001 the Spanish legislature abolished the compulsory retirement age. This gave rise to a number of disputes, particularly concerning the lawfulness of clauses in collective agreements providing for the compulsory retirement of workers. In 2005 the position was clarified by Law 14/2005 on clauses in collective agreements concerning the attainment of normal retirement age. This provided that collective agreements may contain clauses providing for the termination of employment at the retirement age subject to certain conditions.

Mr Palacios was born on 3 February 1940 and had worked for Cortefiel since 1981. In accordance with the collective agreement he was dismissed when he reached the age of 65. The collective agreement stipulated that 'in the interests of promoting employment, it is agreed that the retirement age will be 65 years unless the worker concerned has not completed the qualifying period required for drawing the retirement pension, in which case the worker may continue in his employment until the completion of that period'.

Mr Palacios claimed age discrimination because of his dismissal at the age of 65. The Court held that the national legislation that allowed for automatic termination of employment when a certain age is reached did amount to less favourable treatment and thus amounted to age discrimination. The Court further held that

> It does not appear unreasonable for the authorities of a Member State to take the view that a measure such as that at issue in the main proceedings may be appropriate and necessary in order to achieve a legitimate aim in the context of national employment policy, consisting in the promotion of full employment by facilitating access to the labour market.

Thus it was concluded that a compulsory retirement age was permissible as a means of facilitating access to the labour market for others. There is no evidence that the Court tested the veracity of this justification.

In *Rosenbladt* the German court asked whether a national rule that permitted the state, the parties to a collective agreement and the parties to an individual employment contract to specify the automatic termination of an employment relationship upon reaching a specific fixed age (in this case 65) contravened the prohibition on age discrimination. For 39 years Mrs Rosenbladt worked as a cleaner in a barracks until her contract was terminated on her 65th birthday in accordance with the framework collective agreement for employees in the commercial cleaning sector. The German Government claimed that the lawfulness of clauses on automatic termination of employment contracts of employees who have reached retirement age was

> the reflection of a political and social consensus which has endured for many years in Germany. That consensus is based primarily on the notion of sharing employment between the generations. The termination of the employment contracts of those employees directly benefits young workers

by making it easier for them to find work, which is otherwise difficult at a time of chronic unemployment. (para 43)

The Court of Justice found that this was a legitimate aim within the terms of the Directive and that retirement was an appropriate and necessary means of achieving this. This decision was reached despite the fact that there is little evidence that the termination of older workers does make room for younger workers seeking employment.

A further important case concerning age retirement was the 'Age Concern' case from the English High Court (*The Incorporated Trustees of the National Council on Ageing*). This case arose because the UK government, at the same time as introducing the Employment Equality (Age) Regulations 2006 (now incorporated into the Equality Act 2010) to tackle age discrimination, also introduced a 'default retirement age' which essentially allowed employers to choose whether or not to have a mandatory retirement age. If they chose to have one and followed certain procedures, then any affected employees would not be able to claim unfair dismissal or age discrimination. Age Concern argued that by providing for an exception to the principle of non-discrimination where the reason for the dismissal of an employee aged 65 or over is retirement, then the UK Regulations infringed the principle of proportionality contained in Article 6 of the Directive. In his Opinion the Advocate General stated that 'the possibilities of justifying differences of treatment based on age are more extensive' than those based on other grounds' and the Court held that a high degree of proof was required before justification could be shown. Subsequently, Age Concern lost this case when it returned for consideration by the High Court, although the 'default retirement age' was finally abolished in 2011 (see below).

Upper age limits

In the case of *Wolf* the Court of Justice was faced with an applicant who was turned down for a post in the fire service on the grounds of age. There was an upper limit of 30 years for the posts in question and Mr Wolf was over this limit. The German government stated to the Court that the aim of the maximum recruitment age was 'to ensure the operational capacity and proper functioning of the fire service' (para 33). The German government had also produced evidence that persons over the age of 45 or 50 years did not have this capacity to carry out the required tasks. Thus, someone recruited at the age of 30 years can (after a two year training programme) carry out the activities for 15 or 20 years, whereas someone recruited at the age 40 would only have 5–10 years' possible service. The Court accepted that the measure was therefore appropriate and necessary to fulfil the legitimate aim of maintaining operational capacity. The question to be considered then was whether the setting of a maximum age of 30 years was an appropriate and necessary means of achieving the aim. Finally the Court agreed that the rule setting a maximum age of 30 years for such posts was not precluded by the Directive. The outcome of this decision is, of course, that people of a certain age who are able to carry out the functions of a job may still be rejected as the employer may not be able to maintain its operational capacity by having too many older workers who, apparently, will be unable to carry out the tasks assigned.

Petersen was a German case which concerned a maximum age limit of 68 years for 'panel dentists'. Ms Petersen's authorisation to operate as a dentist expired when she reached this age. The questions from the national court concerned whether this maximum age limit was an objective and reasonable measure to achieve a legitimate aim. The legitimate aim was the health of patients as, 'based on general experience', 'a general drop in performance occurs from a certain age'. The Court pointed out that Article 2(5) of the Directive specifically states that the Directive is without prejudice to a number of measures, including 'the protection of health'. The Court considered the aims put forward by

the German Government in respect of Articles 2(5) and 6(1). It concluded that Article 2(5) precluded a national measure setting a maximum age for practising as a panel dentist where the aim was the protection of patients from the effects of the decline in performance of dentists after the age of 68. The reason for not accepting this as a legitimate aim was that it only applied to panel dentists and there was no age limit for non-panel ones. In terms of Article 6(1), however, where the aim was 'to share out employment opportunities among the generations' (if taking into account the labour market the measure was appropriate and necessary) the measure was not precluded. The outcome of course is that, in a labour market where there is a surplus in a particular profession, it seems to be acceptable to discriminate against older members of the profession in order to facilitate new members of the profession entering.

THE CASE OF THE UNITED KINGDOM

Age discrimination legislation was finally adopted in the UK in 2006, as a result of the EU Framework Directive (2000/78/EC), and is now contained in the Equality Act 2010 (Sargeant 2006). Section 4 of this Act provides that age is one of nine protected characteristics in relation to which there is certain prohibited conduct. The prohibited conduct is direct discrimination (Section 13(1)), indirect discrimination (section 19(1)), harassment (section 26(1)) and victimisation (section 27(1)). Following on from the example set out in Article 6 of the Directive, the age discrimination provisions have a number of exceptions related uniquely to the protected characteristic of age.

Direct discrimination

The protected characteristic of age is the only one of the nine protected characteristics where it is possible to objectively justify direct discrimination, where the aim is legitimate and the means proportionate (section 13(2)). The Code of Practice on Employment published by the Equality Rights Commission states that this is because some age-based rules and practices are seen as justifiable. The Code gives the example of health and safety risks for young people. Where their experience or lesser strength might create risks, then it might be justifiable to have a minimum age for recruitment into a particular job. This is an arguably justifiable reason for discrimination. The problem with this approach is that the legislation provides an exception for justifying direct age discrimination without specifying the particular circumstances. There is no specific list which, for example, contains the exception for young people in respect of health and safety. There is only the blanket possibility of justifying an exception.

Retirement

Regulation 30(1) of the 2006 Age Regulations was concerned with the exception for retirement and stated that 'Nothing in Part 2 or 3 shall render unlawful the dismissal of an employee at or over the age of 65 years where the reason for the dismissal is retirement' (Sargeant 2010a). The Regulations were adopted in order to tackle age discrimination in employment and it is extremely bizarre that at the same time they should introduce a 'default retirement age' of, usually, 65 years. It is clear from the consultation process prior to the adoption of the Regulations that many employers wanted the option of a mandatory retirement age because, it was argued, this was a more dignified way of older employees leaving employment rather than the alternative, which would be a system based on capability. When employee abilities etc. declined with age then dismissal on the grounds of capability might follow (Equality and Diversity 2005). It was an argument based upon stereotypical attitudes of older workers and the result was the introduction of a major piece of age discrimination. This ultimately was removed in 2011 by the coalition government elected in 2010. Nevertheless the possibility

of having an employer justified retirement age remains. If an employer is able to show that having a mandatory retirement age is a proportionate means of achieving a legitimate aim, then it might be possible to impose a retirement age. There will have to be justification of the actual age imposed as well as the reason for having it. In *Seldon* the employer had put forward a number of what it claimed were legitimate aims to the Employment Tribunal which accepted that compulsory retirement was an appropriate means of achieving the 'firm's legitimate aims of staff retention, workforce planning and allowing an older and less capable partner to leave without the need to justify the departure and damage dignity'. After a review of the case law at the Court of Justice of the EU, the Court concluded that two kinds of legitimate aims had been identified. These were inter-generational fairness and dignity. The first of these, which was stated as being 'comparatively uncontroversial' [Para 56 of the judgment] meant various things depending upon the particular circumstances of the employment, but could include facilitating access to employment for young people, but it could also mean enabling older people to remain in the workforce. It can also mean sharing limited opportunities to work in a particular profession fairly between the generations. Two major employers that have adopted this approach are the Universities of Cambridge and Oxford who have adopted a compulsory retirement age of 67 years for their academics.

National minimum wage

The UK has a statutory minimum wage, the effect of which is monitored by the Low Pay Commission. The full adult entitlement does not commence until the age of 21 years. There are two lower bands for young people: one for those aged 16 and 17 years; the other for those aged between 18 and 20 inclusive. There is also a separate rate for apprentices. Without statutory protection, the paying of an age-related lower rate to young workers would amount to less favourable treatment on the grounds of age. This measure only applies to the age bands and pay levels established by the statutory measures on the national minimum wage. Objective justification would be needed to pay a 16-year-old at a different rate to a 17-year-old. Similarly, if an employer were paying rates which were above the levels of the national minimum wage, they would need to justify this, even if the same age bands were used.

In Government evidence to the Low Pay Commission (November 2007) it was stated that the 'Government's aim is to afford very young workers some protection from poverty pay, while maintaining the incentives for 16–17 year olds to remain in education or job-related training and build up their knowledge and future earnings potential.' This measure does exploit young people, however, and is an example of age discrimination written into statute with a business motivation. The issue is that it applies to all those in a certain age group regardless of whether they need the protection. There is a similarity to *Mangold* where a large group of people have employment rights reduced in order to help some.

Provision of benefits based on length of service

This is concerned with the issue of benefits related to length of service and seniority. It is not uncommon for employees to be given extra benefits related to length of service with an organisation. Without further provisions such benefits might constitute unlawful age discrimination, because it will tend to mean that longer serving (and older) receive greater benefits than younger (and less-experienced) colleagues. Schedule 9, Part 2, Para 10(1) of the Equality Act 2010 provides that

> It is not a contravention for a person (A) to put a person (B) at a disadvantage, when compared to another (C), in relation to the provision of a benefit, facility or service in so far as the disadvantage is because B has a shorter period of service than C.

Therefore any benefits associated with length of service are not to amount to age discrimination. There is a further proviso relating to service that is longer than five years. In this case it must reasonably appear to A that the way in which the criterion of length of service is used 'fulfils a business need' (Para 10(2)).

The provision of enhanced redundancy payments

Statutory redundancy payments are calculated using a combination of the length of service and age. The older the employee, then the greater the amount received for each year of service. There is, however, a contradiction between the ability to take length of service into account as a criterion in selection for redundancy and a desire to end discrimination upon the basis of age (Sargeant 2009). Use of this criterion will tend to favour longer serving employees and, therefore, older employees at the expense of younger ones. The same can be said of redundancy payments schemes which provide extra money to those with longer service.

Rolls Royce v *Unite the Union* considered two collective agreements which had an agreed matrix to be used to choose who should be selected for redundancy. There were five criteria against which an individual could score between 4 and 24 points. In addition there was a length of service criterion which awarded 1 point for each year of continuous service. Thus older employees would have an important advantage over younger ones. *MacCulloch* v *ICI plc* concerned a redundancy scheme which had been in existence since 1971. The amount of payment was linked to service up to a maximum of ten years, and the size of the redundancy payment increased with age. The claimant was 37 years old and received 55 per cent of her salary as a payment, but she claimed that someone aged between 50 and 57 years would have received 175 per cent of salary under the scheme.

Loxley v *BAE Systems* had a contractual redundancy scheme in which each employee received two weeks' pay for the first five years of employment, three weeks' for each of the next five years and four weeks' pay for each year after ten years. There was also a further age-related payment of two weeks' pay for each year after the age of 40 years. All this was subject to a maximum of two years' pay. The scheme was amended for older workers approaching retirement when the retirement age was raised, but essentially the claimant, who was 61 years of age, was not entitled to any enhanced payments for voluntary redundancy as he had an entitlement to a pension.

The essential feature of all these cases concerned whether it was possible to have general justification for taking into account length of service or whether it should be justified in each particular case. In fact the general justification argument won, relying substantially on European case law.

CONCLUSION

This chapter has shown that the regulation of age discrimination is not treated in the same way as when other grounds of discrimination are legislated upon. Implementation of the EU Framework Directive in the UK and elsewhere has demonstrated that much needs to be done before justification of age discrimination can be shown as being really an exception, rather than commonplace.

NOTE

1   List taken from EEOC's website (see below) at <www.eeoc.gov>

REFERENCES

Cormack, J. and Bell, M. (2005) *Developing Anti-Discrimination Law in Europe.* Brussels: European Commission

Eglit, H. E (1999) 'The ADEA at Thirty', *University of Richmond Law Review*, 31, 579

Equality and Diversity (2005) Coming of Age; Consultation on the draft Employment Equality (Age) Regulations 2006, *Department for Trade and Industry*.

Mitchell, D. E. (2001) 'Recent cases affecting the role of ADEA in protecting older workers', *Duquesne Law Review*, 39, 437

National Minimum Wage: Low Pay Commission Report (2007) Cm7056, Department *for Trade and Industry*.

Oppenheimer, D. B. (2010) 'Sources of United States Equality Law: the view from 10,000 meters', *European Anti-Discrimination Law Review*, 10(19), 19–30

Sargeant, M. (2005)   Disability and age – multiple potential for discrimination *International Journal of the Sociology of Law*, Vol 33, 17–33

Sargeant, M. (2006) 'The Employment Equality (Age) Regulations 2006: A legitimisation of age discrimination in employment' *Industrial Law Journal*, 35(3), 209–228

Sargeant, M. (2009) Age discrimination, redundancy payments and length of service. *Modern Law Review*, 72(4), 628–634

Sargeant, M. (2010a) 'The default retirement age: legitimate aims and disproportionate means', *Industrial Law Journal*, 39(3), 244–263

Sargeant, Malcolm (2010b) 'Age discrimination and the National Minimum Wage', *Policy Studies*, 31(3), 351–364

Secretary of Labor (1965) *The Older American Worker-Age Discrimination in Employment*. Washington: Department of Labor Cases

Cases

Bartsch v *Bosch und Siemens Hauseräte (BSH) Alterfürsorge GmbH* Case C-427/06 [2008] ECR 1–7245

Beith v *Nitrogen Products Inc.* 7 F.3d 701 (8th Cir. 1993)

Chacon Navas v *Eurest ColectividadesSA* Case C-13/05 [2006] IRLR 706

Commission v *France* Case C-312/86 [1998] ECR 6315 ECJ

Gross v *FBL Financial Services* 129 S. Ct. 2343 (2009)

Hazen Paper Co v *Biggins* 113 SCt 1701, 16 FEP 793 (1993)

The Incorporated Trustees of the National Council on Ageing (Age Concern England) v *Secretary of State for Business, Enterprise and Regulatory Reform* Case C-388/07 [2009] IRLR 373 and [2009] IRLR 1017

Kalanke v *Freie Hansestadt Bremen* Case C-450/93 [1995] ECR 660

European Directives

Statutes

Index